DREAMLAND

DREAMLAND

The Secret History of Area 51

PETER W. MERLIN

SCHIFFER MILITARY
4880 Lower Valley Road · Atglen, PA 19310

Other Schiffer books on related subjects

50 Years of the U-2: The Complete Illustrated History of Lockheed's Legendary "Dragon Lady,"
Chris Pocock, 978-0-7643-2346-1

Lockheed SR-71 Blackbird: The Illustrated History of America's Legendary Mach 3 Spy Plane,
James C. Goodall, 978-0-7643-5504-2

Copyright © 2023 by Peter W. Merlin

Library of Congress Control Number: 2023931203

All rights reserved. No part of this work may be reproduced or used in any form or by any means—graphic, electronic, or mechanical, including photocopying or information storage and retrieval systems—without written permission from the publisher.

The scanning, uploading, and distribution of this book or any part thereof via the Internet or any other means without the permission of the publisher is illegal and punishable by law. Please purchase only authorized editions and do not participate in or encourage the electronic piracy of copyrighted materials.

"Schiffer Military" and the arrow logo are trademarks of Schiffer Publishing, Ltd.

Designed by Christopher Bower
Cover design by Christopher Bower
Type set in Abolition/Minion

ISBN: 978-0-7643-6709-0
Printed in India
5 4 3 2

Published by Schiffer Publishing, Ltd.
4880 Lower Valley Road
Atglen, PA 19310
Phone: (610) 593-1777; Fax: (610) 593-2002
Email: Info@schifferbooks.com
Web: www.schifferbooks.com

For our complete selection of fine books on this and related subjects, please visit our website at www.schifferbooks.com. You may also write for a free catalog.

Schiffer Publishing's titles are available at special discounts for bulk purchases for sales promotions or premiums. Special editions, including personalized covers, corporate imprints, and excerpts, can be created in large quantities for special needs. For more information, contact the publisher.

We are always looking for people to write books on new and related subjects. If you have an idea for a book, please contact us at proposals@schifferbooks.com.

CONTENTS

Preface: Let Perpetual Light Shine in the Darkness 6

Acknowledgments.. 7

Introduction: Desert Dreamland..................................... 8

    Chapter 1   The Angel from Paradise Ranch....................... 16
    Chapter 2   Special Projects 72
    Chapter 3   Roadrunners and Blackbirds 102
    Chapter 4   Dreamland... 128
    Chapter 5   We Have Met the Enemy............................. 190
    Chapter 6   Invisible Airplanes 246
    Chapter 7   Flying Scorpions and Desert Whales 282
    Chapter 8   Mountains of Controversy.......................... 340
    Chapter 9   Unusual Flying Objects 370
    Chapter 10   National Asset 426

Postscript: ... And All That Is Hidden Shall Be Revealed 464

Appendixes
    Appendix 1:   Selected Documents 466
    Appendix 2:   Installation Commanders, 1955-2022................ 476
    Appendix 3:   Test Site Names 477
    Appendix 4:   Test Wing Organization........................... 478
    Appendix 5:   Aircraft Accidents 479
    Appendix 6:   Miscellany....................................... 482

Abbreviations and Acronyms/Initialisms 484
Endnotes 490
Bibliography 538
Index 540

PREFACE
LET PERPETUAL LIGHT SHINE IN THE DARKNESS . . .

The story of Area 51 is like an immense jigsaw puzzle. When I began piecing it together more than three decades ago, there was little publicly available information on the subject. In the pre-internet era, I had to rely on scarce and fragmentary published accounts in books, magazines, and a handful of newspaper articles. Over time I found new sources, both archival and anecdotal, upon which to draw more details. I also met a number of people who felt I was wasting my time because they believed the United States (US) government had thoroughly cloaked Area 51 behind an impenetrable veil of secrecy, as if "the Government" was some sort of monolithic entity, all powerful and supremely capable. Because, in fact, it comprises a multitude of Byzantine organizations made up of ordinary people bound by inefficient policies, the secrecy surrounding Area 51 began eroding even before the first concrete foundations were poured near the edge of Groom Lake, Nevada, in the spring of 1955. Decades later, as various government agencies began declassifying formerly secret Cold War defense programs, the puzzle began to take shape. Sadly, many pieces have been lost over time or remain hidden within Pentagon vaults.

Previous attempts to document the history of Area 51 have been at best incomplete, and at worst fraudulent. Some authors contented themselves with writing primarily about the secret test site's early years or merely covering the details of one specific aircraft development program. Others worked around the edges of the subject to examine the psychosocial aspects of Area 51 in modern popular culture. Too often, supposedly serious narratives veered into the realm of bizarre conspiracy theories with no foundation in verifiable fact. In an attempt to counteract this phenomenon, I have taken great pains to vet my sources and substantiate details of every story in this volume to the greatest extent possible. This proved both challenging and rewarding. If you think you know the story of Area 51 (or even a particular part of that story), expect to be surprised by the material in the ensuing chapters.

To date, I am the first author to attempt to write a comprehensive and scholarly history of Area 51. Note that I use the word *comprehensive* rather than the word *complete*. I have necessarily had to rely entirely on unclassified and declassified source material. As long as some programs remain shrouded in secrecy, there will always be holes in this narrative. Worse still, many of the men and women who served their country in silence during the Cold War passed away before being granted the opportunity to tell their stories. This book is dedicated to them.

Each section begins with a brief vignette that weaves historical facts with some dramatization. These evocative episodes involve real people and events and, whenever possible, actual quotes. Necessarily, some conversations and internal monologues have been reconstructed/invented using the best available documentation along with a combination of logic, common sense, and the author's personal experience. I hope these scenes will help bring the story of Area 51 to life.

LUX PERPETUA LUCEAT IN OBSCURUM ET QUIDQUID LATET APPAREBIT

ACKNOWLEDGMENTS

This book would not have been possible without input and advice from a great many people, some of whom are sadly no longer with us. I would like to give particular thanks to Thornton "TD" Barnes, president of Roadrunners Internationale; researcher and gadfly Glenn Campbell; aviation authors Paul Crickmore, Steve Davies, Jim Goodall, Jay Miller, Curtis Peebles, Chris Pocock, and Jeannette Remak; Dr. James O. Young, Dr. Raymond Puffer, and Joyce Baker of the AFFTC History Office; AFFTC Museum curator Doug Nelson; Dr. James Outzen, historian, National Reconnaissance Office; Bob Biondi, John Stone, and others at Schiffer; Joerg Arnu, Angus Batey, Roger Christensen, Joe Donoghue, Trevor Paglen, Terry Panopalis, Jeff Wedding, and many more; and to my wife, Sarah, for painstakingly editing my manuscript.

Special thanks to Brig. Gen. Robert C. "Woody" Nolan II, USAF (Ret.), and James W. Eastman, chief of the Acquisitions Management Office, NASA Armstrong Flight Research Center, without whom this book would not have been possible.

INTRODUCTION
DESERT DREAMLAND

Groom Lake as seen from the Groom Mine circa 1945. Note the complete lack of man-made structures on the lakebed's distant shore. *Sheahan collection*

July 1871. Coarse gravel crunched and shifted beneath Grove Gilbert's dusty boots as he scrambled up a steep slope at the lower end of central Nevada's Timpahute Range. Pausing at the top of a rugged limestone ridge, he surveyed the barren landscape below, once again marveling at the stark beauty of this high-desert valley that represented a geological and scenic wonderland. A scattering of pinyon and juniper trees at the higher elevations softened the edges of the surrounding mountains while blackbrush, saltbrush, and forests of Joshua trees—their spiky arms upraised as if in mute protest—dotted the valley floor below. Beneath his sweat-stained hat, the geologist squinted into the bright glare reflecting from the vast white expanse of a dry lakebed, several miles distant. Tasting the prehistoric playa's alkali dust on the hot wind, Gilbert stooped to pick up a gray rock and noted the fossilized remains of ancient coral from a primordial sea that once occupied this now-arid landscape.

The story of Area 51 began with an unimaginable cataclysm some 367 million years ago, when an extraterrestrial object pulverized the primitive life forms inhabiting an ancient ocean covering what is now Lincoln County, Nevada. As the small asteroid—or possibly the frozen core of a comet—excavated a crater more than 6 miles in diameter from the shallow seabed, shock-generated mega-tsunami waves and waterspouts ejected debris in a dense slurry. A titanic backwash collapsed the transient crater rim and transported a chaotic mix of sediments down the submarine slope. Impact forces deformed local geology to a radius of at least 60 miles, and ejecta rained down across the entire region, leaving a telltale signature: shocked quartz grains and increased concentrations of iridium, an element proportionately far more abundant in extraterrestrial materials than in terrestrial bedrock.[1]

Over the next several millennia, tectonic forces pushed the seabed upward until it became dry land, and vast fault blocks tilted to form Nevada's characteristic basin-and-range topography. Volcanic basalts and tuff breccias overlaid Cambrian quartzite and Miocene freshwater limestone. The result was a geologist's dreamland of fossiliferous outcrops and precious ores.[2] Approximately 18,000 years ago, a wide valley about 85 miles northwest of modern-day Las Vegas contained a 36-square-mile, rain-fed lake that may have been as much as 38 feet deep during times of maximum precipitation. Climate fluctuations and deposition of sediments from the surrounding mountains eventually caused this pluvial lake to dry out, leaving behind a flat claypan roughly 3 miles in diameter.

Though scant physical evidence remains, humans may have first entered this area (which came to be known in the nineteenth century as Emigrant Valley) some 10,000 years ago, exploiting whatever resources were available near the edge of the lakebed. By the time the first Euro-American settlers arrived, the only remaining Indigenous occupants consisted of scattered groups of Southern Paiute and Shoshone hunters and gatherers who had cleverly adapted to a harsh environment that sorely taxed the newcomers. Moving between seasonal campsites, the natives took advantage of an abundance of pinyon nuts, wild game, and whatever natural springs they could find.

This desolate, inhospitable terrain long discouraged exploration until control of the region passed to the United States of America at the conclusion of the Mexican War in 1848. Following the 1849 discovery of gold in California, an intrepid emigrant party (later nicknamed the "Death Valley Forty-Niners") headed west across the Great Basin under the leadership of Capt. Jefferson Hunt. Near Enterprise, Utah, one group chose to ignore the advice of their guide to follow the Old Spanish Trail and instead turned westward.[3] This splinter group

Robert Groom discovered commercial-grade ore in the mountains north of the lakebed that would eventually bear his name. His claims established the Groom Mining District. *University of Arizona*

eventually passed through the southern end of Nevada's Timpahute Mountains and into Emigrant Valley, but its journey had been arduous.[4] With the help of local Paiutes, the Forty-Niners obtained lifesaving water from nearby springs while recuperating for several days near the eastern edge of the alkali playa. These long-suffering pioneers dubbed the spot Misery Lake, though their trials thus far only foreshadowed the difficulties they would later face in California's Death Valley.[5]

In 1864, the year Nevada gained statehood, a prospector named Robert W. Groom set out from Arizona to Oregon. His journey was interrupted while passing through the Timpahute Mountains, where he discovered ore suitable for mining and decided to stay. Sporadic activity over the next several years led to the formation of the Groom Mining District in 1869.[6] Although his mines never attained the prominence of other nearby operations such as those in Pioche and Delamar, Groom left an enduring legacy. His name was appended to the nearby lakebed and, eventually, to the entire mountain range as far north as Coyote Summit.

Military expeditions followed in the wake of pioneers and prospectors. On one of these, in 1871, US Army lieutenant George M. Wheeler led a Corps of Engineers survey expedition through southern Nevada. Orders from the War Department charged Wheeler with preparing accurate topographical maps of the territory, in part for the purpose of "selection of such sites as may be of use for future military operations and occupation."[7] Wheeler's party stopped briefly at the Groom Mining District, giving geologist Grove K. Gilbert an opportunity to visit the Groom Mine and study local mineral resources. The expedition's chief topographer, Peter W. Hamel, drew a map plotting the route of travel and describing details of the terrain. Although the Wheeler Survey atlas was never fully completed or widely distributed, it produced the first detailed study of the region.[8]

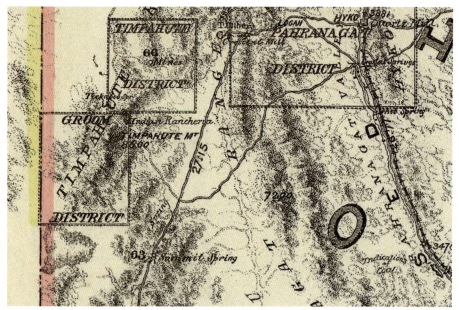

The Wheeler Expedition map created by Peter Hamel showed the location and boundaries of the Groom Mining District. *NARA*

Mining activities gradually increased in the Groom District, spurred in 1872 by the influx of backing from a British mining consortium. Following five years of development, at a cost of $80,000, the effort was abandoned due to the mine's isolated location. Patrick Sheahan, a mining engineer, partnered with lawyer Thomas J. Osborne to acquire the claims in 1885. They soon began leasing sections to other prospectors, but little development occurred until 1915. Sheahan's son Daniel joined the operation four years later. The men hauled ore-laden carts south by tractor along dirt roads through Emigrant Valley to Indian Springs—a three-day journey—to be shipped out on the Las Vegas & Tonopah rail line. Despite its low-grade quality, some 6,145 tons of ore shipped from the Groom Mines between 1915 and 1926 yielded 100,341 ounces of silver and 5,926,371 pounds of lead, as well as about a ton of copper and trace amounts of gold.[9]

After war broke out in Europe and preparations began for American involvement, President Franklin D. Roosevelt signed documents establishing military training sites in Nevada. On October 29, 1940, most of Groom Lake and the surrounding area were subsumed within the boundaries of the Las Vegas Bombing and Gunnery Range, a vast tract of unpopulated desert that had been set aside for mock aerial warfare.[10] Three Army airfields were established near Las Vegas, Indian Springs, and Tonopah, at the edges of this restricted zone. The range boasted excellent year-round flying weather; a sufficient buffer zone to allow for live firing of machine guns, rockets, and bombs; and several dry lakebeds that served as auxiliary airfields, useful as staging areas or for emergency landings. Groom Lake was designated Indian Springs Auxiliary Field No. 1, and an X-shaped set of perpendicular 5,000-foot runways was carved out of the desert scrub just east of the playa.[11] Their use seems somewhat perplexing considering that these sandy strips were never paved and the lakebed itself provided a much-smoother, harder surface for aircraft operations. Why runway outlines were not simply marked directly onto the lakebed is unknown.

Despite the aerial gunnery practice taking place overhead, Daniel Sheahan started full-time operations at the Groom Mine. He built an ore-processing mill west of the mining camp's main house and cabins, as well as a small warehouse and blacksmith shop. Throughout World War II the intrepid miners extracted ore worth $148,200, but they were subjected to nearly constant danger. Spent

A mule train at the Groom Mine circa 1917. The mine produced silver, lead, and copper as well as trace amounts of gold. *Sheahan collection*

.50-caliber shells ejected from aircraft littered the property, stray projectiles damaged a bunkhouse and outhouse, and Army pilots experienced in-flight emergencies—sometimes with fatal consequences.[12]

One such incident took place on July 25, 1945, after an RP-63 with mechanical difficulties made a precautionary landing on the auxiliary airstrip adjacent to Groom Lake. It took almost four hours for a maintenance crew commanded by 2Lt. Donald D. Mon, accompanied by an armed security guard, to drive the 50 miles of rough dirt roads from Indian Springs Army Air Field to reach the stricken plane. They worked throughout the afternoon in gusty winds and occasional rain showers until early evening, when they heard the drone of an approaching aircraft. A two-seat AT-6B, piloted by twenty-two-year-old first lieutenant Benjamin F. Garrett, had been dispatched to pick up the guard and return him to Indian Springs before nightfall. Garrett approached from the south and passed over the airstrip at an altitude of just 300 feet before circling the lakebed and dropping to about 75 feet. To Mon's astonishment, Garrett then executed an aerobatic slow roll directly over the runway. Before completing this maneuver, however, low-altitude windshear hurled his airplane to the ground. The AT-6B exploded in a ball of flame that onlookers vainly attempted to douse using sand and handheld fire extinguishers. Unfortunately, the pilot sustained fatal injuries.[13]

The war's end in 1945 heralded a brief interlude of peace and quiet at Groom Lake, but this would change in the wake of events over the next few years. Increasing geopolitical tensions between the US and the Russian-dominated Union of Soviet Socialist Republics marked the beginning of what became known as the Cold War. In the US, this was seen as an ideological struggle between democracy and Communism that pitted member nations of the North Atlantic Treaty Organization (NATO) against the Soviets and their Communist allies (the Warsaw Pact nations). Two significant events during this period ultimately affected the future of Groom Lake.

First, the US lost its nuclear monopoly in August 1949, when the Soviets successfully detonated an atomic bomb far sooner than most Americans expected. The US still possessed a greater number of bombs, and the Soviets lacked a delivery system with sufficient range to reach American soil, but scientists on both sides raced to develop more-powerful weapons and long-range bombers. Up to this time most US nuclear weapon tests had been conducted on isolated coral atolls in the middle of the Pacific Ocean, but logistical difficulties, adverse weather, and concerns about security and safety sparked a search for a continental test site for all but the most-powerful explosions. Planners from the Armed Forces Special Weapons Project (AFSWP) and the Atomic Energy Commission (AEC) ultimately selected two valleys on the Las Vegas Bombing and Gunnery Range. Frenchman Flat and Yucca Flat were within an hour's drive north of Las Vegas but were sufficiently remote to provide what AEC officials believed to be a reasonable safety buffer. Year-round weather conditions were ideal, and only a sparse population lived downwind in the direction anticipated for clouds of radioactive fallout.[14] In order to ensure protection for the largest population centers, detonations were planned only for times when prevailing winds blew to the northeast, away from Las Vegas. The Groom Mine, directly in the center of the preferred downwind path and roughly 12 miles from the northeastern boundary of the new proving ground, was subject to both blast effects and fallout.

Operation Ranger, the first continental nuclear test series at the Nevada Test Site (NTS), began on January 27, 1951. It consisted of five airdrops with explosive yields ranging from 1 kiloton (equivalent to 1,000 tons of TNT conventional high explosives) to 22 kilotons. By comparison, the bomb dropped on Hiroshima, Japan, during World War II had a yield of 15 kilotons. The first bomb

The wreckage of an AT-6B trainer litters the dirt airstrip adjacent to Groom Lake in July 1945. *Air Force Historical Research Agency*

of Operation Ranger exploded at an altitude of 1,060 feet above Frenchman Flat. Although the blast had a yield of only 1 kiloton, it was felt as far away as Las Vegas and had dramatic effects at the Groom Mine. Daniel Sheahan recalled, "It was quite violent; it broke open the front door of our house and cracked some windows."[15]

Not long afterward, AEC personnel visited the mine to inform the Sheahans of what to expect from future testing. The blasts were going to get larger, and there would be increasing levels of radioactive fallout. Sheahan was advised that any women and children should be sent away as a safety precaution, and that mining operations would need to be suspended for brief periods after each shot. This didn't always happen, however. On many occasions, members of the Sheahan family gathered outside their cabin to watch the bright flash of a nuclear blast, followed by formation of the distinctive mushroom-shaped cloud that threatened their home and livelihood.

Whenever work did cease, it was a costly nuisance that proved only more irksome as nuclear tests occurred more frequently. A shot in November 1951 idled the mine for nearly two weeks. AEC radiation safety, or Rad-Safe, monitor Ed Hyatt told Sheahan that testing in the spring of 1952 would be exceptionally "dirty" (more prone to produce radioactive fallout) due to the number of shots to be fired on 300- and 500-foot steel towers. Detonating closer to the ground than bombs dropped from airplanes, these blasts lofted vast quantities of radioactive soil and debris high into the atmosphere.[16]

Following an outing to Las Vegas on May 5, 1952, the Sheahan family returned home to find a note pinned to their door warning that "a dirty shot will be made early the morning of May 6. We strongly urge that Groom be evacuated by 6:00 a.m., May 6. Return to Groom will be possible by noon, unless informed otherwise." They turned around and went back to the city. Upon checking with the AEC command post the following afternoon, the Sheahans were told there was still too much radiation to permit entry through Tikaboo Valley, through which ran the Groom Mine Road. In a meeting with officials a few weeks later, Daniel Sheahan was told, "There's no question the Groom area is dangerous. No one should live there, especially during the tests." But Sheahan was unwilling to give up on the mine that had been his home for so long. As testing continued, the effects became more pronounced. Sometimes

Dan, Martha, and Bob Sheahan, with their cat Cleo, watch a pre-dawn atomic blast from the Groom Mine in 1953. Shock waves from the explosions occasionally damaged structures at the mine. *Sheahan collection*

An atomic mushroom cloud rises over Yucca Flat, with Groom Lake in the foreground. Dust and radioactive debris from these shots frequently rained down on the Groom Mine area. *Sheahan collection*

the debris clouds rained tiny metal pellets, which were all that remained of the shot tower. The blast wave from one detonation shattered thirty windows and tore metal siding from several buildings.[17]

Eventually, an AEC Rad-Safe team and a monitor from the Public Health Service installed equipment to measure radiation levels at the Groom Mine, placed fallout collection trays, and taught the Sheahans how to use a Geiger counter. In March 1953, a research team from the University of California at Los Angeles (UCLA) set up several cages with live rabbits as test subjects, but the mine's residents also suffered the biological effects of radiation. The family's horses developed clusters of circular burns on their backs, and fallout caused a blister on Martha Sheahan's face that turned into a cancerous sore. Although the family sued the government in 1956 for $75,600, the case was dismissed because the statute of limitations had expired.

The following year, nuclear testing moved temporarily to the Pacific Proving Ground, giving the Groom Mine a brief respite from the radioactive clouds but allowing the Air Force to resume bombing and gunnery practice nearby. In 1954, the mine produced ore valued at $22,000. Unfortunately, the operation also suffered a great loss on June 23, when an Air Force pilot on a training mission destroyed the Sheahans' ore-processing mill, machine shop, compressor room, and power plant with some sort of incendiary device. This time, Daniel Sheahan sued for $650,000.[18] In a letter to Nevada governor Charles Russell, Sheahan wrote of the damage done and of the "almost constant danger we are in from flying machine gun fire, or atomic radiation and blast damage. We have been fired upon by machine guns any number of times. Buildings have been struck by bullets, several people have narrowly escaped being killed and some pilots have even gone so far as to dive down and strafe our workings."[19] The Air Force denied all charges, and the case was eventually dismissed.

The second significant event affecting Groom Lake's future was the publication of a sensational article in the February 15, 1954, issue of Aviation Week magazine describing new Soviet long-range jet bombers capable of carrying nuclear weapons.[20] This spurred public debate about the possibility that the Soviets were quickly surpassing the US in terms of bomber capability, leading to a potential "bomber gap."[21] The most promising avenue toward determining whether such a gap existed was through overhead reconnaissance, but the US did not possess an aircraft capable of covertly penetrating Soviet air defenses.

In November 1954, Edwin Land, president of Polaroid Corporation and a member of President Dwight Eisenhower's Technological Capabilities Panel, sent a memorandum to Central Intelligence Agency (CIA) director Allen W. Dulles advocating procurement of an airborne reconnaissance platform to be operated by the CIA with Air Force support. As it happened, Lockheed Aircraft Company was already studying a concept for what was described as essentially a jet-powered glider with a projected range of 3,000 nautical miles. To ensure survivability against Soviet surface-to-air missiles, the airplane was designed to attain altitudes above 70,000 feet. It would carry a single pilot and a camera capable of resolving objects as small as an individual person. Such a platform, Land suggested, could reveal locations of military and industrial installations, provide for a more accurate assessment of the Soviet order of battle, and allow estimates of Soviet capability to produce and deliver nuclear weapons. Land recognized that the airplane's apparent invulnerability was limited, however. "The opportunity for safe overflight may last only a few years," he wrote, "because the Russians will develop radars and interceptors or guided missile defenses for the 70,000-foot region."[22]

Subsequently, the CIA awarded Lockheed a contract to build twenty examples of their high flier under Project AQUATONE. Agency officials gave this effort the highest priority and made arrangements with the Air Force to provide logistical support for operations and training. Dulles appointed his special assistant, Richard M. "Dick" Bissell Jr., to oversee the project on behalf of the CIA, with Herbert I. Miller serving as his deputy and Col. Osmond J. "Ossie" Ritland acting as liaison between the agency and the Air Force. Ritland's official title was commander, Project Squadron (Provisional), Headquarters Command.[23] His input would ultimately determine the fate of an obscure Nevada lakebed.

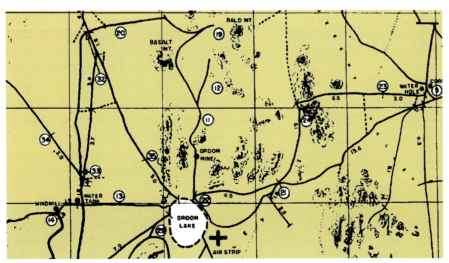

A 1951 map of soil-monitoring stations in the vicinity of Groom Lake and the Groom Mountains. These stations were used to measure radioactive fallout patterns. *DOE*

Lockheed immediately began production at the company's Advanced Development Projects (ADP) division in Burbank, California. ADP chief designer Clarence L. "Kelly" Johnson promised to have the first airplane flying within eight months of signing the contract on December 1. This was no idle boast. Lockheed ADP, better known as the Skunk Works, had previously demonstrated rapid-prototyping capabilities while developing the P-80 and F-104 jet fighters. Johnson selected Anthony W. "Tony" LeVier, who previously served as lead test pilot for the supersonic F-104, to fly the new subsonic reconnaissance plane that eventually came to be known as the U-2. The single-engine aircraft featured a narrow aluminum fuselage and long, slender wings. In order for it to reach the upper stratosphere, Johnson designed the U-2 with the lightest possible structure necessary for minimal airframe strength and low-structural-load factors. It resembled a jet-powered sailplane. LeVier later recalled how he felt upon learning the details of his new assignment. "I switched from flying the plane with the shortest wings in the world to the one with the longest."[24]

Johnson assembled a team of skilled designers and manufacturing personnel, pulling workers from other Lockheed projects without being able to tell their former supervisors why. The production team initially toiled forty-five hours per week, and after the staff grew to more than eighty people, work increased to sixty-five hours per week. Every morning, Johnson met with each member of his team to discuss problems from the previous day and take corrective action. Johnson's U-2 design was a model of simplicity and innovation. The airframe was constructed primarily of aluminum alloys machined to the thinnest gauges allowable within structural strength requirements. Skin thickness varied from just 0.020 to 0.063 of an inch. Structural stiffening consisted of the fewest possible ribs, stringers, and doubler plates. All skin panels were flush-riveted to reduce drag, and the control surfaces aerodynamically balanced with virtually no gaps at any of the hinge points. To further reduce weight, the hydraulic system was simplified and none of the primary flight controls were hydromechanically boosted. Approximately 87 percent of each airframe was fabricated within a single building in Burbank that offered the requisite security but was not fully equipped for all contingencies. Sometimes metal components had to be fed through the company's main presses at night or on Sundays, then hidden from day-shift workers not cleared into the program. Work progressed gradually at the outset, then more rapidly as the first airframe took shape.[25]

All that remained was to find a secure location for testing the new airplane and for training pilots to fly it. The first phase of this task fell to LeVier and Skunk Works foreman and logistics specialist Dorsey G.

Kelly Johnson. *Lockheed*

Tony Levier. *Lockheed*

Kammerer. Johnson explained to them that neither the CIA nor the Air Force wished to test the U-2 at any of the usual locations. Lockheed had a facility at Air Force Plant 42 in Palmdale, about an hour's drive north of Burbank, and the Air Force Flight Test Center (AFFTC) was located nearby at Edwards Air Force Base, but neither offered the requisite security.

In order to find a more remote location, the two men—posing as hunters—surveyed the desert regions of California, Arizona, and Nevada in the company's Beech Twin Bonanza. Between January and March 1955, they examined nineteen candidate sites north and east of the Los Angeles area, focusing primarily on valleys with dry lakebeds (similar to those at Edwards) that could be used as contingency airfields adjacent to a planned paved airstrip. Lockheed prepared a study for the CIA outlining requirements for fuel supplies, ground service equipment, electrical power generators, and other materiel necessary for setting up the flight test facility. This proposal called for construction of two hangars capable of housing one airplane apiece, plus barracks for fifty people and a chow hall.[26] When Bissell and Lt. Gen. Donald Putt, Air Force deputy chief of staff for development, visited the Skunk Works to view the U-2 mockup, Johnson showed them a map of potential locations for the remote test base. He dubbed his first choice "Site I."[27]

Dorsey Kammerer. *Lockheed*

CHAPTER 1
THE ANGEL FROM PARADISE RANCH

A Lockheed-owned Beech Twin Bonanza, similar to this one, was used by company and government officials to scout for potential test site locations. *Beechcraft*

April 1955. Tony LeVier squinted through aviator sunglasses at the blinding-white expanse of clay as he circled above Groom Dry Lake in a red-and-white twin-engine Beech Bonanza. His boss, Kelly Johnson, sat in the right seat. With his blunt nose and dark hair—now iron gray at the temples—slicked back over his domed forehead, Johnson looked more like an aging boxer than one of the world's foremost aeronautical engineers. "It would be a lot easier at the other site, Ossie," he shouted over the drone of the propellers, "and I don't like the idea of working next door to those A-bombs!" Col. Ritland, military bearing obvious despite his civilian attire, gave a short, barking laugh. "Yeah, but this is much better from a security standpoint. We can hide our operation behind the AEC restrictions." Seth Woodruff, the local AEC site manager, nodded emphatically. Dick Bissell, his lanky frame wedged uncomfortably into the rear seat next to Herb Miller, peered at the desolate landscape through horn-rimmed spectacles and said nothing. Not for the first time he fervently wished they would soon land, so he could stretch his legs. LeVier made a low pass over the abandoned Army airstrip and, seeing that it was now rough and overgrown, decided instead to land on the lakebed. He shut the engines down as the plane rolled to a stop near the southern shoreline, and the four men stepped into a profound desert silence punctuated only by the tinkling of tarnished brass shell casings beneath their feet. Johnson pointed toward the southwest. "We'll put it right here," he declared. "That's the hangar."

When the CIA drew up the original U-2 contract, it was assumed that Lockheed would undertake testing of the first three or four airframes at a secure, temporary location, after which the company would deliver production articles directly to the agency at an as-yet-unspecified operations site. As plans progressed, Dick Bissell and Ossie Ritland concluded it might be best to build a semipermanent base where all developmental flight testing, equipment checkout, and operational pilot training could be carried out with the greatest possible secrecy. Requirements for the remote site included space for a 5,000-foot landing strip suitable for all-weather operations in an easily secured location out of public view, preferably on government-owned land to facilitate access and eliminate the need for negotiations with local authorities. Living conditions needed to be bearable, though heat and dust were to be expected virtually anywhere within the region under consideration. It was also necessary to avoid placing the site in proximity to the national Air Defense Identification Zone, so as to avoid inadvertently exposing the U-2 to radar surveillance during test flights.[1]

Having thoroughly winnowed the list of potential locations, Kelly Johnson favored a site on the California-Nevada state line east of Death Valley. Estimated costs for construction were only $200,000 to $225,000 for a temporary camp and airstrip. Even when Bissell asked him to design a more permanent facility, about three times the size of his original plan, the projected cost came in under $450,000.[2] Still, the issue of security remained nettlesome. After reviewing Johnson's proposal, Gilbert C. Greenway of the CIA expressed concerns that Site I—located well outside any existing government reservations—was too close to populated areas, where the airplane would be subject to exposure. It was Ritland who came up with a solution. He recalled "a little X-shaped field" near Groom Lake, northeast of Yucca Flat, that he had flown over numerous times while commanding the 4925th Test Group (Atomic) during Operation Ranger. "The location of the field [for the U-2 project] was my selection," Ritland later recalled, "because I was aware of this desolate area where we were dropping atomic weapons, and we were looking for the most isolated part of the United States of America where you could fly this airplane and not cause a lot of curiosity."[3]

On April 6, 1955, Bissell and Miller briefed AEC chairman Lewis Strauss on AQUATONE and secured his concurrence for the use of Groom Lake and its environs as a base of operations. Strauss was more than amenable to the idea and promised the full support of the AEC, including assistance with any cover story necessary to shield the project's true purpose and sponsorship. After going to great effort to design the Site I airfield, Johnson wasn't overly enthusiastic when Bissell told him the site had been rejected. Nevertheless, Johnson agreed to check out the new location, which had been designated Site II. A week later, on April 13, Tony Levier flew Johnson, Bissell, Miller, and Ritland to Nevada in the Twin Bonanza. After picking up Seth R. Woodruff Jr., manager of the AEC Las Vegas Field Office, they headed to Groom Lake and made a low pass over the old auxiliary airstrip. As Ritland later described, "It was a stretched-out thing in the sand, which over the years had got hummocks and sagebrush that wouldn't quit," but the lakebed was a different story. "Man alive, we looked at that lake and we all looked at each other; it was another Edwards."[4]

It was instantly obvious that this was an ideal location for the test site, offering both excellent flying weather and unparalleled remoteness. After landing, Johnson chose a spot just off the southwest corner of the lakebed where they could later construct a few hangars and a 5,000-foot asphalt runway. As an added bonus, the lakebed itself provided an alternative surface for takeoff and landing. Bissell later described the hard-packed playa as "a perfect natural landing field . . . as smooth as a billiard table without anything being done to it."[5] It was, however, littered with shell casings and debris from years of Air Force gunnery practice, which had to be painstakingly removed before flight operations began. Using a Geiger counter, they checked radiation levels, which appeared to pose no hazard. Johnson noted in his diary, "Site was a dandy, but will take much red tape to get cleared."[6]

Upon returning to Washington, Bissell recommended that President Eisenhower approve adding the lakebed and its surroundings to the AEC proving ground. "The [Atomic Energy] Commission's work was already highly classified, and enlarging the site would be the easiest way to prohibit overflights of the new U-2 base without arousing attention from outsiders," he wrote in his memoirs.[7] By the following

Dick Bissell, *left*, and Ossie Ritland. Bissell oversaw the AQUATONE project for the CIA, while Ritland served as liaison between the agency and the Air Force. It was Ritland who recommended Groom Lake as a testing site for the U-2. *NRO*

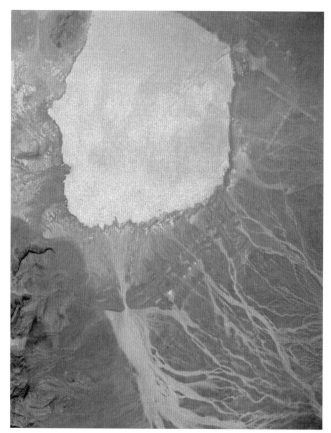

An aerial view of Groom Lake taken in 1952. Three years later, the U-2 test base would be built just off the southwest corner of the lakebed. An auxiliary airstrip, used during World War II gunnery training, is visible east of the lakeshore. *USGS*

Monday, he managed to obtain estimates from the Silas Mason Company, which held the architectural engineering contract for the NTS, and Reynolds Electrical and Engineering Company (REECo). These firms offered to build the specified facility at a cost of $600,000, which was significantly higher than a proposal submitted by a California-based contractor Johnson recommended.

After consideration of REECo's longtime experience at the atomic proving ground, the ready availability of a local workforce with NTS clearances, and the advantages inherent in AEC supervision of the contract, CIA officials concluded that the REECo proposal was more realistic and would be more economical in the long run. It was also more advantageous from a security standpoint. Federal Services, Inc. (FSI), the same contractor that already patrolled the proving ground, would provide most of the permanent security personnel for AQUATONE. Supplies destined for Groom Lake could be routed into the area through regular AEC channels. For all intents and purposes, the new facility would appear to be simply another part of the atomic-testing infrastructure.[8]

Ritland went to see Col. Vincent G. Huston, deputy director of the AEC Division of Military Applications (DMA), to see how they could get control of the land, which was still under Air Force jurisdiction. On Huston's recommendation, Ritland drafted three memos, one each to the AEC, Air Force Headquarters, and the Air Force Training Command that administered the gunnery range. Signed by Trevor Gardner, special assistant to the secretary of the Air Force for research and development, these documents guaranteed that military training activities would not impinge on the U-2 test site.[9]

Birth of a Secret Base

On April 26, Herb Miller sent a memo to all the various AQUATONE project contractors and suppliers, advising them of the site selection and suggesting actions in regard to their preparations for supporting the project's test and training phases. "The test site base has been tentatively located at Groom Lake, Nevada," he informed them, adding that the AEC was planning to extend the boundaries of the atomic proving ground to encompass the lakebed and its surroundings. "Physical security of this site probably cannot be equaled," he noted, "but the fact that it is so remote raises a number of problems which must be settled well in advance in order to properly plan the base." Contractors were advised to submit their requirements as soon as possible because construction was scheduled to be complete, with all necessary equipment installed, by July 1, 1955, and it would be extremely difficult to make any major alterations to the site plan after that date. Allen Dulles wrote to AEC chairman Strauss to formalize the interagency agreement through which the commission would provide any required support through existing contracts with reimbursement by the CIA in accordance with Section 686, Title 31, US Code, under appropriate security safeguards. The agency allocated $650,000 to cover initial construction work.[10]

Kelly Johnson wasn't happy about the idea of conducting a flight test program adjacent to an active nuclear test site, especially since Groom Lake lay directly in the predominant downwind path of radioactive fallout from aboveground shots. Of more immediate concern, however, were the ever-increasing construction costs resulting from the decision to build at the new location. His final estimate for completion of all necessary facilities eventually came to $832,000, almost double what it would have cost to build the same installation at Site I. During the last week of April, he met with CIA officials in Washington, DC, to discuss progress on the base and coordination of logistical issues. Writing in his diary afterward, Johnson noted, "Base location has been decided as Site II, for which they will accept my proposed name of 'Paradise Ranch,'" an ironic choice that he later admitted was "kind of a dirty trick" to lure workers to the program.[11] Soon thereafter, AQUATONE project security officer William H.

Marr Jr. assigned the test site the unclassified nickname SADDLE SOAP, but it never caught on. The Lockheed group had already shortened Johnson's unofficial moniker to "the Ranch," a nickname that soon came into general usage among project staff, Air Force personnel, and support contractors involved in activities at the secret site.[12]

On May 4, 1955, LeVier flew Johnson and Kammerer to Las Vegas for a meeting with Herb Miller and Al Donnell of the CIA, Seth Woodruff, and engineers from the Silas Mason Company. Johnson later noted in his diary that the CIA would now take over responsibility for the base, "except as it affects our particular operation." Miller was assigned responsibility for overseeing construction of the airfield.

Shortly after completion in the summer of 1955, three hangars stood ready to accept the initial batch of U-2 aircraft. The fleet of utility vehicles at left was provided by the AEC. Note the Air Force fire truck parked to the right of the second hangar. *Via Bob Murphy*

According to Johnson, he stated strongly that "the base's primary purpose is for us to test airplanes and 'by gosh' he would see that it ended up that way." Johnson provided Silas Mason representatives with the results of a three-month study on requirements for roads, hangars, offices, and living accommodations. After the meeting, they returned to Groom Lake to break ground for the new test site and realign the proposed runway in keeping with the best available information on prevailing winds. Using a compass and surveying equipment, the three men plotted the outlines of a mile-long airstrip, as well as the general boundaries of the camp area. By placing the north end of the airstrip at the shoreline, it was possible for the lakebed itself to serve as a 3-mile extension for emergency and auxiliary use. Returning to Burbank through restricted airspace above the atomic proving ground, they flew directly over a 500-foot steel tower on which the Apple-2 nuclear device was set to detonate early the next morning, with an estimated yield of 29 kilotons.[13]

For operational purposes, the lakebed was to serve as the primary airfield. The 5,000-foot-long, 100-foot-wide paved airstrip was to be used mainly during the winter months, when the lake was flooded. Designing the runway for relatively moderate usage minimized both specification requirements and construction costs. After grading, construction crews poured a 3-inch layer of cold-mix asphalt over a 4-inch subbase of bank-run gravel, the least expensive compactible fill available. Once fully cured, the paved surface was rated for an 8,000-pound wheel load and 150-pound tire pressure. By the time U-2 airframes started rolling off the assembly line, however, the airplane, with its small wheelbase, sported a much more highly concentrated 10,000-pound load and 250-pound tire pressure. Fortunately, this never created any difficulties.[14]

Groom Lake was still technically part of the Las Vegas Bombing and Gunnery Range, but the AEC was granted a right-of-entry on May 6 and relieved the Air Force of all responsibility for cleansing the area of unexploded or expended ordnance.[15] As agreed, Silas Mason was responsible for drafting detailed plans for the airstrip, but REECo performed the actual field construction. This was no small undertaking. In addition to the runway, the base engineering plan now called for three hangars, a maintenance building, a mess hall, a dispensary and operations building, a wash house, three barracks, and a water tower. The CIA purchased fifteen three-room mobile-home trailers for use as personnel accommodations. Plans for additional infrastructure included access roads, sewage-treatment facilities, and drainage channels. When it became clear to all concerned that it would be impossible to conceal this much activity, CIA officials worked with the AEC to craft a plausible cover story. In a memo to AEC general manager Kenneth E. Fields, public relations chief Richard G. Elliott of the AEC Joint Office of Test Information in Las Vegas stated, "We have primary concurrence in immediate release to local Nevada press of announcement of Groom Lake installation." An early draft included a false claim that the airfield was to be used for continuing research related to the 1955 atomic test series, but officials later removed this assertion, along with the name of the lakebed, prior to releasing the final draft to media outlets throughout Nevada and Utah.[16]

On May 18, the AEC distributed the revised press release to a dozen newspapers as well as four radio stations and two television news broadcasters. The release included a statement by Seth Woodruff announcing he had instructed REECo "to begin preliminary work on a small, satellite Nevada Test Site installation." He noted that work was already underway at the location "a few miles northeast of Yucca Flat and within the Las Vegas Bombing and Gunnery Range." Woodruff said these facilities would include "a runway, dormitories, and a few other buildings for housing equipment," and described the facility as "essentially temporary."[17] This last detail was true since, at the time, officials at both the CIA and Lockheed saw no need to continue using the airstrip beyond completion of the U-2 test and training phases.

The innocuous AEC statement was intended to draw as little media attention as possible while curtailing any speculation as to the purpose of the new airstrip. In this respect, it was somewhat of a failure. Rather than simply printing the statement as written, Las Vegas reporters queried "other sources" that revealed that the new test site was to be located at Groom Lake, a detail Woodruff omitted. Additional "reliable sources" indicated that sufficient dormitory space was being built to accommodate as many as seventy-five to one hundred workers. The morning after the statement's release, the *Las Vegas Review-Journal* splashed the story across the front page beneath a headline that read "Secrecy Cloaks Satellite Test Site Near Yucca," along with speculation that it would be used for experiments of a nonnuclear nature.[18] This ultimately cemented Groom Lake's reputation in the public consciousness as a secret and mysterious place.

The following week, Miller, Ritland, and Donnell met with Dorsey Kammerer to review progress on the base. Dick Bissell had the agency's Real Estate and Construction Division assign an engineer to oversee the project and work directly with the AEC/REECo construction group. Bissell sent a letter to Kenneth Fields on June 2 requesting that the AEC arrange through REECo to provide general housekeeping and maintenance services at the Ranch on a reimbursable basis, and asked for a cost proposal in writing. After two months of negotiations, Bissell and DMA director Col. Alfred D. Starbird signed a Memorandum of Understanding dated August 14, 1955, that established in detail the roles and responsibilities of both agencies with regard to what the CIA had inexplicably dubbed the "Watertown Project."[190]

Plans called for the base to generate its own electrical power using alternating current, with a power plant consisting of three 100-kilowatt diesel generators. Any need for direct current would require special equipment. Air-conditioning would be provided for the barracks and mess hall, but not for the working spaces. Minimal effort would be applied to controlling dust, and only in the immediate camp area. The July 1 forecast for completion of essential facilities slipped several weeks, but the base had begun to take shape by the middle of the month, and REECo officials anticipated completion of essential facilities prior to delivery of the first U-2 on July 25. Obtaining sufficient water supplies was the remaining obstacle. Workers managed to open an old well that was soon delivering 15 gallons per minute, which was considered adequate only for the first month of operations.

Crews started drilling a second well, but progress was so slow that additional water had to be trucked nearly 50 miles from the NTS base camp at Mercury, which itself was located about 75 miles northwest of Las Vegas. Because of the overriding importance of establishing a local water supply, Bissell eventually authorized noncleared drilling crews to continue working throughout the summer, after deliveries of the secret airplane began, but only at night or when the U-2 was inside a hangar. In late September, failure of the pump in the first well left the base without a water supply except for that hauled from Mercury, until a new pump could be installed. Fortunately, the second well was completed quickly and by October 26 was pumping about

A water tower looms over a warehouse and rows of housing trailers that provided accommodations for more than a hundred workers. *CIA*

Each of the 30-foot-long mobile homes housed three people. Boxy air conditioners kept the trailers cool in summertime, and stoves provided heat in winter. Tanker trucks for gasoline and aviation fuel are visible in the background, along with more than half a dozen civilian automobiles. *CIA*

17 gallons per minute. At that rate, estimates indicated, local water resources would likely support a population of two hundred workers at 200 gallons per person per day, using 20,000 gallons stored in the elevated water tank.[20]

To provide secure communications, the CIA connected the Ranch to the agency's HBJAYWALK secure teletype network, assigning the desert base the innocuous and unimaginative cable address KWCABLE, sometimes shortened to simply CABLE. Similarly, the cable address for Project Headquarters in Washington was DYADIC, or ADIC in its shortened form. Additional communications links connected these sites to Lockheed, Pratt & Whitney, and other supporting contractors and agencies. This dedicated network provided for rapid message handling, special security requirements limiting access to message traffic, and flexibility for setting up and controlling short-term circuitry, and allowed Project Headquarters to closely control and monitor all AQUATONE field activities.

The communications station at the Ranch consisted of two trailers containing equipment to support either continuous-wave (Morse code) or radio-teletype circuits, as necessary. Communications specialists monitored signals on a continuous basis, watching for priority and after-hours traffic. Additionally, a VHF radio connected the Ranch with an AEC station at Mercury, which served as a communications relay point. The meteorological unit supporting U-2 operations was based at Mercury as well and had four teletype circuits and one facsimile (FAX) channel for providing up-to-date weather information. On July 21, 1955, Project Headquarters received its first teletype from the Ranch, declaring, "Operations proceeding according to plan," and confirming that delivery of the first U-2 remained on schedule. Within the span of several weeks, cable traffic between the Ranch and Headquarters had reached eight thousand word groups (message components) per week and, by the end of the year, had jumped to thirty-two thousand. A shortage of qualified personnel at the test site made it necessary for teletype operators assigned there to work many hours of overtime.[21]

All U-2 developmental testing was to be undertaken by Lockheed personnel, while the Air Force had responsibility for training operational pilots. The first trainees would consist of several CIA pilot groups, designated Detachments A, B, and C, that would undergo training in series, rather than concurrently. While contemplating a proposed organizational structure for the U-2 test and training phases, Bissell initially anticipated that operational functions at the Ranch would be managed by the commanding officer of whichever detachment was currently training there, and that a civilian in charge of the facility and designated as base commander would concern himself primarily with administrative and support duties.

In June 1955, Bissell accepted a recommendation from the agency's personnel director to appoint Richard D. Newton to serve as resident base manager at the test site. A veteran aviator, Newton had piloted A-26 bombers in the South Pacific during World War II, for which he received numerous honors. After the war, he earned civilian single-engine, multiengine, and commercial pilot ratings and retained the rank of major in the Marine Corps Reserve. Before joining the CIA in 1950, he had a diverse career as a restaurant manager, machinist, insurance salesman, and engineer and worked briefly for an oil company. After reporting to the Ranch with a small cadre of assistants, he worked closely with the agency engineer, REECo, and AEC to make billeting and messing arrangements for incoming personnel, develop bookkeeping procedures for day-to-day operations and maintenance, and bring the installation into a general state of readiness.[22]

View from the water tower with an eighteen-room dormitory and the headquarters building at left. Small buildings at right include security offices and laundry facilities. The runway is visible in the background. *CIA*

An evening scene looking north from behind the headquarters building. *CIA*

Richard Newton relaxing outside his quarters during World War II. *USMC*

FSI guard makes a phone call from Watertown security Post 420. Note radio gear (*at right*) and identification badges for workers hung on the board in the background. *CIA*

Security for the Watertown Project area consisted primarily of FSI guards provided by the AEC along with an additional small force of fifteen security agents under CIA contract. The latter were recruited and trained for duty at Watertown, but with the expectation that they would later deploy overseas with the operational U-2 detachments, as needed. A school for these agents was established at the Ranch to provide training in weaponry, radio and switchboard operation, and the practical application of security methods and procedures. Bissell's secretary, Helen Kleyla, later wrote, "It was considered essential that these young men possess the flexibility to respond to crisis situations, as well as to do well the monotonous jobs required of personnel dedicated to the broad concept of security support."[23]

Primary security duties were numerous: manning two checkpoint gates, conducting roving patrols twenty-four hours a day, apprehension and interrogation of intruders, badge control and maintenance of access lists, briefing and debriefing project personnel, clearance investigations for local-hire employees, checking work areas for improper handling of classified material, coordination of safety response, and destruction of classified material that was no longer needed. Security agents were also responsible for dispatch control of passengers and cargo to and from the test site, courier and escort duties for classified documents and equipment, local implementation of cover stories, and assisting with accident response activities. Agency guards were also responsible for administration of a program to monitor local radioactivity levels through the use of personnel dosimeter badges. The AEC provided FSI guards and patrol vehicles for use in the Watertown cantonment area and maintained Post 385, a guard station at the boundary between the AQUATONE project area and the main portion of the atomic proving ground.[24]

Guards armed with Thompson submachine guns patrolled the rugged terrain surrounding Groom Lake in Willys Jeeps provided by the AEC. *NNSA/NV*

FSI guards at the test site regularly underwent small-arms proficiency training. *NNSA/NV*

After Lockheed made arrangements to acquire a C-47 transport and two T-33A jet trainers, the first test personnel began arriving at the Ranch on July 12. Tony LeVier and fellow Lockheed test pilot Robert L. "Bob" Matye spent several weeks removing rocks and other surface debris from the playa—.50-caliber casings and links, occasional live rounds, bomb fragments, and other detritus left over from when the lakebed had been used for bombing and gunnery practice—to prevent foreign object damage (FOD) during takeoffs and landings. LeVier also drew up a proposal for four 3-mile-long runways to be marked on the hard-packed clay, but Kelly Johnson initially refused to approve the $450 expense, citing a lack of funds.[25] These runways were added later, when additional money became available.

At one point, Johnson flew to Groom Lake in the C-47 to check site status. He came away concerned that the facility would not be ready in time for the first flight, but conceded that it was "an excellent job for only $800,000 in [the] time allowed. I'll bet this is one of the best Air Force bargains they've ever gotten." Meanwhile, final assembly of the U-2 prototype (cryptically designated Article 341) continued at an astounding pace. By July 15, the airframe was essentially complete and over the next several days was subjected to flutter and vibration testing. Johnson's critical eye noted thirty design elements in need of improvement, but the prototype was soon finished, partially disassembled, and readied for transport to the Ranch.[26]

Getting Started

As dawn broke over Burbank on July 24, workers began the three-hour task of loading the U-2 into an Air Force C-124. With its wings removed, Article 341 had been encased in a wooden framework and wrapped in canvas to conceal its shape from unauthorized observers. The fully laden transport had a maximum gross weight of around 216,000 pounds, so it was decided that the C-124 would be landed on the lakebed to prevent wear and tear on the newly paved runway. The lakebed's surface was deemed more than sufficient to support the transport's weight, as determined by dropping a 17.6-pound, 5-inch-diameter steel ball from a height of 6 feet and measuring the resulting imprint. As measured according to this method, a diameter of 3.25 inches or less indicated adequate load-bearing capacity, while anything larger showed the surface to be too soft. At Groom Lake, the imprint typically averaged between 2.25 and 2.63 inches at any given spot as long as the playa remained dry.[27] Unfortunately, by the time Article 341 was secure in the transport's hold, it was raining at the Ranch, so takeoff from Burbank was postponed until the following morning.

The news wasn't any better the next day, and Johnson chafed at the possibility of further delay. Having been informed that the lakebed was now unusable due to the amount of water that had soaked into the clay, he flew to Nevada via C-47 to see what could be done. After landing, he inspected the asphalt airstrip and determined it would be safe to land the C-124 on it if a substantial amount of air was first let out of the tires. Johnson then introduced

C-124 cargo plane over the Watertown runway. View is to the northwest. *CIA*

himself to base commander Richard Newton and explained what he planned to do. Newton immediately rejected the idea because the new runway had not yet been coated with Armor Seal to harden its surface. A heated argument ensued, during which Johnson threatened to call Bissell in Washington. When Newton tried to prevent him from doing so, Johnson "expressed certain dissatisfaction," after which he was finally allowed to contact Project Headquarters.

Demonstrating an apparent willingness to undermine the base commander's authority, Bissell vetoed Newton's decision and said that it was up to Johnson to determine whether the plane should come in. Two hours later, using reverse propeller pitch for braking, the C-124 landed on partially deflated tires. After the dust cleared, the disgruntled base commander noted that the runway was now indented to a depth of a ¼ inch for a distance of 50 feet from the touchdown point, and as much as ⅜ of an inch where the airplane had turned around. Newton wired Headquarters that the airplane had landed successfully "with minimum damage to the runway" despite Johnson's objection to that characterization, since he felt that there really had been no damage to speak of. All the REECo personnel and others not cleared to see the U-2 had been evacuated, and Article 341 was unloaded on schedule and taken into one of the semicompleted hangars for reassembly. Johnson later wrote, "It was real gory for a first meeting with Newton."[28]

Johnson assigned Dorsey Kammerer to oversee remaining preparations at the test site, and Francis A. "Frank" Harvey to supervise the various Lockheed personnel posted to the remote site. He selected Ernest L. "Ernie" Joiner to serve as chief of the flight test program. After Johnson briefed him on the status of the project, which had been underway for six months, Joiner realized significant challenges lay ahead. Not least among these was a challenge faced by all who worked in this secret environment, that of explaining their work to family members. "I knew we were in for a wild ride," Joiner later recalled. That evening he informed his wife, Peggy, that he had accepted a new assignment. Naturally she asked what he would be doing. "I can't tell you," he replied. She glared at him dubiously and asked, "Well, where will you be working?" He looked at her sheepishly and mumbled, "I don't know." Looking back on it some four decades later, shortly after the CIA declassified the U-2 program history, he said, "That was almost the end of a beautiful relationship."[29]

Flight test engineer Glenn C. Fulkerson served as Joiner's right-hand man. Others included structural engineer Henry G. Combs, instrumentation specialist Paul Deal, analysis engineers Mich Yoshii and Robert T. Klinger, and radio technician Jack Reedy. Tony LeVier was charged with making the initial test flights to evaluate airworthiness and handling qualities. Maintenance personnel responsible

Each partially disassembled U-2 airframe was delivered to Watertown inside the cargo hold of a C-124. *CIA*

Loadmasters supervise as trailer carrying the aft fuselage and wings of the U-2 is gently eased down the C-124 cargo ramp. *CIA*

Great care had to be taken when unloading the U-2 forward fuselage, since there were only a few inches of ground clearance. *CIA*

for Article 341 included crew chief Fritz Frye, mechanics Leroy Flynn and Robert F. "Bob" Murphy, and electrician Vernon Buckner. If special components needed to be manufactured, the test site had a metal shop staffed by Carl Herman, Bob Johnson, and "Pop" Christman. Work on the airplane was thoroughly checked by inspectors Dick Padjet and Pete Wilkerson. Frank Cruz was in charge of radio communications. Gene Cuthbert oversaw supply stock. Paul Smith did double duty as clerk and photographer. Frank Harvey and utility electrician Richard "Dick" Hough rounded out the shop personnel.[30]

Joiner and his team were surprised to find the test site still under construction when they arrived. "It was a work in progress," Joiner noted, recalling some relief at seeing that the most important building—the mess hall—was complete. The first hangar was nearly finished but lacked electrical power. "For the first few days our telephone was located outside in the bushes, but we soon had an operational office in one of the portable buildings," he said. Wildlife was an occasional problem. A bobcat took up residence beneath the office floor, and a rattlesnake was found coiled inside an airplane wheel well.[31]

Bob Murphy was struck by the test site's inhospitable character, particularly after Kelly Johnson told him it was called Paradise Ranch. During his first flight from Burbank to Groom Lake, on July 21, 1955, Murphy had no idea where he was headed but soon figured it out. "When we flew over Frenchman Flat, where they blew up the nuclear bombs, [we saw that] the wreckage of the buildings and airplanes they were testing were down there, so we knew where the hell we were then." The plane continued onward over Yucca Flat and finally circled to approach Groom Lake. He later recalled his first impression upon landing: "God almighty, talk about desolate!"[32]

In the beginning, only nineteen Lockheed people were cleared to work on the U-2 flight test project, including pilots, and not all of them were present at the same time. Consequently, shopworkers had to take on multiple responsibilities. Murphy recalled two in particular. "There was one jack-of-all-trades who ran the stock room, supply, and logistics in general, and a guy whose classification was painter but he was also the timekeeper and the aircraft dispatcher."[33]

Ernie Joiner headed Lockheed's U-2 flight test program at Watertown and served as lead flight test engineer. *Lockheed*

Bob Murphy joined the U-2 program as a flight test mechanic and was eventually promoted to flight test supervisor in charge of training operational maintenance crews and managing pilot-training support operations. *Via Chris Pocock*

The team promptly set to work reassembling the various components of the airplane, which they had taken to calling the "Angel" since it was expected to soar nearly to heaven. This process was greatly simplified by the fact that the forward fuselage was joined to the aft fuselage by just three tension bolts. Lightweight landing gear consisted of a bicycle arrangement with a double-wheel main gear and a small tailwheel, both mounted along the centerline. To maintain lateral balance during takeoff, the wingtips were equipped with midspan outriggers or pogos, small rubber wheels on the ends of curved steel legs that dropped away as soon as the plane became airborne. The long, thin wings were among the most efficient in the world. From an altitude of 70,000 feet, the U-2 could glide more than 300 miles. Skid plates on the wingtips protected the airfoils during landing.[34]

After reassembly, which took about two days, technicians prepared the prototype for its first engine run. In order to expedite flight testing, early U-2 sorties were made with a 10,500-pound-thrust Pratt & Whitney J57-P37 engine. Later in the program, this was replaced with the 11,500-pound-thrust J57-P31. Pratt & Whitney engineer Benedict J. Koziol, who played a key role in developing the J57 for the U-2, was on hand to make sure everything went smoothly, but there were initial difficulties with the airplane's special fuel. Most Air Force jets at the time were fueled with kerosene-based JP-4, but the U-2 was intended to run on LF-1A, a special low-vapor-pressure mixture of aliphatic and aromatic hydrocarbon compounds that could be used at extremely high altitudes. When at first the J57 failed to start with the special fuel, the ground crew was forced to improvise. Someone found several 5-gallon drums of conventional JP-4, linked them together, and ran a hose to a fuel valve on the J57. They got the engine running, then disconnected the hose and ran the remainder of the test by using LF-1A. Mechanics later traced the problem to the spark plugs, which were too short.[35] Once this discrepancy was corrected, the Lockheed crew was able to complete engine testing and prepare for taxi trials.

Despite its lightweight construction, the U-2 wing assembly was easily capable of supporting the weight of several men. *CIA*

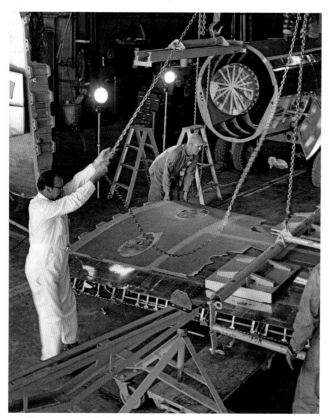

Workers reassemble the U-2 inside a hangar at Watertown. The airframe was built with a minimum number of parts for weight-reduction purposes. Each wing was attached to the fuselage by using twenty-four fasteners. The forward and aft fuselage sections were joined together using just three tension bolts. *CIA*

Two technicians prepare to install the vertical tail on the aft fuselage assembly while several others inspect the engine and exhaust duct. *CIA*

The Angel Flies

On August 1, 1955, Article 341 was towed onto the dry lakebed for initial ground trials. Tony LeVier got the engine running well on his second attempt and began a low-speed taxi run to the north with Ernie Joiner and Kelly Johnson driving along behind in a chase car. At about 45 miles per hour, the wingtips began to lift, but the pogos had been locked into place and remained attached although they were no longer touching the ground. LeVier found that he needed to apply a little rudder to keep the nose straight. He also noted that the pogo wheels trailed satisfactorily and absorbed small lateral loads very smoothly. Maximum speed was about 50 knots, just fast enough to make the ailerons slightly effective. LeVier felt that braking response was somewhat poor, but Johnson assured him the wheel brakes simply needed to be broken in. At the end of the 2-mile run, he made full 90-degree deflections of the tailwheel steering system in both directions before turning 180 degrees and coming to a stop.[36]

Joiner inspected the brakes prior to the second taxi test. This time, LeVier made his run to the south—accelerating to 70 knots in about a ¼ mile—and then pulled the throttle to idle. "It was at this point that I became aware of being airborne," he wrote in his posttest report, "which left me with utter amazement, as I had no intentions whatsoever of flying." He immediately started back toward the ground but had difficulty judging his altitude because there were no markings on the lakebed. Descending from a height of approximately 35 feet, the U-2 made contact with the ground in a 10-degree left bank, and the impact was hard enough that Article 341 bounced back into the air.[37] Fortunately, the second touchdown was gentler, allowing LeVier to regain control, but he found the brakes to be ineffective in slowing the aircraft. After rolling for some distance and finally veering to the left, the U-2 came to a halt with both main wheel tires on fire directly underneath the fuel sump tank. The chase crew promptly extinguished the blaze, which had fortunately caused little damage. A telex sent to Project Headquarters reported, "No ill effects except to Tony's ego."[38]

To prevent further delay, the brakes and tires were replaced that afternoon. An inspection revealed that there had been no significant damage from the fire, so another taxi test was scheduled for the following day. In the meantime, LeVier and Bob Murphy painted some black stripes on the surface of the dry lake immediately north of the asphalt runway to provide a visual reference. "Although this [lakebed] runway was far from adequate in regard to markings," Levier noted, "it was a big improvement."[39]

The U-2 prototype was never assigned a military serial number and was simply designated Article 341. Early in the test program, it was marked with US national insignia and tail number 001. *Lockheed*

A special towing dolly was used to move the U-2 into position on the lakebed prior to takeoff. *CIA*

With a parachute strapped to his back, Tony LeVier climbs into the cockpit of the U-2. Note that he is essentially wearing ordinary street clothes. *CIA*

The next morning, Article 341 was towed back onto the lakebed, and LeVier climbed into the cockpit. "Engine start, OK," he declared, and a few minutes later he radioed, "Rolling." To preclude a repeat of the inadvertent takeoff, he held the control yoke forward and attempted to raise the tail. At 55 knots, the rear wheel lifted off the ground, and LeVier completed a 1-mile run to evaluate directional and lateral control. The results were satisfactory, and with the tail up the airplane reached 85 knots without taking off. LeVier eased off a bit on the yoke and felt the airplane become very light, and it might well have lifted off had he not pulled the throttle to idle. He then activated gust-control spoilers, allowing the tail to settle back to the ground. As the airplane slowed to 70 knots, he applied light wheel braking with little or no effect. Approximately 3 miles down the runway, rapidly approaching the edge of the lakebed, he chopped the power and the U-2 rolled to a stop. The brakes were extremely hot and might have caught fire again if not for quick action by the chase crew.

While allowing the brakes to cool down, LeVier told Joiner he had been bothered by unsatisfactory reflections on the windscreen from some light-colored material forward of the instrument panel. He felt it might have contributed to the visibility problems he experienced during previous tests. He also noted that the cockpit was extremely hot, and recommended installing some sort of sunshade inside the canopy. After the ground crew turned the airplane around, he made a low-speed run to the south with the flaps set at 35 degrees. This time, the U-2 attained a maximum speed of 50 knots, and LeVier didn't bother with the wheel brakes, instead simply allowing the airplane to coast to a stop. Afterward, he concluded that tailwheel steering was of little use and might even be prone to inducing a ground loop. He and Kelly Johnson both agreed that the wheel brakes should not be used at speeds over 30 knots until the airplane's overall gross weight had been reduced by an appreciable degree. LeVier's final comment in the postflight debriefing was "I believe the aircraft is ready for flight."[40]

The test team spent the morning and early afternoon of August 4 preparing for the maiden flight. Johnson kept a close watch as Ernie Joiner, Glenn Fulkerson, Bob Murphy, and several others readied the airplane while LeVier reviewed his test plan. In earlier conversations with the test pilot, Johnson had insisted that the U-2 should be landed with the main gear making initial contact with the runway, followed by the tailwheel. "I disagreed," LeVier later recalled, "and told him it should be stalled in with the tailwheel touching first"; otherwise the airplane would bounce.[41] Nevertheless, he agreed to make the first attempt using Johnson's suggested method.

For the final preparations, Article 341 was towed to the north end of the lakebed and aligned with the runway. As during earlier taxi tests, the pogos were locked in place to provide balance during touchdown. There was a flurry of activity as support personnel repositioned equipment and moved out of the way. Levier—using call sign Angel 1—climbed into the cockpit and began preflight checks. Bob Matye took off in the C-47 with Johnson and Henry Combs on board as observers. Their first task was to check local weather conditions and winds aloft because a storm was moving in. Ernie Joiner (call sign Ground Hog) monitored test activities from his position on the lakebed. Apparently, no one had thought to secure the local airspace in advance of the test flight. A few minutes after the C-47 departed, an Air Force F-86 passed fairly close by overhead on its way to the gunnery ranges. Ray Goudey took off in a T-33 to serve as safety chase, and a fire truck was stationed a mile to the south, adjacent to the runway. All the months of preparation had led to this moment. LeVier reached toward the control panel and flipped a switch to initiate engine start. Nothing happened.

Taken in March 1955, this is thought to be the only surviving photograph of the original U-2 cockpit configuration. *Lockheed*

After two failed attempts to start the engine with LF-1A, Joiner decided they should refuel the airplane with JP-4 and try again. Nearly an hour was lost during this delay, and the observation and chase airplanes had to land to conserve fuel. Rain was already falling north of the lakebed, and a stiff crosswind blew in from the southwest, forcing LeVier to taxi the U-2 to a new starting point farther east than originally planned. Finally, it was time. Pushing the throttle forward, LeVier began his takeoff roll and was airborne in less than a minute. Living up to its nickname, the U-2 took to the air like a homesick angel. "The initial climb-out felt very good," he reported later, "with what appeared to be satisfactory longitudinal stability and control." He noted that the right wing felt heavy, and Johnson told him to hold the wing up to balance the fuel. As he circled the lakebed at an altitude of 5,000 feet and a speed of around 160 knots with the landing gear still down, LeVier declared, "This thing flies like a baby buggy."[42]

"Try gear-up if you want," Johnson suggested. LeVier raised the landing gear, climbed to 8,000 feet, and continued to explore the airplane's handling qualities through a variety of gentle maneuvers, including stalls. He concluded that the U-2 handled fairly well, with very mild stall characteristics. After fifteen minutes of flight, with raindrops spotting his windscreen, he descended, lowered the gear and flaps, and started his landing approach. "It wasn't difficult to realize that this was no ordinary aircraft," he said later. "With the power lever in almost idle, the wing flaps partially down and dive brakes extended, the aircraft had a very flat glide angle and a long float on flaring out."[43]

Attempting to touch the main wheels down first, while pushing forward on the control yoke to lower the nose, produced an erratic and uncontrollable porpoise maneuver. As the U-2 bounced into the air, Johnson yelled, "Go around!" LeVier added power and circled for a second attempt. He made a shallower approach this time, but the airplane just floated in ground effect approximately 10 feet above the lakebed. "Boy, for more drag," he lamented.[44] After several more approaches and go-arounds with similar results, LeVier finally achieved a two-point landing with both the main gear and tailwheel touching down simultaneously. Johnson was forced to agree that LeVier had been right. It was best to land with the tailwheel touching the ground at the same time or just ahead of the main gear. The entire flight lasted less than forty minutes. The storm broke ten minutes later, flooding the lakebed with 2 inches of water. Johnson was astonished, noting in his log that average rainfall had reportedly totaled 4.3 inches for the previous five years. "We have had almost this much in the last two weeks," he wrote. "The lakebed structure is very peculiar, because it remains hard even with water on it." That night, Johnson and his team celebrated, "with beer of all things."[45]

Article 341 descends toward Groom Lake. The unusual bicycle landing-gear configuration proved challenging for the pilot, since both the main wheels and tailwheels had to touch down simultaneously. *Lockheed*

Article 341 on the ground at Watertown as a summer cloudburst drenches Groom Lake in the background. *Lockheed*

LeVier worked to perfect his landing technique during a second flight two days later, with Bob Matye flying chase in a T-33. Rolling northward across the lakebed, the U-2 lifted off at 70 knots and immediately began to porpoise. LeVier added power and pulled up, resulting in a mild stall buffet, but this was less alarming than the porpoising. Matye thought a slight tailwind might have been a factor. After climbing to nearly 7,000 feet, LeVier began the first of several touch-and-go landings. His initial approach was long and shallow, but he cautiously aborted at the last moment. His second attempt was better. At 5 feet above the ground, he established the proper landing attitude and let the airplane settle in. Although this two-point touchdown resulted in mild porpoising, he later described it as "successful and a reasonably good landing."[46] LeVier then raised the flaps, increased power, and held the control yoke forward. The plane started porpoising again on takeoff, and he attributed this motion to low pressure in the main landing-gear shock strut. The third and final landing was about the same. Following the flight, LeVier had several recommendations with regard to adjusting the shock strut pressure and using the gust controls during takeoff to reduce porpoise motion. He also suggested that some method be devised to allow the pilot to establish a proper landing attitude that would result in a two-point touchdown every time. Finally, he recommended fitting the seat with a back cushion. "I'm still using a regular bed pillow," he fumed.[47]

Having proven the U-2's basic airworthiness and solved the difficult challenge of developing a successful landing technique, Johnson scheduled the official first flight for August 8. Representatives of the CIA and Air Force had been invited this time, along with high-ranking Lockheed executives. At dawn, they boarded Lockheed's C-47 in Burbank. These special guests included Bissell and Ritland, along with Richard Horner, who was the assistant secretary of the Air Force for research and development, and Garrison Norton, assistant to Trevor Gardner, who was unable to come. Other dignitaries included Lockheed president Robert Gross and vice president Burt Monesmith (who had seen the airplane for the first time on the assembly line just three days earlier), and Johnson's boss, chief engineer Hall Hibbard. Gen. Thomas S. Power, head of Air Research and Development Command (ARDC), flew in from Nellis Air Force Base on the outskirts of Las Vegas. A viewing area had been set up on the lakebed about a mile north of the hangars. After briefing his guests on the day's schedule, Johnson donned a parachute and climbed into the back of Matye's T-33.[48] The U-2 was readied for flight, remaining in the same configuration as during the previous tests, with the pogos locked onto the wings.

Matye and Johnson took off first, circling the lakebed while LeVier taxied into position for departure to the north. They caught up with LeVier just as the U-2 left the ground. Takeoff was smooth this time, thanks to adjustments that mechanics had made to the gear strut. LeVier made a gentle climb to the left, accelerated to 130 knots, and raised the landing gear. He brought the plane around and passed over the spectators at a moderate altitude before starting a series of planned test maneuvers. Using the T-33 as a pacer, Johnson recorded airspeed calibration data while climbing to cruise altitude, but Matye had difficulty keeping up with the U-2 even though LeVier reported that his engine was practically idling. Soon, the U-2 was nearly 1,000 feet above the T-33, and LeVier noticed his cabin pressure fluctuating wildly. After leveling off at 32,000 feet, he accelerated to 260 knots. The engine seemed to be running a bit rough, so LeVier increased power, lowered the landing gear, and extended the wing flaps. Johnson informed him that the right pogo was shaking a little, and advised terminating the speed run. "Let's get back," he added.[49]

Ford Country Sedan station wagons served as chase cars for the U-2 during takeoff and landing. An experienced pilot in one of the cars used a radio to advise the U-2 pilot with critical information such as altitude above the runway. *CIA*

A U-2 takes off from Watertown Airstrip. Special pogo wheels kept the wings level until the airplane developed sufficient lift, and then fell away as it gained altitude. *CIA*

The tailwheel failed to come down on the first attempt, and while descending at a rate of 1,500 feet per minute, LeVier took a moment to perform a stall test. "It sort of crabs around," he noted. "You can feel it." He recovered quickly and actuated the speed brakes, at which time the tailwheel finally extended. Approximately fifty minutes into the flight, Ray Goudey and Bill Bryden in the C-47 joined up with the U-2 and T-33 to provide additional observers for the landing. LeVier made a low pass for the spectators before coming around for final approach from the south. He had no difficulty setting up his approach angle, but judging the airplane's height above the lakebed remained a problem. "The lakebed *must* have the proper markings," he said afterward. "Otherwise I can foresee trouble at some later date." As touchdown seemed imminent, he activated the gust control mechanism and set power to idle, but he was still a bit high. The ailerons lost effectiveness, causing the left wing to drop suddenly. LeVier realized too late that he should have waited until touchdown to activate the spoilers. The left wingtip struck the ground fairly hard, but he maintained control and, with sparing application of the wheel brakes, managed to bring the airplane to a halt directly in front of the viewing area.[50] The VIP guests were then allowed to inspect the airplane, and Johnson declared that he had successfully achieved his self-imposed eight-month deadline.[51]

Over the next several weeks LeVier completed sixteen additional flights, exploring the airplane's stall characteristics, taking the U-2 to its maximum stress limits (positive 2.5 g and negative 1.5 g), and expanding the performance envelope. He flew the U-2 to its maximum speed of 0.85 Mach, or around 560 miles per hour (487 knots), and in preparation for cruising at altitudes never previously reached in sustained flight, the forty-two-year-old LeVier became the oldest test pilot to complete Air Force partial-pressure-suit training. He expanded the low- and medium-altitude flight envelopes and by August 16 had taken the airplane to 52,000 feet. He then left Project AQUATONE and returned to Burbank to serve as the company's director of flying.[52]

Before departing, LeVier checked out Bob Matye and Ray Goudey in the U-2, and they were soon making at least one flight nearly every day. As the pace of testing increased, test pilots Robert Sieker and Robert Schumacher joined the team to help expand the airplane's performance capabilities and test the reconnaissance systems. Goudey performed in-flight structural test maneuvers, including windup turns to a maximum acceleration of 3 g, measuring wingtip deflections by using a camera mounted atop the fuselage. Schumacher was instrumental in clearing the U-2 for maximum-altitude operations and in demonstrating early sensor systems. By September 8, the U-2 had been flown to 65,600 feet (approximately 12 miles above the earth), and on September 18 Goudey became the first to reach the airplane's design cruising altitude of 70,500 feet. Engine flameouts at high altitudes were becoming a problem, and flights were restricted to within a 200-mile radius of Groom Lake in order to ensure a safe margin for making a dead-stick (unpowered) landing, if necessary. On one occasion Kelly Johnson paid Sieker a $25,000 bonus to intentionally perform such a landing during a test flight.[53]

This still frame from a motion picture provides a close view of the U-2 as seen from a C-47 chase plane during a low-altitude test flight. *CIA*

Ray Goudey, suited up for a high-altitude test flight. *CIA*

Bob Matye performed the majority of U-2 altitude envelope expansion tests. *Lockheed*

Article 342, the second U-2, was delivered to Watertown in September, followed thereafter by the third, fourth, and fifth, at the rate of one per month. As the most thoroughly instrumented airframe, Article 341 was used primarily for airplane and engine performance tests, stability and handling evaluations, systems checkout, and structural demonstrations. This basic development program lasted seven months and encompassed eighty-three flights. Subsequent tests with this airplane were concerned mainly with engine development and miscellaneous items. Articles 342 and 344 were pressed into service for testing camera systems and other mission equipment. Article 342 made twenty-two test flights before being released to the CIA for pilot training. Article 343, first flown on October 27, 1955, served as a dedicated training aircraft. Most of the camera tests were accomplished with Article 344, which was also used for autopilot development and weather research missions. This airplane made eighty-five flights before being released to the training program.[54] At one point, Article 341 received a coat of paint to determine whether a smoother external surface would reduce drag and improve performance. Before and after, this airplane was paced against Article 342, which remained bare of paint or any external markings save its tail number. The results showed only a small performance improvement for the painted airframe, a true airspeed increase of 4 knots at 45,000 feet and just 1 knot at 60,000 feet. Articles 341 and 344 were also flown in loose formation at cruise altitude for two and a half hours, with only a 12-gallon difference in the amount of fuel consumed by the end of the test. Lockheed engineers later calculated this would amount to a savings of just 45 gallons for the painted airplane in the course of an operational mission. They concluded that this trifling advantage did not justify the expense of applying and maintaining the paint scheme, or the attendant weight penalty.[55]

Watertown Airstrip as seen from the Papoose Mountains. Aircraft on the flight line include nine U-2 aircraft, four T-33A jet trainers, one L-20A, and Lockheed's Beech Twin Bonanza. *CIA*

Al Boyd, ARDC deputy commander for systems, sought to acquire several U-2 aircraft for use in high-altitude test projects to be undertaken at Edwards Air Force Base. *USAF*

Pete Everest, chief of flight test operations at Edwards, flew several flights in the U-2 at Watertown. He wrote a detailed evaluation of the airplane and provided a copy to Kelly Johnson. *USAF*

Considering the secrecy surrounding the AQUATONE project, Watertown received a surprising number of visitors. Trevor Gardner arrived on September 19 with the ARDC deputy commander for systems, Maj. Gen. Albert Boyd, and AFFTC technical director Paul F. Bikle. An aerodynamicist and soaring enthusiast, Bikle was impressed by the design of the high-flying U-2, which boasted a lift-to-drag ratio of 25.6:1, better than many competition sailplanes. Several days later, Dick Bissell brought in eighteen more visitors. The airfield then experienced a brief respite from flight operations while the main runway was repaved and the U-2 underwent major modifications.

Boyd returned a few months later, this time bringing renowned test pilot Lt. Col. Frank K. "Pete" Everest Jr., chief of the AFFTC Flight Test Operations Division. On November 8 and 9, the two men took turns flying the U-2 to evaluate the airplane for ARDC, which was scheduled to eventually receive three of the aircraft for use in a variety of high-altitude research projects. The first sortie, in Article 343, was for the purpose of evaluating low-speed handling characteristics at altitudes below 45,000 feet and included several touch-and-go landings. During the next two flights, the same airplane attained higher speeds (up to 260 knots / 0.8 Mach) and a maximum altitude of 70,300 feet. The final sortie was performed in Article 341, which had been painted by then and also had modifications to its vertical stabilizer and fuel controls. During this flight, Everest noted thrust decay at 66,000 feet and aborted further attempts to climb higher. Additionally, he experienced a sudden high-frequency rudder buffet at 0.82 Mach that had not previously been encountered. Following their orientation flights, both pilots professed mostly favorable impressions, although Everest complained of great difficulty landing the airplane. "The approach and landing of this airplane is the most difficult maneuver of any to perform," he later reported. He provided a detailed evaluation to Kelly Johnson, who subsequently took corrective actions wherever feasible.[56]

Chains of Command

The skies above Groom Lake were placed under restriction for the first time by Executive Order 10633, signed into law by President Eisenhower on August 19, 1955, to establish "an airspace reservation over the Las Vegas Project."[57] On September 2, the Air Force chief of staff, Gen. Nathan F. Twining, sent a letter to the AEC establishing "Watertown Airstrip (Unclassified) as a USAF installation assigned for classified functions," emphasizing that its use by any party or agency required prior Air Force approval. A copy of this letter was distributed to the Civil Aeronautics Administration.[58]

Meanwhile, administrative actions necessary to establish base boundaries continued. In September 1955, the Air Force special assistant for installations, John M. Ferry, informed the director of the Bureau of Land Management (BLM) that the AEC had "an urgent requirement for the extension of the Nevada Test Site, which is used in connection with continuing experimental sampling projects." Ferry announced that the Air Force no longer required the 60-square-mile tract of land surrounding Groom Lake as a bombing and gunnery range, and it was forthwith returned to the Department of the Interior. Subsequently, AEC officials submitted a formal request to add the 6-by-10-mile parcel to the Nevada Test Site.[59] As of yet, this block of land had no numerical designation like other test areas on the NTS.

On September 7, 1955, the commander of the 1007th Air Intelligence Service Group, Headquarters Command, USAF, issued General Order No. 1, establishing Project Squadron (Provisional) with subordinate detachments designated Flights A, B, C, and D. The cryptic directive indicated only that this squadron was being activated for the purpose of "providing an organizational structure, operating units, and command channels for the USAF elements of a classified project." The first three detachments were to be activated at the Groom Lake training base prior to overseas deployment in order to cut the direct line between the field organizations and their headquarters components, thus establishing each subordinate unit as a completely separate and self-sufficient entity under the immediate control of its commanding officer. These organizations also served as the original CIA cover units to which Air Force personnel were assigned when selected to staff domestic and overseas field detachments of Project AQUATONE. Under this construct, the Watertown Airstrip staff complement was designated Flight D. This was later renamed Detachment D, Weather Reconnaissance Squadron (Provisional), so as to conform with a cover story that the U-2 was designed for use in meteorological research supported by the Air Force Air Weather Service (AWS).[60]

U-2 pilot deploys a drag chute to slow his landing on the Watertown runway. *CIA*

Gen. Curtis LeMay, chief of Strategic Air Command (SAC), initially showed little interest in the U-2 because it was unarmed, but Gen. Twining felt that the Air Force needed to take a decisive role in the use of such a unique asset for strategic reconnaissance. He therefore ordered twenty-nine more U-2 aircraft be built for the Air Force as a follow-on to the original CIA purchase. These were to be produced under the designation R-17, though the service later decided to stick with the original U-2 designation. Of these, twenty were to be configured as SAC reconnaissance platforms, six would be equipped to collect atmospheric particulate samples for the AFSWP, and three would be used for ARDC test programs. The Air Force U-2 program was assigned the unclassified nickname DRAGON LADY.[61]

Twining eventually signed an agreement with Allen Dulles outlining SAC responsibilities with regard to the U-2 operation, which were to be undertaken as Project OILSTONE. A significant element of this agreement involved the use of SAC instructor pilots to provide training both for CIA and Air Force U-2 pilots. This posed some organizational questions, and by mid-September 1955 Dick Bissell was deeply engaged in discussions with the newly appointed SAC liaison officer, Col. Loran D. Briggs, regarding the chain of command at Watertown. Up to this point, the civilian base commander had been responsible only for administrative and support functions. Bissell expected successive detachment commanders to take responsibility for operations during their training periods, prior to deployment overseas. Briggs disagreed, pointing out, "The officer charged with operational responsibilities should have continuity of tenure at the base, and the detachment commander should not be burdened with operational duties." He suggested instead placing those duties in the hands of the commander of the local SAC training cadre. After due consideration, Bissell decided that the best course of action would be to designate an independent base commander—an Air Force officer—competent to discharge all necessary operational and administrative responsibilities. The current acting commander, Richard Newton, would be reassigned as deputy commander, retaining responsibility for performance of support functions at the base.[62]

Unfortunately, the nominee for permanent base commander was not immediately available, and so it fell to the Detachment A commanding officer, Col. Frederic E. McCoy, to assume that position on a temporary basis. A veteran both of World War II and Korea, McCoy earned his wings with the Army Air Corps in 1940. As a P-38 pilot, he served in the Aleutian Islands immediately after the Pearl Harbor attack and was credited with downing one Japanese aircraft. Later in the war, he conducted reconnaissance flights over New

After disembarking from a C-54 transport at Watertown Airstrip, passengers collect their luggage and prepare to check in with security personnel. *CIA*

Guinea, where he earned a Distinguished Flying Cross for accomplishing the first reconnaissance flight prior to the US invasion of the Philippines. McCoy also participated in the postwar occupation of Germany and flew in the Berlin Airlift. In 1950, he commanded a squadron that specialized in nighttime reconnaissance over North Korea. He was selected for AQUATONE following a staff assignment at the Pentagon.[63]

Upon reporting to Project Headquarters in September 1955, McCoy was hastily briefed before being dispatched to Nevada. As luck would have it, he was immediately thrust into a command position over an extremely heterogeneous organization, without sufficient time to absorb the flavor of the project and fully understand the philosophy behind its joint military/civilian nature. In addition, he had to build his own detachment from scratch and prepare that unit for operational deployment. This, in fact, was his primary concern, and it proved more difficult than expected. Shortly after arriving at the test site on October 1, McCoy clashed with Newton on how the base should be run. This situation spiraled rapidly out of control, to the point where Project Headquarters was constantly being called upon to intervene and to make decisions that should have been quickly and amicably resolved at the local level. Less than two weeks after McCoy's arrival, Bissell was compelled to draft a memo clearly defining the organizational structure and lines of command at Watertown.[64]

Bissell specified that the base commander would be ultimately responsible for management of Watertown Airstrip, control of all air operations at the base, liaison for operational matters with other Air Force installations, and supporting other components sharing use of the Watertown facility. The commander would represent and report directly to Project Headquarters for the coordination of all activities on the base and would monitor test and training activities. Detachment commanders would be responsible for the organization, buildup, and administration of their respective detachments while under the supervision of the project director. The commander of the SAC Training Mission would report directly to SAC Headquarters and would provide specialized guidance to each detachment commander in matters of training. Representatives of Lockheed and other suppliers would be responsible for their own test programs and equipment, with coordination from the base commander. In order to minimize the number of personnel stationed at Watertown, those assigned to the detachment in training would also serve as base staff to the greatest extent possible on an additional-duty basis. Subject to the direction of the base commander, the deputy commander would be responsible for management of base facilities and other support functions.[65]

McCoy balked at continuing to work with Newton and expressed a strong desire to replace the civilian executive with an Air Force officer. If this was not possible, he was willing to have another agency administrative support officer designated deputy commander, if necessary, to maintain agency control and liaison with Project Headquarters. In an attempt to apply pressure, McCoy advised Bissell that unless headquarters took immediate action to fill key positions, Detachment A would likely not deploy on schedule, with consequent adverse effects on the entire program. Bissell's director of administration did not concur with McCoy's suggested change in the command structure. He told Bissell, "If both the Detachment CO and the deputy are of the same cloth, be it CIA or Air Force, you do not obtain that counterbalance and relative objectivity that initially seemed desirable." Bissell agreed and worked toward replacing McCoy as base commander by the end of the year.[66]

Living in Paradise

For official purposes, civil service and military personnel assigned to AQUATONE were given permanent change-of-station (PCS) orders to Los Angeles, where their families were settled, and temporary-duty (TDY) orders to the test site. Those personnel assigned to Watertown for training prior to overseas deployment were given PCS orders to Washington, DC, and TDY orders to Detachment D. In an effort to equalize per diem rates among all categories of personnel, any employee reporting to the test site on or after January 1, 1956, would receive $12.00 a day for the first thirty days and $10.00 a day thereafter. During a visit to Watertown in February, Robert M. Macy of the Bureau of Budget questioned this policy, because individuals were paying only $4.25 for room and board at the base. Project officials eventually convinced Macy of the legitimate need for this policy.[67]

Upon arriving at their assigned station, new personnel often found life at Paradise Ranch to be a paradoxical juxtaposition of restrictions and freedoms. Security was extremely tight, perhaps more so than that of the Manhattan Project during World War II. Workers had to show identification before boarding their commuter flights from Burbank or Las Vegas. Upon arrival at Watertown Airstrip, they lined up to have their identification checked again by a stern-faced security guard, who then issued a "Special Access" badge that was to be turned in upon departure. This procedure ensured that only authorized personnel were admitted to restricted areas and that the identity of all visitors to the remote site was duly recorded. Coded language was used in all radio and teletype communications: pilots were called "drivers," the U-2 was known simply as "the article," and Groom Lake was referred to as either "Home Plate" or "Station D." All the U-2 pilots under contract to the CIA traveled under false names. For example, Francis G. "Frank" Powers was known to his new associates as Frank Palmer, and James G. "Jim" Abraham introduced himself as Jim Allison. The FSI guards, armed with Thompson submachine guns, patrolled the base and the surrounding area at all hours in Willys Jeeps or manned the ubiquitous guard posts and checkpoints.

In later years, Robert Schumacher recalled being very impressed with the secret base. "It was in the middle of nowhere," he said. "They had a couple of small dormitories but the pilots were in a trailer, and there was an eating area with a couple of pool tables at the far end for the evenings. There was one road going in, but we were not supposed to use it." Like most of his colleagues, he found separation from his family especially onerous. "Working away from

Arriving personnel had to check in with security and pick up a special access badge that was to be turned in upon departure. This procedure ensured that only authorized personnel gained entry to restricted areas and that the identity of all visitors was duly recorded. *CIA*

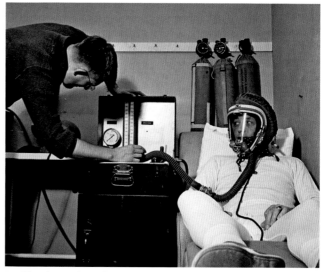

Lockheed test pilot Bob Schumacher prepares for a high-altitude flight. U-2 pilots were required to breathe oxygen for two hours in order to eliminate nitrogen bubbles from the bloodstream. Otherwise, they could experience a painful phenomenon similar to the "bends" sometimes suffered by deep-sea divers during decompression. *CIA*

Frank Powers was among the cadre of CIA pilots who trained for operational missions at Watertown before deploying overseas. *Lockheed*

An Air Force NCO plays a game of pool in the recreation facility during off-duty hours. *CIA*

home [all week long] was the hardest part," he said, because "I had a wife and small kids."[68] Frank Powers had mixed feelings about his new home away from home. "As a place to live, it left much to be desired," he later wrote in his memoir, but "as a secret training base for a revolutionary new plane, it was an excellent site."[69] His opinion about the meals served in the mess hall seems to have been universally shared by everyone who worked at Watertown. "As if to compensate for the lack of other creature comforts, there was an excellent mess, the food exceptional by any standard."[70]

On those rare occasions when they were not working, base personnel had a surprising variety of recreational options. Besides pool and poker, there was a volleyball court, and the mess hall could be converted into a movie theater. Those who remained over the weekend could borrow a jeep and explore some of the abandoned mines in the nearby mountains. At least one worker arrived with golf clubs, and Col. McCoy brought cross-country skis. The latter choice may have seemed counterintuitive considering the location, but the high desert occasionally transformed into a winter wonderland.[71]

Off-duty hours away from the test site presented unforeseen complications. In order to prevent AQUATONE personnel from potential exposure to foreign intelligence collection activities, or even questions from overly curious civilians, the project security officer declared Las Vegas off-limits for

Watertown personnel unload luggage, including a pair of cross-country skis, from a MATS C-54G transport. Despite the absence of a links course, or even a putting green, one man brought a set of golf clubs. *CIA*

recreational purposes. In a memorandum to the deputy project director, he wrote, "Our position on this matter has been based on the fact that publicity in [Las Vegas] has caused undue attention to center upon the Groom Lake area." He noted that any person arriving in the city from Watertown would be an excellent target for penetration attempts by foreign agents, and suggested that it would be better for project personnel to instead visit areas much farther removed from the test site, such as Los Angeles.[72]

Plutonium Valley

Although the inhabitants of Groom Lake had to live with rigorous security protocols, isolation, extreme weather, and spartan accommodations, they had up until now been mercifully free of the ravages of atomic explosions. In the absence of full-scale nuclear testing, AEC planners opted instead to conduct a series of weapon safety trials at the NTS. Because the Department of Defense (DoD) was planning to deploy so-called "sealed pit" weapons, with their fissile cores permanently installed to allow firing at a moment's notice, Los Alamos Scientific Laboratory sponsored several tests to ensure that accidental detonation of a weapon's high-explosive components would not result in a nuclear explosion. The possibility of such an accident during transport or storage also raised the specter of radiological contamination, primarily from plutonium. Isotopes of plutonium—with a half-life ranging from 14,000 to 24,000 years—emit alpha particles, the weakest form of radiation. Although these particles are highly energetic, they are not capable of penetrating a sheet of paper or the dead layers of skin on the surface of the human body. If inhaled, however, even microscopic quantities will damage soft tissues. Once absorbed into the bloodstream, plutonium particles may be deposited in the lungs, liver, lymph nodes, or the surfaces of newly formed bone, where they can cause damage leading to cancer, chronic anemia, osteoporosis, or bone necrosis.[73]

In order to ensure weapon safety and better characterize the effects of a subcritical accident, AEC scientists planned a short series of safety experiments designated Project 56 for the purpose of practicing decontamination and radiation-monitoring techniques. Four test locations were prepared in Area 11, a narrow basin just east of Yucca Flat. Since no nuclear detonations were anticipated, any fallout was expected to remain within NTS boundaries. Nevertheless, Oliver R. Placak of the Public Health Service took charge of off-site monitoring of the surrounding areas. He directed Rad-Safe personnel to set up fallout collection trays and air samplers to record traces of alpha emitters beyond the boundaries of Area 11, including the vicinity of Watertown.[74]

The first three test shots of Project 56 took place in quick succession during the first week of November 1955. Technical difficulties caused the final test to be delayed until January 18, 1956. To the consternation of Rad-Safe monitors, particulate plutonium spread more widely within Area 11 than expected, contaminating more than 1,200 acres. Additionally, two debris plumes—each a mile wide and 10 miles long and containing easily measurable amounts of surface plutonium—stretched to the north and northeast beyond the NTS boundary but remained within the Las Vegas Bombing and Gunnery Range. The entire contaminated sector became known as Plutonium Valley. Although fallout was not expected to be detectable beyond the NTS, the AEC Division of Biology and Medicine suggested an acceptable off-site exposure limit for airborne plutonium of 400 "units" (the ad hoc unit was equivalent to disintegrations per minute per cubic meter of air, multiplied by the number of days of measurable concentration). The highest level detected outside the NTS was a mere 24 units, measured at Groom Lake following the fourth shot. Guards at Post 385, along the test site's northern boundary and on the road to Watertown, were exposed to just 172 units, well below the prescribed threshold.

Since the original Project 56 test plan called for zero nuclear yield (arbitrarily defined as anything less than an energy release equivalent to 4 pounds of TNT), the Rad-Safe teams were not expecting to encounter any gamma radiation, which is a fission product. Los Alamos scientists were therefore surprised to encounter unexpected, slight nuclear yields occurring below the defined 4-pound limit during the early tests, which raised questions about weapon design safety. Consequently, they sought to pinpoint the problem by altering the fourth device to intentionally provoke a slight yield, and it did so to an even-greater degree than expected. The resulting shot produced gamma radiation and other fission products, but the monitors had not been informed of the new hazard. Recovery plans and safety measures were still geared toward alpha rather than gamma protection. Ignoring protocols, four members of a data recovery team approached ground zero too soon after the shot and experienced exposures between 4.3 and 28 roentgens, or up to five times the federal occupational exposure limit per year.[75] These events did not deter operations at Watertown, but it was only a matter of time before the "tall mushrooms" once again grew on Yucca Flat and spread their fallout like spores across Groom Lake.

Death on the Mountain

In order to protect the security of activities at Watertown, officials at Project Headquarters had decided early on that ingress and egress from the remote site would be by air in all but certain special cases. Because of the growing U-2 fleet, increasing site population, and expansion of testing to include cameras and sensor packages, this presented the Air Force and CIA with a significant logistical challenge. Representatives from Hycon Manufacturing (designer of the U-2's camera systems), Baird Atomic, and other vendors had joined Lockheed personnel at Watertown, and groups of pilot trainees were expected to arrive soon. Since the majority of personnel initially traveling to and from the Ranch were contractor employees whose homes were in the Burbank and Palmdale areas, the first air shuttle service consisted of an Air Force C-47 bailed to Lockheed and flown and serviced by Lockheed crews. Increasing visits by contractors and headquarters personnel, as well as cargo deliveries, necessitated acquisition of a second C-47.

Since the agency had no direct control over this service, and because difficulties were anticipated regarding passenger insurance coverage, Dick Bissell made arrangements with the Air Force in September 1955 to transport workers and supplies via somewhat larger C-54 aircraft operated by Military Air Transport Service (MATS). Under this arrangement, MATS provided daily flights throughout the week, except Sundays, as well as for aircraft maintenance, parking, loading, and unloading. The CIA was responsible for maintaining a secure passenger-boarding facility at Burbank, preparation and certification of personnel and cargo manifests, and maintaining communications with suppliers and others who used the shuttle. After regularly scheduled service began on October 3, the project director's executive officer, James A. "Jim" Cunningham, dubbed the operation "Bissell's Narrow-Gauge Airline."[76]

To reach Watertown from Burbank, the MATS transports crossed over the bleak expanse of the Mojave Desert and threaded a narrow flight corridor north from Goodsprings, Nevada, passing just west of 11,916-foot Mount Charleston on the way to Mercury, then due north over Yucca Flat, and finally northeast to Groom Lake. The C-54 pilots maintained a flight altitude of 6,500 feet on the inbound leg and 8,000 feet on the outbound leg to provide safe separation between aircraft. Airspace over the NTS was closed to all aircraft except on special orders from the Air Force chief of staff.[77] During the first month of operation, the MATS shuttle transported 265 people from Burbank to Watertown, including fifty-four CIA personnel, twenty-two Air Force personnel, and 189 contractors. Additionally, the C-54 carried 13,479 pounds of cargo, with average loads ranging from 618 to 791 pounds. The heaviest cargo loads during that period weighed 1,387 and 2,178 pounds. Comparatively, Lockheed's C-47 carried 235 people to the base between October 3 and November 16, including twenty-three CIA personnel, thirty-six Air Force personnel, 170 Lockheed employees, and six others.[78]

A worker uses a forklift to unload a large wooden crate from a MATS C-54. *CIA*

A C-54 takes off from Watertown Airstrip. The transport could accommodate as many as sixty passengers and more than 1,000 pounds of cargo. *CIA*

On November 7, 1955, Richard Newton and two members of the Project Headquarters staff met with Maj. Gen. Howard G. Bunker, the Air Force deputy inspector general, to discuss procedures for handling investigation and news releases in the event of an aircraft crash en route to or from Watertown Airstrip. Bunker was briefed on the nature of the Watertown mission, including the CIA's interest, and was informed that only he and Brig. Gen. Joseph D. Caldara, Air Force director of flying safety research, were cleared for knowledge of the project. After some discussion, they agreed to use the term SANDPAPER ROUGH to denote any accident involving a standard Air Force airplane. The term SANDPAPER TRIPLE-ZERO would be used in the event a U-2 was lost off-site. Upon receipt of either code phrase, Bunker or Caldara, whichever man was on duty, would take charge of the investigation. They would also instruct the nearest Air Force base to secure the crash scene, camouflage the wreckage, and control the release of information to news media.[79]

Although the highly experimental U-2, with its unique flying characteristics, was considered to be at greatest risk of a mishap, there were more-disturbing problems with the routine MATS transport operation. Replacement of one of the Air Force maintenance men assigned to service the C-54 by someone less experienced resulted in several flight delays due to mechanical problems. Newton considered the situation sufficiently serious that he sought assistance from higher headquarters in obtaining competent maintenance personnel.[80] In addition, there were instances of noncompliance with Air Force regulations regarding instrument flight clearances, use of nonstandard forms for passenger and cargo manifests, and confusion due to conflicting regulations. These relatively minor discrepancies foreshadowed a tragedy that struck a major blow to the U-2 project.

As dawn broke over Burbank on November 17, passengers began boarding a MATS C-54M at the Lockheed Air Terminal. They included CIA security personnel William Marr, James F. Bray, Terence J. "Terry" O'Donnell, Edwin J. Urolatis, and James W. "Billy" Brown; Lockheed engineers Richard J. Hruda and Rodney H. Kreimendahl; Hycon camera technician Fred F. Hanks and company vice president Harold C. Silent; and an Air Force life-support technician, SSgt. John H. Gaines. Lockheed flight test mechanic Bob Murphy overslept and missed the flight, an unusual occurrence for him, but the slip-up saved his life.

In the cockpit, 1Lt. George M. Pappas Jr. and 1Lt. Paul E. Winham went through the preflight checklist with the help of the flight mechanic, Sgt. Clayton D. Farris. Flight attendant A/2C Guy R. Fasolas prepared the cabin for departure. Meanwhile, ground crewmen loaded more than 1,000 pounds of cargo and supplies. Just before 7:00 a.m., the transport's four radial piston engines roared to life, and the C-54 lurched toward the runway. Pappas took off under cloudy skies, climbed north over the mountains, and flew toward the Goodsprings homing beacon under Instrument Flight Rules (IFR). Once there, he canceled his IFR clearance and switched to Visual Flight Rules (VFR) for the remainder of the approach to Groom Lake, but this may have been a grievous error. The plane encountered snow showers in

Passenger accommodations inside the C-54 were far from luxurious, consisting of fabric-and-net bench seating. *CIA*

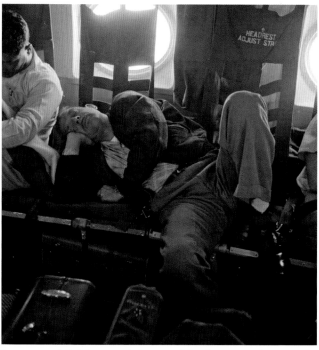

Luggage and freight occupied most of the floor space between the seating areas. Workers made themselves as comfortable as possible. *CIA*

The C-54M crashed near the top of Mt. Charleston, at an altitude of 11,000 feet. *USAF via Steve Ririe*

Members of the recovery team reached the site on horseback but found no survivors. *USAF via Steve Ririe*

the vicinity of Mount Charleston, along with dense clouds broken by occasional "sucker holes," rapidly changing openings in the clouds on the lee side of the mountains. Heavy crosswinds pushed the C-54 off course, and Pappas, faced with decreasing visibility and unaware that he was deviating from his planned heading, turned left to avoid higher terrain amid powerful downdrafts. Suddenly a mountain ridge loomed out of the clouds. Pappas attempted to pull up, but the C-54 struck the snow-covered slope 50 feet below the top, bounced back into the air and nosed in. The airplane slid 20 feet, broke apart, and burned.[81] There were no survivors.

By now, weather conditions at the test site had deteriorated significantly. Snow was falling at Groom Lake, and the Watertown operations officer, Maj. James H. Voyles Jr., contacted Nellis Air Force Base to see whether anyone had heard from Pappas and to suggest that the C-54 should divert to Nellis until the storm passed. But there had been no further radio contact since the pilot canceled his IFR clearance. Watertown officials were not immediately concerned because a message with the plane's takeoff time incorrectly recorded led them to believe the C-54 was not yet overdue. Had they known the correct takeoff time, they might have attempted to divert the plane sooner. Search efforts began as soon as it became apparent the aircraft was missing. At about 3:30 in the afternoon, the pilot of a search plane from Nellis spotted wreckage on a barren, treeless slope. The front end of the C-54 was completely destroyed, and though the rudder showed signs of fire damage, the fuselage from the wings back was largely intact. A rear passenger door was swinging in the high winds that scoured the peak, but there was no sign of life. As soon as the search pilot relayed the location, a rescue team was dispatched to hunt for survivors.[82]

At dawn the next day, searchers began the arduous climb from a base camp near Charleston Lodge in Kyle Canyon. By this time, skies had cleared at the rescue camp, but clouds and snow still shrouded the mountain, and deep drifts covered the trail to the summit. The crew of Dumbo 94, an SA-16A from the 42nd Air Rescue Squadron, circled Mount Charleston in a vain attempt to drop a rescue team by parachute, but that effort was thwarted by high winds and turbulence. The ground team was not expected to reach the wreck for at least another twelve hours.[83] In fact, it took that long just to trudge the first 4 miles on foot and horseback. A second rescue team, led by Clark County deputy sheriff George Dykes, set out several hours later. Both parties were forced to camp in the snow and endure nighttime temperatures that dropped to 20 degrees below zero. By the following morning, five of the eight men in the sheriff's posse had turned back due to exhaustion, leaving Dykes and two Air Force medics to press on without them. Officials asked civilian rescuers not to approach the wreckage until after it had been examined by military personnel, fueling speculation by reporters that the C-54 had been transporting classified cargo.[84] When the searchers eventually reached the crash site, the rescue mission quickly turned into an effort to recover crew and passenger remains.

Although Air Force officials attempted to keep a tight lid on the story, the accident remained front-page news for several days in Las Vegas and Los Angeles. Col. William L. Helmantoler, Air Force spokesman, told reporters the plane was destined for the airfield at Indian Springs, but the commanding officer there told *Las Vegas Review-Journal* reporter Dennis Schieck that the C-54 had not been expected. In his subsequent article, Schieck speculated that the plane might actually have been heading to "a top-secret base" northwest of Las Vegas. Helmantoler vainly tried to quell these rumors. "It's just another plane crash," he said, adding that the C-54 was carrying Air Force personnel and "civilian consultants" to the AEC test area. In a follow-up article two days later, Schieck stated unequivocally that the C-54 was "bound for the super-secret 'proving grounds within the proving grounds'—Groom Dry Lake."[85]

In December, Air Force accident investigators completed an unclassified report confirming that the plane was "on a scheduled transport mission" to "Watertown Airstrip in the Nevada Proving Ground area." This document noted that in accordance with standard operating procedure, the aircraft and crew were "under the operational control of the Commander, Watertown Airstrip." Of all the numerous reports, statements, and supporting documents generated during the investigation, only the Rescue Mission Report was classified secret.[86] Three weeks after the accident, members of the 4602nd Air Intelligence Service Squadron conducted what they described as a "training exercise" at the crash site. A four-man team commanded by Lt. William M. Connor spent three days on the rugged, snow-covered mountain to "aid in the service's knowledge of rescue work in nearly impossible terrain."[87] The 4602nd AISS was one of several elite units tasked with technical investigation and recovery of material from crash sites in all types of terrain and weather conditions. Although their mission on Mount Charleston was officially described as a mock rescue for training purposes, it was more likely an attempt to recover classified material from the C-54 wreckage.

As it turned out, they failed to find everything. While hiking to the top of the mountain on August 5, 1956, some Boy Scouts discovered a briefcase belonging to William Marr, which had lain hidden at the crash scene for more than eight months. Their scoutmaster turned it over to an Air Force Office of Special Investigations (AFOSI) agent at Nellis, who opened the case and discovered Marr's CIA affiliation. The agent immediately forwarded the case and its contents to his regional headquarters in the Los Angeles area so it could be passed to the nearest CIA contact. Agency security personnel contained any potential leaks that might have resulted from this incident by debriefing those involved.[88]

One consequence of the Mount Charleston crash was a temporary suspension of the MATS operation at Watertown. Kelly Johnson expressed a desire to use only the company's C-47, but as the test site workforce grew, it quickly became apparent that this would not suffice. Use of the Air Force C-54s was reinstated on November 28, 1955. In a meeting with Gen. Lew Allen, the MATS commander, Johnson recommended air route changes that would prevent a similar mishap.[89]

Arrival of the Spooks

If officials hoped the AEC statement issued the previous April had quelled further media interest in activities at Groom Lake, they were soon disappointed. Even before the C-54 mishap, a reporter from the *Las Vegas Review-Journal* requested a progress report on the Watertown Project, prompting Col. Alfred Starbird to issue a statement through Kenner F. Hertford of the AEC Albuquerque Operations Office in New Mexico. "Construction at the Nevada Test Site installation a few miles north of Yucca Flat which was announced last spring is continuing," he wrote. "Data secured to date has indicated a need for limited additional facilities and modifications of the existing installation. The additional work which will not be completed until sometime in 1956 is being done by the Reynolds Electrical and Engineering Company, Incorporated, under the direction of the Atomic Energy Commission's Las Vegas branch office."[90] As would be seen in the months and years to come, such innocuous statements merely whetted the appetites of journalists, who suspected that there was something more to the mysterious Watertown Airstrip.

Despite Bissell's desire to operate Watertown on as austere a basis as possible, the need for further improvements became apparent with every passing day as more and more personnel arrived. These included company engineers and tech reps, firefighters, communications specialists, security officers, REECo service people, VIP visitors, and others. At the start of the project, there were sufficient quarters for a maximum of 133 people. Planners expected the base population would likely climb to nearly two hundred by early 1956, and it eventually peaked at 1,250 once U-2 training operations were in full swing.

Workers arrive and depart during shift change at Watertown. The U-2 project was a twenty-four-hour operation. *CIA*

To accommodate this increased activity, Project Headquarters ordered operations suspended for twelve days at the end of November 1955 to allow for construction of additional essential facilities. These included two new eighteen-room dormitories, a control tower, aircraft parking aprons and tie-downs, a new taxiway, classroom and office space for the SAC Training Unit, a 4,000-square-foot warehouse, additions to the dispensary and photo lab, a water pipeline, and an elevated guard post near the top of the water tower. Major structural components for both the control tower and guard shack were manufactured at Mercury and trucked to Watertown for final assembly. Jeeps, sedans, and trucks, on loan from the AFSWP, also had to be brought in from Mercury for use in the base motor pool, along with another twenty three-room mobile-home trailers to provide additional billets for personnel.

During construction, approximately sixty contractors were billeted on-site. Economic considerations and limited on-base housing precluded the use of a larger workforce.[91]

Grading for the taxiway and aprons commenced on November 20, and because temperatures dropped to 6 degrees Fahrenheit at night, these areas had to be paved with hot-mix asphaltic concrete instead of cold road mix, as had been used for the main runway the previous summer. Workers excavated a stockpile of gravel from a pit at the south end of the airstrip and used it to build a 6-inch-thick compacted base for the paved surface. Concrete hardstands equipped with steel tie-downs were spaced on the aprons to accommodate the anticipated number of U-2, T-33, and C-47 aircraft. An additional run-up area was constructed, and the original run-up pad was enlarged to provide parking space for larger aircraft such as the C-54 and C-124. Shortly after the new construction was completed, Secretary of Defense Charles E. Wilson made a one-day visit to the airfield and witnessed a demonstration of the U-2's capabilities. After seeing the results of photographs taken from an altitude of 68,000 feet, Wilson departed with a very favorable impression of the project.[92]

The control tower, located just north of Base Headquarters, was equipped with UHF and VHF radios, and equipment to measure wind speed and direction. *CIA*

Looking north across the roof of a warehouse, several U-2 aircraft are visible on the parking apron, along with a few fuel trucks. *CIA*

Air Force personnel controlled the movement of aircraft on and around Watertown Airstrip. In the event of loss of communication due to radio failure, a light gun, seen here hung from the ceiling, was provided for signaling incoming aircraft. *CIA*

Six U-2 aircraft on the parking apron, each perched on a concrete hardstand. Two are being readied for flight. *CIA*

Col. William R. "Bill" Yancey took charge of the SAC training group at Watertown. During World War II, he led a unit that trained night-fighter pilots for overseas combat and later commanded the 3rd Fighter Group in northern China. Afterward, he and a small number of staff officers remained with the Chinese air force as advisors. Upon returning to the US in late 1947, he was assigned as director of operations, and eventually commander, of the 55th Strategic Reconnaissance Wing, Ramey Air Force Base, Puerto Rico. Following an assignment to SAC Headquarters, Yancey attended the Air War College, where he was assigned to the Advanced Study Group, Evaluation Division, following graduation. Handpicked by Gen. Curtis LeMay, Yancey was tasked with representing SAC interests in the AQUATONE program. LeMay specifically instructed him to evaluate the Lockheed flight test effort, verify that the airplane and reconnaissance equipment performed as expected, and report his findings as soon as possible. Should the results prove satisfactory, Yancey was to train a specified number of CIA pilots for operational missions. Having received his orders, he hurriedly made the 2,500-mile drive to March Air Force Base, in Riverside, California, with his wife, Wilda, and their two sons. He told them only that he would be spending a great deal of time away from home and that he could say nothing about the nature of his work.[93]

Yancey and other members of the SAC training cadre first visited Watertown on October 19, 1955, and held discussions with Kelly Johnson and Project Headquarters personnel to finalize plans. Over the next few weeks, each man underwent a thorough examination at the Lovelace Clinic in Albuquerque, and fitting for partial-pressure suits at the David Clark Company in Worcester, Massachusetts, followed by an orientation at the Lockheed plant in Burbank. They were back in Nevada by the first week in November, flying the U-2 under the supervision of Ray Goudey and Bob Matye. The Lockheed test pilots provided ground instruction and checkout before allowing the SAC pilots to make U-2 familiarization and proficiency flights around the local area. Yancey soon reported to LeMay and Bissell that more personnel were needed to maintain the growing U-2 fleet, as well as the associated fuel trailers and ground-power equipment. He noted a shortage of supply facilities and ramp space for aircraft parking and also requested two additional T-33 trainers to be used for transition training.[94]

Bill Yancey commanded the SAC training group at Watertown. He oversaw the preparation of pilots for operational U-2 missions. *USAF*

The Watertown headquarters building, with a hangar, the control tower, the lakebed, and the Groom Mountains in the background. *CIA*

THE SECRET HISTORY OF AREA 51

Several dozen trailers provided rudimentary accommodations for Watertown personnel. *At left*, after leaning his push broom against the side of a trailer, a custodian carrying a wastebasket stoops beside a pile of bed linens destined for the base laundry. *CIA*

Security guard Richard Mingus makes a radio call from his observation post atop the water tower. *CIA*

The water tower doubled as a security post, providing a commanding perch from which to observe activities on the flight line and in the housing area. *CIA*

This scene inside the Watertown laundry room illustrates the most-mundane details of life on a secret installation. *CIA*

THE ANGEL FROM PARADISE RANCH | 45

For administrative purposes, SAC activated the 4070th Support Wing on December 20, 1955, with Yancey as commanding officer. Although this organization was nominally headquartered at March Air Force Base, all personnel were assigned TDY to Watertown. Yancey's staff included Col. Herbert I. Shingler Jr., deputy commander; Maj. Robert E. Mullin, navigator and classroom instructor; Maj. John E. "Jack" Delap, navigation officer and mission planner; Maj. Arthur Lien, logistics and supply officer development; Maj. Louis A. Garvin and Lt. Col. Phillip O. Robertson, flight test officers; and Capt. John H. "Hank" Meierdierck and Capt. Louis C. Setter, flight instructors. Additional support staff included MSgt. Frederick D. Montgomery, SSgt. Davis N. Sweidel, and SSgt. Paul W. Briest.

High-altitude flying gear was stored in the Life Support shop. Flights above 50,000 feet required use of the MC-3 partial-pressure suits developed by the David Clark Company. Usually worn beneath a light coverall, this garment employed inflatable tubes and cross-stitching to automatically tighten the suit against the pilot's body if the cockpit depressurized, thus counteracting the expansion of gases and bodily fluids. *CIA*

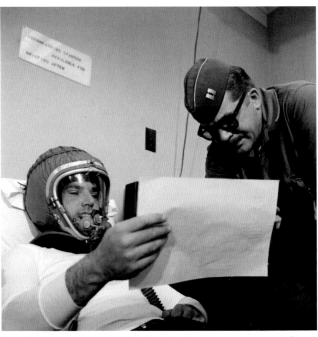

Ray Goudey receives a weather briefing from the base meteorologist while prebreathing oxygen in preparation for a high-altitude flight. Weather briefings were particularly important because the lightweight structure of the U-2 was not designed to withstand heavy turbulence. *CIA*

TSgt. Lewis C. Weldon inspects life-support equipment to ensure safety and readiness for flight. *CIA*

Pilots typically used their prebreathing time to catch up on mission-briefing material or simply relax. Here, Ray Goudey reads the 1955 edition of *Adventures in Time & Space*, a collection of short stories by noted science fiction authors of the day. *CIA*

Because the CIA's Detachment A was not yet a functioning entity at Watertown, the training program was delayed nearly a month. The first three contract pilots finally arrived on January 11, 1956. Martin A. Knutson, Carl K. Overstreet, and Carmine A. Vito had little time to settle in at their new station, since they immediately began U-2 ground school classes and T-33 transition training. Three more agency pilots, Jacob "Jake" Kratt, Glendon K. Dunaway, and Hervey S. Stockman, were qualified by the middle of February, and the detachment operations staff was planning training flights under the supervision of SAC instructors. Progress was being made, but there was still a rough road ahead.[95]

Morale Problems

The arrival of a new commanding officer on December 22, 1955, failed to have the harmonizing effect that Bissell had hoped for. After assuming command of the airbase, Col. Landon B. McConnell had difficulty adjusting to the unorthodox organizational structure and was immediately beset with demands on numerous fronts. By this time the installation was populated by several active organizations: permanent Watertown staff under the base commander, the first CIA field detachment in training, Yancey's group, and the technical staffs of several equipment vendors, including Lockheed, Pratt & Whitney, Hycon, Ramo-Wooldridge, Eastman Kodak, and Firewel. All were trying to function as best they could under Bissell's directive, but with so many disparate organizations and chains of command, not everything went smoothly.

At 1:05 in the afternoon, technicians pause in their tasks. The wings of this U-2 have been mated to the fuselage, but several panels still need to be attached. Pads cover portions of the aluminum skin to prevent damage from accidental tool strikes. *CIA*

Watertown's three hangars are flanked by the control tower and a warehouse. By March 1956, nine U-2 aircraft had been delivered to the test site. *CIA*

The Watertown chow hall was renowned for the quality of its food and served as the facility's social hub. Crates of fresh California oranges are visible in the background. *CIA*

The culinary staff were the unsung heroes of the base, providing tasty sustenance for the workers at all hours. *CIA*

In March 1956, a staff officer reported to Bissell through Col. Jack A. Gibbs, the new deputy project director, that morale at Watertown, once extremely high despite many frustrations and unusual situations, was disintegrating. He blamed a growing sense of factionalism between the permanent base personnel and those assigned to the detachment, particularly its commanding officer, Col. McCoy. "We have two commanders on the station of vastly different personalities," he wrote, noting, "There is little or no common ground of understanding between them." The reporting officer believed that both McConnell and McCoy were equally responsible for fostering discord. "I also feel," he added, "that this poor aspect of leadership is transmitted to their subordinates, which is reflected in their work." An equally baffling situation arose from what the officer described as "an overly paternalistic attitude" on the part of the Detachment A command staff toward the "drivers" (U-2 pilots). When not engaged in ground training, mission planning, or flight operations, the pilots typically enjoyed relaxing in their living quarters. Their off-duty time, however, was frequently interrupted by unscheduled visits from the detachment's two senior officers. Col. Gibbs noted, "The drivers feel that they are almost being spied upon," and that McCoy and his operations officer "actually discuss the drivers as if they were kids, and feel that they should supervise even to the minute when these men should be in bed, etc."[96] Micromanagement of the flight crews was only part of a larger problem.

Many of McCoy's frustrations stemmed from the fact that Project Headquarters components and parent services (SAC, for example) had a tendency to deal directly with Detachment A personnel rather than going through the proper command channels. He complained that if such actions continued, he would request to be withdrawn from the project altogether. In a fiery memo to headquarters, McCoy stressed that "the commanding officer must control all personnel and materiel of his unit." Bissell immediately gave orders to headquarters elements that once a detachment was activated at the test base, its personnel were strictly under the control of the detachment commander and could not receive direction from staff officers outside the proper chain of command. He also sent Ossie Ritland to Nevada to have a frank and thorough discussion with McCoy and McConnell, during which the two officers promised to do everything possible to mitigate the situation. "In my opinion, the base CO has not been fully cooperative in discharging his responsibilities," Ritland reported shortly before ceding his position to Col. Gibbs in preparation for another assignment. He added, "In many cases, morale problems have arisen unnecessarily since [McConnell] had the facilities and authority to prevent them."[97]

Additionally, there were still a variety of personnel shortages, particularly in the areas of physiological training, medical, and life support. As with other critical positions, these personnel were drawn from throughout the Air Force. Medical officers and enlisted medical technicians were particularly difficult to obtain and late in arriving, largely due to the time necessary to get them cleared into the program. The Firewel Company, which subcontracted for the manufacture of partial-pressure suits and auxiliary equipment, was supposed to supply a personal-equipment technician for each detachment, but these specialists first had to be recruited and trained, and none were available by the time Detachment A entered flight training. The original Air Force personal-equipment specialist at Watertown had been killed in the crash of the MATS shuttle on Mount Charleston. Adding to the medical staff shortage, the physiological training officer, Maj. Leo V. M. Knauber, withdrew from the project after suffering a heart attack in the early spring of 1956. By the time Maj. James Deuel reported as Watertown's first full-time flight surgeon on June 1, 1956, the medical and equipment problems were only beginning to be resolved.[98]

The CIA also had great difficulty obtaining firefighting personnel for Watertown. The agency requested in September 1955 that the Air Force provide firefighters for the airbase, which up to that point had been protected by Lockheed firemen. For the first few months of operation, Dick Bissell agreed with Kelly Johnson that "we would not need a fire crew on duty 24 hours a day, but only when landings and takeoffs were in progress; the rest of the time, we would have to rely on security officers to keep watch on the whole staff of the test base to act as an emergency fire crew."[99] Discussions ensued between AQUATONE project personnel and Col. Russell A. Berg, chief of the Reconnaissance Division in the Directorate of Operations at Air Force Headquarters, who complained that qualified Air Force firefighters, once identified and selected, would require months of background checks to be cleared into the program. After several months of fruitless debate, the Watertown personnel officer requested that Lockheed extend its agreement to provide fire protection while the CIA sought to procure civilian firefighters elsewhere.[100]

A technician, *at left*, assists as Ray Goudey checks out the U-2 celestial navigation trainer. *CIA*

Workers push Article 372 into a hangar for reassembly. Another U-2, Article 368, is visible outside on the parking apron. *CIA*

A Hycon technician works on a type B camera with a 36-inch focal length. Used for large-scale, high-resolution photography, it was capable of resolving features as small as 18 inches across from an altitude of 65,000 feet. *CIA*

The type A-2 camera package had to be winched up into the U-2's payload bay, or Q-bay, which spanned the entire fuselage just aft of the cockpit. This package included three 24-inch focal-length cameras on fixed mounts, each carrying 1,800 feet of film and capable of resolving objects from 2 to 8 feet across. *CIA*

Five months later, following a thorough investigation into previous agency experience, it became apparent that recruitment of civilian firefighters was impractical for a variety of reasons. Notable difficulties included the question of which agency to name as the contracting party (CIA, Air Force, or AEC), the fact that billeting requirements at Watertown made a normal schedule—twenty-four hours on-duty and twenty-four hours off—impractical, and that the necessary separation from dependent family members during the term of service was considered a hardship. "This problem," noted the personnel officer, "although certainly not insoluble, is an extremely difficult one for [the] CIA to work out at Watertown." Additionally, there was a question regarding contract duration. Plans called for the CIA to phase out operations at Watertown by late fall of 1956, at which time, agency officials believed, the Air Force might take responsibility for the base. "It is considered practically impossible to secure services of qualified firemen for any period short of a year." After further discussions, Lockheed agreed to continue providing fire protection through June 1956, at which time the Air Force would reconsider assigning its own firemen to the task if the requisite security criteria might be relaxed to some extent. The Watertown personnel officer agreed, conceding, "We believe that firemen do not necessarily have to be fully witting of the Project and can be considered more or less in the same light as REECo employees now utilized as housekeeping personnel on the base."[101]

Another almost constant problem involved the relationship between AQUATONE project staff and the various contractor personnel, as well as the cultural differences among the companies. As prime contractor for airframe manufacturing, flight testing, and systems integration, Lockheed had the largest impact. This was particularly true due to the company's early involvement in selection and design of the test site, and because Skunk Works personnel were the first to arrive. According to Helen Kleyla, they were the "most aggressive group at the base, and with Kelly Johnson as their leader they were prone to grab the ball and run without waiting for signals." Bissell later wrote, "At the beginning of the project, Watertown was for many months in fact a Lockheed facility and we never succeeded in recovering effective control of it, and our efforts to do so gave rise to some unnecessary ill will."[102]

One such example arose after Bissell sent orders to McConnell concerning how to bring the U-2 to operational readiness as quickly as possible. On March 20, 1956, Bissell instructed the base commander to develop a master schedule of test requirements that would make the best use of the available number of U-2 aircraft, taking into account the needs of all suppliers to install, calibrate, and test their equipment. McConnell responded by issuing a memorandum to contractors requesting that they submit schedules of their proposed tests, which could be integrated into the master schedule with sufficient flexibility to allow for any change of emphasis or additional testing that might be required. At a vendor meeting in Los Angeles the following month, Johnson strongly objected to McConnell's dictum. He bristled at the implication that the base commander should be responsible for coordination of test

A technician services a Perkin Elmer T-1 tracker camera for the U-2. This device began operating automatically at engine start and stopped at engine shutdown, capturing panoramic images on 70 mm film every thirty-two seconds. This system was very effective for tracking the course of training missions and for cross-referencing images taken with the B camera. *CIA*

Off the Reservation

Technician inspects a sextant used by U-2 pilots for celestial navigation. The glass-domed instrument was mounted ahead of the cockpit. *CIA*

programs, which he believed was rightfully the manufacturer's responsibility. Following an acrimonious exchange, Johnson was reassured that conduct of developmental flight testing remained Lockheed's primary responsibility, including day-to-day scheduling. However, it fell to McConnell as Bissell's chief representative at Watertown to ensure that priorities desired by Project Headquarters were observed.[103] Johnson seemed somewhat mollified, but Bissell never forgot his dissent.

As each CIA detachment arrived at Watertown, Col. Yancey's flight instructors guided the contract pilots through a training syllabus consisting of ground school classes followed by flight checkouts. Before being allowed to solo in the U-2, each student first flew a number of analog sorties in the T-33 to simulate high-altitude flameouts and restarts, practice U-2 landing-approach techniques, and demonstrate near-stall landings. An instructor pilot in a chase plane shadowed the U-2 each time a student made his first solo, which consisted of a flight to 20,000 feet followed by five practice landings on the lakebed. Students didn't wear the partial-pressure garment until their third solo flight, which was typically a three-hour mission that topped out around 60,000 feet. The next nine sorties introduced trainees to high-altitude navigation and photography, long-duration flight (upward of eight hours), night flying, and landings on the paved airstrip. Each pilot was declared mission-qualified after logging at least fifty-eight flight hours in the U-2 and completing a final eight-hour check ride.[104] "At Watertown we flew the U-2 far more than we would have if we'd been in the Air Force and checking out in a new aircraft," Frank Powers later wrote in his memoir. "As a result, on completing our training we had the utmost confidence in its reliability."[105]

With the Groom Mountains as a backdrop, ground crewmen service Article 361 following landing on the dry lakebed. The tow dolly is visible at right, and a chase car at left. *CIA*

At the end of March 1956, Detachment A was reconstituted as the 1st Weather Reconnaissance Squadron (Provisional), or WRSP-I, by authority of AWS General Order No. 7. As originally envisioned, the quota for each detachment would include ten fully qualified U-2 pilots. However, due to the complex and time-consuming process of getting personnel cleared, only six had so far completed training, and just one more was brought on board the following month. The two subsequent training classes each had a full complement, along with a few extras that would later be given permanent assignments as needed. In addition to ensuring that a sufficient number of pilots completed their U-2 transition training, the 4070th Support Wing was tasked with operational checkout of the airplanes, ground and flight crews, navigation techniques, life-support systems, cameras, and other equipment. The best way to achieve this was to conduct a five-day Unit Simulated Combat Mission (USCM) exercise. This consisted of eight long-duration cross-country sorties, the first of which was flown on April 10. The entire exercise was conducted in the manner of a standard Air Force operational readiness inspection, with Col. Yancey and his staff serving on the USCM Evaluation Board monitoring the squadron's performance. Allen Dulles paid a visit to Watertown on April 13 and seemed very pleased with the operation.[106]

Not everything went flawlessly, however. There were several camera malfunctions, and engine performance remained unreliable. On the final day of the exercise, one of the U-2s suffered a flameout over the Mississippi River. After attempting to restart the engine, Jake Kratt reported violent vibrations and a second flameout. By the time he declared an emergency, the U-2 was somewhere over Arkansas, but Kratt was confident that he could glide as far as Albuquerque. Project officials made a series of urgent phone calls, eventually reaching Brig. Gen. Ralph E. Koon, the Air Force assistant director of operations at the Pentagon. Koon then called Brig. Gen. William M. Canterbury, commander of Kirtland Air Force Base, New Mexico, and told him to expect an unusual aircraft within the next half hour and to get it inside a secure hangar as soon as possible. After about thirty minutes, the crippled U-2 touched down silently at Kirtland. Kratt later reported that from the time of his first flameout until landing, he had traveled more than 900 miles, including some 300 miles without power. Marty Knutson also had a flameout during his long-range mission but was able to successfully relight the engine and recover at Watertown. Despite these problems, the exercise was deemed a success.

Following completion of the USCM, the lead Evaluation Board member, Col. Marion C. "Hack" Mixson, reported to Project Headquarters that WRSP-I was ready for deployment to its first overseas post. Col. McCoy and his deputy, agency staff officer Thomas B. Clendinning, oversaw the move, which took place between April 29 and May 5. In all, more than two hundred personnel and nearly 160,000 pounds of cargo were airlifted from Watertown to a British Royal Air Force base at Lakenheath, England.[107] Additionally, the aeromedical physiologist assigned to Watertown departed with WRSP-I, leaving the medical section short-handed once again for nearly two months.[108]

Watertown personnel undertook some essential housekeeping chores prior to the arrival of the second training group. This included a general cleanup, dust control measures, equipment repairs, and extensive modifications to Hangar 2. Additionally, the agency

The flight surgeon, seen here in the Watertown dispensary, played a vital part in preparing U-2 pilots for their missions. The health and fitness of each pilot were carefully monitored. The flight surgeon was responsible for performing a medical checkup before each flight, and supervising oxygen prebreathing and other physiological support activities. *CIA*

A pilot fills out paperwork in the Watertown operations office. According to the schedule board, a C-54G is inbound from Burbank. Benedict Lacombe (call sign Workhorse 17) landed thirty minutes earlier following an eight-hour flight in Article 361. Raymond Haupt (Workhorse 16) took off at 8:04 a.m. for a training sortie in Article 365, followed by Donald Sorlie in Article 368. *CIA*

allocated $57,500 to REECo for runway resurfacing.¹⁰⁹ This project was expected to take approximately two weeks, during which all takeoffs and landings had to be conducted on the lakebed so as not to interfere with the training schedule. A larger problem was the exposure of the U-2 to more than a dozen uncleared construction personnel. The deputy project director suggested covering any parked airplanes with tarps or shielding them behind fuel trucks or other equipment, but there would be no hiding them during flight operations. In a memo to the project security officer, he admitted, "I doubt whether such workers would be technically inclined enough to gain much information as to the airplane's performance capabilities merely by seeing it towed out."¹¹⁰

Flight planning was a team effort, and the key to success for U-2 missions. In order to maximize target coverage, planners at Watertown carefully studied meteorological data and topographic maps, selected a flight route, and chose appropriate cameras and sensors. *CIA*

U-2 pilot Tony Bevacqua studies navigational charts while planning an upcoming training mission. *CIA*

Detachment B was activated as the 2nd Weather Reconnaissance Squadron (Provisional), or WRSP-II, on May 7, 1956, under the command of Col. Edward A. Perry. An aggressive leader, he demanded the full support and loyalty of his men but spared no effort to achieve the best possible conditions for them. Perry was fortunate to have been selected for his new assignment three months before his detachment was activated. This gave him ample time to be fully briefed at Project Headquarters, visit Watertown and become familiar with operations there, and handpick approximately 60 percent of his staff from men he already knew and trusted. In addition, the base facilities were in a greater state of readiness to receive the next group of trainees, and Yancey's organization had fostered improvements to the aircraft and tailored the training syllabus in accordance with experience gained with Detachment A. Major revisions included the addition of more U-2 sorties as well as greater emphasis on instrument proficiency in the T-33. For his part, Perry spent a good deal of time prior to his arrival working closely with headquarters staff to draft plans and procedures. At one point, he nearly resigned after being told he was not physically qualified for high-altitude flying, but he ultimately chose to remain out of a sense of obligation to his men.

During this period the secret base underwent several significant changes. First, expansion of CIA and Air Force pilot training increased the base population to more than 1,200 personnel. Second, Holmes & Narver, Inc., took over the NTS engineering contract from the Silas Mason Company, becoming responsible for architectural engineering at Groom Lake. Finally, as the U-2 was about to be exposed to the world, the CIA devised a cover story to explain the airplane's unique performance capabilities and to attempt to disguise its true mission.¹¹¹

The growing number of high-altitude training missions crisscrossing the country spurred a tremendous increase in reports of unidentified flying objects (UFOs) by unwitting observers on the ground and in the air. Public and military interest in the phenomenon had grown throughout the early Cold War years due to fears that the unknown aircraft might be some sort of advanced foreign weapon system. The Air Force even created an office called Project BLUE BOOK to collate information on UFO sightings in order to determine whether they posed any threat to national security. Most commercial airlines at that time typically flew at altitudes ranging from 10,000 to 20,000 feet, and military aircraft generally operated below 40,000 feet. Consequently, once the U-2 started flying above 60,000 feet, air traffic controllers and law enforcement agencies started receiving calls from concerned citizens.

A busy day on the Watertown flight line, with several U-2s being prepared for flight. Others are undergoing maintenance in front of the hangar, and one is airborne at upper left. *CIA*

While flying at altitudes above the capabilities of contemporaneous civil and military jets, the U-2 inadvertently caused a number of UFO sightings. *CIA*

These UFO sightings tended to be most prevalent in the early morning or early evening hours, when the sun was below the horizon. This left the observer in darkness, or twilight, while the U-2 at altitude was fully illuminated. The airplane's shiny aluminum skin caught the sun's rays, causing it to glow like a fiery object racing across the sky, high above where any aircraft should be. Even during daylight hours an observer might catch a glimpse of reflected sunlight glinting from the jet's metal surface. When queried, BLUE BOOK spokesmen attempted to explain away such sightings as natural phenomena. Having been briefed into AQUATONE, these investigators routinely attempted to correlate UFO sightings with U-2 flight schedules. This allowed them to eliminate a large number of sighting reports from further investigation, though they could never publicly reveal their true findings. CIA officials familiar with AQUATONE test and training operations later estimated that more than half of all UFO reports from the mid-1950s into the 1960s resulted from flights of manned, high-altitude reconnaissance planes over the United States.[112]

Public exposure of the U-2 was inevitable, so the agency developed what they considered to be a plausible cover story. At the request of CIA Headquarters, the National Advisory Committee for Aeronautics (NACA) drafted a press release regarding the U-2. This followed some debate as to whether the Air Force AWS or the civilian NACA should be named as the prime sponsor for the program. Ultimately, it seemed best to use the civilian agency as a cover, and to paint the project aircraft in NACA markings.[113] On May 7, 1956, NACA director Hugh L. Dryden announced a program in which U-2 aircraft would conduct high-altitude weather research with Air Force support while operating from Watertown Strip, Nevada. The stated goal was to obtain detailed

As part of an elaborate cover story, the U-2 fleet was painted in bogus NACA markings. The fictitious tail numbers (*from left to right*, 311, 302, and 310) correspond to article numbers 371, 362, and 370, respectively. Why the CIA didn't simply use the original article numbers, which were painted on each airplane's nose, remains a mystery. *CIA*

meteorological information at altitudes "as high as 50,000 feet." In order to explain the presence of U-2 operations on foreign soil, Dryden added that "USAF facilities overseas will be used as the program gets underway, to enable gathering research information necessary to reflect accurately conditions along the high-altitude air routes of tomorrow in many parts of the world."[114]

Kelly Johnson was less than impressed with the NACA publicity, calling Dryden's statement "a stupid shambles."[115] Although it was indeed a flimsy cover, it nevertheless carried more than a grain of truth. An instrument package was developed for onboard carriage in place of the normal mission equipment. On days when weather over project targets was such that a photo mission could not be accomplished, pilots could still fly proficiency sorties while carrying out meteorological research for the NACA with a variety of scientific instruments. To further the cover story, data from these instruments were later used to produce unclassified studies for publication and public release. This effort not only shielded the clandestine reconnaissance mission but also provided valuable information to the scientific community.[116]

Article 364, in the livery of NACA 304, is readied for flight. The pilot is seated in the cockpit, and a ground crewman is closing the canopy.

THE ANGEL FROM PARADISE RANCH | 55

Technicians work on a "sniffer" package for installation in Article 372. The U-2 was capable of carrying a variety of particulate sensors, including a sampling system consisting of six 16-inch filter papers that were exposed to air fed from a duct faired onto the left side of the Q-bay hatch. *CIA*

By mid-1956, the U-2 had demonstrated its design altitude, range, and structural limits on multiple occasions and had flown several missions with durations longer than ten hours, each covering more than 5,000 statute miles. To develop a system for accurately determining altitude performance, targets of known dimensions were laid out on the dry lakebed and photographed from an indicated pressure altitude of 70,000 feet. Analysts then determined the true altitude by scaling the target size from the pictures. The maximum altitude achieved during Lockheed flight-testing was 73,300 feet, calibrated and corrected for instrument and position errors. This unofficial record was set on May 5 in Article 350 during a routine production check flight. The airplane had 200 gallons of fuel on board and was not stripped down for a record attempt.[117] One of the SAC pilots flew even higher during a ten-hour training sortie from Watertown to the vicinity of Great Bear Lake, in the Canadian Northwest Territories, and back. Seeing that he still had plenty of fuel remaining, Lt. Col. Phil Robertson proceeded southward almost to the Mexican border before turning around and finally landing back at the Ranch. On the basis of observed altimeter readings, he believed that his maximum altitude had been 72,500 feet. "That evening they recomputed, and my altitude was 74,500 feet," he later recalled. "That record stood for three years until they re-engined the airplane."[118]

Not surprisingly, the intensive training program resulted in a number of mishaps, some fatal. One incident with deadly results was a consequence of the unusual landing-gear arrangement. As originally designed, the pogo outriggers were to be dropped during or shortly after takeoff, using a manual release system. "We soon learned that any delay by the pilot in dropping them would often cause them to hang up," Ernie Joiner recalled. "When that happened, it was wise to stay clear of the airplane's flight path." He also recalled, "We had an unwritten rule that the airplane would not fly over the mess hall with a hung pogo." Presumably this rule applied to other populated areas of the base as well. Bob Murphy and Frank Harvey spent a great deal of time scouring the nearby desert looking for errant pogos that had fallen off after the U-2 was well away from the runway.[119]

The partially disassembled airframe of Article 373 rests on transport dollies inside one of Watertown's three hangars. *CIA*

The airplane's unique design and handling qualities contributed to a series of tragedies and near misses. On May 15, CIA pilot Wilburn S. "Billy" Rose had just taken off for a training flight in Article 345 when he noticed that neither of the outriggers separated when he activated the manual release. He tried again and managed to drop the left pogo, but the other remained stubbornly attached to the right wing. While attempting to shake it loose, he failed to maintain adequate airspeed and altitude. The airplane stalled, banked into a steep right turn, and crashed onto the lakebed. Rose became the first CIA fatality of the program. In order to prevent this problem in the future, the pilot actuation system was removed and the attach point modified so the pogos would fall away automatically as soon as the wings started to lift while the airplane was still on the runway. A spring was installed on the upper end of the pogo to push it away from the wing as soon as the weight of the aircraft was removed. This solved only one problem, however, and trainees continued to suffer a variety of takeoff and landing mishaps. On June 1, John W. "Bill" Strickland somehow allowed Article 344 to run out of fuel. He landed several hundred yards short of the lakebed, miraculously without seriously damaging the airplane. Another pilot made a rough landing in Article 355, but again the damage was only minor.[120]

Article 365 sits on a transport dolly during an engine run. The U-2 was equipped with a turbojet that produced 11,200 pounds of thrust. A metal screen over the air inlet prevented the two crewmen on the ladder from being ingested, and a curved deflector mitigated the amount of dust and debris displaced behind the aircraft. *CIA*

Early on, senior agency officials thought it might be desirable to use foreign pilots for clandestine overflight missions, in order to more effectively insulate the American connection to the U-2 operation in the event one or more of the aircraft were lost over hostile territory. This idea, though largely relegated to a backup plan following selection of a sufficient number of qualified domestic pilots, was not entirely shelved. In case there might still be political conditions preventing the use of an American pilot,

Ground crewmen service Article 367 prior to flight. *CIA*

One crewman monitors flow rate as the special LF-1A fuel is pumped into the right wing of Article 371. *CIA*

eight Greek aviators were recruited under Project OSTIARY and sent to preliminary training at Williams Air Force Base, Arizona. Of these, only four were deemed suited to fly the U-2. They arrived at Watertown in late June 1956, where their poor English-language skills proved to be only one of several stumbling blocks. Yancey's instructors noted that the Greeks had substantial difficulty flying the U-2, and one nearly wrecked an airplane by landing it wing low. Additionally, there was no easy way to fit the foreign pilots into the agency's prevailing cover story involving high-altitude weather research. Over the objections of a few senior officers, Yancey washed them out of the program on July 15 and informed headquarters that they were not qualified to continue flying the U-2. The Greeks were then flown to Washington, where military and agency officials arranged to keep them in the US for a year of additional study and training because of the extensive knowledge of the entire operation they had acquired while at Watertown.[121]

Yancey originally planned to complete training of nine contract pilots for Detachment B by the second week of July, but by mid-May only five had reported for duty, and the others didn't arrive until June. The concurrent training of the four Greek pilots and two casuals, as well as accelerated engine development testing throughout the late spring and early summer, put a heavy burden on the available aircraft. Yancey was facing a potential six-week delay in achieving operational readiness for WRSP-II but was able to make up a great deal of time by adjusting training schedules and by motivating all concerned to put forth maximum effort. Final checkout flights for Detachment B took place during a four-day USCM exercise that began on July 18. This included both daylight and nighttime sorties so that pilots could practice a variety of navigation techniques. Maj. Harry N. Cordes, one of two Air Force officers awaiting assignment to an agency detachment, took off from Watertown in total darkness and flew west toward California, north to Montana, east across the Dakotas, and south over Colorado before completing the final westerly leg back to Nevada. He finally landed after being airborne for eight and a half hours. By the end of the exercise, the unit was declared combat ready. WRSP-II began deployment to Adana, Turkey, on August 13, 1956.[122]

Less than twenty months after the start of the AQUATONE project, a total of fourteen U-2 aircraft had been flown, and the arrival of another at Watertown was imminent. More than 2,200 flight hours had been logged during test and training flights, and total program costs were still well below original estimates. Lockheed transferred Articles 341 and 344 to the training group, only occasionally pressing them into service for flight tests where their unique configurations made it feasible. The original prototype still had most of its test instrumentation and was being used only for landing practice, but plans called for returning Article 341 to Burbank in October to be modified and brought fully up to date in the standard U-2A configuration. This left Article 351 as the only full-time test airplane. It was primarily employed in testing some of the operational equipment packages, including System II (a high-frequency communications and navigation system), System III (a communications intelligence receiver), a side-looking radar, and the type B high-resolution camera.[123]

Detachment C was activated as the 3rd Weather Reconnaissance Squadron (Provisional), WRSP-III, on July 12, 1956, under the command of Col. Stanley W. Beerli. He spent several weeks assigned to Project Headquarters for indoctrination and to work with headquarters staff on the selection of personnel for his new command before finally arriving at Watertown on August 8. He had earlier visited the base to monitor the previous squadron's combat-readiness demonstration. Another World War II veteran, Beerli joined the Army Air Forces after the Japanese attack on Pearl Harbor and eventually logged more than fifty combat missions as a bombardier/navigator on B-17s, primarily over Italy. After the war, he flew several photoreconnaissance variants of the B-17, B-29, and C-54 and participated in some of the early nuclear-testing programs before completing a tour of duty as a jet fighter pilot. Upon taking command of WRSP-III, he immediately began preparing his new squadron for deployment to the Far East. By August 20, seven contract pilots for WRSP-III and one replacement pilot for WRSP-II had arrived at Watertown. Just ten days later, an accident during a training flight put one U-2 out of commission. Fortunately, the pilot suffered no serious injuries, and the airplane was deemed repairable.[124]

Despite the obviously late hour, technicians work on Article 373, which awaits installation of its engine and tail assembly. *CIA*

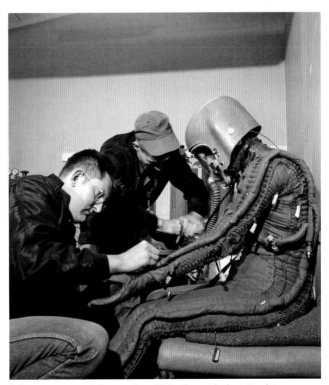

Life-support specialists assist a U-2 pilot with donning his pressure garment in preparation for a flight above 50,000 feet. *CIA*

The very next day, however, the AQUATONE program suffered yet another devastating loss. During a night-training sortie in Article 354, contract pilot Frank G. Grace Jr. climbed too steeply on takeoff and stalled with insufficient altitude for recovery. His airplane dove approximately 50 feet to the ground and disintegrated. Bob Murphy witnessed the accident. "It was pitch black," he recalled. "You can't imagine how dark it is there, where there are no outside lights." Standing by the hangars, he heard the jet take off and then noticed a trail of sparks along the airstrip. At first, he thought it was one of the pogos bouncing down the runway, but it was actually a result of the airplane's wingtip dragging on the asphalt. The U-2 departed the runway and careened toward a telephone pole with a light on it. Upon striking the pole, the airplane's fuselage broke just behind the cockpit. "When we got there," Murphy said, "I thought he was OK; I mean, [the pilot] was in the cockpit and he wasn't hit by anything but he had broken his neck, and he was dead."[125]

To minimize delays, headquarters authorized Beerli to immediately proceed with training operations and to borrow the first Air Force U-2 aircraft, Article 361, as soon as it was delivered in September. One WRSP-III pilot resigned from the program. Those remaining successfully completed a three-day USCM exercise in late October, but the results were not entirely satisfactory. Camera problems prompted Beerli to request additional time for his pilots to increase proficiency, while simultaneously running tests to improve camera reliability. Doing so would not incur further delay, since the deployment date had already slipped to mid-January 1957 due to difficulties in arranging for the use of an overseas base. This put Beerli in the awkward position of having to protect his squadron's franchise for living and working space at Watertown against the encroaching flood of SAC personnel assigned to the Air Force follow-on group (FOG) that would constitute the first operational military unit to fly the U-2.[126]

This was not an inconsequential problem. In September 1956, SAC Headquarters had authorized the FOG commanding officer, Col. William Proctor, to deploy twenty-one officers and enlisted men to Watertown to prepare for the arrival of the Air Force U-2 fleet and pilot trainees. Over ensuing weeks, increasing numbers of SAC personnel were flying in and out of Watertown, sometimes without prior headquarters approval. Base billeting and messing facilities were stressed to their limits, and it was apparent that if WRSP-III were not deployed soon, SAC might be forced to delay phasing in the remaining FOG personnel at the training site. On November 13, Col. Jack D. Nole became the first FOG trainee to be checked out in the U-2. Others soon followed, but due to the influx of SAC trainees and additional support personnel, crowded conditions prevailed at Watertown until the following March, when the CIA reached an agreement with the Air Force to deploy WRSP-III to Atsugi, Japan.[127]

A pilot studies the latest forecast for weather conditions and winds aloft. Groom Lake offered excellent flying weather almost year-round, but U-2 training flights often spanned the country, exposing the airplane to a wide variety of meteorological conditions. *CIA*

A preflight briefing for a long-duration U-2 mission. The base meteorologist presents the latest weather forecast, predicting light turbulence and contrail formation between 27,000 and 37,000 feet, and a cold front pushing down through the central states. A photomap, *at left*, shows the layout of Watertown Airstrip and several lakebed runways. Maj. Richard Heyser stands behind the podium at far right. *CIA*

Color images of the U-2 at Watertown are scarce. Article 368, seen here in NACA livery, sits near the edge of the lakebed. Bald Mountain dominates the skyline at far right. *CIA*

By the first week of December, all U-2 airframes of the initial batch had been delivered to Watertown, along with several from the second batch. Article 355 was undergoing repairs and would soon return to operational status. To improve understanding of the U-2's vulnerabilities, several of the aircraft were evaluated using radar systems operated by Edgerton, Germeshausen, and Grier (EG&G), Inc., at a site approximately 50 miles south of Groom Lake, near Indian Springs Air Force Base.[128] EG&G had long been an integral part of the Nevada Test Site, providing precision test instrumentation, firing systems, and high-speed cameras. The radar site, operated by the company's Special Projects division, would later play a significant part in the history of Groom Lake.

Before the month was out, another agency U-2 had been lost. On December 19, Robert Ericson took off from Watertown on a training mission over northern Arizona. As he climbed to altitude, a slow leak depleted his oxygen supply. Approximately four and a half hours into the flight, Ericson realized that something was seriously wrong, and began an emergency descent, but it was too late. Before he could reach a safe altitude, hypoxia set in, impairing his judgment. As his reaction time slowed and he lost track of the aircraft's speed, the U-2 exceeded the placarded

Ground crewmen prepare Article 368 for flight. Training missions often carried NACA weather research instruments to support the cover story. *CIA*

190-knot maximum, causing excessive buffeting and loss of control. The delicate airframe rapidly approached its load limits and finally disintegrated when it reached 270 knots. Ericson somehow managed to jettison the canopy and was sucked out of the aircraft at an altitude of 28,000 feet. Fortunately, his chute opened automatically at 15,000 feet, and he touched down without injury. The aircraft was a total loss, its wreckage strewn across a sparsely populated section of the Navajo Indian Reservation south of Ganado.[129]

The disintegrating plane left a smoke trail that was visible from the tiny community of Chambers on Highway 66. Lloyd Baker, a traveling salesman, and a trucker named Luther Beasley rushed toward the source of the smoke and found the pilot walking alongside a road. Maintaining his cover, Ericson identified himself as "Robert J. Everett" and said that he had been engaged in high-altitude weather research for the NACA. He also provided his aircraft number (357) and call sign (Workhorse 79) and asked the men to notify officials at Hamilton Air Force Base, California, home of the Western Air Rescue Center, that he was safe and sound. Local law enforcement officers secured the crash scene while Ericson waited to be picked up by Air Force personnel.[130]

A Horse of a Different Color

In 1955, the CIA signed a contract with Westinghouse Electric Corporation of Baltimore, Maryland, for the design and fabrication of high-resolution, single-channel airborne-imaging radar equipment for use on the U-2 and RB-69A/P2V-7. CIA financing for this effort was split between Project AQUATONE and the agency's Air-Maritime Division. The Air Force provided additional funding, with a view toward installing the instrument on RB-47H and RB-57D reconnaissance aircraft. Flight testing was to be carried out at Watertown under Project EQUINE. A World War II–vintage B-17 bailed to Westinghouse Air Arm by the Air Force several years earlier was already being used to provide crew orientation and training. This arrangement was due to terminate on November 30, at which time the airplane was to be scrapped. Agency officials, however, expressed a strong desire to retain the airplane as a test bed under conditions of an extended or transferred bailment, or as a result of direct purchase. Eventually, Westinghouse agreed to purchase the B-17 from the Air Force Wright Research and Development Center at a scrap rate.[131]

EQUINE was well underway by early April 1956, with the completion of the first equipment package. The Westinghouse AN/APQ-56 side-looking airborne radar (SLAR) had been designed to provide 30-meter-resolution imagery from oblique angles at a distance of at least 10 miles and altitudes above 40,000 feet. General Precision Laboratories, Inc., of Pleasantville, New York, was subcontracted to provide a radar navigation system for the test airplane. Westinghouse spent six weeks checking out the first radar-mapping set in the company's DC-3, based at Friendship International Airport in Baltimore. This necessitated approximately 120 hours of flying for shakedown of the equipment and to provide additional operator training.[132] A lightweight model of the APQ-56, weighing just 520 pounds, was specifically developed for use in the U-2. Structural modifications to accommodate this equipment were first incorporated into Article 349.[133]

The first two Westinghouse personnel arrived at Watertown around mid-May. After being cleared into the project, company test pilot Carroll O. "Andy" Andrews, his copilot, and his crew chief flew the B-17 to Nevada. In anticipation of the need to discuss highly classified aspects of equipment performance and test data and to expeditiously resolve any problems, the CIA established a secure

CIA-owned B-17 used for a variety of special projects. This, or a similar aircraft, served as a test bed for the EQUINE radar development program. *Uli Elch*

communications link between Westinghouse Air Arm and Watertown. EQUINE flight testing began the first week of June and continued for nearly a year.[134] All SLAR imagery was captured on film, using a subsystem developed by Eastman Kodak and Photomechanisms, Inc., under another subcontract. A working prototype was available by early November, but because the flight test program was unable to provide the necessary aircraft time or support at Watertown, the processor had to be tested aboard the DC-3. By the time that development and testing were concluded in June 1957, EQUINE project costs totaled $4,768,627.00.[135] The B-17 remained in storage at the test site for the next four years, until it was needed for another project.[136]

When the B-17 was unavailable, components of the EQUINE system were tested aboard this DC-3. *Westinghouse*

Rainbows and Angels

The final months of AQUATONE project activities at Watertown were characterized by intensive training and test sorties that were frequently postponed by inclement weather. Winter rainstorms left the lakebed half covered with water until mid-January 1957, when it froze solid. Next, a blizzard deposited 3 inches of snow on Groom Lake. Flying could be accomplished only by using the asphalt runway, and outdoor maintenance work often had to be done in freezing temperatures.[137] There was no margin for delay because the U-2 operation in Nevada was winding down.

One frigid morning, SAC instructor pilot Louis Setter woke to a snow-blanketed desert landscape. Not surprisingly, U-2 flight operations were canceled for the day. Otherwise, the sky was clear and the winds calm, so, finding himself suddenly free of other obligations, Setter decided to log some local proficiency flying in a de Havilland L-20A Beaver. The single-engine prop plane, normally used for patrolling the test site environs for intruders, was a versatile workhorse favored by bush pilots operating from rough fields in all weather conditions. "As I was flying over the lakebed, I saw someone on skis and landed nearby to investigate," Setter recalled. "It was Fred McCoy, and he asked me if I could tow him behind the plane with a long rope, while taxiing; well, we tried it at just below takeoff speed, but it didn't work too well because the prop wash just blew all the snow back in his face." Setter solved this problem during a second attempt by

The AEC loaned a de Havilland L-20A to the Watertown Project for use as a spotter plane to patrol the test site environs for intruders. *NNSA/LV*

advancing the throttles, taking off, and maintaining an altitude of about 20 feet. He held his airspeed to approximately 70 knots, just about 18 knots above stall speed, while cruising in a wide arc as McCoy held on. "We did one or two circles around the lakebed, then I landed," said Setter. "I think he enjoyed it."[138]

Since the beginning, Project Headquarters had planned on closing the Watertown installation shortly after the departure of WRSP-III at the end of March 1957. The SAC pilots had yet to complete their training, so the base would have to remain open a while longer. Because only the Lockheed flight test organization and Air Force FOG would stay until the end, the project personnel officer asked section heads for estimates of manpower requirements through June 30.[139] Another important consideration was the fact that preparations were once again underway at the NTS to begin full-scale, aboveground atomic testing. Radioactive fallout and shock waves from the powerful explosions would have serious consequences for the secret base.

In mid-March, as the FOG stepped up their training syllabus, Donald C. Downie and James F. Jarboe of Hycon's photographic department arrived to film a documentary for the CIA to use in classified U-2 project briefings. The two men were well qualified for the task. Following a tour of duty as a C-46 pilot in the China-Burma-India theater of operations during World War II, Downie served as chief photographer for the *Independent Star-News* in Pasadena, California, before going to work for Hycon in 1952. A private pilot himself, Downie loved airplanes and during his newspaper career had penned a column called "Flying for Fun." Prior to joining Hycon, Jarboe served as a combat photographer in Korea with the Army's Third Infantry Division. The short film commissioned by the agency was entirely scripted and filmed by Downie and Jarboe. It was titled *The Inquisitive Angel* and covered all aspects of Watertown operations, including delivery, assembly, and testing of U-2 airframes and camera systems, and the loading of disassembled U-2s and support equipment into a C-124 bound for Japan. Additionally, the filmmakers documented pilot-training activities, commuter airlift operations, and daily life at the base. Serendipitously, they also captured an incident in which Article 343 struck the ground short of the runway, shearing off its landing gear. Scenes of crash rescue personnel rushing to the aid of the fortunately uninjured pilot added considerable cinematic drama. Downie and Jarboe wrapped up production within six to eight weeks. Their motion picture and accompanying still photos not only provided historical documentation of the secret project but also included images of startlingly artistic sensitivity that remained hidden from public view until being declassified nearly half a century later.[140]

As the CIA staff diminished and Air Force presence increased, headquarters officials debated whether to continue using AEC contract guards or replace them with approximately twenty air police under the command of a junior Air Force officer who would report to the senior CIA security officer on-site. In an exchange with Dick Bissell, Jim Cunningham declared, "Personally, I have no religion one way or the other as to whether or not we employ contract guards or air police during this twilight period at Watertown." He added, "If the Ranch can accommodate the number of air police suggested, the identifiable costs to the Government would be less than if contract guards were used and, of course, such an arrangement would do no harm to our cover story." On the other hand, he noted, use of contract guards would eliminate the necessity of housing them at Watertown, since most had families in Las Vegas and would commute to work in any case.[141]

It was clear that Watertown's days were numbered. Before the end, Lockheed, Air Force, and CIA officials made the most of the time remaining. One of the final U-2 test projects involved radar cross-section (RCS) reduction. Since the beginning of the AQUATONE project, defense officials had known that the U-2's greatest vulnerability was its radar signature. Although the airplane could fly high above the range of most surface-to-air missiles, it could be easily and accurately tracked, as

Watertown personnel examine the U-2 navigation trainer as Don Downie sets up a shot for *The Inquisitive Angel*. CIA

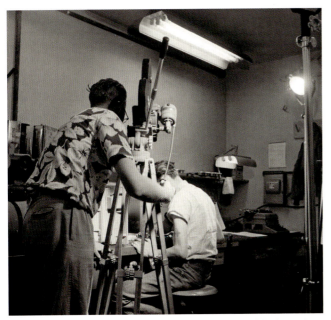

Jim Jarboe films a camera technician at work in one of the base photo labs. *CIA*

A still frame from *The Inquisitive Angel* captures the aftermath of Article 343's crash landing. *CIA*

airplane's radar signature through two vastly different approaches.[143] These were applied to two airplanes in early 1957. The first method, nicknamed "Trapeze," involved stringing copper-plated steel wires with ferrite beads spaced precisely across the aircraft's outer skin at specific distances from the fuselage, wings, and tail to defend against low-frequency radar waves. These wires were strung across laminated wood standoffs bristling from the fuselage, tail, and the leading and trailing edges of the wings.

One attempt to make the U-2 less visible to radar involved stringing copper-plated wires with ferrite beads across the aircraft's outer skin along the fuselage, wings, and tail. *Lockheed*

reconnaissance flights over the Soviet Union demonstrated. Therefore, in July 1956, some two decades before the advent of what later came to be known as "stealth technology," the CIA embarked on an effort to make the U-2 less vulnerable to radar detection through the application of special materials and structures. These treatments would reduce backscatter, the reradiation of incident radar energy back toward the receiver. This pioneering effort, dubbed Project RAINBOW, once again made use of the EG&G radar range at Indian Springs. At the direction of Project Headquarters, EG&G installed additional radars, RCS-measurement equipment, and a hydraulic lift to support test models.[142]

Lockheed engineer Luther D. MacDonald, chemists Melvin F. George Jr. and Perry Merlin, and physicist Edward Lovick Jr. teamed up with Harvard physics professor Edward M. Purcell and Franklin J. Rodgers, associate head of the Radar Division at MIT Lincoln Laboratory, to reduce the

Another view of the so-called Trapeze configuration, showing wires strung on standoffs over the surface of the vertical stabilizer. *Lockheed*

The second approach involved coating the underside of the fuselage with high-frequency radar-absorbent material (RAM), varying in thickness from a ¼ inch to about 1 inch. It consisted of phenolic honeycomb topped by layers of Salisbury Screen, a resistive fiberglass sheet covered with conductive grids of perpendicular lines and isolated squares printed on the surface, using special silver-graphite paint developed by Mel George. Thickness of the honeycomb layer equaled approximately one-quarter of the wavelength of expected incoming radar energy. Since this was a fixed value, it could be tailored only to very specific frequency bands. Technicians nicknamed it "Wallpaper" because of its exterior pattern but also called it "Thermos" because the thick blanket of RAM prevented the normal dissipation of engine heat through the aircraft's skin. The addition of either RAM or beaded wires added excess weight and drag to the U-2, making it aerodynamically "unclean." In fact, the antiradar modifications reduced the airplane's maximum altitude by as much as 5,000 feet and cut its range by 20 percent. Hence, aircraft with the RAINBOW treatments were known as "Dirty Birds."[144]

Robert Sieker conducted tests of the "Thermos" treatment that had been applied to Article 341. His mission on April 4, 1957, was to evaluate aircraft performance relative to engine heating. Sieker planned to fly the first hour at normal engine-operating temperatures, and the second at 68 degrees Fahrenheit above normal. By the time he reached 72,000 feet, the airplane's engine compartment was approaching critical temperature levels due to the insulating properties of the RAM blanket. This caused the hydraulic system to overheat and reduce pressure to the fuel-boost-pump motor. The result was a flameout and loss of cabin pressure. Ordinarily, this would not have been a serious problem because the pilot was wearing his partial-pressure suit. Unfortunately, as Sieker's suit inflated, the clasp on his faceplate failed, causing loss of consciousness when the air rushed out of his helmet. Without the pilot's guiding hand, the airplane soon stalled and entered a flat spin. Upon descending into the lower atmosphere, Sieker eventually regained his senses and attempted to bail out. Struggling to release his harness and the canopy latch, he was finally able to jump clear, but without sufficient altitude for his parachute to fully open.[145]

Sieker's failure to report in to Watertown Operations sparked an intensive search effort. Approximately seventy military and civilian search planes crisscrossed parts of Nevada, Utah, and California in an effort to locate the missing plane and pilot. Searchers from the Western Air Rescue Center and Civil Air Patrol were told to look for a brown airplane with silver wings. Sieker was said to be wearing a red-and-white outer flight garment and had been equipped with a red-and-white parachute. On the ground, law enforcement officers also aided the search. Robert Clark, superintendent of the Nevada Highway Patrol, told reporters the Air Force had requested that in the event it was found, a "maximum security" cordon should be placed around the plane or its wreckage.[146]

Three days later, Ruben Saavedra of the Nevada Civil Air Patrol spotted the wreck while flying over White River valley, southwest of the rural community of Sunnyside.

In another RAINBOW approach, technicians covered the lower fuselage of Article 341 with a layer of radar-absorbent material. One drawback to this configuration was that it acted as insulation, which prevented the normal dissipation of engine heat. *Lockheed*

Lockheed test pilot Bob Sieker. *Via Chris Pocock*

He notified Air Force officials, who immediately dispatched personnel to the scene, but when they reached the crash site they found Sieker dead with his parachute only partially deployed. The airplane was shattered but recognizable. Its tail remained upright and the wings were largely intact, but the engine lay exposed amid the burned-out fuselage. The cockpit had been smashed though not burned. Once officials had been notified and the scene secured, Ben Koziol, Jerry Carney, Glenn Fulkerson, Paul Lehan, and several others were dispatched from Watertown to retrieve the wreckage. Investigators eventually determined that had Sieker's life-support system not malfunctioned, he would have most likely been able to bring the plane home safely. Kelly Johnson called for a redesign of the helmet faceplate latch, a dual oxygen regulator, and an ejection seat that could be used interchangeably with the existing bucket seat.[147]

Despite the tragedy, test and training activities continued at a furious pace. Additionally, several U-2 aircraft had been ordered for use by ARDC at Edwards, but the CIA was still reluctant to allow the aircraft to be flown there. In the interim, Col. Thomas R. Waddleton (ARDC) asked Col. Gibbs to approve clearance for three test pilots and several associated support personnel, all from Edwards, to undergo training at Watertown instead. After Article 368 was delivered in early April, three ARDC pilots, Capt. Loren W. Davis, Capt. Hugh P. "Pat" Hunerwadel, and Maj. Donald M. Sorlie, used it primarily for checkout and familiarization flights. Meanwhile, Articles 344 and 355 were allocated for further RAINBOW studies pending delivery of additional antiradar materials. In the wake of Sieker's mishap, the aft fuselage of Article 344 was instrumented to collect temperature data. Article 351 was equipped to test a signals intelligence package called System IV, and Article 367 was being used to test the type C long-range oblique photography camera.[148] Pressure to complete this work was high due to the forthcoming resumption of nuclear testing.

Atomic Ghost Town

Toward the end of April, shortly before Downie and Jarboe completed filming *The Inquisitive Angel*, the AEC and the DoD began a nuclear test series called Plumbbob. It was scheduled to include twenty-four nuclear detonations and six safety trials. Project 57, the first shot of the series, was a safety experiment similar to those carried out during the earlier Project 56. Defense planners recognized that aircraft crashes and other operational and logistic mishaps could result in the accidental firing of one or more detonators in a nuclear explosive device. Weapon designers strove therefore to make each warhead at least "one-point safe," which meant that if a single detonator fired, there would be no chance of a nuclear yield. Project 56 had demonstrated that the plutonium contamination of the surrounding area had been significant. As a result, Project 57 was undertaken to devise a means of estimating immediate distribution and long-term redistribution of plutonium dispersed during a nonnuclear detonation, collect biomedical data on health hazards associated with plutonium-laden environments, evaluate methods for decontamination of natural and man-made surfaces, and assess a variety of alpha survey instruments and field-monitoring procedures for estimating contaminant deposition promptly. Test objectives included a particle physics study, biomedical program, and decontamination exercise.[149]

The device selected for the test was an XW-25 warhead with a projected yield of 1.5 kilotons. Designed for use with the Douglas MB-1 Genie air-to-air-missile, the warhead was just 27 inches long and 17 inches wide and weighed about 218 pounds.[150] To simulate a one-point detonation during transportation or storage, it was to be fired at ground level, using only the bottom detonator. The warhead was complete and standard in nearly

Members of the recovery crew examine the wreckage of Article 341. The airplane impacted in a flat spin, resulting in a small fire that consumed the center fuselage and Q-bay but left the tail and wings largely intact. *CIA*

all respects, sufficiently representative of operational weapons then in the stockpile. In order to conduct the experiment under the most-ideal conditions, researchers needed test criteria that could not be met inside NTS boundaries. The test had to be located in a broad, flat valley at least 15 miles long with respect to the predicted path of fallout, and with ground zero at least 3 miles from any mountainous terrain. Minimal vegetation was necessary to permit maximum redistribution of contamination during windstorms, which typically occurred on a weekly basis and lasted up to two days. Most important, the test area had to be as free as possible from previous plutonium contamination.[151]

A lengthy discussion at the first project meeting focused on a choice between Papoose Lake, with its adjoining valleys east of Yucca Flat, and the Groom Lake area and Emigrant Valley to the north. Project 57 test director James D. Shreve Jr., Col. Eugene A. Blue of the DMA, William W. Allaire from the AEC Albuquerque Operations Office, and Maynard W. "Bill" Cowan Jr. of Sandia Laboratories conducted an aerial inspection of the candidate sites. Both lay beyond the NTS boundaries and were considered equal from an operational viewpoint, but the decision was ultimately based on existing soil contamination levels from previous nearby testing. Samples taken by UCLA radiation scientist Kermit H. Larson indicated that in the topmost inch of surface cover, the maximum plutonium backgrounds differed by a factor of 60. Soil in the Groom Lake area contained a maximum of 0.5 micrograms of plutonium per square meter versus 30 micrograms per square meter around Papoose Lake. After reviewing these results, according to the meeting minutes, "the choice of Groom Lake Valley went uncontested."[152]

Since the chosen site was under Air Force control, it was necessary for AEC officials to make arrangements to formally acquire the land either as an addition to the NTS or as an off-site adjunct. A check revealed that grazing rights to the area had been extinguished, but Shreve had observed during his aerial inspection that there were between "60 to 80 cattle who hadn't got the word." It was necessary to have them removed prior to the test.[153] The Project 57 test site was designated Area 13, a block of land approximately 10 by 16 miles abutting the northeastern boundary of the NTS and the northern boundary of the Watertown extension. Ground zero for the shot was just 5 miles northwest of Groom Lake and 7 miles from the Watertown cantonment area. The AFSWP chief, Maj. Gen. Alvin R. Luedecke, described the new test area in a letter to the DMA director and noted, "Immediate entry into the area has also been approved and has been coordinated with the agency which has been using the Range."[154]

Originally scheduled for early April, the Project 57 shot was postponed several times due to unfavorable weather conditions. This was problematic because the entire Watertown population had to be evacuated before each planned shot date to avoid potential hazards of plutonium inhalation or an unexpected nuclear yield. At noon on the day prior to the planned detonation, three long siren blasts from two crash trucks signaled that all personnel should immediately secure their work areas and prepare to board the DC-3 and C-54 for evacuation to Burbank. REECo support staff had to secure all foodstuffs, water supplies, and related equipment before departing separately. Following evacuation, designated persons were tasked with checking each day to see whether it would be possible to return to base. The evacuation plan specified that "no one will be advised to return until Watertown is as safe as any other town or city away from AEC."[155]

Finally, on the morning of April 24, conditions were deemed satisfactory and the countdown began. The nuclear device was armed three hours prior to shot time. An observation plane took off from Yucca Flat and climbed to an altitude of 10,000 feet over Groom Lake, but the closest observers were two men assigned to a camera station just 2 miles west of ground zero. Precisely thirty minutes prior to shot time, the test director confirmed that the area was clear and all personnel accounted for. At H-hour, a signal sent

The Project 57 site within Area 13 was fenced and posted to deter entry into the alpha-contaminated zone. *DOE*

to the detonator fired the warhead's high-explosive charge, instantly destroying the weapon and sending a cloud of dust and debris high into the air. The blast distributed plutonium dust and fragments over 895 acres of scrubland. Although there had been no obvious signs of an atomic explosion, the test director dispatched a three-man Rad-Safe team to determine whether any beta or gamma radiation hazard existed from a partial nuclear yield. None was detected, but anyone entering the contaminated area was required to wear full protective suits and respirators to shield themselves from alpha-contaminated particles.[156]

In order to learn about air and surface concentration and dispersal of plutonium, scientists collected data by using air samplers, balloon-borne precipitators, soil samples, photographic methods, and a variable-scale rectangular grid consisting of more than four thousand sticky pans distributed over a 43-square-mile area. They also analyzed the size, shape, and distribution of fallout particles. Biomedical researchers exposed a number of dogs to the fallout cloud and residual contamination to study the effects of acute and chronic exposure. Over a span of several weeks following the shot, test animals were periodically sacrificed and autopsied by veterinary scientists to collect data. By far the largest effort was expended on developing techniques for decontamination of large surface areas. Technicians studied plutonium removal from landscapes, concrete and asphalt pads, and materials used in building construction such as aluminum, steel, galvanized and tar-paper roofing, glass, brick, stucco, and wood. Methods of soil decontamination and fixation included wetting, oiling, leaching and stabilizing agents, and spraying with firefighting foam, as well as disking, plowing, and scraping.[157]

Project 57 Rad-Safe monitors had installed sampling gear at Watertown Airstrip and averaged readings taken every twenty-four hours for the next twenty-eight days. This equipment included two high-volume air samplers in the most heavily populated areas of the base, as well as fallout trays located on the roof of the base weather office and behind the maintenance shop. Initial readings indicated no detectable fallout at Watertown. According to test manager James Reeves, results were to be checked "after a five-day seasoning period and it [was] expected that readings [would] be minor."[158] Samples of rainwater were collected eleven hours after shot time, after a brief shower passed across Area 13 and then over Watertown. These samples contained both alpha and beta particles. Alpha radiation was also detected in the fallout trays and in samples from the Deer Camp watering hole east of Area 13.[159] Minor alpha activity persisted at Watertown for twelve days following the shot, but at well below operational guidelines. Nevertheless, this meant that resuspended plutonium dust was reaching the airbase in small amounts via the prevailing winds, and total amounts may have been underestimated. According to one interim test report, "No consideration was made for wind changes or rain, and the averaged readings ...were lower than is reasonable."[160]

Completion of the Project 57 test programs ended with the decommissioning and decontamination of Area 13. Workers in protective gear scraped the top 2 inches of soil in the vicinity of ground zero and hauled it away for burial at the NTS. Once members of Task Group 57 had mapped the extent and distribution of any remaining traces of plutonium, the contaminated zone was fenced and posted with warning signs. Contaminated equipment was buried in shallow trenches adjacent to Valley Road north of Watertown.[161]

Because Operation Plumbbob was scheduled to include approximately twenty nuclear shots between mid-May and the end of September, Watertown personnel were briefed on what to expect once full-scale testing got underway. More than two hundred people attended two presentations at Watertown by AEC Rad-Safe officers

A Rad-Safe specialist wearing anticontamination garments and a breathing mask measures radioactivity levels on a sample tray in Area 13. *DOE*

Access roads into the Project 57 site were marked with warning signs indicating the presence of alpha particle contamination. *CIA*

Charles Weaver, Oliver Placak, and Melvin Carter on May 14, 1957. At each meeting, the film *Atomic Tests in Nevada* was shown and discussed along with a general overview of nuclear-testing activities, radiation safety, and the possibility of radiation hazards from fallout. In view of the inevitable exposure of the Groom Lake area to radioactive debris, it was clear that the base would need to be evacuated prior to most detonations. If radiation levels were anticipated to be less than 50 milliroentgens per hour (mR/hr.), base personnel would be advised to remain indoors; for higher predicted radiation levels, evacuation would begin at least four hours prior to detonation. In advance of each shot, the Nevada Test Organization (NTO) would notify the Watertown commander of fallout pattern predictions on the basis of the best available weather forecast. Even if the majority of the base population was absent, selected security personnel were required to stay behind to man the guard posts and protect classified material and equipment. If the guards had to be withdrawn to a fallback position due to unusually high radiation intensity, contract or military aircraft would make aerial security sweeps, as necessary. The assistant to the NTO test manager would notify the Watertown commander when it was safe for personnel to return.[162]

Before departing Watertown, the Rad-Safe officers met with Richard Newton and Colonels Nole and Shingler to discuss arrangements for radiation monitors to visit the airbase whenever fallout was anticipated in the Groom Lake area. Newton indicated that he had been instructed to remain at Watertown in the event of evacuation. An agreement between the AEC and Project Headquarters specified that every effort would be made to see that fallout from any given shot would be limited so as to permit reentry of personnel within three to four days without danger of exposure exceeding established off-site radiation safety criteria. It was, however, highly likely that evacuations might be prolonged because tests were often postponed due to weather or technical problems. Newton asked if the NTO planning board might under some circumstances consider delaying a shot in consideration of Watertown operations. This was not an unreasonable request, since by most estimates the U-2 operation was expected to permanently depart Groom Lake by June 30, thus minimizing any interference with Plumbbob. After several delays, full-scale testing began on May 28 with 12-kiloton shot Boltzmann fired from a 500-foot tower on the northern end of Yucca Flat. Next, during the first week of June, were Franklin and Lassen, two small experiments with yields of less than half a kiloton each. More, and larger, shots soon followed.[163]

Maj. James A. Qualls pats Col. Jack Nole on the back as ground crewmen assist with last-minute adjustments to his pressure suit and outer coveralls prior to flight. *CIA*

If any doubt remained that the Groom Lake base should be considered a strictly temporary facility, the proximity of full-scale atomic testing sealed its fate. Because there were additional requirements for development and testing of new aircraft configurations and equipment, the CIA activated Detachment G at the North Base auxiliary field at Edwards under the auspices of ARDC. This was accomplished despite strong objections from the AQUATONE project security officer, who feared that the operation risked exposure due to the relatively open and accessible nature of Edwards and the fact that North Base was located within a mile of a busy highway. The CIA ultimately decided to mothball Watertown Airstrip for one year, after which the agency would make a final decision on whether to keep or dispose of the facility.

Preliminary estimates for closure and maintenance of the base came to $15,723, plus an additional $1,200 per month to pay for a caretaker and provide contingency funding for special repairs and miscellaneous expenses. Detachment G, reconstituted on May 10 as the 4th Weather Reconnaissance Squadron (Provisional), WRSP-IV, began the move to Edwards on June 6. The new squadron was placed under the command of Lt. Col. Roland L. "Cy" Perkins, who had previously served as operations officer for WRSP-II in Turkey. The Air Force opted to move the SAC U-2 training operation to

An observer in a chase plane captured this rare image of a five-ship U-2 formation on its way to Laughlin Air Force Base in Texas. *CIA*

Laughlin Air Force Base near Del Rio, Texas, where it would join the 4080th Strategic Reconnaissance Wing. Col. Nole led a formation of four U-2 aircraft from Watertown to Laughlin on June 10. Six more aircraft followed a few days later, and WRSP-IV completed its move to North Base on June 20. When the Watertown facility was officially shuttered on June 21, 1957, with only two caretaker/security personnel remaining on site, it became the first ghost town of the atomic age.[164]

CHAPTER 2
SPECIAL PROJECTS

A fallout-laden dust cloud from shot Fizeau of Operation Plumbbob rises from Yucca Flat, shifting direction with variations in the winds aloft. *NNSA/NV*

July 1957. Ed Current was lost. The worst part was knowing that it was his own fault. The solo cross-country flight was an important part of his training and necessary if he wanted to earn his private pilot's license. "When you stay near your home airport," his instructor had explained, "you can land and refuel whenever you want, but during a cross-country flight you need to plan ahead. You have to be aware of weather along your route, know the locations of airports, the lengths of their runways, and traffic patterns. Most important of all, you need good navigation skills. You must keep track of where you are, and know how to get to where you want to be." Remembering these words, Current swallowed and stared down at the forbidding landscape. Nothing but deep desert valleys and rugged mountains as far as the eye could see. He had somehow lost his bearings and, to make matters worse, was now low on fuel. As Current lamented his poor planning, the small plane bucked and shuddered violently in the turbulent summer air. Suddenly, he spotted a small airstrip and several hangars on the edge of a dry lakebed. It looked as inviting as an oasis. Current steered toward it and entered what he hoped was the traffic pattern. Circling the field, he saw no airplanes, just a handful of dilapidated buildings and a couple of jeeps. Glancing warily at his fuel gauge, he hoped the field wasn't abandoned, but upon landing he was reassured to see someone driving toward him. Current chuckled with relief as he unlatched his seat harness. "Looks like it's my lucky day," he thought. Glancing up at his presumed rescuer, a friendly greeting died on Current's lips as he stared down the barrel of a Thompson submachine gun.

AEC scientists were quick to take advantage of Watertown's recent abandonment. After the 10-kiloton shot Wilson was detonated from a balloon 500 feet above Yucca Flat on June 18, 1957, the upper part of the debris cloud separated from the stem and drifted northeast, depositing fallout on the Groom Lake area. In anticipation of such an event, Rad-Safe technicians had placed instrumentation in various Watertown buildings, parked vehicles, and open areas to measure radiation levels. Because the airbase included structures made of wood, sheet metal, plaster, and other materials commonly found in an average American town, the resulting data provided information on how well these substances might protect inhabitants against radioactive fallout in the event of nuclear war. In effect, the abandoned base had become a field laboratory for Civil Defense research.

Normal background radiation levels at Groom Lake typically averaged between 0.02 and 0.04 mR per hour. During Operation Plumbbob, readings taken inside one of Watertown's wood-frame dormitory buildings climbed to 30 mR/hr. following the detonation of Diablo, a 17-kiloton tower shot. Radiation levels inside Trailer 10, which had 4-inch-thick aluminum and wood walls, initially went off-scale before gradually dropping to 24 mR/hr. over the next several hours. A warehouse experienced a maximum of 75 mR/hr. indoors, while levels outside the building reached 110 mR/hr. The interior of the base theater received 90 mR/hr. for a few minutes as the cloud passed. Radiation inside the cab of the control tower reached 37 mR/hr., while outside levels were up to 60 mR/hr. Additional readings were taken in several office and storage buildings as well as on the volleyball court. Rad-Safe technicians had also installed monitoring equipment inside several trucks, some with windows closed and others open. The interior of one vehicle, located 9.5 miles west of Watertown in what turned out to be a significant hotspot, received 950 mR/hr. while exterior levels reached an astonishing 1,420 mR/hr. By contrast, another truck, 2 miles west of Watertown, received only 0.3 mR/hr. inside the cab and 0.5 mR/hr. outside.[1]

This O-11A fire truck, built by American La France, carried 1,110 gallons of water-foam solution for extinguishing blazes fed by gasoline or jet fuel and 40 gallons of chlorobromomethane, a vaporizing liquid used to extinguish fires in engine nacelles and other confined areas. *CIA*

Fallout was not the only hazard from Watertown's nuclear neighbor. A shot named Hood, fired on July 5, was sufficiently powerful to produce blast effects that were felt well beyond the test site boundary. The device was lofted by balloon to a height of 1,500 feet over Area 9, about 14 miles southwest of Watertown. With a yield of 74 kilotons, it was the most powerful airburst ever detonated within the continental United States, nearly five times the power of the bomb dropped on Hiroshima. It was also the only aboveground test of a thermonuclear weapon in Nevada and had been detonated despite an informal agreement between the government and the military precluding the use of fusion weapons on American soil.[2] Hood's radioactive cloud drifted over Groom Pass and the Papoose Range, depositing fallout on the Watertown camp, where the blast wave had already left its mark. According to Rad-Safe technician Richard A. Gilmore, damage included shattered windows on the west sides of Building 2 and the mess hall, and a broken ventilator panel on the north side of one of the dormitories. The shock wave also buckled metal doors on a maintenance building and a supply warehouse on the west side of the base.[3]

Vehicles parked outside a building at Watertown include a 1954 Henney-Packard Junior ambulance and a 1953 Dodge M-43 ¾-ton, 4×4, military ambulance. *CIA*

The shock wave from shot Hood shattered windows and caused structural damage at Watertown. The mushroom cloud deposited radioactive fallout as it drifted over the airfield. *NNSA/NV*

Between shots, when radiation levels permitted, two security personnel occupied Watertown. Their task involved guarding any remaining assets and preventing intruders from entering the nuclear proving ground via the few dirt roads entering Emigrant Valley from the north and northeast. For the most part it was an exercise in unrelenting tedium, but this changed on July 28, 1957, when the guards were roused from their torpor by the drone of an aircraft engine. A small civilian plane was circling overhead in violation of the restricted airspace. More surprising, the pilot suddenly brought the plane in for a landing on the asphalt runway. The guards hurried to intercept the unexpected visitor, who was soon identified as Edward K. Current, a Douglas Aircraft Company employee. While being detained overnight and questioned, Current explained that he had been on a cross-country training flight from Torrance, California, to Las Vegas when he became lost, ran low on fuel, and decided to make an emergency landing at Groom Lake. The following day, the AEC Office of Test Information issued a press release describing the incident in detail, adding, "Nevada Test Organization security officials reported the incident to the Civil Aeronautics Board, which administers the air closure over the Test Site." Current's adventure was not yet over, however. Upon release from custody he was allowed to refuel and take off, but shortly after departing Watertown he experienced engine trouble and was forced to make a crash landing at Desert Rock Airstrip near Mercury. Current was uninjured, but the airplane sustained some damage.[4]

Archangel Ascendant

The wheels of bureaucracy turn slowly. Although AEC officials submitted a request in 1955 to formally add the Groom Lake area to the Nevada Test Site, no immediate action was taken. It wasn't until June 20, 1958, one year after Watertown Airstrip was mothballed, that Assistant Secretary of the Interior Roger Ernst signed Public Land Order 1662, legally withdrawing from public access 38,400 acres of land encompassing the Watertown base.[5] Surprisingly, the boundaries of this 60-square-mile parcel left nearly the entire northern half of Groom Lake outside the secure perimeter. A small portion of the lakebed fell within the Nellis Bombing and Gunnery Range, but 1.5 square miles of the playa remained public land, easily accessible from Tikaboo Valley by unpaved roads that were used by miners with claims in the Groom Mountains and by local ranchers seeking errant cattle.

By this time the nuclear-testing program was split between the Pacific Proving Ground and the Nevada Test Site. It ground to a sudden halt at the end of October 1958, when President Eisenhower announced a unilateral moratorium with the understanding that this agreement would hold as long as the Soviet Union also refrained from conducting nuclear weapon tests. The moratorium spared Groom Lake from fallout and blast overpressure and once again made Watertown Airstrip an attractive site for secret aircraft projects. This was fortuitous because it had become apparent that the U-2 would soon be vulnerable to improved Soviet surface-to-air missiles. In preparation for this eventuality, CIA officials sought a successor that could fly higher and faster and be less vulnerable to radar tracking. Unfortunately, such prescient thinking did nothing to avert the loss of a U-2 over Sverdlovsk, Russia, in 1960. Moreover, the capture of its pilot,

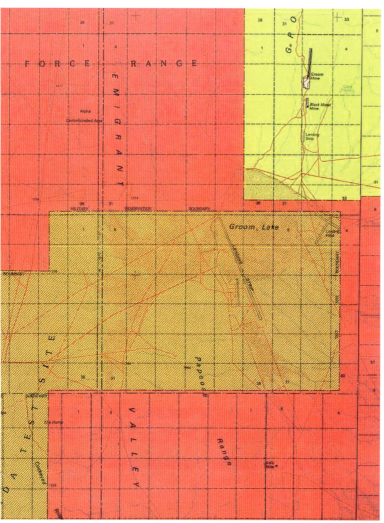

This land use map shows the addition of the Groom Lake area to the Nevada Test Site. Red-shaded sections were under Air Force jurisdiction. The yellow portion at upper right was public land interspersed with small private holdings, including the Groom and Black Metal Mines. *USGS*

Frank Powers, instantly demolished the cover story that the flight had been a research mission sponsored by the National Aeronautics and Space Administration (NASA). Soviet premier Nikita Khrushchev maximized the incident's propaganda value, leading to curtailment of U-2 flights over the Soviet Union and general embarrassment for the American government.

In early 1958, presidential science advisor James R. Killian recommended that the CIA and DoD commence feasibility studies for the development of an advanced manned reconnaissance vehicle to replace the U-2. This effort, which came to be known as GUSTO, focused on theoretical aerodynamic models capable of high-speed, high-altitude operations beyond the capabilities of conventional aircraft. Most important, the new craft was required to have a minimal RCS in order to thwart hostile air-defense systems. Aircraft manufacturers Lockheed and the Convair Division of General Dynamics Corporation, of Fort Worth, Texas, both were invited to submit design proposals. Technical direction for development of anti-radar treatments was assigned to the Scientific Engineering Institute (SEI), a CIA proprietary company in Cambridge, Massachusetts. Scientists at SEI conducted extensive experimentation with radical and exotic materials and designs to assess their effectiveness. Additionally, a number of scale models were shipped to the EG&G test range for signature calibration and RCS measurements. The results were very promising, but it was clear that there would be many technical challenges.[6]

Convair initially proposed building a small, ramjet-powered, high-speed craft designed to be air-launched from beneath the belly of a B-58A Hustler supersonic bomber. The company named it FISH (short for First Invisible Super Hustler) and claimed it would achieve a design cruise speed of Mach 4.2 and an altitude of 90,000 feet with a range of 3,900 miles. By mid-1958, Kelly Johnson's team at Lockheed was well into studies of a variety of design configurations with different combinations of turbojet and ramjet engines. Since he had earlier called the U-2 the Angel because of its high-altitude capabilities, Johnson named his first proposal Archangel 1, later shortened simply to A-1. Each successive design variation was accordingly numbered A-2, A-3, A-4, and so on. These configurations were subjected to extensive testing to evaluate aerodynamics and radar reflectivity. Lockheed proposals for GUSTO focused on configurations that could achieve Mach 3.2 cruise at altitudes from 90,000 to 100,000 feet with a 3,200-mile range. Rather than rely on a complicated arrangement involving a reconnaissance vehicle and mother ship, Johnson preferred an airplane that could take off under its own power. Lockheed teamed up with Pratt & Whitney for propulsion system development, while Convair collaborated with Marquardt.[7]

A subscale model of Lockheed's Model G2A configuration for Project GUSTO. *Lockheed*

Johnson investigated the idea of substituting nonmetallic, radar-absorbent structures for portions of the airframe to reduce RCS at various frequencies. Lockheed eventually subcontracted Narmco, Inc., in San Diego, California, to develop special plastic and high-modulus (elastically stiff) fiberglass materials capable of withstanding a wide range of temperature extremes during different phases of flight. Skunk Works studies examined numerous shapes, including, as Johnson explained, "flying saucers, which fundamentally have a low radar reflection from low viewing angles." One of his "saucers"—the Model G2A—included a metallic fuselage with long, slender plastic wings. Other, somewhat more conventional, configurations featured varying amounts of rubber, plastics, inflated Mylar, and carbon-loaded honeycomb.

At Indian Springs, EG&G evaluated models of both the Convair and Lockheed designs at radar frequencies ranging from 70 to 5,000 megahertz. The lower frequencies represented those used by Soviet early-warning systems, while the higher frequencies were typical of airborne search radar in fighter planes. In order to sufficiently reduce RCS over the representative band of frequencies that might be encountered, designers had to combine the effects of airframe shape, resistively loaded plastics, and other features. According to Johnson, "The very difficult problems of reducing the [radar] return of the air inlet on the engines, from canopies, camera windows, radomes, and antenna installations[,] were satisfactorily achieved after thousands of tests both at model and full scale."[8] After ten months of development, Johnson was sufficiently confident in his progress that he wrote a letter to Lt. Gen. Roscoe C. Wilson, deputy chief of staff for development, proposing that the Air Force authorize Lockheed to build two flying prototypes for evaluation.[9] Unfortunately, the G2A would be capable of only subsonic speeds, and officials favored a high-speed platform.

As the fierce competition between Lockheed and Convair heated up, it became apparent that the FISH concept suffered critical deficiencies. Most notably, the B-58A mother ship was incapable of attaining the required Mach number of 2.7 necessary for its payload to achieve ramjet ignition. The company proposed an uprated model, designated B-58B, but was dealt a setback when the Air Force canceled procurement of the new bomber. Estimated costs and operational complexity of reconfiguring the older B-58A made FISH impractical. Additionally, SAC was reluctant to surrender any of its limited inventory of supersonic bombers to another agency. As a result, Convair opted to pursue a larger craft dubbed KINGFISH that would be capable of taking off under its own power while still meeting operational performance requirements.[10] The company soon had a large-scale model of KINGFISH on the pole at Indian Springs.

Although customer specifications for GUSTO called for the airplane to have a small RCS, Kelly Johnson experienced a great deal of difficulty reconciling that requirement with the structural problems associated with high-speed cruise performance. In February 1959, he submitted his A-10 concept, designed to fly at more than 2,000 miles per hour and cruise at 90,000 feet. Mission radius was estimated at around 2,000 miles, but high RCS was still a concern. But Johnson was more concerned with performance, and the following month he further refined his design. The resulting A-11 was designed to take off from its home base, climb to 93,500 feet, cruise at Mach 3.2, and, with two aerial refuelings, complete an eight-hour, 13,340-nautical-mile mission.

When he pitched his new design to the CIA and reported the results of six months of radar studies conducted by EG&G, Johnson emphasized that expected improvements to Soviet tracking systems would likely enable detection of any airplane that might conceivably fly within the next three to five years. He conceded that the A-11's probability of detection was practically 100 percent. CIA officials deemed this unacceptable for an airplane intended for use in clandestine reconnaissance missions. Johnson went back to the drawing board believing that he had blown his chances with the CIA and that the agency would probably opt to go with Convair's proposal.[11]

Instead, Johnson learned to his astonishment on July 3 that the CIA had offered to accept lower cruising altitudes in exchange for reduced RCS. Then, following a burst of inspiration, he proposed a new Archangel design that combined advanced performance with better survivability. Offering speed, altitude, and low RCS, the A-12 was to be powered by two 34,000-pound-thrust Pratt & Whitney J58 turbojet engines in a midwing arrangement that reduced the airplane's side profile. It would have an unrefueled range of approximately 2,500 nautical miles. Flattened chines along the edges of the forebody softened radar reflection angles while providing additional lift and stability. Twin vertical fins, one atop each engine nacelle, were inwardly canted to further improve RCS characteristics. The airframe structure and most of the outer skin would be manufactured from titanium for strength and to withstand extreme aerodynamic and engine heating. The entire periphery of the airplane (wing edges, tails, and inlet spikes) was composed of composite radar absorbers in a sawtooth pattern varying from approximately 12 to 18 inches (apex to base). This material included electrically resistive asbestos honeycomb sandwiched between phenylsilane/asbestos-silicone laminate panels. Such "plastic" parts had to be capable of reducing radar backscatter as well as withstanding temperatures in excess of 800 degrees Fahrenheit while providing both structural strength and aerodynamic performance. Johnson was gratified to discover that these antiradar treatments reduced the airplane's overall RCS to the single-digit range in some frequency bands, but there was still a problem. Afterburner exhaust plumes from the engines created substantial radar returns from the airplane's aft quadrant. Lockheed radar engineer Ed Lovick suggested adding ionizing cesium salt compounds to the fuel, a development that according to Johnson became a basic part of the company's RCS reduction methods for later projects.[12]

This large, but still subscale, model of Convair's KINGFISH design was mounted inverted on the turntable at the Indian Springs RCS range. The model represents only the airplane's metal structure, without the radar-absorbent plastic inserts along the wing edges. *Convair via Jay Miller*

A subscale model of an early configuration of Lockheed's A-12 design, mounted upright on an inflatable pylon at Indian Springs. Note that the engine inlet spikes are fully retracted to represent cruise conditions. *Lockheed Martin*

Lockheed and Convair submitted final proposals on August 20, and although Convair's design promised better overall performance, the CIA evaluation panel considered it to be technologically riskier. Lockheed offered to produce the aircraft at a much-lower cost than their competitor, and the Skunk Works had prior experience with launching highly classified production efforts without attracting undue attention within the industry. Additionally, Lockheed already possessed a skilled labor pool with the necessary security clearances and a proven track record for producing new state-of-the-art vehicles. As a result, Johnson received a $4.5 million, four-month preliminary contract with the admonition that he prove the viability of his antiradar approach by January 1960 before receiving full go-ahead for production of ten airframes. The CIA terminated Project GUSTO on August 31, and the new development effort was named OXCART, an ironic choice for an airplane designed to fly at more than three times the speed of sound.[13]

Project 51

Lockheed had already tested several subscale models of the A-12 at the EG&G radar range, and work was underway to build a larger model and a full-scale mockup. Facilities at Indian Springs included a rotating platform remotely operated from a single building that contained a radar control room, a data-recording facility, engineering offices, and an electronics laboratory. The low turntable, just a few feet above ground level, was located half a mile from radar transmitters that illuminated the target across a wide spectrum of frequencies. Although this range had been useful while developing antiradar treatments for RAINBOW and GUSTO, Johnson was concerned that the Indian Springs site, located within view of a nearby highway, was not sufficiently secure and that the existing hydraulic lift was incapable of supporting full-scale models. In September 1959, he convinced EG&G's Special Projects division to move the RCS measurement range to Groom Lake.[14]

By this time, Dick Bissell had been promoted to deputy director for plans, and what had previously been the independent Development Projects staff during AQUATONE was transferred to the newly conceived directorate as the Development Projects Division (DPD). When considering reopening Watertown for OXCART, Bissell was mindful of the agency's previous friction with Kelly Johnson over matters of operational jurisdiction. He therefore advised the acting DPD chief, Col. William Burke, to make all necessary arrangements to ensure that Watertown would be operated as an agency facility with Lockheed as a tenant, rather than allowing it to become a Lockheed facility by default.[15]

Watertown Airstrip as it appeared in an aerial survey taken for Holmes & Narver in September 1959, while the base was in caretaker status. The flight line is devoid of airplanes, and all of the housing trailers have been removed. *USGS*

Robert Van Compernolle was ultimately responsible for creating the "Area 51" designation. *REECo*

Even after two years of neglect, the Watertown facilities remained in satisfactory condition to support radar cross-section testing activities. *CIA*

Johnson visited Watertown with Frank Rodgers, Col. Leo P. Geary (OXCART project officer), and the DPD Materiel Branch project engineer to evaluate potential sites for placement of RCS measurement facilities. Rodgers suggested a possible location, but Johnson was largely unimpressed. "There were numerous ditches, 10-foot piles of gravel, depressions, and other impediments," he later wrote. Instead, Johnson proposed placing the radar range on the west side of the dry lake so that the model-support pylons would be on absolutely level ground within clear line of sight from the southwest corner of the lakebed. Inspection of the Watertown site revealed that the runway was in excellent condition, and from the exterior the existing structures left over from AQUATONE appeared to be as well. Inexplicably, the caretaker was absent at the time, so it was impossible to ascertain the interior condition of any of the buildings. The project engineer later reported, "From what we could see by looking through the windows, the buildings appear to be in good shape except for dust."[16]

EG&G provided plans for a radar control center, a data reduction laboratory, and an array of diagnostic systems. Models and mockups were to be stored in the vacant former U-2 hangars. Planned improvements included standardized displays and calibration systems to simplify data reduction, as well as timers to warm up equipment prior to use, and a dual-frequency illumination capability to enable recording radar reflection patterns in both S and L bands simultaneously to reduce setup and recording times. EG&G arranged for REECo to construct several buildings to house radar and data reduction equipment. Cost estimates for constructing the new building and for performing structural, mechanical, and electrical work totaled $120,000.[17] Invoices for work undertaken at the Nevada Test Site were usually charged to project numbers, so, in order to track expenses for the new construction at Watertown, REECo accountant Robert A. Van Compernolle dubbed the effort Project 51. As a result, the project location subsequently became known as Area 51 and was officially designated as such on AEC maps of the NTS.[18]

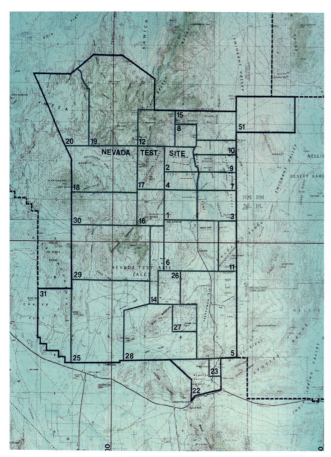

A map of the Nevada Test Site showing all the numbered test areas with the exception of Area 13. Area 51 is near upper right. *DOE*

An unclassified NTS phone directory included Area 51 telephone numbers but affiliated the Groom Lake facility with the Air Force to provide cover for CIA activities there. *Author's collection*

Werner Weiss served as CIA chief of base at Area 51. *Roadrunners*

In order to obscure the true purpose of ongoing activities, the CIA security officer for Project 51 drafted a cover story for Watertown's reactivation. An approved public information release for use in reply to queries from the press or others stated that the AEC had made Groom Lake available to EG&G for radar studies on behalf of the Air Force. The stated reason for selecting the remote site was to reduce the likelihood of any outside interference that might affect instrument calibration or test results. The CIA furnished AEC and EG&G public-relations officials with copies of the statement to use as needed. Requests for additional information were to be referred to the Office of Information Service at Air Force Headquarters, Washington, DC.[19]

By October 1, 1959, the EG&G Special Projects team was working six days a week to prepare for full-scale model testing, and the CIA had placed Werner H. Weiss in charge of Area 51. As "chief of base" at Station D, he oversaw a staff of approximately seventy-five people, mostly contract personnel. Weiss had emigrated from Germany at the age of nine with his family in 1926. He joined the Army during World War II and was stationed in England. Afterward, he became an Army civilian until getting a job with the CIA. Assignments in Germany included involvement with the first U-2 detachment in Wiesbaden, and he later helped organize the U-2 detachment in Japan. He arrived in Las Vegas on January 1, 1960, and while serving at Area 51 earned the nickname "Desert Fox."[20]

The agency's engineer general visited Area 51 for several days to survey construction progress. By this time, a concrete slab had been poured for the radar control center, and the components of the Butler building were expected to arrive no later than October 12. About 6 miles of road had been graded, with the rest due for completion within two months. Workers were drilling a 36-inch-diameter hole on the west side of the lakebed to accommodate a hydraulic lift for full-scale models. Availability of an adequate water supply remained the most significant concern. The two operating wells, drilled to depths of 900 and 1,100 feet, were producing approximately 50 gallons per minute between them. A new pump could nearly double the output, but efforts commenced to locate additional well sites that might produce up to 150 to 200 gallons per minute. Project planners estimated that an output of 250 gallons per minute would be required once the base was fully operational. Jim Cunningham, now chief of the DPD Administrative Branch, learned that a US Geological Survey team was already studying water resources at Mercury, and requested the group be immediately diverted to the Groom Lake area.[21]

Claude E. Cooke, REECo manager for Project 51 construction engineering, foresaw no reason his crews couldn't meet November deadlines for completion of the radar building and pylon lift. They had also been tasked with refurbishing a majority of the original Watertown structures that were being repurposed for the new project. All the old housing trailers for the U-2 workforce had long since been disposed of as surplus, but the remaining dormitory buildings proved more than sufficient to accommodate the first small cadre of Special Projects personnel. Cooke noted that despite the inherent pressures associated with putting the facility into shape on a crash basis under austere conditions, there was still time for occasional levity, such as when he repurposed one of the work trailers as a honeymoon suite. "We had a superintendent by the name of Carl Olson who had just married his wife, Fran," he recalled. "They spent their honeymoon in a trailer that Carl and I located at Groom Lake [for the construction project]."[22]

Increased activities at Area 51 necessitated additional permanent staff assignments, both military and civilian. Col. Burke petitioned Dick Bissell to approve a staffing increase of fourteen positions for the balance of the fiscal year (FY 1960) to meet the estimated minimum number of support personnel necessary to reopen the site for OXCART. He also requested fifty-six additional authorizations for FY 1961. By the time the RCS measurement range was fully operational, agency staffing consisted of forty-seven military and twenty-three civilian personnel. This number did not include either the EG&G cadre or the protective force of fifteen contract security guards.[23]

This was one of several Yagi antenna arrays at Area 51 that simulated Soviet target acquisition and early-warning radar systems. *Via T. D. Barnes*

Radar antennas and a control building were assembled on the edge of the lakebed just north of the aircraft-parking apron. One of the former U-2 hangars is barely visible at lower right. *CIA*

The original EG&G radar facility (*the dark building at left*) was later joined by a second antenna control and data reduction complex. *CIA*

Radar Men

Due to critical need to begin collecting radar data, OXCART project manager John Parangosky gave verbal approval for Lockheed to immediately begin construction of a pylon to support the A-12 mockup. Designed by Henry Combs, the 50-foot pole was assembled from three Navy destroyer propeller shafts welded end to end. A hydraulic piston lowered the top of the pole to ground level for installation of the model and raised it up for testing. Lockheed engineer Leon Gavette designed a mechanism to support and rotate the model during tests. Mounted in the center of a 102-foot-diameter concrete pad 1 mile north of the radar control building, the pole was capable of supporting 20,000 pounds. With the model installed, it could withstand winds of nearly 30 miles per hour. Ideally, testing would not take place under severely gusty conditions, but local desert weather was notoriously mercurial. Shear pins designed to fail in winds of more than 40 miles per hour allowed the model to weather-vane, preventing, it was hoped, serious damage. While preparations continued at the test site, Lockheed assembled the full-scale A-12 mockup, a ⅛-scale model, and a full-scale partial mockup that represented only the forward fuselage and cockpit section.

Two additional radar target installations were set up between the large pylon at the 1-mile site and the radar equipment. To accommodate small-scale models, workers at Area 51 dug a circular pit with a raised lip (which came to be known as the "Swimming Pool") half a mile north of the radar control building. A 22-foot inflatable bag was mounted in the center of the pit to support the ⅛-scale model. The first such device, a translucent pressurized Mylar cylinder with a rounded top, became the butt of numerous phallic-themed jokes and was soon replaced with an opaque tapered cone. Made from neoprene rubber, the new bag was still effectively transparent to radar except along the seam lines, which unfortunately acted as reflectors. Radar engineers solved this problem by redesigning the cone with a single, continuous spiral seam. Calibration tests were then accomplished by mounting a 42-inch metal sphere with a known RCS value atop the bag and measuring backscatter from the bag and surrounding terrain, both of which would later be filtered out to get accurate measurements of the model. For additional calibration, an aluminized sphere sized to provide a 1-square-meter return could be mounted on a fiberglass pole ¼ mile downrange.[24]

Workers prepare to install the 50-foot pole on its pad near the western edge of the lakebed. *CIA*

A ⅛-scale model of the A-12 was mounted atop a 22-foot inflatable pylon half a mile out from the lakeshore radar site. *Lockheed*

The inflatable pylon sat in the middle of a pit nicknamed the "Swimming Pool." This test model included conical structures aft of the engine nacelles to simulate afterburner exhaust plumes. *Lockheed*

For the purpose of obtaining baseline data, radar measurements were taken of the 50-foot pole, with and without antiradar treatment. Ed Rawson of SEI designed much of the necessary instrumentation and supervised its installation. Kelly Johnson met with Dick Bissell in early November 1959 to discuss project status, schedules, and management philosophy. Among other things, they talked about security matters (such as personnel clearances and cover stories), transportation of workers to the site, improvements to facilities, and general logistics. In a follow-up letter to Bissell, Johnson expressed his concern that preparations for testing were behind schedule. "I am very perturbed that the completion of the new site will be delayed at least two weeks," he wrote on November 6, adding, "In any case, we will be ready with our test models."[25]

Workers hold cables to stabilize a full-scale mockup of the A-12 nose and cockpit as it is raised atop the pole prior to taking RCS measurements. *Lockheed*

The full-scale A-12 pole model under construction at Lockheed's Burbank plant. *Lockheed*

Construction of the full-scale A-12 model was completed soon thereafter, and all the major subassemblies were crated and shipped to Area 51 by special convoy. Dorsey Kammerer spearheaded this challenging endeavor, which also served as a dress rehearsal for moving the production airframes from Burbank to the test site. The convoy consisted of four trucks carrying oversize loads under special permit. The largest package, containing the aft fuselage and inner wing/nacelle assemblies, was 65 feet long and 32.5 feet wide. The outer wing panels fit into a 30-by-22-foot container on the second truck. The third, with the forward fuselage section, was 14 feet wide and 63 feet long. A fourth vehicle carried a turnover jig and various fixtures. Departing from Lockheed's Burbank plant in the predawn hours of November 10, the convoy rolled north on Hollywood Way and then west on San Fernando Road to Highway 99, where it met a California Highway Patrol escort. A short break was followed by a steep ascent to the tiny mountain hamlet of Gorman, following the tortuous Ridge Route. Heavy loads meant slow going, with speeds sometimes dropping to less than 5 miles per hour. Whenever traffic built up behind the convoy, the escort pulled the trucks off the highway, allowing other vehicles to pass but making it difficult to regain momentum with the oversize load.

After passing through Gorman, Kammerer steered the convoy east toward the windblown community of Mojave and points beyond. Numerous obstacles had to be bypassed or physically removed, but after logging 185 miles, Kammerer's crew eventually reached the town of Barstow for a planned overnight stay. The second day was a short run of only 120 miles but traversed more hills between the desert outpost of Baker and Shoshone, a settlement near the southern end of Death Valley. Early arrival in Shoshone provided an opportunity to check equipment and fuel, and to service the vehicles. On the third day the convoy covered the final 148 miles via Death Valley Junction and across the Nevada state line to Lathrop Wells. Then, after reaching the AEC base camp at Mercury, the vehicles proceeded north across Yucca Flat, passed through Gate 700, and arrived at Area 51. Nearing the base, one of Kammerer's men had to remove a "No Admittance" sign so the convoy could use a dirt road to reach the lakebed before finally pulling up onto the concrete parking apron.[26]

Less than a week later, a labor dispute generated unwanted publicity that threatened to expose the secret project. The AEC had quietly negotiated a sole-source contract so as not to call attention to any new construction, but problems arose due to the distances involved in commuting to and from the worksite. Because Area 51 was putatively part of the NTS, representatives of Las Vegas Sheet Metal Workers Union Local 88 demanded that workers be paid from the minute they entered the gate

Convoy carrying the A-12 model departs Burbank before dawn to avoid morning rush-hour traffic. *Dorsey Kammerer collection*

Other traffic had to pull off the road to allow the convoy to pass on narrow desert highways. *Dorsey Kammerer collection*

Workers uncrate the A-12 model following arrival at Area 51. *Lockheed*

The process of reassembling the A-12 mockup was nearly as complex as building it in the first place. *Lockheed*

at Mercury rather than when they arrived at Groom Lake, some forty-five minutes later. Not surprisingly, REECo officials balked at paying the extra money even after union representatives threatened not to allow members to work at the site. Subsequently, REECo obtained a court order forcing the union to provide half a dozen laborers, and then, prior to an injunction hearing in district court, agreed to arbitration of the dispute.

As news of this conflict became public, AEC officials attempted to curtail speculation by announcing to the media that "sheet metal workers needed at the Groom Lake Project 51 in the Nevada Test Site are constructing a Butler-type building." Using the approved cover story, a spokesman provided a mundane explanation, saying only that the structure would be used to "house data reduction equipment for use by Edgerton, Germeshausen, and Grier in an Air Force program." At least one local journalist surmised that there was more to the story. In an article for the *Las Vegas Review-Journal*, the writer noted that Groom Lake was "ideally suited to secret projects because experimental aircraft can take off and land without detection from any outside point."[27]

Lockheed technicians reassembled the A-12 mockup, then moved it out to the lakebed and had installed it on the pole by November 18. Subsequent testing included RCS measurements of the small-scale and full-sized models to provide standard reference patterns from all possible angles at various frequencies, with and without application of antiradar materials to the airframe. For

The A-12 model was mounted atop the pole inverted and is seen here raised to full height. The vertical tails have not yet been installed. *Lockheed*

Workers install vertical tails on the A-12 model's engine nacelles. *Lockheed*

purposes of comparison, an untreated U-2A (Article 352) also underwent RCS pole testing. At one point Johnson even considered mounting an actual F-94C jet fighter on the pylon and running its engine with and without afterburner in order to study radar reflections resulting from exhaust ionization. He eventually abandoned this idea in favor of modifying the A-12 model's engine outlets with extensions that mimicked the predicted shape of the exhaust plume. By the end of the month, Johnson expressed satisfaction at the considerable progress being made. "I think a fine job has been done by all in getting the base ready and the model up and tests underway," he later wrote. But this didn't mean anyone could relax. In December, the CIA issued approval for the Special Projects team to work forty-eight-hour weeks through January 15, 1960, along with $28,000 in extra funding for improvements to the pole. Results of RCS testing proved more than satisfactory, and by the end of January, Bissell had authorized Johnson to proceed with production of a dozen A-12 aircraft plus one static-test airframe.[28]

Test articles could be mounted on the pole upright or inverted. This made it possible to obtain proper viewing angles simulating the cruising angle of attack (AOA) at the line of sight from an early-warning radar approximately 300 miles away. Results accurately characterized the grazing angle of incidence for a radar beam as if it was striking an A-12 flying at its design altitude. The EG&G cadre experienced considerable difficulty during early tests because of radar returns from the post supporting the model, as well as from ground reflections. To solve the first problem, a retractable shield that could move up and down with the model was placed around the post. Unwanted ground reflections were controlled with carbon-loaded-hair pads placed on the ground under the model. Frank Rodgers invented particularly useful tools for full-scale ground testing. This device, nicknamed the "railroad," consisted of a traveling corner reflector mounted on a rail alongside the pylon. Technicians used it to locate radar "hotspots" by determining the phase relationship between the reflector and the test article and then drawing two bearing lines that intersected at the source of the high return.[29]

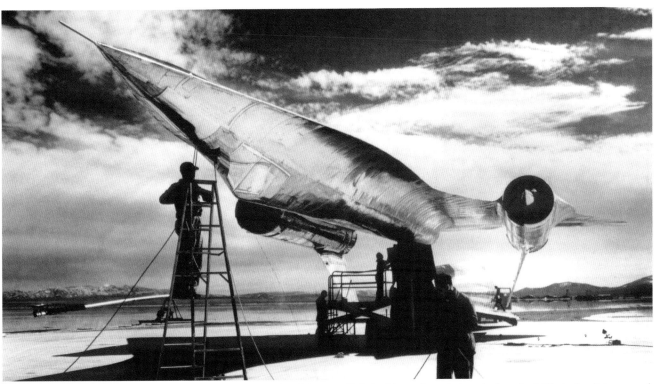

A work crew prepares to raise the full-scale model, now with tail fins installed. In this southward view, the base is visible in the distance, and the nearby hills have a dusting of snow. *Lockheed*

A man standing next to a Willys M38 Jeep provides scale in this photo of a full-size A-12 mockup in its final external configuration, with all-moving rudders on stub fins. For some reason the model has been entirely painted in a camouflage pattern, perhaps to conceal its shape from ground observers. *Lockheed*

The full-scale A-12 model was fitted with radar-absorbent structures in the chines, wing edges, tails, and inlet spikes. Cylindrical frameworks covered with reflective material mimicked radar returns from ionized exhaust plumes. A special shield prevented radar backscatter from the pole and rotator mechanism. *Lockheed*

Johnson also advocated providing the RCS range with equipment to measure an actual A-12's radar signature during flight once the program got fully underway. Getting the most-accurate data would entail detecting the airplane with acquisition radar and then locking on with fire-control radar, similar to the types used by potential Warsaw Pact adversaries. For the acquisition system, EG&G purchased a 60-foot-diameter dish antenna from the D. S. Kennedy Company in Cohasset, Massachusetts, and installed it on the edge of the lakebed in early 1961. This radar simulated Soviet S-band long-range tracking systems. The fire-control system consisted of narrow-beam X-band radar of the same type used with the Nike air-defense missile. The Nike radar was slaved to the dish to facilitate target lock, something never done in an operational environment, where acquisition and fire-control radar antennas were not typically collocated. To precisely determine the airplane's attitude, the A-12 was equipped with a telemetry system designed by Brint Ferguson of SEI and built by Wayne Pendleton of EG&G Special Projects. All data were recorded using magnetic tape and printouts inside the radar control building on the edge of the lakebed.[30]

In March, the agency formed Information Fidelity, Inc. (IFI), another CIA proprietary company, under the leadership of Herb Miller. The primary function of this scientific management group was to oversee and coordinate radar range activities in support of Project OXCART. Although nominally headquartered in Las Vegas, IFI had a field office at Area 51, where representatives provided advice and consultation to Lockheed, EG&G, SEI, and others and monitored their progress. As the agency's scientific and technical representative for OXCART, either Miller or his chief scientist was required to be present for all testing.[31]

The EG&G radar facilities at Area 51, with the Papoose Mountains in the background. Note the new water tower at far right. *Via T. D. Barnes*

The EG&G radar range continued to evolve and expand throughout the OXCART program, and the Special Projects organization eventually split into two sections. By late 1964, the test site cadre was under the management of Lee Wilder, with Harry Phiffer supervising a small engineering team. The G-Systems group, under Jim Tarver, used pylon-mounted models (up to full scale) to identify radar return hotspots and evaluate mitigation techniques. Wayne Pendleton was in charge of the F-Systems group, which was responsible for RCS measurement of aircraft in flight, primarily using the S-band radar and the 60-foot dish. Engineers analyzed radar returns for different frequencies, angles, and altitudes and with various types of RAM installed on the airplane's chines to minimize RCS. According to former radar engineer Jules Kabat, the chief engineer at the EG&G Las Vegas office was very skeptical of anything done by the people at Area 51, and directed that all "real engineering" be handled by his group "Downtown." This didn't sit well with Kabat, who enlisted the aid of lead technician Bill McCloud. "I set out to rectify this arrangement and met with quite a bit of hostility," he recalled. "We eventually got it sorted out, and once McCloud was on my side, nobody else was allowed to touch the system without my OK, which was a real shock to the Downtown guys."[32]

X-15 Support

The CIA was not the only government agency interested in Groom Lake. A team of NASA, Navy, and Air Force personnel headquartered at Edwards was testing the X-15 rocket-powered research plane. This revolutionary vehicle was capable of speeds in excess of Mach 6 and altitudes of more than 50 miles, which was generally considered to be the edge of outer space. In order to achieve desired flight profiles, the X-15 had to be carried to an altitude of around 45,000 feet beneath the wing of a modified B-52 bomber. A few seconds after release, the X-15 pilot ignited the craft's liquid-fueled rocket engine and set whatever climb angle was called for, depending on whether the mission was a speed or altitude run. Fuel was typically exhausted within about eighty seconds, and the remainder of the flight was flown without power, using only the available energy of the vehicle's momentum. With judicious energy management, a skilled pilot could bring the X-15 in for a precision landing on a lakebed runway at Edwards. But the liquid-fueled rocket engines were notoriously unreliable, often shutting down prematurely or failing to light altogether.

To prepare for these contingencies, mission planners designated a series of alternate landing sites along the X-15's flight path. Each launch took place above a dry lakebed, so that if the engine failed within the first forty-three seconds, the pilot could jettison remaining fuel and immediately make an emergency landing. Each mission required that several contingency-landing lakebeds be designated between the launch lake and Edwards. Not all dry lakebeds were suitable; some were too soft to support the weight of the X-15. In order to evaluate each playa, technicians from NASA's Flight Research Center (FRC) at Edwards, assisted by the Air Force, surveyed dozens of lakebeds and tested surface hardness by using the steel ball method.[33]

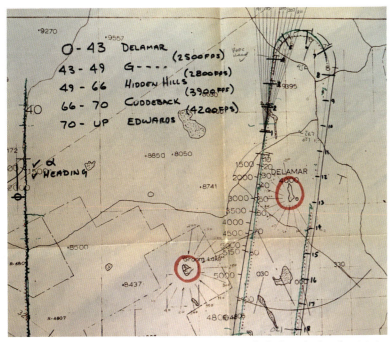

A portion of a radar-tracking chart for a NASA X-15 flight launched in the vicinity of Delamar Lake. Had the vehicle's rocket engine failed to ignite or burned for less than forty-three seconds, the pilot would have been forced to land at Delamar. A burn time of forty-three to forty-nine seconds would have made Groom Lake the next-best option. Additional contingency landing sites were selected on the basis of successively longer burn times. Note that although Groom is clearly labeled on the chart, planners were unwilling to fully spell out the name in the handwritten notes. *NASA*

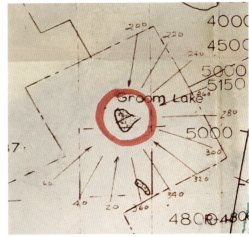

X-15 pilots had a wide variety of approach options for landing at Groom Lake, if necessary. *NASA*

NASA personnel test lakebed hardness by dropping a 17.6-pound steel ball from a height of 6 feet and measuring the resulting imprint. Up to 3.25 inches across was considered acceptable. *NASA*

Maj. Robert M. White, deputy chief of the AFFTC Flight Test Operations division, was designated as the Air Force's primary X-15 pilot. In preparation for testing, he embarked on a two-day survey trip to investigate potential contingency landing sites in Nevada. He and several other AFFTC personnel crowded into the narrow cabin of a single-engine L-28A and departed Edwards on July 13, 1959. After visiting four other lakebeds, White received clearance to land on Groom Lake. "The surface is very smooth and extremely hard," he later reported. "All approaches are good, and runways can be used in any direction with just over three miles of lake available. This lake is considered excellent for emergency use."[34]

Recovery operations from Groom Lake would necessarily require special clearance for personnel to enter Area 51, making this option less desirable than any of the others. Although Groom was ultimately accepted as a contingency landing site for X-15 missions, particularly those launched from above Delamar Valley, none ever aborted to the secret base. An aerial survey photo of Groom Lake, taken for Holmes & Narver in September 1959, showed as many as ten runways crisscrossing the playa. Whether any of these were specifically made for use by the X-15 or if they were simply left over from the U-2 program is unknown.

Occasionally the X-15 contingency lakebeds had to be revisited, especially following wet weather. Landing clearance was not always granted for Area 51. At least one Air Force survey crew had to be content with a low-altitude flyby during which they noted water on the eastern half of the lakebed.[35] Another survey mission, on December 17, 1959, became infamous after a NASA R4D-5 landed without prior clearance. FRC flight operations chief Joe Vensel, along with research pilot Forrest Petersen and engineer Jim McKay, apparently assumed this would be permissible as long as their plane remained on the northernmost end of the lakebed, just outside the restricted boundary of Area 51. They noted the marked runways and determined surface hardness by taxiing the airplane across the northeast section of the playa and observing the depth of their tire tracks.

A few miles to the south, swirling dust clouds rising from the lakebed heralded the approach of vehicles, but the Area 51 Security Force arrived only just in time to watch the white-and-orange plane take off, and to note the distinctive NASA insignia painted on the side of the fuselage. The survey plane visited several other lakebeds in Nevada and California, and by the time it touched down at Edwards there had been a heated exchange of phone calls among various government officials on both coasts. NASA deputy administrator Hugh Dryden eventually phoned Paul Bikle, then FRC director, to find out if he had such an aircraft and what it was doing in a highly classified restricted area. Shortly after Vensel and his crew returned to Edwards, Bikle gave them a stern dressing down, but no other official action was taken.[36]

Mission controllers followed all X-15 flights through using the High-Altitude Continuous-Tracking Radar Range, or High Range. Completed in 1959, this integrated system of instrumentation facilities, data-recording equipment, and communications gear stretched more than 400 miles from California to Utah. It included two hilltop radar stations near the Nevada towns of Beatty and Ely, connected to one another and to Edwards by a series of data acquisition units and microwave relay units. One of the latter, designated MRU-4, was installed 14 miles north of Groom Lake and about 2,100 feet below the summit of Bald Mountain.[37] FRC and AFFTC officials also discussed the idea of using the airspace just north of Area 51 as a launch site for the X-15, which would make Groom the primary abort site in the event of engine failure early in the flight. Area 51 had advantages over Mud Lake near Tonopah because there were a greater number of intermediate contingency landing sites available between Groom and Edwards. Also, using Groom Lake meant a reduction in AFFTC support requirements since there was already an airfield with emergency equipment and personnel at the site. After some discussion, however, Groom was removed from consideration as a launch site due to difficulty obtaining clearance into the area.[38]

A technician services microwave relay equipment at MRU-4 on Bald Mountain. *USAF*

When contingency lakebed status was again reviewed in March 1961, AFFTC air operations officer Capt. James Varnadoe reported that Groom Lake security restrictions appeared to be easing. This was good news, since Maj. White asserted that the available landing surface at Groom made it preferable to Delamar Lake if there was a clear choice between the two in an emergency situation. Varnadoe indicated that agreements with other agencies would be renegotiated and brought up to date, and promised to investigate any changes in security status at Groom Lake and their potential effect on the X-15 program.[39]

A Permanent Base

As soon as radar testing was underway at Area 51, OXCART project officials began seeking a permanent base from which to test and operate the A-12 fleet. As with the U-2, a secure location was most desirable since the mere existence of the new plane was classified top secret. The OXCART operational concept called for missions to be flown from a domestic base, with range extension accomplished as necessary by aerial refueling en route. Security requirements precluded basing the clandestine detachment at an active military installation, where the A-12 would be subject to widespread scrutiny. Criteria for site selection dictated that the test base be remote from metropolitan areas, be easily accessible by air yet far enough away from civil and military airways to preclude aerial observation or midair collision hazards, have good year-round weather, provide accommodations for large numbers of personnel, have adequate fuel storage facilities, and possess an 8,000-foot runway capable of supporting an aircraft weighing more than 117,000 pounds.[40]

Unfortunately, the old Watertown airstrip was unsuitable. The existing 5,000-foot runway was woefully insufficient, and the airbase lacked the necessary support infrastructure. Because of the substantial expenditure that would be required for upgrading the Groom Lake facility, OXCART planners initially contemplated converting one of several Air Force bases then programmed for closure as possible alternatives. It soon became clear that none of these provided adequate security, and the annual operating costs for most were prohibitive. Officials briefly considered the idea of basing the A-12s at Edwards because all necessary support facilities were available there. This plan was rejected almost immediately because the secret plane would be exposed to too many uncleared observers on base as well as in nearby communities.

Ultimately, Area 51 seemed like the only logical choice; it already had adequate security and a remote location, and a moderate construction program could provide whatever else was needed. Lockheed provided the CIA with a list of requirements for hangar space, maintenance facilities, housing, monthly fuel consumption, and runway specifications. The agency then produced a plan for construction and engineering.[41] According to early estimates, it would require a little over $3.8 million to build a new concrete runway and parking aprons, hangars large enough to accommodate the A-12, fuel and water storage facilities, paved roads, and other essentials.[42]

Not everyone considered this a good idea. Use of Area 51 as a radar range had necessarily deferred the CIA's decision on whether to retain the property as a physical asset of the agency. Now the matter was at hand, and there were compelling arguments on both sides. The OXCART project security officer worried that erosion of the security cover surrounding the earlier U-2 program—particularly due to the Powers shoot-down—had branded the Groom Lake site as a "spook base" and that it would be best to separate the new program, to the greatest extent possible, from any connection whatsoever to the U-2. To minimize speculation by unwitting persons, all earlier terms of reference to the base (such as Watertown, Groom Lake, and the Ranch) were ordered eliminated from the vocabulary of OXCART-cleared personnel. Instead, they were to immediately adopt the term "Area 51," since it was the acknowledged official AEC designator for that portion of the NTS. Additionally, every effort was to be made throughout the OXCART program to disassociate

Several types of radar are visible in front and to the left of the EG&G control building, including a 60-foot dish antenna, seen here in its resting position. *Via T. D. Barnes*

the CIA from any interest in the Nevada base. Ultimately, the final decision on whether the agency would continue to manage Area 51 was made on the basis of fiscal and operational considerations. Thanks to the rehabilitation of the Watertown facilities, much of the framework for the new installation was already in place. Developing a clandestine test site from scratch would have required essentially unlimited time, funding, and personnel resources, which were simply not available.[43]

On December 23, 1959, Dick Bissell approved establishment of Area 51 as the primary domestic base for OXCART, subject to concurrence of the Air Force and AEC. His decision, however, did not immediately result in a large program of improvements and new construction. Until Lockheed received final go-ahead for A-12 production, expenditures for improvements to the former Watertown facilities were limited to only those necessary to sustain the RCS measurement project. When final approval was granted in January 1960, the civil-engineering staff at Project Headquarters already had an orderly plan to ready the base to receive aircraft and all associated equipment and personnel on schedule. To preserve cover and security, the CIA continued to maintain the fiction that the AEC managed the Groom Lake facility. The agency also renewed agreements with REECo to provide construction, maintenance, culinary, and housekeeping services. This was both convenient—REECo personnel were qualified and possessed the necessary clearances—and helped support the cover story that Area 51 was simply another part of the atomic test site.[44]

The agency dispatched a staff civil engineer to provide guidance to Werner Weiss and act as liaison between Project Headquarters and REECo. Construction began in earnest in September 1960 and continued on a double-shift schedule until June 1964. Initial work included surface grading, road improvements, and drilling for a new well. By the end of the first year, the base population had grown to 150, including the EG&G Special Projects cadre and REECo construction crews, and immediate logistical needs were fulfilled on an as-needed basis. With the new airfield taking shape, workers found they were afforded few necessities and none of the amenities of life. Even after renovation, the leftover buildings from the U-2 days were dilapidated. REECo had to procure additional trailers from Kit Manufacturing Company, Long Beach, California, to billet construction workers as they arrived. Recreational facilities were extremely limited, and the movement of workers to and from the site posed numerous difficulties.

With the exception of EG&G and REECo employees, contractors working at Area 51 were prohibited from maintaining residences in Las Vegas. Lockheed provided a C-47 shuttle service to Burbank on a nonscheduled basis, while the Las Vegas–based EG&G contingent used a chartered Lockheed Model 18 LodeStar. Daily commuting by automobile was impractical not only because of the distance, but also because the only decent road into the area had deteriorated considerably since 1957. Instead, many workers remained on-site throughout the week. As a result, program security was jeopardized when it was discovered that Nevada law required that the names of all contract workers remaining in the state for more than forty-eight hours be reported to state authorities. This would apply not only to construction workers but to all the various support contractors providing equipment for the top-secret spy plane. OXCART security personnel worried that providing these names and their company affiliations would reveal too much about the nature of the work going on at Area 51. This crisis was ultimately averted when the CIA's general counsel discovered an exemption for federal employees and thenceforth appointed all Area 51 contractor personnel as government consultants.[45]

Building the new runway was among the highest priorities and presented both fiscal and engineering challenges. Kelly Johnson initially suggested simply extending the northern end of the old U-2 runway by 3,000 feet and

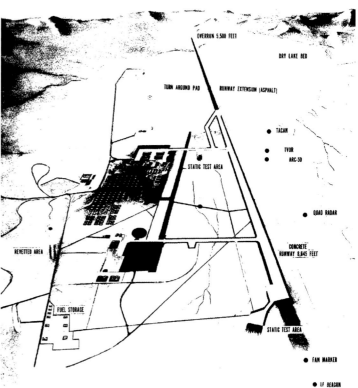

An official map of Area 51 created by the National Photographic Interpretation Center included the basic airfield layout and general locations of navigational aids and select facilities. *CIA*

widening it by 50 feet, at a total cost of $200,000. Rather than build an entirely new airstrip, he reasoned, it would be less costly to pour concrete for a transition from the asphalt portion onto the lakebed and for about 1,000 feet beyond where the A-12 was expected to rotate for takeoff; a concrete turnaround pad would be installed at the southern end of the runway.[46] This design proved less than ideal, not only because the heavyweight A-12 might eventually wear grooves in the asphalt but because the original airstrip was not properly aligned with prevailing winds.

Instead, surveyors plotted a new airstrip starting from a point about 1.5 miles south of the southern shoreline and running northwest on a magnetic heading of 320 degrees. Additionally, after considering the A-12's long, flexible airframe, Johnson was reluctant to build a standard Air Force runway with expansion joints every 25 feet because he feared that as it rolled over the joints at high takeoff and landing speeds, the airplane would experience undesirable vibrations. At his suggestion the airstrip was assembled in segments, each consisting of six 25-foot-wide, 150-foot-long longitudinal sections. These sections were staggered to put most of the expansion joints parallel to the direction of aircraft roll and reduce the frequency of perpendicular joints. Construction of what came to be known as runway 14-32 began on September 7, 1960, after REECo subcontracted WMK Transit Mix, Inc., of Las Vegas to set up batch plants and pour some 25,000 cubic yards of reinforced concrete. When completed on November 15, the airstrip was 8,645 feet long and 150 feet wide. Air Force runways at most bases were typically 200 feet wide, but cost-saving measures dictated a narrower width for the one at Area 51.[47] The southern end included a 1,000-foot emergency overrun with a 50,000-square-foot concrete parking pad nearby for use during final preflight preparations.

Required runway length is typically a compromise among such factors as airfield elevation, ambient temperature, aircraft gross takeoff weight, and available thrust. The A-12 was expected to need no more than 8,500 feet for its takeoff run, and the lakebed was expected to provide sufficient landing surface for an aborted takeoff. But by November 1961, concerns had been raised regarding anticipated increases in the airplane's gross weight. These were brought to the attention of Jim Cunningham, who sent a memo to the chief of the DPD's Development Branch expressing his understanding that reduced vehicle loads would compensate for increased design weight, at least during the OXCART test phase. "I believe [that operational missions] are scheduled for launch in the night hours when ambient air temperature is well within reason," he wrote, adding, "The only time you could really come close to violating the minimum safety factor would be in a maximum gross weight takeoff under high ambient temperatures." He suggested simply not flying under such conditions but admitted that escalating aircraft weight due to design changes might eventually become a serious problem.[48]

Work crews from Las Vegas pour and smooth concrete strips for the new Area 51 runway. *Dorsey Kammerer collection*

Consequently, Cunningham asked for a cost estimate to build a runway extension, which he thought would have to be added to the southern end of the existing airstrip. This posed a few difficulties, first because the question needed to be resolved before installation of permanent runway lighting. "I also wish you to note," he added, "that any extension to the southeast end would mean that the aircraft readiness pad would end up being somewhere other than at the end of the runway." Nevertheless, Cunningham remained reluctant to proceed immediately, telling the Development Branch chief, "While I would agree that if in the last analysis we must increase the length of the bloody thing that we should do it sooner rather than later, I believe that to do it now might well be premature." Winter was fast approaching, and he noted, "The weather, after first freeze, will prevent us from taking positive action until the spring."[49]

Funding was eventually approved, but agency airfield engineers decided to extend the airstrip to the northwest instead of the southeast. This necessitated construction of a raised causeway to bring the surface of a 6,000-foot asphalt extension level with the northern end of the concrete runway, gradually sloping down to the elevation of the lakebed and terminating in a concrete turnaround pad. Later, a second 5,500-foot asphalt section, for emergency use only, was added as overrun beyond the midlake turnaround pad. In the event that an aircraft departed this overrun, a 2-mile-diameter Archimedes curve (nicknamed "the Hook") was marked on the lakebed surface in a gently tightening spiral to aid with deceleration. Although the main runway surface was just a little over 8,600 feet long, the various extensions made it appear from the air as though it ran on for more than 4 miles. Cunningham later described the extended airstrip as "a monstrous runway that went all the way from hell to breakfast."[50]

Since the prevailing winds blew mainly from the northwest, takeoff and landing usually took place toward the lakebed on runway 32. This was considered the preferred runway on calm days, when surface wind velocity was less than 10 knots. When winds were blowing from the southeast, or if traffic conditions permitted, the control tower operator could advise takeoff on reciprocal runway 14. Smaller, propeller-driven aircraft such as the C-47 or Twin Bonanza could be cleared for takeoff from intermediate taxiway intersections, provided there was sufficient room for the aircraft to reach decision speed and yet safely come to a stop on the remaining runway if the pilot aborted takeoff. Jets using runway 14 were required to begin takeoff roll from the midlake turnaround pad in order to establish an adequate safety margin. If necessary, a pilot could choose to land on the dry lake from any direction, but the lakebed surface west of the runway, occupied by the radar range, was to be used only in dire emergencies. Two unpaved airstrips were marked on the lakebed surface in case crosswinds were too severe to permit landing on the paved runway. Runway 09-27 crossed the lakebed from southwest to northeast, and runway 03-21 was aligned from northwest to southeast. The two strips formed a V with its apex pointing toward a spot between the midlake turnaround and the beginning of the Hook. If using these airstrips for crosswind contingency or training purposes, pilots were directed to take off or land adjacent to either side so as to preserve the marked runway surface for aircraft landing under emergency conditions.[51]

Provisions were made for coordinating air traffic into and out of the secret base. Headquarters, Air Force Communications Service, assigned twenty-five air traffic controllers to man the Area 51 control tower and the ground-controlled approach (GCA) trailer and, whenever necessary, a desk at the Nevada Test Site's main command post (CP-1) at the southern edge of Yucca Flat.

The new runway and its lakebed extension became the dominant features of the Area 51 installation. The loop road on the west side of the lakebed provided access to the RCS pole. *USAF*

Controllers in the tower used the call signs "Bud" and, later, "Apex," while the call sign "Saucy" was assigned to the GCA. Once fully staffed, the air traffic control unit was activated on February 1, 1961. Airfield navigation aids included VHF omnidirectional radio range (VOR) and tactical air navigation (TACAN) systems. Due to the anticipated performance of the A-12, requirements for the VOR included a capability for providing the pilot with an accurate fix at a range of 160 nautical miles while the plane was cruising at or above 70,000 feet. Initially, a single-channel TRN-6 portable TACAN was used until it could be replaced with a permanent, dual-channel GPN-9 unit. Several radio beacons were also installed at various nearby locations, including Mercury.[52]

The CIA responded to impending transportation requirements for a larger workforce by procuring a Lockheed Constellation aircraft to provide scheduled service to and from Area 51. During a telephone conversation with Jim Cunningham on October 5, 1960, Kelly Johnson offered to sell the agency the original L-1649 Starliner Constellation prototype on an "as is" basis for $305,000. This would be a bargain price, he said, since comparable used L-1649 models were then going for between $750,000 and $1 million, depending on their condition. To sweeten the pot, Johnson said Lockheed would furnish parts for the aircraft, adapt the forward cabin to accommodate fifty passengers and the rear section for cargo, and install a small galley to provide light refreshments aloft. Additionally, the company would operate the commuter service at a modest per-mile cost. Work began as soon as the purchase was approved on November 30. The airplane, initially dubbed the "White Whale," was in poor shape after having been stored at Burbank for some time. Having served primarily as a test aircraft, it also lacked the more comfortable seats found on Constellations in commercial service. Despite the additional expenditure of $37,000 to put it into satisfactory condition, it was derisively nicknamed "the Hog" or "Cattle Car" by its unlucky passengers.[53] Two additional Super Constellations joined the fleet in the summer of 1963 to meet the increasing pace of the OXCART program. In June of that year, Lockheed reacquired an eighty-eight-seat L-1049G that had briefly been leased to Capitol Airways. The following month, under the cover of the agency's covert airline, Air America, the CIA purchased a 120-seat L-1049H from Flying Tiger Line for $472,850 and immediately leased it to Lockheed.[54]

The main control room at CP-1 in Area 6 of the Nevada Test Site. Though not labeled with its number, the outline of Area 51 is visible on the large NTS map on the wall at right. *DOE*

A Lockheed Constellation used to ferry workers to and from Area 51, seen here at Lockheed's Burbank plant. *Via Curtis Peebles*

All three Constellations of the Lockheed commuter fleet at Burbank. *Lockheed*

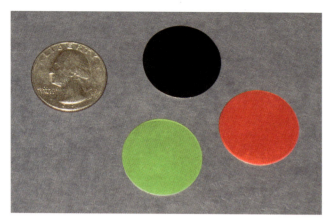

Anodized aluminum chits for flights on the Constellations. When approaching the aircraft, passengers matched the color of their chits to that of a sign next to the boarding stairs. *Author*

Following two years of flight testing, the CL-329 JetStar prototype was reassigned to serve as Lockheed's Burbank-based corporate jet. Kelly Johnson used it for trips to Area 51, often accompanied by VIP guests. *Lockheed*

When boarding, each passenger presented the flight attendant with a thin anodized aluminum disk, slightly smaller than a quarter. Possession of a black chit foreshadowed an uncomfortable ride aboard the decrepit Starliner. More-fortunate passengers who received red or green chits boarded the Super Constellations. Each transport made several flights a day ferrying personnel from Burbank and Las Vegas to Area 51. Between January 1961 and May 1968, the three Constellations completed 11,495 flights, logged 12,897 flight hours spanning approximately 3,669,900 miles, and carried 492,205 passengers and 4,328,073 pounds of cargo.[55] Carco Air Services (purchased by Ross Aviation, Inc., in 1969) provided additional transportation, mostly to EG&G Special Projects personnel, using two C-47s. Meanwhile, Kelly Johnson and other VIPs traveled in style when visiting Area 51, arriving in Lockheed's CL-329 JetStar prototype, which had been reassigned for use as the company's corporate jet.

Essential facilities at Area 51 were complete by August 1961. The new main cantonment area overlay the site of the original Watertown camp and included all the existing permanent structures. Older buildings were refurbished and repurposed for the new project. The three T-hangars that once housed the U-2 took on new roles: one became a machine shop, another served as a maintenance bay for aerospace ground equipment (AGE), and the third housed a precision measurement equipment laboratory (PMEL) and photo lab. Warehouses on the west side of the original flight line were now occupied by the motor pool and automotive service shop. Base engineering offices, dormitories, and REECo shops remained, but many new facilities had been built and more were still under construction. Since commercial electrical power was unavailable, additional generators had to be trucked in to provide electricity for the growing installation.[56]

To the greatest extent possible, streets were laid out in an orderly grid. Most of those oriented north–south were numbered. Several east–west thoroughfares bore the names of presidents: Truman, Grant, Washington, and Lincoln. Following the November 1963 assassination of John F. Kennedy, the main road into Area 51 from the NTS was named in his honor. By this time, the base population had climbed to 1,423, necessitating construction of additional personnel quarters and a new mess hall. A new base headquarters building housed the Command Post along with offices for administration, communications, finance, security, and civil engineering, as well as a dispensary and one of several fire stations. The original control tower remained, but the old headquarters became a flight operations center with provisions for flight planning and scheduling, crew briefing and debriefing, flight safety, academic training, and weather forecasting.[57]

For expansion of personnel accommodations, Project Headquarters turned to the Naval Ammunition Depot at Hawthorne, Nevada, and the adjacent community of Babbitt, which was built in the 1940s to house depot workers supporting the war effort.[58] The result of a low-cost defense housing project, Babbitt consisted of more than 570 prefabricated, wood-framed, gable-roofed duplexes clad in asbestos-composition shingles. Built on concrete perimeter-footing walls, these structures were considered semipermanent and could be moved to new locations as warranted. Each one-story duplex had a rectangular footprint, roughly twice as long as it was wide (27 by 55 feet). These buildings were identical on the exterior, and the architect had designed two floor plans to accommodate various family sizes: Plan-A contained two units, one side with a single bedroom and the other with three bedrooms, while Plan-B contained twin two-bedroom units. Each unit also contained a single bathroom and a basic kitchen with standard equipment, including a stove and refrigerator. Units within each duplex mirrored one another, with adjoining front doors facing the street and entering into living rooms that shared a common wall. A second door at each end opened through the kitchen to the outside. Entirely utilitarian, the duplexes were plain, undifferentiated, and singularly lacking in decorative detailing or architectural adornment.[59]

A close view of the North Ramp and main cantonment area. The brown-roofed structures are the Babbitt houses. A nearby cluster of mobile-home trailers provided additional accommodations. Recreation facilities, visible at far right, include a tennis court and indoor swimming pool. *Via Bob Hughes*

and ejected just 2,500 feet above the ground. His parachute deployed successfully, and he touched down twenty seconds later. The airplane continued in a slow, wings-level glide until it contacted the ground and disintegrated 3.5 miles north of the lakebed. Area 51 personnel soon arrived on scene, determined the pilot was uninjured, and transported him to another location where he could be picked up by a rescue helicopter from Nellis.[62]

The following year, airspace above Groom Lake became part of a new restricted area called R-4808 (replacing the former Prohibited Area P-275), which covered both the Nevada Test Site and Area 51. It was established on August 11, 1961, and the rules governing R-4808 prohibited unauthorized overflight below 60,000 feet. There was, as of yet, no prohibition against flying over the mountains immediately northeast of Groom Lake, but this was just one of several potential security threats facing OXCART. Others were brought to light in late September, when CIA inspector general Lyman B. Kirkpatrick Jr. conducted a three-day inspection tour of Area 51. The CIA officer managed to make a surprisingly thorough inspection of the facility environs despite being confined to a wheelchair. Area 51 staff personnel were extremely helpful in ensuring he received a comprehensive overview of current activities, but the visit left Kirkpatrick with reservations on several key aspects of the overall program. Afterward, he offered some critical comments regarding both Area 51 security and OXCART project management.

In his preliminary assessment, Kirkpatrick stated, "The 'Area' in my opinion appears to be extremely vulnerable in its present security provisions against unauthorized observation. The high and rugged northeast perimeter of the immediate operating area, which I visited in order to see for myself, is not under government ownership." He was particularly alarmed by the Groom District mineral claims, which he warned included "sites of unoccupied buildings or cellars which together with the terrain in general afford excellent opportunity for successful penetration by a skilled and determined opposition." Kirkpatrick felt Area 51 was "already demonstrably

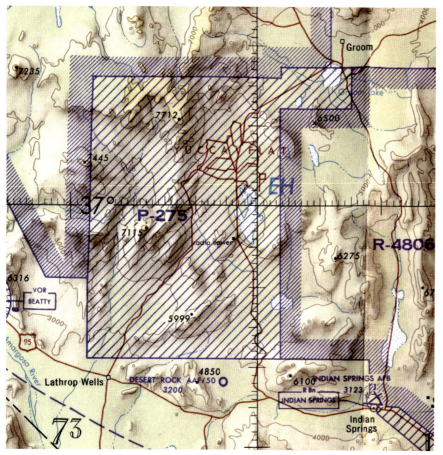

An Air Force operational navigation chart published in November 1960 defines the prohibited airspace over the Nevada Test Site and Area 51. *USAF*

vulnerable to air violation including landings," that "major installations are not rigorously protected against sabotage," and that construction of facilities had been undertaken before the building contractors had received a full security clearance. Dick Bissell agreed that these points were valid, and the assistant to the CIA's deputy director of plans later noted that Bissell "was particularly interested in why we have not yet been able to eject the various citizens holding property around the Area." This referred primarily to the Sheahan family and the Groom Mine.[63]

As during AQUATONE, the OXCART operation at Groom Lake was threatened with safety concerns and potential delays resulting from the resumption of nuclear testing. President Kennedy had optimistically hoped to negotiate the testing moratorium into a nuclear test ban treaty, but it was not to be. After the Soviets broke the moratorium and began conducting an ambitious test series, the president directed the AEC to resume operations in Nevada, though all detonations would now take place underground. The AEC military applications director, Brig. Gen. Austin W. Betts, told his staff, "We are authorized to proceed with the readiness program without the unusual security procedures which have previously applied to our planning efforts," and he emphasized that "something must be tested as soon as possible."[64] Increasing activity over the hill from Groom Lake prompted Werner Weiss to fire off a memo to Betts in which he expressed his hope that the AEC had planned for and would initiate additional safety and security measures at the NTS. "As you are aware," he wrote, "the implementation of any such measures will directly affect those . . . personnel located in Area 51; therefore, in order that we may gear our planning accordingly, we would appreciate being advised of your anticipated actions in this regard." Weiss asked that the AEC provide for an educational program in radiological safety measures and hazards, issue dosimeter badges to all Area 51 personnel, and assign a radiological safety officer to the area whenever test conditions involved the potential for fallout in the vicinity of Groom Lake. Betts assured him that he would do everything possible to ensure these measures were taken.[65]

Building an organization to fly the new airplane proved complicated. Kirkpatrick asserted that top-level administration of Area 51 needed to be consolidated with clear and precisely defined authority, particularly with regard to Weiss as senior on-site agency representative and manager of Project 51. While he considered Weiss both competent and conscientious, Kirkpatrick believed that his authority and his ability to oversee the complex relationships among various contractors and others working at Area 51 were seriously inadequate. "The organizations responsible for testing and instrumentation were in disagreement or misunderstanding on key aspects of their program," he wrote, "and no one at the 'Area' seemed to be in a position to bring their issues into focus with Headquarters and to expedite their resolution." Kirkpatrick warned that this situation would likely prove increasingly detrimental as OXCART moved into the testing phase.[66] This apparently came as news to Bissell, who decided that the problem could be solved with the addition of another layer to the command structure. Specifically, this entailed assigning an Air Force officer as commander with a CIA deputy.

For political reasons it was considered important that covert spy flights not be conducted by US military services or personnel, but the agency lacked the necessary organizational infrastructure and manpower to run a flying operation on its own, especially one with the scope of OXCART. To resolve this dilemma, the CIA worked with Air Force Headquarters Command at Bolling Air Force Base in Washington, DC, to create the 1129th Special Activities Squadron to operate both the OXCART aircraft fleet and the Area 51 installation. Pilots, maintainers, operations and administrative staff, and others were drawn from other Air Force units. Project pilots (once again referred to simply as "drivers") resigned their military commissions, effectively becoming employees of the CIA in a process colloquially known as "sheep dipping," but aircraft assigned to the squadron, including the A-12, were painted in standard Air Force markings and serial numbers.

Although the new squadron was nominally headquartered at Bolling, the permanent duty station for most 1129th SAS personnel was Detachment 1 at Groom Lake. All agency staff and contract personnel assigned to the detachment were given appropriate Air Force documentation to support their cover. Travel orders admonished, "Las Vegas is in excess of 100 miles from your duty station, which is a classified location." Those bringing family members were advised that Las Vegas was the closest city in which all dependent facilities and conveniences were located, and that they would normally be able to return to the city on weekends. Upon arrival in the Las Vegas area, each person assigned to Detachment 1 called a local telephone number and received specific reporting instructions. As with the earlier U-2 program, assigned personnel were prohibited from discussing their assignments with friends or family members. A typical tour of duty lasted about three years.[67]

On November 15, 1961, Col. Robert J. Holbury was named commander of the secret base, with Weiss reassigned as deputy commander for support.[68] During World War II, Holbury served as a fighter pilot in both the P-38 Lightning and P-51 Mustang, distinguishing himself by flying seventy-six combat missions in Europe. After the war he served in a variety of command and staff positions in the US and overseas. In the two years prior to his selection as the OXCART detachment's commanding officer, Holbury led the Reconnaissance Branch of the Operations Plans Division at SAC Headquarters. Now, he was tasked with overseeing flying operations at Groom Lake, maintaining an operationally ready unit, and coordinating Air Force support of OXCART. As chief of base at Area 51, Holbury reported to the DPD chief, the deputy director for plans, and the director of central intelligence (DCI). His deputy managed the challenging tasks associated with base maintenance, project security, staffing, logistics, labor union relations, transportation, housing, and liaison with local, state, and federal officials. Weiss was also responsible for establishing on-base recreation facilities, a rod-and-gun club, and anything else he could think of to keep the troops happy at such a remote post.[69]

On January 15, 1962, the FAA expanded the restricted airspace above Groom Lake to encompass approximately 516 square miles. To the south and west lay the Nellis Air Force Range and the NTS. Certain FAA air traffic controllers were briefed into the OXCART program so that they would be better prepared to coordinate A-12 flight operations in such a way as to prevent these missions from being observed by pilots or passengers of other aircraft. Briefings and clearances were also necessary for North American Air Defense Command (NORAD) personnel to preclude the scrambling of interceptors in reaction to the detection of high-speed, high-flying unidentified aircraft.[70]

Once the A-12 began flying, it seemed unlikely that such a large and complex operation could be shielded against exposure resulting from questions by uncleared military and industry personnel and members of the news media. The CIA, therefore, worked with representatives of the DoD, NASA, and the Federal Aviation Agency[71] (FAA) to develop an interdepartmental cover story for OXCART. Primary goals were to conceal the aircraft's mission, state-of-the-art technology and performance characteristics, and any involvement with the intelligence community. One early draft of the cover legend proposed describing the airplane as an experimental vehicle (dubbed "X-19") with an "advanced engine" of unspecified type.

Robert Holbury was named commander of Area 51 in November 1961. *USAF*

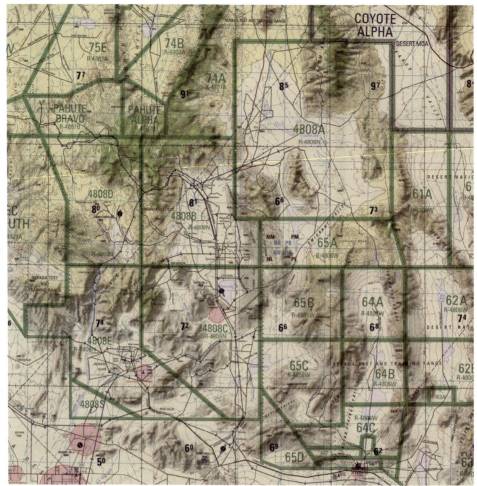

The restricted airspace above Groom Lake, identified here as R-4808A, was expanded in 1962 to provide a larger buffer zone for classified flight activities. *USAF*

National security concerns and use of an exotic fuel would supposedly justify the need for a remote test facility, which was to be named as the Flight Test Center for Advanced Propulsion Development. Someone even suggested releasing an aerial photo of the Groom Lake base along with a news release.[72]

It was immediately apparent to critics that this fiction would not suffice. To begin with, Air Force responsibility for propulsion research typically fell within the purview of ARDC. Revealing the existence of a propulsion laboratory not under the cognizance of ARDC might provoke questions from authorities who perceived a threat to their personal fiefdoms. Additionally, the term "advanced engine" could be construed to imply either nuclear or rocket propulsion. Neither would necessarily warrant such isolation for safety considerations, and President Kennedy had already announced the cancellation of nuclear-powered aircraft programs. Moreover, nearly all previous experimental research aircraft up to this point—even Navy programs—had been tested at Edwards. This would inevitably raise the question of why the X-19 had to be flown from Groom Lake. Greater complications would arise as soon as interested parties realized that more than a dozen airframes had been procured, under a sole-source contract no less, when research aircraft projects typically resulted in no more than two or three vehicles.[73]

A revised version of the cover plan described the new high-performance aircraft as a DoD-sponsored system for launching small satellites into low earth orbit. Assigning the vehicle to the realm of space operations explained why it might not be tested at Edwards, and the elevated security conformed to existing policy for restricting information concerning military satellite programs. Additionally, the DoD could realistically claim that classified procurement was accomplished for security reasons and in the national interest. Lockheed's involvement would be explained by the company's prior experience with developing multi-purpose advanced aircraft in a secure environment at minimum cost. Jim Cunningham and Eugene P. Kiefer, DPD special assistant for technical analysis, met with Hugh Dryden at NASA Headquarters in June 1962 to discuss the new cover story. The deputy administrator suggested that the agency might wish to reconsider the wisdom of identifying the OXCART vehicle as a satellite-launching system "for the simple reason that this statement carries the responsibility to explain what kind of satellite this aircraft is capable of launching." Dryden pointed out that critics might be quick to infer that the vehicle was capable of providing a covert launch capability for military hardware or clandestine satellite reconnaissance, or both. As an alternative, he suggested claiming the aircraft was being used to investigate experimental air-launched ballistic missile (ALBM) systems, which would have been consistent with ongoing military research efforts.

Even this version had obvious deficiencies. Dryden and Cunningham were forced to concede that use of the ALBM cover story would unequivocally associate the OXCART aircraft with offensive weaponry "to a degree that may well be inconsistent with subsequent disavowal of any hostile purpose for this system." Ultimately, rather than make any sort of public announcement at all, officials decided to adopt a "no comment" policy in response to all queries, along with a concise statement simply affirming that this was a classified government project. FAA chief Najeeb Halaby praised the simplicity of this new approach. He commented that as he saw it, his response to any unauthorized sighting reports involving the OXCART vehicle would be to state that he was unaware of "any strange aircraft flying in the desert." In the event of an accident or forced landing, he would simply refer all press inquiries on the subject to the secretary of the Air Force without further comment.[74]

The task of safely and securely operating an officially nonexistent supersonic aircraft from an equally nonexistent base required unusual and highly specialized procedures. In early 1963, the FAA established the Yuletide Special Operations Area (SOA) to restrict the use of designated airspace north of Area 51 to OXCART and associated support aircraft at altitudes between 24,000 and 60,000 feet. Authorized aircraft approaching Groom Lake from the north and east first entered Yuletide SOA under control of OXCART-cleared air traffic control personnel located at CP-1, the AEC command post at Yucca Flat. After being cleared into R-4808, aircraft were handed over to the Area 51 control tower. Covert procedures were also established for designated arrival/departure corridors for support aircraft operating from Area 51. These procedures allowed the pilots of such aircraft to file for clearances ostensibly from Nellis, though the aircraft were, in fact, flying from Groom Lake. Prior to July 1965, all A-12 sorties were undertaken without any clearance whatsoever. After that date, each OXCART pilot filed for takeoff clearance as if they were departing VFR from Edwards to a fix within Yuletide SOA, there picking up an IFR clearance for a route above 60,000 feet, returning to the SOA, canceling the IFR flight plan, and ostensibly returning to Edwards VFR for landing (but actually touching down at Area 51). Yuletide SOA boundaries and procedures were periodically revised due to changing requirements.[75] According to a January 1962 notice posted in the *Federal Register*, "The Department of the Air Force has stated that this alteration and inclusion of additional airspace is required in support of a classified project and has justified this requirement as a matter of military urgency and necessity, and in the interest of national defense."[76]

With the test site ready and security assured, only one task remained. It was nearly time to transport the first A-12 airframe, dubbed Article 121, to Groom Lake for flight testing. During a planning session in Burbank, Kelly Johnson stood before a chalkboard and sketched out the final steps under the heading "Schedule for 121." He announced that assembly was expected to be complete by February 17, 1962. The airframe would be subjected to a rigorous battery of engineering tests, and then, as Johnson noted with a flourish, "Feb. 26—4:00 a.m.—Move out to Area 51."[77]

Kelly Johnson presents the schedule of activities for completion and delivery of the first A-12 airframe. *Lockheed*

CHAPTER 3
ROADRUNNERS AND BLACKBIRDS

The convoy transporting the first A-12 to Area 51 rolls through the desert somewhere north of Baker, California, on the way to Nevada. *Dorsey Kammerer collection*

December 1961. Col. Holbury leaned into the doorway of the Command Post and called out, "O.B." Rising from his chair, TSgt. Oren B. Harnage replied, "Yes, sir!" TSgt. Billy Pryor stood as well, listening attentively. What could the brass want? "Colonel Nelson and I are going to try out the new radios in the staff cars. I want you to listen in and let me know how it sounds." Harnage relaxed. "Yes, sir. Will do." A short while later, Pryor and Harnage listened as the two officers spoke to each other and then requested a radio check from the Command Post. "You're coming in loud and clear, sir," Harnage replied. Pryor said, "They need call signs." Harnage thought for a moment and said, "How about Roadrunner One and Roadrunner Two." They ran it by the brass later and no one objected, so Pryor subsequently assigned Roadrunner call signs for all the other command staff personnel. Eventually, "Roadrunners" was also adopted as the official name for the 1129th Special Activities Squadron.

The ordeal of moving the radar model to Groom Lake taught Dorsey Kammerer some valuable lessons. "We could save considerable money and man-hours by having a special trailer built to move the main portion of the article in one piece," he noted in a report to Kelly Johnson. "This cuts down on having to dismantle the forward section and then reassemble it at the Area on arrival."[1]

He then tasked Leon Gavette with designing an ingenious transport system. The lower portion consisted of a steel framework for mounting carriage wheels and towing equipment and to support the airplane, which rested on the framework on its landing gear to allow the airframe structure to safely carry the load on rough road surfaces. A removable upper framework surrounding the aircraft was assembled from 4-inch-square aluminum tubing, covered with canvas fabric along the sides and top and a corrugated aluminum shield on the forward end. When complete, the box was 35 feet wide and 105 feet long and oriented so the airplane was traveling tail end first. Steerable wheels operated manually from two stations at the back of the vehicle allowed the carriage to negotiate tight turns.[2]

Convoy requirements for moving Article 121 to Area 51 were far more extensive than the previous effort and required a dozen different vehicles. The operation began three hours before sunrise on February 26, 1962, with personnel coordinator Frank Harvey taking the lead and driving on ahead to arrange for food and lodging along the way. Kammerer rented two sedans, two pickup trucks, and a station wagon to provide transportation for Lockheed security personnel, mechanics, a woodworker, and an electrician. Another station wagon carried company photographers Joseph Gulli and Paul E. Smith to document the journey. R. A. "Bud" Rice and the Lockheed plant security chief made sure that identifying markings or company names were removed from all convoy vehicles.[3]

At dawn, near the edge of the San Fernando Valley, the convoy paused by the California Aqueduct to await the arrival of a California Highway Patrol escort. From there the schedule was similar to the previous trip with the radar model, and the journey proceeded smoothly with the exception of one brief delay when the rear wheels of the main carriage sank into soft soil during a turn. On the third day the convoy crept up Highway 127 to Death Valley Junction, where the Nevada Highway Patrol took responsibility for escort duty as far as the NTS boundary. While entering the AEC test site through Mercury, the procession was joined by two trucks carrying Area 51 security personnel William A. Mullan, Lloyd G. Wiggins, Thomas J. Stanks, Victor G. Cibello, Marshall L. Edwards, and Richard P. Kallman. With red lights flashing, the security vehicles fell in behind and ahead of the convoy and proceeded across the nuclear proving ground. Upon arrival at Groom Lake, the transport carriage was immediately moved into Hangar 5, where Kammerer supervised the unloading of Article 121. The various components of the transport system were carefully dismantled for later use as each of the remaining A-12 airframes rolled off the assembly line.[4]

Three "First" Flights

Over the next few weeks, Lockheed technicians reassembled the A-12 and checked out its systems. Since the airplane's J58 engines were not yet available from Pratt & Whitney, Kelly Johnson decided to use J75 engines in the interim. The less powerful J75 was incapable of propelling the A-12 to its design speed but was sufficient for use in the initial stages of handling-qualities testing. To prevent delay in the test schedule, three of the first five A-12 airframes were initially powered by the J75.

At Death Valley Junction, the Nevada Highway Patrol accepted responsibility for escorting the convoy as far as the entrance to the Nevada Test Site. *Dorsey Kammerer collection*

Following reassembly, the A-12 underwent a battery of systems tests in preparation for initial engine runs and taxi testing. *Lockheed*

During fueling tests, two forklifts were used to raise the airplane's nose to simulate attitude during high-speed cruise. *Lockheed*

Kelly Johnson's basic philosophy for flight-testing the A-12 was essentially the same as that employed with the U-2. All test activities were aimed toward the earliest possible successful demonstration of operational capabilities. Safety was given the highest priority, followed by reliability. The next-highest priorities were demonstration of aircraft performance, and development of mission equipment and camera systems. Performance goals included successful demonstrations of low radar and infrared (IR) signatures, and measurement of aircraft noise patterns on the ground when the A-12 flew overhead at cruising speeds and altitudes. Of least but not insignificant importance was the need to develop optimum training procedures both for flight and ground crews. Early flights would focus primarily on pilot familiarization, basic airplane-handling qualities, checkout of flight test equipment, and general operation of aircraft systems. During initial sorties, the stability augmentation system (SAS) would be operable but not turned on unless deemed absolutely necessary. After several flights the pilot would test the SAS by turning it on, one channel at a time. Most early sorties would be used for collecting data on stability and control, structural loads, investigation of flutter regimes, and operation of the fuel management system, communications gear, and other equipment.[5]

Prior to engine testing, the A-12 was secured to a thrust stand, using thick steel cables. *Lockheed*

Ejection seat testing for the A-12 consisted of towing a mockup of the nose section and cockpit behind a rented 1961 Ford Thunderbird speeding across Groom Lake. The seat was occupied by an anthropomorphic dummy. *Lockheed*

Johnson and Col. Holbury met with FAA officials at Area 51 on March 31, 1962, to finalize plans for flight routes to be used for high-speed envelope-expansion sorties that would allow for ground-based measurement of sonic boom effects. This would require flying beyond the boundaries of the Nellis Air Force Range and crossing airspace frequented by commercial air traffic. "The matter of crossing two active air lanes must be given due consideration," Johnson noted, "not only from a safety standpoint but also from a security point of view." In order to make communications more secure, code names were assigned to various natural landmarks so that project pilots could make position reports over the radio without providing unauthorized listeners with any meaningful information. Additionally, more than a dozen dry lakebeds were surveyed for use as contingency landing sites, just as had been done for NASA's X-15. In fact, many of the same lakebeds were selected.[6]

While preparing Article 121 for its maiden flight, technicians had great difficulty sealing the airplane's fuel reservoirs. The rubbery, gray sealant material did not adhere properly to the titanium interior surfaces of the integral fuel tanks that occupied much of the space inside the wings. "When we first poured fuel in the aircraft, it developed 68 leaks," Johnson recalled. "We had to strip the sealant from the aircraft and reseal it with another, which we knew was not as good at high temperature."[7]

Johnson's plans for the first two weeks of testing were completely disrupted while technicians worked around the clock to fix the leak problem. But to mitigate the delay, he devised an innovative short-term solution that allowed the team to proceed with engine runs and low-speed taxi testing. As soon as the wing tanks had been resealed, allowing top cover panels to be reinstalled, the Lockheed crew rigged two 300-gallon external tanks on wooden stands, one atop each wing. These provided fuel to the engines via gravity feed and were designed to withstand taxi speeds of up to 80 miles per hour. To further reduce schedule delays Johnson considered resealing only three of the six fuel tanks prior to making the first flight. Engine runs were accomplished with Article 121 parked on a concrete pad adjacent to the north taxiway and a wooden barrier erected on one side to prevent unauthorized Area 51 personnel from observing the test. Firefighters stood ready because the J75 engines were fueled with JP-4 instead of the high-flash-point JP-7 that would be required once the J58 power plants were installed. Although the A-12 and its successors became notorious for dripping fuel even under the best of circumstances, a new sealant eventually solved the problem of major leaks.[8]

In 1959, Johnson assigned Lorris M. "Larry" Bohanon to act as on-site manager of Lockheed flight test operations at Area 51. He then selected Louis W. Schalk Jr. and William C. "Bill" Park Jr. as primary A-12 project pilots. A fighter pilot by training, Schalk attended the Air Force

The Area 51 fire chief, standing by his pickup truck, observes preparations for an engine run on a pad adjacent to the North Taxiway. The engine inlets have been covered with screens to prevent ingestion of foreign objects, and fuel is fed from external tanks that were used during ground testing only before tank sealant problems had been resolved. *Lockheed*

Test Pilot School in 1954 and graduated at the top of his class. He served as a test pilot at Edwards until 1957, when he joined Lockheed as an engineering test pilot, flying advanced versions of the F-104 Starfighter and other Lockheed aircraft. Two years later he was appointed chief test pilot for the Skunk Works. Park was a distinguished combat veteran with service in World War II and Korea. He resigned from the Air Force in 1956 to take a position as a test pilot with Convair, where he flew production acceptance tests of the F-102A and TF-102A. In 1957, he joined Lockheed as an engineering test pilot and was assigned to work on early development of the F-104, including performance envelope expansion, structural, and flutter tests. Park transferred to Lockheed's Advanced Development Projects Division in 1961.[9] His initial OXCART test duties involved providing safety chase in an F-104, during which he observed the A-12 for problems, checked the operation of the landing gear, and provided standby communications in case of radio failure.

Schalk's first task in the A-12 was to conduct low- and medium-speed taxi tests. These went as planned, and on April 25 he was ready for the first high-speed taxi run. Starting from the southern end of the runway, he pushed the throttles forward and accelerated to what he thought was just under takeoff speed. He intentionally left the SAS off, since it could be properly tested only in flight, and he had no intention of leaving the ground. The desert landscape was a blur as Article 121 rolled down the concrete strip and Schalk felt the airplane shudder and vibrate.

Then, suddenly, near silence with just the dull roar of the engines behind him. To his astonishment, Schalk realized that he was airborne and that the airplane's nose was swinging to the right. He fought the controls while flying for about a mile at an altitude of 20 feet as the A-12 rocked wildly from side to side. Kelly Johnson watched in horror as his prototype got off the ground with the rudders swinging first right then left, again and again, to their limits. "This set up lateral oscillations that were horrible to see," he later recalled.[10]

By the time Schalk wrestled the A-12 back to the ground, he was on the emergency overrun beyond the departure end of the runway. From Johnson's perspective the airplane immediately disappeared in a cloud of dust. "The tower controllers were calling me to find out what was happening," Schalk said later, "but the UHF antenna was located on the underside [of the fuselage] and no one could hear me." He finally slowed down enough to turn onto the lakebed, and as he emerged from the dusty haze, everyone breathed a sigh of relief.[11] A postflight inspection revealed that the nosewheel steering and rudder pedals had been improperly hooked up, causing the aircraft to turn in the opposite direction from that desired. This was soon corrected, and Schalk agreed to attempt a planned flight the following day.

Lou Schalk settles into the cockpit of Article 121 to begin preflight cockpit checks. An F-104 chase plane is visible in the background, and Kelly Johnson can be seen leaning into frame at far right. *Lockheed*

Lockheed test pilot Lou Schalk. *Lockheed*

Article 121 is readied for flight next to Lockheed's F-104 chase plane. Two F-101 Voodoos are visible in the background. *Lockheed*

The true maiden flight on April 26 was generally successful but revealed a few minor problems. As the A-12 reached an altitude of about 300 feet, it began shedding fillet panels from the lower fuselage. This had little effect on flying qualities, so Schalk completed a brief checkout of the airplane's basic handling characteristics. Per standard practice for a first flight, he left the landing gear down and locked, and touched down without incident thirty minutes after takeoff. It took the Lockheed team several days to fix the fillet problem, by which time Johnson had scheduled the official first flight for April 30.[12]

On that day, Schalk flew a one-hour sortie in front of an audience of dignitaries including Herbert "Pete" Scoville Jr., the CIA's deputy director for research; Lockheed chairman Courtlandt Gross; National Reconnaissance Office (NRO) director Joseph Charyk; FAA chief Najeeb Halaby; and Dick Bissell, even though he had resigned from the CIA following the Bay of Pigs debacle.[13] Within three minutes of takeoff, Schalk had leveled off at 30,000 feet. He reported that the airplane responded well to control inputs and was extremely stable in all aspects with or without stability augmentation. Bill Park kept pace in an F-104 while Schalk made several passes over the airfield before descending for a low flyby over the old Watertown runway for the benefit of observers. He then made a flawless landing, with a planned rollout onto the lakebed extension. Johnson, perhaps with some irony, later described it as "the smoothest first flight in his experience."[14]

Article 121 lifts off the runway as Schalk applies takeoff power on one of the airplane's three "first" flights. *Lockheed*

Schalk smiles at a comment from FAA chief Najeeb Halaby while shaking hands with former CIA deputy director for plans Dick Bissell. Other VIP observers included Herbert "Pete" Scoville (*far left*), Joseph Charyk, Courtlandt Gross, and, *at right*, John Parangosky. *Lockheed*

Schalk retracts the landing gear as he begins his climb on April 30, 1962, for the official first flight. *Lockheed*

Just four days later, Schalk expanded the airplane's flight envelope beyond Mach 1.0, and he continued to explore its handling characteristics over the next few months. He also tested the airplane's brakes, which were subject to chatter and asymmetrical braking. A drag chute tested on the eighth flight significantly reduced landing roll and marked the first time the lakebed runway extension was not required for deceleration.[15] With testing well underway, preparations began for training operational project pilots.

Into the Black

Lt. Col. Houser Wilson of the Pentagon's Special Activities Office (cryptically designated AFCIG-5) and Col. Jack C. Ledford, the CIA's Air Force liaison officer, oversaw the pilot selection process for OXCART. Candidates were required to have a minimum of two thousand flight hours, with at least a thousand hours in high-performance jet fighters. Each underwent an extensive background check and a rigorous medical examination. Potential candidates were summoned to secluded hotel rooms, where they were interviewed by anonymous civilians offering unspecified employment at a classified location. Those few candidates who met selection criteria had to decide immediately whether to take the assignment, without knowing what they would be doing, or where, or for how long. Many didn't make the cut for physiological or psychological reasons. One candidate in particular was rejected largely due to concerns about his "very inquisitive, intelligent, and domineering wife." During his second screening interview, the subject said he would have difficulty keeping the truth of his assignment from his spouse. He was ultimately dissuaded from accepting the assignment and sworn to secrecy.[16] Those who agreed to the terms and met the medical criteria found themselves ushered into the so-called "black world" of covert operations.

The OXCART project pilots included William L. "Bill" Skliar, Alonzo J. "Lon" Walter Jr., Kenneth S. Collins, Mele "Mel" Vojvodich Jr., Walter L. Ray, Jack W. Weeks, Ronald J. "Jack" Layton, Dennis B. "Denny" Sullivan, David D. Young, Russell J. Scott, and, eventually, Francis J. "Frank" Murray.[17] Scott, Young, and Skliar remained with OXCART for only a short time before returning to the regular Air Force, and Skliar and Scott later flew an interceptor variant of the A-12. Murray spent three years at Area 51 as a safety chase pilot before being selected to join the A-12 pilot cadre. As soon as the project pilots were accepted, the Air Force took measures to document appropriate transfers to cover their new assignments. Each pilot was also given a pseudonym. Collins became known as "Mr. Maltravers," Weeks as "Mr. Farenkoff," Ray as "Mr. Kempiak," Layton as "Mr. Dickhurst," and Murray as "Mr. Vanagunas." Other

OXCART project pilots and Roadrunners administrative personnel pictured are, *from left*, Jack Layton, Dennis Sullivan, Mel Vojvodich, Burt Barrett, Jack Weeks, Ken Collins, Walt Ray, Jack Ledford from CIA Headquarters, Bill Skliar, Cy Perkins, Robert Holbury, John Kelly, and Hugh Slater. *CIA*

false names included Treske, Frienmuth, Kielhack, and Sazausky.[18] Selectees were instructed to arrange for housing in Las Vegas for their families and given instructions for reporting to their new duty station.

Upon arrival at Area 51, they reported to base headquarters at the corner of 5th Street and Kennedy. The two-story, H-shaped structure provided office space for Col. Holbury and the 1129th SAS administrative staff, Weiss and his staff, base security, the medical dispensary, and one of several fire stations. As with other personnel who remained at Area 51 throughout the course of the week, the project pilots were assigned quarters in the Babbitt houses. One of these, house 6, eventually came to serve as an informal gathering place after duty hours where the men could unwind with a drink and a game of cards. During the day the main hub of activity was inside the operations building, known as Base Ops, where Col. Douglas T. Nelson served as director of operations with Lt. Col. Maynard Amundson as his assistant. Other key staff included Lt. Col. Burton S. Barrett, training and operations officer; Maj. Raymond L. Haupt and Maj. Harold E. Burgeson, standardization and evaluation (Stan/Eval) officers and instructor pilots; Lt. Col. Blair J. Davis, support pilot and A-12 maintenance officer; and Lt. Col. John R. Kelly Jr., materiel officer. Base Ops consisted of briefing rooms and space for the mission-planning section, Stan/Eval, communications, meteorology, and the Command Post. Air Force meteorologists at Area 51 were assigned to Detachment 1, 3rd Weather Wing, commanded by Lt. Col. Daniel B. Mitchell, and after May 1965 by Maj. Ralph W. "Bill" Thomas. Maj. Robert L. Seymour, a meteorologist, and Maj. Samuel E. Pizzo, navigation officer, designed a squadron patch for the 1129th SAS that featured a cartoon roadrunner on a yellow field with the words "Beep, Beep" in the border. A similar patch for the weather detachment included the same roadrunner, but holding an umbrella.[19]

The emblem of the 1129th Special Activities Squadron. *Author*

Visitors and Observers

As the A-12 test program was getting underway, Area 51 received several distinguished visitors. On May 14, 1962, Kelly Johnson and Col. Leo Geary escorted a delegation from SAC Headquarters that included Gen. Thomas S. Power, the commander in chief; Maj. Gen. Keith K. Compton, director of operations; and Col. Patrick E. Montoya.[20] After receiving an OXCART briefing, they watched an A-12 takeoff and then toured the facilities. Power seemed very impressed with the airplane and its antiradar characteristics and queried Johnson as to the adaptability of the A-12 to bombardment or reconnaissance/strike missions. As it turned out, Johnson had already considered this possibility and had drawn up a proposal for a bomber, which he called the RB-12, which would be capable of carrying four 400-pound bombs or a single large weapon inside the airplane's fuselage without compromising the fuel load. He also suggested an interceptor variant, dubbed AF-12, that would be capable of firing as many as three air-to-air missiles while cruising at Mach 3.2 and hitting airborne targets at any altitude. Johnson explained that he ultimately envisioned a "common market" version of the A-12 with a single configuration for the aft fuselage, wings, tails, and engines but a different forward fuselage assembly (reconnaissance, recce/strike, or interceptor), depending on customer requirements.[21] The SAC delegation was then treated to a low flyby before departing to Las Vegas for further discussions. A week later, Col. Wilson visited Area 51 with Fred Payne, the DoD deputy research director for strategic and space systems. Payne asked about the possibility that high-altitude contrails might make the A-12 vulnerable to visual detection. He suggested it might be worthwhile to conduct a study on this problem under the guise and funding for the XB-70 program, a defunct bomber prototype that had been transformed into a research aircraft.[22]

While invited guests surveyed Area 51 from ground level, uninvited visitors threatened from above. OXCART security personnel were frequently concerned with military aircraft operating within the Nellis Range boundaries adjacent to the Groom Lake test site. In a telex to the program director on May 15, the Area 51 security chief noted that Schalk's April 30 flight had been concurrent with an X-15 mission, and that subsequent NASA publicity mentioned that unidentified objects were captured on film during the flight. He suggested reviewing the film to determine whether the A-12 had been inadvertently recorded by the research vehicle's camera.[23] On the X-15 flight in question, civilian research pilot Joseph A. Walker reached an altitude of 246,700 feet over southern Nevada while a rear-facing camera filmed the horizon and the landscape below. After a thorough examination, NASA officials determined the unidentified objects seen in some of the frames were simply ice particles flaking off the sides of the rocket plane's fuselage.[24] Other traffic across the range resulted from normal military training activities. Another telex on May 19 noted, "There were four unidentified aircraft in the flight-test area today. However, we do not feel that any of them were near enough to compromise security."[25]

A rocket-powered X-15 research vehicle drops away from the wing of its B-52 mother ship. *NASA*

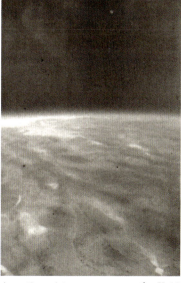

A motion picture camera on the X-15 captured an unidentified object, the white dot near the top of the frame, at an altitude of around 270,000 feet while passing approximately 20 miles southeast of Groom Lake. Subsequent analysis suggested it was simply frost flaking off the vehicle's fuselage. Delamar Lake is visible at lower right. *NASA*

Portion of a Soviet military map of southern Nevada that was produced from satellite imagery in 1980. A small dirt airstrip just south of the Groom Mine is clearly identified. Surprisingly, although a number of man-made structures are noted just off the southwest corner of Groom Lake, the concrete runway and its asphalt extension are identified here as an extension of the road from Indian Springs. *Author's collection*

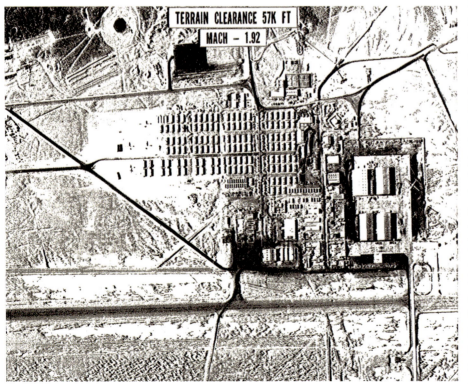

The Area 51 cantonment was photographed from an A-12 at 57,000 feet. Aircraft visible on the North Ramp include an A-12 and a Constellation next to Hangar 6, and another A-12 on the run-up pad by the taxiway. The dark circular feature near the upper left is the Crash Pit. *CIA*

Unauthorized observation from the air was only one security concern because intelligence collection had entered the space age. By this time, both the US and the Soviets had begun launching reconnaissance satellites, but because they followed predictable orbits it was easy to anticipate when one would be in a position to obtain coverage of Area 51. Base security was responsible for notifying project personnel of "Sputnik cover" times (another term for a spy satellite was "Ashcan"), and standard operating procedures were developed to protect assets from inadvertent exposure. During daylight cover times, all aircraft and related equipment deemed to be "sight-sensitive" were to be placed inside a hangar or otherwise camouflaged to conceal their identity or configuration. In some cases, when it was suspected that a Soviet spacecraft might have an electronic intelligence (ELINT) capability, all signal-producing electronic equipment had to be inactivated as well.[26] By 1966, the Defense Intelligence Agency had instituted a formalized program called Satellite Reconnaissance Advanced Notice (SATRAN), also known as STRAY CAT.[27]

While it was easy to conceal airplanes and other mobile equipment, there was no way to hide permanent facilities and infrastructure from overhead reconnaissance. John Parangosky discussed the problem with DPD executive officer John N. McMahon and came up with two proposals. First, they suggested having a U-2 take photographs of Area 51 and then pass the images on to CIA photo interpreters, without briefing them on the target, and asking them to determine what type of activity was being conducted at the site. Second, they proposed having a CORONA reconnaissance satellite make a pass over the Nevada Test Site area and again subjecting the images to interpretation. "This would give us," McMahon wrote in a memo to the acting DPD chief, "a pretty fair idea of what deductions and conclusions could be made by the Soviets" from their own reconnaissance capabilities.[28]

Support and Chase

Support aircraft began arriving at Area 51 in the spring of 1962. These included six F-101B and two F-101F Voodoo two-seat fighters for proficiency flying and safety chase. Additionally, the F-101F model was equipped as a trainer with dual controls, and its radar was replaced with lead ballast. There were two T-33A trainers for proficiency flying and other support duties, one Lockheed C-130 cargo transport, a U-8A for administrative use, and a Cessna 180 for liaison use (later replaced with a Cessna 210D). Lockheed supplied two F-104A/G fighter-interceptors as chase planes during the OXCART flight test program. These were equipped with telemetry relays to provide test data to engineers on the ground. Capt. Donald J. Donohue, maintenance officer for the 1129th SAS, arranged for periodic maintenance support from Ogden Air Logistics Center (OO-ALC) at Hill Air Force Base, Utah, for the F-101 and T-33 aircraft. He also arranged for similar support for the C-130 from Warner-Robins Air Logistics Center (WR-ALC) at Robins Air Force Base, Georgia. In addition to his maintenance duties, Donohue regularly flew chase for the A-12 during test and training sorties.[29]

The Voodoo fleet served several purposes. Because it closely approximated the flying characteristics of the A-12, the F-101 could be used as a surrogate trainer for OXCART pilots as well as for maintaining flying proficiency. The Voodoos were also used for safety and photo chase for A-12 sorties during the low-altitude portions of flight, immediately after takeoff and prior to landing, and during aerial refueling. It was the duty of a safety observer in the F-101 to check the A-12 for indications of fuel leaks, loose panels, or other problems.[30] Dennis Sullivan recalled one flight chasing Bill Park when an unexpected problem cropped up. During acceleration to Mach 1.5 shortly after takeoff, Park abruptly cut the afterburner and turned back toward the airfield. Sullivan asked if there was a problem, and Park replied tersely, "Aft bypass!" Sullivan was puzzled, since the aft bypass doors on the engine nacelles—used to reduce aerodynamic drag at higher Mach numbers—wouldn't come into play at that speed. Back on the ground, Park sheepishly admitted he had turned back to make an emergency trip to the bathroom, since the alternative would have been to soil his pressure suit.[31]

Maintenance personnel pose next to one of the F-101B Voodoos that were used for safety chase, proficiency flying, and weather support missions. *Roadrunners*

Support aircraft at Area 51 included a U-3B, *left*, and a Cessna 210D, seen here parked adjacent to Hangar 8 on the South Ramp. *Roadrunners*

Observers in an F-101B watch as Lou Schalk dumps fuel from Article 121 during a test flight. *Lockheed*

DREAMLAND

Hooked up to an MD-3 ground power unit, an F-101B is readied for flight. *Roadrunners*

Chopper Ops

The CIA also procured a helicopter for search and rescue, mission support, and use in special construction projects. On March 2, 1962, the agency's deputy for special-projects materiel staff received a call informing him that a twin-rotor Kaman HH-43B was being reassigned from a squadron at Holloman Air Force Base, New Mexico. Although it would be available within a few days, the 1129th SAS did not yet have a helicopter pilot or maintenance crew. Arrangements were made to transfer the chopper to Nellis, where it would be maintained in flyable condition until such time as it could be moved to Area 51.[33]

Sometimes the rear seat in the F-101 accommodated a photographer to shoot still or motion pictures for engineering documentation purposes. On long-range missions the Voodoos were also used for weather reconnaissance. The weather scout took off in advance of the A-12, flying the same planned route and taking note of any areas of significant turbulence or clouds near refueling rendezvous points. On occasion, chase or weather scout pilots would scrutinize suspicious air traffic within nearby restricted areas. Frank Murray was once directed to investigate an airplane that had been picked up on radar in the vicinity of Delamar Dry Lake, about 40 miles east of Area 51. "When I got there," he recalled, "I saw an F-104 in NASA markings making very steep, diving approaches toward the lakebed." It was a memorable day for NASA research pilot and X-15 astronaut William H. "Bill" Dana as well. "Delamar was one of the contingency landing sites for the X-15, and I was practicing my approach technique when all of a sudden there was a Voodoo flying just off my wing."[32]

Capt. Charles E. Trapp Jr. joined the Roadrunners in September, following an assignment to a helicopter rescue detachment at Charleston Air Force Base, South Carolina. At first, when his commander asked if he would be interested in joining a mysterious unit at a classified location somewhere in the US, he wasn't sure, but it was a flying job and it sounded interesting, so he said yes. He never regretted his decision.

Trapp's first task upon arrival in Las Vegas was to pick up the HH-43B from Nellis and fly it to his new duty station. The chopper, which had been used at Holloman for retrieving parachute payloads in midair, had seen some rough treatment and was in poor shape. When Trapp called the Area 51 Command Post to report the problem, Col. Holbury got on the phone and asked what he needed. "I recommended that factory maintenance folks and a test pilot come to Nellis," he recalled, "and they flew in two days later from the Kaman factory in Connecticut."

Charlie Trapp poses with the HH-43B helicopter that was used for mountaintop construction and maintenance projects, search and rescue, survival training, security, and other utility purposes. *Via Charles Trapp*

Trapp worked closely with the factory technicians and the Air Force maintenance crew and explained that he had been told the helicopter was needed for a high-altitude construction project of some sort. The Kaman pilot made some suggestions for adjustments to improve altitude performance. These changes were soon implemented, and, following a brief check flight, the HH-43B was declared ready. Trapp then called Holbury, who came down to Nellis and flew with him to Area 51. To Trapp's surprise, the colonel directed him to bypass the airfield and fly to the 9,380-foot summit of Bald Mountain for a brief tour of the proposed construction site, a barren expanse of windswept rock. Holbury explained that this would be the location for a communications antenna array, and, since there were no roads, all necessary personnel, tools, food, water, tower sections, wire, cement, welding equipment, generators, and other equipment had to be flown to the site.

The HH-43B hovers over the Bald Mountain antenna site. The helicopter was also used to transport metal poles, welding equipment, generators, and tools, as well as food and water for the construction crew. *Via Charles Trapp*

It was an onerous task. The construction contractor dug three holes, which had to be filled with 30,000 pounds of wet cement transported by helicopter 1,000 pounds at a time. Each hole contained four embedded steel rods supporting a steel plate serving as a foundation for an antenna tower. The three towers formed an isosceles triangle, with thirty-three parallel wires strung horizontally across one long side and the short side, forming a curtain array. "Because of the heavy weight of each of the poles and the high altitude, we had to reduce the fuel load with only the pilot on board," Trapp said. "We used a hundred feet of intercom cable so the crew chief could direct the pilot from the ground to raise the poles from the horizontal to the vertical position and place them on the concrete bases." Operating the helicopter at such a high elevation was extremely hazardous due to low air density, which made hovering difficult, gusty winds, and poor visual reference in relation to the steep terrain along the sides of the mountaintop. While Trapp used the chopper to hold each antenna tower vertical, four people on the ground struggled to tether it with ropes until the bolts could be secured to the base and permanent guy wires installed to anchor it. "We were pretty much at the red line for power during the lift," Trapp later recalled. Holbury personally supervised the first operation and was reportedly very pleased with the results.[34]

When not involved in construction projects, the HH-43B was assigned to the Rescue Section, and Trapp shared piloting duties with Capt. Keith Spencer. "We had only two helicopter pilots for a while, so we didn't always get home every weekend," Trapp said, adding, "We wouldn't know until late Friday if we had to stick around for a Saturday A-12 flight." Eventually, three more pilots were assigned, including captains Keith A. Spencer, Theodore E. "Ted" Angle, Joseph H. Pinaud, and Samuel J. Scamardo. As crew chief, MSgt. Bill "Flash" Walters oversaw the maintenance staff. Pararescue personnel included Technical Sergeants Earl Casto and Frederick W. Schneider and Master Sergeants Gordon C. "Beetle" Bailey, William W. Thomas, and Coy V. Staggs.[35] The Rescue Section provided not only search-and-rescue support for A-12 test flights but also survival training for the OXCART pilots. This included exercises in traversing desert and mountainous terrain, as well as water survival training in the Area 51 swimming pool and at Lake Mead, where parasail-equipped pilots were towed aloft by boat and dropped into the water.[36] Casto distinguished himself in a series of jumps to test the A-12 crew escape system parachute. Drops of an instrumented dummy from an NB-66B over the Navy's parachute test range near El Centro, California, at altitudes from 25,000 to 45,000 feet, were interspersed with Casto's live jumps, some while wearing a full-pressure suit.[37]

Crewmen attach a load to the HH-43B for use in a construction project atop Bald Mountain. Fire Station No. 2 is visible in the background, and the Personal Equipment Building is at left. The tower is part of the parachute rigging and repair facility. *Via Charles Trapp*

During water survival training at Lake Mead, *from left*, Coy Staggs, flight surgeon Ted Dake, Charlie Trapp, and Earl Casto. *Via Charles Trapp*

Survival trainees were lofted over the lake, using a parasail towed by a boat, and then released to float down to the water. *Via Charles Trapp*

Jack Layton, in full-pressure suit, is prepared for water survival training at Lake Mead. Plans to attempt this by using the parasail were abandoned as being too risky. *Via Charles Trapp*

With water dripping from his boots, Ken Collins swings gently in a harness over the Area 51 swimming pool. In the background, Charlie Trapp (*seated*) chats with a life-support technician. *Via Charles Trapp*

Trapp and his team were occasionally called upon to provide photographic and security support for activities at the NTS, and for search-and-rescue missions involving Air Force planes that crashed in the vicinity of the Nellis range. They flew airborne alert when President Kennedy toured the Nuclear Rocket Development Area at the NTS in December 1962. They also trained Area 51 firefighters on the use of 1,000-pound extinguisher bottles carried aboard the HH-43B. Such exercises were undertaken at the Crash Pit, a simulated aircraft wreck in a cleared space west of the housing area, where controlled burns provided realistic training conditions. The helicopter crew had to fly close to the flames and drop off two firemen with an extinguisher, then hover overhead, cooling the area with the chopper's rotor wash and clearing away the smoke. This gave the firefighters an opportunity to lay down a trail of fire-retardant foam for the purpose of extracting potential survivors from the simulated crash site. Other helicopter missions involved placing radar targets on the lakebed or hovering with a hollow metal radar calibration sphere dangling below the chopper on a long cable. After ground observers complained that they had trouble seeing the helicopter at altitude, Trapp asked Flash Walters to find a solution. The next day, Walters installed a pressurized extinguisher bottle filled with oil, with a tube running to the engine exhaust pipe. Trapp demonstrated the device during a 115-knot maximum-speed pass over the taxiway, releasing the pressurized oil as he pulled into a steep climb. This resulted in a spectacular smoke trail that was visible for miles.[38]

One mission entailed positioning color-coded reference markers at specified distances and headings from the EG&G test complex, to aid in the location and recovery of test items to be dropped from a C-47. Joe Pinaud was flying the HH-43B with two firemen and two paramedics on board. One of the firefighters, strapped into a gunner's belt (safety harness) at the open cabin door, served as acting drop master for the mission. Guidance to the drop locations was provided by monitors at the EG&G radar complex. Pinaud took off and climbed to 5,500 feet to get clear of ground clutter while being vectored to a position 6 miles north of the radar dish. Once over the spot, he descended steeply to an altitude of less than 10 feet above the ground and hovered while the drop master wrestled the first of eight markers, made from painted automobile tires, over the edge of the doorway. The chopper crew repeated this procedure without incident, making another drop at a second location. Dust devils swirled across the valley floor as Pinaud maneuvered to the next drop point. The third approach seemed normal until the HH-43B was about 200 feet above the ground, at which point the chopper dropped like a stone.

Pinaud fought to slow his descent, but the helicopter struck the ground and bounced back into the air. After confirming that his crew had sustained no injuries, the pilot requested a visual assessment of the damage. The drop master reported that the right landing gear was badly damaged and partially missing. At this point the mission was terminated and Pinaud declared an emergency. The remaining markers were jettisoned on the South Ramp, and three of the crewmen were lowered to the ground, using the chopper's hoist. Pinaud climbed to a higher altitude to conserve fuel and circled south of the base while ground crews readied a makeshift landing cradle from mattresses, wooden pallets, and tires. Once this task had been completed at the center of a taxiway, well clear of any parked aircraft, he lowered the chopper slowly to the ground. It took several attempts to achieve a stable landing before it was safe to shut down the engine. Investigators later concluded that the HH-43B rapidly lost altitude as a result of a downdraft encountered when Pinaud descended through a dust devil vortex.[39]

Firefighters train at the Crash Pit. Trapp uses the HH-43B's rotor wash to cool the area, clear away smoke, and flatten the flames to enable firemen to extinguish the blaze by using handlines. *Via Charles Trapp*

Eventually, the Rescue Section acquired a UH-1F helicopter. According to Trapp, "It was faster than the HH-43B and we were able to load and unload people and cargo from both sides of the cabin, which made our job easier and safer." He and Walters picked up the new chopper from the Bell Helicopter plant in Fort Worth and flew it back to Area 51. "We maintained both helicopters until the crews were checked out in the UH-1," Trapp said. Both choppers were used to support continuing construction efforts and other projects at the base. Installation of P-1, a communications facility on the highest peak in the Papoose Mountains, just west of the base, was accomplished with the UH-1. As Trapp proudly recalled, "Our aircrews were awarded 10 Air Medals and several Air Force Commendation Medals for meritorious achievements while participating in aerial flights at the Ranch."[40]

The UH-1F helicopter was used to install a communications antenna at the top of Papoose Mountain, southwest of Groom Lake. *Via Charles Trapp*

Crewmen with the UH-1F. *From left, front row*: unknown, MSgt. Baker, Fred Schneider, unknown; *middle row*: Coy Staggs, Joe Pinaud, Ted Angle, Gordon Bailey. Bill Walters is standing at center rear. *Via Charles Trapp*

Lurching Toward Mach 3

While awaiting the arrival of J58 engines, the A-12 fleet continued to operate with the J75 and fixed inlet spikes. This created some difficulties because the engine and inlet were mismatched, resulting in duct rumble (inlet airflow vibrations) as the airplane approached Mach 2.0. Pratt & Whitney delivered the first J58 in mid-June 1962, and by the end of August it was undergoing static testing in one of two test cells near the southernmost end of the base. In the meantime, the test team did what they could with the J75.

After receiving ground instruction from Lou Schalk, Bill Park made his first flight in the A-12 on June 21. After that, the two pilots alternated flying duties, which included aerial-refueling practice in which an F-104 served as a surrogate for the tanker. A KC-135 Stratotanker arrived from Castle Air Force Base, California, and was prepared to handle the special fuel while its crew was briefed on rendezvous procedures. Schalk first performed dry hook-ups with the KC-135 on July 10, and the following day Park accomplished the first fuel transfer. Brig. Gen. Bill Yancey, former commanding officer of the 4070th Support Wing and now commander of the 47th Air Division at Castle, accompanied the tanker crew and later described the entire procedure as "very stable and controllable."[41]

Although the second A-12 airframe, Article 122, arrived by convoy on June 26, 1962, and was quickly reassembled, it was not immediately used for flight testing. Instead, the airplane was raised, inverted, on the EG&G radar range pylon for several months of RCS measurement testing prior to engine installation and final assembly. "It was quite an experience to see such an expensive piece of machinery that far up in the air," Kelly Johnson later recalled.[42]

Article 122 was finally removed from the EG&G pylon and flown for the first time on January 15, 1963. It was used primarily for performance envelope expansion and propulsion studies. Many early flights of this airframe were devoted to solving the duct rumble phenomenon. Lockheed engineers addressed the problem by devising improved inlet controls.[43] Article 122 was the first A-12 to make its initial flight with J58 engines, which the pilots found considerably more responsive than the J75. Lockheed and project pilots were soon conducting tests to expand the speed envelope and learn the peculiarities of the J58, because, unlike the J75-equipped airplanes, those with J58s had movable inlet spikes to control the position of the shock wave, a necessity for preventing a violent airflow interruption called "unstart." This phenomenon occurred with unnerving frequency during the early years of the program. Unstart resulted in a violent yawing motion that pilots described as like "being in a train wreck."[44] Replacement of manual spike controls with a computer-controlled system eventually eliminated this problem, but at the time, it was a serious issue.

Article 122, the first A-12 to make its initial flight with J58 engines, approaches a KC-135Q tanker for a refueling rendezvous. *Lockheed*

The OXCART flight test program was occasionally interrupted by activities at Yucca Flat despite the fact that after 1957, nearly all nuclear testing in the continental United States had moved underground. With the exception of excavation experiments for Project Plowshare, a program involving peaceful applications of nuclear explosives, all tests in Nevada were then being conducted in shafts and tunnels. The largest excavation shot was Sedan on July 6, 1962. The 104-kiloton thermonuclear explosion created a crater 320 feet deep and 1,280 feet across, along with a billowing cloud of radioactive dust that drifted northeast over Groom Pass toward Area 51. Although the underground shots were supposed to be completely contained, radioactive material occasionally vented into the atmosphere through natural fissures or because of failed containment measures. During 1962 at least twenty-one underground nuclear tests vented radioactivity, which occasionally drifted over the hills northeast of Yucca Flat and deposited fallout on the Groom Lake area.[45]

As a result, test operations were necessarily halted from time to time, and the base evacuated. Area 51 personnel were indoctrinated in a radiological defense plan that called for notification of all tenants and staff whenever there was a possibility that a radiation hazard might occur. If evacuation became imminent, all classified equipment and material had to be secured. All vehicles suitable for providing transportation were to be parked next to the mess hall, which served as the assembly point. Air traffic controllers remained on duty until all departing aircraft had taken off, and then closed the control tower and joined the remaining personnel leaving with the vehicle convoy. The designated convoy leader and other key staff personnel rode aboard the Mobile Command Post, at least one ambulance and medical technician accompanied the convoy, and the financial officer carried sufficient funds to provide support in an emergency. The mess hall

With the Groom Mountains dominating the distant horizon, the road to Area 51 becomes visible as dust settles around Sedan crater. *NNSA/NV*

supervisor may have had the most important duty of all: loading one of the vehicles with water jugs and nonperishable food items such as donuts and sweet rolls.[46]

When Area 51 personnel weren't busy evacuating or chowing down on sweet rolls, they were hard at work pushing the A-12 toward its specified design goals. Lou Schalk made the first full-pressure-suit flight on August 8, 1962, while using Article 121 to determine the airplane's maximum speed and altitude capabilities with the J75 engines. Nearly two months later, after technicians installed a J58 in the right-hand engine nacelle, he made a test flight to check out the new power plant. By January 1963, he was satisfied that the engine was performing as expected, and the airplane made its first sortie powered by two J58s.[47]

The Sedan thermonuclear device was buried at an optimum depth so as to maximize the amount of earth displaced by its 104-kiloton explosive yield. *NNSA/NV*

Workers begin the task of uncrating Article 123 shortly after its arrival at the test site. Each A-12 airframe was built by hand, with every component carefully tracked during construction. Skin panels on the stub fin atop the nacelle are marked "123 RH" to indicate which aircraft they belong to and where they should be installed. *Kammerer collection*

Article 123 is slowly extracted from its transport crate. The composite chines are covered by protective panels and marked "Fragile." *Kammerer collection*

The third A-12 arrived at the test site in August 1962 and made its first flight on October 9 with Bill Park at the controls. When Park made the fourth flight of Article 123, he was accompanied by two chase planes, an F-101 and an F-104. EG&G technicians using X-band radar had no trouble distinguishing between the three aircraft as they circled within 40 miles of Groom Lake. Surprisingly, the A-12 presented the largest signature despite its antiradar treatments.[48] Several weeks later, the same equipment was used to conduct RCS measurements of a U-2 flown by a Lockheed test pilot.[49]

Jim Eastham. *Author's collection*

James D. "Jim" Eastham, who had been recruited by Lockheed from Hughes Aircraft Company, had been flying chase for the A-12. He received his checkout and transition flight in Article 123 on October 31 and was immediately pressed into service testing the airplane's inertial navigation system (INS) and reconnaissance payload. During subsequent flights, Eastham made photo runs over targets on the lakebed and elsewhere at the base to test the camera package, which had been designed and built by Eastman Kodak. Prior to conducting one such test on November 17, he joined up with Article 121 and an F-104 chase plane to make a three-ship flyby of the airfield for the benefit of the visiting secretary of the Air Force, Eugene M. Zuckert.

Kelly Johnson kept a close eye on the A-12 assembly line, pushing his workers to meet production goals, while Dorsey Kammerer's convoys continued to make the laborious journey from Burbank to Groom Lake. The fourth airframe arrived at Area 51 in November, followed by the fifth on December 17. In an effort to meet production deadlines, Article 125 arrived at the test site without engines. As Johnson noted in a December 1962 diary entry, "We delivered the fifth airplane to Area 51, meeting our schedule requirements for the year."[50]

Titanium Goose

Up this point, when each pilot was checked out in the A-12 for the first time, it was a solo flight. He had to rely solely on his simulator training and knowledge of the pilot's handbook. In order to improve training capabilities, Lockheed built a single A-12T (Article 124) with a second cockpit for an instructor pilot behind and above the regular crew station. As with Article 121, the trainer was an all-metal airframe, lacking antiradar treatments. The

This three-ship flyby was staged for VIP visitors to Area 51 on November 17, 1962. *CIA*

The A-12T takes to the air. The trainer lacked the composite radar-absorbent structures found on the operational airframes. *Lockheed*

sleek elegance of the single-seat A-12 had earned it the nickname "Cygnus," after the constellation of the swan. By contrast, the awkward appearance of the A-12T saddled it with the moniker "Titanium Goose." When Article 124 arrived at the test site, it was equipped with J75 engines, which it retained throughout its entire service life. This meant the Titanium Goose never attained Mach 3 speeds, but it provided OXCART pilots with basic handling-qualities familiarization and aerial-refueling practice.

Bill Park flew the first flight of Article 124 on January 6, 1963. During takeoff the F-101 chase pilot reported seeing fluid leaking from the left engine, and Park shut off both afterburners while continuing to climb to 20,000 feet in altitude. He noticed the left-hand hydraulic-system pressure was fluctuating, indicating a loss of hydraulic fluid, and the aircraft had begun oscillating laterally. Park aborted the flight and dumped approximately 10,000 pounds of fuel while returning to base. By this time the A-12T was in a descending right-hand turn at about 6,000 feet, approximately 15 miles northeast of Groom Lake and trailing a spectacular plume of vaporizing fuel. As Park maneuvered into a southeasterly heading, entering a normal downwind leg for landing on runway 32, the control tower reported sighting an Air Force T-39B flying at a nine o'clock position relative to the A-12 and about 3 to 5 miles out. Park couldn't see it, so the F-101 was dispatched to intercept the airplane and get its tail number. Area 51 security personnel notified the Nellis Command Post and made arrangements for AFOSI agents to meet the T-39 upon landing and debrief the crew. The airplane had been engaged in a routine training mission over the range, and none of the crew admitted seeing anything

unusual.[51] This was to be a continuing problem, since each flight over the Nellis range increased the chances of exposing the A-12 to unauthorized observers. Additionally, the need to test the airplane's speed and range capabilities would soon necessitate flying off-range over considerable portions of the United States.

Six days later, Park flew the A-12T with Lockheed FTE Keith L. Beswick riding in the instructor's cockpit. Following several additional checkout flights, Article 124 was deemed ready for use as a trainer. On January 24, Park checked out OXCART project pilots Bill Skliar and Lon Walter. The following day he practiced making dry hookups with a KC-135 but cut the flight short due to excessive commercial airline traffic in the area. On February 6, Schalk checked out Ken Collins, and then Mel Vojvodich and Walt Ray the following day. Five days later, Skliar and Walter were flying the Titanium Goose with Walter in the rear seat, wearing a full-pressure suit. The A-12T was cruising at 22,000 feet, accompanied by an F-101. When the pair was approximately 30 miles north of Groom Lake, the chase pilot spotted a flight of four F-105s approaching on a converging course. The fighters were operating within their authorized airspace, which restricted them to 15,000 feet or below, and as they passed directly underneath the A-12T there was no question as to whether the secret plane had been spotted. Upon notification of the incident, Area 51 security officer Ed White immediately called Brig. Gen. Boyd Hubbard Jr., commander of the 4520th Combat Crew Training Wing at Nellis. Hubbard personally met the F-105 pilots as soon as they landed, and admonished them not to talk about what they had seen.[52] The pilots acknowledged the sighting, but the general's warning was enough to keep them quiet.

Twin cockpits gave the A-12T a distinctive profile. The instructor's position is above and behind the student's cockpit. *Lockheed*

Even with his face partially hidden beneath an oxygen mask, Kelly Johnson appears to have a pleased expression as he sits in the student cockpit of the A-12T. This was Johnson's only flight in his creation. *Lockheed*

Over the next several months, Schalk and Park continued to act as instructor pilots, checking out Dennis Sullivan and Lockheed test pilot Robert J. Gilliland. Following several flights in the A-12T to gain experience with the airplane's basic handling characteristics and to practice aerial-refueling rendezvous procedures, each new pilot transitioned into the single-seat A-12 for operational training and cross-country navigation sorties. The Titanium Goose was also used to give rides to select VIP visitors, including Col. Jack Ledford, FAA test pilot Joseph J. Tymczyszyn, and Najeeb Halaby. After the FAA chief's flight, Kelly Johnson noted in his diary that Halaby "was quite non-committal about it, but I know he was impressed."[53] On August 27, 1963, Johnson himself got a ride from Lou Schalk, who later recalled, "I took off, cleaned it up, then gave it to Kelly. He climbed the airplane, leveled off with the afterburners and accelerated to Mach 1.4. That was the first time he had ever been supersonic, and he was delighted."[54] Surprisingly, Johnson never mentioned the flight in his diary.

The First Loss

By this point only Article 123 and the A-12T retained their J75 power plants, all the other aircraft having been equipped with J58s. Due to their midwing installation, which put the inlets close to the ground, both types of engines were highly susceptible to FOD. When ingested into a jet engine, even a small pebble could cause considerable—and expensive—harm to the turbojet's compressor blades. Some FOD incidents were traced to careless maintenance, but most resulted from debris on the runway, particularly from tiny rocks blown off the desert by the wind. Since mechanical runway sweepers were not available during the early days of flight testing at Groom Lake, officers and enlisted men alike formed a "broom crew" to cleanse the airstrip manually.[55] Col. Holbury encouraged such activities; it was important to keep operations running smoothly, since the OXCART program was receiving intense scrutiny from the highest levels. Distinguished visitors in early 1963 included Assistant Secretary of the Air Force Joseph S. Imirie and Brig. Gen. David L. Carter from Air Force Systems Command (AFSC) headquarters.[56]

Article 123 as it appeared in early 1963. This airplane represented the operational antiradar configuration but was still powered by J75 engines with fixed inlet spikes. *Lockheed*

While the first and second airplanes were engaged in performance envelope expansion, Article 123 was used for testing the INS and camera package and also set several significant milestones. The first of these occurred on January 26, 1963, when Schalk piloted the airplane's thirty-fifth flight. Troubled from start to finish (the INS failed during takeoff, and the drag chute malfunctioned on landing), it nevertheless marked the one hundredth A-12 sortie. On April 3, Article 123 became the first A-12 to accrue a hundred flight hours, during a mission piloted by Jim Eastham. Nine days later, Schalk logged the program's two hundredth flight in the same airplane.[57] Unfortunately, Article 123 was also destined to set the program's most dubious milestone: the first A-12 to crash.

On May 24, 1963, Ken Collins (using mission call sign Dutch 26)[58] took Article 123 aloft for its seventy-ninth flight to test a velocity-to-height (V/H) sensor and to practice INS navigation. Integral with the camera package, the V/H sensor compensated for aircraft motion in order to prevent image blurring. The mission was to follow a planned course that had been flown before, with a route chosen to fulfill equipment test requirements. Following a mission briefing, Collins was driven to the South Trim Pad, where he boarded the aircraft under cloudy skies. Weather was a serious concern, since rain and thunderstorm activity was predicted along the flight path, and the pilot had been advised to abort the mission if he encountered IFR conditions or any undercast that would prevent visual observations for the INS or V/H sensor.[59] As he completed his preflight checks, Collins was grateful for one thing. Because he was planning to remain at an altitude of around 30,000 feet, he wouldn't have to wear a bulky pressure suit; a standard flight coverall and lightweight helmet would suffice.

Dutch 26 departed Area 51 with Capt. Don Donohue (call sign Boxer 11) flying safety chase in an F-101B. They climbed to an initial cruising altitude of 25,000 feet and made a right turn over the small mining community of Austin, ascending to 27,000 feet to get above the clouds. But it wasn't high enough. The jets were battered by turbulence as they passed through cloudy patches and finally climbed out into clear skies about 30 miles from the town of Wendover on the Nevada-Utah state line. Collins and Donohue entered a restricted area on the edge of Utah's Great Salt Lake Desert, turned, and proceeded southwest toward Area 51. As the two airplanes completed one circuit of the training route, Jack Weeks (call sign Boxer 10) relieved Donohue, and the formation headed north again, the pilots vigilant for increasing cloudiness.

Nearing the Utah state line, Dutch 26 and Boxer 10 cruised at 0.85 Mach while maintaining an altitude of around 34,000 feet. Weeks stayed in close formation with the A-12 as the two jets skimmed through the tops of the clouds. At the Wendover checkpoint, Collins started a planned left turn and climb, but about a third of the way through the turn, Weeks felt a slight buffeting and heard a warning horn that signaled his airspeed was getting too slow. To avoid stalling the Voodoo, Weeks extended his turn and accelerated, intermittently losing sight of the A-12 in the cirrus overcast. Meanwhile, as Collins pulled away from his escort, he noticed some curious instrument readings. Although his throttle setting was constant and the airplane was apparently climbing, the indicated airspeed and Mach number appeared to be increasing. The A-12 was, in fact, decelerating into a dangerous corner of the flight envelope. "I think my airspeed is fouled up," he told Weeks.[60]

Article 123 cruises over Nevada during a low-altitude training mission. For such flights, the pilot had no need to wear a bulky pressure suit. *Lockheed*

Soon the A-12 began to shudder and stall. "I got troubles," Collins noted calmly as he attempted to lower the airplane's nose, using only the flight instruments. By this point he had entirely penetrated the cloud deck, losing all outside visual references. At around 30,000 feet, Article 123 suddenly pitched up, rolled to the right, and entered an inverted flat spin. After several attempts to right the aircraft, Collins realized his efforts were in vain. Weeks heard him say, "I'm in a spin and I don't . . ." The rest was garbled. Passing through 25,000 feet, Collins snapped his helmet visor shut, pushed his head back firmly against the seat headrest, and pulled the ejection handle. He felt a blast of icy cold air as the canopy opened and tumbled away, and searing heat from the small rocket motor that propelled his seat out of the cockpit. Seconds later, Collins was pushed away from the seat and felt a tug as his drogue chute opened. With almost surrealistic calm, he took a moment to look at his watch, which read 12:05. At about 15,000 feet, the drogue separated and the main parachute opened, slowing his descent. A few minutes later, Collins released his survival kit, allowing it to swing freely from its lanyard. He raised his fogged helmet visor and saw the A-12 still spinning, inverted, toward the desert below. Descending through light rain and occasional snow flurries, Collins oscillated beneath his chute, and when next he saw the airplane, it was shattered on the desert floor a few miles away beneath a column of orange flame and black smoke.

Rapidly approaching the ground, Collins prepared for touchdown. He landed on his feet and fell to the left, rolling on his back and shoulder. The wind was blowing, threatening to drag him through the scrub, and he struggled to unlatch his right riser to collapse the chute, but it would not open. He finally unlatched the left riser, removed his harness, and gathered up the parachute. He also collected checklist pages that had broken loose and various other aircraft items lying in the immediate vicinity. Making two trips, Collins moved his gear to another hill in an attempt to get closer to the remains of his airplane. As he started toward the drogue chute, which lay on the ground nearly ¼ mile away, he spotted a red pickup truck bouncing across the rugged terrain with its headlights on.[61]

Loyd A. Hewitt of Salt Lake City had been driving north toward Wendover when he spotted Collins descending in his parachute and thought he might need help. Along the way, the thirty-eight-year-old geophysicist and his three companions stopped just long enough to pick up the airplane's ejection seat and throw it in the back of their vehicle. Upon reaching Collins, the men were relieved to see the pilot was unharmed. After placing his flight gear into the truck, Collins asked Hewitt to take him to the nearest Highway Patrol station. But as soon as the men reached the highway, they encountered Elko County deputy sheriff Ed Boyce and transferred Collins and all his equipment—except the ejection seat—to the officer's station wagon. Collins used Boyce's radio to contact the Highway Patrol and provided a phone number to call to alert the proper authorities regarding his status. The two vehicles then drove to weigh station no. 8 in Wendover, where patrolman Roger Skougard coordinated efforts to assist Collins and set up a security cordon for the crash site.[62]

Shortly after losing sight of the A-12, Weeks began circling above the clouds, trying in vain to raise Collins on the radio. He switched to National Guard frequency and broadcast a mayday distress signal to the Salt Lake air traffic control center but got no answer. After several attempts, Weeks eventually raised the radar station near Cedar City, Utah, and asked someone to relay a message to Boxer Control that "Boxer One Zero's wingman was in trouble approximately 70 nautical miles southeast of Elko." Unable to see the crash site through the clouds, he then headed back to Area 51. By this time, several ground stations were responding to his mayday, but he told them to disregard his earlier transmissions. As soon as Weeks got within radio range of Groom Lake, he called the control tower and advised that he had lost visual and radio contact with Dutch 26.

Weeks transmitted, "Bud Tower, Boxer One Zero." At first, SMSgt. James C. Green struggled to make out the garbled transmissions from the F-101, but after a few minutes Weeks's voice came in loud and clear: "I have lost contact with Dutch Two Six and I think he's in trouble." Green had TSgt. Billie Brown activate the emergency telephone circuit to notify the crash crew, headquarters, base hospital, and Boxer Control of the developing emergency situation.[63]

The underside of Article 123 displays a distinctive pattern of black-painted radar-absorbent inserts along the leading and trailing edges of the wings. The forward fuselage chines were also made of antiradar composites. *Lockheed*

The response was immediate. Col. Holbury went to the Command Post and established a teleconference with Project Headquarters in Langley, Virginia. All available aircraft were dispatched from Area 51 to search for Collins, including the Starliner Constellation, C-47, T-33, U-3B, and two F-101s. A third Voodoo took up a position between Groom Lake and Wendover to serve as a radio relay. The Cessna 180 and HH-43B helicopter remained on standby alert to transport medical personnel. Cloud cover thwarted the search effort, but about an hour after Collins ejected, a Highway Patrol dispatcher called via Yuletide Control to report that an aircraft had crashed 14 miles south of Wendover and that the pilot was uninjured. This was excellent news, but there was still the problem of top-secret airplane wreckage lying unprotected, in proximity to a significant population center and a public highway.

As soon as it had been confirmed that Collins was safe, the search aircraft were recalled and all efforts turned toward securing the crash scene and recovering debris. Over the next several hours, a C-47 and a Lockheed Constellation arrived at Wendover Auxiliary Air Force Base with security personnel and crash investigators. Kelly Johnson followed in the JetStar after stopping at Area 51 to pick up Holbury, Maj. Bruce K. Kimbel (flight surgeon), and several security personnel. In response to a request from Collins, the Hill Air Force Base commander, Col. Elwood P. Donohue, dispatched an air policeman, SSgt. Lloyd D. Gregory, to secure the accident scene and had a helicopter standing by at Wendover.

When Holbury arrived, he found that Collins, who had not given his name or provided any other information to authorities, was being held in semi-isolation and guarded by Ed Boyce along with the Tooele County, Utah, deputy sheriff, G. Lewis Young. Collins assured Kimbel that he felt pretty good except for some minor back pains. Following a brief medical examination, he answered questions from Holbury and Johnson before flying back to Area 51 aboard the Constellation. The next day, he was transported to the Lovelace Clinic for a more comprehensive evaluation.[64]

After questioning the pilot, Holbury and Johnson proceeded to the crash site via helicopter, along with Col. Charles L. Wimberly and Arthur E. Smith of the Air Force Directorate of Aerospace Safety. Earlier in the day, a T-33 pilot made a pass over the crash scene to photograph the wreckage. He reported that the front of

Wreckage of Article 123 covers a hillside 14 miles southwest of Wendover. Area 51 security forces scrambled to secure the site. *CIA*

In a scene surprisingly devoid of recovery vehicles or personnel, the largest and most-recognizable components have been covered by tarps. The impact crater, *in the foreground*, retained the shape of the airplane's planform. *CIA*

the airplane was completely destroyed, but that the aft section was still identifiable as a twin-engine, delta-wing configuration. The A-12 had impacted nose down while still inverted, leaving an impression of the twin tail fins and aft fuselage before tumbling across a ravine and spreading parts over a wide area. Both tails had separated and were lying some distance away from what remained of the fuselage, engine nacelles, and wings. In the rapidly fading daylight, ground crews made arrangements to cover any large pieces with canvas tarps. Because the A-12 crashed in a remote area with no roads, and no electric lighting was available, work halted after nightfall. Meanwhile, senior leaders discussed how to proceed.

Recovery personnel use heavy equipment to break down and remove the wreckage of Article 123 and transport it to an auxiliary airfield at Wendover prior to taking it back to Area 51. *CIA*

Debris is hoisted by crane and lifted onto a flatbed truck for transport to Wendover. Despite claims by the on-scene commander that all traces of the aircraft were removed, many small but identifiable pieces remained. *CIA*

Brig. Gen. Jay T. Robbins, director of aerospace safety for the Air Force, arrived in Wendover to coordinate the accident investigation. Col. Donohue supplied flatbed trucks, a crane, and other equipment from Hill to recover the debris. There was some debate over whether to dynamite the largest sections of wreckage to make identification by unauthorized personnel more difficult. The suggestion to use explosives came from NRO director Brockway McMillan, who felt that the accident investigation was subordinate to the security of the program. McMillan urged that recovery operations continue throughout the night if at all possible. Johnson felt that such extreme measures were unnecessary, since the airplane was sufficiently destroyed as to prevent identification. He did, however, insist that removal of the wreckage proceed as rapidly as possible despite objections that it might impede accident investigators in determining the cause of the accident. The cause could best be learned through detailed debriefing of the pilot, Johnson argued, rather than by "digging around in the wreckage."[65]

Security personnel from Area 51 maintained a tight cordon around the scene, but no unauthorized persons attempted entry during the night. Recovery crews began loading and removing debris early the next morning under iron-gray skies. The A-12's fuselage and wings were too large to easily transport and still retained their distinctive shapes. Workers cut them into smaller pieces by using acetylene blowtorches, then hoisted the sections onto flatbed trucks along with the tails and other large pieces. Smaller debris was packed into hastily constructed plywood boxes, and all of it was moved to a secure hangar at Wendover. Jim Cunningham, now serving as deputy director of the Office of Special Activities, received a telex stating unequivocally that "all traces of [Article] 123 had been removed from [the] crash scene . . . by late afternoon on 25 May."[66]

That same day, two C-124 cargo planes arrived at Wendover, one from Hunter Air Force Base, Georgia, and the other from Travis Air Force Base, California, to pick up the wreckage. Workers spent the afternoon and evening loading boxes and pallets into the immense cargo bays, and guards were posted to watch the planes through the night. Security personnel debriefed the truck drivers and equipment operators before releasing them to return to Hill. In the morning the wreckage was transported to Area 51, where it was unloaded and placed under tarps in a hangar with a guard in attendance, awaiting disposition by the accident investigation board.[67]

Some consternation resulted from the fact that one item was not immediately recovered. During his bailout, Collins lost an emergency kit containing several official letters and $1,000 cash. Nine people, including Col. Holbury and Area 51 security officer Ed White, searched the crash area for two full days after the cleanup effort ended. Driving three trucks spaced 75 to 100 yards apart, with two observers standing in the back of each vehicle, they covered an area 4 miles long and 2 miles wide centered on the impact location of the airplane's canopy. When this failed to produce the packet, they spent the next two days with all nine men walking in a line, abreast, about 50 feet apart, covering the same area, with similar results. A low-level aerial reconnaissance utilizing the Cessna 180 also proved fruitless. Officials decided that since the letters contained no information regarding the airplane or its mission, configuration, or manufacturer, their exposure would not endanger the program. Additionally, it seemed that anyone finding the packet would be more likely to keep the money than to publicize the letters. Nevertheless, efforts to find the packet continued, this time on horseback. In early June, three paramedics and a first sergeant from the 1129th SAS started from the impact point and systematically covered the surrounding area with the assistance of local wrangler Ray B. Peterson. On the second day, using calculations supplied by Kelly Johnson, they finally found the packet, intact, about 1.25 miles northeast of where Collins had landed. It was opened and inventoried by Col. Holbury, who determined it had not been compromised.

Security concerns necessitated creating a cover story to prevent public exposure of the OXCART program, so Brig. Gen. Hubbard announced to news media that an F-105 operating from Nellis had crashed and that the pilot was a Hughes Aircraft Company employee contracted for testing electronic equipment. Wright-Patterson Air Force Base, Ohio, was given as the home base for the fictional aircraft, but the pilot's name was not released. It was a flimsy cover story that held together only through the good fortune that the airplane had crashed in an isolated area, out of sight of the lightly traveled highway, thus preventing unauthorized personnel from getting a view of the airplane's configuration. Also, since the mission had been flown at low altitude, Collins wore an ordinary coverall instead of a full-pressure garment. Had he been picked up wearing a space suit, it might have raised unwanted questions about his airplane's performance capabilities.

Although the incident initially drew little attention from the media, not immediately releasing the pilot's name led to speculation that he may have been a famous test pilot or astronaut. Another mistake was Hubbard's failure to sufficiently backstop the story. Attempts by reporters to follow up on various details led to confusion when personnel at Nellis, Wright-Patterson, and the Pentagon denied any knowledge of the aircraft or even of the accident itself. In spite of such glaring inconsistencies, the cover story held up, and news coverage, which was carefully monitored by OXCART security personnel, was minimal. An after-action report to CIA Headquarters on June 4 noted, "Press interest in the affair . . . appeared mild and died quickly after Collins' name was released."[68]

The only notable security threat came from television reporter Art Kent of KUTV News in Salt Lake City, who claimed to have flown over the crash site on the afternoon of May 24 and taken pictures that he planned to show on the evening news. Col. Holbury discussed with Project Headquarters how best to approach the newsman in an attempt to suppress the photos, and then he made arrangements with Brig. Gen. Hubbard to provide Ed White and his deputy with AFOSI credentials. The two men drove to Salt Lake City in a rented car, met with Kent, and explained that the incident was classified and it would be "in the best interests of national security to withhold publicity." Kent said that he was a former agent of the Army Criminal Investigative Division, had served six years on the Salt Lake City police force, and was well versed in security requirements. He explained that he had learned of the crash while monitoring the Utah Highway Patrol circuit and thought it had news potential, so he contacted a photographer, then hired a pilot with a private plane to fly them over the accident scene. After taking the photos, which had yet to be developed, he requested additional information about the crash from personnel at Nellis.

Now, faced with a potential security violation, Kent agreed to surrender the film in exchange for a $60.00 reimbursement for the aircraft rental and film costs, and as long as any images unrelated to the crash were returned to him. White thought this was reasonable, and agreed. The reporter refused, however, to give the names of either the photographer or the pilot, because in order to get the shots they had to fly 5 miles inside restricted airspace, and he didn't want to get anyone in trouble. How the plane had penetrated the restricted area undetected by radar and unobserved by anyone at the crash site remained an open question. Since Kent had willingly relinquished the film, the matter was initially dropped, but White returned to Salt Lake City the following day via C-47 and, after assuring Kent that no flight violations would be filed, convinced him to provide the names of the photographer and the pilot. White contacted and debriefed both men, but the matter didn't come to an end until the pictures were developed and it became apparent that they were of such poor quality that it was unlikely they would have presented any sort of threat to the security of the OXCART program.[69]

Col. Wimberly headed the accident investigation board. He took sworn statements from Collins, Weeks, and others and coordinated the collection of supporting documentation. In addition, Collins submitted to an intensive interrogation while under the influence of sodium amytal (a drug used to enhance memories following a traumatic event) to ensure that he recalled all pertinent details.[70] Lockheed engineer Norman E. Nelson determined that the primary cause of the accident was inadequate pitot tube heating that allowed entrapped moisture to freeze, blocking the total-pressure ports and resulting in erroneous reading on both primary and secondary airspeed indicators. This caused the automatic flight control system to increase the airplane's AOA, bleeding off airspeed and driving the plane into a stall. In addition, the pressure ports may have become unblocked, causing speed indications to suddenly revert to correct readings, further confusing the pilot. Upon reviewing the board's findings, however, Col. Ledford made it clear that he did not agree that material failure was primarily to blame. Instead, he asserted, "The true cause for this accident was pilot error in that the pilot failed to take adequate corrective action in a deteriorating airspeed situation," and that Collins continued to operate the aircraft in IFR conditions despite being briefed to abort the mission should such conditions prevail. Ledford felt that had Collins applied full power and afterburner or pushed the nose down to achieve a shallow dive, he could have built up sufficient airspeed to recover. Moreover, he believed that had Collins simply aborted the test and climbed above the cloud deck, it would have likely precluded the accident altogether.[71]

Design Cruise Speed

The loss of an airplane slowed the test program only briefly. DCI John A. McCone was considerably agitated by Lockheed's lack of progress in attaining the stated design goals for project OXCART, so there was a great deal of urgency in expanding the A-12 performance envelope. Additionally, training flights for project pilots were conducted concurrently with test flying, a calculated risk that occasionally had serious consequences. In one incident, Mel Vojvodich was scheduled to perform engine tests in Article 122 but somehow inadvertently skipped an important checklist item prior to takeoff. As soon as the airplane left the ground, one engine suffered a series of compressor stalls. Vojvodich immediately aborted his takeoff, touching down at the end of the runway near the North Taxiway. The 96,000-pound airplane rolled onto the overrun at 170 knots, and when Vojvodich hit the brakes, he blew all six main tires. He popped the chute and swerved onto the lakebed, grinding to a halt on bare wheel rims. A subsequent inspection of the aircraft revealed additional damage, including a stressed panel on the upper surface, some popped rivets, and bending on the airplane's lower surfaces. The A-12 had to be defueled and jacked up to replace the wheels before being towed back to the hangar for repairs.[72]

Finally, on July 20, 1963, Lou Schalk attained Mach 3.0 for the first time in Article 121. He maintained this speed for no more than a minute while cruising at 72,000 feet. By the end of September, the A-12 was being flown at sustained triple-sonic flight speeds, but there were substantial difficulties with inlet control and transonic drag. Lockheed engineers solved the problem by improving the engine controls, increasing the penetration speed for Mach 1.0 by 50 knots, and making numerous structural improvements to the exhaust ejector flaps, which were subjected to extreme loads and temperatures. Test crews continued to expand the airplane's performance envelope, and on February 3, 1964, Jim Eastham flew Article 121 to 83,000 feet and logged fifteen minutes above Mach 3.2.[73] The A-12 had at last met its specified performance goals.

Ground crewmen prepare to hook up start carts in preparation for starting the engines. Article 121 is seen here on the North Ramp, with Hangar 5 visible at left and Hangar 6 on the right. *Lockheed*

Article 121 cruises north over Emigrant Valley shortly after departure from Area 51. Mud Lake is visible at upper right, just beyond Cactus Flat. *Lockheed*

From 70,000 feet, OXCART pilots viewed Earth's curvature against deep-indigo-blue skies. *USAF*

A subsequent increase in OXCART test and training sorties resulted in a flood of noise complaints from residents of Ely and other northern Nevada communities, where sonic booms reportedly caused property damage. Air Force officials at Nellis bore the brunt of these grievances, and Brig. Gen. Hubbard attempted to deflect protests by requesting that complainants provide detailed aircraft descriptions along with time and date, and any justification for believing the booms had been caused by Air Force planes rather than by jet fighters operating from Naval Air Station Fallon in Churchill County. He asked the CIA for guidance as to what public position he should take. Venting his frustration, Hubbard suggested that perhaps he should simply advise citizens that putting up with a little noise from sonic booms was preferable to the sound of Russian bombs. More realistically, he considered simply sending representatives from the Nellis legal office to investigate and settle any valid claims, in keeping with Air Force policy.[74] In an attempt to characterize and mitigate the effects of shock waves generated by the A-12, the CIA enlisted the help of a team of NASA researchers led by acoustic scientist Domenic J. Maglieri. Over the course of three days in August 1963, a variety of sonic boom pressure measurements were obtained during eleven passes. Data were collected from directly beneath the aircraft and along a line at right angles to the flight path, using microphone arrays and observers stationed at specified intervals. The most distant observer was located 33 miles from the flight path. The NASA scientists paid particular attention to booms generated at Mach numbers ranging from 1.4 to 2.5 at altitudes between 41,000 and 64,000 feet. Plans to obtain data points at higher speeds were temporarily shelved due to conflicts with the OXCART flight schedule. The results precipitated a directive from Project Headquarters that overflights of populated areas at altitudes below 70,000 feet be avoided whenever possible. Additionally, mission flight paths were not to pass within 30 miles of communities the size of Ely or larger unless absolutely necessary due to operational or test requirements.[75]

Article 130, parked in front of the Southend hangars, displays the initial operational paint scheme in which the edges, cockpit, tails, and inlet spikes were black while the rest was left unpainted. *Lockheed*

CHAPTER 4
DREAMLAND

The fleet lined up on the North Ramp in April 1964 included eight single-seat A-12s, the A-12T and, barely visible at the far end, the first two AF-12 interceptor prototypes. Article 121 takes place of pride in the foreground, in front of the Titanium Goose. The fourth airplane is Article 122. *CIA*

May 1967. Mechanics bustled about in the cool stillness of the desert morning, preparing Article 122 for a functional check flight. Unnoticed, a lone moth flitted to and fro beneath the open canopy, eventually alighting in the shadows of the instrument panel. A dark-blue van pulled up alongside the A-12. The door slid open and several life-support technicians helped Jack Weeks climb a metal stair in his bulky pressure suit and settle into the cockpit. Soon the 400-pound canopy was closed and sealed, and the silence was shattered by the roar of twin V-8 start carts spooling up the jet's mighty J58 engines. Within minutes, Weeks roared aloft into the cerulean sky to rendezvous with a tanker. After refueling, he pushed the throttles forward and began to climb, but the airplane seemed sluggish. Accelerating through Mach 2.2, the pilot was battered—his head slammed side to side—as first the right inlet unstarted, and then the left. Weeks fought for control as the A-12 yawed, pitched, and vibrated before finally smoothing out at more than two and a half times the speed of sound. Climbing to 83,000 feet, he pushed the airplane to a speed of Mach 3.2, faster than a rifle bullet. Weeks sustained cruising speed for forty minutes, exposing the airframe to tremendous temperatures. The canopy became heated to more than 620 degrees Fahrenheit, and Weeks, comfortable within his air-conditioned pressure suit, watched a strip of red silicone sealant peel away from the interior edge and fall to the cockpit floor. Weeks throttled back, slowed the airplane, and descended to a lower altitude. Dropping through 10,000 feet on final approach to Groom Lake, he noticed a moth fluttering around inside the cockpit.

When designing the Archangel, Kelly Johnson quickly recognized the potential for expanding the airplane's capabilities. As early as March 1960 he had discussed with Air Force officials the possibility of developing a long-range interceptor version of the A-12, using the same basic airframe. Designated AF-12, the interceptor featured a pulse Doppler radar system and launch bays for three air-to-air missiles. A second crew position, located just behind the cockpit, accommodated a fire-control officer (FCO) to operate the missile launch system. Secretary of Defense Thomas S. Gates Jr. approved Johnson's proposal, and with the assistance of the CIA, the Air Force entered into an agreement with Lockheed to build three prototypes under Project KEDLOCK. Just as with OXCART, procurement of the AF-12 was undertaken with the greatest secrecy in order to achieve an operational capability without providing any potential enemy an early opportunity to develop defenses or countermeasures.[1]

Long-Range Interceptor

Work began in October 1960, when Johnson assigned J. Rus Daniell as project engineer and made arrangements to build the first AF-12 prototype in place of the seventh A-12 airframe. A separate work area was set up in Burbank, partitioned off from the A-12 assembly line, and only those personnel cleared for work on "Plan 3A" were allowed inside. Although the AF-12 shared many of the A-12's design features—overall configuration and structure, power plants, etc.—there were distinct differences. First, in order to improve visibility, the pilot's seat was raised along with the canopy. This added a slight hump to the airplane's profile. Second, the typically flat, sharklike nose assembly was replaced with a conventional conical radome to accommodate a Hughes AN/ASG-18 radar system. Third, the interceptor lacked the antiradar treatments that had been considered of such critical importance to the A-12 configuration. As with the A-12T and Article 121, the AF-12 had all-metal chines, tails, and inlet spikes. Finally, the most notable change was the addition of three ventral fins: two fixed strakes on the undersides of the engine nacelles, and a single, hydraulically actuated fin beneath the aft fuselage that was so large it had to be folded during takeoff and landing. These surfaces were deemed necessary after wind tunnel testing revealed directional-stability problems resulting from the revised nose and canopy configuration.[2]

Construction of the first AF-12, designated Article 1001, was complete by July 1963, and the airplane was convoyed to Area 51 for final assembly and checkout. Technicians spent several weeks installing the engines, conducting leak checks, and testing various systems. Jim Eastham flew the maiden flight on August 7, with Lou Schalk flying chase in an F-104. He found that the AF-12 performed much like its predecessor, and flight testing proceeded with no unpleasant surprises. A second airframe, Article 1002, joined the fleet a few months later and made its first flight on November 23, just one day after the assassination of President Kennedy. Col. Robert L. "Silver Fox" Stephens visited Area 51 on December 31 and became the first Air Force pilot to fly the new interceptor. The following month, with a third AF-12 under construction, the prototypes were temporarily grounded for inlet upgrades and installation of more-powerful engines.[3]

For security reasons, the AF-12 airframes were cordoned off in a separate corner of the hangar from the A-12 assembly line during construction. *Lockheed*

Jim Eastham lands the AF-12 following its maiden flight as Lou Schalk flies chase in the F-104. *Lockheed*

The AF-12 was characterized by its raised cockpit and large nose radome. It also lacked the antiradar treatments found in the A-12. *CIA*

After resumption of flight testing, Lockheed and Air Force test pilots continued to expand the airplane's performance envelope and build confidence in its handling characteristics. The results were of great interest to those authorities responsible for overseeing US air defenses, and so, on October 3, 1963, a number of high-ranking military officers arrived at Area 51 for the purpose of witnessing an AF-12 test flight. This group included Gen. John K. Gerhart, the NORAD commander in chief, and his deputy, Air Marshal Charles R. Slemon; Maj. Gen. William H. Wise, NORAD deputy chief of staff for plans and policy; Brig. Gen. Richard S. Abbey, NORAD director of plans and policy; Brig. Gen. Henry C. Huglin, deputy US representative to the NATO Military Committee and Standing Group; and Brig. Gen. Horace A. Hanes, assistant chief of staff for plans, Air Defense Command (ADC).[4] Presumably, they were as impressed by the AF-12 as previous distinguished guests had been with the A-12.

Plans for fully exploring the AF-12's capabilities generated some controversy even before its maiden flight. The problem centered on a proposal to conduct the tests at Edwards rather than at Area 51. Proponents argued that as long as the AF-12 remained a covert asset, it could never be used operationally. Moreover, some senior Air Force officials felt that surfacing the interceptor would provide additional cover for the clandestine OXCART operation, which was already in danger of exposure due to unauthorized sightings and the increasing circle of people within government and industry who had some knowledge of the program. Indeed, after the loss of Article 123 it seemed inevitable that another accident or an emergency landing at an off-range airfield would blow the lid off the whole effort. Others, including Leo Geary, were adamant that disclosing information on any version of the airplane would reveal its unique design innovations and compromise its defensive capabilities. Geary also felt that upon learning of the new airplane, the Soviets would surely mount a propaganda campaign, tarring the AF-12 with the same brush as they had the U-2 following the Powers incident. In a discussion with Deputy DCI Marshall S. Carter, he even suggested enlisting the aid of aerospace industry leaders to help keep the airplane's existence secret as long as possible. "Most leaders in the aircraft business," he argued, "know that something is up, and we stand to gain more by asking their help than by trying to pull the wool over their eyes."[5]

The first AF-12 undergoes radar systems ground testing on the North Ramp on October 8, 1963. The planned test flight was postponed due to a hydraulic-pressure gage malfunction. *Lockheed*

Two fixed strakes on the engine nacelles and a hydraulically actuated ventral fin beneath were added to offset directional-stability problems resulting from the revised nose and canopy. The pods with conical ends contained cameras to record missile launches. *Lockheed*

By this time, the Air Force had also authorized procurement of the R-12 (code name EARNING), a new variant of the A-12 with expanded reconnaissance capabilities and a second crew position to accommodate a sensor operator. President Kennedy's successor, Lyndon B. Johnson, and his new defense secretary, Robert S. McNamara, had been briefed on OXCART, KEDLOCK, and EARNING, and the potential of the latter two programs to expose OXCART. Every effort was being made to segregate the Air Force activities from those of the CIA, but as with the AF-12, Air Force plans called for testing the R-12 at Edwards. As an alternative, Kelly Johnson suggested to acting assistant DCI Jim Cunningham in December 1963 that Lockheed could conduct flight testing on both new aircraft at Area 51 until January 1965, by which time the OXCART unit was expected to be operational. Cunningham noted, "We do need time to plan for hangar, shop, and living quarters for the additional people who would be sent to Area 51 if this course of action is adopted."[6]

Geary had hoped to keep the airplanes secret for another year, but powerful forces were in play. In a February 1964 meeting of the National Security Council, McNamara told the president that surfacing the AF-12 would pave the way for sharing Lockheed's innovative manufacturing techniques with the aviation industry at large, something deemed critical for developing a proposed supersonic transport (SST) that could revolutionize commercial aviation. Lessons learned from Lockheed's years of experience with fabricating titanium aircraft structures would greatly facilitate construction of the SST and other future high-speed aircraft. McNamara argued that information about Lockheed's clandestine projects was already leaking out, and that the magnitude of the program—estimated to total $1.5 billion for more than two dozen airplanes—made it virtually impossible to keep it hidden much longer. Better, he felt, to orchestrate a controlled release of information.[7]

As a result, the public first learned of the AF-12 on February 29, 1964, when President Johnson announced its existence in a carefully prepared statement that had been approved by McNamara, John McCone, Najeeb Halaby, and Secretary of State Dean Rusk. By prior agreement with Kelly Johnson, the president intentionally misidentified the aircraft as an "A-11," after Lockheed's early proposal for a high-speed aircraft that lacked anti-radar characteristics, and no mention was made of OXCART or the A-12. The president described the A-11 as "an experimental aircraft, which has been tested in sustained flight at more than 2,000 miles per hour and at altitudes in excess of 70,000 feet." The president noted that development of the aircraft had been made possible by major technological advances that would be of great significance both in military and commercial applications. There was no mention of Area 51; in fact, the president explicitly stated that the aircraft were being tested at Edwards. This was not yet the case, so, to backstop the president's claim, Lou Schalk and Bill Park flew the two AF-12s from Area 51 to Edwards.[8]

The second AF-12, Article 1002, in February 1964. The drag chute bay doors are open on top of the aft fuselage. *Lockheed*

Article 1001, *at left*, with Article 1002. The second AF-12 is not equipped with camera pods. *Lockheed*

Despite public acknowledgment of the program, the airplanes were still considered sight sensitive to some degree. Schalk and Park arrived without fanfare and, immediately after landing, taxied the planes into a hangar to shield them from view. Hopes for discreetly establishing the birds in their new nest were dashed when the heat radiating from the J58 engines activated the hangar's fire sprinklers and set off alarms that summoned the base fire department. Kelly Johnson, who was present, noted ruefully that at least "we got a free wash job."[9]

When Air Force and CIA officials convened a meeting on April 1, 1964, to finalize policy and define responsibility for the development of emergency and operational procedures, Col. Geary commented that OXCART operations at Area 51 should take full advantage of the cover provided by the test activities at Edwards. In addition, the so-called A-11 received a new designation in accordance with standard DoD nomenclature. Col. Horace A. Templeton of the Wright Air Development Center announced that effective immediately, the interceptor prototype was officially designated YF-12A.[10] Air Force test crews evaluated the airplane's radar and weapons over test ranges off the coasts of California and Florida and one at White Sands, New Mexico. A third YF-12A prototype was used to set several official speed and altitude records in 1965, none of which reflected the airplane's maximum capabilities. But the interceptor's days were numbered. McNamara, at that time, was engaged in a bitter feud with the Air Force over appropriation of defense funds. His cost-cutting measures specifically targeted the planned procurement of the production model of the interceptor, the F-12B. One of the three prototypes was damaged beyond repair in a landing mishap. The other two were temporarily mothballed. They were later used in a joint NASA–Air Force research program, during which one crashed. The sole surviving example was eventually placed on public display at the Air Force Museum at Wright-Patterson.[11]

President Johnson also revealed SAC's imminent acquisition of the R-12, by now officially designated SR-71.[12] During a press conference on July 24, 1964, he announced "the successful development of a major new strategic manned aircraft system" that would provide a long-range, advanced worldwide reconnaissance capability. He noted that the Joint Chiefs of Staff had reviewed an earlier proposal for a reconnaissance aircraft with a bomber strike capability, designated RS-70, and had chosen instead to emphasize the importance of the strategic reconnaissance mission. "The SR-71 aircraft reconnaissance system is the most advanced in the world," Johnson said, without acknowledging the A-12. He confirmed that the new airplane would use the same J58 engines as the interceptor and would be capable of flight at more than three times the speed of sound and altitudes in excess of 80,000 feet.[13] Geary's fears proved unfounded, since the president's revelations failed to erode the veil of security surrounding OXCART. Public attention, such as it was, focused on Edwards, leaving the Roadrunners to labor in obscurity at Area 51.

Unwelcome Guests

Remaining out of the public eye was only half the battle. The Roadrunners still had to contend with military training activities over the Nellis Air Force Range and within the boundaries of Yuletide SOA. One notable incident occurred on October 8, 1963, when a flight of three F-105 fighter jets led by British Royal Air Force (RAF) exchange pilot Anthony "Bugs" Bendell was on a practice nuclear weapon delivery sortie about 80 miles north of Las Vegas. When one of the aircraft suffered an oil pressure malfunction, Bendell ordered the third airplane to return to Nellis while he led the stricken craft to the nearest airfield—Area 51.

Security guard Jim Noce poses with two "captured" F-105s on the Area 51 flight line in October 1963. *Tim Zarrella via Jim Noce*

After circling once over Groom Lake with no response to distress calls, Bendell advised the other pilot to make his emergency landing on the long concrete runway. Once assured his wingman was safely on the ground, Bendell prepared to head for Nellis. Suddenly, however, he found himself boxed in by two F-101s while a voice on the radio tersely requested his nationality. Upon learning that he was a British citizen, Bendell was ordered to land immediately. He was instructed not to look to his left while taxiing along the airstrip, but it was too late. Bendell had already spotted a sleek, futuristic craft with enormous engines and inwardly canted tail fins. After parking near the southern end of the airfield, he was met by two security guards and Col. Holbury, then hastily escorted to a small, dark room where he underwent an intensive interrogation to verify his identity and his story. The other pilot underwent a similar debriefing in a separate room. As the session drew to a close, Bendell was admonished in the strongest possible terms not to discuss what he had seen at the secret base. "I gave my word as an RAF officer that I would remain silent," he later recalled, but that didn't seem to impress his interrogators, who still seemed suspicious about his reasons for diverting to Area 51.[14]

While the hapless fighter pilots were being questioned, security guards Jim Noce and Tim Zarrella grabbed a Polaroid camera from their office and drove down the flight line to where the F-105s were parked. Noce picked up one of the pilots' flight helmets and posed for a few photos beside the planes.[15] A short while later, Bendell was escorted to the defective airplane, with instructions to make a ground check of the engine. If the oil pressure remained steady, he planned to swap aircraft with his student and the two would return to Nellis together. After a few minutes the oil pressure began to fluctuate, indicating that the airplane needed more-extensive maintenance. Bendell flew south in his original aircraft, leaving the student stranded until he could return to Las Vegas aboard the Area 51 commuter shuttle. The incident caused quite a stir at Nellis. Brig. Gen. Hubbard was very unhappy about a foreign national landing at Area 51, but Bendell's commanding officer, Maj. Warren Foss, supported his actions. After his experience the student pilot was so overawed by events that he scarcely spoke a word to his colleagues. Bendell noted that "even after two weeks, it was difficult to get a civil 'Good morning' out of him."[16]

Anthony "Bugs" Bendell poses with an F-105 at Nellis in 1963, around the time of his close encounter with Area 51. *USAF via A. Bendell*

Military air traffic wasn't the only problem. According to Dennis Sullivan, a civilian pilot once landed at Area 51 with his girlfriend. He had lost his way during a night flight from Reno to Las Vegas and was desperately low on fuel by the time he spotted runway lights in the otherwise featureless darkness. Security guards immediately detained the two civilians after they landed. While the pilot was being questioned, Sullivan recalled, his girlfriend started berating him for his stupidity and hit him with her purse.[17]

On another occasion, Frank Murray was late completing a functional check flight (FCF) in an A-12 and missed the last Friday evening flight to Burbank. Consequently, he had to remain at Area 51 over the weekend, which gave him an opportunity to work on his radio-controlled (R/C) model airplane—a popular pastime during off-duty hours at the test site. His anticipated Saturday morning recreation was interrupted by the sound of a light aircraft flying overhead. Minutes later, a small airplane landed on the taxiway, and Murray jumped into a truck with some security men and headed out to greet the unexpected guest. As it turned out, the pilot was a student (ironically, a former Air Force navigator) who had become lost during a solo cross-country training flight from Apple Valley, California. After the ranking Area 51 security guard on duty checked his story, the plane was refueled and the hapless aviator was allowed to resume his journey with nothing more than a stern warning.[18]

Not All Work

Quite a few of those working at Area 51, particularly some of the Lockheed employees, had been there since Project AQUATONE and still referred to the test site as "the Ranch." The base, however, soon acquired yet another in the long string of names, the status of which shimmered, mirage-like, in a twilight zone somewhere between official and unofficial. During the latter half of the 1960s, Yuletide SOA was renamed Dreamland, a designation that initially pertained to a vast swath of airspace to the west, north, and east of Area 51 but was later reduced to cover only the airspace above the NTS and Emigrant Valley. Eventually it was further reduced to a 516-square-mile block centered on Groom Lake. The name pertained to the restricted airspace and served as a radio call sign when contacting Approach Control personnel for clearance. The origin of the name has been lost to history but may have been inspired by the Edgar Allen Poe poem "Dream-Land," which describes "lakes that endlessly outspread" with waters "lone and dead." More to the point, Poe admonished that "the traveler, travelling through it, may not—dare

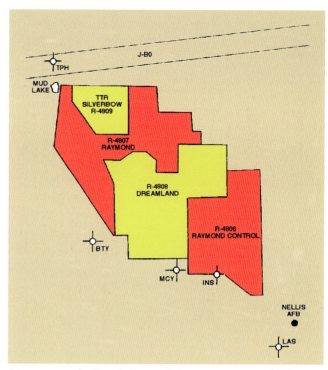

Airspace over the Nevada Test and Training Range was divided into several distinct restricted areas. Groom Lake is in the upper right portion of R-4808, better known as Dreamland. *USAF*

not—openly view it; Never its mysteries are exposed, to the weak human eye unclosed."[19] This certainly seems an apt description of Area 51 but may merely be a coincidence. Whatever its origins, the name came to be associated with the secret facility as well as with the airspace overhead, and in some official documents it was used to identify the operating organization.[20]

Daily life in Dreamland was not all about work. Area 51 personnel with free time during the week, or those remaining over the weekend, enjoyed numerous recreational activities. To occupy nonduty hours in the evening, OXCART project pilots converted house 6 into a bar and established a running poker game. Movies, provided by the Armed Forces Motion Picture Service, were shown in the base theater every night of the week except Saturday for a nominal fee of 25 cents per person (increased to 50 cents for "higher-grade movies"). The base morale, welfare, and recreation facility included a beer bar, library, television lounge, and hobby room, as well as offering snooker, pool, ping-pong, and shuffleboard. For the athletically inclined, there was a full-size gymnasium, basketball and badminton courts, a squash court, and an indoor swimming pool. Brunswick Corporation installed a six-lane bowling alley with automatic pinsetters and ball returns. A softball field was located adjacent to the canteen and recreation center, along with four tennis courts, volleyball and handball courts, and a golf cage. Eventually, the Roadrunners arranged for construction of a three-hole golf course.[21]

Team sports were very popular. The Area 51 bowling league included teams with names such as the Great Ones and Pinsplitters. Throughout the 1960s, the *Bulletin Board*, an unclassified newsletter published by REECo, regularly posted articles about NTS sporting events, with such headlines as "Area 51 Wins Slow-Pitch Tournament." In fact, with players such as Harry Martin, Tom Lewis, and "Big Clem" Byzewski, the Area 51 8-Ballers proved formidable, routinely crushing such opposing teams as the Area 12 Mets and the Mercury All-Stars.[22] The 8-Ballers demonstrated equal skill in basketball. Thanks to top scorers Fo Jordan and Odis Thompson, they easily bested the Motor Pool Truckers and others.[23] While the 8-Ballers consisted primarily of OXCART project and support personnel, EG&G Special Projects fielded its own sports teams. According to radar engineer Jules Kabat, the company's softball team was good, but its football team was truly outstanding, eventually competing in the Las Vegas city-sponsored league in 1965. It was an opportunity for the Area 51 workers to blow off steam, though a friendly game of flag football could occasionally get out of hand. "Needless to say," Kabat recalled, "it got pretty nasty and evolved into tackle without pads because everybody was tying the flag to their belt loop. We won the championship undefeated thanks to our fabulous quarterback Dick Wilson and our very fleet-of-foot ends/pass-defenders, Carl Newmiller and Bob Pezzini."[24]

About a mile north of the main cantonment there was a reservoir and fishing pond named "Slater Lake" in honor of Col. Hugh C. "Slippery" Slater, Roadrunners operations officer (and later commander). Building and operating R/C model planes and cars were also popular, as was "boondocking," the practice of checking out a jeep and exploring the surrounding hills for old mining camps and artifacts. One who took advantage of these outdoor pastimes was William A. "Bill" Goodwin, who arrived at Area 51 in 1963 as an employee of Baird Atomic to maintain the A-12's periscope viewfinder, map projector, and sun compass systems. He lived in Santa Monica and commuted to Area 51 via Burbank during the week but occasionally found himself stranded at the area over the weekend, listening to the last Constellation depart while lying on his back inside one of the OXCART aircraft, preparing the Baird systems for a Monday flight. He made the best of his situation by using his free time to explore the surrounding desert. "Early on in the project, the Weather Group and I traded vehicles," Goodwin recalled. "They preferred my early version of a minivan, and I preferred their four-wheel-drive International Harvester." Goodwin's friendly relations with the flight planners proved especially rewarding when Sam Pizzo arranged an incentive ride for Goodwin in the back seat of an F-101B. In fact, Goodwin took advantage of this privilege on many occasions despite a propensity for airsickness. "After the first flight I always took a helmet bag with me," he recalled wryly, "The bumpy final approach sequence, when cockpit cooling was at a minimum, got to me every time." As a result, someone eventually changed his desk nameplate to read "Barf Goodwin."[25]

Protecting the Blackbird

To further secure the Groom Lake installation, the Area 51 Security Force was augmented in 1963 with a squad of Air Force K-9 handlers and their dogs for perimeter patrol. A kennel with six enclosures was established in a remote location nearly a mile from the cantonment area, so few Area 51 residents were even aware of the dogs' presence. TSgt. Ira C. Crowder supervised a team of five handlers that included Ronald Stump, Cecil W. Hopper, Alva E. McMillion, Cyrus W. Newton, and Walter K. Koopman. Another handler, Jack Starcher, lost an eye while watching a machinist press a bearing in the machine shop; it shattered and a fragment struck him, causing severe injury and costing him his job. Each patrol consisted of a handler in a covered Dodge pickup, with a dog secured in back. Personnel assigned to K-9 duty worked three days on and three days off, policing the range during the nighttime hours. "We patrolled the perimeter from dusk until midnight," Koopman recalled. "The second handler then relieved us, and he and his dog would work until daylight." Although the kennel also housed an illicit distillery, few Area 51 inhabitants exhibited either the desire or fortitude to sample its dubious products. After three fairly uneventful years, the Air Force decided to phase out K-9 patrols at Area 51. Koopman and one of the other handlers, both finishing their second tour of duty, elected to transfer to the government contract guard force and remain at Area 51, while Crowder and the rest accepted new Air Force assignments elsewhere.[26]

Personnel assigned to the Area 51 Security Force wore this type of badge during the 1960s and early 1970s. *Author*

Physical security at the test site was only one challenge. It was also necessary to ensure the survivability of the A-12 while it was flying. Ultimate responsibility for this fell to Albert D. "Bud" Wheelon, who replaced Pete Scoville as the CIA's deputy director for science and technology in January 1964. With degrees in engineering and theoretical physics, the thirty-five-year-old Wheelon was considered something of a whiz kid by his colleagues and eventually became one of the architects of the nation's reconnaissance satellite program. He visited Area 51 for indoctrination into the OXCART operation and discussed his concerns about the airplane's vulnerability to Soviet tracking and threat radar. It was decided that prior to operational deployment, the A-12 fleet would be equipped with a variety of electronic countermeasures (ECM) capable of defeating every known Eastern Bloc threat system. Wheelon also sparred with Kelly Johnson over the need to replace the hydraulic inlet spike control system with a faster one driven electronically. Reluctant to make this change, Johnson pointed out that $35 million had already been invested in developing the hydraulic unit and that it would be foolhardy to throw this investment away. As Wheelon later recalled, "I pointed out that we threw $35 million away every time a plane crashed."[27]

That summer brought a number of changes to the Skunk Works test organization and the OXCART detachment, one of which earned the A-12 and its successors their signature nickname. When Article 121 took to the air for the first time, it was entirely bare of paint, but it soon became clear that this would result in adverse aerodynamic heating effects during high-speed cruise, especially for subsequent airframes equipped with composite antiradar materials. To solve this problem, Lockheed engineers exploited Kirchoff's law of thermal radiation, which states that an efficient heat absorber—such as any extremely dark object—is also an efficient heat emitter. Initial efforts involved application of high-emissivity black paint only to areas subjected to the highest temperatures, including the airplane's nose, chines, inlet spikes, and wing leading and trailing edges. This greatly improved the airframe's heat-radiation characteristics, reducing thermal stresses, but the OXCART project went a step further. By mid-1964, all aircraft in the A-12 fleet, with the exception of the A-12T, were painted overall matte black. Besides improving heat emission, it made the airplanes less visible from the ground during high-altitude cruise. This paint scheme was quickly adopted for the YF-12A and subsequent variants as well, thus giving rise to the sobriquet "Blackbirds."[28] Another change came after Lou Schalk left the Lockheed flight test organization in July. Kelly Johnson appointed Bill Park chief test pilot for the A-12 and its derivatives, and Bob Gilliland was directed to concentrate on engine testing with Article 122.[29]

By June 1964, A-12 production was complete and the final airframe—Article 133—had been delivered to Area 51. On July 9, Bill Park made the tenth flight in this airplane. The mission plan called for a maximum afterburner climb and sustained Mach 2.8 cruise at 78,000 feet along a northerly route called Copper Bravo. The weather was exceedingly good, and all preflight preparations were accomplished on schedule. Crew chief Arthur Patnode gave Park the thumbs-up and watched the A-12 taxi toward the runway. At takeoff the Blackbird climbed steeply away from Groom Lake with afterburners at full power. Once at cruise altitude, Park adjusted engine thrust to maintain Mach 2.8 along a straight course until he began his turn just short of the Canadian border. Now heading south, he started having problems with the left engine and the SAS. Park notified the Area 51 radar flight controllers, "Bungalow, this is Dutch Three Three. I got a problem here. I can't get my left duct pressure up." The duty officer passed on the information to the control tower: "He's having a little engine trouble; he just shut his left one off." Tower personnel activated the Crash Net when the A-12 was about 370 miles out, and Park called in five minutes later. "I'm going to abort going around the course. I'd say about 15 minutes, maybe 10."[30]

Article 121 displays the new all-black paint scheme that was designed to improve surface cooling. *CIA*

Lockheed test pilot Bill Park survived several close calls during his career. *Lockheed*

The lower portion of the right windshield frosted up during the descent, so Park turned the antifog system up to full. A few minutes later he entered the landing pattern at around 30,000 feet, making a sweeping left turn over the airfield and spiraling down as he would for a single-engine approach. At 15,000 feet he opened his helmet visor to eliminate distracting reflections and turned off the oxygen feed. By this time, Boxer 14, an F-101 piloted by Col. Holbury with Capt. Richard J. Roussell in the back seat, was racing to rendezvous with the balky Blackbird. The chase plane followed the A-12 into the downwind leg, giving its crew ample time to look the Blackbird over for any visible signs of difficulty. Everything appeared normal, and it was obvious that Park had the landing gear down and locked before turning onto final approach. Holbury maintained a loose formation about 500 feet away and closing slowly. He was checking his own airspeed and fuel quantity when Roussell exclaimed, "My God, look at him!"[31]

Park had throttled back to 200 knots, with the Blackbird flying straight and level and the runway less than 2 miles ahead. Suddenly the A-12 began rolling precipitously to the left. The pilot tried to correct but found the airplane unresponsive. He added power and considered attempting to climb and go around, but the airplane continued to roll. With less than 250 feet in altitude, Park had only moments to make a critical decision. By the time he pulled the ejection seat D-ring, the A-12 had tipped into a 45-degree bank. The next few moments were a blur as the canopy jettisoned with a loud bang and spun away, and in a flash the seat's rocket motor pushed Park up and out of the cockpit. He tumbled end over end, having barely enough time to separate from the seat before his parachute blossomed, fully opening just as his feet touched the ground. Park heard the hiss of oxygen from his emergency bottle and felt intense heat on his face as the airplane struck the ground nearby and exploded. Caught by the wind, his still-inflated chute was dragging him toward the fireball, and Park was concerned that there wasn't sufficient time to open his quick-release harness. Fortunately, he managed to collapse the chute before getting close enough to the flames to ignite the oxygen flowing from his pressure suit.

Mel Vojvodich was situated on the west side of runway 32 about 1,000 feet from the approach end, serving as mobile control officer. He watched in horror as the A-12 began to roll, then he saw the pilot eject and witnessed the airplane flip upside down and crash about a mile short of the runway. Flames, black smoke, flying debris, and billowing dust obscured his view, and he lost sight of Park's parachute. Fearing the fireball had engulfed his friend and colleague, Vojvodich jumped into his station wagon and sped to the scene. When he arrived, Park was covered with dust and struggling to stand up. "I shook his hand and congratulated him on getting out," Vojvodich later told investigators. "I thought he'd bought the farm."[32]

Constant training ensured that the base fire department and crash rescue personnel were ready to respond to an aircraft accident at a moment's notice. *Via Charles Trapp*

Badge worn by Area 51 firefighters during the 1960s. *Via Glenn Campbell*

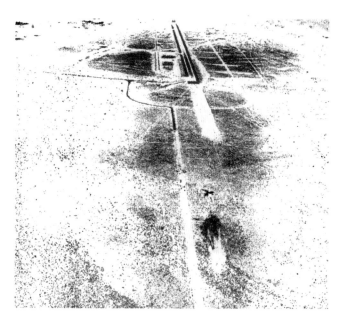

Park's A-12 left a scar in the desert on the approach path to the runway's southern end. *CIA*

More vehicles converged on the scene, including a fire truck, a staff car driven by Lt. Col. Cy Perkins (the assistant deputy commander of operations), and a pickup with two communications technicians who had been servicing a radio beacon south of the airfield. SMSgt. Paul Fout and TSgt. Thomas Law assisted Vojvodich with removing Park's pressure suit, and three minutes later the dazed pilot—dressed only in his long johns—was sitting in Perkins's car. Vojvodich asked, "What the hell happened, Bill?" Park shook his head. "I just lost control," he muttered. "I lost complete control." By this time, an ambulance had arrived, but Park told the corpsman that other than experiencing slight soreness in his left shoulder, he felt fine. He insisted he wished to be debriefed as soon as possible while events were still fresh in his mind. Perkins immediately drove him to the Flight Test Engineering office and also alerted life-support personnel and the flight surgeon. Meanwhile, firefighters extinguished the flaming wreckage, and armed guards secured the scene. The control tower cleared Holbury to land his F-101 on runway 14 in order to stay clear of emergency response activities, which included Capt. Scamardo circling over the crash site in the HH-43B helicopter. Holbury and Roussell were climbing out of the cockpit when Perkins drove by with Park and flashed an "OK" signal to let them know the pilot was all right.[33]

An accident investigation board led by Col. Arthur F. Jeffrey from the 1002nd Inspector General Group at Norton Air Force Base, California, examined numerous potential causes for the mishap but eventually focused on the behavior of the right outboard elevon. Available data indicated that the control surface was deflected fully downward immediately prior to impact. After subjecting the right outboard elevon servo valve to exhaustive testing at Lockheed-Burbank, investigators concluded that the valve had become stuck in a partially open position. This failure was the result of warping incurred through operational use combined with a rapid change in temperature during descent, as well as from metal particles within the servo valve (probably accumulated during manufacture). Binding of a metering spool allowed the passage of fluid under pressure to the mechanical actuators, gradually lowering the elevon and creating a rolling tendency beyond the capability of the control system to counteract. There was nothing Park could have done, and only the single-step escape system saved his life.[34]

All A-12 aircraft were grounded pending the outcome of the investigation and, ultimately, necessary changes to the flight control system's servo valves governing elevon operation. The accident also postponed plans for an interim operational capability for OXCART. Known as SKYLARK, this effort would have provided for contingency overflights of Cuba at Mach 2.8 and 80,000 feet, somewhat less than the airplane's full design capabilities. In order to achieve emergency operational readiness, the Roadrunners pursued an ambitious flight schedule to validate camera performance, qualify OXCART project pilots for Mach 2.8 flight, and coordinate supporting elements for possible deployment. Detachment aircraft underwent extensive modifications, and pilots flew training missions that simulated Cuban overflight sorties. By November the unit had achieved a state of interim readiness and was working to develop the capability for sustained operations.[35]

By now, the A-12 fleet had logged more than nine hundred test and training sorties and over 1,200 flight hours since the maiden flight in 1962. Test pilots had achieved a maximum speed of Mach 3.27 and a maximum altitude of 83,000 feet and demonstrated sustained Mach 3.1 cruise for thirty-two minutes. Perkin Elmer supplied three camera packages and Eastman Kodak two more, all of which performed well at speeds up to Mach 2.35, which had been the restricted maximum speed for the aircraft to this point. Kelly Johnson was concerned with deficiencies in the airplane's transonic and cruise performance, but the SKYLARK flights provided an opportunity to extend the camera test envelope to encompass higher speeds and temperatures than had previously been encountered.[36]

The airplane's most serious deficiency was its lack of sufficient ECM gear to protect the A-12 from Soviet tracking and missile guidance radar systems. So far, only one of several planned ECM devices had been installed, and the others were not expected to be forthcoming anytime soon. Ironically, the delay in fully equipping the A-12 resulted largely from Air Force concerns that should an OXCART aircraft be lost over hostile territory, items recovered from the wreckage might allow the Soviets to devise counter-countermeasures of their own, thus compromising similar equipment being used in American fighters and bombers.[37]

In an effort to provide the A-12 with additional protection, the CIA hired former Boeing engineer Nick Damaskos to run Project KEMPSTER, which involved development of a unique approach to active stealth. Tests demonstrated that the airplane's engine inlets produced significant radar returns, and there had been much discussion among the Lockheed team of how to mitigate this problem. Ed Lovick suggested there might be a way to project streams of electrons ahead of the inlet spikes to ionize the air and scatter any incoming radar energy. He envisioned something along the lines of the type of electron gun used in a television's cathode ray tube. Westinghouse Research Laboratories, in Pittsburgh, Pennsylvania, was contracted to design and build the equipment, and Benjamin Delacroix was assigned as lead engineer. In order to understand the potential effects of the device, the ⅛-scale A-12 model

Building 120, one of the original U-2 hangars, was converted into a nose dock for servicing the A-12's sensitive avionics and camera systems without exposing them either to the elements or unauthorized observation. *CIA*

Two aircraft could be serviced simultaneously. The forward fuselage of Article 125, *foreground*, is enclosed by a set of conformal doors. The other airplane is Article 130. *CIA*

was equipped with assemblies made of lossy foam, nicknamed "puff balls," that simulated the estimated size, shape, and frequency attenuation that might be obtained when electron guns were activated. The model underwent testing on the EG&G RCS range at Area 51, and the data were passed on to the Westinghouse engineering team.

Optimistic designers initially estimated that the electron guns would weigh between 25 and 50 pounds and use only 5 kilowatts of power. As it became clear how much power would actually be needed to produce a useful amount of radar attenuation, the KEMPSTER equipment gradually evolved into a 300-pound monstrosity that took up the entire Q-bay and consumed 125 kilowatts, nearly all the airplane's available power supply. Ground testing was undertaken inside a hangar. One KEMPSTER gun, pointed straight down, was mounted in Article 125 and energized while a portable x-ray inspection unit was moved around the airplane. Results indicated that the cockpit would require additional radiation shielding (in the form of lead foil) to protect the pilot from x-rays. Initial flight testing involved pulsing the electron beam on and off one hundred times per second, which caused the radar return to fluctuate at the same rate between the normal RCS and a markedly lower reading. The results were sufficiently promising that the CIA directed Westinghouse to proceed with designs for an operational version that could operate continuously yet require less power and space. The new device, called KEMPSTER A, was configured to project streams of electrons sideways from the chines in front of each inlet. It was installed in Article 131, and by August 1964 the preliminary findings from two test sorties indicated the equipment was performing as specified. Further testing was concluded in March 1965. There were continued efforts to reduce the system's weight and volume for an operational version called CAT NAP, but cost overruns and schedule slips plagued the program. Carl E. Duckett, who succeeded Bud Wheelon as the CIA's deputy director for science and technology, ultimately terminated the KEMPSTER project.[38]

Eventually, the A-12 was equipped with several defensive avionics systems. BIG BLAST was designed to prevent the Soviet's S-75 Dvina (NATO reporting name SA-2 Guideline) surface-to-air missile from accurately acquiring the range of its target, forcing the missile to arm too soon. RED DOG was a passive missile liftoff indicator. BLUE DOG was capable of recognizing guidance activity and then transmitting false commands to the missile's guidance systems. The PIN PEG system passively intercepted radar frequencies in order to locate the position of the missile's SNR-75 (NATO reporting name Fan Song) tracking-radar site. Finally, the colorfully named MAD MOTH denied the tracking radar accurate angle information, causing the missile to miss its target by a large distance. Redundancy between recognition and jamming systems provided 100 percent overall systems reliability, effectively lowering the vulnerability of the airplane to insignificant levels.[39]

In further preparation for operational deployment of OXCART, technicians continued to assess the airplane's RCS using the EG&G radar range. In-flight measurements were compared with data obtained from tests using the

Ed Power, *left*, and Keith Root install a high-power traveling-wave tube in a RED DOG ECM system. *Sylvania*

ground pylon. According to Ed Lovick, some of these tests were used to evaluate the efficacy of the basic anti-radar treatments under normal operating conditions. Other flights involved tests of various fuel additives on the conductivity of the exhaust plumes. Measurements using high-frequency emitters (3,000 megacycles) yielded a 0.2-square-meter RCS at low depression angles. The A-12 proved most vulnerable to low frequencies (70 to 90 megacycles), at which the aircraft showed up on the radar screen with a 6-square-meter RCS. Lovick noted that there was good correlation between flight test results and those from ground tests of the full-scale A-12 mockup. "Sometimes we would test at night," he recalled, explaining that waiting for data to stream in could be tedious. "I and a few others would go outside and howl and try to make contact with the coyotes," he said. "It never worked, but you could have heard a lot of howling."[40]

Radar engineer Ed Lovick. *Lockheed*

Lovick was also responsible for developing devices to protect the A-12 from lightning strikes. In early 1964 one of the plastic rudders on an A-12 suffered delamination after entrapped air expanded under high-altitude flight conditions. Both fins were removed so that a few tiny holes could be drilled through the silicone-asbestos skin to allow the pressure to equalize during ascent. Lovick happened to be in the hangar with Kelly Johnson when the tail fins were lifted off their metal pivot posts. Looking at the airplane silhouetted against the bright desert sky through the open hangar doors, he asked Johnson if the twin pivot posts looked like lightning rods. They did indeed, Johnson realized. He immediately directed Lovick to work with fellow engineer Peter Gurin to devise a lightning protection system for the A-12.

Gurin arranged to have one rudder fin airlifted to General Electric's High Voltage Engineering Laboratory in Pittsfield, Massachusetts, where he, Lovick, and GE's Albert F. Rohlfs and Edward R. Uhlig set to work on the problem. Established in 1949, the world's largest man-made-lightning lab occupied a humble tin shed known simply as Building 9. There, on April 11, 1964, the team simulated typical lightning strikes and their discharge through the aircraft structure to a maximum intensity of approximately 5 million volts at 30,800 amperes. A second series of tests two weeks exposed the fin to higher currents and lower voltages. To mitigate damage, Lovick initially arranged a large number of 1-inch-long segments of copper wire around the leading edge of the fin, across the top, and down the trailing edge to the rudder's metal base. Each conducting segment was separated from its neighbor by a ½-inch gap. This arrangement carried electrical currents away from the vulnerable graphite-coated asbestos assemblies to more-durable metal components. Artificial lightning discharged into the test article generated spectacular arcs of ionized air around the fin's perimeter.[41]

Having proven the basic principle, Lovick's team replaced the wires with patches of paint containing dielectric materials (silver and graphite) on strips of armament tape. The results were very satisfactory, and the patches performed just as well after being covered with black copper-oxide paint. This treatment was subsequently applied to the tails of an A-12 back at Area 51, where radar backscatter measurements showed no adverse consequences to the airplane's RCS. Encouraged by his success with the tail fins, Lovick set about developing similar protection for high-frequency communications equipment in the nose of the A-12, as well as for the plastic edge structures on the chines. After several successful demonstrations in the summer of 1964, he was satisfied with the results. "I know of only one lightning strike to an A-12 aircraft," he recalled. "The only evidence, aside from the pilot's comments, was some discolored spots on the right-hand side of the fuselage."[42]

A-12 Performance and Deployment Plans

Project OXCART activity at Area 51 peaked in 1965 with completion of the physical growth of the facility. The base population grew to 1,835, and commercial power finally reached the site, eliminating the need to rely on generators. The Special Projects group had recently acquired a surplus radar system from Fort Fisher, North Carolina, to simulate the threat capabilities of the Soviet Fan Song radar. This equipment was subsequently employed in A-12 ECM systems flight testing.[43] Lockheed technicians were working three shifts per day modifying the A-12 fleet, on the basis of lessons learned from flight test experience. This resulted in substantial systems improvement and demonstrated the capability to repeatedly fly at design cruise conditions for prolonged duration and at sustained altitudes above 80,000 feet. With additional systems refinement and simulated mission sorties, CIA officials believed that OXCART would achieve operational capability by the end of the year.

A lightning generator was used to simulate lightning strikes on the A-12's rudder fin. *General Electric*

An aerial photo taken on August 28, 1968, shows how much the base had expanded since the early days. One of the lakebed crosswind runways is partially visible at upper right. A B-52H is parked on the North Ramp. Two commuter transports, a Super Constellation and F-27F, are parked on the South Ramp. *USGS*

Flight testing revealed numerous technical obstacles that had to be overcome. Although the airplane's RCS had been considerably reduced, data indicated the A-12 could still be detected by Soviet radar systems. Defensive ECM equipment considerably reduced risk to the aircraft in hostile environments, but efforts were underway to further reduce RCS and to develop improved countermeasures. Fully two years of testing had been expended before the engine air inlet controls demonstrated acceptable reliability to permit consistent Mach 3 flight. Development of fuel tank sealants capable of withstanding continuous exposure to temperatures exceeding 750 degrees Fahrenheit came slowly and caused considerable program delays. Problems with the durability of electrical wiring and connectors at high temperatures plagued the airplane's communications equipment. Engine power control accuracy was critical at cruise speeds, and the associated equipment was required to operate reliably at temperatures from subzero to more than 800 degrees with widely varying fuel flow rates. As flight testing uncovered various problems, engineers and technicians developed necessary modifications to fix them, and subsequent tests demonstrated considerable improvements in aircraft and system performance.[44]

Throughout 1965 the A-12 fleet set several performance milestones. On May 8, Article 125 was flown to a maximum speed of Mach 3.29 (approximately 2,175 mph). That same day, Article 129 demonstrated a 123,750-pound maximum gross weight takeoff. Three months later, on August 14, Article 129 was flown to a maximum altitude of 90,000 feet. On October 18, Article 127 was used to demonstrate a maximum endurance mission lasting seven hours and forty minutes, with four aerial refuelings. On December 21 the primary test airplane, Article 121, sustained speeds at or above Mach 3.2 continuously for three and a half hours. By this time there were eight operationally ready detachment pilots, each averaging more than three hundred hours of flight time in the A-12.[45] The Blackbird was nearly ready to leave the nest.

In order to demonstrate operational readiness, three of the detachment aircraft (Articles 126, 127, and 128) were scheduled to fly twelve simulated missions over the span of seven weeks. Prior to commencement of this exercise, these aircraft had been engaged in a series of performance and systems reliability tests with satisfactory results. For this operational readiness inspection, they were flown mostly in standard configuration, but with the addition of two cockpit cameras used to photograph the instrument panels, an oscillograph to record engine inlet duct performance, and a voice recorder to capture pilot comments. Between October 7 and November 20, 1965, the Roadrunners accomplished nine successful sorties consisting of three per airplane. Six missions included three aerial refuelings

One A-12 stands by for departure clearance. In the background, an F-101B waits to take the runway while another A-12 is readied for flight on the South Trim Pad. *Lockheed*

with four high-speed cruise legs, for a total of approximately six hours each. Three sorties included two refuelings each while flying four-hour transcontinental routes. Three additional flights had to be aborted following takeoff, one due to low oil pressure and the other two because of radio communications failure. Inspectors gave the unit an overall satisfactory rating of 75 percent, which was considered a great improvement in performance and reliability for the A-12 at that time. Had the radio problems not occurred, officials noted, the rating would have been 90 percent. Most important, the A-12 was now considered operationally ready for deployment on overseas missions.[46]

With US military activities increasing in Vietnam, CIA mission planners developed a deployment strategy for OXCART under the cryptonym CAROUSEL and the unclassified nickname IRON MAIDEN, later changed to SUPER MAIDEN. Once all detachment aircraft, materiel, and personnel were settled at their forward base, they would commence operational reconnaissance overflights under the cryptonym PINWHEEL and the unclassified nickname BLACK SHIELD. These missions would employ the A-12 to provide photographic coverage of critical targets in Southeast Asia and possibly China, where several U-2 aircraft flown by CIA-trained Taiwanese pilots had been shot down. Expanded use of SA-2 missiles and MiG-21 jet fighters made the U-2 increasingly vulnerable, and although satellite reconnaissance programs provided satisfactory imagery, they lacked the quick-reaction capability of manned aircraft. Only the A-12, operationally ready and pre-positioned at a forward operating location, could maintain the necessary on-call capability required by top intelligence and military analysts.

Unfortunately, much work still needed to be done to prepare the A-12 for operational use. A seemingly endless series of malfunctions in the inlet controls, communications equipment, defensive avionics, and cockpit instruments were in many cases traced to failures of electrical wiring and connectors. There were also problems with fuel tank sealants and evidence of serious maintenance deficiencies. Officials at Project Headquarters felt that Lockheed needed to take prompt corrective action to ensure delivery of an aircraft with sufficient reliability to meet operational requirements. John Parangosky met with Kelly Johnson in early August 1965 and had a frank discussion regarding the measures necessary to get the program back on track.[47]

A few weeks later, Johnson recorded in his diary, "The situation regarding our operational capability is critical." He decided the only way to proceed was to spend the next several months making daily trips to Area 51, where he could take matters in hand personally. "I uncovered many items of a managerial, materiel and design nature," he later wrote. Areas of greatest concern included the delivery schedule of A-12 aircraft to the test site, fixing problems with the airplane's electrical system, improving vendor quality control, and increasing supervision. About a third of the problems with the airplane resulted from poor engineering, complicated by the addition of numerous systems that were not part of the original design. Johnson assigned Abner L. Baker, assistant to Skunk Works chief inspector Ron Harris, to Area 51 full time. "We tightened up inspection procedures a great deal," Johnson recalled.[48]

Johnson's firm and effective management did the trick, and by the fall of 1965 the 1129th SAS had successfully demonstrated OXCART's operational readiness. The concept of operations for BLACK SHIELD called for deployment of approximately 225 people and three A-12 aircraft, along with all necessary support equipment to Kadena Air Base, on the Japanese island of Okinawa. SAC's 903rd Air Refueling Squadron provided a tanker task force for aerial refueling. All operational missions would be planned, directed, and controlled by CIA Headquarters as approved by higher authority. Initially, the OXCART detachment would deploy for two sixty-day tours per year before establishing a permanent presence at Kadena. In preparation for this eventuality, the DoD allocated $3.7 million to provide support facilities and secure communications capabilities. In late November, the 303 Committee, the National Security Council's special group for reviewing sensitive intelligence operations, met to consider authorizing the first deployment, but there was insufficient support among the members. BLACK SHIELD was temporarily shelved, though the committee directed the CIA to maintain a quick-reaction capability, with the OXCART detachment ready to deploy to Okinawa within twenty-one days following an approval notification.[49]

Fire and Ice

In lieu of operational deployment, test and training operations continued at Area 51. One such sortie was scheduled for the afternoon of December 28, 1965, when Mel

On the North Ramp, Article 121 is flanked by workstands as ground crew personnel stand by a start cart, *at right*. CIA

Vojvodich was to fly a performance check flight in Article 126. The mission plan included a rendezvous beacon test with a KC-135 tanker. Bill Skliar planned to fly chase in an F-101 during the low-speed and low-altitude portions of the flight. Both pilots received briefings from the operations staff, then Vojvodich computed the necessary takeoff data and went to the life-support ready room to don his pressure suit. A short while later, he was driven to the South Trim Pad and strapped into the cockpit.

The weather was generally good, with scattered clouds beneath a high overcast. Winds were light, though somewhat gusty, and by midafternoon the temperature had risen to only 40 degrees. Although the runway was dry, rainwater from the previous week had frozen, covering the adjacent lakebed surface with a thin sheet of ice. Skliar took off first in the F-101. Vojvodich then taxied the A-12 to runway 32 and began trimming the engines. A compressor stall on the left engine caused a brief delay, but the pilot made some adjustments, completed his checklist, and, having received clearance, advanced the throttles. With a gross weight of 118,300 pounds, the A-12 ate up nearly 7,000 feet of runway before the nosewheels lifted off the concrete.[50] At 210 knots the main gear left the ground, and an otherwise normal takeoff suddenly became a terrifying fight for survival.

As Vojvodich pulled back on the stick to raise the nose, the jet yawed to one side. He tried to correct with the rudder pedals but instead pitched upward. Suddenly the jet lurched into the air, pitching and yawing in defiance of all control inputs. The pilot desperately tried to tame the beast, to no avail. Less than thirty seconds after takeoff, with the airplane gyrating wildly, Vojvodich pulled the ejection handle while he was at the apex of a pitch maneuver. By this point he was only about 150 feet above the ground and probably at the last possible moment to make a safe escape. The pilot separated from the ejection seat, and his parachute blossomed immediately before his feet hit the ground. "I never felt the parachute-opening shock," he later recalled. "I tried to disconnect my survival pack but hit the lakebed before I could get it clear."[51]

Feeling a jarring pain as he struck the frozen ground, Vojvodich feared he had fractured his right leg. Fortunately, he suffered no broken bones, but the impact left him temporarily paralyzed from the waist down. At nearly the same moment, the A-12 exploded just west of the runway overrun, breaking into pieces that slid across the icy lakebed for nearly a mile. With agonizing slowness, the injured pilot used his arms to drag himself away from the conflagration and toward rescuers who were now rushing to the scene.

Aircraft technician Daniel Beaulieu, who witnessed the accident from the northern parking apron, later recalled, "We were upgrading Article 122 in the north hangar when I went out front under the old tower to have a smoke. Suddenly here comes Article 126 right toward me. I couldn't believe what I was seeing." He watched in horror as the A-12 pitched up and down wildly, nearly striking the runway several times before the pilot bailed out. "I was glad he waited to eject because as soon as he cleared the cockpit, that monster turned left and hit the ground in a clear spot at the end of the runway," Beaulieu said. "It was one big fireball, and if he had ejected a second or two sooner, I'd have been cooked and the north hangar would have been gone."[52]

Maj. Burgeson was on duty in Base Ops when the accident occurred, and immediately ran to the parking lot. Just as he reached the outside gate, Col. Holbury screeched to a halt in his staff car and picked him up, and they headed to the crash site together. Dennis Sullivan, having been positioned near the runway as mobile control

Article 122, *at left*, and Article 126 undergo maintenance inside one of the Southend hangars. *Lockheed*

Mel Vojvodich had a harrowing escape from an out-of-control A-12. *Roadrunners*

Area 51 firefighters use water cannons and handlines to extinguish a blaze. *Via Randall Gooding*

officer, got there first. In his haste to reach the scene, he skidded on the ice, narrowly missing Vojvodich. Shortly afterward, Maj. Roger Andersen arrived from the Command Post. "Heavy black smoke and orange flames boiled from the wreckage until the fire trucks gained control," he recalled. Fuel from the airplane's shattered tanks flowed across the lakebed's frozen surface and seeped underneath. "It was burning under the ice with an eerie bluish white flame," Andersen said.[53]

Following a thorough medical examination, Vojvodich was immediately cleared for flight duty in support aircraft and would eventually fly the A-12 again, pending a full recovery. All things considered, he was in excellent physical shape after his ordeal, though he still complained of some discomfort in his right hand and foot. After he returned home, his wife asked why he was limping. Vojvodich told her that he had sprained his ankle while playing tennis.[54]

An accident investigation team from Norton, headed by Col. James Fussell, arrived at Area 51 just six hours after the accident and began work determining the cause. The crash scene had been secured and remained under guard. Investigators interviewed witnesses, recovered the pilot's checklist, and impounded all relevant maintenance and training records. Film from an over-the-shoulder camera inside the canopy was found to be overexposed, but as a result of requirements instituted following Park's earlier crash, investigators were able to review 16 mm motion picture footage of the takeoff. All A-12 aircraft were grounded until further notice, while the twisted wreckage of Article 126 was stored and examined inside Hangar 9.[55]

Detailed examination and analysis of all available data revealed that a maintenance technician had reversed the wiring for the pitch and yaw gyros in the SAS, a circumstance that rendered the aircraft completely uncontrollable as soon as the wheels left the ground. The results of this mistake were twofold. First, the airplane had no stability in either pitch or yaw axes. Second, every input by the pilot into one axis induced a command into an opposing axis. Whenever Vojvodich attempted to pitch up or down, the airplane yawed right and left, and any yaw commands resulted in pitching motions.[56] Things happened so quickly that the pilot did not have sufficient time to save the airplane, which would have required intuitively recognizing the nature of the malfunction and overcoming his natural instincts and training.

Negligence on the part of the electrician responsible for reversing the wiring harness was listed as the primary cause of the mishap, but investigators also noted that both the electrical supervisor and inspector failed to perform their duties properly. In a letter to Brig. Gen. Jack Ledford, now director of the Office of Special Activities, Kelly Johnson acknowledged the design deficiency that made it possible to physically connect the wiring harnesses in reverse order. He proposed redesigning the connector fittings, as well as adding color coding and easily readable labels. He also promised to devise improved ground-testing techniques and written inspection procedures and noted that the A-12 design was already being reviewed for other features with similar vulnerabilities. Johnson lamented, "We are finding as our aircraft become more and more complex that we have an increasing problem training even experienced people to follow good practice." In fact, the inspector who signed off on Article 126 was considered quite competent, having seventeen years' experience. Johnson also noted with some chagrin, "The mechanic who connected up the wires improperly had seven-years experience and much of it on aircraft with complicated electrical systems, such as the Constellation."[57]

All OXCART mechanics and supervisors were subsequently ordered to receive refresher training, and by the time Col. Fussell's team departed on January 6, 1966, the airplanes were once again cleared to fly. That same day, Col. Holbury fired off a telex to Ledford advising him that he had admonished senior representatives of all contractors at Area 51 for immediately leaking information about the crash, something he considered a serious breach of security. Word of the accident had spread quickly, and Holbury noted bitterly, "My Command Post was queried by your Headquarters within three minutes of the crash and prior to the time I'd even had time to reach the crash scene in my car."[58]

A-12 vs. SR-71

As normal operations resumed, Lockheed and CIA pilots continued testing the A-12 and developing its capabilities. Seven operationally configured aircraft were now available, along with two test aircraft and the trainer. OXCART detachment pilots were constantly engaged in flying proficiency and training sorties in preparation for eventual deployment.

Although no such orders were forthcoming, the Roadrunners honed their procedures, logistical requirements, and mission planning to the point where the time needed to go from notification to deployment had been reduced from twenty-one days to just fifteen.[59] In July, Holbury was transferred to Laon, France, as commander of the 66th Tactical Reconnaissance Wing. At the same time, Col. Hugh Slater assumed command of the 1129th SAS.

In the hope of convincing officials in Washington of the operational readiness of OXCART, Lockheed and Roadrunners aircrews endeavored to demonstrate the A-12's endurance capabilities. On December 21, 1966, Bill Park flew 10,198 statute miles in six hours at an average speed of 1,659 miles per hour (including slowdown and descent for aerial refueling). After departing Area 51, he headed northeast over Yellowstone National Park, then eastward across North Dakota and Minnesota before turning south to Tampa, Florida. He then turned northwest, making a dash to Portland, Oregon, and then southwest to Nevada. Again, he flew eastward, passing Denver and St. Louis, before turning around at Knoxville, Tennessee, and passing Memphis in the home stretch back to Area 51. This flight established a performance record then unattainable by any other aircraft. John Parangosky later noted that Park's sortie "began at about the same time a typical government employee starts his workday[,] and ended two hours before his quitting time."[60]

Unfortunately, opposition to OXCART threatened to terminate the program before it ever performed its intended mission. For several years, William R. Thomas III of the Bureau of Budget sought to discontinue funding for the A-12 in favor of its younger sibling, the SR-71. For reasons that remain unclear, he saw OXCART as superfluous and claimed that the SR-71 would achieve operational readiness by July 1966. There was, in fact, no basis for such a claim. Ignoring that the A-12 had already demonstrated design performance capabilities, the SR-71 was 20,000 pounds heavier than the A-12 and would therefore attain altitudes about 3,000 feet lower at any given point in a mission profile of the same range. Moreover, the SR-71 was still in the early stages of testing at Edwards and was currently available only in limited numbers. Thomas also saw no value in maintaining a covert, non-military reconnaissance capability. "We do not believe this distinction is meaningful," he wrote in a memorandum to bureau director Charles L. Schultze. "It is certainly not worth the cost of maintaining the A-12 program."[61]

Despite the A-12's apparent advantages, President Johnson approved termination of OXCART just one week after Park's record-breaking endurance flight. The CIA was immediately directed to develop a schedule for orderly retirement of the A-12 fleet, an operation that became known as SCOPE COTTON. According to this plan, all of the OXCART aircraft were to be placed in long-term storage by the end of January 1968. Deputy Secretary of Defense Cyrus Vance began making plans to prepare the SR-71 for use over Cuba and Southeast Asia. In the meantime, the 1129th SAS was to remain ready for deployment with seven to fifteen days' notice.[62]

The SR-71 looked nearly identical to the A-12, with the exception of wider nose chines, an extended tail cone, and a slightly raised cockpit. *Lockheed*

Hugh Slater, *left*, and Werner Weiss enjoy a day of boating on Lake Mead near Las Vegas. *Roadrunners*

Out of Gas

OXCART mission training continued unabated at Area 51, but tragedy befell the program on January 5, 1967, when another A-12 was lost, this time along with its pilot. Walt Ray, using call sign Dutch 45, took off in Article 125 about 1:00 p.m. for a routine high-altitude training sortie with two scheduled aerial-refueling rendezvous. The first of these took place within Yuletide SOA. Upon reaching the rendezvous point, Dutch 45 made contact with Cute 62, a KC-135Q piloted by Maj. Billy Bristow and 1Lt. Stephen Gemlich of the 903rd Aerial Refueling

Squadron. Ray successfully hooked up with the tanker and waited patiently while TSgt. George Chope pumped 31,000 pounds of JP-7 fuel into the Blackbird's tanks. After scanning his instruments Ray notified the tanker that he had room for more fuel. Chope then transferred an additional 5,000 pounds, at which point Ray indicated that he had onloaded about all he could take. After breaking contact, Dutch 45 continued his planned route and climbed to altitude.

During ascent, Ray encountered turbulence between 48,000 and 52,000 feet, forcing him to adjust his climb schedule. By the time he reached 66,000 feet, the fuel gauge indicated a total of 45,000 pounds of fuel on board. A little more than an hour into the flight, Ray reported that he had 36,700 pounds of fuel, 600 pounds more than he had expected on the basis of his flight plan. Approximately forty minutes later, he began descent with 260 nautical miles to go before his second aerial-refueling rendezvous in Yuletide SOA. When Ray leveled off at 29,000 feet, about 52 nautical miles from the next rendezvous point, he had 14,000 pounds of fuel remaining. The second tanker, Cute 57, piloted by Lt. Col. Clarence Thomas and 1Lt. James Curd, was already on station and transferring 3,800 pounds of fuel to Boxer 17, an F-101B assigned to chase Dutch 45. About 30 miles short of the rendezvous point, the Blackbird's fuel had dropped to less than 11,500 pounds, and Ray was becoming anxious. He was a few minutes behind schedule and had to wait for Boxer 17 to clear the boom before hooking up with the KC-135Q. SSgt. George McCabe, the boomer on board Cute 57,

The loss of Article 125, seen here ready for departure from runway 32, resulted in the OXCART program's first fatality. *Lockheed*

immediately transferred approximately 3,800 pounds of JP-7 to the A-12. He then informed Ray that the tanker pilot wanted to begin a shallow climb to gain an additional 3,000 feet of altitude while maintaining hookup. Ray acknowledged and said he would "give it a try."[63]

Light turbulence during the climb caused the A-12 to disconnect from the tanker on several occasions, but McCabe didn't notice significant spillage. Eventually, he completed his task and informed Dutch 45 that the Blackbird had received 61,000 pounds of fuel. Although this was 1,000 pounds more than originally briefed in the flight plan, Ray complained that he was 4,000 pounds short. Unfortunately, nothing could be done to remedy the situation. As Lt. Col. Thomas later recalled, "We told him that our tanks were dry and we had transferred all of our fuel."[64]

An F-101B chase plane prepares to take on fuel from a tanker. *Via Charles Trapp*

A-12 moving in for rendezvous with a KC-135Q. In-flight refueling was critical for long-duration flights. *Lockheed*

Ray then contacted Bungalow and reported to MSgt. Raymond Short that he would have to shorten the second leg of his flight. But, he added, he was glad to do so because the Blackbird's autopilot was inoperative and he had been hand-flying the A-12 all day and was getting tired. Short acknowledged Ray's transmission and continued to track Dutch 45, now headed eastbound toward Utah. By the time Ray leveled off at around 80,000 feet, the airplane's instruments indicated a little more than 40,000 pounds of fuel remaining, or a bit more than 2,000 pounds less than expected. Almost three and a half hours into the mission, Dutch 45 contacted Raybold Control, the Area 51 Command Post, and stated that he was rolling out of a turn over Little Rock, Arkansas, at the easternmost end of his flight track and heading home. Ray noted that he had apparently lost some fuel. "I'm running 800 to 1,000 pounds short," he said, apparently unconcerned. "I don't think it's any problem at all, I can make it up." He sounded considerably more worried when he contacted Raybold Control again about twenty-four minutes later. "I've got a little bit of a problem here," he said, giving his latest position as abeam of Farmington, New Mexico, "I've lost about another thousand, ah, I think I can make it but..." The rest of his transmission was lost in a confusion of static.[65]

The Command Post struggled with Dutch 45's garbled transmissions for several minutes, asking, "What are your intentions and are you having any difficulty?" Exasperated, Ray called back, "I've been trying to tell you all along, I don't know where my fuel is going." By this time, he had only 4,600 pounds of fuel remaining and was still 200 miles from Area 51. Raybold Control advised that he would have to decide whether to land the top-secret jet at Kirtland Air Force Base, which shared its runway with Albuquerque International Airport, or press on for home. By this point, Ray felt he was closer to Groom Lake than to Albuquerque, so he decided to take a chance. "I'm trying to stretch it out as far as I can," he said, noting that he was 130 miles out with 4,000 pounds of JP-7. "Unless I'm losing it someplace, I should be able to make it," he added hopefully. But his hopes died a few minutes later, with the A-12 still 85 miles from home. "It's just sucking up too much fuel," he reported worriedly.

Ray's attention was suddenly drawn to the instrument panel, where two yellow warning lights indicated low fuel pressure readings for both engines. He immediately contacted Apex, the Area 51 control tower, to give his final position. "I'm 70 miles out, on a heading of one-zero-zero. I'm going to stay with it as long as I can make the engines run." A few moments passed, then, "They both flamed out, I'm going to have to get out now."[66]

Ray tucked his legs in, sat up straight, and grabbed the ejection handle. His helmet pressed against a custom headrest extension that he had requested installed because, as the shortest of the OXCART pilots, he found the standard headrest uncomfortable. As soon as he pulled the handle, the canopy sailed away and Ray was blasted out of the cockpit. Tumbling in his seat, he caught glimpses of the dark-blue sky above and a nearly solid deck of white clouds below. At this point the man-seat separator, a gas-driven rotary actuator and strap assembly colloquially known as the "butt snapper," was supposed to forcibly separate Ray from his ejection seat. Instead, constant pressure pushing the pilot upward jammed the top of Ray's parachute pack firmly against the underside of his headrest-spacer extension. He was trapped.

Boxer 17 was trailing behind Dutch 45 at a distance of about 10 to 15 miles. The chase pilot could see the A-12 as little more than a distant black speck at the head of a long white contrail. Then, the contrail abruptly disappeared and the Blackbird nosed over and plunged into the clouds.

Beneath the overcast at a much-lower altitude, Capt. James C. Sharp and an instructor pilot from the 4526th Combat Crew Training Squadron flew a two-seat F-105 over the rugged desert landscape. Their mission had begun as a "Dollar Ride" range orientation flight designed to acquaint new students with the local area, but the Nellis Command Post diverted the F-105 toward the vicinity of Caliente to help search for a downed F-4C. Cloudy conditions below 10,000 feet made it impossible to safely search the mountainous terrain, and darkness was fast approaching. Sharp made a right-hand turn and glanced out through the top of his canopy just in time to see an airplane plummet through the clouds trailing streamers of white vapor. As it struck the ground, a great cloud of gray smoke billowed upward and quickly dissipated, leaving behind several small fires that burned brightly in the waning daylight. Sharp immediately radioed Nellis to report what he had seen.[67]

Search-and-rescue operations began when the crash alarm sounded at Area 51, and all key personnel reported to the Command Post. The deputy chief of security notified four guards and one shift captain to stand by for deployment to the crash scene. Several charts were marked with the estimated coordinates of the ejection point, and winds were plotted for the accident area from ground level up to flight altitude for estimation of the aircraft impact point and pilot touchdown. Two four-wheel-drive crew-cab pickup trucks were loaded with extra gasoline, water, spare tires, and emergency radio communications gear. Extra food was ordered from the mess hall, and departing personnel were equipped with cold-weather clothing and sleeping bags provided by the Security Office as part of standard emergency response kits. By the time the rescue team departed, a little more than an hour after Ray's ejection, overnight temperatures in the search zone were forecast to be below 10 degrees Fahrenheit.[68]

Searchers in the HH-43B scoured the area in a vain attempt to locate Walt Ray. *Via Charles Trapp*

As soon as Apex activated the Crash Net, the Area 51 Command Post scrambled several aircraft, including two T-33 jets and the UH-1F helicopter, as well as an F-101B that served as a radio relay over a search zone that extended from Groom Lake to Cedar City. The HH-43B was already in the area, assisting Air Force search teams that were looking for the F-4C. Additional observers went aloft in a C-47, U-3B, and Cessna 210D. An HU-16 was dispatched from Hamilton Air Force Base. Capt. Sharp's report shifted the searchers' focus to the Meadow Valley Mountains south of Caliente, but rescue teams had no luck and the HH-43B was soon running low on fuel. Poor weather and the onset of nightfall ultimately curtailed flight operations until the following day.

Ground search operations started at the town of Caliente, where the Area 51 rescue team met with searchers from Nellis and learned that a local rancher believed he might have heard a plane crash that afternoon. The incident commander asked Caliente's chief of police to guide the rescue team into the rugged mountains to the south. He consented, and the group headed to the rancher's house, where they learned that the man had most likely heard only a sonic boom several hours before Ray's accident. Searchers therefore focused on the plots and fixes established earlier by the Command Post. In order to cover more ground quickly, the rescue team was forced to split up at Elgin, a section station along the Union Pacific Railroad some 20 miles south of Caliente. One group drove west while another went south toward Moapa, and the rest headed east into the Mormon Mountains. Despite freezing temperatures, ground units searched through the night in these areas, hoping to spot a strobe light or hear a radio call from the downed pilot. Unfortunately, the twisting canyons blocked both radio and visual signals. By midnight, no trace of Ray or his aircraft had been found.[69]

Operations resumed at dawn with additional security and medical personnel in several ground vehicles en route to the search area. Once again, the Area 51 Command Post dispatched all available aircraft and requested an additional UH-1F helicopter from Indian Springs. After the chopper arrived, the crew received a briefing from the deputy security officer and signed a memorandum of understanding that included nondisclosure agreements. Lt. Col. Barrett flew to Nellis to speak with Lt. Col. Maynard R. "Dusty" Rhoades from the Western Aerospace Rescue and Recovery Center, who was coordinating additional search efforts. Before departing, Barrett arranged for William O'Donnell, special agent in charge of the Nellis AFOSI office, to join him in the meeting so as to impress upon Rhoades the importance of security aspects surrounding the incident. Meanwhile, steps were taken to brief all personnel departing Area 51 on commuter flights as to the security embargo on any discussion of the crash. Ground rescue teams established a base camp at Leith, an abandoned railroad siding located near the geographic center of the assumed ejection/impact area. There, they were fed and given an opportunity to rest while communications were established with the Command Post. Eventually, each team was provided with new instructions, and the search continued.[70]

Taking advantage of all available resources, the CIA authorized use of a U-2 from Detachment G to take high-resolution images in the hope that photo interpreters might spot the crash site or the pilot's parachute.[71] No lead was overlooked. Charles Trapp flew the UH-1F to Nellis, where he picked up Capt. Sharp and an Air Force flight surgeon. Sharp was fairly certain he knew where the plane went down, and in fact his estimate proved to be within 1 mile of the actual impact crater. When he spotted the crash site late in the afternoon, the airplane's wreckage was strewn across several gullies at the edge of a long canyon through scrub-covered rolling hills. The airframe had completely disintegrated; the largest remaining pieces included a 4-by-5-foot fragment of one of the tail fins, and a lower-fuselage fillet panel that separated prior to impact. There was little evidence of fire, and the impact point was scarcely distinguishable from natural erosion features in the surrounding terrain. Trapp dropped two of his pararescue jumpers at the scene, where they quickly determined that the canopy and ejection seat were missing. At this point, they still held out hope that the pilot had ejected successfully.[72] It was now late afternoon, but they continued searching for Ray until nightfall, again without success. A C-130 remained airborne throughout much of the night, looking for visual or radio signals from the missing pilot.

On the morning of January 7, guard schedules at Area 51 were revised to ensure adequate coverage on base as well as availability of personnel who could be on standby for any eventuality. As the day wore on with no positive results in the field, Col. Slater requested more men be deployed. Robert Bennett and four other security guards departed for the search area while aerial observers continued to scour the region in the hope of finding Ray. In the HH-43B, Trapp followed the A-12's flight path backward from the impact point, crisscrossing hills and gullies. Finally, the crew of another search plane reported seeing something about 8 miles east of the crash site. Swooping as low as possible over the unknown object, observers on board the plane identified it as a parachute but reported they were unable to spot the missing airman. "Later in the day," Trapp recalled, "the C-47 guys saw sunlight reflecting from the pilot's suit or visor and they directed us to the site."[73]

Ray was lying on a steep hillside, partially wrapped in his parachute, with the ejection seat nearby. He wasn't moving. Trapp landed as close to the scene as possible and dispatched TSgt. Gordon Bailey to check the pilot's condition. "I had to proceed about a half mile on foot," Bailey later told investigators. He quickly ascertained that Ray was dead, and then made a detailed examination of the seat and other equipment that lay scattered across the rocky slope. The ejection seat had apparently struck the ground on its left side and bounced twice before coming to rest. The automatic lap belt disconnect mechanism had functioned, and there was evidence that the butt snapper had functioned properly. He noted that the pilot's body was in proximity to the seat and wrapped in several feet of parachute material, as if he had been thrown from the seat and rolled up in the chute as he traveled downhill. "The only conclusion I can draw from this is that he was still in the seat when he hit," Bailey said.[74]

He notified Trapp, who passed word back to the Command Post. A second helicopter soon arrived on the scene, carrying TSgt. Fred Schneider along with a medical officer, a photographer, and two members of the accident investigation board. With darkness fast approaching, Capt. Gary L. Randolph, Area 51's chief of public health and occupational medicine, examined Ray's body before it was airlifted to Nellis. Over the next several days, investigators made a detailed search of the scene to recover the seat, survival equipment, and various small components and pieces of debris that might explain how Ray perished.[75]

To preserve the secrecy surrounding OXCART, several CIA and Air Force officials worked together to develop a cover story and draft a statement for news media. Agency representatives submitted two proposed drafts even before the crash site and pilot were located. The first stated only that an SR-71-type aircraft was missing and presumed down east of Las Vegas. This text was approved by Carl Duckett and NRO director Alexander Flax, as well as by the Air Force director of special activities, Brig. Gen. Paul N. Bacalis, and the director of information, Maj. Gen. Eugene LeBailly. Upon being informed of the planned release, Kelly Johnson objected strenuously to the use of the term "SR-71," suggesting instead ascribing the mishap to some unspecified "experimental model." After further discussion, the principals agreed to compromise by calling the airplane "an experimental model of the SR-71" based at Edwards. A statement issued by Col. James Smith, the Edwards public information officer, also claimed that the missing aircraft was being operated by Lockheed Aircraft Corporation and flown by a civilian test pilot on loan from Hughes Aircraft Company. The pilot's name was not released until after his next of kin had been notified.[76]

For the most part, this cover story shielded OXCART and Area 51 from media scrutiny, but the *Las Vegas Review-Journal* noted, "There were some reports that the plane was not an SR-71, but some other secret Air Force plane."[77] Col. Smith denied these allegations and fended off additional queries from *Los Angeles Times* aviation editor Marvin Miles, who expressed dissatisfaction with the Air Force account of the accident and the paucity of information that had been released. Miles seemed particularly provoked by use of the term "experimental" aircraft and threatened that unless he was given firm reason to believe it would be contrary to national interests, he intended to publish an article exposing the entire incident.[78] He must have ultimately been convinced, or otherwise discouraged, because no subsequent exposure was forthcoming. Nevertheless, base security conditions underwent constant evaluation throughout the days following the loss of Article 125. The Area 51 security chief eventually noted with some relief that there had been no breaches or leaks and that through AFOSI sources in Las Vegas and other areas in Nevada, "It has been determined that the cover story concerning Cygnus 125 has been accepted as gospel."[79]

Exhaustive search-and-rescue efforts rapidly turned the normally quiet Meadow Valley Wash into a bustling hive of activity. As the nearest major town, Caliente was soon bulging with government and contractor personnel, and every motel was full to capacity. The sudden demand for food, fuel, housing, and other necessaries brought a brief economic boom to eastern Lincoln County. As one of the Air Force men told a reporter, "We're going to get this plane out no matter what it costs."[80]

Security remained paramount throughout the search-and-recovery operation. Armed guards were posted near Elgin and as far south as Carp, another section station along the railroad tracks running between Caliente and Las Vegas, to prevent unauthorized entry into the area. Inquisitive security personnel politely queried all travelers in the vicinity of Meadow Valley Wash as to their business and destination in the area. They even went so far as to interview a rancher who happened to be working in his own pasture at the time. "We've had military airplane crashes around here," said one Caliente resident, "but we've never seen anything like the security for this crash." Rumors that the wrecked airplane might have been of a type not previously acknowledged as being among the Air Force arsenal brought only blank stares from officials, who implausibly suggested that perhaps some military men were using incorrect designations in their conversations with civilians. Over the next few weeks, approximately eighty government men were constantly moving in and out of the community, searching by day and resting at night, but few would say anything about their activities. "It hasn't been like other crashes," said another resident. "Everything is hush, hush."[81]

Activity on the night of January 7 was confined to efforts to retrieve two disabled vehicles with ground searchers aboard. Circling overhead, the crew of a C-130 passed directions to rescue teams, and once the vehicles had been located, a mechanic made sufficient repairs to move them. This operation was not completed until nearly an hour after midnight, at which time the C-130 returned to Area 51. The next morning, orders arrived from the Command Post to break camp at Leith and move the base camp to a new location closer to the main crash site. Within an hour, all fires were extinguished and equipment loaded, and the convoy was on its way. At the new site they rendezvoused with Mobile 7, commanded by Col. James Anderson, who had arrived from Area 51 with a large task force to begin retrieving the wreckage. Some personnel began this work immediately, while others erected tents and established areas for vehicle repair, parking, a garbage dump, a fuel depot, a communications center, and a heliport. A few days earlier, deputy chief of security Nicholas R. Zubon arrived from Area 51 with grading equipment needed to cut a path to the impact site. He surveyed the landscape surrounding the scene and then directed blade operators to carve a 4-mile-long road, the shortest possible route from the new base camp at Kane Springs Wash.[82]

At this point, the only major component left to find was the canopy, which had separated from the aircraft in the normal manner following initiation of the ejection sequence. Observers in helicopters had been unable to spot it from the air, so ground search parties were deployed to search the rugged terrain surrounding the seat impact point. Ironically, when the canopy was finally located on the fifth day after the accident, it was first sighted by one of the crewmen aboard the UH-1F, call sign Hobard 1. Investigators were distressed to learn, however, that two over-the-shoulder cameras that would have provided valuable information about Ray's final moments had been torn off by the airstream and were still lost in the desert. Searchers were ordered to continue looking for them, but freezing temperatures, rugged terrain, and the distance over which wreckage was scattered promised to extend the hunt for as much as several weeks.[83]

As evening fell on January 8, Col. Anderson departed for Area 51 on the last helicopter, leaving Zubon in charge of ground search operations. Glenn Fulkerson of Lockheed was responsible for wreckage retrieval with the help of two dozen members of the OXCART ground crews and twenty additional Air Force personnel. Together, they spent many hours gathering pieces at the scene and loading them onto pickup trucks that hauled the material out of the narrow canyons to the base camp. Once there, debris was sorted and placed in bins aboard flatbed trucks for transportation back to Area 51. At the suggestion of Project Headquarters, these trucks delivered their cargo after dark and were accompanied by security surveillance teams to ensure they were not followed. Recovery crews continued picking up bits and pieces until sundown on January 11, at which time the effort was terminated, base camp was disassembled, and all personnel and equipment returned to Groom Lake.[84] Nick Zubon later reported that the entire operation was completed securely, without incident. He advised, however, that due to the rugged nature of the terrain, it would be extremely difficult to be ensured that all the wreckage had been recovered.[85]

Making use of available resources, Air Force officials hired local ranchers at $5.00 per day to provide horses and riders to continue the search for the missing cameras. After being dropped off by helicopter at Elgin, one airman led four civilians into the foothills on horseback while twenty others continued the search on foot. Attempts over the ensuing two days yielded no results, and on January 12, fresh horses and riders were brought in. This pattern continued until the weekend, when crews were finally given a much-needed rest.[86]

Bill Goodwin and one of his colleagues from Baird Atomic also participated in the search for the cameras. Hauling a camping trailer along rough dirt roads behind a Cadillac proved an adventure. On the way they had a flat tire and ended up spending one night under a railroad trestle. The next day they joined other searchers scouring the area. "We searched for the cockpit cameras for the better part of a week," he recalled. They saw numerous wild horses, but no sign of the missing equipment, and eventually exited the area in the teeth of a snowstorm as part of a ragtag convoy of military and civilian vehicles.[87] The cameras remained lost.

Sunlight shines on Joshua trees in Tikaboo Valley as a late-winter snowstorm sweeps into the Groom Mountains. *Author*

Accident investigators were ultimately unable to conclusively determine why the A-12 ran out of fuel 70 miles short of its destination. They concluded that the most probable cause was a fuel-gauge malfunction resulting from a faulty measurement device in one of the tanks that inadvertently became grounded to the aircraft structure. This resulted in an error that varied in proportion to the amount of fuel in the tank; the more fuel in the tank, the greater the error. Initially the pilot thought he had more JP-7 than he actually did, then, after a certain amount was consumed, the indicated total returned to normal and Ray was suddenly faced with an unexplained apparent loss of fuel.[88] Investigators felt that Ray should have safely recovered the A-12 at Kirtland when he had the opportunity instead of initiating a descent toward Area 51 under known low-fuel conditions, and into a strong headwind, earlier than called for in his flight plan. Restrictions were imposed on flying the remaining OXCART aircraft until fuel-quantity validation flights had been performed. Headrest spacers were removed from all aircraft to eliminate the possibility of interfering with man-seat separation.[89]

Controlled Flight into Terrain

Routine operations resumed at Area 51, but just five days after the loss of Article 125 a schedule for placing the remaining airframes in long-term storage at Lockheed's Palmdale facility had already been presented to project managers. CIA officials continued fighting to employ OXCART's unique capabilities, at one point proposing a joint operation that would take advantage of the best capabilities of both the A-12 and U-2 acting in concert. Agency planners suggested an ambitious mission called Project SCOPE LOGIC (its classified name was Operation UPWIND) to determine the exact nature of a series of Soviet missile installations near Tallinn, Estonia. Attempts to photograph these sites by using satellites had been thwarted by persistent cloud cover over the region. The UPWIND scenario called for an A-12 launched from Area 51 to rendezvous with a U-2 over the Baltic Sea. The A-12 would then be flown along the Soviet-Finnish border, never violating Soviet airspace but skirting the coasts of Estonia, Latvia, Lithuania, Poland, and East Germany before turning west for the return leg to Area 51. The entire eight-and-a-half-hour mission would cover 11,000 nautical miles and require four aerial refuelings. It was hoped that Soviet radar operators, believing the A-12 was preparing for an overflight in the vicinity of Leningrad, could be provoked into activating radar equipment installed at the Tallinn complex to track the intruder. The A-12 pilot would be using the airplane's high-resolution camera to photograph the entire coastal region, while counting on the plane's speed and electronic countermeasures for protection against surface-to-air missiles. Meanwhile, the U-2, flying farther out to sea, would be able to collect electronic signals data from the Tallinn radar systems. Although both CIA and DoD officials supported SCOPE LOGIC / UPWIND, Secretary of State Dean Rusk strongly opposed it, and the proposal was never forwarded to President Johnson.[90]

In a desperate bid to save the OXCART program, Kelly Johnson proposed converting half the SR-71 fleet then under construction to bombers, thus eliminating any perceived surplus of reconnaissance aircraft. He had already attempted to counter criticism that the SR-71 was superior to the A-12 by modifying Article 122 with upgraded systems in accordance with SR-71 standards, following the airplane's 157th flight in March 1966. Johnson's efforts were in vain. Article 122, now designated A-12B, was redelivered to Area 51 in April 1967 but made only five more flights before being retired. Improvements to the airplane's electronic-warfare suite, chine compartments, etc. only complicated matters. Existing flight and maintenance manuals for the A-12 did not include material pertinent to systems peculiar to the modified airframe, and it was estimated that it would cost $125,000 and take two months of additional work to produce a set of Article 122–specific supplements. This added cost had not been included in the budget forecast. Additionally, some flight testing was needed to determine whether fuel system modifications might be required to optimize center-of-gravity control. Project Headquarters decided instead to mothball Article 122, which was flown to Palmdale on September 16, 1967, making its last hop at subsonic speed and never flying above 20,000 feet.[91]

Just ten days later, Jack Layton was scheduled for a nighttime navigation training mission in the A-12T with Harold Burgeson as instructor, and using Burgeson's call sign, Dutch 12. Chase was to be provided by Lt. Col. James S. Simon Jr. in an F-101B. During the premission briefing the A-12T crew went over the assigned navigational training route, which included one aerial-refueling rendezvous. Simon was instructed not to refuel or fly close formation, except immediately after takeoff if sufficient light remained. Layton and Burgeson took off thirty-six minutes after sundown. Simon joined up in close formation, looked over the A-12T, advised that Dutch 12 appeared to be in good shape, and then broke formation to take up position in a holding pattern over Area 51. "I'll see you later," said Simon as Article 124 disappeared into the dusk.

When Dutch 12 returned, Layton descended toward Area 51 under the control of Saucy GCA and requested permission for a low approach over runway 32. As the A-12T entered the downwind leg at an altitude of about 4,000 feet, Burgeson contacted the chase aircraft and advised Simon that Dutch 12 would be landing shortly. Simon indicated that he could not see Article 124. Burgeson reported the airplane's position and advised Simon that all systems were normal and there was no further requirement for chase, but Simon responded that he would rendezvous to establish visual contact.

As Dutch 12 turned onto final approach, Simon entered a position in trail behind and to the left of the A-12T. He informed Dutch 12 that he was moving over to the right side. An observer on the ground noted that the Voodoo lost some altitude during the maneuver but regained it prior to leveling off on short final. At this point, Simon was approximately 1 mile to the right of the A-12T, in trail, and at a slightly lower altitude. Dutch 12 flew over the runway at an altitude of 500 feet and at 190 knots indicated airspeed. Witnesses near the South Trim Pad saw Simon's F-101B strike the

In the spring of 1966, Article 122 underwent substantial modifications to the point that some company documents referred to it as the A-12B. *Lockheed*

An F-101B chase plane shadows the A-12T Titanium Goose during a training flight. *Lockheed*

ground some 4,000 feet south and 2,000 feet east of the approach end of the runway. The Voodoo was in a wings-level attitude, with its landing gear retracted and flaps up. It slid approximately 1,600 feet, exploding in a fireball that streaked across the desert. Simon apparently made no attempt to eject.[92]

Jim Simon joined the Roadrunners in the summer of 1966. *USAF*

The crew of the Titanium Goose also saw the bright flash of the explosion and felt the concussion. Thinking it might be the trouble with his own aircraft, Layton instinctively stop-cocked the right engine, lit the left afterburner, and said, "Burgie, be ready to bail out."

"That wasn't us, Jack," said Burgeson. "It had to be the chase." With the right engine shut down and the left afterburner on full, the Titanium Goose developed a pronounced yaw. "If you can keep this thing flying straight," Burgeson told Layton, "I'll restart the right engine." Once both turbojets were operating, Layton circled for a landing. Both crew members of Dutch 12 avoided looking at the fire near the runway.[93]

A thorough investigation determined that the primary cause was most likely pilot error, a type of mishap referred to as controlled flight into terrain. Simon somehow lost situational awareness and flew his plane into the ground. Although no supervisory factors were cited as contributory causes, investigators noted that standard operating procedures for the 1129th SAS failed to differentiate between day and night chase procedures. To enhance safety, further nighttime chase activities were suspended except in emergencies, or at the specific request of an OXCART pilot.

Although the accident occurred at night in the heart of the nation's most secret military facility, Simon's death threatened to publicly expose elements of the OXCART program. Obituary notices published in Las Vegas and in Simon's hometown of Osawatomie, Kansas, noted that he had been assigned to Detachment 1 of the 1129th SAS in July 1966. Though the squadron was said to be located in Las Vegas, an Air Force spokesman told reporters the unit was not attached to the local base and that no Voodoos were stationed at Nellis. A front-page headline in the *Las Vegas Review-Journal* trumpeted, "Super-Secret Base Jet Crash Kills Pilot," and the accompanying article revealed that the crash site was within what was "known to Nevada Test Site workers as Area 51 . . . the same area where the Air Force developed and tested the U-2 spy plane and its successor, the SR-71." A follow-up story noted that the F-101B had crashed "near the runway of the Air Force's secret Groom Lake experimental station."[94] Fortunately for the sake of program security, there was no mention of either the CIA or the A-12.

Drones and Mother Ships

OXCART was not the only project underway at Area 51 at this time. Kelly Johnson's ongoing efforts to sell the government new designs based on the A-12 resulted in discussions, as early as 1962, of converting the airplane into an unmanned drone. Johnson opposed this idea on the grounds that the A-12 was much too large and complex. Instead, he proposed launching a smaller vehicle, which he referred to variously as the AQ-12 and Q-12, from a modified OXCART aircraft. On July 31, following a meeting at Area 51, he returned to Washington and presented a Lockheed-funded study to NRO director Joseph Charyk and Eugene Fubini of the DoD Office of Research and Engineering, outlining the possibility of designing a drone aircraft capable of operating in the same speed and altitude range as the A-12.[95] Such a vehicle would give the US president a choice between manned or unmanned reconnaissance platforms for overflying sensitive areas.

Charyk saw no inherent political value in using a drone and said he felt the vehicle's capabilities would be no better than those of the A-12. He recognized, however, that such a scaled-down vehicle would be significantly harder for enemy radar to detect. By October 5, Robert McNamara and DCI Allen Dulles agreed to proceed with development of the drone under Project TAGBOARD. Program management responsibility was assigned to the CIA despite the agency's apparent lack of enthusiasm, and Pete Scoville assigned managerial oversight of TAGBOARD to Jack Ledford.[96]

Several days later, Johnson submitted a written proposal for a feasibility study regarding the Q-12, as he finally settled on calling the drone. This was accepted, and he drew up plans for a ramjet-powered vehicle that would be launched from a dorsal pylon atop the fuselage of an A-12-type aircraft modified with provisions for a launch control officer (LCO) seated in a compartment behind

Kelly Johnson experimented with several different configurations for the Q-12. Though promising, this early version was ultimately rejected in favor of a more conventional arrangement. *Via T. D. Barnes*

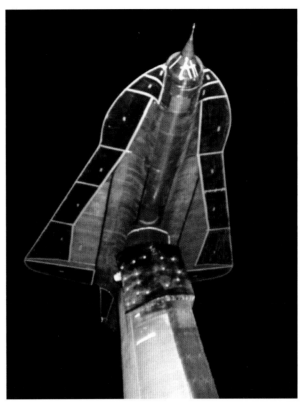

This full-scale Q-12 mockup, seen here in its final configuration, incorporated antiradar treatments similar to those used on the A-12. *Lockheed*

the cockpit. The launch pylon was to be situated on the airplane's centerline between the twin vertical stabilizers. Johnson was aiming for a craft with a 3,000-mile range and 425-pound payload capacity. He sought Hycon's help with providing a camera capable of obtaining 18-to-24-inch resolution imagery from up to 90,000 feet. Each drone would be expendable, designed for one-time use with parachute recovery of the camera package.[97]

Although Johnson was already in negotiations with Hycon, John Parangosky also sought input on the camera question from Eastman Kodak and Vidya, a small research-and-development company working on development of optics for satellites. Litton and Minneapolis-Honeywell were queried regarding guidance systems, and Van Nuys–based Marquardt offered an impressive demonstration of an engine that could be shut down for as much as forty-five seconds and restarted during flight.

While this was going on, the Skunk Works team in Burbank built a full-scale Q-12 mockup complete with antiradar treatments like those applied to the A-12. The mockup was delivered to Area 51 on December 10, 1962, and over the next two weeks was subjected to testing on the EG&G radar range. Initial results were somewhat disappointing. "Its cross-section is surprisingly high compared to the A-12," Johnson wrote in his project diary. "We still have a great deal of work to do on this A.R. [antiradar] configuration."[98] The problem was resolved through numerous design refinements, resulting in a final configuration with a frontal RCS of just 0.2 square meters at a 15-degree depression angle.[99] At the time, the Q-12 represented the most "low observable," or stealthy, aircraft ever built, and Lockheed's experience with TAGBOARD ultimately laid the foundation for future design efforts.

Johnson received approval to produce twenty drones and two launch aircraft. To avoid confusion with the single-seat reconnaissance jet, he designated the mother ship M-21, reversing the numerals. The drone then became the D-21, and the mated combination was called MD-21. When not carrying the drone, the M-21 had the same performance and handling characteristics as the A-12. The D-21 was almost 43 feet long, with a nearly 20-foot wingspan, and about 7 feet tall at the tip of the tail. The vehicle had an empty weight of 5,130 pounds and a maximum gross takeoff weight of approximately 10,330 pounds. Design specifications called for launch at an altitude of 75,000 feet while the mother ship was cruising at Mach 3 speeds. The D-21 would then climb to an initial mission altitude of 80,000 feet and eventually top off above 95,000 feet while cruising at Mach 3.3.[100] The MD-21 was limited to maneuvering loads of no more than 2 g, and most rolling maneuvers were prohibited to prevent adverse side loads on the drone. The only aileron maneuver allowed for the mated configuration consisted of a gentle, steady turn, performed well within specified load limits.[101]

The D-21 was a sleek craft, with chines and rounded delta wings blended into the fuselage. Like the A-12, the drone featured a semimonocoque design using rib and skin construction and was built primarily of titanium with radar-absorbent edge panels. No internal space was wasted. The forward section included a circular air inlet with a fixed spike and air-bypass system. Behind this, the equipment bay contained navigational and guidance avionics, and a removable hatch housing the camera and its parachute recovery system. The third section contained three integral fuel tanks, interconnected to provide fuel efficiently to the engine. The aft section housed a Marquardt XRJ43-MA20S-4 ramjet, designed for stable combustion at extremely high altitudes and low atmospheric pressures. The engine inlet duct extended from the nose section aft through the fuselage to the engine section. A rudder and two elevons provided aerodynamic control.[102]

On June 4, 1963, following a political tug-of-war between the Air Force and CIA, primary responsibility for TAGBOARD was shifted from the agency to the Air Force under NRO Program D. Consequently, the service canceled an existing order for five A-12 airframes, previously approved in January 1962 under the cryptonym WEDLOCK. Three of these (Articles 131 through 133) were transferred back to the OXCART program in November 1963, and the remaining two (Articles 134 and 135) were scheduled for conversion to the M-21 configuration. This was logical, since WEDLOCK had become superfluous when the secretary of defense–approved Air Force procurement of the R-12.[103]

Throughout 1963, Skunk Works engineers were struggling with MD-21 aerodynamic-loads problems. Johnson noted in his log that wind tunnel data indicated there would be difficulties during launch, when the drone passed through the shock wave generated by the mother ship's nose section. "Going through the fuselage shock wave is very hard," he wrote. "I am insisting on launching at full power, but there are problems regarding fuel-air ratio to the engine and engine blowout in this condition." Subsequent wind tunnel tests indicated the need for the M-21 pilot to initiate a pushover at launch because the pylon was, for structural reasons, necessarily shorter than would be aerodynamically desirable. For enhanced safety, Johnson also resolved to equip the D-21 with an emergency destruct system. "I am very concerned about how we fly the drones during test stages," he wrote, "so that we can be sure we don't bomb Los Angeles or Portland."[104]

While the drones and mother ship were being built in Burbank, testing of the camera recovery system was underway at Area 51. The D-21 was programmed to automatically jettison its camera package at a preplanned rendezvous point over the ocean, where—far below—the crew of a JC-130B Hercules waited to spot its parachute and snatch it from the sky, using the same Mid-Air Retrieval System (MARS) that had been employed with the CIA's CORONA satellite film capsules. To test the TAGBOARD recovery system, a D-21 camera pallet was dropped from a B-66 flying at its maximum altitude capability while the Hercules orbited below, flying a racetrack pattern around the Groom Lake area at around 24,000 feet. Lockheed engineers wanted motion picture documentation of the tests, but neither the F-101 nor the T-33 was suitable because the JC-130B would be flying as slow as possible, well below the jets' stall speeds. Frank Murray thought he could accomplish the task by using the Cessna 210, though it would be pushing the single-engine prop plane to its performance limits. Murray reviewed the pilot's handbook, which indicated he should be able to reach 24,000 feet at 125 knots thanks to the engine's turbocharger. At that altitude it would be necessary to use supplementary-breathing oxygen. He made an initial test flight with Lockheed's photographer and everything checked out, so he then scheduled a chase mission to accompany the first MARS test.

A truck delivers the first D-21 to Hangar 5 at Area 51, inside a special container to conceal the drone's shape. *Lockheed*

The crew of a JC-130B snatches a payload in midair. This method had been perfected during retrievals of film capsules from reconnaissance satellites. *USAF*

"I took off first, rendezvoused with the C-130, and the game was on," he recalled years later. The B-66 dropped the package on schedule, and a radar beacon began transmitting as soon as the parachute opened. Murray's Cessna performed an aerial dance with the JC-130B as the Hercules crew repeatedly attempted to snag the chute, without success. They eventually gave up after losing too much altitude, and the package landed near the north end of the lakebed. The second MARS sortie resulted in a successful recovery, and Murray managed to get into position to film the catch despite the Cessna being "tossed around like a rag doll" in the transport's wake.[105]

As of May 1964, the D-21 design configuration was still plagued by transonic drag deficiencies and other problems, but Johnson was confident these problems could be overcome. Construction of the first M-21 was well underway, and a launch pylon had been developed to carry the 10,000-pound drone. Fit checks of the mated MD-21 configuration took place in June, using Article 134 and the first production D-21, Article 501. The second drone to roll off the assembly line, Article 502, was designated solely for use as a structural test article. Article 134 was delivered to Area 51 for checkout and ground testing on August 12, and the second M-21 followed a few months later. By November 12, Johnson reported that the first M-21 was ready to fly.[106]

Over the next several weeks the mother ship was put through its paces during six airworthiness and functional check flights. Not surprisingly, the aircraft performed identically to the A-12; even with the extra crew compartment there was little change to the basic configuration. By the fourth flight, Bill Park had expanded the M-21 performance envelope to Mach 2.67 and an altitude of 75,000 feet. The fifth flight, one week later, provided an opportunity for a second crew member to begin familiarization with the LCO station behind the cockpit. On December 15, the day before the final shakedown flight, Article 503 became the first drone to be delivered to the test site. There followed three ground taxi runs at increasing speeds with the D-21 mounted on top of the mother ship. Finally, on December 22, the two vehicles were ready for their first mated flight. Aerodynamic fairings were placed over the drone's inlet and exhaust to

Workers prepare to mate the D-21 to the M-21 mother ship inside Hangar 5. Protective fairings have been installed over the drone's inlet and exhaust. For extra security, MD-21 activities were separated from other A-12 projects by a wooden partition. *Lockheed*

Red McDaris, *lower left*, pulls a work platform away from the MD-21, which is being readied for its first mated flight. *Lockheed*

reduce drag during captive flight conditions, and the aircraft were towed onto the North Ramp. While Park listened to preflight briefings and completed final preparations, Kelly Johnson and other Lockheed officials attended the maiden flight of the SR-71 at Palmdale, a surprisingly public setting for a Blackbird's debut. Johnson's party finally arrived at Area 51 very late in the afternoon, and Park started the engines, taxied the MD-21 to the end of the runway, and took off as the sun dipped toward the horizon.

Ground crews ready Article 134 for flight as firefighters stand by. This image provides a good view of the launch pylon and the drone's exhaust fairing. *Lockheed*

"I climbed straightaway up to 20,000 feet without making a turn or any pitch change at all," Park reported afterward. Despite the additional weight and drag from the drone, he found the MD-21 flight characteristics and handling qualities to be quite satisfactory. He accelerated to Mach 1.03 and reached a maximum altitude of 25,000 feet. The drone's presence was most noticeable whenever the pair hit turbulence. "It feels like it's clanking around back there," Park said, though he later admitted the sensation may have been exacerbated by his ejection seat rocking a bit on its rails. Chase pilot Bill Weaver confirmed Park's impression, noting, "In turbulent air I noticed the 'D' was jittering and shaking in conjunction with the aircraft movement."[107]

Bill Park in the MD-21 and Bill Weaver in the F-104 chase plane wait, side by side, for clearance to taxi on a frosty December afternoon. *Lockheed*

The second mother ship, Article 135, completed its maiden flight two days later on Christmas Eve. Preparations immediately began for a series of captive tests leading up to the first drone launch. On January 18, 1965, Article 134 was once again mated to Article 503 and flown to a speed of Mach 1.8 to check pylon loads and acceleration performance. That same day, Article 135 completed an FCF and drag chute evaluation before going into layup for fuel-transfer modifications and installation of test instrumentation. Flight planners scheduled the two mother ships to fly a series of mated and unmated flights over the ensuing weeks to practice launch maneuvers and extend the mated flight envelope to Mach 2.6. Additional sorties were slated for early February to check out the drone's systems and evaluate handling characteristics during aerial refueling. Other test flights were used for extending the speed envelope to Mach 3.2, practicing D-21 engine starts, and completing prelaunch systems checks.[108] Johnson hoped to schedule the first launch for his birthday, February 27, but it was not to be.

"We have all kinds of troubles," Johnson complained as his planned launch date came and went. Problems mounted when Minneapolis-Honeywell failed to deliver a guidance system on time and within budget. Captive flight testing continued, but events conspired to push the first free flight ever further out. During one test mission in April 1965, severe control-surface flutter resulted in loss of the drone's elevons. Lockheed technicians fixed the problem by adding locking devices and counterweights. By May, Bill Park had cleared the MD-21 performance envelope to Mach 2.6, considerably short of the desired Mach 3.2 launch speed. He had found that the additional weight and drag of the drone atop the fuselage caused the M-21 to have poor transonic acceleration, particularly on hot days. Additionally, there were problems with the Hamilton-Standard inlet controls for the mother ship's 32,000-pound-thrust J58 engines. Johnson managed to secure some uprated 34,000-pound-thrust power plants and had the inlet controls replaced with Lockheed models.[109]

By the first week of May the two mother ships had logged fifty-four flights, including twenty-one in the mated configuration. Article 135 was designated the primary launch aircraft, while Article 134 was to be used only for captive-carry flights and chase missions. Difficulties with acceleration through the transonic region were

The maiden flight of the mated MD-21 configuration validated Kelly Johnson's concept for TAGBOARD. *Lockheed*

mitigated after engineers developed a shallow-dive maneuver that allowed the mated configuration to more quickly accelerate to supersonic speeds. The drone's inlet and exhaust covers, designed for explosive separation, also caused problems and were ultimately eliminated after Article 503 suffered considerable damage due to being struck by flying debris during a test of the system.[110]

Johnson's engineers doggedly overcame each technical obstacle, but his supervisors weren't communicating well with one another. "I am beset by managerial problems," Johnson lamented in October 1965. Resolving to take a more direct hand in matters, he scheduled a meeting with his engineering and flight test groups to coordinate efforts for accelerating the test program. Jack Ledford stationed Col. Frank W. Hartley Jr. at Area 51 to serve as assistant project director and CIA liaison. Arrangements were made to test the D-21 over the Pacific Missile Range, west of Naval Air Station Point Mugu, California. All arrangements were complete by the end of January 1966, and the test was initially scheduled for early February.[111]

That target date slipped nearly a month, but at last, on March 5, 1966, Article 135 took to the air carrying Article 503. The M-21 was piloted by Bill Park with Keith Beswick serving as LCO. The test plan called for launching the D-21 about 250 miles off the California coast and allowing it to fly approximately 1,600 nautical miles to a recovery zone near Hawaii. Unfortunately, though the drone separated smoothly from the mother ship following engine start and achieved a speed of Mach 3.3, it flew only 150 nautical miles before pitching over and plummeting into the Pacific Ocean. Even so, Johnson was quite pleased. "Mainly," he noted in his diary, "we demonstrated the launch technique, which is the most dangerous maneuver we have ever been involved in, in any airplane I have worked on."[112]

The MD-21 prepares for refueling, as seen from the boomer's position aboard the KC-135. *Lockheed*

Article 135, the second M-21 built, is ready to taxi on June 16, 1966. The airplane is carrying the fifth D-21, Article 505. *Via T. D. Barnes*

Article 135 awaits takeoff clearance. For some reason, the airplane's rudders have been replaced by ones borrowed from Article 127 but switched so that the tail number is displayed on the inward-facing side. *Lockheed*

During the second flight, on April 27, things went better. This time, Park was accompanied by Ray Torick, a thirty-year-old engineer who had joined Lockheed in 1963 following five years of service as a carrier-based naval aviator.[113] Article 506 flew 1,120 nautical miles and attained an altitude of 90,000 feet and a speed of Mach 3.3 before falling out of the sky due to a hydraulic-pump malfunction. Despite this setback, the overall flight results represented significant progress.

The inherent dynamics of the launch maneuver continued to haunt Johnson. The necessary flight profile required the M-21 pilot to attain a speed of Mach 3.12 at an altitude of 72,000 feet and commence a gentle pull-up before pushing the nose over to maintain a steady force of 0.9 g. With the drone's ramjet operating, the LCO initiated pneumatic separation of the drone somewhere between Mach 3.2 and 3.25.[114] It was a hazardous operation. If the drone malfunctioned during separation, the M-21 crew would be in grave danger. The potential risks worried Johnson to the point that on May 19, 1966, in the wake of an order for a second batch of drones, he made a formal proposal to SAC Headquarters for a modified drone (eventually designated D-21B) that would be launched from beneath the wing of a B-52H. This, he said, would provide greater safety, reduced costs, and expanded deployment range.[115] In order to propel the D-21B to ramjet ignition speeds, the drone would require a rocket booster to provide initial acceleration to Mach 3.

Seen through a rear-facing camera behind the M-21's cockpit, a D-21 lifts away from its launch pylon. *Lockheed*

Three drones were successfully launched from Article 135, the only one of the two mother ships to be used for live launches. *Lockheed*

Park and Beswick made another flight over the Pacific on June 16, carrying Article 505. This time, the M-21 crew found the drone's launch characteristics to be somewhat unsettling. During separation, the D-21 lifted slowly off the pylon and seemed to float just above the mother ship as if reluctant to depart. After a few seconds that felt like an eternity, it finally climbed away and flew nearly 1,600 nautical miles. The drone followed its planned course perfectly—successfully making eight programmed turns—but then failed to eject its camera package due to an electrical malfunction.

The TAGBOARD program finally seemed to be on track, but on July 30, Johnson's worst fears were realized. Park was flying with Torick during the fourth launch sortie when Article 504, the first D-21 to carry a full fuel load, suffered an asymmetrical engine unstart during launch. Rising slowly through the mother ship's shock wave, the drone suddenly rolled sideways and dove into the M-21. Keith Beswick, filming the launch from Article 134, could only watch in horror as his airplane's sister ship pitched up and disintegrated, raining debris over the Pacific. When Article 135 broke apart at a speed of Mach 3.25, the forward fuselage and cockpit section snapped off at the wing root and began to tumble, decelerating rapidly. Miraculously, the crew managed to eject despite the wild gyrations, and Park was picked up by a chopper after floating in his life raft for nearly an hour about 150 miles off the California coast. Injured during bailout, Ray Torick was apparently unable to inflate his life vest or climb into his raft, and he drowned before rescuers arrived on the scene.[116] Most of the aircraft wreckage sank in deep water and was never recovered.

Project SENIOR BOWL

As a result of this tragedy, Kelly Johnson prohibited further use of the M-21 as a launch platform and once again lobbied to replace it with a B-52. An assessment by CIA project managers determined that Lockheed should proceed on a limited basis with implementing Johnson's proposal. Of the initial batch of twenty drones, fifteen flightworthy vehicles remained. These could be easily retrofitted to D-21B configuration, and Lockheed eventually received authorization to build nineteen more. The surviving M-21 was placed in storage at Palmdale on September 29, 1966, after completing a total of ninety-four flights. Leo Geary arranged for a B-52H to be delivered to Lockheed's Palmdale facility from Kelly Air Force Base, Texas, on December 12, 1966. The bomber required a number of modifications, most notably installation of launch control panels in place of the ECM and tail gunner's stations, telemetry and communications gear and associated wiring, high-speed cameras to document the launch sequence, and special pylons to carry one drone under each wing. Reconfigured as a mother ship, the former bomber was designated JB-52H, signifying a temporary modification. Initial D-21B flight testing was to be conducted from Area 51 before transitioning to Beale Air Force Base near Marysville, California, where the stateside contingent of the operational SR-71 fleet was based.[117] The JB-52H/D-21B program eventually came to be known as SENIOR BOWL, though the drone was still referred to as TAGBOARD.

Technicians prepare to install a launch pylon on the first JB-52H, AF serial no. 61-0021, following its arrival at Groom Lake. *Lockheed*

Trailing fuel vapor, debris from the M-21 and D-21 tumbles through the stratosphere following a midair collision. This image was captured by Keith Beswick from Article 134, which served as a high-speed chase plane. *CIA*

This view of the mated D-21B/DZ-1 stack shows how little ground clearance existed between the booster's folded ventral fin and the concrete. The twin-bladed ram-air turbine on the booster's nose provided the drone with hydraulic pressure and electrical power prior to launch. *Lockheed*

The first D-21B, Article 501, stacked with a DZ-1 booster, has been mated to the left wing of the JB-52H for a series of captive-carry tests. *Lockheed*

Switching from a supersonic to a subsonic launch platform necessitated major changes to the drone's airframe and power plant. First, engineers provided the D-21B with a less sensitive inlet to mitigate the unstart problem that contributed to the fatal mishap. New dorsal mounting points enabled it to hang from the wing pylon. The most significant challenge was providing sufficient acceleration after drop to allow for ignition of the Marquardt ramjet. Using the M-21 made it possible to launch at Mach 3.2, but the JB-52H had a maximum speed of around 0.84 Mach (639 mph). So, Johnson tasked Lockheed Propulsion Company (LPC) in Redlands, California, with developing a booster to be mounted on the underside of the drone. Due to the highly secret nature of the program, uncleared LPC designers were forced to work from a set of unclassified requirements and specifications and were prohibited from knowing anything about the customer or the end use of the hardware. The company named their solid-propellant rocket motor the Avanti, which was the name of a popular sports coupe produced by Studebaker in the early 1960s, but the rocket motor was more often simply called the A-92.[118]

The completed 44-foot-long booster assembly, designated DZ-1, consisted of the steel-cased, three-segment Avanti motor with a single ventral stabilizer fin on the aft end, and a steel nose cone containing hydraulic and electrical systems driven by a Marquardt B-4 ram-air turbine to provide power and hydraulic pressure to the drone during the captive-carry and launch phases of flight. The DZ-1 weighed 13,286 pounds and produced approximately 27,300 pounds of thrust during an eighty-seven-second burn. Accelerating rapidly to Mach 3 speeds, the D-21B/DZ-1 combination experienced sudden aerodynamic heating that rapidly raised surface temperatures from −58 degrees Fahrenheit at launch to 428 degrees at cruise, putting severe thermodynamic stress on the airframe.

The D-21B had a complex flight profile. Each sortie began with the JB-52H being flown to a specified launch point. For testing, that meant somewhere over the Pacific Missile Range; operational missions could be staged from anywhere in the world, with aerial-refueling support for the B-52. The LCO would release the drone/booster stack from the pylon at an altitude of about 40,000 feet. About five seconds later, booster ignition propelled the D-21B to a speed of Mach 3.3 while climbing to altitude. The drone's self-destruct mechanism was not designed to arm until the vehicle climbed above 63,000 feet, allowing the LCO to manually destroy the D-21B if it went off course. Below this altitude, no manual or automatic destruct was possible. Ramjet ignition was programmed for 74,000 feet, and booster burnout and jettison were set to take place at an altitude of about 80,000 feet. The drone's course was preprogrammed. As with the original D-21, following completion of its mission the D-21B would fly to friendly territory and jettison its camera package for midair recovery before automatically self-destructing.[119]

In August 1967 a second B-52H was assigned to SENIOR BOWL and delivered to Palmdale for modification and checkout. This work was scheduled for completion sometime in December. Meanwhile, the first JB-52H was flown to Area 51 for integration with the drone and the beginning of captive testing.

On the North Ramp, ground crewmen preflight the JB-52H with two D-21B drones slung underneath its wings. *Lockheed*

Unplanned Launch

Technicians at Area 51 attached launch pylons to the JB-52H, using existing hardpoints installed for SAC's AGM-28 Hound Dog missile. Following loads tests using sandbags to simulate the weight of the drone/booster stack, fit checks were conducted with Article 501, the engineering test article. For initial captive-carry flights, Article 501 was mated to an inert DZ-1 rocket booster, designated Unit 1 and containing no actual propellant. These flights allowed engineers and flight crews to evaluate the handling characteristics of the mated aircraft and study the drone's low-speed aerodynamics.

In late September 1967, test planners scheduled the JB-52H to carry two drones simultaneously on a captive-carry flight for a total in-flight checkout (IFCO). Because the mission called for complete end-to-end systems compatibility and integrity testing, the drones were fully configured for an operational mission. Live rocket boosters were installed even though they were not to be launched during this flight. Article 501 was attached to the left wing pylon and mated to DZ-1 Unit 2. A second D-21B/DZ-1 stack was mounted beneath the right wing. Upon experiencing difficulty mating Article 501 to the pylon, a technician attempted to retap a stripped nut for one of the forward attachment bolts. Although this facilitated the connection, it also weakened the threads on the nut, leaving it vulnerable to stress.[120]

Two airmen marshal the JB-52H out of the parking area as it taxis toward the runway. The ventral fins of each rocket booster are folded, allowing a very small amount of ground clearance. *Lockheed*

On the morning of September 28, ground crews readied the JB-52H and its experimental cargo for departure. Maj. Hal Rupard and Maj. Jack G. Reed, Air Force project officers for TAGBOARD, oversaw preparations and then went to the control room to monitor the flight. The eight-engine jet, crewed by Lt. Col. Marvin R. Leitzel, his copilot and navigator, and two LCOs, took off from runway 32 and passed over Groom Lake. As the plane climbed over Emigrant Valley, the pilot executed a gentle turn to the north-northeast on a direct heading toward the Currant VOR. Once there, Leitzel began flying a racetrack pattern between Currant and Austin while gradually climbing to an altitude of 20,000 feet.

Banking over southern Nevada, the JB-52H enters an oval racetrack pattern while climbing to cruising altitude. *Lockheed*

The booster's A-92 rocket motor was programmed to fire approximately five seconds after the stack was released. *Lockheed*

As Lockheed's senior flight test engineer for the D-21B, John R. Wallis Jr. was responsible for Article 501. He performed IFCO procedures while a second LCO checked out the drone on the right wing. About 50 nautical miles north of Area 51, the JB-52H was climbing at about 1,500 feet per minute on an easterly heading at a speed of around 225 knots. As the bomber leveled off, Wallis was conducting a procedure that required manual activation of the drone's control surfaces to check their movement. The subsequent increase in aerodynamic loading apparently proved too much for the damaged nut, which abruptly failed. With a groan and a snap, the left-hand D-21B/DZ-1 stack pivoted, shearing the aft attachment and then the forward bolt as well. Wallis watched helplessly as the vehicle fell away from the B-52. Five seconds later, the rocket engine ignited as automatic sequencing took over.[121]

Because the mission was a planned captive carry, the drone's INS had not yet been programmed and the unguided vehicle shot off through the skies over central Nevada. As designed, the Avanti rocket motor pushed the vehicle to supersonic speeds, but instead of ascending, the stack lost altitude. It never climbed high enough to allow either arming of the destruct mechanism or ignition of the drone's ramjet engine. Minutes later, the vehicle plunged into the desert and exploded, scattering parts of the secret drone and its booster across the landscape.

Leitzel immediately notified the Area 51 Command Post, aborted the mission, and returned to base. A helicopter was readied to transport a team of security personnel to the crash site while Rupard and Reed procured a vehicle from the motor pool and began the long drive north. As soon as the JB-52H pulled into its parking space on the North Ramp, John Wallis disembarked and boarded the chopper, which then departed for the crash scene.[122]

In Railroad Valley, rancher Carl Hanks was out riding when he heard a sound like thunder, but there were no storm clouds to be seen. He urged his horse into a gentle trot up a scrub-covered slope. Emerging from the ravine, he confronted a strange sight. Something was burning intensely a few miles away. Approaching cautiously, he saw scattered metallic debris and other material he couldn't immediately identify. Soon, other locals arrived on the scene by truck and horseback. They included several ranch workers and some men from a county road crew. Bill Gibson arrived with his wife, Miriam, and took several pictures.

They soon heard the rotors of an approaching helicopter. The Air Force chopper flew in over Cherry Creek Summit and dropped down into the valley. As soon as it landed, several armed men disembarked, ushered the civilians back, and took control of the crash site. As Hanks recalled years later, "The government people that were involved in the cleanup were very concerned about picking up every piece of wreckage." He particularly remembered that Air Force personnel told the locals that "it would be better if they forgot this ever happened."[123]

The D-21B/DZ-1 stack drops away from the left wing of the JB-52H. *Lockheed*

At this point, Rupard and Reed were still trying to find the best route by which to reach the scene. After a few wrong turns, they were eventually pointed in the right direction by some locals who were cutting firewood. When they finally arrived, the Air Force officers joined other Area 51 personnel examining the wreckage, which was scattered over a wide area. The largest remaining pieces were those of the steel-cased DZ-1 booster and its Avanti motor, while the D-21B had largely disintegrated. To recover as much material as possible, search teams lined up in a shoulder-to-shoulder search of the debris field.

For the remainder of the afternoon, the helicopter flew back and forth between the crash site and Area 51, ferrying personnel and supplies. Col. Hartley personally took charge of the cleanup detail. A temporary bivouac was set up, and trucks were brought in to haul the wreckage back to the test site. The only harrowing moment came early on, when the drone's destruct package suddenly exploded. Cleanup efforts ended when darkness fell, and resumed at first light.

Hartley somehow learned about Bill Gibson's unauthorized photos. He knew he had to get his hands on them but was reluctant to strong-arm the civilian. Instead, he chose a diplomatic approach, asking Gibson if there was anything he might like in exchange for the film. The man thought it over for a few moments. "Well," he said, "I kind of have a hankering for cream pie." So, Hartley made some calls. A pie soon arrived on one of the helicopter supply flights, and Gibson traded his film for the dessert.[124]

By early afternoon, the operation was complete. The wreckage was loaded onto trucks, the base camp was dismantled, and Air Force personnel had departed. Railroad Valley was quiet again. Nearly four decades later, after the desert's scars had time to heal, Norman Sharp of Nyala Ranch recalled the prodigious recovery effort.[125] "They spent days policing the area," he mused. "There is nothing left to indicate it ever happened."[126]

Mixed Results

Flight testing of the D-21B officially began on November 6, with the launch of Article 507 over the Pacific Missile Range. Mission goals required the drone to fly westward toward Hawaii, turn north around the islands, and then

Debris from the drone and rocket booster littered the desert. Note how impact forces crushed the booster's steel nose cone like a stomped beer can. Part no. DZ82-29 and the words UNIT 2 are stenciled on the interior surface, and a mass of electrical- and hydraulic-system components has been exposed. The bent panel at left is part of a dorsal fairing that housed hydraulic lines connected to a ram-air turbine on the tip of the booster's nose. *Author*

Test launches were conducted over the Pacific Ocean. D-21B drones flew twelve test missions and four operational sorties. *Lockheed*

turn west to a recovery point near Johnson Island after covering a total distance of 3,000 miles. Both the drop and boost phases were successful, but the vehicle traveled less than 150 miles downrange before pitching over and diving into the sea. Investigators suspected that the inlet cone's plastic skin delaminated, causing unstart.

Another attempt took place three weeks later. The JB-52H left Area 51 carrying Article 508 and Article 509, but the mission aborted. Article 509 finally flew on December 2, maintaining the desired speed but falling short of the programmed altitude for some reason. After cruising for nearly 500 miles, the D-21B quit flying prematurely due to hydraulic-system failure. Two successive attempts to launch Article 508 were aborted due to difficulties with the auxiliary power unit and the INS. This drone was successfully launched on January 19, 1968, and flew 550 miles. The mission terminated prematurely when the vehicle pitched downward and rolled left. Telemetry was lost, but engineers suspected an electrical malfunction.[127]

Kelly Johnson organized an independent team to analyze the failures and to seek a solution. Careful study of all available data revealed that even with the rocket booster, drones launched from the JB-52H reached altitudes 6,000 to 10,000 feet lower than had those launched from the M-21. There were also quality control and design problems. As a result of this analysis, Johnson resolved to make a number of procedural improvements and redesign the mission profile. Frank Hartley returned to Washington to take over Geary's job as head of Program D, overseeing all NRO aerial-reconnaissance programs. Col. Richard "Dick" Baldwin replaced Hartley at Area 51.[128]

Johnson was more than a little concerned at the lack of progress on the D-21B. The program suffered yet another setback on April 30 following the launch of Article 511. The drone achieved a speed of Mach 3.22 before suffering unstart about six and a half minutes into the flight. Spike failure was again suspected as the cause. Consequently, the next drone was fitted with a metal inlet spike assembly, and the launch of Article 512 on June 16 went off without a hitch. This time the drone successfully achieved its 3,000-mile design range, reached an altitude of 90,000 feet, and cruised at a maximum speed of Mach 3.25. There were several instances of engine flameout during turns, but each time the ramjet reignited. Most important, the camera hatch was successfully recovered in midair by the JC-130B crew. It was a great cause for celebration at Area 51 and in Burbank.

Unfortunately, the next test on July 1 was considerably less successful. Article 514 experienced violent roll-yaw coupling immediately after launch. At separation, the booster struck the D-21B, rupturing the drone's fuel tank. The camera hatch ejected upon command and was recovered from the water in good condition. Despite this failure and continuing quality control deficiencies, Johnson still hoped the program was getting back on track. He was on vacation during another attempt on August 28, in which two D-21B drones were carried from Area 51 to a launch site near the island of Kauai. Article 516, the first to carry a camera package instead of ballast, failed to accelerate following separation and was lost at sea. The hatch ejected at excessive speed and was not recovered. When Johnson returned from his trip, he initiated an independent review panel headed by Jim Plummer of Lockheed Missiles and Space Company (LMSC) in Sunnyvale, California.[129]

The booster produced 27,300 pounds of thrust during an eighty-seven-second burn, propelling the drone to the Mach 3 speeds needed for starting the ramjet engine. *Lockheed*

The second JB-52H, AF serial no. 61-0036, takes off carrying two drones in August 1968. *Lockheed*

Johnson implemented the panel's recommendations and was gratified when a flight on December 15, 1968, proved highly successful. Article 516 not only completed its assigned route but also became the first D-21B to acquire images with its Hycon camera. Additionally, as it turned out, this was the final

D-21B sortie flown from Area 51. Since January 1968, for security reasons and due to lack of facilities at Beale Air Force Base, all SAC personnel assigned to TAGBOARD / SENIOR BOWL had been detailed to Area 51 under the designation A-Flight, 14th Air Division. In March 1969, this organization moved into permanent facilities at Beale as the 4200th Support Squadron.[130]

These changes did not bring an end to the program's woes. In early February an autopilot malfunction resulted in the loss of Article 518 and its camera package. This delayed the next attempt to May 10, at which time Article 519 performed the most successful mission to date, demonstrating a speed of Mach 3.3 and a maximum altitude of 96,588 feet. The flight of Article 520 on July 10 also yielded impressive results, leading Johnson to proclaim, "We have now met our design objectives to the point where the Air Force can consider the program successful and completed up to the operational phase."[131]

Responsibility for deciding whether to deploy the drones operationally fell to President Richard Nixon, who subsequently approved an overflight of southern China on November 10, 1969. On that date, Article 517 was launched from somewhere west of the Philippines. The drone attained the programmed altitude of 84,000 feet and cruising speed of Mach 3.27. Unfortunately, during the terminal phase of flight the drone failed to appear at the rendezvous point and was presumed lost. CIA officials were concerned it might have crashed in the People's Republic of China after exhausting its fuel supply, though they presumed it probably self-destructed after descending to the requisite altitude of 52,500 feet. An INS failure apparently caused the drone to miss a planned turn, and the D-21B flew straight across China into Kazakhstan. If it continued flying until fuel exhaustion, analysts concluded, it would have eventually crashed in an isolated region approximately 75 miles east of the Aral Sea.[132]

Whether or not the destruct system activated is unknown, but the drone apparently did fall into the hands of the Soviets. Designated "Object R," it proved to be of great interest to the Soviet aircraft industry. Engineers from many leading organizations involved with the development of aircraft, missiles, electronics, and defense technology eagerly studied the wreckage—since it had broken into several large pieces—to determine what lessons might be learned. Then, in accordance with Directive No. 57 of March 19, 1971, passed by the Presidium of the Soviet Council of Ministers for the defense industry, the Tupolev Design Bureau was ordered to build an equivalent system based on the American design but using Soviet structural materials and propulsion technology. The vehicle was named Voron (Raven) and was to be launched from either a Tu-95 or Tu-160 carrier aircraft.

The reverse-engineered craft strongly resembled its American counterpart, though the wing planform was closer to a true delta, lacking the D-21B's chines. The Voron had an operating profile similar to that of the D-21B. After separation from the carrier aircraft, it would be accelerated to high supersonic speed by a 104,720-pound-thrust solid-fuel rocket booster, providing sufficient velocity to ignite the drone's RD-012 ramjet engine. Like the D-21B, the Voron would follow a programmed course and jettison its camera package for parachute recovery. Though its flight history is unknown, Tupolev's work on the Voron program continued for several years and provided a great deal of interesting and useful data for the further development of advanced hypersonic aircraft. The remains of the wrecked D-21B were ultimately stored at the Zhukovsky flight test and development base (the Soviet equivalent of Area 51 or Edwards), 30 miles southeast of Moscow.[133]

The loss of Article 517 spurred Lockheed to institute INS software changes to prevent another such incident. The updated system was tested on February 20, 1970, during a 3,000-mile sortie nicknamed Long Drive. Article 521 performed superbly, reaching a speed of Mach 3.32 and a maximum altitude of 95,700 feet while hitting every checkpoint to an accuracy within 2 or 3 miles. The drone completed its route and obtained good imagery. Aerial recovery of the camera hatch was successful despite some broken parachute risers.

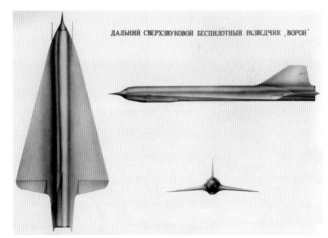

The Soviet Union's Tupolev Design Bureau reverse-engineered the D-21B from a crashed example recovered in Kazakhstan. *OKB Tupolev*

Tupolev's D-21B clone, known as Voron, included a solid-fuel rocket booster similar to the DZ-1. *OKB Tupolev*

Another operational mission was attempted on December 16. On this occasion, Article 523 completed is programmed route over China and dropped its camera package at the rendezvous point. But the JC-130B crew failed to capture the camera hatch because its parachute disintegrated. This was not the end of difficulties for the troubled program. Article 526 was launched on March 3, 1971, also completing its mission. Once again, the parachute was damaged during deployment. The camera package fell slowly into the sea, where a naval vessel was waiting as a backup recovery vessel. After spending forty-five minutes making unsuccessful attempts to fish the hatch out of the water, the ship ran it over and caused it to sink. The camera was never found. Another naval vessel located the drone, surprisingly still afloat, but was unable to effect recovery before it, too, sank.[134]

Although the recovery phase had been a dismal failure during two critical intelligence-gathering missions, the D-21B was apparently operating as designed. Consequently, the president approved another overflight of China. Launched on March 20, Article 527 was tracked through the first fifteen checkpoints along its planned route. It disappeared with sufficient fuel to sustain flight for another 1,100 miles.[135] The drone's loss remained a mystery for nearly four decades. In 2008, Gen. Ma Jiesan, retired commander of the People's Liberation Army Air Force's Yunnan Air Defense Center, claimed the D-21B was downed over Yunnan Province. After crashing in a forest, it was recovered largely intact by Chinese military forces. Following much study by defense and aerospace specialists, the remains of Article 527 were secretly stored for many years before finally being placed on public display in the China Aviation Museum at Shahe Airbase on the outskirts of Beijing. In his memoirs Ma wrote, "This D-21 was a great American gift for China and inspired many technological breakthroughs in China aviation and aerospace areas."[136]

Soldiers of the People's Liberation Army pose with a D-21B after it crashed somewhere in Yunnan Province, southwestern China. *PLA via Lin Xu*

Not surprisingly, the devastating loss of yet another D-21B over denied territory proved fatal for TAGBOARD and SENIOR BOWL. The end, however, did not come quickly. Over the next several months there was another independent review and a major shake-up within Skunk Works management of the program, and Kelly Johnson personally oversaw altitude chamber tests at Lockheed's Rye Canyon facility in Santa Clarita, 20 miles northwest of Burbank. By this point Lockheed had only three people officially assigned to the project, and the budget was extremely tight. Approximately 160 Air Force personnel were assigned to the 4200th Support Squadron. Johnson estimated that over a ten-year period of development and flight operations at Area 51 and Beale, the drone program had cost $184 million, including seven years of field service support. Undertaking nine more launches, Johnson estimated, would likely cost another $31 million.

When, on July 8, 1971, Col. Hartley asked what could be done for something like $4 million in the upcoming fiscal year, Johnson pointed out that the cost of any single launch had been running at a minimum cost of $5 million. One week later, he received a message from Hartley announcing termination of the program. The seventeen remaining D-21B drones were to be placed in nonflyable storage; the static-test article had been scrapped in February 1969, and the residue buried at Area 51. The end was bittersweet. Johnson's disappointment was tempered by pride in what his team had accomplished. "We did an excellent job on a program of the most difficult nature," he wrote in his diary. "The remarkable part of the program was not that we lost a few birds due to insufficient launches to develop reliability, but rather that we were able to obtain such a high degree of performance with such low cost compared to any other system."[137]

Leaving the Nest

But what of OXCART? For a while it appeared that the A-12 would be the greatest reconnaissance system never deployed. Project personnel at Area 51 were preparing to place the fleet in long-term storage even though the SR-71, the A-12's putative replacement, was not yet fully operational. Finally, in the spring of 1967, US policymakers and intelligence officials came to an agreement to employ OXCART for tactical reconnaissance missions over North Vietnam. The primary purpose would be detection of medium-range surface-to-surface missiles, though the imagery collected would also provide a wide variety of other valuable intelligence data. On May 15, DCI Richard Helms submitted a plan for deploying three OXCART aircraft and all necessary support personnel from Area 51 to Kadena, thus allowing for a minimum of nine operational sorties per month, depending on weather.[138] President Johnson approved the plan the following day, and within twenty-four hours the Roadrunners were headed for Japan to begin Operation BLACK SHIELD. With the deployment of more than 250 people, approximately half of whom worked for Lockheed or the various support contractors, the population of Area 51 temporarily dropped to 938.[139]

Col. Slater accompanied the airlift of personnel and equipment to Kadena that began on May 17, while ground crews readied three A-12s to follow several days later. Mel Vojvodich departed first in Article 131 on the morning of May 22. After topping off his fuel from a tanker, he climbed to 79,000 feet and cruised at Mach 2.9 before descending to meet a second tanker near Hawaii. The second leg of his journey was much like the first and included another refueling rendezvous near Wake Island. He then accelerated to Mach 3.1 for the final leg and landed at Kadena just six hours and ten minutes after leaving Area 51. Jack Layton duplicated this feat two days later in Article 127, but with a cruising altitude of 81,000 feet. He nearly aborted his flight due to failure of a critical instrument shortly after takeoff but decided to proceed, making the necessary calculations manually. Jack Weeks departed in Article 129 on May 26 but had to land at Wake Island four and a half hours later as a precautionary measure after having trouble with his INS and communications equipment. A pre-positioned contingency recovery team repaired the airplane, and Weeks continued his journey the following day. His final leg was subsonic, in the company of a KC-135, and lasted five hours and fourteen minutes.[140] Other personnel already in place at Kadena included OXCART pilots Ken Collins, Dennis Sullivan, and Frank Murray. Maj. Weldon "Walt" King headed the meteorology group that would provide critical weather data for Sam Pizzo's mission planners. In place at last, the OXCART detachment was ready to demonstrate the A-12's capabilities in an operational environment.

BLACK SHIELD sorties commenced on May 31 with a 3.5-hour flight that included multiple passes over North Vietnam (a typical pass lasted only about 12.5 minutes). Vojvodich photographed seventy known missile sites and nine additional high-priority targets, including airfields, ports, military barracks, and training areas. Throughout the mission the Blackbird's ECM gear picked up no radar signals, indicating that Article 131 successfully penetrated North Vietnamese airspace completely undetected. Over the ensuing eleven months the OXCART detachment was placed on alert for fifty-eight potential missions and performed twenty-nine, including twenty-four over North Vietnam, two over Cambodia and Laos, and three over North Korea. Flight assignments were divided fairly evenly among the pilots. Layton and Collins each flew six;

Reviewing mission results are, *from left*, Lt. Col. Blair Davis, Jack Weeks, Ken Collins, Col. Hugh Slater, and Col. James Anderson. *Roadrunners*

Vojvodich and Weeks, five; Murray, four; and Sullivan, three. The A-12 and its camera systems proved very reliable, and twenty-seven sorties were deemed successful on the basis of the quality of imagery obtained. A few missions were unsuccessful or only partially successful due to cloud cover over the targets or camera malfunction. One mission was cut short due to engine trouble. Most of the canceled alerts resulted from inclement weather, while the remainder were canceled due to operational decisions. Average mission duration was around four hours and required two or three aerial refuelings. Data collected during Operation BLACK SHIELD made it abundantly clear that North Vietnam never deployed any medium-range surface-to-surface missiles, but these missions provided valuable information for bomb damage assessment, analysis of enemy air defenses, supply routes, and troop deployments.[141]

This artwork is based on a line drawing from official CIA briefing material. The colors are notional. *Author*

Despite routinely overflying heavily defended areas, no A-12 aircraft were lost to hostile fire. North Vietnamese forces launched SA-2 surface-to-air missiles at the Blackbirds on several occasions but failed to down their targets. During the 16th BLACK SHIELD sortie, Dennis Sullivan detected the launch of an SA-2 while approaching Hanoi in Article 131 at a speed of Mach 3.15 and an altitude of 83,500 feet. Due to the tardiness of the launch and the efficacy of the Blackbird's ECM suite, Sullivan was never in danger. He faced North Vietnamese missiles again a few days later while making two passes between Hanoi and Haiphong. Although he detected two missile sites preparing to launch during his first pass, neither did. Article 129 was cruising at Mach 3.1 at 84,000 feet on the second pass when Sullivan's radar detection alarms again sounded a warning. Peering through his rearward-facing periscope, he saw vapor trails of at least six SA-2 missiles stretching up to about 90,000 feet, arcing over, and reaching toward his airplane like skeletal fingers. Several of these projectiles converged on the Blackbird at Mach 3.5 and closed to within 100 to 200 yards before exploding. Sullivan felt at least three detonations close by, but his airplane was apparently unharmed. A postflight inspection at Kadena revealed that two small metal fragments, probably debris from an exploded missile, had penetrated the airplane's titanium skin on the bottom of the right wing and lodged near one of the fuel tanks.[142] Consequently, flights over North Vietnam were temporarily suspended while the OXCART fleet's defensive avionics were checked out.

The BLACK SHIELD A-12s were tasked to overfly North Korea three times in early 1968 following the seizure of a US Navy ship that had been engaged in collecting signals intelligence from the safety of international waters in the Sea of Japan. On January 26, three days after USS *Pueblo* and its crew were captured, Jack Weeks flew a

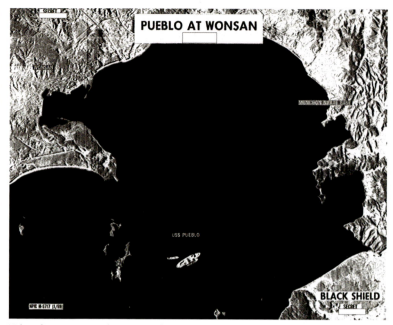

Taken from an A-12, this image of Wonsan Harbor, North Korea, shows the location of USS *Pueblo*. North is to the right. *CIA*

three-pass mission over the southern part of North Korea and the demilitarized zone to determine whether North Korea was mobilizing for hostilities. Weeks reported that he had been tracked by Chinese radar, but no missiles were fired. His intelligence take provided new insight on North Korea's armed forces, revealed no signs of a military response to the incident, and located *Pueblo* in a small bay north of Wonsan. Frank Murray flew the next mission on February 19, but scattered clouds concealed the area where *Pueblo* had been spotted. On May 6, Jack Layton made the third flight, which turned out to be the final BLACK SHIELD mission.[143]

Two missile fragments and a segment of damaged titanium wing structure from Article 131. This was the closest the Vietnamese forces ever got to shooting down a Blackbird. *CIA*

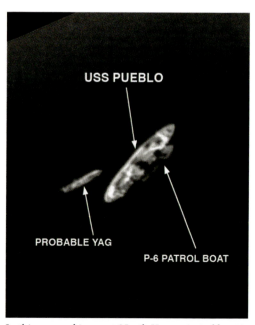

In this cropped image, a North Korean patrol boat is moored next to *Pueblo* while a utility vessel stands by. *NARA*

Despite these exceptional accomplishments achieved against almost overwhelming odds, the Roadrunners did not come through Operation BLACK SHIELD completely unscathed. In fact, they suffered two devastating losses during noncombat missions. The first occurred at the beginning of what was to be a weather observation flight on June 1, 1967. On this occasion, Bill Goodwin was scheduled to ride in the back seat of an F-101B piloted by Maj. Walt King, but Goodwin was unavoidably delayed. "I was in a staff car by the runway waiting to film an A-12 taking off," he recalled, "Somehow, Maj. King contacted me, saying he couldn't wait any longer." Goodwin watched the F-101B taxi past and saw King wave. A few minutes later, during takeoff rotation, the Voodoo's tail came off. The pilot ejected at extremely low altitude but probably would have survived if the airplane hadn't landed on top of him when it crashed.[144]

Little more than a year later, the program suffered another blow. By this point the detachment was awaiting redeployment to Nevada, and the OXCART pilots were flying about once a week to maintain currency and ensure the airplanes remained in peak operating condition. Each A-12 also underwent a thorough FCF in preparation for its final overseas flight. During one flight in Article 129, Frank Murray experienced problems with the right engine, leading to flameout while descending to a lower altitude.[145] The troublesome engine was replaced, and Jack Weeks performed the next checkout on June 4, 1968. He was in good spirits as he rendezvoused with a tanker twenty minutes after takeoff from Kadena. When the boom operator commented that he was ten minutes early, Weeks responded glibly, "I was just sitting on the ground with nothing to do, so I thought I might as well come on up."

Following disconnect, the tanker crew watched Article 129 climbing normally, on course. A telemetry system called Birdwatcher constantly monitored vital A-12 systems and equipment, providing information to the pilot and transmitting coded signals to a ground station that indicated normal equipment activity or flagging anomalies in the event a system exceeded established limits. Weeks was cruising at Mach 3.1 some 76,000 feet above the Philippine Sea when his Birdwatcher chirped, warning of excessive exhaust gas temperature in the right engine. Ground monitors saw the same signal, followed by another chirp seven seconds later indicating engine fuel flow had dropped below 7,500 pounds per hour. A final transmission repeated the two previous warnings and indicated the A-12 was rapidly descending below 68,500 feet. Monitors in the Kadena Command Post frantically attempted to contact Weeks via radio and Birdwatcher channels, but without success. These efforts continued until it was calculated that the Blackbird's fuel would have been exhausted, but no further transmissions were received. A massive air-sea rescue operation focused on a wide stretch of ocean some 500 nautical miles east of the Philippines and 600 nautical miles south of Okinawa. No trace of Article 129—or its pilot—was ever found. Without any physical evidence to examine, investigators were unable to conclusively determine the primary cause. Catastrophic failure of the right engine was deemed the most likely explanation.[146]

Jack Weeks flew four BLACK SHIELD missions over Southeast Asia and one over North Korea. *Roadrunners*

Article 129 was the last A-12 to crash and the only one not recovered following the mishap. The wreckage presumably sank in the Philippine Sea. *Lockheed*

End of an Era

OXCART advocates fought long and hard to save the A-12 from being mothballed. Battles between the CIA and Air Force centered on agency claims that the A-12 flew higher and faster than the SR-71 and had superior cameras (though it could carry only one per mission). Air Force officials countered that the SR-71 was more capable because it was equipped with a better sensor suite, including three different cameras (area search, spotting, and mapping), IR and radar-imaging equipment, and special gear for collecting electronic-signals intelligence. Administration officials sought to resolve the question by pitting the two airplanes against one another in a fly-off competition called NICE GIRL in late 1967. Over the course of two weeks, A-12s and SR-71s flew three identical routes over the Mississippi River at one-hour intervals. Analysts from the CIA, National Photographic Interpretation Center (NPIC), Defense Intelligence Agency (DIA), and other military intelligence organizations found the results inconclusive. The A-12's camera covered a wider swath and had higher resolution, but the SR-71's sensors collected unique intelligence not yet available from the A-12. In light of Dennis Sullivan's BLACK SHIELD experiences, Air Force officials were forced to admit that some SR-71 sensors would have to be removed to make room for additional defensive avionics.[147] Aircraft performance was nearly identical. Both planes were designed to cruise at Mach 3.2; somewhat lower performance resulted from conservative operational practices with respect to redline temperature limits and fuel reserves. Because it was lighter, the A-12 had an altitude advantage of between 2,000 and 5,000 feet over the SR-71 at any given speed, though the SR-71 had slightly better range performance. Both had a relatively low RCS, with any vulnerabilities offset through the use of ECM gear.[148]

On May 16, 1968, despite the A-12's stellar performance in Southeast Asia, the new secretary of defense, Clark Clifford, reaffirmed the decision to terminate the OXCART program and mothball the aircraft. The president concurred a few days later, and the remaining Roadrunners at Kadena began packing up and preparing to return home to Area 51. Project Headquarters directed the squadron to continue phasing out all A-12 aircraft and support equipment under the SCOPE COTTON directive. Other than the J58 engines, few A-12 components could be salvaged for use with the SR-71 fleet. Even the exceptional OXCART cameras were unusable because they were too large to fit inside the SR-71's equipment bay.[149] So, one by one, the remaining A-12s were ferried to Palmdale for long-term storage, an exercise the Roadrunners nicknamed SCOPE BARN. The A-12T left first on May 29, followed three days later by Article 132. By macabre coincidence, Article 130 made its final flight the same day its sister ship, Article 129, was lost at sea. Oldest in the fleet, Article 121 was put out to pasture on June 6, followed days later by Article 128. As each airplane arrived, it was drained of fuel and squeezed into a tightly packed secure hangar at Lockheed's Site 2 facility.

The two surviving BLACK SHIELD airplanes were ferried back to Area 51 before going to final disposition at Palmdale. On June 9, Dennis Sullivan made the trip from Okinawa in Article 127, crossing the Pacific Ocean, California, and southern Nevada in just five and a half hours. Three days later the airplane made its final journey to Palmdale. Ken Collins departed Kadena in Article 131 on June 7 but was forced to land on Wake Island due to a severe fuel leak in the right engine nacelle. A recovery crew was dispatched to make basic repairs sufficient for the pilot to reach Hickam Air Force Base in Hawaii, where the A-12 could be fully serviced. Once the leak was fixed, Collins flew Article 131 at low altitude and subsonic speed, in the company of a tanker to top off his fuel from time to time. Over the course of several days, mechanics at Hickam struggled to solve the problem. Collins flew back to the mainland via commercial airline to attend Jack Weeks's funeral, leaving Frank Murray

The surviving A-12s were tightly packed into a building at Lockheed's Site 2 in Palmdale. Article 131 is in the immediate foreground. The second plane, Article 127, is wearing a bogus tail number as was typical during BLACK SHIELD missions. *Lockheed*

to deal with the balky airplane. Two attempts to fly Article 131 home were thwarted by a repeat of the fuel leak problem, which mechanics eventually traced to an unbalanced accessory drive that vibrated hard enough to crack an adjacent fuel line. With repairs complete, Murray was able to depart Hawaii for good and make a high-speed run to Area 51, finally bringing Article 131 home eleven days and forty minutes after departing Kadena.[150]

A few days later, in the predawn hours of June 21, 1968, Maj. Willys D. "Bill" Wuest briefed Murray on the weather for the final SCOPE BARN mission. To avoid drawing unwanted attention, the short subsonic flight was routed over the most sparsely populated regions of Death Valley, Owens Valley, and the southern Sierra Nevada. Wuest, also known as "the Bard of Beatty," read a poem he had written for the occasion, bringing a poignant emotional note to the proceedings. Afterward, Murray bid farewell to the duty officers in the Command Post before heading to the personal-equipment room to don his pressure suit. Life-support technicians then transported the pilot to the South Trim Pad and assisted him as he climbed into the A-12's cockpit for the last time. It was still dark when he took off, and after climbing to 40,000 feet, Murray couldn't resist turning back for a supersonic pass over Area 51 before decelerating and dropping to 30,000 feet to follow his planned route. In a relaxation of program security, the other OXCART project pilots brought their families to Palmdale to view the mission's climax. Upon reaching Palmdale, Murray performed two flybys, one while climbing in afterburner following a low approach. He then landed and taxied to Site 2. Murray later recalled, "This was the first and only time the family members saw the A-12 in flight."[151]

Though they could share their achievements with no one, the Roadrunners received numerous accolades presented by the deputy DCI, Adm. Rufus L. Taylor, at a secret ceremony held at Area 51 on June 26. Surprisingly, the pilots' wives were also allowed to attend this event. Kelly Johnson gave a moving address lamenting the demise of OXCART, which he considered his pinnacle achievement. The six pilots who participated in Operation BLACK SHIELD were awarded the CIA Intelligence Star for Valor, while squadron commander Hugh Slater and his deputy, Maynard Amundson, received the Air Force Legion of Merit.[152] Air Force Headquarters presented all members of Detachment 1, 1129th SAS, with the Air Force Outstanding Unit Award for exceptionally meritorious service in support of military operations from April 1966 to April 1968.[153]

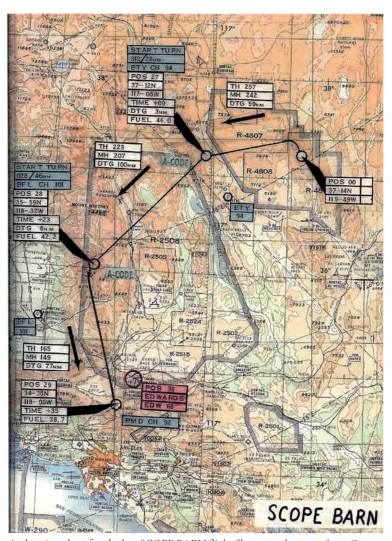

A planning chart for the last SCOPE BARN flight illustrates the route from Groom Lake, *at upper right*, to Palmdale. *Roadrunners*

Frank Murray made the final A-12 flight in Article 131 on June 21, 1968. *Roadrunners*

Adm. Rufus Taylor presented the CIA Star for Valor to BLACK SHIELD pilots Mel Vojvodich (*out of frame at left*), Dennis Sullivan, Jack Layton, Ken Collins, and Frank Murray. A posthumous award to Jack Weeks was accepted by his widow. *Roadrunners*

And so, Project OXCART came to a close, having never been employed for its intended purpose of strategic reconnaissance, a role then increasingly being assumed by imaging satellites. Though BLACK SHIELD yielded useful tactical-reconnaissance imagery, it contributed little to the CIA's strategic intelligence mission. Additionally, the A-12 lacked the affordability and quick-response capability of the U-2 and required substantially greater logistical support. In the end, OXCART's greatest legacy was one of technological achievement. Kelly Johnson's A-12 demonstrated unprecedented speed, range, and altitude, but the program's most important contributions lay in aerodynamic design, materials, engine performance, camera technology, electronic countermeasures, life-support systems, antiradar techniques, use of nonmetallic composite materials for major aircraft subassemblies, and improvements in manufacturing. Perhaps most important, it laid the foundation for future stealth research and development.[154]

Life after OXCART

Termination of OXCART had serious ramifications for the future of Area 51. To begin with, it was necessary to disband a joint organization comprising more than two thousand people, including over four hundred CIA and Air Force personnel and some 1,600 contractors. According to the writer of a February 1967 briefing note to DCI Helms, "Our main problem during the year will be to keep the disengagement of people under strict control, otherwise our operational capability may be jeopardized." He was particularly concerned with the possibility of a mass exodus of workers who might still be needed. "In any such termination," he wrote, "self-preservation impels people to want to jump ship."[155]

In April 1968, the CIA's deputy director for special activities noted that Helms agreed with Carl Duckett that it would be a good idea to shop around within the agency to see if they could come up with reasons to retain Area 51 beyond the end of OXCART. Duckett proposed a study to determine the least amount of funding necessary to keep Area 51 open on a modest scale, and he also suggested looking into the Air Force's interest in using the Groom Lake facility for future ad hoc programs.[156] Helms endorsed these recommendations at a meeting of the President's Foreign Intelligence Advisory Board the following week.[157] At that time, the TAGBOARD drone was still undergoing testing at the site, and the Air Force already had a modest project underway in one of the hangars on the North Ramp.

Project managers made an assessment of requirements and available assets and determined, at least, that they anticipated no need for construction of new facilities. Building 204, the existing Area 51 headquarters, would suffice to support base administration, finance, communications, security, civil engineering, and the dispensary, message center, and post office. Building 119, the Flight Operations facility and Command Post, remained available for flight planning and scheduling, crew briefing/debriefing, weather forecasting, flight safety, academic classrooms, and operations staff offices. The expected flight operations tempo also necessitated continued use of the Personal Equipment and Aircrew Survival facility, control tower and GCA, aircraft and facilities maintenance, dining facilities, billets, medical services, and recreation facilities and equipment. Fuel storage requirements included motor vehicle fuels and lubricants, aviation gasoline for the Constellations and U-3B, JP-4 for military aircraft, and PF-1/JSP-100 for the D-21B.

Some facilities were consolidated to reduce maintenance costs. A proposal to continue use of Hangar 17 for receiving, buildup, and checkout of D-21B camera packages was not approved. Instead, this operation was moved to Building 120, a former U-2 hangar that had been repurposed as the base Precision Measurement Equipment Laboratory (PMEL) and photo lab. The concrete flyaway pad adjacent to the north taxiway was designated for parking and servicing of the JB-52H, while the asphalt parking ramp near the Southend was allocated for personnel and cargo transport aircraft. Planners determined that a sizable fleet of ground vehicles were required, including three radio-equipped automobiles, one staff car, nine station wagons or crew buses, ten pickup trucks, at least one aircraft tug and one Coleman tractor, fire engines, and an assortment of fuel trucks.[158]

After OXCART, base administration remained in Building 204, visible at upper right, next to the dining facility. Base supply warehouses are at upper left. Operations was located behind Building 120, the hangar near lower left. The Quonset hut on the right side of the picture occasionally served as the base movie theater. *CIA*

Remaining OXCART ground support equipment was pressed into service for a variety of follow-on projects. *CIA*

Manpower requirements included Air Force maintenance staff, contractor technicians, life-support and medical personnel, test engineers, and flight crews. Civil engineers would be responsible for maintenance, utilities, and fire protection. Contract guards would provide physical and administrative security twenty-four hours a day, seven days a week, with limited peripheral patrols on weekends. Planners expected to support one B-52 sortie per week and as many as five each for the U-3B and UH-1F. As had been the case during OXCART, the helicopter was to be used mainly for search and rescue. One C-130 was retained as primary support aircraft for transporting supplies and equipment to and from Area 51. To reduce costs further, use of the three Lockheed Constellations for shuttling workers was set to end by about July 15, 1968. Shuttle service for remaining personnel would continue using C-47-, F-27-, and DC-6-type aircraft furnished by Carco. By mid-August the former A-12 maintenance section had been closed down, and all services and utilities were terminated. The support aircraft function moved to the north end of the base, resulting in improved management and utilization of resources, personnel, and facilities. Personnel supporting the TAGBOARD project took over the major portion of the old Operations Building, relegating the remaining 1129th SAS officers to that portion of the building previously known as the Base Operations and Training Area.[159]

As things began to wind down, Col. Slater was reassigned as vice commander of the 20th Tactical Fighter Wing at RAF Wethersfield in England.[160] A small cadre of 1129th SAS personnel remained at Area 51 to oversee the closeout of OXCART and the final test flights of TAGBOARD / SENIOR BOWL before that program was moved to Beale in January 1969. As the last of the Roadrunners, they dubbed themselves the "Damn Few Of Us Left Society," or DFOULS. Lt. Col. Gilmore L. Sanders was the ranking Air Force officer at the site and shared C-130 crew duty with Lt. Col. Walter T. Smith, Maj. George W. "Robbie" Robinson, and Capt. Ronald L. Girard. Having first arrived at Area 51 in December 1962, Maj. Harold

Detachment 1, 3rd Weather Wing, commanded by Maj. Ralph "Bill" Thomas (*bottom row, second from left*) from 1965 to 1968, provided meteorological data to flight planners at Area 51 and Kadena. This photo was taken at Area 51 on July 2, 1968. *Roadrunners*

Murphy Greene of the REECo culinary services branch reportedly ran the mess hall with an iron fist, often scolding officers and contractors—regardless of rank—for violating one of his rules. He also provided an excellent meal selection, including steak and seafood, which was much appreciated at the remote outpost. *Roadrunners*

On April 6, 1965, Greene posed as a fisherman for a gag photo of the flooded west side of Groom Lake. This picture appears to have been taken from the edge of the concrete RCS pylon pad. *Roadrunners*

Burgeson was dubiously honored with "Old Timer rating #1." Maj. Forrest W. Calico shared flight surgeon duties with Maj. Theodore "Ted" Dake Jr.; a relative newcomer, Calico had arrived at the Area only in May 1968. Majors Bill Thomas and Bill Wuest constituted the entire weather detachment. Captains Ted Angle and Joe Pinaud remained to fly the UH-1F. Maj. George W. Atkinson, Hal Herring, Rick Richter, and Arnie Williams rounded out the remaining DFOULS membership.[161]

In the spring of 1969, the CIA assigned Richard A. "Dick" Sampson as the new commander of Area 51. He was a good choice, already having been deeply involved with the OXCART project as an agency security officer. After joining the CIA in 1951, following graduation from Michigan State University with a bachelor of science degree in police administration, he spent the next thirteen years in domestic and foreign assignments as a special agent, inspector, and security officer attached to the Security Services Division, Office of the Secretary of Defense. In 1964, Sampson was assigned to the Services and Support Group, Headquarters Command, at Bolling Air Force Base, where he worked with fellow agency security officers Joe Murphy and Herb Saunders to handle program security for the U-2, A-12, and SR-71. Among other accomplishments, they had developed a forty-eight-hour preliminary background investigation that streamlined the process of screening new employees without unnecessarily slowing work on those high-priority programs.[162]

To reduce travel costs and bureaucracy, Sampson suggested setting up a West Coast office for the Services and Support Group. His boss, William Kotapish, passed the recommendation to Jack Ledford, who subsequently approved the plan. Since it had been Sampson's idea, he was transferred to California in 1965 to establish and manage the new organization, which focused on industrial security for various CIA contractors but primarily monitored Lockheed's security performance in Burbank with regard to OXCART. With Kelly Johnson's assistance, he oversaw the growth of his group's workspace from a 10-square-foot closet in a hangar to a slightly larger office adjacent to the company's communications center. In 1966, he arranged for a new operating location in the basement of the Tishman Building near downtown Los Angeles that came to be known as the Western Industrial Liaison Detachment, or WILD. In his capacity as OXCART security officer, Sampson also provided assistance to the families of Walter Ray and Jack Weeks following their fatal accidents.[163]

Immediately upon assignment to Area 51, he moved to Las Vegas with his wife, Janet, and their two children. An avid outdoorsman who enjoyed sailing and camping,

Dick Sampson, while in command of Area 51, changed the commuter shuttle's call sign to "Janet," after his wife. *Roadrunners*

Sampson spent his free time at Groom Lake collecting rocks and minerals and land-sailing across the dry lakebed on a modified Aqua Cat catamaran. Before departing Nevada in 1971 for a stint at the Air War College at Maxwell Air Force Base, Alabama, Sampson left his most indelible mark on the secret base when he assigned the call sign "Janet" to commuter flights transporting workers between Las Vegas, Area 51, and Burbank.[164] Surprisingly, despite many changes of command, use of this call sign endured into the twenty-first century.

In an interesting postscript to the OXCART era, project officer John Parangosky (writing pseudonymously as Thomas P. McIninch) documented the program's history in "The OXCART Story" for *Studies in Intelligence*, a classified CIA periodical. There was some initial resistance prior to publication. In May 1971 an official at Air Force Headquarters sent a letter to NRO director John McLucas, stating, "I cannot concur with the CIA intention to publish subject story in a collateral security channel which will obviously be disseminated outside of NRO agencies." The official was particularly concerned that "the article exposes the existence of Area 51, ADP covert methodology, and names of individuals with extensive backgrounds in covert reconnaissance."[165] Certainly, covert "sources and methods," as they are known in intelligence community parlance, are sensitive issues. The existence of Area 51, however, was already widely known and publicly acknowledged. Ultimately, "The OXCART Story" was first published in the Winter 1971 issue of *Studies*, and again in the Summer 1982 issue after the existence of the A-12 had been officially declassified. A redacted version of the article, lacking many names and all references to Area 51, was declassified and publicly released several years later.

A Bird in the Hand

Advances in miniaturization of electronic components and other technologies led some at the CIA to contemplate development of small, unmanned reconnaissance aircraft that might, with sufficiently low radar, visual, and acoustic signatures, reconnoiter areas of interest without detection. Existing airborne collection systems such as the U-2 and A-12 were large and had to fly very high and very fast to survive within contested airspace. They were also expensive to produce and operate and carried human crew members who might be killed or captured if an airplane were shot down. Alternatives under consideration included smaller, cheaper unmanned vehicles capable of flying at low altitudes while carrying or emplacing small, lightweight, low-power, solid-state sensors. This system concept required using the most-advanced microelectronics, microminiature sensors and power sources, communications, and control systems available.

Agency planners envisioned a new level of capability for photographic-reconnaissance missions as well as for emplacement of electronic intelligence-collection payloads at strategic targets hundreds of miles inside China, Russia, Cuba, North Vietnam, and other denied areas. Proposed targets included missile ranges, nuclear test facilities, biological and chemical weapon test areas, and other highly restricted sites. Collected information would be stored on board for later retrieval via radio transmissions to overhead platforms such as a U-2 or relay satellite. The resulting development of a vehicle and associated component subsystems was organized under the cryptonym AQUILINE and fell under the purview of the agency's Office of Research and Development (ORD). In 1965, the ORD began work on a concept for an inexpensive remotely piloted aircraft (RPA) about the size and appearance of a large bird. By mid-November, only one company had responded favorably to a request for proposals (RFP). One year later, following a $96,000 study effort to analyze system and vehicle-performance requirements, and to provide preliminary designs, the CIA awarded Douglas Aircraft Company of Santa Monica, California, the first of several contracts for development of an operational RPA system.[166]

The agency established the ORD to conceive and devise intelligence applications from scientific and technical advances and discoveries, and to support intelligence collection by advanced technical means. It was staffed with dynamic and creative individuals, including Applied Physics division chief David L. Christ and his deputy, Donald Reiser, who helped pioneer the development of low-voltage transistors and micropower electronics. Other team members included audio-surveillance expert Cadwallader V. Noyes, who transferred from the Radio Physics division in 1965, and Charles N. Adkins, a talented physicist and aerodynamicist. In May 1966, Frank A. Briglia of the ORD's new Special Projects Group was designated AQUILINE project manager. According to Adkins, Christ frequently delighted in recounting his first RFP meeting at Douglas. "I told them we wanted an unmanned aircraft that would fly over 1,000 miles; have an autopilot with complete onboard navigation, a payload of a few pounds for taking pictures or collecting intelligence of one kind or another, and a wingspan of only 10 feet or so; and look like a bird," he reportedly said.[167]

The Douglas engineers were probably incredulous, but they valiantly tackled the problem. They built upon foundational studies by researchers from the ORD and Naval Weapons Center China Lake near Inyokern, California, for a very small RPA that—even from a short distance—would look very much like a large bird in gliding flight. Conceptually, the platform could loiter for long periods of time in target areas while going virtually unnoticed. It would be designed to blend into the natural physical signal environment of living birds. Extended loiter time would permit detailed examination of targets of interest and allow a wide variety of technical intelligence missions, from signals intercepts to air-particulate sampling. Being unmanned, unarmed, and less expensive than conventional aircraft, it could essentially be considered expendable and therefore deployable against heavily defended targets. Additionally, in the event that one was shot down or captured, the small size and innocuous nature of the vehicle would make it more politically palatable to employ than a conventional aircraft. It could also complement existing high-altitude collection systems by providing more-detailed examination of selected targets, especially those hidden beneath cloud cover.

Technical goals for AQUILINE were challenging but not insurmountable. After considering a wide range of aerodynamic-lift devices including balloons, ballistic and powered gliders, and helicopters, the ORD team settled on the powered-glider concept. This offered a small, aerodynamically clean vehicle that would easily contain the kinds of miniature payloads and subsystems required for desired missions. There were a variety of practical and available propulsion systems powered by two- and four-cycle internal-combustion engines or fuel cells, any of which could potentially propel the vehicle to a maximum range of 1,200 to 2,400 nautical miles. Available miniature radioisotope-powered systems offered a range of 25,000 to 36,000 nautical miles or flight duration of up to thirty days. There were even plans for an advanced radioisotope power source that would allow the RPA to loiter over its target for as long as 120 days.

Tests of mockup models demonstrated that the birdlike craft should have sufficient low observability (visual, acoustic, radar, and IR signatures) so as to be immersed in the indigenous signal environment of the target area, loitering unobtrusively while performing a mission. Existing guidance and navigation systems including over-the-horizon (OTH) radar, radio direction finding, satellite navigation, and global-range radio were capable of directing the RPA to within a few miles of its destination. A subminiature television camera was available that could provide visible-light and IR imagery for both navigation and surveillance. Secure communications for data transmission and vehicle control were easily achievable at line-of-sight ranges and were at least feasible over longer ranges using airborne or satellite relays or OTH radar systems. Several ORD divisions labored to develop photographic, audio, ELINT, air-sampling, and other sensors that could be carried on board or dropped over a target to maximize AQUILINE's diversified potential. Researchers also examined a variety of deployment options that included launch from a boat, airplane, ground vehicle, or man-portable system.

In 1967, Douglas merged with McDonnell Aircraft Company to become McDonnell Douglas Corporation, and the AQUILINE effort was assigned to McDonnell Douglas Astronautics Company (MDAC) in Huntington Beach, California. During this time, ORD and MDAC designers strove to develop an initial operational-capability prototype. The AQUILINE Mk.1 looked more like a conventional R/C model of airplane than a bird. The configuration featured a cruciform tube-and-wing planform with straight, tapering airfoils that curved upward toward the tips. A dorsally mounted V tail provided directional stability. A two-stroke engine powered a twin-bladed pusher propeller on the aft end, and a slow-scan television camera eye dominated the nose. Internal space in the forward fuselage was devoted to fuel tanks, navigation and communications equipment, a remotely controlled autopilot, and sensor payloads weighing as much as 5 pounds. The Mk.1 prototype was designed to climb as high as 10,000 feet, with a maximum range of 600 nautical miles. Concurrent development programs focused on aerodynamics, propulsion, navigation, communications, survivability, intelligence-collection payloads, and ground-based control systems. To test the vehicle, the CIA established a secure, instrumented test range at Randsburg Wash within the vast expanse of the Naval Weapons Center. Instrumentation was supplied and maintained by MDAC personnel.[168]

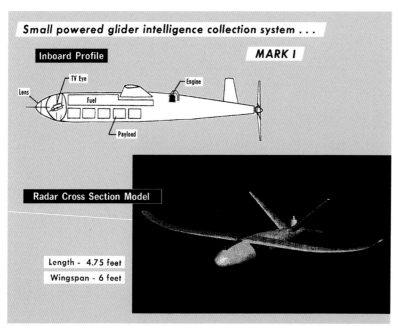

The AQUILINE Mk.1 was powered by a two-stroke engine driving a twin-bladed pusher propeller. It was designed to carry payloads up to 5 pounds as high as 10,000 feet, with a maximum range of 600 nautical miles. *CIA*

The MDAC prototype systems development program resulted in design and fabrication of three Mk.1 vehicles, each with increased capability. They were intended to be test-flown for proof of concept and to collect basic flight performance data. These vehicles were also intended to carry developmental subsystems for experimental flight testing. The RPA was designed to be catapult-launched from an inclined rail and recovered with a net strung between two poles. Initial flight testing began in October 1967 and almost immediately ran into difficulties.

When the first flight ended in a crash, Adkins warned Briglia that the MDAC team "knew nothing of the sport of making and flying R/C aircraft." Vehicle #1 was repaired and made three additional flights to verify launch and recovery techniques and general handling characteristics. Unfortunately, two of those flights also resulted in crashes. Briglia, therefore, decided to forego further R/C testing and opted to push ahead on autopilot development with Vehicle #2 in the hope of averting further problems of human error. The Randsburg Wash facilities had proven more than adequate, and, despite the mishaps, early testing yielded useful data. The next flight was to be fully automatic, and the MDAC team was confident that an impending success would vindicate past failures and seemingly excessive costs that had plagued the project to this point.

Adkins and Reiser were on hand to observe the first autopilot flight. Preparations for takeoff seemed to drag on forever, but eventually Vehicle #2's engine started and the tiny plane vaulted into the sky. Moments later it entered a steep dive and disappeared from view over a cliff. An examination of the model's shattered remains revealed that the longitudinal accelerometer had been subjected to exceptionally high acceleration as the vehicle moved along its launch rail. This caused the autopilot to erroneously register a nose-up attitude and compensate by moving the control surfaces to pitch nose down. Reiser requested the test data and autopilot schematics from MDAC and directed Adkins to perform a complete stability-and-control analysis as soon as possible. "I told Frank [Briglia] that the analysis showed [that the airplane had] no stability margin at all and that, in all probability, the vehicle would have crashed in the last test even if the accelerometer had been properly locked out during launch," he reported. Engineers at MDAC agreed with this assessment and admitted they had overlooked the necessity of giving the latest autopilot parameters to their control system analyst.[169]

The mishap effectively ended AQUILINE Phase I testing. The original plan for the second phase called for design, fabrication, and testing of a small airplane with improved subsystems and a four-cycle engine, as well as demonstration of a limited operational capability. In the wake of the accident, the agency's Science and Technology Panel conducted a thorough program review, ultimately concluding that there was no technical reason not to proceed directly to Phase III. The Phase II program would

Designers intended the AQUILINE to resemble an actual living bird. This full-scale model was even painted to look as if it had feathers. *CIA*

not have produced a birdlike vehicle and would therefore have had a significantly lower order of penetration survivability. Proceeding directly to Phase III would, by establishing a single well-defined goal, be more efficient from a cost standpoint and move the program forward toward the desired operational concept. The new target date for the maiden flight of AQUILINE Mk.2 was set for April 1970, more than two years ahead of schedule.[170]

That did not mean everything was going smoothly. Although the vehicle's visual and acoustic signatures met expectations, its RCS was still considered too high. At low frequencies the RCS was less than 0.10 square meter, providing a radar signature smaller than that of an eagle, but spikes of backscatter in the VHF band increased the likelihood of detection. Studies showed that this was not an insurmountable problem. Deficiencies with the navigational system represented a more serious concern. AQUILINE still lacked a programmable autopilot and had to be remotely operated. Additionally, once it flew beyond line of sight, all navigational commands had to be relayed through a high-flying aircraft. Signals transmitted from a medium-altitude platform such as a DC-6 loitering at 25,000 feet would give the RPA a range of 250 nautical miles; transmitting from a U-2 at 70,000 feet would extend the vehicle's range only to 350 nautical miles. These issues required resolution in order to meet desired operational requirements.[171]

In January 1969 the Office of Special Activities (OSA) was working in close coordination with the ORD to resolve problems associated with evolving AQUILINE from a developmental test article into a practical and viable intelligence tool within the next two years. Facilities at the Randsburg Wash range were not considered adequate for ORD-directed flight testing of the new vehicle or for subsequent operational training to be conducted by the OSA, but program managers felt that Area 51 was ideal for such activities. The agency now focused efforts on logistical requirements for preparation of selected portions of the Area 51 facilities, and on procurement of support equipment including the first AQUILINE ground control station

(AGCS-1) and associated specialized communications gear. A Cessna 210D, previously used by the Roadrunners, was selected for use as a chase plane and airborne communications relay. Plans called for equipping another aircraft—possibly a U-3B, T-33, or C-130—with a satellite communications (SATCOM) link for longer-range relay duties.[172]

OSA personnel were integrated into the program in such a way that as AQUILINE began to produce an operational capability, they would already have had the required training and experience necessary for a smooth transition from research and development to intelligence collection. Under the revised program plan, the OSA continued to participate with ORD in these development efforts. During joint planning and coordination meetings with the OSA, Dave Christ proposed procuring seven prototype AQUILINE vehicles as engineering-development articles but ultimately accepted a decision to build only six. He further recommended that at the conclusion of testing, the remaining prototypes be rehabilitated and turned over to OSA for use in training, follow-on testing, and refinement of operational concepts.

Anticipating a high attrition rate among flight test vehicles, Christ assumed that only three RPAs would likely be available for these purposes. He therefore proposed that four additional vehicles be procured during FY 1971 to ensure the capability of OSA to attain an initial marginal operational posture by the end of that year. Additionally, he suggested purchasing a mobile ground-control unit for operational use by the OSA. Planners determined that manpower requirements to support AQUILINE training, testing, development of operational concepts, and possible deployment would comprise seventeen positions. These included a field program director (FPD), three flight planners / vehicle operators, two administrative personnel, two support personnel, two contract security guards, five automation technicians, one weather specialist, and one medical technician. Agency comptrollers determined there was sufficient funding available to support the AQUILINE program at Area 51 on an austere basis, plus coverage of deployment contingencies.[173]

All AQUILINE vehicles instrumented as flight test articles were to be under ORD control until such time as they were no longer required for developmental efforts. They would then be retrofitted for operational missions, as would AGCS-1, and management and control of the system would be transferred to the FPD. Planners in the OSA envisioned a requirement for as many as eighteen operational AQUILINE vehicles to support intelligence missions worldwide. As during OXCART, all operational vehicles would be stationed at Area 51, which would serve as a permanent training and support base for forward deployments, as required. Four of these would be maintained in a state of operational readiness for immediate deployment. At least one of the remaining aircraft would be used for training purposes. At the conclusion of training, Project Headquarters would subject each deployable field team to an operational-readiness evaluation before certifying that team ready for overseas deployment. Upon receipt of mission requirements from Project Headquarters, the FPD at Area 51 would direct accomplishment of mission planning and preparation of the mobile AQUILINE teams to satisfy the levied mission requirements. Deployment teams would practice their operational missions at Area 51 prior to departure. All necessary ground-control and support personnel would then be deployed to the forward operating location. Mission-ready AQUILINE vehicles and spare equipment were to be ferried to the forward base from Area 51, along with all necessary mission flight-planning materials.[174]

The OSA staff drafted a security plan for the upcoming operations at Groom Lake. Under the new guidelines, AQUILINE became known as RECHARTER within OSA areas of responsibility, and was given the unclassified nickname Project 274. These designators were to be used in all verbal and written correspondence with Area 51. Confusingly, the unclassified nickname was later changed to Project M277, and the ORD continued to use the term AQUILINE within its own areas of responsibility and communications channels. Project Headquarters directed that following completion of flight testing, operational activities would transition to the cryptonym AZANA.

The OSA was responsible for all aspects of security at the test site. Project Headquarters and the Area 51 Security Office maintained permanent records of names of project personnel and approved visitors. Access to sensitive information was restricted to an absolute minimum number of persons, each briefed only to the extent necessary to make possible their maximum contribution to the project effort. In order to be granted clearance, individuals from the CIA, other government agencies, and industry partners were subject to at least a fifteen-year background investigation. Assuming they had legitimate need to know, project personnel with access to Area 51 could be briefed into the general purpose of the AQUILINE/RECHARTER system, mission equipment, configurations and capabilities, aircraft performance characteristics, and identification of other contractors, suppliers, and vendors. Very few of these individuals were ever granted official confirmation of the true identity of Project Headquarters, details of broad mission objectives, operational mission details, future plans, or the project's relationship to other classified programs. A staff security officer was assigned to assist the program manager in Project RECHARTER facilities at Area 51 with protection of project assets and personnel, and to provide liaison and coordination with the base commander. Contingency and cover plans were developed for flight activities, particularly those that would take the RPA off-range.[175]

As of March 5, 1969, arrangements for use of test facilities at Area 51 were progressing rapidly. Requirements for billeting and messing of personnel were expected to be sporadic until the spring of 1970, by which time the project anticipated having approximately twenty-five personnel on-site. The west half of Hangar 6 was partitioned off as a work area for maintenance and secure storage of the aircraft and ground station equipment. A lean-to on the north side of the building provided adequate shop and office space to meet MDAC specifications. The concrete parking apron between the hangar and the lakebed would serve as an RPA launch site. The base provided three 4×4 pickup trucks with ground-to-air radios, and two jeeps were borrowed from Detachment G at Edwards. The agency established a secure communications link between Area 51 and Project Headquarters (cable address: ABEAM). Additionally, arrangements were made to provide airlift of MDAC personnel from Huntington Beach to the test site on a weekly basis once flight testing got underway. The Cessna 210D proved unsuitable as a chase aircraft and was subsequently replaced with a UH-1F helicopter. Planners still needed an airborne communications relay capable of six to eight hours of sustained flight at altitudes between 17,000 and 25,000 feet and sought to lease a Carco C-47 for that role.[176]

In August 1969, the agency established an AQUILINE Division within the OSA Operations Directorate. This new organization comprised five positions, foremost among them the division chief, Col. James W. Cherbonneaux, a former U-2 pilot who had received his training at Watertown in the summer of 1956. His deputy was Lt. Col. Hank Meierdierck, former Watertown U-2 instructor pilot and OXCART administrative officer. Meierdierck would serve as FPD throughout the AQUILINE/RECHARTER flight test program at Area 51. Other personnel included an operational planning officer, an Automatic Data Processing programs officer from the Office of Computer Services, and a secretary/stenographer. Andrew J. Frisina was assigned to head Meierdierck's administrative staff at the test site. Walter Smith was one of several ground-based pilots trained to remotely fly the rail-launched RPA from its ground-based control station.[177]

The final air vehicle configuration was about 5 feet long and had a 7.5-foot wingspan and a maximum design gross weight of 86 to 105 pounds, though the prototypes weighed slightly less, each averaging about 78 pounds. Twin ventral fins at the aft end provided lateral directional stability. Instead of having the desired four-stroke engine, the vehicle was powered by a McCulloch MC-101 single-cylinder, 12.5-horsepower, two-stroke engine. This power plant drove a twin-bladed pusher propeller that provided enough thrust to allow for a maximum speed of 60 to 65 knots. Average loiter speeds ranged from 43

Hank Meierdierck served as field program director for AQUILINE at Area 51. *USAF*

to 50 knots, and the craft had a 40-knot stall speed. The vehicle was designed to be capable of maintaining 60-knot airspeeds at an altitude of 1,000 feet for up to thirty hours, while carrying a 15-pound sensor payload. This was due, in part, to the engine having extremely high fuel efficiency, approximately 480 nautical miles per gallon. Although the RPA had a design service ceiling of around 11,800 feet on a standard day, engineers predicted an absolute ceiling of up to 13,000 feet under ideal conditions.[178]

Meierdierck's team was in place at Area 51 by mid-June 1970, with a view toward completing all necessary developmental flight testing to establish the air vehicle's total-system parameters within six to eight months. Before flying the RPA, they first tested the launch-rail system to make sure it would propel the vehicle with sufficient speed to become airborne, approximately 60 knots. The director of special activities, Brig. Gen. Harold F. Knowles, and several OSA staff were on hand to observe one such test on July 23. "The rail testing was delayed one day for our benefit," he later reported. Overall it was successful, but the recovery net broke during capture. While at Area 51, Knowles took some time to try to smooth out friction that had developed between personnel from the two agency offices involved. "I made it perfectly clear to everyone that AQUILINE responsibility presently rests with ORD . . . and that OSA personnel will not interfere," he later wrote, adding, "Everyone assured me that there would be no sovereignty problems."[179]

During his two-day visit, Knowles also reviewed an agreement between the agency and the Air Force that would allow SAC to use Area 51 as a dispersal base for the SR-71 and a support fleet of KC-135Q tankers during periods of national emergency. Such an action would take place only in the event of DEFCON 2, a wartime defense posture just one step short of nuclear war. The last time SAC had been ordered to DEFCON 2 was during the Cuban Missile Crisis in 1962. In accordance with a pact signed in October 1969, the 9th Strategic Reconnaissance Wing had already stored a variety of spare parts and ground-support equipment in base facilities previously dedicated to OXCART. "Some of their equipment was pre-positioned in this area, I believe, in hopes of getting squatters rights because we had denied SAC use of some parts of [the base]," Knowles noted. Although the desert test site was nearly ideal for SAC deployments in terms of cost and adequacy of facilities, the necessity for regular equipment maintenance placed an undue burden on the base security force. Following his inspection, Knowles hoped to negotiate a better agreement that would minimize, if not eliminate, periodic SAC maintenance visits and reduce the quantity of stored materiel so as to afford the agency ample use the facility. Although Area 51 workspaces were increasingly being devoted to Air Force tenant activities, the CIA asserted its claim on Hangar 6 for AQUILINE and Hangar 8 for another project.[180]

Over the next ten months, only six sorties were accomplished with four flightworthy AQUILINE prototypes, and three of these were destroyed in crashes. Initial launch tests involved dummy air vehicles, or QTVs, that were unpowered and uninstrumented. The first fully functional flight vehicle, designated FV-1, completed its maiden flight on August 10, 1970. It successfully demonstrated basic handling qualities but suffered minor damage during recovery. The second craft, FV-2, stalled and spun into the ground the following month due to erroneous airspeed readings. On the third flight, the first vehicle (now redesignated FV-1A) was flown again with improved control system gains to correct the problem encountered on the previous flight. It was also equipped with stall strips on the wings and enlarged ventral fins for greater stability, modifications later incorporated into the remaining airframes. The only difficulty encountered on this flight came when the drone missed the net during recovery.

In December, FV-3 made the fourth flight, reaching an altitude of 10,800 feet at a gross weight of around 80 pounds. Elation at this success was marred somewhat when, after transferring from automatic control to manual via the chase helicopter, a specious command shut down the engine and the vehicle was lost. The fifth flight, in March 1971, was a total success. Ground pilots practiced visual approach with the help of the onboard television camera and demonstrated constant-attitude, no-flare landings ending with successful net recovery. Landing approaches were accomplished with the assistance of the Area 51 GCA and beacon. Observers on the ground and in chase planes had difficulty spotting the diminutive craft while it was airborne. "It really looked like an eagle or buzzard when it was in the air," said Meierdierck. Though this attribute was promising for operational use, it was exceedingly frustrating for test personnel. In fact, chase observers had difficulty seeing the AQUILINE vehicle even after its entire upper surface had been painted bright orange. The following month, FV-4 performed the first flight outside the local area. Unfortunately, this vehicle crashed off-range some five hours into the ambitious demonstration.[181]

Overall test results were decidedly mixed. The landing sequence, for example, was very hard on the vehicles even under the best of circumstances. The net-recovery method nearly always resulted in damage to the wings or propeller. Consequently, one or more prototypes were undergoing repair almost constantly, and the sortie rate was less than one flight per month. A technical consultant finally recommended an alternative "nose bump" belly-landing method, which was successfully demonstrated following a minimal test series using dummy vehicles. Although this technique apparently yielded substantial savings—presumably as the result of reduced downtime and repair costs—program managers still favored using the net. Flight performance, on the other hand, was generally satisfactory. The vehicle's lift-to-drag ratio was 10 percent better than predicted, and in operational testing one AQUILINE vehicle flew 130 miles and obtained high-resolution imagery of its target before successfully returning to the launch site. At least

An AQUILINE flight test vehicle swoops past the northern edge of the Papoose Mountains, looking every inch the bird of prey it was meant to resemble. *CIA*

one program manager lamented that the airplane's mission capabilities and overall reliability were never satisfactorily demonstrated. Moreover, no significant effort had been made to put any of the machines into a truly operational configuration, or to simulate a realistic operational life cycle. Program officials estimated that necessary improvements to make AQUILINE into a practical long-range reconnaissance system would take an additional two to three years and cost another $35 million.[182]

That didn't sit well with Project Headquarters. From the beginning, funding for the program had been provided in piecemeal fashion, project by project, as various program areas were defined. Funding for AQUILINE was based on a master ORD agreement with MDAC. Several individual support contracts with other companies and a moderate number of AQUILINE-related projects (mainly payload development) were monitored by other CIA divisions and funded separately. The basic program structure supported tasks involving subsystem development, environmental studies, mission analysis, and flight testing. Individual funding of these tasks in FY 1967 created unnecessary complications in contract negotiations and management and increased the problems of coordinating and synchronizing technical development of each subsystem.

The agency comptroller introduced a new arrangement for program funding and control in FY 1968. A master contract established quarterly funding limitations, under which MDAC requested funds on a task basis against estimated costs, technical milestones, and delivery schedules. This plan provided the necessary flexibility for program development while assuring adequate control of expenditures. It didn't work as well as hoped, however, and schedule slippage led to increased expenditures. Anticipated extension of the flight test program into the spring of 1971 led the ORD to request another $1.1 million from the OSA for contractor support and $270,000 for logistical and materiel support at Area 51. As delays and costs mounted, according to Meierdierck, a series of meetings between the CIA and MDAC became increasingly heated, with the contractor wanting to charge the agency ten times the amount of the approved budget allotment. Subsequent to an extensive program review, headquarters canceled AQUILINE in November 1971.[183]

Termination and closeout activities began almost immediately and were anticipated to be complete by about January 15, 1972. All AQUILINE assets then in the possession of MDAC and various subcontractors were inventoried, packaged, and shipped to Area 51 for semipermanent storage along with materiel already on-site. Four RPAs remained: three fully functional flight vehicles (FV-1A, FV-5, and FV-6) and one QTV dummy vehicle. The OSA retained custodial responsibility for this property and for providing relevant documentation to potential future users. CIA officials briefed key individuals in the Air Force, Navy, Army, and Marine Corps on the AQUILINE program, emphasizing the agency's willingness to turn over all remaining assets to any interested organization. The OSA planned to maintain these assets, intact, until June 30, 1972. After that date, if there were no offers to adopt the program as a whole, the material was to be redistributed on a piecemeal basis. There were only a few low-key inquiries as to the availability of component parts, technology, and mission payloads as the deadline approached, so the OSA moved to release these items for redistribution.[184]

Before this could happen, however, someone at the agency determined there might be an urgent need for the birdlike RPA, after all. The OSA sent a cable on November 22, 1972, announcing the possible reactivation of the program as AQUILINE II. Within two weeks, plans were well underway for a crash program to check out the three existing flight vehicles and retrofit the remaining QTV to the same configuration as FV-5. All work was to take place at Area 51, including two test flights using FV-1A. The first of these was intended to demonstrate that all equipment was still functional after more than a year in storage. The second flight was to be a full mission dress rehearsal to an altitude of 5,500 feet while carrying a video sensor payload, radar altimeter, miniature navigation transponder, and compact S-band radar tracker. Aircraft configuration requirements included the nose skid, large tail fins, and extended wingtips. The agency solicited bids from MDAC and EG&G, but AQUILINE II was apparently canceled even before the field unit deployed to the test site.[185]

Just over six months later, the OSA approved a request to downgrade the highly sensitive AQUILINE program from top secret to secret, so the agency's training department could use information about the program in a management training course. The final nail in AQUILINE's coffin was driven home on September 13, 1973, when the director of special activities, Brig. Gen. Wendell L. Bevan Jr., advised the OSA director of logistics that all remaining program assets were to be turned over to the Army Electronics Command for its burgeoning Remotely Piloted Vehicles program. This transfer was to be accomplished on a nonreimbursable basis, with the Army paying only the cost of shipping. It was an anticlimactic end to a revolutionary research-and-development effort. Evolution of the AQUILINE concept required agency scientists to take a hard look at the future of technical intelligence collection and create innovative solutions to challenging problems. The resulting efforts were catalytic in generating a variety of new technologies. Small IR scanners, microminiaturized receivers, recorders, communication and navigation equipment, and more not only had applications within the AQUILINE program but also met more-general needs of the intelligence community as a whole.[186]

Specter of the Bomb

Despite having moved nuclear testing underground, activities at the NTS continued to affect Area 51 operations. In particular, two cratering tests planned for October 1969 posed a serious threat of potential blast damage and fallout at Groom Lake. Designed to excavate enormous amounts of hard rock, both were part of the Plowshare program. Scientists at Lawrence Radiation Laboratory (LRL), Livermore, California, hoped that resulting data would be applicable to the use of nuclear explosives for large-scale excavation projects such as constructing harbors along shorelines lacking sheltering coves, or even for digging a second Panama Canal. The first shot, called Sturtevant, was to be fired about 800 feet below ground, with a yield of 170 to 250 kilotons. Researchers expected the explosion to produce a crater 300 to 500 feet deep and up to 1,400 feet across. This was to be followed by shot Yawl, with a yield of 750 to 900 kilotons. Buried nearly 1,000 feet underground, this device would blast a crater 500 to 700 feet deep and as much as 1,500 feet across.[187]

LRL geologist Larry Ramspott was tasked with scouting the best locations in which to conduct these tests, no easy task because the physicists wanted nonlayered, uniformly hard, dense rock such as granite. To simplify their calculations, they also required that the test site have relatively level ground contours. Since much of the NTS consisted of alternating layers of soft and hard volcanic rock, Ramspott was forced to consider areas along the easternmost boundary of the NTS and beyond. He studied geologic maps to find quartzite outcrops surrounded by sufficiently flat ground to a radius of several thousand yards. The best candidates were located a few miles east of Groom Pass and just south of Groom Lake Road, placing them closer to the Area 51 cantonment than any previous full-scale nuclear experiments. Some four decades later, Ramspott wrote, "It took several months of negotiations before permission was obtained to carry out exploratory drilling at the [Sturtevant] site, without any agreement that the test would be allowed."[188]

In April 1969, an exploratory hole for Sturtevant was drilled in the southwest corner of Area 51, just 6 miles west of the main camp. Ramspott selected a candidate site for Yawl just over 1 mile farther west, at the edge of Area 15. Workers drilled several narrow holes to determine how deeply buried the quartzite was beneath a layer of alluvium. A larger drill rig was then used to bore a 900-foot-deep exploratory hole that might later serve to contain test instrumentation. Core samples indicated the site would be acceptable, so the work crew drilled a 1,250-foot instrumentation hole and a 900-foot emplacement hole for a nuclear device. The project gave Ramspott an appreciation for the hydrologic situation that made Yucca Flat ideal for nuclear testing. "When we drilled in Groom Lake Valley, the depth to the water table was a few hundred feet," he wrote. "In nearby Yucca Flat it was more than 1,500 feet."[189] While the Yawl site's shallow water table was somewhat less than ideal, it was apparently not considered a deal breaker.

To ensure personnel safety at the nearby installation, E. O. Dahle of Sandia Laboratories analyzed the predicted effects the blasts would have on Area 51. Predictive models for both shots focused on atmospheric overpressures, radiation hazards, base surge and ejecta, possible damage to Groom Lake Road, potential evacuation of workers from Area 51, and possible firing delays. Predicted effects of both shots proved similar. According to Dahle's safety analysis for Sturtevant, "Anticipated ground motion at Area 51 Camp is below the damage threshold for structures, therefore, only minimal architectural damage is expected to occur to buildings, utilities or other camp facilities."[190]

Air blast in excess of 15 millibars had the potential to damage doors, window glass, ceiling-mounted light fixtures, and delicate instrumentation within unhardened structures. Dahle calculated that peak overpressures of as much as 30 millibars might be expected at Area 51 under unfavorable wind and temperature conditions. Although test planners promised to fire the shot only under more-ideal atmospheric conditions, he recommended removal of window panels where feasible, or at least opening windows to mitigate changes in air pressure. The same conditions held true for Yawl.

Each explosion was expected to produce a massive base surge, a cloud of dirt and debris towering nearly a mile high with a radius of 4 to 6 miles. "With the Area 51 Camp more than eight miles distant [from Yawl ground zero]," Dahle wrote, "the base surge is not expected to reach the camp."

A drilling crew prepares an emplacement hole for subterranean detonation of an experimental nuclear explosive device. *NNSA/NV*

The Papoose Mountains would provide additional shielding to protect the airbase from flying debris. Portions of the access road between the NTS and Groom Lake were considered likely to be damaged by ejecta over a distance of 5 to 6 miles and contaminated by radioactive dust for as much as 15 miles. Power lines for the airbase passed within a scant 2.5 miles of Sturtevant ground zero, prompting a recommendation to deenergize the lines prior to the shot.[191]

Radiation was also an important consideration. Neither shot would have been fired if winds were expected to cause the "hot line," the area of highest radiation, to pass near the airbase. According to Dahle, "Wind conditions at detonation time will be chosen such that predicted contamination at Area 51 Camp will be less than 6R total dose including shine and redistribution." The dose rate was expected to fall below 6 mR/hr. within five days. He strongly suggested covering windows and other openings with plastic or plywood to minimize the amount of radioactive contamination inside buildings.[192] Luke Vortman of Sandia's Underground Physics Division made arrangements to install an outdoor ground-level air-blast measurement station at Area 51. In a letter to William Allaire he wrote, "We need permission for Henry G. Lauritsen to have access to Area 51 Camp for installation, maintenance, and recovery of the equipment at the station."[193]

As with so many previous shots, personnel were to be evacuated to reduce risk of radiation exposure. "Detonation . . . will require evacuation of the entire Area 51 on D-day," Dahle noted. Additionally, the duration of the evacuation would depend on reliability of contamination predictions and in-field measurements. According to his best estimates, "Re-occupancy is expected by [the fifth day] although field conditions may require short work shifts for several days, possibly two to three weeks." This assumed that everything went according to schedule. The possibility of successive firing delays due to unforeseen technical problems raised the specter of evacuation for days or even weeks, potentially delaying critical work at Area 51. As always, weather was the determining factor. Dahle's reports specified that it might "be necessary to delay detonation on a day-to-day basis awaiting favorable atmospheric conditions." In the end it was moot. By late 1969, both shots had been canceled.[194]

Area 51 personnel still had to deal with the consequences of ongoing underground nuclear testing at Yucca Flat, Rainer Mesa, and Pahute Mesa. Automated air-sampling stations continued to operate at Groom Lake and within the surrounding areas to detect any accidental radiation release due to venting. In addition, observers were stationed at numerous locations, including the secret airbase, to record ground motion caused by subterranean detonations. When shot Tijeras was fired on October 14, 1970, with an explosive yield between 20 and 200 kilotons, Donald Bruskert recorded his observations from an outdoor post at Area 51. According to his subsequent report, there was no violent jolt; he felt the motion in rolling waves beginning five seconds after detonation and continuing for nearly half a minute. Following shot Artesia on December 16, observer William Moore felt a distinct shock while waiting inside the Area 51 security building, but Bruskert, standing outdoors, scarcely felt any motion at all.[195]

Although ground motion caused little concern, subterranean shots occasionally vented radionuclides into the atmosphere due to containment failure. The most spectacular such incident took place on December 18, 1970, after the 10-kiloton Baneberry shot was detonated at the bottom of a 910-foot-deep shaft in Area 8 on Yucca Flat. Shortly afterward, radioactive gases erupted from a surface fissure. The plume of dust and debris reached an altitude of more than 8,000 feet before dispersing to the northeast as well as to the west. Fallout descended on Groom Lake an hour later, where a dosimetry station (one of ninety-nine monitored by the Southwestern Radiological Health Laboratory) registered above-normal background radiation on three EG&G TL-12 thermoluminescent dosimeters. Within twenty minutes, radiation levels at Area 51 had reached a peak exposure rate of 0.18 mR/hr., compared to a normal background reading of 0.02 mR/hr. Within another hour the cloud had passed.[196]

Preshot meteorological reports indicated that northeasterly winds were expected at zero hour, making it necessary to evacuate Area 51 ahead of time. The nine hundred workers at Area 12 camp, near the base of Ranier Mesa, were not so fortunate. Baneberry was supposed to be contained, and, in the event of inadvertent venting, the prevailing winds should have carried any effluents away from Area 12. Unexpected changes in wind direction left Rad-Safe personnel scrambling to evacuate all personnel, and in the time it took to alert the camp and clear everyone out, a number

Venting from the Baneberry underground nuclear shot deposited radioactive fallout on the Groom Lake area. *NNSA/NV*

of people were exposed to radiation. Several later died of leukemia. Although there had been a number of other shots that same week (including six devices fired in three separate tests in a single day), Baneberry was the only shot during which Area 12 camp was not evacuated in advance.[197]

The Black Bats

One night in early October 1968, a C-130 landed at Area 51 and taxied to the North Ramp. The droning wail of its four turboprop engines drew the attention of the few workers still on duty. They watched the transport's rear ramp open and disgorge a troop of what appeared to be Chinese soldiers who marched off into the darkness, disappearing in the direction of the dormitories.[198] Though isolated from and scarcely seen by the majority of the base population, this band of Republic of China air force (ROCAF) personnel from the island of Taiwan spent more than six months at Area 51 training for a highly secret and extremely hazardous mission.

The CIA had long sought to drop sensors into the northwestern part of Communist China to monitor activities at the Lop Nur nuclear test site, and the urgency of this desire only increased with the detonation of China's first hydrogen bomb in June 1967.[199] Within a year of this event, scientists at Sandia Laboratories had devised a sensor package that could collect radiological and other data, then send the information to an orbiting satellite via burst transmission. The greatest challenge was how to deliver the large device, undetected, deep inside the borders of the heavily defended Chinese mainland.

Lt. Col. Robert L. "Bob" Kleyla of the CIA Special Operations Division Air Branch suggested flying a C-130 from Thailand, crossing over the Himalayas, then hugging the rugged terrain and staying below Chinese tracking and acquisition radar. After dropping a sensor package, the crew would have to return the same way.[200] In order to maintain deniability for the Americans in the event the aircraft was shot down, the C-130 would be crewed by ROCAF personnel of the 34th Squadron, known as the "Black Bats." This Taiwan-based unit was charged with flying clandestine low-altitude reconnaissance flights—mostly in the dark of night—over Communist territory to photograph military infrastructure, collect ELINT, and drop agents and propaganda packages. So dangerous were these sorties that each member of the squadron was asked to write his will before he began flying operational missions. Squadron personnel were also dispatched to Southeast Asia to support American efforts during the war in Vietnam. The Black Bats flew 838 missions between 1955 and 1969 (including 586 over mainland China), during which more than a dozen aircraft were downed and 142 crewmen lost their lives.[201]

Members of the 34th Squadron Black Bats pose with an American adviser. Operating from Taiwan, this unit performed numerous clandestine reconnaissance flights over Communist territory. *ROCAF*

At a meeting in early 1968, 34th Squadron commander Liu De-qi was asked to select two crews for a special high-priority mission called Qi Long (Magic Dragon) by the ROCAF and HEAVY TEA by the CIA. Most of the pilots, navigators, flight engineers, radio and electronic-warfare operators, and loadmasters were drawn from C-123 operations in Vietnam. Others were transferred from assignments flying antiquated C-119 and C-46 transports. In late September, Col. Sun Pei-zhen and twenty-four airmen of the 34th Squadron were sent to Sewart Air Force Base, Smyrna, Tennessee, for an accelerated training course in flying the C-130E. Next, they went to Area 51, becoming only the second contingent of foreign nationals to train at the secret Nevada airfield.[202]

They remained segregated from most other workers at the base and were instructed to ignore other activities going on around them. "Our movements were strictly controlled," navigator Lt. Col. Feng Hai-tao recalled in the squadron's official oral history. "We were only allowed to go to the bathrooms, the gym, the laundry, and the cinema, but we were very comfortable." Their American hosts provided the Black Bats crews with free meals and drinks, even flying in specialty Chinese food. They also kept a close eye on their foreign guests. As Feng later recounted, "The base commander joined some of our leisure activities, an American flight surgeon lived with us full-time, and I remember four other Americans who were always around; I guess that they were sent by CIA to watch over us."[203]

Sun and his men were shown a C-130E that had been specially modified by Lockheed for covert insertions. To facilitate deployment of the special sensor pallets, it had been equipped with a high-speed delivery system for low-altitude cargo drops. For low-level navigation at night, there was a forward-looking infrared (FLIR) sensor and improved terrain-following radar, as well as an inertial navigation system. Sun divided his airmen into two twelve-man crews that took turns flying long-range daylight practice missions as far as the Mexican and Canadian borders. They practiced navigation and learned to use the C-130's defensive systems against Air Force fighters sent to intercept them. Next, they began flying low-level nighttime navigation training missions and dropping cargo pallets. Mountainous terrain in Oregon and Washington provided a reasonable surrogate for the eastern Himalayas, and the desert landscape surrounding Groom Lake approximated that of the desolate Xinjiang Province in northwestern China. By the time the Black Bats departed Area 51 in April 1969, Sun had selected his primary and backup crews for Magic Dragon / HEAVY TEA.[204]

They were soon deployed to Takhli Royal Thai Air Force Base, about 144 miles northwest of Bangkok. As at Area 51, the group was isolated for maximum security. Col. Sun led the primary crew, and Col. Yu Chuan-wen was assigned to command the backup crew. The special C-130E arrived three weeks later, leaving just enough time to get in a few nighttime training flights before the first operational sortie. Finally, on May 17, the Black Bats received the authorization they had been waiting for. Sun and his crew took off and flew for six and a half hours, mostly at low altitude and in the dark. All the training and secrecy paid off when the loadmaster opened the rear cargo door and deployed two battery-powered sensor pallets over the target area precisely as planned. After another harrowing six and a half hours, they arrived safely back at Takhli. CIA analysts were overjoyed when the sensors began transmitting data to a US intelligence satellite. The two sensor packages functioned as designed for six months before their batteries finally wore out. During that period, the Chinese conducted two nuclear tests in September 1969.[205] One was China's first underground detonation, a 19-kiloton device fired inside a sealed tunnel; the second was a 3-megaton thermonuclear airburst. Venting from the tunnel test, and fallout from the airburst, dispersed radionuclides that were detected by the CIA sensors, providing valuable intelligence.[206]

Following the remarkable success of Magic Dragon / HEAVY TEA, CIA officials began planning a second mission. This time the drop zone would be 280 miles farther west, still close to Lop Nur but farther away from the air defenses surrounding the Shuang-ch'eng-tzu missile test center, where China's first satellite, Dong Fang Hong 1, was undergoing launch preparations. The new mission was dubbed Golden Whip, and in March 1970 the Black Bats C-130 crews, now led by Col. Yu, returned to Area 51 for refresher training. Other than improvements to the airplane's FLIR system to improve image quality, aircraft equipment and procedures were substantially the same. Training proceeded according to plan, but for reasons never explained to the 34th Squadron, the mission was called off while the team was still training in Nevada.[207]

This did not end the Black Bats' association with Area 51. While the US was withdrawing troops from South Vietnam, a covert campaign to harass North Vietnamese forces was launched from Laos at the direction of National Security Advisor Henry Kissinger. Sabotage operations, nicknamed COMMANDO RAIDER, were carried out by Hmong tribesmen with planning and support from the CIA. In early 1971, the agency again called upon the 34th Squadron for its unique talents, and for the deniability offered by using non-American agents in covert operations. As a result, Yu found himself back in Nevada with eight other Chinese airmen, this time learning to fly a de Havilland DHC-6 Twin Otter equipped with a LORAN long-range hyperbolic radio navigation system. Yu and his team spent three months at Groom Lake practicing precision nighttime navigation and airdrops over mountainous terrain before returning to Taiwan. They were then deployed to Pakse Site, or PS-44, an isolated guerrilla encampment high on a mountain plateau in southern Laos, to support missions designed to disrupt enemy activity along the Ho Chi Minh Trail, a major strategic supply route for North Vietnamese forces.[208]

Meanwhile, on Taiwan, the 34th Squadron selected twelve pilots for helicopter training in support of commando missions in Laos. Since few of these airmen had rotary-wing experience, they were sent to the US Army's Fort Rucker in Alabama for a basic course in helicopter operations. Upon completion of training, six of the newly minted chopper pilots deployed to PS-44. The rest were sent to Area 51 for a special assignment flying an extensively modified OH-6A light observation helicopter called the Hughes 500P ("P" stood for penetrator), dubbed "the Quiet One."[209]

The quest to develop a near-silent helicopter began with a May 1968 meeting at the Institute for Defense Analyses in Washington, DC, after which the Defense Advanced Research Projects Agency (DARPA) initiated a $200,000 feasibility study with technical management by the Army's Air Mobility Research and Development Laboratory at Fort Eustis, Virginia. The following year, DARPA modified three helicopters—a Kaman HH-43B, Sikorsky SH-3A, and

A C-130 Hercules takes off at dusk. The Black Bats typically flew missions at low altitudes and in the dark of night. *USAF*

Hughes OH-6A—for low-noise operation. Noise output comparisons conducted at NASA Langley Research Center in Hampton, Virginia, clearly indicated that the OH-6A offered the most-promising results. In fact, by simply replacing the chopper's twin-blade tail rotor with a four-bladed unit and installing a low-speed gearbox, researchers achieved an overall sound-pressure-level decrease of approximately 73 percent.[210] Upon learning of this study, the CIA immediately ordered two quiet choppers for field use and pledged the resources of the agency's Technical Services Division to aid in development.

In April 1970, DARPA awarded Hughes Tool Company of Culver City, California, a contract to design and build a helicopter with its acoustic signature reduced to an unprecedented minimum. This proved no easy task; nearly everything on a helicopter generates noise: the engine, spinning rotors, vibrating fuselage panels, etc. Blade vortex interaction alone, in which oncoming blades strike tiny whirlwinds formed by the spinning rotor tips, creates a sharp slapping noise that can be heard several miles away. After a stock OH-6A (serial number 65-12968) was bailed from the Army to serve as a prototype, a team of thirty Hughes engineers and craftsmen tackled the seemingly insurmountable technical challenge.

First, rotor speed (revolutions per minute) had to be significantly slowed to reduce total rotor noise output. Designers compensated for the attendant loss of lift by adding a fifth main rotor blade and replacing the standard twin-bladed tail rotor with a scissors-style four-blade assembly. They minimized tip vortex noise by replacing the usual square tips on the main rotor blades with trapezoidal tips with a 2-degree twist. Next, technicians modified the main gearbox and rotor gearboxes with silicone inserts to reduce contact noise and improve the mechanism's ability to sustain increased horsepower levels. Minimizing these noise sources drew attention to those emanating from the transmission system, which necessitated providing gears with a soft coating and reducing tolerances so that gear teeth would mesh more smoothly. Noises that would never be noticed on a standard OH-6A suddenly became significant while developing the Hughes 500P. These included a noisy relief valve in the fuel system and rotating inverters that were eventually replaced with lighter, quieter, solid-state devices.[211]

The final challenge was development of an exhaust muffler. After several weeks of unproductive work with an acoustical-engineering company in Boston, the team turned to Leslie S. Wirt, a Lockheed acoustical engineer. Although Lockheed declined a request for his services because he could not be spared from his ongoing projects at the company's Rye Canyon laboratory, he agreed to work on the problem at home in his spare time. Within a week he had produced a design that was nearly perfect. Additional

The Hughes 500P was a modified OH6A, redesigned to fly almost silently. The results were remarkably effective, even at close range. *US Army*

airframe modifications included lead-vinyl pads to deaden skin vibrations, and a baffle to block noise from the engine air intake. By this point the chopper's overall acoustic signature was almost entirely dependent on the aircraft's speed; its quietest mode was at about 85 knots, but it was still difficult to detect when flying at as much as 120 knots.[212]

For operational purposes the designers also made provisions for improved propulsion, range, and navigation. Out of several hundred Allison 250-C18 engines tested, only the six with the highest power output and lowest fuel consumption were selected, providing two for immediate use and four spares. To increase range, each chopper was equipped with two foam-filled, semipliable auxiliary fuel tanks that were both lightweight and crash resistant. In order to operate in pitch-dark conditions during low-level, cross-country flight over varied terrain, the Hughes 500P was equipped with a FLIR night vision system. Developed by two Hughes engineers, it was not only lighter than any such system yet produced but also provided substantially better image quality. In fact, when using this equipment, pilots were able to recognize the faces of individual ground crew members as they walked in front of the aircraft. Additionally, Singer-Kearfott Corporation provided an extremely precise INS.[213]

Thanks to an accelerated development program, the prototype Hughes 500P was ready for flight testing within sixty days of project go-ahead and attained full operational capability within just six months. Upon completion of a safety-of-flight review, the chopper was transported to Wallops Island, Virginia, where NASA researchers from Langley conducted an acoustic evaluation. Results indicated an overall sound-pressure-level reduction of 14 to 16 decibels during level flight, and as much as 17 to 20 decibels in hover compared to a typical OH-6A.[214]

Following the adage that it's best to hide in plain sight, most flight testing took place at Hughes Airport in Culver City. On one occasion, CIA general counsel Larry Houston stopped in to observe a nighttime demonstration flight. A standard OH-6A first made a low-level pass over the airfield to establish a baseline noise measurement. When the Hughes 500P made a similar pass three minutes later with no lights, Houston was chatting with project officers and never even noticed it. He realized it was there only during a second pass, when the pilot turned on the chopper's running lights while directly over the viewing area.[215]

Upon completion of testing in April 1971, two more choppers (civil registrations N351X and N352X) were modified to the 500P configuration. After CIA instructor pilots Lloyd G. A. Lamothe Jr. and Daniel H. Smith underwent flight training at Culver City, the prototype was shipped to Area 51. In Nevada's high desert, ROCAF crews practiced low-level flying, maneuvering at close quarters, and night landings on mountain peaks in preparation for missions in Southeast Asia. By October, N351X and N352X had been transported to Taiwan, where the 34th Squadron continued training until June 1972.[216] The Quiet Ones were then shipped to Tahkli, reassembled, and flown to PS-44 by the American pilots. Five ROCAF airmen followed, commanded by Col. Lu Wei-heng.

It was a critical time in the Southeast Asia conflict; negotiations were underway between Henry Kissinger and North Vietnamese politburo member Le Duc Tho that would eventually lead to complete withdrawal of US troops from South Vietnam. Kissinger worried that the North Vietnamese might be planning a full-scale invasion of the South, so the CIA developed plans for a daring mission to place a wiretap on a military communications telephone line along the Ho Chi Minh Trail. The scheme called for having two ROCAF pilots fly the Hughes 500P to a spot where the line ran through remote, rugged terrain and insert two Laotian commandos to secure the tap while the helicopter crew dropped a radio relay antenna on top of a nearby tree.[217] Unfortunately, this task proved too much for the ROCAF crews.

Lamothe and Smith spent several months trying to train the Nationalist Chinese, but Lu and his team complained of insurmountable difficulties with the FLIR system as well as with negotiating the steep terrain surrounding PS-44. After chronic poor performance culminated in a botched landing that severely damaged N352X, CIA project managers decided to send the Black Bats home to Taiwan and ordered Lamothe and Smith to fly the crucial mission themselves. Several early attempts had to be aborted within enemy territory due to inclement weather. Persistent difficulties with the FLIR and night-vision goggles caused additional delays, and a scorpion stung one of the commandos.[218]

Finally, on the night of December 5, the Americans and their Laotian allies made a death-defying nighttime flight across jungles and mountains to the planned

The Hughes 500P, seen here at a forward operating location in Southeast Asia, was used for only a single but crucial clandestine mission. *US Army*

wiretap site. While the commandos set the tap, Lamothe and Smith flew to the top of a 1,000-foot mountain to deploy the relay antenna. Upon completing this task, they extracted the commando team and exfiltrated to Laos without incident. The tap operated perfectly for several months, yielding sufficient intelligence from the North Vietnamese high command to allay Kissinger's fears, and the Paris Peace Accords were signed in January 1973. The surviving Hughes 500P was relocated to Edwards, where CIA pilots Allen Cates and Robert Mehaffey flew it for a short while. But the Quiet One never flew another operational mission. Without explanation, it was abruptly decommissioned, stripped of its unique features, and transferred to a CIA holding company. N351X was eventually sent to the Army's Night Vision Laboratory at Fort Belvoir, Virginia, for use as a test platform. According to James Glerum, who oversaw the chopper's single historic mission, "The Agency got rid of it because they thought they had no more use for it."[219]

Despite this seemingly ignominious end, the Hughes 500P program had long-term benefits for aircraft designers. Development of the FLIR system alone laid the foundation for future generations of night-vision devices used in aircraft and ground vehicles. Use of composite materials to construct the main rotor resulted in substantial reduction of the chopper's radar signature, a characteristic with future applications for military helicopters. Analysis of methods for evading hostile radar led to the realization that it was possible to exploit "blind spots" in certain systems that were unable to detect objects moving at low speeds and altitudes. Most important, the Hughes/CIA team proved that helicopters could be quieted to a truly remarkable degree, and that missions could be configured to minimize detectability.[220] These capabilities were eventually employed in future special-mission helicopters, greatly improving survivability under hostile conditions.

CHAPTER 5
WE HAVE MET THE ENEMY

An American pilot flies a Chinese copy of the Russian-designed MiG-17, one of the most feared and versatile fighters in service with Communist armed forces during the 1960s and 1970s. *Al Walker*

February 1969. *Feng Hai-tao sat in the back of the classroom at Area 51, struggling to follow the instructor's words. Feng's English was poor, and the tall man with short-cropped hair had a tendency to speak too fast, making the lesson hard to follow. It didn't matter; the training program at the secret American base had prepared him as well as possible for his dangerous task to navigate a C-130 deep into Communist China and drop a sensor package over a target. The trick would be flying low enough to avoid being detected and shot out of the sky. It may not have been a suicide mission, but there were so many threats including antiaircraft guns, missiles, and the dreaded MiG-17 jet fighters. But all of that waited on the other side of the world. Best not to think about it now. The window behind Feng rattled as a jet took off. He was tempted to turn and look, but the Americans had sternly instructed the Nationalist Chinese students to disregard all activities not directly pertaining to their mission. The other training base in Tennessee hadn't been like this. What could they possibly have here that warranted such secrecy? As a second jet roared aloft, Feng's curiosity got the better of him. Glancing quickly outside, he turned deathly pale. In a heartbeat, the instructor was beside him, pulling the blinds, and barking, "Don't look outside!" Feng stammered, "I saw a MiG-17." The man just stared at him coldly and said, "No, you didn't."*

In the early years of the Vietnam War, American airmen found themselves at a severe disadvantage, in part because they had received little instruction in aerial combat tactics. Fighter pilots were increasingly trained to rely on air-to-air missiles, and although most fighters were equipped with guns, there was little emphasis on dogfighting. And though technical difficulties were eventually overcome, it didn't help that early-model Sidewinder and Sparrow missiles suffered from poor reliability and performance limitations. More important, North Vietnamese pilots were flying Soviet-built MiG-17 and MiG-21 fighters. Both were small and difficult to see from a distance, especially since they lacked the distinctive smoke trails common to many American jets. This was a serious concern because the established rules of engagement required visual identification of enemy aircraft prior to firing upon them. Additionally, the MiGs were highly maneuverable. In a close-in dogfight, a MiG-17 could easily outmaneuver a heavier F-4 or F-105.

During the Korean conflict, American pilots had a greater than 10-to-1 kill ratio, but in the skies over Southeast Asia between 1965 and 1968, this had dropped to only slightly better than 2 to 1. This meant that for roughly every two North Vietnamese MiG-17 or MiG-21 jets shot down, one American F-4, F-8, or F-105 was lost. Worse yet, the percentage of US Air Force and Navy fighters being lost during air-to-air combat engagements was growing, rising from 3 percent in 1966 to 22 percent in the first three months of 1968. Those were merely averages; occasionally, US fighters suffered an adverse kill ratio, as occurred between August 1967 and February 1968, when eighteen American aircraft were lost for only five North Vietnamese MiGs.[1] Something had to change. Increasing awareness of this problem among senior US military leaders led to the establishment of what was to become the largest and longest-running secret program at Area 51.

Acquisition and technical analysis of foreign military aircraft was not a novel concept, having been ongoing since World War I, but during the Cold War its importance increased by orders of magnitude. In July 1961, AFSC, the major command responsible for Air Force flight-test and evaluation activities, established the Foreign Technology Division (FTD) at Wright-Patterson, where most of the service's foreign materiel exploitation (FME) programs were being conducted. Military leaders recognized that scientific and technical analysis of foreign—particularly Soviet—aerospace equipment would not only reveal the vulnerabilities of a potential adversary but also provide a valuable yardstick against which to measure the progress of American research and development. In time, FTD personnel gained a reputation throughout the Air Force as experts in Soviet aircraft, missiles, space systems, and related equipment. Earlier FME efforts during and after the Korean War resulted in the acquisition of North Korean Yak-9, Yak-18, and Il-10 aircraft. Additionally, Polish and North Korean defectors provided opportunities for American airmen and analysts to examine MiG-15 jet fighters.[2] By the mid-1960s, all of these aircraft represented antiquated technology. The FTD wanted examples of the latest Soviet aircraft.

Toward this end, AFSC established a program called Go-Gam / Little Sam (later renamed HAVE BRIDGE) in which a test pilot assigned to the AFFTC Directorate of Flight Test was tasked to serve as an on-call specialist for limited technical analysis of such foreign materiel as became available, wherever it might be. On August 29, 1967, Maj. Fred J. Cuthill accepted this assignment, taking over from Lt. Col. Don Sorlie. Specific duties included foreign travel, and Sorlie was once sent to Germany. Cuthill received orders for what proved to be an abortive mission to examine a MiG in Cuba. "It had an advanced radar that we wanted to study," he recalled in a 1999 interview. A contact at the CIA directed him to fly to Mexico City, using a passport with the name "Fred Carter." He waited there for the final order to proceed to Cuba, but it never came. "The operation was called off for some reason," he said. "I never found out why."[3]

Don Sorlie was on call to conduct limited technical analysis of foreign aerospace materiel that became available by chance or through more-direct means. *USAF*

Fred Cuthill followed in Sorlie's footsteps as HAVE BRIDGE project officer before moving on to more in-depth exploitation efforts. *USAF*

A Golden Opportunity

American authorities were not the only ones interested in obtaining a MiG for study. Israel, pressed all around by enemies, had long sought to acquire a MiG-21 because it was the most advanced fighter being exported by the Soviets to their Middle East allies. In 1966, Israeli intelligence agents induced an Iraqi air force colonel, Munir Redfa, to defect with a MiG-21 under the condition that the Mossad (Israel's spy agency) exfiltrate his family from Iraq, where they would otherwise surely be punished for his actions. Though a member of an oppressed Christian minority in his own country, Redfa still considered himself patriotic. He was, however, violently opposed to his government's persecution of Kurdish tribesmen in northern Iraq. As deputy commander of his squadron, Redfa was deeply troubled by orders to conduct bombing missions against the nearly defenseless Kurds.[4]

On August 16, Redfa delivered on his promise, flying to Israel's Hatzor Airbase in a MiG-21F-13 (NATO reporting name Fishbed E).[5] There he helped familiarize an Israeli air force (IAF) test pilot, Lt. Col. Daniel "Dani" Shapira, with the fighter's systems and operation. Not least of Shapira's challenges was the fact that all the instruments were labeled in Russian and Arabic. "We posted notes all over the aircraft, so I could safely and efficiently operate the plane," he recalled nearly four decades later. "We translated the entire starting procedures, from climbing into the cockpit to the flight itself."[6]

Shapira spent several weeks learning the aircraft's systems, perplexed by the peculiar human-factors engineering decisions that had gone into designing the cockpit. "It seemed completely irrational, as if the engineer just piled [equipment] up inside the cockpit," he noted, though, "On the other hand, it was a very simple and reliable jet; just refuel and go." It soon became apparent that maintenance would be a serious problem. The ejection seat had exceeded its service life, and several components required replacement. Somehow, the Mossad arranged to acquire the necessary items. Shapira was soon ready to become the first Westerner to fly a MiG-21. A maintenance crew stripped the aircraft of Iraqi markings and serial numbers and painted IAF roundels on the wings and fuselage so no Israeli air defense gunners or fighter pilots would mistake Shapira for the enemy during his test flight. Once in the air, he rapidly gained familiarity with the MiG's handling characteristics. To his delight, he found the lightweight fighter highly maneuverable, with good acceleration capabilities.[7] It was immediately apparent why the MiG-21 was such a formidable adversary.

Not surprisingly, US intelligence agencies were anxious to examine Israel's prize. "The Americans were stunned when they heard of our achievement," Shapira recalled, adding, "They reported [to Hatzor] immediately with a large technical crew and asked to test and fly the jet." Israeli authorities saw this as a golden opportunity. According to the former test pilot, "We said, not so fast! First, we will test it ourselves, then you will provide us with information about the [Soviet] SA-2 [antiaircraft] missiles and supply us with Sidewinder missiles, and then we will talk."[8]

Once he had logged a number of flight hours, Shapira began writing a technical report describing the jet's performance characteristics and highlighting its strengths and vulnerabilities. IAF officials, meanwhile, drew up plans for a series of mock combat engagements pitting Shapira against several of Israel's top fighter pilots, each of whom would fly a different type of aircraft in order to evaluate the MiG's performance against a variety of threats. Simulated air battles revealed that the MiG-21's greatest advantage—speed—could quickly become its greatest weakness. Through repeated engagements, the IAF pilots learned that they

This MiG-21 was examined by Israeli military authorities at Hatzor Air Base following the defection of an Iraqi pilot with his airplane in 1966. *IDFAF*

Israeli test pilot Dani Shapira evaluated the MiG-21's performance capabilities and wrote a detailed technical report. *IDFAF*

needed to force the opposing MiG-21 down to lower altitudes, where it lost maneuverability at high speeds. They discovered the MiG pilot's blind spots and studied technical descriptions that showed the most-critical locations on the airframe to hit with cannon fire; a fuel tank just behind the pilot's seat was particularly vulnerable. Most important, the MiG-21 was no longer a mysterious foe. The experience of flying the MiG and learning how it performed during air combat maneuvers provided valuable lessons that paid off handsomely during the Six-Day War of June 1967, in which airpower was a decisive factor.[9]

By this time, the Israeli government was finally ready to deal with the Americans, so Headquarters, Tactical Air Command (TAC), dispatched Lt. Col. Joe B. Jordan to Israel for familiarization with the MiG-21. At the time, Jordan was assigned to Detachment 1 of the 831st Air Division at Edwards as part of the F-111 Joint Test Force. He was a graduate of the Aerospace Research Pilot School and had a great deal of experience in jet fighters. According to Shapira, who briefed Jordan at Hatzor, "It was all top secret. No one could know that an American pilot was there, and learning to fly the MiG-21 jet." Whenever he was outside on the airfield, the American pilot had to wear an IAF flight suit and keep his helmet on to hide his features. At first, he flew chase in a Mirage III, carefully observing Shapira's demonstrations. Next, Jordan switched places with his counterpart and flew four sorties in the MiG-21, with the IAF test pilot chasing in the Mirage. As Shapira later recounted, "He communicated with me on one channel and I communicated with the control tower on another, and so it seemed [to anyone listening] as if I was the one flying the MiG." Eventually, in exchange for the opportunity to borrow the MiG for an extended test program, and under some amount of political pressure, the US government agreed to provide Israel with the requested Sidewinder missiles and technical information on the SA-2 system.[10]

Detailed studies of the MiG-21F-13 by the US military were carried out under a highly classified project, ridiculously dubbed HAVE DOUGHNUT. This unclassified nickname was created from a list of approved terms, which taken singly or together had no inherent meaning relative to the project. The first word, HAVE, was specifically allocated for use with AFSC-sponsored programs. AFSC officials then randomly selected the second word. Previously, this process had saddled a program for airborne measurement of missile heat signatures from a U-2 with the name HAVE COFFEE. Unlike code words, nicknames were never classified, even if the subject was a top-secret special-access program (SAP).

The FTD had overall management responsibility for HAVE DOUGHNUT. As the organization's on-site representative at Area 51, Lt. Col. Vincent C. Rethman led a team of specialists drawn from throughout the Air Force and Navy for exploitation of what was sometimes euphemistically referred to as "the asset." Maj. Everett J. Henderson served as lead FTD analyst. AFSC was responsible for a thorough technical evaluation under the supervision of Fred Cuthill, now a lieutenant colonel and chief of the AFFTC Fighter Branch. Responsibility for tactical evaluations was split between Lt. Col. Jordan, representing TAC, and Cmdr. Thomas J. Cassidy Jr., Navy project officer of Naval Air Test and Evaluation Squadron Four (VX-4). Other Air Force project pilots included Maj. Gerald D. Larson, Maj. William T. "Ted" Twinting, and Maj. Robert G. Ashcraft. Lt. Dennis A. Sullivan was the only other Navy pilot to fly the MiG-21 during HAVE DOUGHNUT. A joint Air Force / Navy committee developed flight profiles to be flown in the MiG-21 and determined the order in which these sorties would be flown. Cmdr. Robair F. Mohrhardt served on the committee and headed up a select group of Navy pilots who flew simulated combat missions against the MiG in A-4, F-4, and F-8 aircraft. AFFTC civilian personnel included project engineer Charles E. "Pete" Adolph, flight test engineers Richard R. Hildebrand and Robert C. Tucker, and instrumentation technician Donald G. Thomson. Stanley F. Kulikowski from the FTD oversaw a ground crew that included the TAC maintenance lead, MSgt. Richard F. "Dick" Sinclair; the crew chief, SSgt. Ronald W. Syphers; and four technicians (SSgt. Elmer Richardson, SSgt. Robert Hutchins, TSgt. Lou Baird, and C. C. Zedeker).[11]

Joe Jordan represented Tactical Air Command interests in the HAVE DOUGHNUT project. *USAF*

Tom Cassidy served as Navy project officer for HAVE DOUGHNUT. *US Navy*

In the deliberately ambiguous language of secret programs, Phase 1 of HAVE DOUGHNUT concerned transportation of the asset from the acquisition site to the exploitation site. This began on January 12, 1968, with a briefing for the thirteen-man team that boarded a C-141 Starlifter bound for Israel the following day. The cargo transport also carried an assortment of equipment, including a flatbed truck, three 10-ton aircraft jacks, several generators, lighting, a large supply of plywood and lumber, six tarpaulins, twenty overalls, and a wide selection of tools. The team arrived at midafternoon on January 15, but, for security reasons, their supplies were not unloaded until after nightfall. At midnight, the Starlifter was flown to a staging site to await recall when its secret cargo was ready to be loaded aboard. As it turned out, the C-141 developed maintenance problems and had to be replaced with a larger C-133A commanded by Maj. Carl E. McDonald.

Disassembly of the MiG-21 was scheduled to take an entire week but was completed in just five days. First, the airplane had to be defueled and raised on jacks. Technicians retracted the landing gear, disconnected the pitot tube from the nose, and removed the gear doors, tail cone, and several fairings and actuators. They also detached the wings, the horizontal stabilizers, and the aft fuselage assembly. Using the raw materials they had brought along, they constructed wooden cradles to support the fuselage and wings, as well as crates for the external fuel tanks and an assortment of small items. On the evening of the fifth day, the various components of the MiG-21 were loaded onto trucks and subsequently transferred to the C-133. The entire disassembly operation including loading onto the transport took forty-one hours.[12]

The massive cargo plane landed at Area 51 three days later, on the evening of January 23, and disgorged its cargo into Hangar 5. The next morning, the maintenance team uncrated all the parts and inspected them for damage. Reassembly, completed on February 7, was a complicated process since it involved not only putting the MiG back together but also simultaneously adding test instrumentation to the vehicle, conducting the equivalent of a fifty-hour phase inspection and adjusting, repairing, and checking out the airplane's various components.[13]

The MiG-21 in Hangar 5 following reassembly. Note US national insignia, and the bogus tail number. *USAF*

Two teams from the Aeronautical Systems Division (ASD) at Wright-Patterson were responsible for subsystem exploitation, the first element in the analysis of any captured enemy aircraft. This involved detailed examination of the airplane's systems and individual parts. Analysts found the MiG-21's hydraulic and pneumatics systems to be of conventional design, comparable to those of most Western fighters. The fire suppression system was considered unusual, however, since it used highly toxic methylene bromide and required a bulky plumbing system. The MiG-21's radar and gunsight systems were somewhat outdated, similar in capabilities to US equipment of the early 1950s. An optical sight consisted of little more than a gyro system that provided lead computation for air-to-air gunfire and rockets, and an aiming reference for missile launch, air-to-ground gunnery, and bombing. The Mikoyan-Gurevich Design Bureau's most significant improvements included increased radar range gained through the use of a novel antenna design, and a missile launch computer that signaled the pilot when he was within range to fire IR-guided missiles. One notable weakness was that the radar lacked any equipment to counter jamming.

For the most part, examination of the airplane's structure, materials, and construction methods revealed no unique manufacturing techniques. Aluminum alloys used in the MiG were comparable to those typically found in US aircraft. The only somewhat unusual features were the use of large aluminum panels in the construction of the airplane's nose section, and the amount of heavy steel components elsewhere in the aircraft. Inspectors found no indications of structural weakness or metal fatigue. The airplane's aerodynamic smoothness was marginal. Surprisingly, many of the rivet heads protruded well above the airframe, and there was a general waviness to the structure between frames, as well as gaps and mismatches between sections of the aircraft's skin. Analysts felt this reflected a Soviet design philosophy of focusing primarily on engineering and construction of components critical to operation, reliability, or maintainability, while other elements received little care or attention.[14] Examination of markings such as part numbers and data plates also provided a wealth of information. Analysts determined, for example, that the MiG's jet engine was manufactured at Plant 26 in Ufa, capital city of the Russian republic of Bashkortostan, during the fourth quarter of 1963. It bore production number 065 and was part of the sixth series of R11F-300 engines produced at that factory. Markings indicated that most of the MiG's other components had also been built in 1963.[15]

Prior to the first checkout flight, the MiG-21 was given US national insignia, boldly painted on the sides of the forward fuselage. A bogus serial number—80965—was stenciled on the tail. This number was taken from an actual Air Force serial previously assigned to an AIM-4D Falcon air-to-air missile, one that had most likely been expended during a training exercise and was no longer considered part of the service's inventory. Most important, the airplane itself needed an unclassified designation.

Every military pilot logs his flight hours in an Individual Flight Record document, the Air Force version of which is called AF Form 5. As Fred Cuthill recalled, "We realized right away that we couldn't call the plane a MiG-21 on our Form 5 because the project was secret, but the flight records were unclassified."[16] Ground crews had a similar problem when filling out maintenance records, which were also unclassified. Cuthill discussed the problem with Joe Jordan, and the two came up with a novel solution that served not only HAVE DOUGHNUT but many future programs as well. Per DoD standards, they needed an alphanumeric mission design series (MDS) designator that included a basic mission indicator (such as "F" for fighter or "B" for bomber) followed by a unique number-letter combination to identify the specific variant. Prior to 1962, the Air Force and Navy used completely different designation systems, but these were replaced that year with a single, unified MDS system for all US military services. This both simplified the numbering system and effectively ended use of "Century Series" fighter designations, so called because they began with F-100. One result of these actions was that Navy and Air Force production models of the McDonnell Phantom II, respectively known under the old system as F4H-1 and F-110A, became the F-4B and F-4C. Additional status prefix letters could be added to designate modified aircraft such as the JC-130B, or service test and prototype vehicles such as the YF-12A. Cuthill and Jordan had to come up with an MDS designator that had never been used for any existing US military aircraft and that would never be needed for any future aircraft. Their solution was to return to the abandoned Century Series and refer to the MiG-21 as YF-110B.[17] This terminology was adopted for use in all flight and maintenance documentation and served as a foundation for documenting later special-access test programs at Area 51.

Unique to the Air Force inventory, the MiG-21 posed special challenges. Maintainers had no previous experience with this airframe, and spare parts were scarce. There was a very real possibility that the airplane might be damaged during testing and rendered unflyable. Any given sortie might be its last. Therefore, data collection objectives were strictly prioritized. Most important was the need to obtain performance comparisons between the MiG-21 and the F-4 and F-105. The second-highest priority involved quantitative flight testing for

Joe Jordan logged his first flight in the MiG-21, identified here as a YF-110B, on this Aircraft Status and Maintenance Record form on February 8, 1968. Someone has scribbled out "Area 51" in the location block and replaced it with "Nellis" but forgot to remove three additional references to Area 51 next to the crew chief's signature at the bottom of the page. Via Ken Jordan

performance, stability and control, and maneuverability. Finally, TAC leadership wanted to pit the MiG against as many different US tactical aircraft as possible in mock combat maneuvers.[18] Secondary objectives included RCS and IR signature measurements, and air-to-air still and motion picture photography. As chief test pilot, Jordan was responsible for standardization of all flight procedures. He conducted an intense ground-training-familiarization course for the other pilots who checked out in the airplane, gave daily briefings and debriefings, and monitored all aircraft changes and modifications.[19]

Every effort was made to minimize wear and tear on the aircraft. With few exceptions, the MiG-21 was usually towed to the active runway prior to each sortie, to reduce the possibility of a ground mishap. Similarly, after each landing the pilot shut down the engine, and the plane was towed back to the hangar. As an added benefit, this prevented unnecessary brake and tire wear. Prior to the first test flight, on the morning of February 8, 1968, Jordan performed a ground evaluation and taxi test. He found the cockpit arrangement less than ideal but essentially satisfactory. With the canopy closed, forward visibility was poor, and aft visibility was restricted by aircraft components and structures. Engine response was poor during taxi and while checking engine trim. Wheel brake performance was only fair, steering with differential braking proved difficult, and the brakes failed to hold during a full-power engine run-up.[20]

Safety chase aircraft were required for every test mission, and each chase pilot had to be familiar with all details of the flight plan, characteristics of MiG-21 operation, and emergency procedures. The initial HAVE DOUGHNUT sortie was accompanied by two chase planes: an Air Force F-4D piloted by Fred Cuthill for tactical comparisons and a Navy F-8E with Tom Cassidy as safety observer. Following takeoff and climb to 10,000 feet, Jordan had some difficulty retracting the landing gear. After finally succeeding on his third attempt, he performed functional checks of all systems and investigated the airplane's basic handling characteristics. The remainder of the thirty-minute flight was primarily devoted to a qualitative acceleration performance comparison between the MiG-21 and F-4D, though Cassidy also took the opportunity to compare the MiG's performance with that of the F-8E.

Jordan quickly discovered that the MiG-21 suffered from slow engine response at all power settings and that he was unable to engage the afterburner until engine speed reached 100 percent. When the trio began a 350-knot maximum-rated-thrust climb to 12,000 feet, Cuthill was able to keep up while flying the F-4D at a 93 percent power setting. Cassidy, flying trail in the F-8E, could not maintain position and began to drop back. He rejoined the formation in time for a level acceleration from 300 to 450 knots, during which the F-4D passed the MiG-21 with power to spare, and the F-8E again failed to match the MiG's acceleration capabilities. During a second level-acceleration run, this time in afterburner, it was Jordan's turn to drop behind. Toward the end of the flight he practiced turning, deceleration, and stalls, noting that he was comfortable at speeds of 300 to 500 knots but that when flying below 200 knots, "the airplane feels squirrelly."[21] Return to base was uneventful. Jordan made a celebratory low pass over the Area 51 runway before circling for landing.

Maintenance technicians work on the MiG-21, which has been fitted with a belly tank for extra fuel and dummy missiles mounted beneath the wings. *USAF*

The MiG's clean, simple lines are on display in this photo, taken on the North Ramp between flights. *USAF*

Several days later, following another handling-qualities and performance sortie, tactical evaluations began in earnest, with Jordan and Cassidy flying the MiG against the F-4, F-8, and F-105 in one-on-one engagements to practice both offensive and defensive air combat maneuvers. Of particular interest were simulations of attack conditions similar to those being employed in Southeast Asia. Mission planners devised air combat scenarios that simulated the Southeast Asian operating environment, and participating aircrews flew various tactical maneuvers in order to validate their effectiveness against the MiG-21. The MiG's acceleration capabilities and zoom climb performance were compared against those of the US fighters while the results were recorded by each participating pilot, safety chase, and other observers. Qualitative assessment of the MiG's stability and control characteristics while performing air combat maneuvers was limited to the airplane's normal operating regime. To gather additional data, Cuthill flew a series of stability-and-control-evaluation sorties that included pushing the MiG-21 to its maximum performance limits.[22]

Overall, the MiG-21 proved easy to fly and lacked any inherently dangerous characteristics. The jet had excellent turning performance and roll response throughout the entire flight envelope. The MiG's basic stability was generally good, too, though at altitudes below 15,000 feet and at airspeed Mach numbers between 0.96 and 1.15, the airframe vibrated so much the MiG pilot could not accurately engage a target. Instrument panel vibrations under these circumstances were so severe that the cockpit appeared to the pilot as little more than a blur. Engine response was poor even at high power settings, precluding precise formation flying. Instruments and controls were antiquated by American standards, and labeling of the various switches and dials was inconsistent. Pilots also complained that "it was not possible to enter the cockpit with any degree of urgency because of the time-consuming tasks associated with donning the parachute harness and hooking up the necessary leads."[23]

By the first week of March the three test pilots had flown nearly fifty sorties. Over the next several weeks they checked out Larson, Twinting, Ashcraft, and Sullivan. Testing then expanded to include a wide variety of US tactical aircraft, gathering of electronic intelligence, air-to-air IR signature measurements taken from a highly modified NT-39A, and evaluation of the effectiveness of ECM systems used on the B-52 and B-58 bombers. Two sorties included firing the MiG-21's 30 mm cannon at targets on the ground, including a derelict bulldozer. Flight operations were, for the most, fairly routine, but one incident nearly compromised project security.

Cuthill was performing a level acceleration run at high speed and altitude when he started having controllability problems. "The airplane had a free-floating rudder, and near Mach 2 it seemed to want to fly sideways," he recalled, "so I was just trying to keep the nose pointed forward." It was then that he noticed the contrails of two approaching airliners headed his way. Under the circumstances, turning was not an option, so he decided to keep flying straight and level and slip between them. Closing speed between the three airplanes was so rapid that the civilian pilots probably saw little more than a blur as the MiG passed by. Cuthill breathed a sigh of relief, but he wasn't out of the woods yet. His speed run had used up a significant amount of fuel, so he made a tight turn over Mount Charleston and practically coasted back to Groom Lake, landing with very little fuel remaining. "Later, I was chewed out because they were worried that the airline pilots might have seen the MiG," he said, "but nothing ever came of it."[24]

All the pilots and maintainers agreed that the airplane's reliability was outstanding; 76.5 flight hours were logged during 102 missions. Often, three or even four missions were flown in a single day. More sorties could have been flown but for the fact that operations were limited to daylight hours, and briefing and debriefing time was required between flights. At no time during the evaluation period was the MiG-21 flown as often as would have been possible during an operational maximum-effort flying schedule. Nevertheless, there were many obstacles to fulfilling the project's ambitious schedule. The airplane remained at the test site for seventy-five days; it was available for flying on fifty-two days but actually flown on just forty. At the beginning of the project, several days were lost not due to aircraft problems but to

Gerald Larson observes as Fred Cuthill prepares for a test flight in the MiG-21. Larson flew eighteen tactical-evaluation sorties, while Cuthill conducted two dozen technical-evaluation flights. *USAF*

lack of test equipment, lack of specific training in jury-rigging ground-servicing equipment, and practically nonexistent logistical support. Other flight opportunities were scrubbed because of inclement weather, mechanical problems, or administrative reasons. Overall, analysts for HAVE DOUGHNUT were extremely impressed. They extrapolated that if a small team with extremely limited resources could operate the MiG-21 with such success, then the Soviet air force could easily field large numbers of airplanes with potentially devastating results. As one analyst later noted in a report published by the DIA, "Considering the conditions under which the evaluation was conducted, the reliability record of the airplane was not only unbelievable, but was a rather sobering fact."[25]

Aircraft maintainability was excellent, thanks in part to the airplane's design but more due to the outstanding efforts of the ground crew. Overall simplicity of the MiG-21's arrangement, system reliability, and a minimum complement of backup systems and equipment were key factors. The airplane's small size necessitated significant internal equipment density, but removable panels provided ready access to equipment bays and internal systems, fittings, and service points. This made it possible for the airplane to be turned around—the time from touchdown to wheels up—between flights in less than thirty minutes, excluding armament servicing, by just two maintenance men. On one occasion when a quick turnaround was required, the maintenance supervisor allocated forty-five minutes, but ground crewmen accomplished the task in just twenty-five, including the fifteen minutes required to tow the aircraft from the runway to the hangar and back to the runway again. Malfunctions were kept to a minimum by thorough postflight and preflight inspections and preventive maintenance. Two of the most significant challenges included the ground crew's initial unfamiliarity with the aircraft and the lack of replacement parts, particularly for the brakes and the exhaust-gas temperature indicator system.[26]

The first of these hurdles quickly diminished as maintainers gained experience with the airplane. The second required innovation on the part of maintenance chief Stan Kulikowski. According to Cuthill, "Stan was probably the foremost civilian expert on Soviet aircraft," and he did

Awaiting takeoff clearance on the runway at Area 51. The MiG-21 proved rugged and easy to maintain, allowing the test team to fly as many as three or four flights per day. *USAF*

whatever was necessary to keep the airplane flying. As the accelerated pace of the project took its toll on the MiG's airframe and systems, Kulikowski traveled the world to scrounge replacement parts. If he couldn't find the necessary items, he made what he needed or used off-the-shelf hardware. On one occasion, he replaced the MiG's tires with those from a civilian aircraft. They worked fine, Cuthill recalled, but didn't last as long as the original Russian tires.[27]

Kulikowski's growing experience with the MiG-21 may have prevented a tragedy or at least averted a serious accident. On February 28, 1968, Cuthill was performing a series of flights involving windup turns to as much as

Kawich Valley and Belted Peak form a backdrop as the MiG-21 climbs northwest out of Area 51 on a test sortie. *USAF*

8 g. The ambitious flight schedule called for an unprecedented six sorties that day, placing both the pilot and airplane under exceptional physical stress. After the fourth flight, an exhausted Cuthill complained to the mechanic that the brakes felt spongy. "Stan reached down under the seat and traced the brake cable from the handgrip on back," Cuthill recalled. He found it was almost completely worn through in one spot. "It was hanging on by a strand," said Cuthill. "If it had broken, the brakes would have failed and the airplane could have been seriously damaged or destroyed."[28]

Part of the HAVE DOUGHNUT evaluation included a study of pilot visibility from within the MiG-21's cockpit in order to determine the aircraft's areas of vulnerability due to blind spots. One method for determining visibility restrictions involved mounting the MiG-21 atop a pedestal on the surface of the dry lakebed while a photographer took pictures from a "cherry picker" at heights of up to 40 feet above the ground. A pilot sat in the cockpit, simulating flight conditions by wearing a helmet, oxygen mask, and parachute. As the airplane was rotated through 360 degrees, the pilot attempted to spot the photographer. Whenever he was unable to see the photographer even with body and head movement, the pilot gave a signal and a picture was taken. These photos identified aspect angles from which the MiG-21 pilot could not see attacking aircraft, information that later proved vital during the air campaign in Southeast Asia. HAVE DOUGHNUT project pilots also performed airborne visibility evaluations in which they reported the various positions at which the chase aircraft was no longer visible.[29]

On the night of March 29, Cuthill flew the MiG-21 to Edwards, where project officials showed it to specially cleared representatives from the aerospace industry. He landed in the dark and quickly taxied to a secure hangar that was being used at the time by the SR-71/YF-12 Test Force. After the secret briefing he spent the night at Edwards, flying back to Area 51 at dawn the next day.[30] Project HAVE DOUGHNUT was now complete.

Disassembly of the MiG-21 began at noon on April 3 and continued for three days. On Sunday, April 7, an Air Force transport crew loaded the crated components and other equipment aboard a C-133B. Afterward, the fourteen-man team received an Area 51 "site security debriefing" before being released to overnight accommodations at the secret base. The C-133 departed the test site at shortly after noon the following day and arrived in Israel on the morning of April 10. As during the acquisition phase, the unloading of the MiG was postponed until after sundown for security reasons. Not everything went smoothly. The reassembly and acceptance process was dogged by technical problems, the need for rechecking various equipment, and bad weather. Finally, on the afternoon of April 24, the MiG-21 underwent a forty-minute FCF, and the "host country" accepted its return.[31]

Throw a Nickel on the Grass

By late 1968, Air Force and Navy analysts had completed three reports on HAVE DOUGHNUT. The first, a six-hundred-page volume describing the technical exploitation, included a Navy structural-vulnerability evaluation, an AFFTC performance and stability evaluation, a SAC evaluation of the MiG-21's effectiveness against electronic countermeasures, RCS measurements, propulsion system evaluations, findings from the assembly and disassembly of the MiG-21, an instrument evaluation, a list of modifications made to the MiG for the test program, records of all maintenance work, aircraft weight and balance calculations, markings analysis, cockpit visibility observations, and acoustic and IR signature analyses. The primary objective was to determine the level of technology employed in the Soviet Union at the time of the airplane's design. Analysts studied the MiG's hydraulic, electrical, and armament systems and collected data on the airplane's structural

Looking east, with White Sides Hill in the distance as the MiG-21 banks over Groom Lake. The diminutive jet was highly maneuverable and difficult to spot during combat maneuvers because its engine did not produce a heavy smoke trail. *USAF*

characteristics, flight control systems, corrosion protection, airframe-propulsion integration, aerodynamic design, and avionics systems. They concluded that the MiG-21's aerodynamic design was impressive, considering it had been developed during the mid-1950s. The fuselage had a high fineness ratio with a small frontal area, minimizing transonic and supersonic drag, and the delta wings had a thin symmetrical airfoil. It became clear, through subsequent engineering studies and reduction of flight test results, that the MiG-21 was optimized for flight within the supersonic region and was particularly vulnerable when flying below 15,000 feet, where its airspeed was limited to less than 0.98 Mach.[32]

The 310-page tactical exploitation report detailed results of the mock dogfights between the MiG-21 and all types of US fighter and attack aircraft. This volume contained separate evaluations by personnel from the Navy, TAC, and ADC. A third, "Special Distribution," volume consisted primarily of the technical evaluation, including a lengthy description of the acquisition and return phases but without the SAC material. Although these highly detailed reports (more than 1,400 pages) contained extremely valuable data, they were not published in a form easily accessible to those with the most direct need for the information—the pilots and aircrews fighting the MiG-21 over North Vietnam. This was instead provided through briefings to combat crews, as well as in a training film titled *Throw a Nickel on the Grass* that was shown to American fighter, interceptor, and attack pilots being deployed to Southeast Asia. The short documentary, named for a drinking song popular among fighter pilots, revealed the fact that the US had come into possession of a MiG-21, and outlined the goals and accomplishments of Project HAVE DOUGHNUT. The film's narration began tantalizingly with the words "An ideal way to develop combat skill against an enemy aircraft would be to fly the enemy aircraft yourself before you had to fight it. Of course, that's an impossible idea. Or is it?"[33]

Motion picture and still images showed the MiG-21 in US markings at an unnamed desert test site. Joe Jordan and Tom Cassidy acted as narrators, providing commentary on their experiences battling the MiG in mock combat. They began with a brief technical description of the MiG-21 and then moved to its vulnerabilities. Next, they detailed the strengths and weaknesses of different US aircraft against the MiG as indicated by the results of simulated dogfights. The MiG-21, they noted, was highly maneuverable at speeds below 500 knots, where it could easily outturn US aircraft. However, the MiG's low-speed acceleration was poor, requiring several seconds for the engine to reach full power. In contrast, the US aircraft with more-powerful engines could easily overtake the MiG-21 at low altitudes.

Jordan and Cassidy took their show on the road, conducting briefings at the Pentagon as well as to Air Force and Navy air units stationed overseas. They outlined the best tactics for use against the MiG-21. Rather than getting into a low-speed dogfight, where the MiG pilot held the maneuvering advantage, American fighter pilots were advised to keep their speed above 0.95 Mach and drive the fight to lower altitudes, where the MiG-21 was vulnerable to severe airframe vibration in the transonic region. Forcing the MiG-21 into a hard turn would cause it to slow abruptly, leaving the enemy pilot struggling to accelerate. This would give the US pilot an opportunity either to attack or outrun the MiG. Exploitation of the MiG-21's blind spots would allow an attacker to get into position and fire cannons or missiles before the enemy pilot became aware of the threat.[34] All of this information, and more, eventually saved numerous American lives in the skies above Southeast Asia.

On landing approach with gear down. Without the MiG-21 having a reliable supply of spares, tire and brake problems proved among the most troublesome maintenance issues. *USAF*

The MiG-21 was flown against nearly all types of US combat aircraft. Here, it flies in the company of two Navy fighters from VX-4, an F-8E and F-4B. *US Navy via Bob Dorr*

But showing *Throw a Nickel on the Grass* to pilots who would soon be flying combat missions over North Vietnam involved a calculated risk with regard to the security of US efforts at foreign-materiel evaluation. Despite formidable efforts to keep HAVE DOUGHNUT and other FME programs secret, a fighter pilot captured by the enemy might break under interrogation and talk about the film. But intelligence is valuable only if it is used. Had knowledge gained from the MiG-21 evaluation been withheld from tactical planners and frontline combat crews, aircraft and personnel would have been lost unnecessarily, rendering the whole effort pointless.[35]

The increasing number of people with knowledge of HAVE DOUGHNUT—participants, analysts, test site personnel, others briefed into the project, and the hundreds of airmen who saw the film—made a leak to the media inevitable. Such a leak occurred in the February 17, 1969, issue of *Aviation Week & Space Technology*. A brief article in the magazine's "Industry Observer" section matter-of-factly declared that a "Soviet MiG-21 fighter was secretly brought to the US last spring and flight[-]tested by USAF pilots to learn first-hand its capabilities and design characteristics. The aircraft, which engaged in simulated combat against US fighters, was highly regarded by the pilots who flew it." The anonymous staff writer noted that the MiG-21 was particularly impressive at altitudes above 25,000 feet, and suggested that the evaluation was likely part of a broad effort by the Air Force to analyze the threat of Soviet airpower while planning new aircraft, such as the McDonnell Douglas F-15 air-superiority fighter then under development.[36] Ironically, publication of the *Aviation Week* article came on the same day that another secret MiG was making its debut at Area 51.

Two for the Price of One

The MiG-21 was not the only significant peril facing US airmen in the skies above Southeast Asia. According to FTD analysts, "One aircraft of utmost concern is the MiG-17F, which has been widely exported and operationally deployed to Far Eastern nations within the Communist sphere." Though capable of subsonic flight only, the small, single-seat, swept-wing interceptor was extremely maneuverable. American combat losses up to that time further stressed the MiG-17 threat and demonstrated the urgent need to conduct both technical and tactical evaluations of this weapon system, as had been done with the MiG-21.[37] As luck would have it, such an opportunity arose just four months after the completion of HAVE DOUGHNUT.

On the morning of August 12, 1968, the residents of Western Galilee near Israel's northern border were startled to see two Syrian MiG-17s circling to land at Betzet Airfield,

Israeli soldiers inspect two Syrian MiG-17s after their pilots got lost and accidentally landed in Western Galilee. *Moshe Milner via National Library of Israel*

a largely abandoned former British aerodrome then used occasionally by civilian crop dusters. Farmers working nearby watched as the first plane touched down and overshot the end of the runway, plowing through a field and coming to rest just short of a stand of cypress trees. The second plane circled the strip again and made a better landing. A large crowd of curious onlookers quickly gathered, and someone alerted Israeli defense authorities. It was initially unclear whether the Syrians were defecting or if they had simply gotten lost. At first, the befuddled Syrian pilots seemed quite relaxed; one was reported to have been seen reclining beneath the wing of his jet while sipping a cold drink that had been offered to him by an Israeli security policeman. Both were armed with pistols but made no hostile moves, nor did they try to escape.

The young airmen, Lt. Walid Adham and 2Lt. Radfan Rifai, were eventually hustled away for interrogation at an undisclosed location. Statements issued by the Israel Defense Forces, later that day, said an investigation was underway. A Syrian military spokesman in Damascus suggested that the pilots had lost their way in bad weather and were forced to make emergency landings after running out of fuel. Israeli military sources disputed this account, pointing out that skies over the region were clear and that both Syrian planes still had fuel in their tanks. Yossi Yitzhak, an Israeli youth who had been working with his tractor in a nearby hayfield, said the MiG pilots thought they were landing in Lebanon, just a few miles north. As the boy later explained to reporters, "When I told them they were in Israel, they both went white with shock."[38]

Israeli authorities seized the airplanes and had them moved to Hatzor Air Base. As with Munir Redfa's MiG-21 two years earlier, Dani Shapira was assigned to test-fly the MiG-17. Both aircraft were stripped of all Syrian markings and painted in Israeli national insignia with white-bordered red recognition stripes on the nose, aft fuselage, tail, and wingtips.[39] They were also given new numbers, 002 and 055, painted on the airplanes' noses in large white numerals. It wasn't long before US officials arranged to borrow the airplanes for another joint Air Force–Navy evaluation at Area 51.

Once again, the exploitation effort was managed by the FTD with support from AFSC, TAC, and the Navy. Fred Cuthill and Lt. Col. Wendell H. Shawler were assigned as AFSC project pilots. TAC project pilots included Maj. Maurice B. "Duke" Johnson Jr., Maj. Robert Ashcraft, and Maj. Thomas S. Swalm. The Navy contingent once again included Tom Cassidy, along with Lt. Cmdr. Foster S. "Tooter" Teague, Lt. Cmdr. Jerry B. "Devil" Houston, Lt. Cmdr. Ronald E. "Mugs" McKeown, and Lt. John M. "Mike" Welch. AFFTC civilian personnel from the Directorate of Systems Test included Teddy A. Goff, Edward I. Seto, Walter A. Lipe, Joseph F. Stroface, and Don Thomson, as well as Navy civilian Harry W. Down. Stan Kulikowski once again served as maintenance lead. Additional ground crew detailed from the 6515th Field Maintenance Squadron at Edwards included TSgt. Charles A. Socci, TSgt. Evander Lucus, Sgt. Michael C. Morris, and civilians William J. Moreira, Frank Brandon Jr., and Jesse R. Jones. SSgt. Normal E. Wilson and SSgt. Arville G. Barnett of the 6505th Supply Squadron provided logistical support.[40]

The primary test aircraft was nicknamed HAVE DRILL. The second MiG-17, called HAVE FERRY, was assigned a backup role but was later used effectively during two-ship tactical maneuvers. Although the two airplanes were identical in configuration, they received different MDS designations for no other reason than the fact that, at the time, AF Form 5 had no provision for tail numbers. To keep a clear record of how many hours each pilot logged in each airframe, the HAVE DRILL airplane was designated YF-113A and HAVE FERRY was designated YF-114C. Both were eventually transported to Area 51 in the same manner as the MiG-21 had been.

Before either MiG-17 was disassembled, Cuthill and Kulikowski traveled to Israel to inspect one of the airplanes and obtain baseline flight data for later comparison to make sure that the aircraft had the same flight characteristics before and after reassembly. Their visit was shrouded in secrecy. All orders were transmitted verbally; there was nothing in writing. "The clandestine nature of the situation was very intriguing," Cuthill remembered. "During my visit, I wasn't allowed to talk to or contact anyone whose name I didn't already know."[41]

At an appointed time, a casually dressed Israeli official met Cuthill at his hotel in Tel Aviv. The American was blindfolded and driven for about fifteen or twenty minutes, eventually arriving at the airfield where the MiG-17 was concealed within a concrete revetment. Shapira briefed him on the airplane's controls and discussed his experience flying the MiG. "I spent the entire day in the cockpit, labeling the instruments in English so that I could read them," Cuthill recalled. He was then blindfolded once again and taken back to his hotel, expecting to fly the following day. To his surprise, several days passed before he was contacted again. Cuthill spent the time reviewing his test cards and mentally planning his flights. Finally, his handler picked him up and drove him to the airbase, repeating the blindfold ritual.

After being issued a flight suit and helmet, Cuthill flew two sorties in the MiG-17, with Shapira flying chase. The airplane handled well and Cuthill had no difficulty mastering the controls. He maintained radio silence during both flights, having been instructed to use a designated channel only in the event of emergency. After familiarizing

Wendell Shawler was primary AFSC project pilot for the MiG-17 exploitation. *USAF*

Duke Johnson served as TAC's project pilot during HAVE DRILL. *USAF*

Mike Welch, seen here about to climb aboard the HAVE DRILL aircraft, was project officer for Naval Air Test and Evaluation Squadron Four. *US Navy*

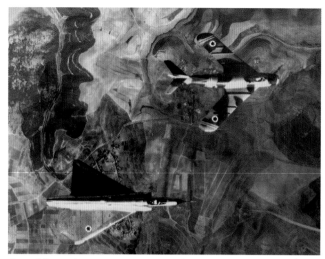

One of the ex-Syrian MiG-17s, painted in Israeli markings and flying in the company of a Mirage IIIC. *IDFAF*

The HAVE DRILL MiG-17 is reassembled and analyzed at Area 51. Numerous components had to be repaired or replaced, and special flight test instrumentation installed. *USAF*

himself with the MiG's basic handling qualities, he landed without incident. Upon returning to his hotel, Cuthill looked forward to some relaxation. This was easier said than done. He had been warned to avoid the US embassy and to keep a low profile. That night, however, his Israeli contact invited him to a party. He went but resolved to remain tight-lipped about the reasons for his visit to Israel. One of the guests was Maj. Gen. Mordechai Hod, commander of the IAF, who greeted Cuthill with a broad smile and asked, "So, what did you think of the MiG-17?"[42]

Over the course of the next several days, an American team disassembled the HAVE DRILL MiG-17, number 055, and loaded it aboard a cargo plane. Cuthill wrote a short but detailed qualitative flight test report before boarding a commercial flight to Washington, then traveling to Wright-Patterson for debriefing at FTD Headquarters.[43] The MiG-17 was delivered to Area 51 on January 27, 1969. Uncrating and assembly began two days later. As with the MiG-21, the airplane's components and systems were thoroughly examined and studied. Analysts soon discovered that the airplane was actually a Lim-5M, a Polish-built copy of the MiG-17F (NATO reporting name Fresco C). Both the airframe and engine had been manufactured in Poland sometime in 1956 or 1957, using many Soviet-built components, particularly electronics.[44] After being reassembled, the MiG-17 was subjected to a fifty-hour phase inspection, during which numerous discrepancies were identified. Each problem component had to be repaired and operationally checked out, a process that took nearly three weeks.[45]

For the maintenance crew, the litany of woes seemed nearly endless. The right-hand brake line was damaged beyond repair. Hydraulic hoses supplying the actuators for both main gear doors were badly deteriorated. The trailing edge of the left horizontal elevator was damaged. The radar was inoperative, and several associated components were loose or broken. Technicians discovered leaks in transfer and vent lines for the aft fuel tank. More leaks were discovered in the pilot's oxygen line, speed brake selector valve, and a hydraulic line in the left wing. Additionally, there was minor damage to the gun, and the seat ejection cartridge was outdated.[46]

In addition to these repairs, AFFTC requirements necessitated installation of flight test instrumentation. Don Thomson and his team expended approximately 960 man-hours between January 29 and February 16 fitting the airframe with equipment to collect quantitative performance and stability data, temperature and pressure probes to measure engine inlet conditions during ground runs, cockpit cameras, and voice recorders. Additionally, they had to fabricate special adapters, fittings, fuel lines, and other components. Many of these items had to be built or calibrated at Edwards, using AFFTC facilities and capabilities that were unavailable at Area 51.[47]

On February 17, as readers of *Aviation Week & Space Technology* were learning about the Air Force's secret MiG-21 test project, Fred Cuthill was conducting the first two FCFs of HAVE DRILL. All went well until the right main tire blew out during the second landing. The ground crew installed a new tire, repacked the wheel bearings, checked the brakes and gear retraction mechanism, and examined the hydraulic system. Mechanics discovered a damaged pneumatic line in the gun package, a hydraulic leak in the left wing flap, and a leaky brake selector valve. They repaired or replaced these items, manufacturing parts whenever necessary.[48]

"Damned Effective"

HAVE DRILL advanced much as HAVE DOUGHNUT had previously. Cuthill flew a series of performance, stability and control, and handling-qualities sorties, but the tactical evaluation was given top priority. The first Navy tactical

Fully reassembled and wearing US national insignia, the HAVE DRILL aircraft stands ready in front of Building 120. For documentation purposes, this airplane was designated YF-113A. *USAF*

mission took place on February 19, and the first Air Force tactical mission followed one week later. An aggressive flight schedule often included several sorties per day. Mission planners designed most of these tactical missions with parameters chosen to simulate as closely as possible the air-combat-maneuvering environment encountered in Southeast Asia. As with HAVE DOUGHNUT, Air Force and Navy pilots flew a wide range of their services' tactical aircraft against the MiG-17. One-on-one encounters provided good basic combat experience as well as a chance to collect comparative performance evaluations. Later scenarios involved multiple aircraft for the purpose of evaluating existing tactics and developing new ones.[49]

Qualitative data were gathered during pilot debriefs after each sortie and were used to optimize, modify, and refine tactical techniques through repeated engagements. All briefings, debriefs, and airborne communications—comments by the MiG-17 pilot, opposing combatants, and airborne observers—were recorded. During discussions following each mission, the participants reconstructed each engagement in detail in order to verify maneuvers and recommend adjustments to the conduct and rationale for future engagements.

Standard rules of engagement required a positive visual identification of the target prior to any simulated gun or missile shot. To maximize engagement time, all simulated AIM-7 Sparrow missile shots were assumed to be misses, and engaging airplanes continued to maneuver after a visual sighting. Captive AIM-9 Sidewinder missile lock-on tones were used in conjunction with gun camera footage to verify Sidewinder launch parameters. A satisfactory gun kill was assumed when the offensive airplane maintained

The HAVE DRILL MiG-17 accelerates down the runway at Area 51 during one of its 172 test and evaluation sorties. *USAF*

continuous tracking within 2,000 feet for Navy and TAC aircraft, and 4,000 feet for the MiG-17. A designated minimum fuel state (called "Bingo") limited the MiG-17 to operating within 25 miles of Groom Lake, and other tactical airplanes to between 60 and 75 miles. All engagements terminated with a simulated kill, loss of two-way communications, or when an airplane reached Bingo fuel.[50]

A cargo plane bearing the second MiG-17 arrived at Area 51 on March 12, but the reassembly process did not begin until March 20. For all practical purposes, the HAVE FERRY airplane was identical to HAVE DRILL in every respect and required just as much work to get it into shape for flying. Technicians spent twenty days inspecting, repairing, and assembling the components to make the airplane ready. In fact, the YF-114C did not make its first FCF until April 9, little more than a month before the project ended. Nevertheless, it was flown more than fifty times during that period, including twenty-five dual tactical missions with the YF-113A.[51]

Throughout the HAVE DRILL / HAVE FERRY project, the agile Soviet fighter proved a formidable adversary for its more technologically advanced American challengers. Analysts noted that the MiG-17 demonstrated outstanding maneuvering capabilities. It was easy to fly, and undesirable features such as spin and accelerated stall were easily handled. A small internal fuel capacity limited the MiG-17's range and endurance. Its combat intercept radius was 115 nautical miles with no external stores, assuming a five-minute warm-up and taxi, a military climb on heading to 20,000 feet and cruise at that altitude, three minutes of combat using afterburner near sea level, a return-heading military climb to 20,000 feet, and idle descent, allowing for a 5 percent fuel reserve. With wing tanks, the combat radius could be extended to 215 nautical miles. Longitudinal stick forces increased significantly beyond 0.85 Mach and were excessive above 0.90 Mach. Lateral-directional damping was generally weak, and roll rate capability

The HAVE DRILL jet flies in formation with an F-105D from the 4537th Tactical Fighter Training Squadron at Nellis during a tactical-evaluation sortie. *USAF*

A two-ship formation with the YF-114C in the lead and the YF-113A trailing in the wingman's slot. *USAF*

The HAVE FERRY MiG-17, which carried the designation YF-114C, primarily served as a backup to the YF-113A but was also used for multiple-ship air combat scenarios. *USAF*

was low, only 100–130 degrees per second. Nevertheless, the pilots who flew the airplane generally agreed that with proper knowledge of its maneuvering capabilities and limitations, the MiG-17 could be a very effective interceptor or air-superiority daylight fighter throughout most of its subsonic flight envelope.[52] This was demonstrated dramatically during tactical encounters over the Nevada desert.

Although substantial information concerning MiG-17 capabilities was available prior to HAVE DRILL, the airplane's performance level could not be duplicated or realistically simulated by using any existing US aircraft. As a result, none of the American pilots were accustomed to fighting an airplane with the turn performance of the MiG. Additionally, the antiquated design and relative age of the Soviet fighter led US aircrews to be generally overconfident prior to their first engagement.[53] The results were devastating. According to Mugs McKeown, "Nobody beat the MiG-17 the first time out."[54]

None of the US fighters could match the diminutive jet's extremely tight turning radius, so the Navy pilots began using lag pursuit tactics—staying to the rear of the opposing MiG—or employing a barrel-roll maneuver during attack to maintain separation. This experience served McKeown well three years later, during a deployment to Southeast Asia. "We were jumped by six MiGs," he recalled, "and one of them was really chewing me up." McKeown applied the same lag pursuit tactics he had practiced in the skies above Nevada. "The MiG-17 shot by me within about 15 feet," he explained. "I got him into a position where I knew he couldn't see me, and I shot him down." McKeown then set off in pursuit of a second MiG, and "he rolled away but I knew what his rotation rate would be, and I used the roll maneuver that we had developed [during HAVE DRILL] and got him, too."[55]

For situations in which these techniques proved ineffective, McKeown devised what he called the "Bug Out" maneuver for use in the F-4 Phantom II. This involved waiting until a pursuing MiG-17 was close enough to look dangerous, then to feint one way and immediately reverse direction. With the F-4's throttles advanced to full power, he pushed the stick forward, yanked it back, and then pushed it all the way forward again before pulling the stick back as hard as possible, raising the Phantom's nose while simultaneously reversing rudder. This generated sufficient yaw to make the F-4 seem to float in midair while the MiG-17 overshot, becoming a target.[56] The hunter had become the hunted.

On March 26, the Navy conducted a two-on-one tactical-evaluation sortie with two Phantoms against one MiG-17. Though assigned to VX-4, McKeown and his radar intercept officer, Lt. Peter G. Gilleece, were flying a brand-new F-4J on loan from VF-121, a naval replacement air group (RAG) that operated the newly formed Navy Fighter Weapons School (better known as TOPGUN) at Naval Air Station Miramar, California. The TOPGUN founder, Lt. Cmdr. Dan "Yank" Pedersen, and Lt. Cmdr. John "JC" Smith crewed the second F-4 while Tooter Teague piloted the MiG-17. At the end of the tactical mission, McKeown determined he had plenty of fuel remaining and requested an opportunity to try out his new maneuver.

Formation flight prior to a two-versus-two engagement between the MiG-17s and Navy A-7E Corsair II attack jets assigned to VA-122. *USAF*

Naval aviators Mugs McKeown, *left*, and Tooter Teague stroll through Hangar 5 while a maintenance crew works on the YF-113A in the background. *Via Paul Crickmore*

He began with a straight and level acceleration run at 11,000 feet altitude, with the MiG approaching from behind. As Teague prepared to track the F-4J with his guns, McKeown feinted, reversed, advanced his throttles to full, and stood on the Phantom's rudder while pulling up into a vertical scissors maneuver. Just then the Phantom suffered a compressor stall and one engine flamed out. Then the second engine flamed out, and the $4 million jet slid into a flat spin and plummeted earthward. Just as McKeown had hoped, Teague shot past in the MiG-17, but there wasn't time to celebrate. Teague called out, "Hey, that was damned effective!" Then, noticing his comrade's predicament, he added, "Are you all right?"[57]

With some difficulty, McKeown recovered from the spin and restarted both engines, but the heavy Phantom still needed more forward airspeed to begin climbing. Looking out through the forward windscreen, McKeown saw the desert landscape coming up fast and realized he lacked sufficient altitude to save the aircraft. He and Gilleece ejected at around 600 feet above the ground, and their chutes opened just before they touched down, both narrowly missing the fireball from the exploding jet. In fact, McKeown landed right next to the flaming wreck. Crews in the other airplanes initially thought their friends had been killed. Teague saw a column of dense black smoke rising from the desert floor and radioed frantically, "Did anybody get out?"[58]

Pedersen replied uncertainly, "I thought I saw a couple of chutes." He dropped down to make a low pass over the crash site and felt greatly relieved when he finally spotted the downed pilots. "I have two standing up! Two standing up, both waving at me," he reported. On the ground, McKeown and Gilleece were enthusiastically giving the "one-finger salute."

Within minutes, a helicopter from Area 51 crewed by Capt. Clark E. Lovrien Jr. and Teddy Goff arrived on the scene. McKeown and Gilleece were immediately returned to the base, where a flight surgeon checked them over and asked how they were feeling. The bruised but apparently otherwise uninjured airmen replied that they were "pissed off and thirsty." McKeown also complained of back pain, and it soon became apparent that he would need further treatment at a better medical facility. "They gave us a six-pack of beer and put us back in the chopper," McKeown recalled, adding, "We thought we were going to Las Vegas, but they dropped us off at the crash site again."[59]

McKeown and Gilleece were then told that in order to protect the security of the program, they would have to wait to be "rescued" by a helicopter from Nellis.[60] After cooling their heels in the desert for about twenty minutes, they heard an approaching Air Force chopper. Capt. Gary Robertson then transported the two aviators to the Nellis Hospital for a routine examination.[61] While a doctor examined his crushed vertebra, McKeown worried the physician might smell alcohol on his breath from his previous rescue.

Meanwhile, Teague informed Capt. Jim Foster, VX-4's commanding officer, about the accident. Foster eventually contacted RAdm. Edward L. "Whitey" Feightner, director of the Naval Aviation Weapons Systems Analysis Group, and arranged through unorthodox channels to retroactively transfer the wrecked airplane from the RAG to VX-4 so the test squadron would bear ultimate responsibility for the mishap.[62]

The accident did little to slow the pace of tactical sorties and other important tasks. Maj. Thomas Swalm, an aerial-tactics instructor from Nellis and veteran of 220 combat missions in Southeast Asia, made two orientation flights in the MiG-17 that were also used to accomplish aerial photography for a cockpit visibility study. Two ADC pilots were checked out in the MiG as part of a thirteen-sortie trial that pitted the jet against the F-106, a supersonic, all-weather interceptor. There were four IR-signature-measurement flights using the NT-39A. Several missions were devoted to air-to-air gunnery practice in which the MiG pilot fired the plane's 23 mm and 37 mm cannons at a towed dart target. In air-to-ground gunnery tests, a total of 560 rounds of 23 mm and seventy rounds of 37 mm ammunition were expended against ground targets that included a previously serviceable Air Force flatbed truck. The Soviet weapons had a low firing rate and low muzzle velocity, and even small, inadvertent control disturbances degraded the pilot's ability to maintain lateral-directional tracking. "When I fired the 37 mm and 23 mm cannons simultaneously, the aircraft practically stopped in midair," Cuthill noted, adding, "It really kicked, and the smell of cordite filled the cockpit."[63]

Though light and maneuverable, the A-4 Skyhawk was primarily designed as a ground-attack platform. Only once was it credited with a MiG-17 kill in Vietnam. *USAF*

Cuthill logged a total of seven flights in both MiG-17 aircraft, including six in the YF-113A and one in the YF-114C, before he was reassigned to a tour of duty in Southeast Asia. He made his last flight in the YF-113A on April 18, the same day that Wendell Shawler made his first in the YF-114C. As chief of the 6512th Test Squadron's Special Projects Branch, Shawler would oversee the next round of FME projects at Area 51.[64]

The MiG-17 proved very reliable, and its operational availability was exceptional. The test team easily accomplished as many as four to five flights, day after day. Analysts noted that this operational record resulted directly from a deliberate design approach toward airframe, engine, and system simplicity and reliability. The airplane's most attractive features included dependable in-flight gun clearing and charging, a rearview periscope, and a smooth, well-balanced flight control system. Particularly impressive was the lack of engine exhaust smoke at lower altitudes, which made the tiny jet extremely difficult to see from a distance.[65] A total of 224 evaluation flights were flown during HAVE DRILL / HAVE FERRY. The YF-113A accumulated 131.3 flight hours during 172 sorties. The YF-114C accumulated 37.7 flight hours during fifty-two sorties.[66] The final flight of the project took place on May 14, 1969. Disassembly of the YF-113A began the next day, and that airplane was subsequently returned to Israel. The YF-114C remained at Area 51 for use in future evaluation programs.

As with the previous project, all data and lessons learned were compiled into a set of reports by the various services, as overseen by the FTD. The first volume, detailing the results of technical exploitations, was issued in November 1969. A second volume, containing the results of all Air Force and Navy tactical exploitations, followed six months later. Once again, every effort was made to convey the lessons learned to all frontline air combat crews.

Permanent Presence

Though still modest in scope at this time, the joint Air Force–Navy FME program at Area 51 was destined to forever change the history of Groom Lake. This resulted from a simple administrative action that paved the way for the Air Force to have a permanent presence at Area 51. Recognizing the benefit of continuing to use the secret test site, AFFTC leadership entered into a host-tenant relationship with the CIA for Project HAVE GLIB, which would serve as an umbrella program for follow-on testing of foreign military equipment. The original agreement was signed in March 1970, though it underwent subsequent minor revisions over the next several years.[67]

On November 25, 1970, Col. Jesse E. Green, AFFTC deputy chief of staff for plans and programs, signed directives assigning responsibility for two unspecified test projects. In both cases, all information regarding background, scope, and even project schedule was classified. The first was HAVE GLIB, for which Green designated the 6512th Test Group at Edwards as the responsible test organization. Wendell Shawler was assigned as project officer.[68] He planned to begin by picking up where HAVE DRILL / HAVE FERRY left off, flying additional evaluation flights in the YF-114C when not involved with his normal duties at Edwards.[69] But that would have to wait. The second project, HAVE PRIVILEGE, had a higher immediate priority. The AFFTC vice commander, Col. William W. Gilbert, was designated project officer, and, though not mentioned in the directive, Shawler was assigned to serve as project pilot.[70] The American government had arranged through diplomatic channels to borrow a J-5A (a Chinese copy of the MiG-17F) from Cambodia's Khmer National Air Force (KNAF). Unfortunately, the airplane would be available only for a limited time and was to remain in Southeast Asia. There would be no opportunity to ship the fighter jet to Area 51.

This patch was created to commemorate participation in the HAVE DOUGHNUT and HAVE DRILL projects at Area 51. *Author*

This Cambodian J-5A was flown to Phu Cat Air Base, Republic of Vietnam, in December 1970 for evaluation by an American pilot. *USAF via Marty Isham*

In mid-December, Shawler and a small team of FTD analysts flew to Phu Cat Air Base in the Republic of Vietnam. One morning, a KNAF pilot took off from Pochentong Air Base near Phnom Penh in a brand-new J-5A with only twenty hours on its airframe. He flew northeast and crossed the border, from which point he was escorted to Phu Cat by a pair of American F-4D Phantom jets. Shawler, by now very knowledgeable about the operation and handling characteristics of MiG-17-type aircraft, prepared to fly a series of missions to compare the Chinese-built jet to the Polish-built examples he had flown previously. Time was short, and Shawler's frustration mounted when engine troubles delayed the first flight for three days. Once he finally got airborne, Shawler began performing a routine handling-qualities and performance evaluation. He did not attempt any tactical maneuvers, nor did he have an opportunity to fire the cannons. Shawler flew a total of five flights in the J-5A, each lasting about thirty to thirty-five minutes. Since these sorties were flown in the Southeast Asian theater of operations, he was able to log them as combat missions. In his AF Form 5, Shawler later identified the aircraft type as YF-113C.[71]

Because an unwitting observer might easily mistake the Cambodian J-5A for a North Vietnamese MiG-17, each of Shawler's missions was accompanied by at least one F-4D flying safety chase. All went well during the first four missions, but, unknown to Shawler, the Phantom aborted on the fifth flight due to a mechanical problem. He was now alone, flying through South Vietnamese airspace in an "enemy" aircraft. The J-5A was equipped with a UHF radio for communications during the tests, but it had very limited range. Fortunately, the flight ended without incident. As soon as the HAVE PRIVILEGE tests were complete, the Cambodian pilot flew the J-5A home to Phnom Penh, and the American analysts returned to the US.[72]

Back in Nevada, tests continued with the remaining ex-Syrian jet, for the moment HAVE GLIB's only asset. The MiG-17F/YF-114C was flown only sparingly for limited performance and tactical evaluations, and to familiarize select Navy TOPGUN instructors with the MiG's capabilities. Occasionally, high-ranking military officers were invited to Area 51 for orientation flights. These VIP guests included aviators whose experience entailed flight in a wide range of high-performance aircraft, from propeller-driven World War II fighters to modern supersonic jets and rocket planes. Vice Adm. Thomas F. Connolly, a decorated war veteran and test pilot with more than eight thousand flying hours, who had served as the first director of the Naval Test Pilot School, logged his final active-duty flight in the MiG-17. On another occasion, Marine Corps general Marion Carl, a fighter ace and test pilot who had set world speed and altitude records at Edwards, was flown to Area 51, where he logged 1.7 hours of flight during two sorties in the MiG-17. While there, he witnessed some of the area's security precautions. At about midday, all flight operations ceased and ground crews pulled the MiG into a hangar. Carl was later told that this was done to prevent the airplane from being photographed by a Soviet reconnaissance satellite that was scheduled to pass overhead.[73]

The J-5A was a Chinese copy of the MiG-17F. Wendell Shawler used the designation YF-113C when he logged his flights in the airplane. *Al Walker*

Two F-4D Phantom jets stand ready to escort the J-5A, which is being readied for flight behind a protective revetment. *Al Walker*

Shawler lifts off the runway at Phu Cat for one of his five evaluation sorties. *Mike Jacobssen*

Following the conclusion of HAVE DRILL / HAVE FERRY, the YF-114C remained at the test site for use in follow-on projects. *USAF*

In 1971, Shawler checked out about a dozen Edwards test pilots in the MiG-17. Because the MiG was a single-seat aircraft, every pilot's first sortie was a solo flight. Shawler briefed each airman on the plane's operation and systems and then flew chase in a T-38A while acting in the role of instructor. Keeping the MiG flyable remained the greatest challenge; every malfunction and maintenance discrepancy left the mechanics scrambling to find or build replacement components. Eventually, the Air Force sent a small delegation to Cambodia to pick up some spare parts.

Shawler's many duties included serving as HAVE BRIDGE project officer and being on standby to evaluate foreign aircraft anywhere in the world whenever they became available. In June 1971, for example, he was directed to fly to New York with open-ended travel orders. There, he met an FTD representative who gave him tickets to fly to Iran. In the expectation that he was going to have an opportunity to fly a foreign jet, he had already packed a flight helmet that was compatible with Soviet life-support systems. Shortly after arrival, he met Gen. Mohammad Khatami, the commander of the Imperial Iranian Air Force, and learned why he was there. At an airfield near Hamadan, Shawler examined an Iraqi Su-7BKL that had been flown in from the neighboring country through a clandestine diplomatic arrangement. Built by the Soviet Union's Sukhoi Design Bureau, the Su-7BKL was a single-engine, swept-wing fighter-bomber. The variant exported to Iraq was designed for rough-field operations and equipped with skids beside the main wheels, and provisions for two 13,000-pound-thrust rockets for short-field takeoffs. "For political reasons, I was never allowed to fly the Su-7," Shawler recalled. "I only made some engine runs and ground tests." He found the throttle quadrant confusing and was unable to get the engine up to full military power, but the brief opportunity provided useful data not previously available to the West. Testing was completed several days later, and with Shawler observing from the airfield, an Iraqi pilot took off and flew the airplane home. Shawler returned to the US but, traveling on a tourist visa, encountered some difficulty getting his Russian flight helmet through Customs.[74]

Maj. Norman L. Suits joined the Special Projects Branch in May 1971, assuming command of the unit two months later, when Shawler was reassigned as director of the F-15 Joint Test Force (JTF). A combat veteran, Suits had flown a hundred missions in Southeast Asia and earned the Silver Star. Having faced the MiG-17 in combat, he was now tasked with performing propulsion, performance, systems, stability and control, weapons, and avionics testing in the airplane. Shawler checked him out in the YF-114C on May 13 during a two-hour sortie over the Groom Lake area. Suits had to split his time between Edwards and Area 51 and didn't have another opportunity to fly the MiG until mid-August. As time permitted, he commuted to Groom Lake in any available F-104 or T-38, flew one or more MiG-17 sorties, and returned to Edwards for his primary duty, testing the F-111. Typically, he flew the MiG only once or twice a month. In the fall of 1972, he was joined by Maj. Charles P. "Pete" Winters, who served as his deputy and shared flying duties in the MiG-17.[75]

Winters had flown 298 combat missions in Southeast Asia and accumulated 478 combat hours in the F-100 before being selected to attend the Aerospace Research Pilot School. Upon graduation in July 1970, he remained at Edwards with the F-111 JTF, where he performed a variety of tests involving stability and control, expansion of the nuclear weapon

Norman Suits assumed command of the Special Projects Branch and HAVE GLIB in 1971. *USAF*

delivery envelope, engine icing, and weapon system development. While F-111A stall and spin characteristics were being evaluated, the airplane entered an uncontrolled spin and crashed, but Winters and his flight test engineer, Sgt. Patrick S. Sharp, ejected safely. Winters was also one of two pilots to participate in HAVE LEMON and HAVE LIME, both projects for developing an armed remotely piloted vehicle (RPV) for suppression of enemy air defenses.[76]

In September 1972, Suits was tasked to act as AFFTC project manager in support of a high-priority project called RIVET HASTE.[77] Air Force leaders initiated this effort after identifying training and equipment deficiencies plaguing fighter forces deployed to Southeast Asia. The effort was designed to mitigate these problems through a combination of aircrew training and aircraft modifications. The first phase of the project called for equipping the F-4E with wing slats, improved cockpit switches, and an electro-optical target identification system. The second and more important element emphasized pilot experience and training. Under the aegis of RIVET HASTE, TAC selected a number of handpicked crews made up of seasoned combat veterans to form an elite force of MiG killers. During an extensive training program at Nellis, these crews were introduced to the modified Phantoms and began practicing aerial-combat tactics. Each crew, consisting of a pilot and a weapon systems officer (WSO), was paired up to remain together throughout training and deployment, in order to develop coordination and camaraderie. Three groups, each consisting of six pilots and six WSOs, went through training at one-month intervals. Those that had already completed the course passed lessons learned on to the new trainees.[78]

Although all the RIVET HASTE crews experienced aerial combat in Southeast Asia, none had ever faced their adversary in a controlled environment. Therefore, as part of their training in Nevada, each crew flew three sorties against the HAVE GLIB MiG-17. Following arrangements by Lt. Col. Glenn F. "Pappy" Frick of the 57th Fighter Weapons Wing, two TAC pilots, Capt. Gaillard R. "Evil" Peck Jr. and Maj. Dawson R. "Randy" O'Neil, soon arrived at Area 51 to act as adversaries against the F-4 crews. Initially, Norm Suits objected to their assignment to the project and made it clear that they were not welcome on his turf. O'Neil stood up to the senior officer during a verbal altercation witnessed by the young captain. "Randy ate Norman's lunch," Peck later wrote in his memoirs. "From then on all was cool and we had a great time checking out and flying the MiG."[79]

Each tactical sortie involved the single MiG versus two or four Phantoms. The F-4 pilots quickly learned to take advantage of the Phantom's climb capabilities, and to avoid trying to match the MiG-17 in a turn. Being able to fly these sorties in a controlled environment allowed the Phantom crews to absorb each lesson and afforded them the luxury of experimenting with new tactics without the life-or-death stress of actual combat. One of the participants, Capt. Huey H. "Hugh" Moreland, later told an Air Force historian that those were the best training missions any of the RIVET HASTE crews ever experienced.[80]

Upon completion of training, they were sent to Udorn Royal Thai Air Base in Thailand with extensive knowledge of new aerial-combat tactics, and with aircraft that had been modified to alleviate previous shortcomings in handling qualities, weapons employment, and target identification. Unfortunately, the concept was introduced too late to do any good. Deployed RIVET HASTE crews flew only a handful of combat missions before the air war over Southeast Asia ended, and they never shot down a single enemy plane.[81]

Another significant event in 1972 was the formation of a training program at Nellis that simulated Warsaw Pact air combat scenarios in an effort to filter the lessons from black-world tactical exploitation programs into a "white world" (unclassified) environment. Initially equipped with T-38s and later F-5Es, airplanes that approximated the performance of the MiG-21—the Aggressors, as they became known—flew using Soviet tactics to simulate as accurately as possible what US aircrews might face in any conceivable conflict. Fighter pilots from units throughout the Air Force met the Aggressors in mock combat in the skies above Nevada in what came to be known as Red Flag exercises. Cleared for top-secret/special compartmented information, the Aggressors had access to the latest and most accurate intelligence available on Soviet equipment and tactics.[82] Randy O'Neil was selected to be operations officer for the new unit and, using connections he had made with AFSC during RIVET HASTE, made sure that several of the Aggressor pilots were checked out in the HAVE GLIB MiG-17. Among the first of these were Capt. Joe Lee Burns and Maj. David "DL" Smith, each of whom was sent "up-range" to the classified location to fly "the asset."[83]

The F-5E served as a reasonable analog for the MiG-21 and provided an unclassified alternative for equipping the Aggressor squadrons at Nellis. *USAF*

THE SECRET HISTORY OF AREA 51

The HAVE GLIB project acquired a MiG-17PF, like this one, which was given the designation YF-114D. *Via Curtis Peebles*

Following several years in Israel, the former HAVE DOUGHNUT MiG-21 returned to Area 51 as YF-110B, tail number 007. *National Library of Israel*

Efforts to expand the MiG evaluation project at Area 51 were rewarded in late 1972, when the FTD acquired an all-weather fighter variant of the MiG-17 designated MiG-17PF (NATO reporting name Fresco D). This model was equipped with search and ranging radar. The most significant characteristic distinguishing the MiG-17PF from the MiG-17F was a bulbous radome affixed to the inlet splitter and an extension on the upper lip of the intake. The new airplane was dubbed the YF-114D and assigned tail number 008. When Norm Suits made his first flight in the airplane on December 8, the forty-minute sortie was marred only by minor problems with the fuel pump. The mechanics soon resolved the problem, and by the end of January 1973, Suits had begun an accelerated flying schedule involving both the YF-114C and YF-114D.[84]

Around this time, a C-141 arrived at Groom Lake to deliver the same MiG-21F-13 that had been previously flown during HAVE DOUGHNUT. For documentation purposes, it still bore the designation YF-110B, but the Israelis had given the airplane a new tail number: 007. Suits checked out in the airplane over the course of two flights, the first on February 13 and the second—a night sortie—on February 23.[85] While Suits and Winters continued to conduct their technical evaluation of the MiGs, Navy and TAC authorities sought to expand tactical-exploitation opportunities. Meanwhile, the FTD worked quietly to acquire more airplanes and spare parts. As the program expanded, AFSC Headquarters put the Area 51 FME projects under the authority of a new blanket program called HAVE IDEA. The old name, HAVE GLIB, remained in use for the purposes of the joint AFFTC/CIA agreement.

More with Less

AFFTC support for HAVE IDEA was authorized per directive from the Air Force deputy chief of staff for plans and operations. As responsible test organization, the 6512th Test Squadron was tasked with planning, directing, documenting, and coordinating the program, which formally began on May 30, 1973, with the signing of Project Directive 73-115. The first flight was scheduled for June 4. At about the same time, Pete Winters was assigned as lead test pilot for the F-15 JTF. He continued flying the MiGs at Area 51 whenever necessary, but Maj. David L. Ferguson took over as Suits's deputy.[86]

During two combat tours in Vietnam, Ferguson flew more than a hundred missions in the F-105—first as a strike pilot and later flying "Wild Weasel" sorties for suppression of enemy air defenses. His squadron was responsible for missions within Route Pack Six, a region that included the heavily defended Hanoi corridor in North Vietnam, one of the most hazardous duty assignments for combat pilots in all of Southeast Asia. After returning to the US, he entered the Air Force Test Pilot School, graduating in 1972. His first assignment was to the Special Projects Branch, where he was checked out in the U-2. He spent several months flying the high-altitude reconnaissance jet in a variety of programs,

Dave Ferguson started as Suits's deputy and eventually became commander of the secret MiG squadron at Groom Lake. *USAF*

WE HAVE MET THE ENEMY | 213

Pete Winters, *left*, and Skip Anderson holding a plaque with two control sticks, one from a MiG-21 and the other from a MiG-17. *Via Dave Ferguson*

including Projects TRIM (Target Radiation Intensity Measurement) and HAVE COFFEE, both of which involved measuring the IR signatures of missile launch plumes, satellites, and reentry vehicles. Temporarily assigned to the Fighter Branch, he also flew in test projects involving the F-105B and F-4E. Suits checked him out on both the MiG-17 and MiG-21, but the latter was to be Ferguson's primary responsibility.

While with the Fighter Branch, Ferguson had worked closely with Maj. Leslie B. "Skip" Anderson III in several F-4 test projects. Anderson held a bachelor of science in astronautics from the US Air Force Academy, as well as a master's degree in aerospace engineering from the California Institute of Technology. Anderson was also a 1972 graduate of the Test Pilot School, and Ferguson thought his friend and former classmate would be well suited to the challenges inherent in Special Projects. Anderson was assigned to HAVE IDEA in September 1973 and began flying the MiGs the following month. Ferguson also recruited Lt. Col. Michael V. Love for HAVE IDEA. He had combat experience in Vietnam and had served two years as an instructor at the Test Pilot School before transferring to the Fighter Branch. Love divided his duty time between Special Projects activities in Nevada and a joint Air Force–NASA program to test wingless lifting-body research vehicles at Edwards.[87]

American airmen examine Indonesian MiG-21s at Iswahyudi Airport. These airplanes are in better shape than the ones acquired for the exploitation program. *Via Robert D. Young*

Following a CIA-sponsored overthrow of Indonesia's Communist dictatorship in 1970, the Indonesian air force retired five dozen MiG-17, MiG-19, and MiG-21 fighters. Lacking further Soviet engineering and maintenance support, the aircraft had swiftly broken down and been abandoned to the elements. Most were left outdoors or simply pushed into a ditch. The FTD saw this as an irresistible opportunity. Starting in 1973, the American government agreed to provide Indonesia with airplanes and helicopters in exchange for the derelict Soviet fighter jets.[88]

The first shipment of four MiG-21F-13 airframes soon arrived at Area 51 for inspection. All of them were in fairly poor shape, but Stan Kulikowski, Dick Sinclair, and their talented team of mechanics managed to assemble a single flightworthy airplane, which was given tail number 004. Because it was virtually identical to 007, and since the AF Form 5 now had space for tail numbers, the new MiG-21 was designated YF-110B, as were several others when they eventually became available.

As primary pilot for 004, Ferguson was scheduled to fly the airplane's first sortie on August 23 with Suits as chase. It was not an uneventful flight. The MiG's engine quit immediately after takeoff, forcing Ferguson to make an emergency landing on the lakebed, where the MiG-21 left a long, curving trail in the clay. Asked why he didn't just roll out straight ahead, Ferguson said he made the turn because he was "trying to avoid hitting a rock." Later, according to Suits, Ferguson was presented with a small rock as a souvenir of his ill-fated flight. Such incidents were rare, however. "We flew all the time, sometimes three or four flights a day," Suits recalled. "I never had an abort."[89]

In the summer of 1973, Pete Winters was detailed to a nine-month assignment as project pilot for HAVE IDEA, during which he flew eleven sorties in the MiG-21. Several of these involved flying simulated combat maneuvers against a preproduction F-15A in a project nicknamed HAVE DRY. Born out of the lessons learned in Vietnam, the McDonnell Douglas F-15 was an advanced, twin-engine, air-superiority fighter with a high thrust-to-weight ratio and the very latest radar and weapons technology. Though comparatively antiquated, the MiG-21 remained one of the most widely exported of all Soviet fighters, and one that F-15 pilots might reasonably expect to encounter in combat.

As chief of F-15 flight test, and with his intimate knowledge of the MiGs at Area 51, Wendell Shawler recognized a valuable opportunity when he saw one. Pursuant to a request from the F-15 System Program Office, most likely at Shawler's behest, AFFTC leadership authorized a limited comparative evaluation of the F-15 and MiG-21 to be conducted jointly by F-15 JTF and Project HAVE IDEA test personnel. Plans confined the two-day HAVE DRY evaluation to a limited number of comparative performance maneuvers consisting of side-by-side level accelerations, turns, and climbing pull-ups, as well as qualitative evaluation of the F-15's radar. Airplanes selected for the trials included the sixth preproduction F-15A and 007, the better of the two available MiG-21s. Both aircraft were instrumented and equipped with X-band radar beacons to facilitate tracking, but security restrictions precluded using telemetry systems to send data to test controllers on the ground. Maj. Roger J. Smith and Col. Frank W. Bloomcamp took turns flying the F-15, while Winters flew all of the MiG-21 sorties. Maj. Lloyd A. Edwards, F-15 project engineer, was responsible for analyzing the results.[90]

A portion of Norm Suits's personal flight record, AF Form 5, illustrates how pilots logged their time in the MiGs using the bogus MDS designations. *Via Norman Suits*

Project HAVE DRY pitted this antiquated MiG-21 against a modern air-superiority fighter. *USAF*

A preproduction F-15A proved more than a match for the MiG in one-on-one combat. *USAF*

On August 22, Smith rendezvoused with Winters over the Nellis Air Force Range. During this and each successive encounter, Smith tested the F-15's radar acquisition and lock-on capabilities. Flying in close formation at an altitude of 15,000 feet, each pilot accelerated with maximum afterburning thrust in order to evaluate the F-15's capability to increase separation distance from the MiG-21 in level flight. During the first tactical engagement, with the F-15 trailing approximately 1,500 feet behind the MiG-21, Winters entered a turn using maximum afterburner and maintained constant altitude while increasing power until he achieved the airplane's thrust-limited maximum turn capability. After completing a series of similar maneuvers, he broke off and landed at Area 51 to refuel. Smith, meanwhile, departed the test area to rendezvous with a KC-135 aerial tanker.[91]

The second engagement began with a 0.25 g unloaded acceleration, but this maneuver was terminated when Smith saw that his left engine oil pressure caution light had illuminated. Once the problem appeared to be resolved, Smith and Winters resumed thrust-limited turning maneuvers before switching to maximum-power vertical climbs. As expected, the F-15, with a better than 1:1 thrust-to-weight ratio, demonstrated superior climbing performance. Each maneuver was initiated with the two aircraft approximately side by side at 0.65 Mach and an altitude of about 15,000 feet. Winters accelerated to 0.87 Mach and pulled back on the stick, climbing in a 60-degree pitch attitude while gradually increasing his load factor to 3 g at a rate of 0.22 g per second. Approximately 7.5 seconds later, Smith initiated an identical maneuver at 0.88 Mach. After descending back to 15,000 feet, both pilots repeated the maneuver in a 45-degree climb, increasing the load factor to slightly more than 4 g. Unfortunately, quantitative comparison data for this maneuver were lost due to an instrumentation failure on the MiG-21. Once again, Winters was forced to land and top off his fuel while Smith rendezvoused with the tanker.[92]

Prior to the third engagement, Smith and Winters started another level acceleration run. This time, however, the MiG-21 suffered a series of compressor stalls when Winters attempted to light the afterburner. Disconcerted by the malfunction, and not wanting to subject a scarce asset to unnecessary risk, he elected to abort the remainder of the mission and return to base.

Three more sorties were scheduled for the following day. This time, Bloomcamp flew the F-15. Like Smith, he began each encounter with a radar evaluation. The first engagement of the day, and the fourth overall for HAVE DRY, included a level acceleration run to acquire data that were not collected the previous day, followed by a series of turns and climbs. Typically, the mission terminated with both airplanes going their separate ways for refueling. A fifth engagement consisted of more turning maneuvers and level acceleration. This time, however, upon landing at Area 51 for fuel, mechanics informed Winters of a serious maintenance issue. It was of sufficient significance that the planned sixth sortie was canceled.[93] Thus, Project HAVE DRY came to an end. Information gained during the brief study was subsequently applied to the development of operational tactics for the F-15.

By this point, TAC leadership was seeking increased access to the MiGs. Randy O'Neil spearheaded this effort with the help of Pappy Frick, who, as commander of Detachment 1, 57th FWW, served as TAC's liaison to HAVE IDEA test managers. Initially, TAC pilots detailed to HAVE IDEA were restricted to flying a single MiG-21. Norm Suits and other AFFTC authorities were concerned that allowing too many different people—particularly those who weren't test pilots—to fly the MiGs would increase the risk of damaging or crashing one of the scarce assets. Despite this strangely adversarial relationship, both sides eventually came to trust one another, and the TAC pilots were granted access to the other airplanes.[94]

Capt. Michael "Bat" Press was briefed into HAVE IDEA in 1973, shortly after accepting an assignment with the Aggressors. He was worried at first when the squadron operations officer called him into his office. "I thought I was in trouble," Press recalled, "but he said, 'Mike, you have been selected for a classified project, and I want you to show up at base operations tomorrow morning; pack a bag for a week. Someone will meet you in an F-4 and take you where you need to go. I can't tell you anything more than that, but don't tell anyone, not your family, your squadron mates or anyone else, where you are going or what you are doing.'"[95]

The following day at sunrise, with O'Neil's cryptic warning still echoing in his ears, Press met Norm Suits and climbed into the back seat of the senior officer's F-4. "We stayed in afterburner on the deck at about 500 feet, heading north out of Nellis, and then at about 50 nautical miles farther north, we dropped down to about 10 feet off the deck," Press remembered. Speeding over the desert, he felt as if he was looking up at the passing desert scenery, cactus, and Joshua trees as the Phantom turned westward and headed directly toward the dreaded "Box," the block of restricted airspace known as Dreamland. "I was always told to remain as far away from [that area] as possible on the threat of court-martial or worse," Press noted. After topping a ridgeline, he saw a vast lakebed, a long runway, and a cluster of hangars and buildings. Suits then dropped to treetop level again, lit the afterburners, and streaked over the lakebed at just above the speed of sound. "He proceeded to cross the base and boom every window, door, and person on the field," Press recalled. "He said this was their normal wake-up call in the morning."[96]

Press spent the next four years as part of the initial cadre of Aggressor pilots who were granted the privilege of flying the foreign assets. He started out flying the MiG-17 and eventually transitioned to the MiG-21, sharing these duties with DL Smith, Joe Lee Burns, and Capt. Ed "Pigpen" Clements. According to Press, "We started out flying against the Edwards chase planes under the leadership of Randy O'Neil, then we flew against F-4 Phantoms from the Fighter Weapons School and the 422nd Test and Evaluation Squadron." As leader of the project, Pappy Frick worked for the Tactical Fighter Weapons Center (TFWC) commander at Nellis, a two-star general. According to Press, for HAVE IDEA the TFWC commander reported directly to the TAC commander and then to the Air Force chief of staff. "Besides the MiG pilots and F-4 pilots from Nellis that flew in the program," said Press, "those were probably the few officers in the Air Force that even knew about the existence of HAVE IDEA [outside FTD and AFFTC]."[97]

In order to derive better value from TAC's exploitation of the assets, O'Neill, Peck, and others worked tirelessly to convince senior Air Force leaders that more TAC pilots, and specifically more Aggressor pilots, needed to fly the HAVE IDEA MiGs so they could accurately replicate Soviet tactics and transfer that knowledge to the rest of the Aggressor pilots and the fighter community as a whole. From about 1974 to 1976, HAVE IDEA tactical sorties advanced from simple one-versus-one engagements to more-advanced tactics development against F-4s and F-15s flown by the Fighter Weapons School and 422nd TES. Press, along with Maj. Robert "Kobe" Mayo, Maj. Gene Jackson, Maj. Alvin D. "Devil" Muller, and others, flew two-versus-two, two-versus-four, and sometimes four-versus-four engagements with MiG-17 and MiG-21 aircraft involved simultaneously.

According to Press, his most memorable mission during HAVE IDEA came one afternoon when he flew the MiG-21 against two F-4s within the Dreamland restricted area: "I was in military power to conserve fuel, as this was the last setup and I wanted to complete the engagement before reaching Bingo fuel." He vividly recalls being near the east end of the Box at about 20,000 feet when he merged with one of the Phantoms and entered into a slow, rolling scissors maneuver with his opponent. To his distress, Press noticed his MiG-21 was losing altitude and airspeed with every roll. "As these were tactics tests, there were *no* rules of engagement," he said. "If you thought you were going to hit the ground before the other guy hit it, then you would try to disengage by rolling out, separating, and trying to run away." He added that there were no knock-it-off provisions, and "The only end to the engagement was either a shot to a kill or a successful cut and run."[98]

Training-mission participants at Nellis were briefed to avoid the dreaded Dreamland box, nicknamed "Red Square," at all costs or face dire consequences. *Author*

The MiG-21, seen here in a steep climb over the range, was considered a formidable adversary. *USAF*

Still locked in a tight rolling scissors with the F-4, Press saw that his airspeed had dropped to about 150 knots and was rapidly decreasing as he plummeted toward the desert floor. Recognizing he could not disengage without taking a simulated heat-seeking missile or gun-shot, his only choices were to roll out and be "killed" and keep from crashing, or to light the afterburner and continue the engagement. "So, like the young foolish captain that I was, who had no fear or regard for the fact that he was flying a national asset," he explained, "I slammed the throttle full forward while at about 50 knots, [the airplane's] nose almost straight up in the air." His gambit paid off when the afterburner roared to life at approximately 200 feet above the ground, and Press practically scorched the tumbleweeds while making his escape. "I still wake up at night in a cold sweat, some forty years later, dreaming about this mission."[99]

Navy involvement in HAVE GLIB / HAVE IDEA began with the assignment of Marine Corps captain Peter B. Field from the Weapon Systems Test Directorate at the Naval Air Test Center, Patuxent River, Maryland. A recent graduate of the Naval Test Pilot School, he was designated HAVE GLIB project pilot in the summer of 1971 and performed this task as an additional duty through June 1974. During his three-year assignment, the MiGs were being flown against Navy F-4 jets to collect radar signature data. Field had the opportunity to fly the MiG-21 and was very impressed with the airplane's flying qualities and simple, rugged design. American pilots had always been quick to show disdain for the relatively crude—by Western standards—production quality of Soviet hardware, but Field found the MiG-21 to be a highly capable airplane. Even low-time pilots could operate it without great effort. Field appreciated the designer's attention to cockpit ergonomics and marveled at the airplane's speed and maneuverability. "It was not as smooth or as pretty as ours," he recalled, "but it was doggone effective."[100]

Throughout the program, Navy operational test and evaluation was conducted primarily by pilots from VX-4 at Point Mugu, the same squadron that participated in the earlier exploitation efforts. The first of these, Lt. Cmdr. John K. "Jack" Ready, was assigned to HAVE GLIB in August 1972. He was checked out in the MiG-21 by Dave Ferguson and remained with the project until July 1974.[101] Lt. Cmdr. Thomas A. Morgenfeld became VX-4's HAVE IDEA test director in January 1976. A graduate of the RAF's Empire Test Pilots' School, he was initially disappointed about his assignment to Point Mugu, but a friend told him that VX-4 was the only place where exciting things were happening. He was soon running a number of classified programs concerned with Soviet tactics and hardware, and was tasked with making sure that the Navy and Air Force were following the same approach with regard to intelligence on Soviet tactics, weapons, and equipment. As he later recalled, "We would read the latest threat assessments to come out of the FTD and I would make sure that we were being consistent and correct about what we were doing."[102] Morgenfeld ultimately flew a variety of Soviet fighters.

Naval aviator Tom Morgenfeld was detailed to HAVE IDEA in 1976. *Lockheed*

But airplanes were only one part of the exploitation effort. The FTD was also studying the characteristics of Eastern Bloc radar equipment. Among the highest intelligence priorities for the US and NATO military allies was the collection of up-to-date information on Soviet long-range tracking, target acquisition, and fire control systems that were widely distributed among the Communist states and their allies in Asia and the Middle East. Once again, Israel was a key player.

On October 6, 1973, Egypt and Syria attacked Israeli outposts in the Sinai Peninsula and the Golan Heights. In what came to be known variously as the Arab-Israeli War or the Yom Kippur War, the US backed Israel while the Soviets supplied Egypt and Syria with weapons and equipment. By the end of the month, the brief conflict had ended with an Israeli victory but had driven the US and the Soviet Union closer to nuclear war than at any time since the Cuban Missile Crisis. It also provided a rare opportunity for US intelligence analysts. Later that year, a team of FTD personnel visited an Egyptian airbase at Fayid on the Suez Canal, which had been captured by Israeli forces. While there, they cataloged a variety of equipment, each piece designated with a colorful NATO reporting name. They examined and removed SA-2, SA-3, and SA-7 missile systems, as well as an SA-6 transporter-erector-launcher and its Straight Flush control radar. They also appropriated P-10 Knife Rest, P-12 Spoon Rest, and P-35 Bar Lock early-warning radar systems, SNR-75 Fan Song and SNR-125 Low Blow missile control radars, and a ZSU 23-4 tracked antiaircraft battery along with its Gun Dish fire control radar. All were subsequently transported to Area 51 for testing.[103]

Additional threat systems were acquired from other sources as well. This endeavor spawned an ever-growing number of FTD exploitation projects with nicknames such as HAVE JEEP, HAVE HEAT, HAVE OUT, and HAVE LIST.[104] When actual hardware was unavailable or inoperable, technicians reverse-engineered and replicated the foreign equipment. Much of this materiel ended up

Operationally, the Fan Song radar was used in conjunction with the SA-2 Guideline surface-to-air missile. *DoD*

at Area 51, where a complex of actual Soviet systems and replicas began to grow around Slater Lake and throughout the valley northwest of the main cantonment area. Ranging in size from the Spoon Rest's simple Yagi antenna to the massive P-14 Tall King early-warning radar, they were arranged to simulate a Soviet-style integrated air defense system (IADS).[105] Both fixed and mobile threat systems were available. Height-finder radar worked in conjunction with early-warning search and acquisition systems to provide azimuth and range data to the IADS network. Several AN/MPQ-47 Quick Kill track-while-scan radar simulators replicated SAM target acquisition systems. These were capable of acquiring multiple targets while simultaneously providing an overall view of the surrounding airspace to maintain situational awareness.

A P-37 Bar Lock search-and-acquisition radar system near Valley Road, north of Groom Lake. *DLR via Joerg Arnu*

The P-14 Tall King early-warning radar was the largest system acquired for exploitation by the US. An array similar to this one was installed 3.5 miles southwest of Groom Lake. *DoD*

Ultimately, the Groom Lake radar complex allowed analysts to identify threat signals, develop jamming systems and defensive tactics, and devise weapons and procedures for defeating electronic threats. Equally important, it served as the basis for an airborne RCS range that played a vital role in the development of future tactical and strategic aircraft. Notwithstanding the grave character of this enterprise, each of the radar systems was given a name such as Mary, Kay, Susan, and Kathy, after flight attendants on the Area 51 commuter shuttles, some of whom had been known to spend off hours sunbathing on the shore of Slater Lake.[106]

Though temporarily mothballed in 1967, the original EG&G radar site played a vital role after being reactivated to measure the RCS of the MiG-21 and MiG-17. Now relegated to the company's Microwave Department, this facility was for a time manned by a mere skeleton crew under the supervision of John W. Grace in support of the expanding exploitation program. Then, in 1972, the RCS measurement project at Groom Lake began ramping up and the Microwave Department split from the main company to become EG&G Special Projects, Inc., under the direction of William T. "Billy" Barrett. Other key personnel included David B. Haen, who had conducted airborne telemetry work with the A-12. He subsequently set up the first radar repair and calibration lab at Area 51. During the mid-1970s, EG&G Special Projects security and safety manager Denise Rodreick visited the site on numerous occasions, an experience she said was very rewarding. "Having been briefed on the programs and now being able to see where it all occurred, and to actually see where our employees worked, made my job much more worthwhile and interesting," she said. Though not permanently assigned to the test site, Rodreick's presence at the Groom Lake facility foreshadowed coming organizational and cultural changes. As she explained years later, "In the early days, there were no facilities for women at the Area and, little by little, women started being hired to work there."[107]

By this time, three dedicated AFSC pilots, six maintenance personnel, and a handful of engineers and technicians assigned to HAVE IDEA were beginning to see an increase in the tempo of their own tasks. On the basis of the comparatively small scale of the Special Projects Branch's activities, their involvement was initially limited to only part-time or additional-duty efforts. But this was about to change. Plans were underway to acquire more airplanes, conduct a greater number of sorties per week, and assign additional support personnel. Those assigned to the program took to calling themselves the "Red Hats" in acknowledgment that their mission involved operating Communist aircraft and other Eastern Bloc military hardware.

Skip Anderson was the first among them to suggest that their secret organization needed a distinctive insignia for morale purposes and esprit de corps. His wife, Karen, designed a unit emblem consisting of a black-bordered yellow disk with two tabs. In the center of the disk, a growling Russian bear perched atop the hemisphere of a globe, rendered simply and with no detail other than latitude and longitude lines. The bear wore a broad-brimmed red hat and was surrounded by six red stars. The upper tab displayed the name RED HATS, while the lower tab contained the organization's motto, MORE WITH LESS, symbolizing the team's ability to consistently produce useful data despite the challenges of operating from a remote location with a small cadre and having to scrounge or manufacture spare parts to keep their aircraft

Billy Barrett, *left*, head of EG&G Special Projects, and airborne telemetry specialist Dave Haen. *Roadrunners*

Denise Rodreick managed security and safety for EG&G Special Projects. She eventually married Dave Haen. *Roadrunners*

Skip Anderson's wife, Karen, designed the original Red Hats emblem. *USAF*

flyable. Mike Love offered an idea for a second emblem to be applied to the pilots' flight helmet visor shields. One afternoon he sat down with Ferguson and Anderson, and the three sketched out several circular designs with various arrangements of stars. The final result was a 4-inch-diameter white disk with a tight grouping of six five-pointed red stars, five with points touching to enclose a pentagonal space in the center in which the sixth star nestled inverted relative to the others. One star was slightly larger than the others, giving the arrangement an asymmetrical appearance. "That particular skewed star arrangement looked really good on a curved surface," Ferguson recalled, "so we decided to make our visor covers with that design." It could be easily painted onto the red helmet by using a simple stencil, or applied as a decal.[108]

In December 1974, Norm Suits left Edwards to attend the Air Warfare Course at RAF Cranwell, England, after which he was assigned to serve as a senior advisor to the British aircraft test organization at RAF Boscombe Down. That same month, Anderson was reassigned to the 436th Tactical Fighter Training Squadron at Holloman, having logged a total of forty-seven HAVE IDEA sorties. Dave Ferguson was immediately promoted to chief of the Special Projects Branch, which thus far had only four flyable assets: two MiG-21F-13s, the MiG-17F, and the MiG-17PF. Ferguson had been offered a choice between Special Projects and the Lightweight Fighter program, a fly-off competition between the General Dynamics YF-16 and Northrop YF-17 to determine which would be selected for acquisition as the Air Force's newest jet. The latter should have seemed like a dream job for a fighter pilot like Ferguson, but he saw things differently. "I chose Special Projects," he recalled, "because the branch chief had total control of the program and flew most of the missions himself."[109]

At Edwards, the CIA had recently closed down Detachment G at North Base because the agency's U-2 program had come to an end. Ferguson saw this as an opportunity. The auxiliary field had a 6,000-foot runway, several hangars, and a fire station. Additionally, it was very remote from the Edwards Main Base complex, providing unparalleled privacy at the busy test site. In 1975 the Red Hats took over the largest hangar at North Base, along with the chow hall and several other buildings. These were soon enclosed within a fenced compound with its own security gate. Armed guards ensured that curious visitors would keep their distance. North Base served as the Red Hats headquarters and workspace when the unit was not deployed to Area 51.[110]

By that time, Devil Muller, Kobe Mayo, and Capt. Ronald W. Iverson had replaced Joe Lee Burns and DL Smith as TAC representatives assigned to the Red Hats. Occasionally, other TAC pilots were allowed to fly the MiGs as well. Nellis Aggressors Ed Clements and Gene Jackson, for example, each made one orientation sortie in the MiG-17. At first, they were permitted to fly the MiG only in one-versus-one combat-maneuvering sorties against other experienced Aggressors. But these missions

A second emblem, specifically created for use on the Red Hats flight helmets, was designed by Mike Love, Dave Ferguson, and Skip Anderson. *USAF*

were infrequent, and the assets were sometimes grounded for months due to maintenance issues or spare-parts shortages. Eventually, the TAC syllabus was expanded to include engagements of two versus two or more. When Capt. Francis K. "Paco" Geisler joined the Aggressors in 1975, his instructor was Muller, who immediately recognized his potential. Geisler was soon teaching academics to the fighter squadrons at Nellis, and, before long, Muller informed him that he would be receiving additional training. Geisler had no idea what this meant until he was "read in" to HAVE IDEA. "First, they showed me a MiG in a hangar [at Groom Lake]," he recalled, "and then they had me exposed to one in the air."[111]

As the program grew, more AFSC pilots were assigned. Capt. John H. Casper and Maj. Steven R. Nagel joined the Red Hats in 1976. A Vietnam veteran with 229 combat missions, Casper had served as a test pilot with the 6512th TS at Edwards since 1975, where he performed weapons delivery and avionics testing in the F-4 and A-7. Nagel had also served with the 6512th. Prior to assignment to HAVE IDEA, he performed engine testing in the A-7 and release testing of the B77 nuclear weapon shape from an F-4. As a testament to the caliber of personnel selected for Special Projects duty, both pilots were destined to become astronauts, and each eventually flew four space shuttle orbital missions.

Casper's first sortie was in 007, and he found the MiG-21 a joy to fly. "I was impressed," he recalled, declaring that "the aircraft felt fast and nimble, with light control stick forces and good harmony between pitch and roll control." In the summer of 1977, after a Communist Chinese pilot defected to Taiwan with a Shenyang J-6 (a Chinese copy of the Soviet MiG-19), Casper was sent to examine it. He and several Red Hats maintenance personnel flew to Taiwan and made a thorough inspection of the aircraft. Although he was not permitted to fly the jet, Casper checked out the controls and made some taxi runs while the technicians measured engine heat and radar signatures.

Steve Nagel initially flew HAVE IDEA sorties as an additional duty above and beyond his work at Edwards, but eventually he joined the Red Hats full time. While his work with the MiGs was laudable, he became infamous for an incident that, according to Norm Suits, resulted in damages to the test site valued at approximately $50,000. On the morning in question, Nagel made a high-speed, low-altitude pass over the runway in full afterburner. Without intending to, he exceeded Mach 1 and caused a sonic boom that shattered the control tower windows and dislodged ceiling tiles and fluorescent lights in some of the buildings. "Fortunately for Steve," said Casper, "his aircraft was found to have a faulty airspeed/Mach indicator, so he didn't get into official trouble, but he was ribbed about the incident for much of his career."[112]

The AFFTC commander, Maj. Gen. Thomas P. Stafford, took a personal interest in the FME programs for which he was responsible. He was extremely impressed with the ever-growing collection of foreign airplanes, radar, and surface-to-air missile systems being tested at Groom Lake, and the "handpicked team of super-talented NCOs [noncommissioned officers] and test pilots" known as the Red Hats. "The NCOs did a tremendous job of keeping the Soviet aircraft in top flight condition," he later recalled in his autobiography. Besides performance testing and tactical evaluation of the MiGs, SAC occasionally sent B-52 bombers into Dreamland on simulated penetration bomb runs to evaluate the capabilities of Soviet radar and fighters to track and intercept them. Stafford loved flying with the Red Hats whenever possible, especially after one of the maintainers painted "General Tom Stafford" in Russian Cyrillic characters on the canopy rim of the MiG-17F.[113]

In July 1976, Col. Charles J. Luther, AFSC deputy chief of staff for intelligence, arranged for CIA director George H. W. Bush to visit Area 51 to see the Red Hats facilities and assets for himself. While there, Bush received several briefings and a tour of a hangar full of MiGs and had the opportunity to witness a flight demonstration by Maj. Ferguson. Bush seemed quite impressed with the operation and later sent letters of appreciation, thanking his hosts for the opportunity to observe the operation firsthand and for their contributions to what he described as a "significant national effort."[114]

CIA director George H. W. Bush visited Area 51 in 1976 for a tour of the Red Hats facilities. *CIA*

A Gift from the East

Later that year, the Red Hats had an opportunity to examine one of the most mysterious Soviet fighters. First revealed nearly a decade earlier, the MiG-25 (NATO reporting name Foxbat) was reportedly capable of cruising at Mach 3.2 and reaching altitudes above 80,000 feet. This perplexed Western experts, who wondered how the Soviets had apparently achieved unexpected breakthroughs in metallurgy, engine and airframe design, and perhaps even avionics. In 1973, Air Force secretary Robert C. Seamans asserted that the MiG-25 was "probably the best interceptor in production in the world today." Records set in 1967 with stripped-down prototypes achieved a speed of 1,852 mph and a zoom-climb altitude of 118,898 feet. If the MiG-25 proved to be as formidable as analysts believed, the American government would be forced to respond with costly and urgent defense appropriations. If, on the other hand, Western fears proved unfounded, then the DoD and Congress could more efficiently and intelligently allocate resources to counteract real threats. FTD analysts were desperate for answers.[115]

Those answers were delivered on a silver platter on September 6, 1976, when Lt. Viktor Ivanovich Belenko, with the Soviet air force, departed from his assigned flight plan during a training sortie, dove to treetop level to avoid being tracked on radar, switched off his radio, and flew toward Japan. Flying at low altitude rapidly depleted his fuel supply, and throughout his harrowing journey he worried that he might be spotted and shot down by Soviet interceptors or missile batteries. With only thirty seconds of fuel remaining, Belenko broke through the clouds near the island of Hokkaido, where his only option was to land immediately at Hakodate Airport. On approach he narrowly missed a departing commercial airliner before touching down at high speed, skidding off the runway, and blowing a tire. The MiG-25 came to rest in the grass beyond the end of the runway. As soon as he exited the cockpit, Belenko tried to communicate to airport officials that he was requesting political asylum in the United States.[116]

Upon learning of this momentous event, Dave Ferguson called Maj. Gen. Stafford to request an urgent meeting to discuss the exploitation possibilities. Belenko's defection had ignited a political firestorm. The Soviets were furiously demanding that both plane and pilot be immediately returned. Though it was unlikely that such a valuable defector would be denied asylum, US authorities would probably agree to return the MiG-25 as a matter of diplomacy. Ferguson made a strong case that if the Red Hats were to examine the plane, then time was of the essence. As Stafford recalled, "Twenty minutes later, I was signing special travel orders for him and several senior Red Hats NCOs to fly to Japan to examine Belenko's MiG."[117]

Ferguson traveled to Hakodate with SMSgt. Robert O. "Bobby" Ellis and other maintenance technicians and a team of FTD analysts, eleven men in all. The mission, dubbed Project STABLEMATE, was carried out under the remit of HAVE BRIDGE. Ferguson hoped to fly the MiG-25, but due to political sensitivities he was allowed only to conduct ground evaluations. Nevertheless, engine runs and checkout of the avionics suite and radar systems proved immensely valuable. Once it became clear that the Japanese government would soon accede to the Soviets' demands, American analysts pressed ahead with a quick, five-day exploitation as they hastily disarmed and disassembled the Foxbat. This provided a quick-look study of the airplane's propulsion system, structures and materials, cockpit, and weapons. Ferguson studied the control panels, examining switch and instrument locations in order to estimate pilot workload. Western diplomats fended off Soviet entreaties long enough for the Red Hats to airlift the MiG-25 via C-5A from Hakodate to Hyakuri Japan Air Self-Defense Force Base, east of Tokyo, for a more comprehensive exploitation.[118]

Belenko's plane had been manufactured between December 1975 and February 1976 and was thus one of the Soviets' latest, most sophisticated production aircraft. The engines, radar, computer, automatic pilot, weapons-fire control mechanism, electronic-countermeasures, hydraulic, communications, and other systems were removed, measured, x-rayed, sampled, and photographed in detail.

Belenko's MiG-25 on the grass beyond the end of the runway at Hakodate Airport. *NARA via Gerald Ford Presidential Library*

Exploitation of the MiG-25 had to be accomplished rapidly, and there was no opportunity to fly the airplane. *NARA via Gerald Ford Presidential Library*

Technicians even made acoustic recordings of engine noise. The results of mechanical, electronic, and metallurgical analysis surprised FTD specialists. The airplane's electronic systems still used vacuum tubes instead of transistors. Analysts surmised that the Soviets must have reasoned that vacuum tubes would not be affected by electromagnetic pulse in the event of nuclear attack, were more resistant to temperature extremes than transistors, and were easier to replace at remote airfields where transistors might not be readily available. All welding was done by hand, and rivet heads were left exposed in areas not subjected to critical levels of parasitic aerodynamic drag. The airplane's metal skin was flecked with rust; it had been made from steel alloys rather than titanium, although strips of titanium were used in areas subject to the most-severe heating.

Information provided by the pilot's flight manual and data supplied by Belenko himself under initial interrogation by the CIA seemed surprising and, at first, contradictory to what was already known about the MiG-25. "You cannot safely exceed Mach 2.8, but actually we were forbidden to exceed Mach 2.5," Belenko explained. "At high speeds the engines have a very strong tendency to accelerate out of control, and if they go above Mach 2.8, they will overheat and burn up." Three years earlier, according to intelligence reports, a MiG-25 was tracked overflying Israel at Mach 3.2 and reportedly landed in Egypt with its engines completely wrecked. Western analysts had thought this was a freak accident, but Belenko assured his interrogators that it was simply the inevitable consequence of operating the Foxbat's Tumansky R15D-300 engines to maximum performance capability.[119]

Flying at optimum altitude, without maneuvering or using afterburner, the MiG-25 could fly in a straight line for 744 miles. The Foxbat's operational combat radius was only 186 miles. It was not an air-superiority fighter, but rather an interceptor designed to climb at tremendous speeds, fire missiles during a single pass, and then land. Being limited to 2.2 g turns with full fuel tanks and less than 5 g with nearly empty tanks, it was not well suited to air combat maneuvering. Although the airplane's search-and-tracking radar had a range of 56 miles and was virtually jam-proof, it was incapable of distinguishing targets at altitudes below 1,600 feet due to ground clutter. The MiG-25 was also equipped with a superb autopilot and digital communications system.

With a gross weight of 64,200 pounds, the MiG-25 could carry a weapons load of two missiles to a maximum operational altitude of 78,740 feet for a maximum duration of two minutes; carrying four missiles reduced the maximum altitude to 68,900 feet. Although experts had feared that the MiG-25 would be a threat to the SR-71, Belenko assured them this was not the case. The Blackbird flew too high and fast to be caught in a trailing pursuit. Additionally, Soviet air-to-air missiles lacked sufficient velocity to overtake a target cruising at Mach 3 speeds, and in the event of a head-on intercept the missile's guidance system could not adjust to the high closure rate of the SR-71.[120]

Not at all surprising either to the Red Hats or FTD analysts were Belenko's claims that the MiG-25 had been remarkably free of mechanical problems. Like other Soviet airplanes, it had been designed for ease and simplicity of maintenance. Even a mechanic with modest skills and training could quickly check critical systems by inserting plugs from portable test sets. All components most likely to require maintenance were contained in an easily accessible rack situated behind the cockpit. Simply by turning a hydraulic valve, a mechanic could raise the rack and by turning smaller valves could gain access to each separate component for repair or maintenance.

Once the Americans and Japanese had finished methodically mining the MiG-25 of its secrets, they finally agreed to return the plane to the Soviets. On November 12, more than two months after Belenko's defection, a convoy of eight tractor-trailer trucks delivered the airplane—in pieces—to the port of Hitachi, where the Soviet freighter *Taigonos* waited with a crew believed to be augmented by military technicians and KGB (intelligence) agents. Before departing, the Soviets took several days to inventory the parts, making sure that all were accounted for. For the next two years, FTD analysts gleefully pored over their trove of data under a scientific and technical-exploitation effort dubbed HAVE RIDE, and produced detailed reports describing their findings.[121]

Critics, most notably Rep. Milton R. "Bob" Carr of the House Armed Services Committee, were quick to disparage the MiG-25 as being barely equal to the aging F-4 Phantom and "hopelessly outclassed by our new[-] generation McDonnell [Douglas] F-15 and General Dynamics F-16 . . . our two newer Air Force fighters [that] can out-climb, out-accelerate, out-turn, out-see, out-hide, and out-shoot the Foxbat by margins so wide that our expected kill-ratio advantage is almost incalculable."[122]

Technicians examine the cockpit and inner workings of the MiG-25. *NARA via Gerald Ford Presidential Library*

Yet, having closely examined one during its brief visit to Japan, some American analysts were very impressed with the MiG-25. One reportedly said that some aspects of the plane were brilliantly engineered. Though relatively crude by Western standards, the plane seemed likely to be capable of performing its mission effectively at a fraction of the cost of a US equivalent, should one have been built. "We thought it was a damned good plane, and that's what it turned out to be," another analyst commented. "We're belittling it because it's unsophisticated or because it rusts; in fact, it can fly higher, faster, and with a bigger payload than any plane in the world." As had been seen during previous exploitation of Eastern Bloc military hardware, it was readily apparent that Soviet designers were efficient cost managers who used only as much quality as was needed to accomplish a task. One expert summed up the situation: "They [Soviet designers] seem to ask, 'Why go to the expense of developing something new when we have something proven and cheaper on the shelf?' They could come over here and teach us something in the way of cost-conscious management and design."[123]

Red Eagles

Both the TAC and AFSC exploitation efforts underwent significant reorganization due to the exponential growth of FME flight testing and expanded emphasis on passing on lessons learned to US tactical aircrews. The latter resulted in a program that eventually exposed more than six thousand American airmen to simulated combat with a variety of Soviet fighter planes in the skies over Nevada.

On April 1, 1977, the TAC exploitation team was organized into a more formalized unit called the 4477th Test and Evaluation Flight. Although this unit was actually squadron sized, the 4477th TEF was initially designated a "flight" in order to conceal its significance and scope of operations. Lt. Col. Glenn Frick commanded the initial cadre, which included Maj. Ron Iverson (operations officer), Lt. Cmdr. Charles J. "Heater" Heatley III, Maj. Gerrald D. "Huffer" Huff, Lt. Cmdr. Tom Morgenfeld, Maj. Joseph L. "José" Oberle, and Maj. Don "Devil" Muller (who doubled as project security officer) as the six pilots; Maj. Jim Keys and Capt. Bud Horan as ground-controlled intercept (GCI) radar controllers; SSgt. Gary Lewallen as Operations NCOIC; and a team of aircraft maintenance technicians headed by Bobby Ellis, whom Frick hired away from the Red Hats.[124] Heatley was the driving force behind naming the newly minted unit the "Red Eagles," largely on the basis of his belief that the Soviet air force had a fighter weapons school of that name.[125]

The original Red Eagles unit emblem. *Author*

Rather than simply perform tactical evaluations of each aircraft type, the Red Eagles set out to acquire as many airframes as possible of as many different types as they could get their hands on. The purpose of these acquisitions was to build a fleet of fully operational Soviet fighters to use in dissimilar air-combat training over the Nevada ranges. Unlike the Aggressors, who used the F-5E as a surrogate for the MiG-21, the Red Eagles planned to expose US fighter pilots to more-realistic simulated combat against actual MiG-17s, MiG-21s, and other types. The unit's first airplanes included two MiG-17s, 002 and 008, and six MiG-21s. This program, dubbed CONSTANT PEG, was initiated at the direction of Air Force Headquarters in January 1978. As with earlier FME programs, the Navy also played a significant role. TAC would have overall control, but the funding was to be split, with the Air Force providing 70 percent and the Navy 30 percent.[126] Plans for CONSTANT PEG called for continuous operation of a large number of aircraft, and with a growing contingent of support personnel it was clear that the Red Eagles would soon need a new home away from Area 51.

A MiG-17 leads a four-ship formation, trailed by a MiG-21. The two accompanying F-5E jets from the 64th Aggressor Squadron at Nellis were used to simulate MiG-21 performance characteristics, as well as Soviet tactics, in mock aerial combat during annual Red Flag training exercises. *USAF*

The obvious choice of location was Area 52, the Tonopah Test Range (TTR) complex, approximately 65 miles northwest of Groom Lake at the northwest corner of the Nellis Air Force Range.[127] Nearly two decades earlier, the AEC had chosen this area, known as Cactus Flat, for use as a ballistic test range for nuclear weapon shapes. In 1956, the Air Force issued a permit to Sandia Laboratories to operate the range, and testing began in February 1957. The Tonopah site proved more than adequate both for high- and low-altitude bombing operations. It was remote and isolated, air and ground traffic caused few interruptions, and the weather was reasonably good throughout the year. By late 1958, the AEC had decided to make the TTR a permanent facility, and its mission rapidly evolved to include rocket launch capability for testing parachute systems and shock-resistant components, high-explosive studies, and emplacement of 155 mm and 203 mm guns to test artillery-fired atomic projectile designs. Research at TTR included the study of underground blast effects, explosive case ruptures, shock wave propagation, cratering, and overpressure measurements. Additionally, in the spring of 1963, several nuclear safety experiments similar to the earlier Project 56 and Project 57 took place on Cactus Flat. Over the course of the next several years, Sandia transformed TTR into a highly instrumented outdoor laboratory.[128]

During the 1960s a crude 5,000-foot airstrip was constructed, mainly for delivery of supplies. Sandia Strip, as it was known, wasn't even equipped with runway lights until 1969. Establishment of the airfield was necessary because most of the Sandia employees at TTR had moved to Las Vegas and subsequently began commuting daily to the range by air. The runway was extended to 6,600 feet in 1970 and equipped with a VOR localizer and nondirectional radio beacon the following year. By the spring of 1975, the Air Force had begun to take a greater interest in TTR. Col. Joseph Salvucci, a senior TFWC leader, announced the creation of the Tonopah Electronic Combat Range (TECR), also known as Site 4, in the eastern portion of Cactus Flat. He assured local residents of the nearby towns of Tonopah and Goldfield that they would scarcely be aware of jets conducting electronic-warfare training at the range and that they would seldom see any of the aircraft involved. The TECR provided a diverse selection of simulated and real-world threats, from long-range tracking systems to fire control radars. Activities at Site 4 not only enhanced US tactical capabilities but also served as a cover for the eventual arrival of the Red Eagles. If queried about their presence in Tonopah, squadron personnel could simply claim they worked at the TECR. According to Dave Haen, who transferred to the TECR as EG&G section head in the early 1980s, "Site 4 began with 20 technical employees and increased to well over 200 in a matter of years."[129]

The old Sandia airstrip needed substantial improvement before it could serve as a viable base of operations. In May 1978, the deputy secretary of defense approved $7 million to fund Phase I construction of a new airfield and support facilities for the 4477th TEF. Initial efforts included the addition of a maintenance hangar, concrete parking apron, taxiway, propane tank, a few permanent outbuildings, and sixteen mobile homes for use as personnel accommodations. The original runway was extended to 10,000 feet, with a 1,000-foot overrun on each end, and widened to 150 feet. Runway 14-32 (so numbered because it had the same magnetic heading as the runway at Area 51) was equipped with two arresting barriers as well as equipment for navigation and instrument landings.[130]

Lt. Col. Gaillard Peck assumed command from Frick on October 1. Up to this point, the 4477th TEF had continued to operate from Groom Lake, but now it was time for the Red Eagles to move into their new roost. On July 17, 1979, Peck climbed into the cockpit of a MiG-21 and bade farewell to Area

A MiG-21 taxiing at TTR following the Red Eagles' move from Groom Lake in 1979. The new airfield facilities provided the 4477th with ample room for growth. *USAF*

51. Joe Oberle taxied out behind him in the former HAVE FERRY MiG-17. Following the short hop to TTR, the pair made several low passes over the new runway before landing. Five more MiG-21s and the other MiG-17 arrived at TTR in short order, and the 4477th was soon ready to commence training operations.[131]

Phase II construction began at TTR in September 1980. At a cost of $18 million, it included expansion of the parking apron, construction of another taxiway, fuel and water storage tanks, a dining hall, a warehouse, support utilities, and a 42,000-square-foot hangar. When completed in January 1982, this phase began the transition of the TTR airfield from a bare base to a standard Air Force installation.[132] But the Red Eagles were not the only tenant to occupy the facility. In March 1981, Phase III construction began in preparation for the arrival of the even more shadowy 4450th Tactical Group. Against all logic or reason, this supersecret unit appeared to have been formed to conduct classified avionics and electronic-warfare testing, using antiquated A-7 Corsair II attack jets. Like the Red Eagles, they were to be based at TTR, and so additional facilities had to be built at a cost of $79 million. These included fifty-four hangars grouped together in several sets of double rows dubbed "canyons," where each hangar would house only a single aircraft. Unlike the portion of the base allocated to the Red Eagles, the 4450th TG flight line was surrounded by a double set of tall fences topped with barbed wire and intrusion-warning sensors. Authorized personnel had to submit to a palm print scan for entry. These measures seemed highly unusual considering their alleged purpose.

The 4450th TG was activated at Nellis in October 1979 and began moving personnel to TTR in June 1981. During the interim, airmen assigned to the unit made a show of surrounding their aircraft with armed security guards and warning signs while ground crews bustled around a strange-looking pod installed beneath the wing. This spurious device, festooned with flashing lights and venting peculiar vapors, had been ginned up by TSgt. Philip "Tin Man" Barta and TSgt. Charles "Bags" Baggerly, using the shell of a surplus BLU-27 incendiary bomb. They immediately nicknamed it the "Klingon cloaking device." The forward end featured a lens from an electro-optically guided glide bomb with a pulsing red light, while the body of the pod bristled with UHF and VHF blade antennas, and several faux blowout ports similar to those used on some nuclear weapons. According to Doug Robinson, a former maintenance officer for the 4450th, "It was truly an awesome[-]looking thing when mounted under the wing of an A-7D."[133] It was all, of course, an elaborate subterfuge. Although the unit actually did operate A-7s, they also flew something else—a mysterious black airplane that emerged from its Tonopah hangar only in the dead of night. That airplane would eventually spawn numerous rumors—many of them true—as well as UFO sightings.

Variable-Geometry Fighter

Exploitation of the MiG-17 and MiG-21 provided the opportunity to examine Soviet first- and second-generation fighter technology. Although they represented 1950s-era designs, both aircraft represented significant threats because they not only were employed by the Soviet air Force but had also been widely exported to Communist allies around the globe. By 1970, the Mikoyan-Gurevich Design Bureau was producing a third-generation fighter called the MiG-23 (known in the West by its NATO reporting name: Flogger). It was a single-engine jet with variable-geometry wings swept forward for low-speed flight, such as during takeoff and landing, and swept back for high-speed flight at speeds up to Mach 2.35. Two major variants and more than a dozen subvariants were produced in large numbers, with export versions being sold to Cuba and Soviet allies in Europe, Asia, and the

An A-7D in the livery of the 4450th Tactical Group. This organization's alleged purpose was to test classified avionics, but this was just part of an elaborate cover story. *USAF*

One example of the so-called Klingon cloaking device carried beneath the wing of the A-7D was really just a dressed-up luggage pod. *Author*

Middle East. One variant, the MiG-23MS, was optimized for air-to-air combat. It was equipped with a twin-barrel 23 mm cannon, advanced air-intercept radar, and a variety of air-to-air missiles. A second variant, designated MiG-23BN, was optimized for air-to-ground attack and met Soviet requirements for a lightweight fighter-bomber. This model retained the 23 mm gun but lacked radar. Instead, it was equipped with a laser rangefinder and bombsight, armored windscreen, and a raised pilot seat to improve visibility. FTD analysts were extremely anxious to get their hands on a MiG-23 of any type.

An opportunity finally arose as a result of improved diplomatic ties between the US and Egypt. The two nations had sustained a rocky relationship for nearly two decades, but things improved after Egyptian president Anwar al-Sadat came to power in 1970. Seeking to improve his nation's economy and security, he secretly approached US secretary of state William Rogers in May 1971 with an appeal for friendship, even offering to end Egypt's fifteen-year alliance with the Soviet Union in favor of restoring relations with the United States. In a bold move toward that end, al-Sadat expelled thousands of Soviet advisers from Egypt in July 1972. Equally important, he made unprecedented efforts to establish peaceful relations between Egypt and Israel with help from Rogers's successor, Henry Kissinger.[134]

After the US resumed economic aid to Egypt, American officials began negotiating to acquire examples of the military hardware Egypt had purchased from the Soviets. The architect of this endeavor was James R. Fees, CIA station chief in Cairo. Since assuming his post in 1974, he had worked tirelessly to build trust and establish relationships with officials at the highest levels of the Egyptian government. His first major achievement was enlisting the aid of Vice President Hosni Mubarak in obtaining copies of technical manuals and pilot handbooks for the MiG-21 and MiG-23. Next, Fees arranged for Brig. Gen. Richard V. Secord, then serving as chief US military adviser to Iran, to visit Egypt for an orientation flight in a MiG-23. Finally, he lobbied Mubarak to convince al-Sadat to provide the US with some Floggers in exchange for a variety of Western military items that included Sidewinder missiles.

Jim Fees, CIA station chief in Cairo, examines an Egyptian MiG-23MS. American analysts were anxious to get their hands on an example for technical exploitation. *Fees collection*

Fees successfully arranged the acquisition of more than a dozen Floggers that eventually found their way to the Red Hats and Red Eagles. *Fees collection*

For their part, the Egyptians were not averse to disposing of the airplanes, which had been grounded since the Soviets stopped providing logistical and technical support. By late 1975, all Egyptian MiG-23s had been placed in storage at Bani Suwayf Air Base, in the Nile River valley about 60 miles south of Cairo. Some of these were eventually traded to China for spare parts and support for Egypt's MiG-17 and MiG-21 fleets. The rest went to the US, thanks entirely to Fees's persistence. Negotiations were finalized by July 1977; all that remained was to complete the acquisition. Gen. William G. Moore Jr., commander in chief of Military Airlift Command (MAC), authorized operations orders for two classified airlift missions dubbed VOLANT CAT and VOLANT QUILT. A few months later, two C-5A transports touched down at Bani Suwayf on the night of September 21 carrying teams of Red Hats and FTD analysts. They collected a dozen partially disassembled Floggers (eleven MiG-23MS models and one MiG-23BN), loading six into each C-5. Arrangements were made to collect five more of the MiG-23BN type at a later date.[135]

Lockheed Aircraft Service Company (LASC) in Ontario, California, won a contract to overhaul the MiG-23s, and the first flightworthy airframe was made ready for use in an exploitation project nicknamed HAVE PAD. Throughout this process, analysts inspected the disassembled airframe and all of its subsystems as part of the usual technical-exploitation effort. They found that the manufacturing methods used circa 1974, when the plane was built, employed essentially the same materials and manufacturing techniques found on earlier Soviet aircraft. However, certain methods were more extensively used and in such a manner as to indicate a considerable effort to produce an economical, lightweight design geared for a long production run. The airframe was composed primarily of high-strength aluminum alloys, though stainless steel was used in certain areas such as fuel tanks because its improved weldability characteristics provided leakproof sealing. Lightweight structures, heat-treated to high strength, were used wherever possible to reduce overall gross weight. The strength-to-density ratios of the stainless-steel components compared favorably with Soviet low-strength titanium alloys found in Belenko's MiG-25. Additionally, there was a considerable amount of machine-sculptured, spot-welded, seam-welded, weld-bonded, and riveted structure throughout the entire airframe. Analysts found similarities between some of the spot-welded structure in the MiG-23's wing box and that of the MiG-25. In the latter case, it had been found to represent at least a 50 percent cost reduction when compared with a heavier riveted structure.[136]

On at least one occasion, Kelly Johnson visited LASC to see how the overhaul project was going and to personally examine the MiGs. Although Johnson had officially retired from Lockheed in 1975 and had been succeeded by Benjamin R. Rich, he continued to serve as a consultant to the Skunk Works. He and Rich, along with engineers Rus Daniell and Henry Combs, inspected the MiG-23 on December 7, 1977. "We were all impressed with the [original] manufacturing [qualities] of the aircraft," Rich noted in his diary.[137]

Once reassembled and delivered to Area 51, the MiG-23MS was given the designation YF-113E. The Red Hats subjected it to a variety of ground tests and systems checkouts and took jet engine modulation and acoustics measurements. The flying phase of HAVE PAD began in March 1978, with the primary objective of determining performance and handling qualities. Secondary objectives involved tactical evaluations to determine the Flogger's combat effectiveness against US aircraft. Project pilots from AFSC included Dave Ferguson and Maj. Edward

A partially disassembled MiG-23 in a hangar at Bani Suwayf Air Base is prepared for shipment to the US. *Fees collection*

Like most contemporary Soviet fighter planes, the MiG-23 was ruggedly built from high-strength aluminum alloys and stainless steel. It was designed for durability and ease of maintenance. *OKB MiG*

T. "Tom" Meschko. Tom Morgenfeld was the Navy project pilot and test director, performing exploitation flights on behalf of VX-4. He eventually flew a total of nineteen sorties in the MiG-23, two in March and seventeen in May, exposing it to virtually every type of Navy combat aircraft then in service. Ron Iverson headed TAC's team, which was developing plans to use the additional MiG-23 airframes in CONSTANT PEG as they became available from LASC. Project engineers included Don Thomson, Walter Lipe, Charles V. Van Norman, Edward N. Bradfield, and John Kuramoto.[138]

Throughout the spring of 1978, the HAVE PAD technical exploitation team flew the aircraft to collect data on basic handling qualities, stability and control, IR and radar signature measurements, and operation of navigation and radar-warning systems. Of particular importance, examination of the MiG-23MS offered analysts an unparalleled opportunity to study and test the most-current examples of Soviet avionics equipment. Every effort was made to determine the level of technology, operational capabilities, and areas for potential improvement. Many of the MiG subsystems could not be exploited due to component malfunctions that rendered them inoperable, and some had been installed with downgraded capabilities for the export model. Analysts found a peculiar mix of older technologies, such as vacuum tubes and oversized resistors and capacitors, with newer ones such as hybrid and integrated microcircuits. Some systems employed analog processing, while others used digital techniques. The only armament available for examination was the fixed, fuselage-mounted gun installation containing one twin-barrel 23 mm cannon and a two-hundred-round ammunition container. Technicians removed the gun pack from the aircraft and fired it on an instrumented test range.

The MiG-23's Tumansky R29-300 turbojet engine was evaluated both on the ground and in the air. During the HAVE PAD flight test program, total engine operation time was approximately eighty-seven hours, with no major propulsion problems or operator complaints. Pilots found the cockpit well laid out, with ample attention to human factors. Flight controls were conventional and closely matched those of other Mikoyan-Gurevich models such as the MiG-21 and MiG-25. Most switches, controls, and indicators were easy to see and use. Weapon fire-control switches were conveniently located except for a rotary armament selector. Because it was mounted on a lower panel in the center console, between the pilot's legs, switching from one weapon to another—such as missiles or bombs to guns—required a head-down action that distracted the pilot's attention. As with earlier Soviet aircraft, forward and rear cockpit visibility was restricted. Externally and internally mounted rearview mirrors mitigated this problem slightly but were of little use during a maneuvering dogfight.[139]

Tom Meschko banks an F-16 over the Nevada Test and Training Range. *USAF*

Ron Iverson poses beside an Aggressors F-5E. *USAF*

Western analysts expected the MiG-23 to be a formidable adversary in a dogfight, but it performed poorly during low-speed maneuvers and had dangerous spin characteristics. *Dimitriy Vinogradov*

Stripped of its Egyptian markings, this MiG-23 leads a pair of A-10 Warthogs over the Nevada ranges. The MiGs were pitted against as many different US combat aircraft as possible, but this seems an odd pairing since the A-10 was specifically designed to destroy heavily armored ground targets such as battle tanks. *USAF*

Prior to HAVE PAD, many analysts believed that the MiG-23 would prove to be an excellent dogfighter. During tactical exploitation, however, pilots discovered that despite its small size, excellent engine response, nearly jam-proof radar system, and formidable weapons capacity, the Flogger was significantly less capable than expected. From a pilot's perspective, "Its turning performance is unimpressive, cockpit visibility is poor, the engine smokes, flight control forces are high, and the variable wing sweep system is not automated nor [*sic*] optimized."[140] Additionally, the MiG-23 performed poorly in low-speed maneuvering flight, had dangerous spin characteristics, and was unstable in yaw both during transonic flight and when the aircraft exceeded Mach 2. Mike Press noted that it was also "squirrelly at high angles of attack" and had a tendency to depart controlled flight very suddenly. Most pilots who flew the Flogger said that it was dangerous under the best of circumstances and that it "flew like a pig." Maj. John B. Saxman, who eventually logged 116 sorties in the MiG-23 during CONSTANT PEG, was considerably less charitable. He contended, "It was a piece of shit."[141]

Ron Iverson hired analyst Robert E. "Darth" Drabant for a portion of the HAVE PAD tactical exploitation that provided critical data for later use in CONSTANT PEG. Drabant had done groundbreaking work on energy maneuverability (EM) theory, a quantitative model of aircraft performance first developed by Col. John Boyd and civilian mathematician Thomas Christie in 1964. In simple terms, EM theory defined the capability to change direction, altitude, and airspeed to outflank an opponent. Drabant's application of EM theory allowed combat capabilities of various aircraft or prospective design trade-offs to be predicted and compared, but the complex equations involved were often obscure to nonmathematicians. His most significant contribution was converting the concept into performance graphs that were easily understandable to the average fighter pilot. Using EM graphs, tactical aviators could compare the performance characteristics of dissimilar fighters engaged in air combat maneuvers and highlight relative strengths and weaknesses. The Red Eagles needed this capability for use with their tactical-training syllabus, but Drabant also created EM graphs for the MiG-17 and MiG-21 to be used by AFSC and FTD in Project HAVE IDEA.[142]

According to Drabant, "The exploitation started out slowly to find out what the aircraft could and could not do . . . based on data supplied to us by the intelligence community." Without prior hands-on experience, assumptions about the Flogger's capabilities were based on guesswork. Prior to HAVE PAD, analysts predicted that the MiG-23 would turn very well and have reasonably good acceleration

A good visual comparison from the forward aspect of a MiG-23 flanked by an F-15, *at left*, and F-16. *IDFAF*

capability. Drabant further noted, "The early flights proved these [assumptions] were wrong in that the airplane did not turn well at all and, in fact, when it approached high angles of attack the MiG-23 became very unstable." It did, however, accelerate well, and he observed, "As the aircraft got faster and faster the stability issues resurfaced, even in straight and level flight."[143] This characteristic later proved to have deadly consequences.

Once the tactical exploitation began in earnest, the MiG-23 was flown against the F-4E and F-15A. The Phantom was crewed by Capt. Ronald E. Keys, an instructor from the F-4 Fighter Weapons School, and his WSO, Capt. Robert T. Newell III. Maj. Timothy F. O'Keefe Jr., commander of the F-15 Weapons School, and Maj. Ed Clements, now an instructor pilot at the school, took turns flying the F-15. They began with basic offensive and defensive engagements and then progressed to more-complex air combat maneuvering. The evaluation concluded with a variety of tactical intercepts. Results confirmed that the MiG-23MS was ill equipped to be a dogfighter and could be easily defeated by either the F-4 or F-15. The only time this was not the case was when either aircraft approached the Flogger in a head-on pass and the MiG pilot decided to run for it. "By the time the F-4E or the F-15A got turned around to pursue," Drabant recalled, "the MiG-23 was 2 to 3 miles away and was rapidly accelerating well outside any missile envelope." It soon became obvious that the MiG-23MS was best suited to the role of point defense interceptor, good only for doing hit-and-run attacks.[144]

Throughout HAVE PAD the reliability, maintainability, and serviceability characteristics of the Flogger were evaluated from an overall system effectiveness viewpoint, with emphasis on the design, manufacturing, and operating environments. The MiG-23 exhibited typical Soviet design features but with increased emphasis on serviceability. These features were clearly based on a practical awareness of Soviet operational maintenance conventions and the inherent reliability resulting from use of practical or functional design approaches, and from extensive use of off-the-shelf or proven equipment. However, the optimum reliability and maintainability characteristics that might have been realized through exemplary subsystem design were degraded by the typical Soviet airframe integration process, as well as labor-intensive manufacturing with only marginal quality control.

Data obtained over the course of HAVE PAD's 115 technical and tactical exploitation sorties demonstrated that the Flogger, when operating in a controlled operational environment, was very reliable and easy to maintain. Factors that tend to contribute to malfunctions, or lack thereof, include aircraft condition, flight profiles flown, weather, maintenance procedures, and the skill level of maintenance personnel. During HAVE PAD, all of these elements combined to provide an environment conducive to reliable operations. Under conditions prevailing in a typical Soviet operational environment, these factors would certainly have been less than ideal, and the airplane's operating reliability would have been less than that demonstrated during testing.[145]

Ultimately, exploitation of the MiG-23MS by the Red Hats and Red Eagles at Area 51 provided many valuable lessons, all of which were captured in a series of technical reports. Many of these lessons were subsequently applied by the Red Eagles throughout the ensuing decade during the CONSTANT PEG program, which ultimately employed a total of ten MiG-23s at TTR, though not all were flyable simultaneously. Among the most-important results of HAVE PAD was that the Flogger's air-intercept radar, identical to that used in nearly all later MiG-21 and MiG-23 variants, was now well understood in quantitative and qualitative detail. MiG-23 subsystems were representative of those at the heart of nearly every contemporaneous Soviet domestic and export fighter aircraft. As noted in the HAVE PAD final report, "The technology benchmark recorded on this 1974 production aircraft, coupled with the 1976 MiG-25 exploitation, provides a unique database upon which to better judge current and future Soviet capabilities."[146]

6513th Test Squadron

By 1977, the 6512th TS Special Projects Branch had greatly expanded its Red Hats mission. The original organization started out with one or two pilots and six maintenance technicians, who occasionally traveled to the remote operating location for relatively infrequent test missions. Their involvement was limited to a part-time or additional-duty effort based on the comparatively small scale of the branch's activity. But over the ensuing five years,

The MiG-23 was equipped with rugged gear, allowing it to take off and land on unimproved dirt airstrips. *USAF*

circumstances changed drastically. The team's responsibility now included project management for all phases of developmental test and evaluation, as well as some phases of operational test and evaluation for certain specified aircraft. The Red Hats evaluated foreign aircraft not only at Area 51 but at other locations as well. With more than a dozen aircraft and increasing sortie rates, additional support personnel were needed. The unit's strength rapidly increased to two officer test pilots and thirty-eight maintenance, operations, and administrative enlisted personnel. The Red Hats were now managing an operating budget in excess of $670,000 per fiscal year and were flying an average of 25 percent of all sorties charged to AFFTC. By this point, the Special Projects Branch was responsible for an integrated AFSC/TAC/Navy joint test team, while maintaining overall operational control of the assets and management of test activities. Project personnel commuted to Area 51 on a continuous basis throughout the week, with additional weekend duty as required to accomplish special missions.[147]

The AFFTC commander felt that because of its diversified and expanded mission, the classified nature of its projects, and geographic separation from its parent squadron, the Special Projects Branch should become more self-sufficient than other units of similar, small size. Therefore, on October 21, 1977, Maj. Gen. Stafford drafted a proposed organizational change and sent it to Detachment 28, AFSC Command Management Engineering Team, at Edwards. He recommended that the Special Projects Branch be removed from the 6512th TS, reorganized, and elevated to full squadron status. Stafford felt this had become necessary due to problems encountered under the original organizational structure. Perhaps the worst of these was a noticeably misaligned chain of command. The chief of the Special Projects Branch was functionally responsible to the AFFTC deputy commander for operations rather than to his own squadron commander. Coordination with the commander of the 6512th TS served no functional purpose and, in some cases, actually impeded the rapid response needed for immediate action on critical projects. In fact, due to the "limited access" nature of most Red Hats activities, the commander of the 6512th TS was rarely privy to project status or test results.

The second problem was organizational fragmentation. Since project personnel typically deployed to Area 51 throughout the workweek, they were already operating as a self-contained unit. In actual practice, the 6512th TS provided no tangible support other than administrative assistance. This resulted in misaligned responsibilities and job definitions. As the on-site representative of the AFFTC commander, the chief of the Special Projects Branch—stationed at Area 51—was responsible for ensuring that the HAVE IDEA / HAVE GLIB mission was accomplished effectively and safely. He was directly responsible for test scheduling, flying safety, day-to-day flight operations, personnel matters, aircraft maintenance and refurbishment, and granting security clearances. In other words, he had all the duties and responsibilities of a squadron commander. Although the Special Projects Branch was, for all practical purposes, operating as a squadron and was tasked with a critical mission, it lacked the organizational status that other squadrons enjoyed. Requests for support and resources, therefore, had to go through administrative channels that frequently imposed significant delays.[148]

Stafford believed that elevating the Special Projects Branch to the squadron level would eliminate these problems and officially reflect the role that Dave Ferguson and his Red Hats had already unofficially assumed. To simplify matters, the new organization required no additional manpower authorizations. The new unit was to be staffed with existing branch personnel—the two officers and thirty-eight NCOs—with job titles adjusted to reflect their new squadron duties. The squadron's command section, consisting of an operations officer and one

The growing inventory of foreign assets flown by the Red Hats and Red Eagles included multiple examples of the MiG-21F-13 (YF-110B), *left*, and its Chinese twin the J-7 (YF-110C). The most notable difference was the location of the canopy hinge. *USAF*

Project HAVE UP involved the exploitation of a Sukhoi Su-22M, an export model of the Su-17 then in service with frontline Soviet air forces. *US Navy*

operations NCO and two administrative NCOs, was responsible for administration, operations, training, test and evaluation activities, and logistics to ensure accomplishment of the unit's mission. The squadron's Shop Maintenance Branch and Flight Line Maintenance Branch were staffed by a combined total of thirty-five NCOs to provide aircraft repair and maintenance, AGE, and aircraft servicing for the special assets and support aircraft. The most notable organizational change was at the topmost level, where the branch chief's position had previously been designated for a major's billet. Because the squadron commander's slot required a lieutenant colonel, Ferguson was promoted so he could retain his duty position.

AFSC Headquarters approved Stafford's request on November 22, 1977, and the 6513th Test Squadron was officially activated on December 1 under the command of Lt. Col. Ferguson, with Maj. John Casper as his deputy. Organizationally, the 6513th TS reported directly to the AFFTC commander, but this changed on March 1, 1978, when the squadron was reassigned to the newly formed 6510th Test Wing (TW). Reorganization and integration into the wing necessarily cast a bit of light onto the shadowy world of the Red Hats, but the unit's mission was still carefully shielded behind equivocal bureaucratic language. If anyone asked, they were simply informed, "The 6513th TS is tasked with accomplishing specially classified test projects for Air Force Headquarters at the direction of the Headquarters AFSC Special Projects Office."[149]

Necessarily, the Red Hats developed their own special terminology for discussing the classified assets. Initially, the MiG-17 was referred to as the Type I aircraft, the MiG-21 was Type II, and the MiG-23 was Type III. Suffix letters were added whenever it became necessary to distinguish between different models of the same type. For example, Russian-built MiG-21F-13 (YF-110B) aircraft were called Type II, while the nearly identical Chinese copy, the J-7B (YF-110C), was designated Type IIA. When the squadron acquired a later-model MiG-21MF (YF-110D), it was called Type IIB.[150]

In July 1978, the squadron began preparations for Project HAVE UP. This effort involved technical and tactical exploitations of an Su-22 (NATO reporting name: Fitter), an improved fighter design based on the Su-7B but with variable-geometry wings. Sukhoi produced it for frontline Soviet forces as the Su-17, but the export model was designated Su-22M. The Fitter was a high-speed, medium-range, single-engine jet capable of carrying a variety of stores for precision strike, reconnaissance, and suppression of enemy air defenses. Standard armament included two 30 mm cannons and various combinations of air-to-air and air-to-ground munitions. It had a maximum speed of 1,380 mph (around Mach 2) and a service ceiling of 49,869 feet. The Soviets exported the Su-22M to Vietnam, Poland, Syria, Yemen, Bulgaria, and the Czech Republic. A final export version, designated Su-22M4, saw extensive service in Europe and the Middle East.

MiG-23MS, US designation YF-113E, with its wings swept forward for low-speed flight and landing gear partially retracted. This variant was designed for foreign export and was less capable than domestic Soviet versions. *USAF*

Naval aviator Tom Morgenfeld, assigned to the 4477th TEF as an exchange pilot in January 1979, became project pilot and test director for HAVE UP. He made fifteen flights in the Fitter during May and June 1979, while continuing to fly various other HAVE IDEA special projects aircraft. Both Lt. Col. Joe Oberle and Col. Gaillard Peck had opportunities to fly chase for HAVE UP, but Oberle was the only TAC pilot to fly the Su-22. Pilots found that this aircraft exemplified key traits that had come to be synonymous with Soviet military equipment, including simplicity of design and operation as well as structural strength. Both the airframe and its Lyulka AL-21 F-3 engine were optimized for ease of maintenance and trouble-free use under the most-demanding operating and environmental conditions.[151]

Around this time, the Red Hats also embarked on additional MiG-23 exploitation projects. One such effort, called HAVE LIGHTER, involved performance and flying-qualities evaluation of a Type IIIB aircraft, most likely a MiG-23ML. Initial preparations began in June 1978, and by the end of April 1979 the project had been paired with another called HAVE DOWN. A seven-month in-flight exploitation of HAVE LIGHTER / HAVE DOWN began in May 1980. Because these were not the only Red Hats projects, Don Thomson's team of instrumentation specialists struggled to meet the twin challenges of increasing demand for their services and dwindling manpower. Thomson lamented that his people were having difficulty designing special instrumentation for HAVE LIGHTER / HAVE DOWN due to lack of detailed information on the Type IIIB aircraft, particularly wiring diagrams and technical manuals. He noted that "available information/documentation is incomplete or insufficient to enable determination of how to measure, or even if it is possible to measure, certain flight parameters." Additionally, he had only four installation and maintenance personnel, two military and two civilians. "It is considered marginal," he told superiors, "that they can maintain [the] current flying project and instrument another [aircraft] at the same time." The number of available qualified personnel was limited, and although he interviewed several acceptable candidates in January 1980, all but one refused to accept the assignment, citing personal reasons.[152] These refusals most likely had to do with security constraints and anticipation of the excessive amount of time spent away from home and family.[153]

On July 5, 1979, AFSC Headquarters authorized a project to exploit a Type IIIA (MiG-23BN) under the name HAVE BOXER and the designation YF-113B. This aircraft was designed primarily as an export fighter-bomber for close air support of ground engagements. Its secondary air-to-air role was extremely limited due to lack of sophisticated ranging and sighting equipment. The pilot could therefore employ missiles or cannon only in a rudimentary fashion. HAVE BOXER was an important exploitation effort because it was the first time that Western analysts had unlimited access to a MiG-23BN. The project offered an unparalleled opportunity for comparison with other Flogger variants, as well as access to subsystems peculiar to the ground attack role. Among several previously unexploited pieces of electronic equipment, the most significant was an inertial navigation system, the first of its kind operationally employed on a Soviet aircraft.

In the MiG-23BN ground attack variant, US designation YF-113B, the nose radar was replaced with a laser rangefinder / target seeker. More than six hundred BN models were produced, with most exported to countries in the Middle East, Europe, Asia, and Africa. An improved version was introduced into service as the MiG-27. *USAF*

A MiG-23BN flies in formation with an F-15 over a snowy Nevada landscape. *USAF*

Two swing-wing fighters together. A Navy F14 Tomcat shadows the MiG-23BN. *USAF*

Teams of technicians examined airframe materials and construction techniques, avionics and electrical systems, hydraulics, power plant, landing-gear, cockpit, and flight control systems. The flaps and engine inlets were not designed for high-AOA maneuvers, suggesting that designers optimized the MiG-23BN for high-speed dash operations. Basic aircraft-flying qualities were implemented primarily through aerodynamic means coupled with an elaborate fuel management system. Flight controls were mechanically actuated with very little electronic augmentation. In outward appearance the aircraft differed from the MiG-23MS only in that it had a more sharply tapered nose section due to lack of an air-to-air radar system. In fact, FTD analysts assessed the MiG-23BN to be essentially identical to the newer MiG-27 fighter-bomber then in service with the Soviet air force. Test instrumentation design, calibration, and installation took place from January to March 1980, following completion of the initial scientific and technical evaluation. Flight testing of HAVE BOXER began in April and continued through late September. The airplane was then transferred to the Red Eagles and flown to TTR on November 1, where it was eventually joined by at least two additional MiG-23BN models.[154]

Some Red Hats projects involved weapon separation testing. Capt. Joe M. Roberts, an armament engineer with the 6513th TS, was responsible for designing and overseeing construction of a small weapons test range (WTR) approximately 4 miles east of Groom Lake. The WTR included two circular targets with diameters of 350 feet and 1,000 feet, as well as tracking cameras and scoring instrumentation. In March 1981, the squadron began testing a Type IIID aircraft, described as "HAVE LIGHTER–Modified." The seven-month effort apparently involved a MiG-23MLD, a modified version of the MiG-23ML incorporating improved avionics, armament, and aerodynamic features. The FTD reportedly obtained one such aircraft that had been legally sold to a Finnish company by a Russian general, allegedly to raise money to feed his troops. In 1983, the squadron tested a two-seat MiG-23UB trainer, or Type IIIT, under the project name HAVE FIREMAN.[155]

Several other projects involved MiG-21 variants. One of these, dubbed HAVE COAT, was a scientific and technical exploitation of an ex-Egyptian MiG-21MF. Whereas earlier projects had involved testing first-generation MiG-21 daylight air-combat fighters, the HAVE COAT aircraft represented a third-generation, radar-equipped, all-weather interceptor with a more powerful engine. The MiG-21MF was significantly larger and heavier than the MiG-21F-13 and had noticeably different handling qualities. The Soviets produced the MiG-21MF in large numbers from 1968 to 1975, widely exporting the jets to Warsaw Pact allies, the Middle East, Vietnam, and Cuba. Additionally, India produced about 160 under license between 1975 and 1981. The primary purpose of HAVE COAT was to validate the already fairly extensive US intelligence database on the MiG-21MF, and to confirm estimates concerning similar later models in the MiG-21 series. The exploitation effort began with a five-month engineering examination of the airframe structure and systems prior to flight testing.

FTD analysts at Wright-Patterson led a series of multiservice engineering and laboratory studies carried out by teams across the country. When received, the overall condition of the HAVE COAT aircraft (by now designated YF-110D) was generally good. The ten-year-old airframe showed signs of rough use and appeared to have been overstressed on several occasions, but visual and x-ray inspections revealed no signs of structural damage. With only minor exceptions, all subsystems appeared to be in working order. Technicians examined, photographed, and tested numerous components and systems. The basic airframe differed little from earlier models except for an extra fuel tank in the upper fuselage behind the cockpit, giving the jet a thicker spine than that of the MiG-21F-13. Soviet avionics technology appeared to be about two decades behind Western standards. The flight control system resembled earlier models but for the addition of a two-axis autopilot and SAS. Designed for close air support, interdiction, and air defense, the MiG-21MF was armed with a twin-barrel 23 mm gun and equipped with two hardpoints

The Flogger's wings could be fully swept back during high-speed flight, sacrificing stability for velocity. *USAF*

An Egyptian MiG-21MF was acquired for the HAVE COAT exploitation project. This model was widely exported by the Soviets from 1968 to 1975. *DoD*

on each wing, plus one on the underside of the fuselage, for carrying ordnance and external fuel tanks. The plane was powered by a Tumansky R13-300 augmented turbojet engine capable of providing 8,900 pounds of thrust (or 14,000, with afterburner engaged). The MiG-21MF "appears to be a rugged and reliable aircraft based on proven components," analysts concluded. "It is readily maintainable in the Soviet operational system and is available in quantities that represent a considerable threat."[156]

On October 6, 1980, Don Thomson visited FTD Headquarters with fellow instrumentation cadre members Thomas Zaloga, Arlow K. "Butch" Hyland, and Richard "Dick" McQuillan to examine the MiG-21MF. Thomson's group studied the airplane's electrical system for several days to determine the best locations for installing test equipment. They took pictures and measurements, occasionally using mockup instruments to get a better feel for what they needed to do. Four weeks later, they met at the test site to present their results to an avionics specialist, CMSgt. Ray C. Welch; the crew chief, SMSgt. Ron Syphers; and the squadron operations officer, Lt. Col. George K. Muellner, who approved a projected schedule. Some original equipment needed to be removed to accommodate test instrumentation, but items such as the radar-warning receiver and the identification friend or foe (IFF) system had to remain in place. This meant finding alternate locations for some of the new instrumentation, but that would not have an adverse schedule impact.[157]

The next step was flight testing, and the team spent the next several months figuring out how and where to install a variety of instruments on the airframe and engine. At a status meeting on July 1, 1981, Thomson discussed progress with Hyland, SSgt. Dave Hollingsworth (maintenance deputy), MSgt. Joseph J. Laskowski (machinist), Tom Ackerman (avionics technician), SSgt. Thomas W. Savidge (instrumentation technician), and SMSgt. Charles E. "Chuck" Neuwohner (weapons specialist). Several weeks later, they conducted a final instrument checkout. The laborious process began early on Monday, July 27, and continued into the evening. The maintenance crew also defueled the HAVE COAT aircraft and collected complete weight and balance data. It was almost 8:00 p.m. by the time aircraft power was turned on and Thomson could finally begin checking the instrumentation. Calibration and troubleshooting continued into the following week. Finally, on August 5, the YF-110D was towed onto the parking apron in front of the hangar for its first engine run. Attempts to collect data at maximum thrust were unsuccessful, and Thomson decided to recalibrate some of the equipment. Once the problem was resolved, ground and flight testing continued on schedule.[158]

Concurrently with HAVE COAT, the Red Hats had been charged with the additional task of carrying out another project dubbed HAVE BLANKET. This high-priority effort spurred a whirlwind of activity that took the project from initial approval by AFSC Headquarters to testing in just seven days. These tests were accomplished from April 13 to December 22, 1981, and earned Thomson a Certificate of Merit from AFSC. Maj. Gen. Philip J. Conley Jr., AFFTC commander, presented it to Thomson with a letter of appreciation praising his dedication, initiative, and technical expertise. Conley added, "The results of this test program will have significant impact on future development of fighter aircraft and weapons systems."[159]

The MiG-21MF was larger and heavier than the MiG-21F-13 examined in earlier exploitation efforts, and had significantly different handling qualities. *DoD*

At this time, both the Red Hats and Red Eagles were still flying several MiG-17 airframes, including the YF-114C and YF-114D, but the end was near. Lt. Melvin H. "Hugh" Brown, a Navy exchange pilot with the Red Eagles, lost control of the YF-114C while performing air combat maneuvers against a Navy F-5 over TTR. Brown entered a spin from which he was unable to recover. He apparently never attempted to bail out, and he died when the aircraft struck the ground.[160] This was the same airframe previously used in HAVE FERRY and HAVE GLIB. The YF-114D, another HAVE GLIB veteran, suffered catastrophic damage in a nearly fatal accident at Groom Lake on March 11, 1981. George Muellner was just taking off when a hydraulic accumulator cap ruptured. Fragments of metal penetrated the fuel tank directly behind his ejection seat, sparking a fire. Acting quickly, Muellner immediately landed and exited the burning aircraft and was doused with fire extinguishers thanks to the rapid response of base firefighters. Capt. Mark F. "Toast" Postai, a Red Eagles pilot, had the dubious distinction of making the last MiG-17 flight on April 8, 1982. The jet's engine casing cracked during takeoff from TTR. Several turbine blades broke, with fragments slicing through fuel lines. Postai made a gear-up landing on the desert, but the MiG nosed into a shallow wash, where it caught fire. He managed to extract himself from the wreck, unharmed though badly shaken. This final mishap resulted in the immediate and indefinite cessation of further MiG-17 operations.[161]

The dynamic pace of operations brought numerous personnel changes to the Red Hats organization. Dave Ferguson transferred command of the 6513th TS to John Casper in July 1979. The following year, several new pilots came on board, including Maj. Paul D. Tackabury, Capt. Jon S. Beesley, Lt. Col. Roger A. Moseley, and Maj. James W. Tilley II of AFSC, and a TAC pilot, Capt. Norman D. Keator. In 1981, the squadron welcomed three AFSC pilots, Capt. Marvin L. "Roy" Martin, Capt. James H. Wisneski, and Maj. John A. "Ashby" Taylor, and a naval aviator, Lt. Fred D. Knox Jr. Another Navy pilot, Lt. Cmdr. David R. Bryant, arrived in October 1983. Duty tours lasted from several months to several years, and some, such as Beesley and Tackabury, later became involved with other projects at Groom Lake.

This elite cadre continued to accrue superlative achievements in performance, flying-qualities, and tactical evaluations, as well as radar and electronic-warfare (EW) systems testing, with a diverse fleet of airplanes including the YF-110B, YF-113B, YF-113E, and YF-114D. Though highly classified, such efforts did not go unrecognized. Knox was awarded a Meritorious Service Medal for his work, and the 6513th TS earned the Air Force Outstanding Unit Award for activities performed from January 1979 through December 1980 and another for activities performed from January 1983 through December 1984.¹⁶² George Muellner took command of the Red Hats in April 1981 and was succeeded by Jim Tilley on July 18, 1982. The new squadron commander's career was nearly cut short one day while performing windup turns in a "Type III aircraft," when the engine broke loose of its mounts and flamed out. With few available options, the pilot attempted a dead-stick landing on a dry lakebed in Sand Springs Valley. During touchdown the jet struck a low dune, collapsing the landing gear, and then slid across the desert, broke apart, and caught fire. Tilley managed to extract himself from the wreck, suffering only minor injuries. Rescue personnel arrived quickly via helicopter, and armed guards secured the scene, which was attracting unwanted attention. Residents of the nearby hamlet of Rachel, a small community of alfalfa farmers and prospectors, were admonished, "You have one minute to turn around and leave the area." Cleanup efforts continued through the night and into the next day and were reportedly quite thorough. Air Force recovery personnel then attempted to slip away quietly after finishing their work but were thwarted when the flatbed truck hauling the wreckage got stuck in the sand, and then the driver became lost in Rachel while trying to find the road back to the test site.¹⁶³ Remarkably, this event was kept quiet, but another mishap generated adverse publicity that cast a shadow over the squadron's accomplishments and threatened to publicly expose the clandestine exploitation program.

Death in the Desert

On April 26, 1984, Lt. Gen. Robert M. "Bobby" Bond, the AFSC vice commander, visited Groom Lake for a briefing on Red Hats activities. He requested and was granted permission to be checked out in the MiG-23MS (YF-113E) and make two orientation flights. Developed by the Red Hats on the basis of experience from HAVE PAD, the MiG-23 training syllabus normally included extensive ground schooling followed by taxi runs and six flying-qualities and systems familiarization sorties, the last of which was the formal qualification check ride. Bond's hasty checkout consisted of a quick review of the MiG-23 flight manual followed by cockpit familiarization. An instructor pilot briefed Bond on the airplane's normal operating procedures, handling qualities, operating limitations, and departure/spin characteristics. Bond also underwent egress training in the event he might need to eject due to an in-flight emergency, as well as briefings on local-area traffic patterns and navigational aids.¹⁶⁴

Using a standard Bandit call sign, Bond then prepared for takeoff. Following a supervised engine start, he taxied out in the MiG-23, followed closely by an instructor and observer in a T-38, call sign Alpha. Test personnel monitored the flight's progress with full uplink-downlink telemetry from the Current Operations Center (also known as the "White Room" or by its call sign, Chainsaw). This facility served as the command-and-control center for all aircraft ground tests and flight test missions within the Dreamland box and the surrounding Nellis range complex. Test conductors and engineers in the White Room had access to real-time collection and display of flight test information, and equipment for postflight data processing and analysis.

Bond accomplished his initial sortie without incident, taking some time to become familiar with the controls. Powered by a 27,500-pound-thrust engine, the MiG-23 was fast, but the swing-wing fighter was notoriously unstable in yaw while passing through the transonic regime. Pilots were also warned to avoid spinning the airplane, since this could lead to catastrophic engine damage due to side loads. Introduction of any sideslip when turning at high angles of attack could result in loss of directional stability, causing the jet to snap-roll in the opposite direction.¹⁶⁵

Plans for Bond's second sortie included a supersonic acceleration to speeds in excess of Mach 2.0, followed by systems and radar familiarization. Once again, engine start, taxi, and takeoff were normal. Trailed by the T-38, Bond climbed to 40,000 feet and leveled off. Chainsaw verified that both planes were broadcasting on Mode 3 with their radar transponders, and advised Bond that he would need to turn soon to remain within restricted

Bobby Bond was vice commander of Air Force Systems Command at the time of his visit to Groom Lake. *USAF*

airspace. When the MiG-23 was less than 2 miles from the edge of the range, Chainsaw told Bond to turn right to 210 degrees. The chase pilot advised him to check his fuel level and airspeed. "We've got you down [to] about 36–37,000 feet, so you might run into your calibrated [airspeed] limit first."[166]

Bond acknowledged that he had descended a bit and stated his intention to climb back up to 40,000. Once level he accelerated to more than twice the speed of sound, rapidly outdistancing the T-38. Within half a minute he was again approaching the edge of the range, his chase pilot lagging more than 20 miles behind. Chainsaw advised him, "Turn now, right zero-two-zero," and he acknowledged with a double click of his microphone button. Alpha had lost sight of the MiG-23 and missed Bond's next transmission: "I'm out of control; I'm out of . . ." Bond's radio call was interrupted by a transmission from Chainsaw repeating the order to turn and alerting the chase pilot to Bond's current distance and heading. Alpha acknowledged and, apparently unaware of Bond's dire situation, requested he provide the MiG's fuel status. "I've got to get out," Bond repeated, "I'm out of control."[167]

Now some 25 miles distant, Alpha still had no visual contact with the MiG-23, but Chainsaw's radar track indicated he was over Area 25 of the Nevada Test Site. Following a frantic discussion between the chase pilot and test conductor, Chainsaw noted that radar contact had been lost. Bond failed to respond to further transmissions. Witnesses at a café in nearby Lathrop Wells reported hearing an explosion and seeing black smoke rising from the vicinity of Jackass Flat. A search eventually located wreckage from the MiG-23 near Little Skull Mountain. Bond's lifeless body was found about 2 miles away.

The MiG-23 was dangerous to fly under most conditions, but particularly at high speeds with its wings fully swept. *DoD*

The loss of a senior command staff officer was a devastating blow, as was the destruction of a scarce and valuable aircraft. It also brought unwelcome publicity to the secret projects being undertaken within the test and training ranges. The incident was front-page news the following day, with reporters noting that Air Force officials at Nellis did not confirm Bond's death until more than seven hours after he died, and that they would not say what type of "specially modified test aircraft" he had been flying.[168] Some speculated that Bond had been at the controls of a long-rumored radar-evading "stealth" fighter or bomber prototype said to be under development at Area 51. Publicly, Pentagon sources denied this and even refused to acknowledge the existence of such a program, but off-the-record comments to journalists indicated that Air Force sources were quite concerned that the crash might have compromised what, until then, had been a well-shrouded secret.[169]

Brig. Gen. Gordon E. Williams from the Air Force Inspection and Safety Center at Norton presided over an accident investigation board, with Pete Winters, recalled from duty at AFSC Headquarters, as his deputy. Williams assigned Maj. Timothy J. Shaw, also from Norton, to serve as principal investigator, while other members were selected to represent such fields as aerospace medicine, maintenance, flying qualities and performance, and engineering.[170] Maj. James Wisneski, the board's sole pilot member, flew with the 6513th TS from June 1981 to July 1986 both as project pilot and operations officer. During his tour of duty, he made 321 flights in five foreign aircraft, including various models of the MiG-21 and MiG-23. He was responsible for performance, flying-qualities, avionics and systems tests, and operational-suitability evaluations. "The MiG-21 was a real sports car," he recalled, "but the MiG-23 had poor lateral stability." As it happened, Wisneski was tapped to serve on the Bond mishap board because he had been on vacation and was the only Red Hats pilot not present at the test site at the time of the accident.[171]

An intensive investigation determined that the airplane was functioning properly at the time of the mishap. With a little more than 392 hours of test flying on its airframe, the MiG-23 was in good shape, having undergone its last scheduled fifty-hour inspection six weeks earlier. Investigators examined wreckage from the tail assembly, engine compressor section, and engine inlets. There was no evidence of overheating, fire, or structural failure prior to ground impact. Bond was determined to have been turning when he lost control, but examination of the mangled remains of the engine showed no sign of damage due to any violent aircraft maneuver. On the basis of the evidence, the engine was operating normally at a high cruise power setting and did not suffer a compressor stall.[172] Officially, no definitive cause for the accident was ever identified, but unofficially it was blamed on pilot error. Bond exceeded the MiG-23's flight envelope, with catastrophic results.

For an inexperienced pilot the MiG-23 could be a deathtrap. In order to safely decelerate from speeds above Mach 1.7, the pilot had to bring the throttle to idle and leave it there for nearly half a minute. It took at least twenty seconds to decelerate to Mach 1.66, at which point the pilot could gently raise the nose to 20 degrees to reduce velocity to Mach 1.5. Below that speed, the engine would eventually spool down to idle, but it did not do so gently. For that reason, the propulsion system was equipped with a hydromechanical inhibitor called the "speed coast-down interlock" that actively prevented the engine from throttling back too quickly, even when the throttle lever had been retarded. Its sole function was to gradually reduce thrust output, thereby preventing the pilot from decelerating so rapidly that the engine might tear free from its mountings. When Bond retarded the throttle in an attempt to slow the MiG-23, he would have been alarmed to discover that the engine was apparently not responding, and would not even have come out of afterburner. He lacked sufficient experience in the airplane to know that he simply had to wait for the engine to spool down to the point where the inhibitor would disconnect automatically.[173]

Worse still, according to former Red Eagles pilot James D. "Thug" Matheny, the wings would have necessarily been swept back to 72 degrees, and Bond would have had only limited pitch authority via differential stabilator. "Above Mach 2 it didn't want to turn at all," Matheny recalled of his own experience in the MiG-23, which he had flown at speeds up to Mach 2.5. In short, Bond would have found himself in a situation where he was accelerating toward the airplane's placarded limits with reduced pitch control while being unable to slow down to a safe airspeed. Additionally, according to Matheny, he might have experienced "inlet buzz," a phenomenon caused by instabilities due to shock wave and boundary layer interactions within the air intakes. When this occurred on only one side, it caused so much drag that the airplane yawed sideways, pushing one wing forward into a higher AOA. This produced sufficient lift to induce a rolling motion. "With that much drag," Matheny noted, "differential stab[ilizer] and opposite rudder would not have been sufficient to stop the roll." The MiG-23 was not equipped with ailerons, but if the roll rate was sufficiently low, Bond could have attempted to slow down by raising the nose, decelerating to a point where he could bring the wings forward and deploy spoilers to arrest the roll. As a last resort, he could have pulled the throttle all the way back, entirely cutting off fuel flow, and then attempted to restart the turbojet. "It could have damaged the engine," said Matheny, "but the alternative was almost certain death."[174]

Serving as safety chase, Bond's instructor pilot should have been close enough to observe the situation and provide advice. Unfortunately, with a top speed of Mach 1.3 the T-38 was not ideally suited to chasing the MiG-23 during the supersonic acceleration run. In order to do so effectively, it would have been necessary for Bond to begin accelerating while the T-38 was positioned ahead instead of behind, so that when he passed by, the chase pilot would have visual contact with the MiG-23.[175] "He probably should have flown a modified flight profile to allow the T-38 chase plane to keep up," said Wisneski. "An F-4 would have been a better chase for the MiG-23, but one was not available for some reason." Lacking sufficient experience to save the airplane on his own, or outside guidance from his instructor, Bond lost control and decided to abandon the aircraft. He ejected while still flying at supersonic speed, well beyond the safe envelope for egress. The airstream caught the forward lip of his helmet, pulling his head up and back and breaking his neck. It may be noted—perhaps with some irony—that unlike their Soviet counterparts, the flight helmets worn by US airmen lacked venting holes in the helmet shell to relieve positive pressure from sudden windblast effects during a high-speed ejection.[176]

Although he was a command pilot with more than five thousand flying hours, primarily in tactical fighter aircraft, many people felt that the fifty-four-year-old Bond had no business being in the cockpit of the MiG-23 in the first place. Congressional sources questioned why a senior command officer was permitted to fly a high-performance aircraft alone, since pilots over the age of forty-five are usually not allowed to fly solo in service aircraft.[177] Several Red Hats and Red Eagles pilots were among those quick to criticize his actions, accusing Bond of recklessness for insisting on flying the MiG without

A memorial to Bobby Bond on the spot where his body was recovered in Area 25 of the Nevada Test Site. *Author*

completing the standard checkout process. Others felt he was just trying to pad his flight log with another exotic aircraft type. "He was about to retire," one commented caustically, "and this was his going-away present."[178] But he was also widely respected and well liked. According to Wisneski, "Bond was a good pilot and liked to mingle with the troops."[179] Those who remembered him fondly erected a small black-granite marker at the scene of his death. Deep within Area 25 and seen by few, its inscription reads: BOBBY BOND, APRIL 26, 1984, HE WAS A MAN OF GREAT STRENGTH, A WARM AND FAITHFUL FRIEND WHO GAVE HIS LIFE FOR THE COUNTRY HE LOVED.[180]

Bond's accident failed to harm the Red Hats' record of achievement in any meaningful way, and the squadron pressed on. Fortunately, the mishap had not resulted from any fault in the squadron's operations or maintenance procedures. In fact, those were areas in which the unit excelled.

Maintenance and Engineering

The key to keeping the Red Hats and Red Eagles airborne lay in the almost miraculous abilities of the maintainers and engineers. Technical documentation for the diverse stable of foreign fighters was virtually nonexistent. Spare parts had to be scrounged from around the globe or built from scratch by using "Yankee ingenuity," according to Dave Ferguson. Fortunately, there was sufficient commonality among the different Soviet types that many parts were interchangeable with available supplies. Scarcity of replacement tires meant that landing gear sometimes had to be modified, but nothing was ever done that might alter aircraft performance or flying qualities.[181] Lead FTD representative Stan Kulikowski acquired spare parts wherever he could find them, even pulling some from a MiG-15 on display at the Air Force Museum.[182] Living up to the squadron motto, "More with Less," the

Red Hats maintenance personnel circa 1969, *from left*: Kenny Leach, Stan Kulikowski, Afta [last name unknown], Dick Sinclair, Josef Elazar, Ron Syphers, and Bill Mattson. *Via Dick Sinclair*

50. Huntington D. Sheldon, "Summary Report of Major Aircraft Accident Resulting in the Loss of A-12 Number 126, 28 December 1965," BYE-2300-66, March 10, 1966.

51. Jim Tuttle, *Eject! The Complete History of US Aircraft Escape Systems* (St. Paul, MN: MBI, 2002), 152.

52. Roadrunners Internationale historical files.

53. Ibid.

54. Ibid.

55. Memorandum for the director regarding arrival of Accident Investigation Team, December 29, 1965, CIA-RDP71B00590R0000100060018-1, released August 25, 2000.

56. Sheldon, "Summary Report of Major Aircraft Accident Resulting in the Loss of A-12 Number 126, 28 December 1965."

57. Clarence L. Johnson, letter to Gen. Jack Ledford, "Lockheed Recommendations on Changes in Operating Procedures Resulting from Aircraft #126 Accident," January 4, 1966.

58. Robert Holbury, memo to Gen. Jack Ledford regarding communications security, January 6, 1966, CIA-RDP71B00590R000100060013-6, released August 25, 2000.

59. Robarge, *Archangel*, 33.

60. McIninch, "The OXCART Story," 41–42.

61. Assistant for Programs, R&D, Office of Special Activities, memorandum for Jack C. Ledford, director of special activities, "Comments to W. R. Thomas III, Memorandum to the Director, BOB," July 27, 1966, 10.

62. Pedlow and Welzenbach, *The Central Intelligence Agency and Overhead Reconnaissance*, 310.

63. James G. Fussell et al., "USAF Investigation of Major Aircraft Accident, A-12, S/N 125, 5 January 1967," OXC-0261-67, CIA-RDP71B00590R000100010001-4, approved for release August 29, 2001.

64. Ibid.

65. Ibid.

66. Ibid.

67. Ibid.

68. Memorandum for chief, Security Staff, Station D, from deputy chief, Security Staff, "Accident, Dutch 125," January 12, 1967, approved for release March 21, 2011; and Memorandum for chief, Security, OSA, from chief, Security, Station D, "Aircraft Accident on 5 January 1967 involving Cygnus 125," January 13, 1967, approved for release March 21, 2011.

69. Ibid.

70. Memorandum for chief, Security Staff, Station D, from deputy chief, Security Staff, "Accident, Dutch 125," January 12, 1967.

71. Project IDEALIST, Mission GT 67-11 from Edwards AFB, North Base.

72. Fussell et al., "USAF Investigation of Major Aircraft Accident, A-12, S/N 125."

73. Memorandum for chief, Security Staff, Station D, from deputy chief, Security Staff, "Accident, Dutch 125," January 12, 1967; and Trapp, "History of Helicopter Operations at Area 51."

74. Fussell et al., "USAF Investigation of Major Aircraft Accident, A-12, S/N 125."

75. Ibid.

76. Paul N. Bacalis, briefing memorandum for the acting deputy director for science and technology, "A-12 Accident Status Report," BYE-2016-67, January 9, 1967; and Special assistant, Office of Special Activities, Memorandum for the Record, "News Release on A-12 Loss," BYE-2065-67, January 9, 1967.

77. Colin McKinlay, "No Clue as to Parachute," *Las Vegas Review-Journal*, January 8, 1967.

78. Special assistant, Office of Special Activities, memorandum for the record, "Marvin Miles, Aviation Editor, Los Angeles Times," January 10, 1967.

79. Memorandum for chief, Security, OSA, from chief, Security, Station D, "Aircraft Accident on 5 January 1967 Involving Cygnus 125," January 13, 1967.

80. "Spy Plane Mishap—Probe Crash Scene," *Las Vegas Review-Journal*, January 15, 1967.

81. Ibid.

82. Ibid.

83. Fussell et al., "USAF Investigation of Major Aircraft Accident, A-12, S/N 125."

84. Memorandum for chief, Security Staff, Station D, from deputy chief, Security Staff, "Accident, Dutch 125," January 12, 1967; and Memorandum for chief, Security, OSA, from chief, Security, Station D, "Aircraft Accident on 5 January 1967 Involving Cygnus 125," January 13, 1967.

85. [DELETED], Memorandum for the Record, "Return of Wreckage of A-12 #125 to Area 51," January 10, 1967.

86. Memorandum for chief, Security, "Aircraft Accident on 5 January 1967 Involving Cygnus 125."

87. William A. Goodwin, "The Crash of Walter Ray," Roadrunners Internationale collection, 2008.

88. John Parangosky, memorandum for acting director for science and technology, "Loss of Article 125 (OXCART Aircraft)," BYE-2028-67, January 25, 1967.

89. Fussell et al., "USAF Investigation of Major Aircraft Accident, A-12, S/N 125."

90. Pedlow and Welzenbach, *The Central Intelligence Agency and Overhead Reconnaissance*, 302–04.

91. Memorandum to [DELETED], "Definition of FY-68 OXCART Program Requirements," June 9, 1967, CIA-RDP33-02415A000800290004-7, approved for release August 25, 2000; Merlin, *From Oxcart to Senior Crown*, 180; and OXCART flight records.

92. Accident report and supporting documents, "F-101B (AFSN 56-0286) Accident, September 26, 1967," CIA release May 5, 2005.

93. Roadrunners Internationale collection.

94. "Super-Secret Nevada Base Crash Kills Jet Pilot," *Las Vegas Review-Journal*, September 27, 1967; "Lt. Col. J. S. Simon Killed in Crash," *Osawatomie, Kansas, Graphic News*, October 5, 1967; and "Jet Crash Victim's Rites Set Friday," *Las Vegas Review-Journal*, October 5, 1967.

95. Clarence L. Johnson, "Q-12 Drone Log, 1962–1971," Lockheed California Company, 1.

96. Ben R. Rich, interview with Stuart F. Brown, senior editor, *Popular Science*, July 1, 1994.

97. Herbert Scoville Jr., memorandum for secretary of defense and director of Central Intelligence, "Q-12 Ramjet Drone," BYE-2192-63, February 6, 1963, SC-2018-00037_C05114703, approved for release November 16, 2018.

98. Johnson, "Q-12 Drone Log," 2.

99. Frank W. Hartley Jr., memorandum for the director, National Reconnaissance Office, "TAGBOARD Background Notes," March 18, 1970, SC-2018-00037-C05114882, approved for release November 16, 2018; and Memorandum for assistant to the president for National Security Affairs et al., "TAGBOARD Missions," CIA-RDP79B01709A000100050007-9, approved for release May 28, 2005.

100. Art Bradley, "D-21 Manufacturer's Model Specification," SP-582, Lockheed Aircraft Corporation, Advanced Development Projects, 1963; and Ben R. Rich interview.

101. Gordon J. Angerman, "Structural Criteria and Design Loads, M-21," SP-727, Lockheed Aircraft Corporation, Advanced Development Projects, 1966.

102. ADP staff, "D-21 Technical Manual," SP-790, Lockheed Aircraft Corporation, Advanced Development Projects, Burbank, CA, 1971.

103. Kleyla and O'Hern, *History of the Office of Special Activities*, chap. XX, p. 71; and Memorandum for the record, "Project WEDLOCK—Status," October 14, 1963, CIA-RDP63-00313A000500140021-9, approved for release June 29, 2004.

104. Johnson, "Q-12 Drone Log," 5.

105. Crickmore, *Lockheed Blackbird: Beyond the Secret Missions*, 80–82.

106. Johnson, "Q-12 Drone Log," 6.

107. Bill Park, "Postflight Comments," Article 134, Flight 7, Test 10, December 22, 1964; and Cables to director from OXCART FLTEST OPS dated December 5 through 24, approved for release May 13, 2004.

108. Larry M. Bohanan, memo to Clarence L. Johnson, "M-D Flight Planning," January 19, 1965.

109. Johnson, "Q-12 Drone Log," 7.

110. Memorandum from director of advanced systems, Air Force Systems Command, to Gen. Osmond J. Ritland, "SR-71 and TAGBOARD," May 12, 1965, SC-2018-00037_C05115152, approved for release November 16, 2018.

111. Johnson, "Q-12 Drone Log," 8–9.

112. Ibid., 9.

113. "Flight Engineer Dies in Calif., Former Pittsburgher Drowns Testing Plane," *Pittsburgh Post-Gazette*, August 2, 1966; and "Services Set in Mysterious Flight Death," *Twin Falls Times-News*, August 2, 1966.

114. Merlin, *From Oxcart to Senior Crown*, 50.

115. Johnson, "Q-12 Drone Log," 10.

116. Ibid.

117. John Parangosky, memorandum for deputy director for science and technology, "TAGBOARD Program," BYE-2559-67, August 17, 1967.

118. Robert L. Geisler et al., "Unlocking the Mystery of the D-21B Solid Rocket Boosted Air-Launched Mach-3 UAV," AIAA 2007-5761, American Institute of Aeronautics and Astronautics, July 2007, 3–4.

119. Merlin, *From Oxcart to Senior Crown*, 51.

120. Hal Rupard and John Wallis, interview with author, June 28, 2005.

121. Ibid.

122. Ibid.

155. Joe M. Roberts biographical data via SETP, circa 1990; USAF Fact Sheet, "Mikoyan Gurevich MiG-23MLD (Flogger K)," National Museum of the US Air Force, Dayton, Ohio, n.d.; and Undated notes and project schedules from the Donald G. Thomson Collection.

156. [DELETED], "Project HAVE COAT Report," FTD-1320X-500-81, Headquarters, Foreign Technology Division, July 1981, xxvii–xxix, I-1–I-3, III-1, IV-1, V-1, and IX-32.

157. Undated notes and project schedules from the Donald G. Thomson Collection.

158. Ibid.

159. Philip J. Conley Jr., letter to Donald G. Thomson re: HAVE BLANKET I, April 13, 1982, from the Donald G. Thomson Collection.

160. Davies, *Red Eagles*, 97–99.

161. Ibid., 174–75.

162. AFPAM 36-2801V3, "Unit Decorations, Awards, and Campaign Participation Credits Approved, 1 Jan 1981–31 Dec 1991," May 1984; and Maj. Eric M. Schneider, Special Order G-61, Headquarters, Air Force Flight Test Center, July 13, 1982, AFFTC History Office collection.

163. Charles P. Winters, comments to author, March 13, 2022; and Harold Singer and LaRue Fletcher, residents of Rachel, NV, comments to Glenn Campbell, 1995.

164. Gordon E. Williams, "[YF-113E] Accident, Nevada Test Site, April 26, 1984," Headquarters, Air Force Inspection and Safety Center, Norton Air Force Base, CA, May 1984.

165. Davies, *Red Eagles*, 146–48.

166. Williams, YF-113E accident report.

167. Ibid.

168. Phil Pattee, "General Killed in Crash of Secret Plane," *Las Vegas Review-Journal*, April 27, 1984.

169. Wayne Biddle, "General Killed in Nevada Crash Flew Soviet Jet," *New York Times*, May 3, 1984.

170. Williams, YF-113E accident report.

171. James H. Wisneski, comments to author, October 13, 2006.

172. Williams, YF-113E accident report.

173. Davies, *Red Eagles*, 257–58.

174. Ibid., 258.

175. Ibid., 257.

176. Wisneski comments.

177. Biddle, "General Killed in Nevada Crash Flew Soviet Jet."

178. Davies, *Red Eagles*, 239–40.

179. Wisneski comments.

180. Author's visit to the Bobby Bond memorial in Area 25 of the NTS on October 7, 1999, with DOE escort La Tomya Glass and Wackenhut security officer Marvin "Lee" Morris.

181. David L. Ferguson interview.

182. Suits interview.

183. George Gennin, "Fellow Red Eagles: Commander's Call," *Red Eagles Newsletter* 5 (March 2010): 2.

184. Suits interview; and "Red Hats Comprehensive Recall Roster," November 25, 1993, Donald G. Thomson Collection.

185. Earl Henderson, "Reflections on Bobby Ellis," *Red Eagles Newsletter* 3 (September 2009): 1.

186. Ibid.

187. Ibid.

188. Ben Galloway, "The Way I See It," *Red Eagles Newsletter* 7 (September 2010): 3.

189. Gaillard Peck, "Fellow Red Eagles: Commander's Call," *Red Eagles Newsletter* 2 (July 2009): 1.

190. Thomas Zaloga, memorandum to all engineers and technicians, 6520th Test Group, Engineering Instrumentation, "Getting Our Act Together and Taking It on the Road," n.d. (circa 1984), from the Donald G. Thomson Collection.

191. Donald G. Thomson, draft proposal, "Instrumentation Special Projects," n.d. (circa 1984), from the Donald G. Thomson Collection.

192. Lt. Col. William D. Carson Jr., Special Order G-45, Headquarters, Air Force Flight Test Center, June 6, 1985, AFFTC History Office collection.

Chapter 6: Invisible Airplanes

1. Dwayne A. Day, "Astronauts and Area 51: The Skylab Incident," *Space Review*, January 9, 2006, http://www.thespacereview.com/article/531/1, accessed January 15, 2006.

2. Richelson, *The US Intelligence Community*, 539.

3. Clayton D. Laurie, *Leaders of the National Reconnaissance Office: 1961–2001* (Washington, DC: Office of the Historian, NRO, 2002).

4. Robert D. Singel, memorandum for chairman, COMIREX, "[Area 51] Skylab Photograph," National Reconnaissance Office, April 11, 1974.

5. [Deleted], memorandum for the director of Central Intelligence, "Skylab Imagery [of Area 51]," April 19, 1974, CIA-RDP80M01048A000800210008-5, approved for release October 12, 2004.

6. Ibid.

7. Enno H. Knoche, deputy director of Central Intelligence, letter to Gen. David C. Jones, chief of staff, United States Air Force, August 26, 1976, RG 340 National Archives and Records Administration, RG340, Records of the Office of the Secretary of the Air Force.

8. Ibid.

9. Ibid.

10. Stafford and Cassutt, *We Have Capture*, 202–03.

11. Air Force Pamphlet 11-6, "Administrative Practices: Nicknames and Exercise Terms." Former security guard Fred Dunham confirmed information about SCORE EVENT in a 1994 interview with the *Las Vegas Review Journal*. Additionally, a US Department of Energy Nevada Operations organization and personnel directory (dated June 1990) listed a mail stop for SCORE EVENT.

12. Fred M. Dunham Jr. interview with Angus Batey, October 7, 2011; Troy E. Wade, comments to author, October 3, 2007: Wayne Maynard, comments to author, May 30, 2016; McClain interview; and Charles P. Winters, email to author, March 13, 2022.

13. Ernest D. Campbell, EPA, memorandum to Troy Wade, Roger Ray, Leon Silverstrom, Dave Jackson, Paul Dunaway, Bruce Church, and Mary G. White, "Dead Cattle in Area 51," June 24, 1977.

14. Donald D. Smith, memorandum to files, "Field Investigation of Dead Cattle in Area 51," June 23, 1977.

15. Ibid.

16. Ibid.

17. Michael J. Lippitz and Richard H. Van Atta, "Stealth Combat Aircraft," in *Transformation and Transition: DARPA's Role in Fostering an Emerging Revolution in Military Affairs*, vol. 2, IDA Paper P-3698 (Alexandria, VA: Institute for Defense Analysis, November, 2003), I-1.

18. Ibid., 2:I-2 and 2:I-3.

19. Johnson, "Reduction of Radar Cross Section of Large High-Altitude Aircraft," 1–4.

20. Harvey model photos circa 1975 in the Ben R. Rich Papers collection, Huntington Library, San Marino, CA.

21. David C. Aronstein and Albert C. Piccirillo, *Have Blue and the F-117A: Evolution of the "Stealth Fighter"* (Reston, VA: American Institute of Aeronautics and Astronautics, 1997), 15–20.

22. Little Harvey Concept B drawing 1016-4 in "Progress Report No. 2, High Stealth Conceptual Studies," Lockheed Advanced Development Projects, May 1975.

23. Robert C. Loschke, interview with Peter J. Westwick, January 9, 2012, Aerospace Oral History Project, Huntington Library, San Marino, CA, 6.

24. Aronstein and Piccirillo, *Have Blue and the F-117A*, 20; Richard Scherrer, letter to Stuart F. Brown, senior editor, *Popular Science*, December 16, 1994; Richard Scherrer, letter to Louis Dachs, Lockheed Advanced Development Company, June 1, 1994; and Rich, "XST Log," 1.

25. Drawing of intermediate XST design, Lockheed Martin Skunk Works, Palmdale, CA, circa 1975; Aronstein and Piccirillo, *Have Blue and the F-117A*, 23; Rich, "XST Log," 1; Ray Passon, "Have Blue Contract History," n.d., excerpted from "F-117A Cost Performance and Contracts History," Lockheed white paper WP40532, declassified in accordance with F-117 Security Classification Guide (January 15, 1991), Ben R. Rich Papers, Huntington Library, San Marino, CA; and Ben R. Rich and Leo Janos, *Skunk Works: A Personal Memoir of My Years at Lockheed* (New York: Little, Brown, 1994), 26.

26. Aronstein and Piccirillo, *Have Blue and the F-117A*, 29–30; and Paul F. Crickmore and Alison J. Crickmore, *F-117 Nighthawk* (Osceola, WI: MBI, 1999), 14.

27. Lippitz and Van Atta, "Stealth Combat Aircraft," I-3.

28. Aronstein and Piccirillo, *Have Blue and the F-117A*, 24.

29. Tony Chong, *Flying Wings & Radical Things: Northrop's Secret Aerospace Projects and Concepts, 1939–1994* (Forest Lake, MN: Specialty Press, 2016), 196–97.

30. Rebecca Grant, *B-2: The Spirit of Innovation* (Falls Church, VA: Northrop Grumman, 2013), 8–9.

31. Ibid., 11–12.

32. Aronstein and Piccirillo, *Have Blue and the F-117A*, 31–32.

33. Kenneth Perko, interview by Ruth Williamson, March 27, 2001, *Living in the "Black World"—Conversations with the Early Pioneers of Stealth* (Dayton, OH: Aeronautical Systems Center History Office, 2004), sec. 1, p. 13.

34. Edward F. Martin Jr., memo to Ben R. Rich, "Comments on XST May 19th ARPA Review," May 26, 1976, Ben R. Rich Papers, Huntington Library, San Marino, CA.

35. Nomination of the Pioneers of Stealth National Aviation Hall of Fame Spirit of Flight Award, http://www.pioneersofstealth.org/NAFH%20Award%20Writeup.pdf, accessed December 23, 2015.

36. Ben R. Rich, "SENIOR PROM Advanced Tactical Cruise Missile (ATCM)," handwritten notes dated September 9, 1992, from the Ben R. Rich Papers, Huntington Library, San Marino, CA, 2.

37. Aronstein and Piccirillo, *Have Blue and the F-117A*, 34; and AFP 11-6, "Administrative Practices: Nicknames and Exercise Terms."

38. Rich and Janos, *Skunk Works*, 41–44; and Keith Beswick, comments to author at Roadrunners Internationale Reunion, Las Vegas, NV, October 2, 2007.

39. Ben R. Rich, handwritten notes on HAVE BLUE, circa 1992, Ben R. Rich Papers, Huntington Library, San Marino, CA, 1–2.

40. Ibid., 2–3.

41. HAVE BLUE Utility Flight Manual (HB-1), December 1, 1978, declassified on December 31, 1990.

42. Rich, handwritten notes on HAVE BLUE, 3–5.

43. Ibid., 5–6.

44. Ibid.

45. HAVE BLUE Utility Flight Manual, sec. 1, p. 51.

46. Rich, handwritten notes on HAVE BLUE, 7–9.

47. Ibid.

48. HAVE BLUE Utility Flight Manual, sec. 1, p. 3.

49. Rich, handwritten notes on HAVE BLUE, 7–9.

50. Ibid., 10; and HAVE BLUE Utility Flight Manual, sec. 5, pp. 7–8 and sec. 6, p. 7.

51. Aronstein and Piccirillo, *Have Blue and the F-117A*, 37; Rich and Janos, *Skunk Works*, 48; and Robert Murphy interview with Volker Janssen, 30.

52. Rich, "XST Log," 13–25.

53. Keith Beswick, comments to author, October 2, 2007; Wayne Maynard, comments to author, May 2, 2016; and Office of Special Activities, "Memorandum of Agreement: Project [DELETED]," OSA-1855-6-71, July 31, 1974, CIA-33-02415A000400390001-7.

54. Rich, "XST Log," 27; and Crickmore and Crickmore, *F-117 Nighthawk*, 17–18.

55. Rich and Janos, *Skunk Works*, early draft, Ben R. Rich Papers, series 6: Memoirs, box 6, folder 7, Huntington Library, San Marino, CA, 1–2.

56. Ferguson interview; and Bill Park interview by Ralph Vartabedian, "Now It Can Be Said—He Has the Right Stuff," *Los Angeles Times*, September 29, 1989.

57. Allen Atkins, interview by Ruth Williamson, May 8, 2002, *Living in the "Black World,"* sec. 1, p. 30.

58. William J. Fox, comments made during the Contractors Forum at the National Atomic Testing Museum, Las Vegas, NV, Roadrunners Internationale Reunion, October 6, 2005.

59. Crickmore and Crickmore, *F-117 Nighthawk*, 18.

60. Eugene "Red" McDaris, interview with author, July 12, 2001.

61. Ibid.

62. Richard Burton, "HAVE BLUE Program Overview," AIAA-94-2122-CP, American Institute of Aeronautics and Astronautics, 1994, 5; Rich, "XST Log," 28; and Norman K. "Ken" Dyson comments at National Museum of the US Air Force, August 28, 2015.

63. Robert Murphy interview with Volker Janssen, 30–31; and Rich, "XST Log," 28.

64. Ken Dyson, interview with Peter J. Westwick, January 9, 2012, Aerospace Oral History Project, Huntington Library, San Marino, CA, 17.

65. Rich and Janos, *Skunk Works*, 57; and Herbert J. "Skip" Hickey, interview by Ruth Williamson, April 7, 2000, *Living in the "Black World,"* sec. 4, p. 7.

66. Rich, "XST Log," 28–30.

67. Aronstein and Piccirillo, *Have Blue and the F-117A*, 40–41.

68. Rich and Janos, *Skunk Works*, early draft, 4–6.

69. Ibid.

70. Ibid.

71. Dyson, interview with Peter J. Westwick, 72.

72. Dyson, comments at National Museum of the US Air Force.

73. Keith Beswick, comments to author at Roadrunners Internationale Reunion, Las Vegas, NV, October 2, 2007.

74. Loschke and Dyson, interview with Peter J. Westwick, 58–59.

75. Rich and Janos, *Skunk Works*, 59; and Dyson, comments at National Museum of the US Air Force.

27. Rhodes, "Nighthawk Memories," 24; and Eldred D. Merkl, interview by Ruth Williamson, *Living in the "Black World,"* sec. 3, p. 25.

28. Merkl, interview by Ruth Williamson, *Living in the "Black World,"* sec. 3, pp. 25–26; Aronstein and Piccirillo, *Have Blue and the F-117A*, 88; and Eldred D. Merkl, "First Flight Remembrances," http://www.f117sfa.org/f117_look_back.htm, accessed 20 April, 2013.

29. Leslie B. "Skip" Anderson III, "The Tale of the Too-Small Tails," *Stealth Fighter Association Newsletter* 10, no. 4 (Winter 2013): 3–5; and Crickmore and Crickmore, *F-117 Nighthawk*, 58.

30. Crickmore and Crickmore, *F-117 Nighthawk*, 58–59.

31. Ferguson interview.

32. Kevin Helm, "SENIOR TREND (FSD)," April 1, 2002, http://www.f-117a.com/Senior.html, accessed June 23, 2010.

33. Moseley, "F-117 Flight Test Program from Design to Initial Operational Capability," 12; and Crickmore and Crickmore, *F-117 Nighthawk*, 61.

34. Crickmore and Crickmore, *F-117 Nighthawk*, 62–64.

35. Anderson, comments during the Gathering of Eagles 2016 discussion panel.

36. Crickmore and Crickmore, *F-117 Nighthawk*, 4; and Aronstein and Piccirillo, *Have Blue and the F-117A*, 91.

37. Morgenfeld interview.

38. Ibid.; and Moseley, "F-117 Flight Test Program from Design to Initial Operational Capability," 13–14.

39. Klein interview.

40. Thomas A. Morgenfeld, comments during the Gathering of Eagles 2016 discussion panel, Lancaster, CA, October 1, 2016.

41. John Garman, "Moving the Night Hawks," *Stealth Fighter Association Newsletter* 10, no. 2 (Summer 2013): 4–7.

42. Phil Drake, "It's Here Again: 'Secret' Night Flights Draw Burbank Fans to Edge of Tarmac as Huge Jet Roars In," *Burbank Leader*, January 7, 1987, A-4.

43. Ibid.; and Garman, "Moving the Night Hawks," 4–7.

44. Moseley, "F-117 Flight Test Program from Design to Initial Operational Capability," 8.

45. Blazek, *Nighthawks*, 49; and Michael E. Cawthon, comments on C-141 Heaven website, http://www.c141heaven.info/dotcom/patches/mystery.php, accessed April 15, 2016.

46. Lockheed, F-117A Flight Test Log, June 1981–December 1999; and Rhodes, "Nighthawk Memories," 24.

47. Aronstein and Piccirillo, *Have Blue and the F-117A*, 91; Crickmore and Crickmore, *F-117 Nighthawk*, 64; and Moseley, "F-117 Flight Test Program from Design to Initial Operational Capability," 14–15.

48. Randy Meathrell, "T-38 First Flight," *Star Dusters Newsletter*, January 2013.

49. Moseley, "F-117 Flight Test Program from Design to Initial Operational Capability," 13.

50. Thomas A. Morgenfeld and Charles P. Winters, comments during the Gathering of Eagles 2016 discussion panel, Lancaster, CA, October 1, 2016.

51. Moseley, "F-117 Flight Test Program from Design to Initial Operational Capability," 13; Hickey interview, sec. 4, p. 11; and Ferguson interview.

52. Moseley, "F-117 Flight Test Program from Design to Initial Operational Capability," 16.

53. Lou Gum, "Board of Directors Introduction," *Stealth Fighter Association Newsletter* 9, no. 3 (July–December 2012): 3; and Breslin and Myers, "History and Lineage of the F-117A Stealth Fighter Organizations," 54–55.

54. Moseley, "F-117 Flight Test Program from Design to Initial Operational Capability," 11–12.

55. Ron Constable, "A Tribute to Pete Barnes—from the Creation Times," *Stealth Fighter Association News Letter* 10, no. 3 (Fall 2013): 3–5; Breslin and Myers, "History and Lineage of the F-117A Stealth Fighter Organizations," 54; and Blazek, *Nighthawks*, 27.

56. Edward B. Hart and Richard H. Bryan, "Modern Dynamic RCS and Imaging Systems," presented at the 10th Annual Antenna Measurement Techniques Association Symposium, Atlanta, GA, September 12–16, 1988.

57. Paul F. Crickmore, *Lockheed's Black World Skunk Works* (Oxford: Osprey, 2000), 93–94; Program Element 0605809F, "Program 06 Research and Development," *Future Years Defense Program (FYDP) Structure*, DoD 7045.7-H, Department of Defense, Office of the Director, Program Analysis and Evaluation, April 2004, E-1157; Malcolm W. Browne, "Will the Stealth Bomber Work?," *New York Times*, July 17, 1988; F-117A Flight Test Log; and Moseley, "F-117 Flight Test Program from Design to Initial Operational Capability," 11.

58. Aronstein and Piccirillo, *Have Blue and the F-117A*, 105–06.

59. Ibid., 107–11.

60. Ibid., 111.

61. Paul D. Tackabury, biographical information via SETP, circa 1990.

62. Robert C. Loschke, interview by Ruth Williamson, March 26, 2001, *Living in the "Black World,"* sec. 4, p. 80.

63. F-117A Flight Test Log; and Red McDaris interview.

64. Crickmore and Crickmore, *F-117 Nighthawk*, 143.

65. F-117A Flight Test Log; and Jay Tweed, "F-117A Milestones" graphic, released December 4, 1990, revised May 9, 1995.

66. Loschke interview by Ruth Williamson, sec. 4, p. 73; and Aronstein and Piccirillo, *Have Blue and the F-117A*, 147–48.

67. Crickmore and Crickmore, *F-117 Nighthawk*, 146–57; and Dave Southwood interview with Steve Davies, *10 Percent True*, episode 8, "Flying the Stealth Fighter at Area 51," February 8, 2020, YouTube video, https://www.youtube.com/watch?v=7mvlmgNznkY, accessed May 15, 2022.

68. At the time, the McDonnell Douglas F-18 Hornet possessed the highest-numbered MDS designation of any operational fighter. Northrop had been trying to market a self-financed, updated, export version of the company's venerable F-5 as the F-5G. Unfortunately, this designation called to mind a Vietnam-era airframe that had been in production since the first F-5A rolled off the assembly line in 1959. In order to make the new product seem more modern and state of the art, Northrop officials requested the designation be changed to F-20. The Air Force approved this request in late 1982, leaving a gap (F-19) in the numerical MDS sequence. This made it very easy for armchair analysts to conclude that the missing number had been assigned to a secret aircraft, the existence of which was well supported by circumstantial evidence.

69. Jim Cunningham, "Cracks in the Black Dyke: Secrecy, the Media, and the F-117A," *Airpower Journal* 5 (Fall 1991): 16–34; and Paul Ciotti, "Tempest in a Toy Box," *Los Angeles Times Magazine*, October 19, 1986, 24.

70. Marc R. Marchesseault, "USAF Aircraft Accident Investigation, F-117A 81-0792, 11 July 1986," Headquarters, Tactical Air Command, January 1987; Knight-Ridder Newspapers and Reuters, "Hush Fuels Reports That Doomed Plane Was Stealth," *Seattle Times*, July 17, 1986; and "USAF Aircraft Destroyed in Crash Believed to Be Stealth Fighter," *Aviation Week & Space Technology*, July 21, 1986, 22–23.

71. "USAF Aircraft Destroyed in Crash Believed to Be Stealth Fighter," *Aviation Week & Space Technology*, July 21, 1986, 22–23; Staff writer, "Air Force Crash Remains Shrouded in Secrecy," *Ridgecrest Daily Independent*, July 14, 1986; Robert Lindsey, "Pilot's Cover Story," *Daily News*, July 15, 1986; and David Holley, "TV Crew Finds Debris at AF Jet Crash Site," *Los Angeles Times*, August 12, 1986.

72. John T. Manclark, "USAF Aircraft Accident Investigation, F-117A 83-0815, 14 October 1987," 57th Fighter Weapons Wing, Nellis Air Force Base, December 1987; Christopher Beall, "Stealth Crash Kills Pilot," *Las Vegas Review Journal*, October 16, 1987; Associated Press, "Stealth Aircraft Crashes at Base," *Daily News*, October 16, 1987; and Christopher Beall, "Crash Pulls Veil Aside for Glimpse of Stealth Program," *Las Vegas Review Journal*, November 1, 1987.

73. "F-117 Archives," *Stealth Fighter Association Newsletter* 13, no. 1 (Spring 2016): 26; US Air Force News Release, November 10, 1988; and Melissa Healy, "Pentagon Ends Long Silence on Stealth Fighter," *Los Angeles Times*, November 11, 1988.

74. Jeff Rhodes, "Nighthawk Memories," 25.

75. Crickmore and Crickmore, *F-117 Nighthawk*, 85; and Breslin and Myers, "History and Lineage of the F-117A Stealth Fighter Organizations," i–ii.

76. Breslin and Myers, "History and Lineage of the F-117A Stealth Fighter Organizations," i–ii; and Charles A. Horner, "The Air Campaign," *Military Review* 71, no. 9 (September 1991): 26.

77. Steven A. Green, 410th Flight Test Squadron historical reports, AFFTC History Office, 1993.

78. Grant, *B-2: The Spirit of Innovation*, 15–16; William J. Perry, testimony before US Congress, Senate Committee on Armed Services, Department of Defense Authorization for Appropriations for FY 1979, part 8: Research and Development, February 28 and March 7, 9, 14, 16, and 21, 1978, 5506–5937; and Robert R. Tomes, *US Defense Strategy from Vietnam to Operation Iraqi Freedom* (New York: Routledge, 2007), 65–81.

79. Tomes, *US Defense Strategy from Vietnam to Operation Iraqi Freedom*, 82; United States Air Force Fact Sheet: Tacit Blue, 1996; and Grant, *B-2: The Spirit of Innovation*, 15.

80. Scale models floating in a shallow saltwater pond underwent RCS testing in a remote part of the China Lake Naval Weapons Center near Ridgecrest, California. The Skunk Works eventually designed a full-scale experimental prototype, dubbed Sea Shadow (IX-529), which

was built by LMSC inside the Hughes Mining Barge at Redwood City. The faceted, small-water-plane-area, twin-hull (SWATH) craft was powered by two Garrett AiResearch diesel-electric motors. It had a low RCS and negligible wake and was very stable in rough seas.

81. Ibid., 18; and Rich, "XST Log," 18–26.

82. Rich, "XST Log," 26–27; Bill Sweetman, *Inside the Stealth Bomber* (Osceola, WI: Motorbooks International, 1999), 14–17; and Photo of radar model identified as SENIOR PEG, but more likely BSAX, published in *Aviation Week & Space Technology*, February 14, 2005, 68.

83. Grant, *B-2: The Spirit of Innovation*, 18–19.

84. Rich, "XST Log," 28–29.

85. Chong, *Flying Wings & Radical Things*, 213.

86. Dennis W. Jarvi, interview with Diana Cornelisse, August 15, 1996, *Living in the "Black World,"* sec. 3, p. 66; Richard G. Thomas, interview with author, February 8, 1997; Atkins interview, sec. 1, p. 33; and Michael A. Dornheim, "Testbed for Stealth," *Aviation Week & Space Technology*, May 6, 1996, 20–21.

87. Irving T. Waaland, letter to managing editor, *Aviation Week & Space Technology*, May 15, 1996, Curtis L. Peebles collection; and Twigg interview by Diana Cornelisse, May 23, 1996, sec. 3, p. 11.

88. Twigg interview by Diana Cornelisse, May 23, 1996, sec. 3, pp. 21–22; Peter Grier, "The (Tacit) Blue Whale," *Air Force Magazine*, August 1996, 52–54; and Ralph E. Grimm, interview with Ruth Williamson, May 9, 2001, *Living in the "Black World,"* sec. 4, p. 35.

89. Thomas interview with author; Dyson, comments at National Museum of the US Air Force; and Hickey interview, sec. 4, p. 8.

90. "Tacit Blue Flight Tests Lead to E-8 Radar System," *Flight International*, October 16–22, 1996, 37; Dyson, comments at National Museum of the US Air Force; and David P. Maunder, interview by Ruth Williamson and Diana Cornelisse, January 2001 and September 2003, *Living in the "Black World,"* sec. 4, p. 128.

91. Maunder, interview by Williamson and Cornelisse, January 2001 and September 2003, *Living in the "Black World,"* sec. 4, p. 128; Hickey interview, sec. 4, p. 8; and "TACIT BLUE Flight Test Program," June 1996, Richard G. Thomas collection, 1.

92. "TACIT BLUE Flight Test Program," June 1996, Richard G. Thomas collection, 1–2; and Thomas, interview with author.

93. Maunder interview, sec. 4, p. 128.

94. Ibid., sec. 4, pp. 127–28.

95. Dyson, comments at National Museum of the US Air Force; and Klein interview.

96. Klein interview; Ferguson interview; and Maunder interview, sec. 4, pp. 134–37.

97. Maunder interview, sec. 4, pp. 135–36.

98. Donald Murray, "The TACIT BLUE Project," presentation at Western Museum of Flight, Torrance, CA, December 9, 2021; and Dyson, comments at National Museum of the US Air Force.

99. Dyson, comments at National Museum of the US Air Force; "Tacit Blue Flight Tests Lead to E-8 Radar System," 37; Thomas interview with author; and Maunder interview, sec. 4, pp. 134–35.

100. Maunder interview, sec. 4, pp. 134–36.

101. Ibid., sec. 4, p. 136–37.

102. Ibid., sec. 4, pp. 135–36.

103. Grier, "The (Tacit) Blue Whale," 54; Thomas interview, *Living in the "Black World,"* sec. 5, pp. 14–17; John K. "Jack" Twigg, comments to author, June 8, 2016; and Thomas, interview with author.

104. Thomas, interview with author; Maunder, sec. 4, p. 133; "TACIT BLUE Flight Test Program," 3; and Thomas interview, *Living in the "Black World,"* sec. 5, pp. 16–20.

105. Thomas interview, *Living in the "Black World,"* sec. 5, p. 20; Thomas, interview with author; Hickey interview, sec. 4, p. 8; and Donald A. Cornell, interview with author, November 11, 2006.

106. Maunder interview, sec. 4, p. 137.

107. Ibid., sec. 4, p. 138.

108. Ibid.

109. "TACIT BLUE Flight Test Program," 3, Dick Thomas collection via Cynda Thomas; and Thomas interview, sec. 5, pp. 17–18.

110. Thomas interview, sec. 5, p. 15.

111. Ibid., sec. 5, pp. 15–16.

112. Dyson comments at National Museum of the US Air Force; and Maunder interview, sec. 4, pp. 138–39.

113. Jarvi interview, sec. 3, p. 64.

114. Thomas interview, sec. 5, p. 19; and "TACIT BLUE Flight Test Program," 2.

115. Maunder interview, sec. 4, p. 139.

116. Ibid., sec. 4, p. 139; and Dornheim, "Testbed for Stealth," 20–21.

117. Maunder interview, sec. 4, p. 139.

118. Cornell interview; Maunder interview, sec. 4, p. 140; and Thomas interview, sec. 5, p. 21.

119. Maunder interview, sec. 4, p. 140.

120. Cornell interview; Daniel R. Vanderhorst biographical information via SETP; Thomas interview with author; and Jarvi interview, sec. 3, p. 72.

121. Jarvi interview, sec. 3, p. 72; Daniel R. Vanderhorst biographical summary, 2004 Gathering of Eagles awards banquet program, October 1, 2004, 22; and Thomas interview with author.

122. Chong, *Flying Wings & Radical Things*, 213.

123. Grier, "The (Tacit) Blue Whale," 52–55; and John M. Griffin and James E. Kinnu, *B-2 Systems Engineering Case Study* (Dayton, OH: Air Force Center for Systems Engineering, Air Force Institute of Technology, 2007), 15.

124. Rich and Janos, *Skunk Works*, 304; and Susan J. Bodilly, "Case Study of Risk Management in the USAF B-1B Bomber Program," RAND Note N-3616-AF, RAND, 1993, 5.

125. Rich and Janos, *Skunk Works*, 302–04.

126. Rich and Janos, *Skunk Works*, early draft manuscript, Ben R. Rich Papers, series 6: Memoirs, box 6, folder 7, Huntington Library, San Marino, Calif., 423.

127. Griffin and Kinnu, *B-2 Systems Engineering Case Study*, 16.

128. Ibid., 22; and Rick Atkinson, "Stealth: From 18-Inch Model to $70 Billion Muddle," *Washington Post*, October 8, 1989.

129. Griffin and Kinnu, *B-2 Systems Engineering Case Study*, 15–18.

130. Ibid., 20–21.

131. John M. Griffin, interview by Diana Cornelisse, July 19, 1996, *Living in the "Black World,"* sec. 4, pp. 103–04.

132. Griffin and Kinnu, *B-2 Systems Engineering Case Study*, 24–25.

133. Richard Halloran, "Washington Talk: Military Aircraft; Stealth Sheds Secrets, but Its Cost Stays Hidden," *New York Times*, December 14, 1988; and Robert C. Toth, "Odds Favor Stealth Bomber Despite Flaws," *Los Angeles Times*, June 28, 1981.

134. Author's personal observations, and comments to author by several aviation enthusiasts; and Atkinson, "Stealth: From 18-Inch Model to $70 Billion Muddle."

135. Thomas interview with author; Douglas A. Joyce, comments to author, March 22, 2011; and Photos of TACIT BLUE cockpit via National Museum of the US Air Force.

136. Clarence A. Robertson Jr., "Bomber Choices Near," *Aviation Week & Space Technology*, June 1, 1981, 18–22; Rick Atkinson, "Unraveling Stealth's 'Black World,'" *Washington Post*, October 9, 1989; Toth, "Odds Favor Stealth Bomber Despite Flaws"; and Peebles, *Dark Eagles*, 248–49.

137. Secretary of the Air Force for Public Affairs, "Air Force Unveils Stealth Technology Demonstrator," Release No. 01-04-96, April 30, 1996.

138. Odgers letter.

139. Wendell L. Bevan Jr., director of special activities, memorandum for deputy director of science and technology, "Area 51 Aircraft Support Requirements," September 20, 1971.

140. [DELETED], telex regarding "Utilization of Otter Aircraft for HAVE GLIB and Other Tenant Airlift Support Requirements," December 5, 1972, CIA-RDP75B00326R000100110006-7, approved for release June 24, 2002; Frank E. Bucher and Ulrich Klee, *Airline-Fleets International 1994/1995*, 28th ed. (Zurich, Switzerland: Editions JP, 1994); and Author's conversations with members of Roadrunners Internationale.

141. Charles L. Pocock, interview with author, September 1, 2019.

142. Ibid.; David N. Keller, ed., "Alumni News," *Rainbow of Delta Tau Delta* 93, no. 2 (Winter 1970): 31; "Lieutenant Wins Wings," *Casa Grande Dispatch*, February 20, 1974, 3; and Robert Bradford Richard Jr. obituary, *Las Vegas Review Journal*, August 14, 2014.

143. Pocock interview; Stewart Maus, interview with author, August 25, 2019; Edward K. Raschke obituary, *Las Vegas Sun*, June 30, 2000; NTSB Aircraft Accident Brief, Accident No. DCA00MA030, "Southwest Airlines Flight 1455, Burbank, California, March 5, 2000," National Transportation Safety Board, Washington DC, June 2002; and Thomas C. Losh obituary, *Las Vegas Review-Journal*, November 19, 2006.

144. Pocock interview.

145. Maus interview; and "Red Hats Comprehensive Recall Roster."

146. Pocock interview; and Lockheed Aircraft Service Company, "Eclipse Program Operations Manual," Revision 2, January 1983.

147. Pocock interview.

148. Ibid.

149. Maus interview; and F. Tucci, AirCal interoffice correspondence to Dee Lewis, manager of in-flight training and scheduling, "In-Flight Training for Lockheed Aircraft Personnel," April 15, 1982, from the collection of Stewart Maus.

150. Maus interview; EG&G Special Projects, Inc., "Airlift Flight Attendant Manual," Revision 1, June 1984; and Lockheed Aircraft Service Company, "Eclipse Flight Attendant Manual," n.d. (circa 1980).

151. Charlie Pocock, Eclipse senior program manager, letter to Eclipse personnel following one-year contract inspection, August 1, 1981, from the collection of Stewart Maus.

152. Pocock interview; and Robert B. Richard, letter to Stewart Maus, September 30, 1984.

153. Maus interview.

154. Morgan C. "Clark" Hampton, vice president, Airlift Operations, EG&G Special Projects, letter to Airlift staff, March 1, 1985, from the Stewart A. Maus collection.

155. Trevor Paglen, "Unmarked Planes & Hidden Geographies," *Vectors* 4, University of Southern California, http://vectors.usc.edu/issues/04_issue/trevorpaglen/page2.php?primaryId=2&secondaryId=3, 2006, accessed August 1, 2017; Joerg Arnu, "Janet Fleet," https://www.dreamlandresort.com, accessed August 3, 2017; John "Hank" Henry, LinkedIn profile, accessed March 4, 2017; and "Airline and Commercial Aircraft Report," *Airways International*, June 1994, 24.

156. Secretary of the Air Force, "Manpower and Organization," Air Force Instruction 38-101, January 2017; Online discussion, "Do Aliens Bowl?" Google Group Alt. Conspiracy.Area 51, May 2010, https://groups.google.com/forum/#!topic/alt.conspiracy.area51/TrN5MoQwuUw, accessed 24 June 2010; Michael D. Jackson, assistant fire chief, Det 1, AFEREG, "Change Mismanagement—a Study of Why the Range Complex Fire Department Isn't Using Its Accountability System," Executive Fire Officer Program, National Fire Academy, 1996; and United States Department of Energy, "Security Instructions: Personnel Security System," US DOE Nevada Operations Office, various editions (May 1978, September 1981, January 1985, July 1991), copies provided by DOE Public Reading Room, Las Vegas, NV.

157. Trevor Paglen, "Unmarked Planes & Hidden Geographies"; FAA Aircraft Registration, N6563C, February 29, 1994; FAA Aircraft Registration, N654BA, August 14, 1996; FAA Aircraft Registration, N6564C, February 29, 1994; FAA Aircraft Registration, N661BA, August 14, 1996; FAA Aircraft Registration, N20RA, August 14, 1996; and FAA Aircraft Registration, N27A, August 14, 1996.

158. Air Force Materiel Command, "Aircraft Accident Investigation, Beechcraft 1900C, UB37, N27RA, Tonopah Air Force Auxiliary Airfield, Nevada, 16 March 2004," July 31, 2004; Keith Rogers, "Nellis: Five Die in Crash of Plane," *Las Vegas Review-Journal*, March 17, 2004; Brian Haynes, "Five Killed in Plane Crash on Nellis Range Identified," *Las Vegas Review-Journal*, March 24, 2004; Keith Rogers, "Crash Report Points to Pilot," *Las Vegas Review-Journal*, July 31, 2004; and "Safety Rules Boosted for Flights on Air Force Range at Nellis," *Reno Gazette-Journal*, August 24, 2004.

159. Observations by various individuals posted to Dreamland Resort website, June 2021; and Ben Smithson, "How Do Those Dimming Dreamliner Windows Work?," The Points Guy, August 17, 2019, https://thepointsguy.com/guide/how-do-those-dimming-dreamliner-windows-work/, accessed June 10, 2021.

Chapter 8: Mountains of Controversy

1. Dunham interview, 2011.

2. Reno and Pippin, *An Archeological Reconnaissance of the Groom Range, Lincoln County, Nevada*, 3; and Paine, "A Mine, the Military, and a Dry Lake," 34–35.

3. David F. Miller, memo to files, "Request for Information about Area 51 from Bob Stoldal, KLAS-TV," Department of Energy Nevada Operations Office, Las Vegas, NV, March 6, 1978; and Ned Day, "What's Going On at That Secret Test Site Base?," *Las Vegas Review-Journal*, 1979.

4. Ed Vogel, "Officials Continue Search for Protesters," *Las Vegas Review-Journal*, April 18, 1983; and Paine, "A Mine, the Military, and a Dry Lake," 35.

5. Paine, "A Mine, the Military, and a Dry Lake," 35; and Ed Vogel, "Reid Mum on Visit to Secret Defense Base," *Las Vegas Review-Journal*, July 7, 1984.

6. Ed Vogel, "Reid Mum on Visit to Secret Defense Base," *Las Vegas Review-Journal*, July 7, 1984.

7. Ed Vogel, "Nevadans Question Air Force Seizure of Land," *Las Vegas Review-Journal*, May 20, 1984.

8. Ibid.; and "Secret Range," *Aviation Week & Space Technology*, August 13, 1984.

9. Chris Chrystal, "AF Admits to Illegality of NTS Land Grab," *Las Vegas Sun*, August 7, 1984.

10. Ibid.; and United Press International, "Gov. Bryan Fires at AF," *Las Vegas Sun*, August 7, 1984.

11. James M. Parker, associate director, Bureau of Land Management, statement before the Subcommittee on Public Lands, Committee on Interior and Insular Affairs, March 11, 1986; Christopher Beall, "Air Force

Will Seek Continued Access Restriction to Secret Base," *Las Vegas Review-Journal*, October 11, 1987; and Paine, "A Mine, the Military, and a Dry Lake," 36.

12. Paine, "A Mine, the Military, and a Dry Lake," 36; and James F. Boatwright, deputy assistant secretary of the Air Force for installations, environment, and safety, letter to Patrick Sheahan, July 6, 1984.

13. Robert W. Smith, director, USAF/DOE Liaison Office, letter to Patrick Sheahan, April 24, 1986; Daniel R. Sheahan and Patrick Sheahan, letter to Col. Robert W. Smith, April 27, 1986; and Col. Charles L. Meyer, director, USAF/DOE Liaison Office, letter to Patrick Sheahan, April 15, 1987.

14. Ibid., 36; Mary Manning, "Groom Mtn. Land Withdrawal Protested," *Las Vegas Review-Journal*, November 24, 1985; Christopher Beall, "Air Force Will Seek Continued Access Restriction to Secret Base," *Las Vegas Review-Journal*, October 11, 1987; and David Koenig, "Congress Extends Fed Takeover of Groom Area," *Las Vegas Review-Journal*, April 2, 1988.

David Koenig, "House Separates Groom Mountain Pact from Wilderness Issue," *Las Vegas Review-Journal*, June 15, 1988; Associated Press, "Group Stakes Claims during Lapse," *Las Vegas Review-Journal*, June 17, 1988; and Laura Wingard, "Feds Battle Environmental Group," *Las Vegas Review-Journal*, June 23, 1988.

16. "Four Plead Not Guilty in Groom Rap," *Las Vegas Review-Journal*, August 25, 1988; "Trial in Fed Site Trespass Continues," *Las Vegas Review-Journal*, December 8, 1988; and Elmer R. Rusco, "Native Americans and State and Local Governments," State of Nevada Agency for Nuclear Projects, Nuclear Waste Project Office, NWPO-SE-043-91, October 1991, 8.

17. "Input on Public Land Sought," *Las Vegas Review-Journal*, February 16, 1985; and Beall, "Air Force Will Seek Continued Access Restriction to Secret Base."

18. Beall, "Air Force Will Seek Continued Access Restriction to Secret Base."

19. Edward U. Condon, "Appendix A: Special Report of the USAF Advisory Board Ad Hoc Committee to Review Project Blue Book," in *Scientific Study of Unidentified Flying Objects* (Boulder: University of Colorado, 1968), 1282–1286.

20. Mike Hunt, letter to David L. Dobbs, April 20, 1980, Curtis Peebles collection.

21. Memorandum for the record from OSA Contracting Officer, "Concurrence in Amendment No. 1 to Contract No. SH-511 with Shell Oil Company, New York, NY, Project REDLIGHT (OXCART)," OXC-5152, June 27, 1963, CIA-RDP67B00074R000500400013-5, released January 6, 2009; Memorandum for the record from OSA Contracting Officer, "Concurrence in Amendment No. 1 to Contract No. SH-512 [AF33(657)-8582] with Shell Oil Company, New York, NY, Project OXCART," OXC-5735, September 30, 1963, CIA-RDP67B00074R000500410002-6, released January 6, 2009; and Precontract Approval Record, Mobil Oil Company, Contract MO-15042, Amendment No. 1, OXC-6183, December 13, 1963, CIA-RDP67B00074R000500340001-5, released January 6, 2009.

22. In his autobiography, Kelly Johnson mentioned Project SHOEHORN in relation to the shipment of a jet engine for the U-2 from the supplier; the CIA's online FOIA Reading Room contains numerous declassified Project AQUATONE work orders and shipping documents citing SHOEHORN.

23. Thornton "TD" Barnes, comments to author, October 2013.

24. Timothy Good, *Alien Contact* (New York: William Morrow, 1993), 150–52; and David Darlington, *Area 51: The Dreamland Chronicles* (New York: Henry Holt, 1997), 61–92.

25. Darlington, *Area 51: The Dreamland Chronicles*, 61–92 and 258.

26. Ibid., 61–92.

27. Fred Dunham, comment posted on May 18, 2014, in response to article by Lee Spiegel, "We're About to Learn a Lot More about Area 51," *Huffington Post*, May 17, 2014, http://www.huffingtonpost.com/2014/05/17/area-51-exhibit-re-opens_n_5341248.html, accessed April 12, 2015.

28. Sarah Knapton, "Area 51 and Extra-terrestrial Life Both Exist Says Head of NASA," *The Telegraph*, June 19, 2015.

29. Shannon Sands, "Believers Are Not Alone," *Los Angeles Times*, March 20, 1991; and Glenn Campbell, *Area 51 Viewer's Guide*, edition 2.0, September 8, 1993, 74–77.

30. Fred M. Dunham Jr., interview with Angus Beatty, December 5, 2008.

31. Campbell, *Area 51 Viewer's Guide*, 78.

32. Glenn Campbell, "Groom Lake: The Base That Isn't There," *Covert Action Quarterly* 52 (Spring 1995): 35–40.

33. Glenn Campbell, "Sensor Wars," *Groom Lake Desert Rat* 17 (October 13, 1994); and Glenn Campbell, "The Groom Range Land Grab—Part II," *Citizen Alert*, Spring 1994, 7.

34. Campbell, "Groom Lake: The Base That Isn't There," 35–40.

35. Keith Rogers, "Seven People Arrested in Groom Lake Incident," *Las Vegas Review-Journal*, January 5, 1994.

36. Ann J. Morgan, Bureau of Land Management, state director, Nevada, "Caliente Management Framework Plan and Nellis Air Force Range Resource Plan: Proposed White Sides Land Withdrawal Amendment and Environmental Assessment," BLM Las Vegas District, November 2, 1994.

37. Ibid., 3–22.

38. "No Peeking from Peak: Air Force Wants to Seize Mountain to Protect Secret Base," *Salt Lake Tribune*, October 17, 1993.

39. Stuart F. Brown, "Searching for the Secrets of Groom Lake," *Popular Science*, March 1994, 52–59.

40. Ibid., 54 and 85.

41. Letters to the editor, "Readers Talk Back," *Popular Science*, June 1994, 6.

42. Glenn Campbell, "End of an Era," *Groom Lake Desert Rat* 25 (April 15, 1995): 1.

43. Campbell, "The Groom Range Land Grab—Part II," 1.

44. Dunham interview, 2011.

45. Ibid.

46. Ibid.

47. Ibid.

48. William J. Fox, comments made during the Contractors Forum at the National Atomic Testing Museum.

49. Klein interview.

50. Dunham interview, 2011.

51. Ibid.

52. Ibid.

53. Ibid.

54. Steve A. Mizell, George Nikolich, Greg McCurdy, Craig Shadel, and Julianne J. Miller, "Project 57 Air Monitoring Report: October 1, 2013 through December 31, 2014," DOE/NV/0000939-27, Nevada Field Office, National Nuclear Security Administration, US Department of Energy, Las Vegas, NV, February 2016, 4.

55. Ibid., 21.

56. Tsuneo Tamura, "Characterization of Plutonium in Surface Soils from Area 13 of the Nevada Test Site," presented at the Plutonium Information Conference, Las Vegas, NV, October 8–11, 1974.

57. Evan M. Romney, Arthur Wallace, Richard O. Gilbert, and Jean E. Kinnear, "239-240 Pu and 241 Am Contamination of Vegetation in Aged Plutonium Fallout Areas," in *The Radioecology of Plutonium and Other Transuranics in Desert Environments*, NVO-153 (Las Vegas, NV: US Department of Energy, Nevada Operations Office, 1975), 43–88.

58. Richard O. Gilbert, "Revised Total Amounts of 239-240 Pu in Surface Soil at Safety-Test Sites," in *Transuranics in Desert Ecosystems*, ed. M. G. White, P. B. Dunaway, and D. L. Wireman, NVO-181 (Las Vegas, NV: US Department of Energy, Nevada Operations Office, 1977), 423–29.

59. A. E. Fritzsche, "An Aerial Radiological Survey for the United States Department of Energy of Area 13, Nevada Test Site," EGG-1183-1752, EG&G Energy Measurements, Las Vegas, NV, 1979.

60. Robert R. Kinnison and Richard O. Gilbert, "Estimates of Soil Removal for Cleanup of Transuranics at NAEG Offsite Safety-Shot Sites," in *The Radioecology of Transuranics in Desert Ecosystems*, ed. M. G. White, P. B. Dunaway, and R. G. Fuller, NVO-224 (Las Vegas, NV: US Department of Energy, Nevada Operations Office, 1982).

61. Arden E. Bicker, field task proposal/agreement, Project 57 (Area 13) Decontamination and Decommissioning, US Department of Energy Surplus Facilities Management Program, February 27, 1981.

62. Earl R. Sorom, "Project 57 Decontamination Program," US Department of Energy, September 1983.

63. Frank R. Standerfer, assistant manager for defense and energy programs, Department of Energy, Richland Operations Office, draft memo to Mahlon E. Gates, manager, Department of Energy, Nevada Operations Office, "Project 57 (Area 13) Decontamination and Decommissioning," July 14, 1981.

64. Ibid.

65. NASA Landsat imagery, circa 1987 and 1988; and Soviet satellite imagery, circa 1988.

66. Peter K. Fitzsimmons, letter to David D. McNelis regarding "Interim Emergency Response Plan for Aircraft Crash in Air Force Alpha Area (AFAA) near the Nevada Test Site (NTS)," Department of Energy, Nevada Operations Office, April 13, 1989.

67. T. Longo, M. Merkhofer, D. Layton, L. Barker, B. Deschler, and R. Jacobsen, "Cost/Risk/Benefit Analysis of Alternative Cleanup Requirements for Plutonium-Contaminated Soils on and Near the Nevada Test Site," DOE/NV-399, US Department of Energy, Nevada Operations Office, Las Vegas, NV, May 1995.

68. Mizell et al., "Project 57 Air Monitoring Report: October 1, 2013 through December 31, 2014," 1–4.

69. Ibid., 4–5.

70. Ibid., 8.

71. Ibid., 34.

72. Trevor Paglen, *Blank Spots on the Map: The Dark Geography of the Pentagon's Secret World* (New York: Dutton Books, 2009), 146–51.

73. Keith Rogers, "Groom Lake Toxic Burning Alleged," *Las Vegas Review-Journal*, March 20, 1994; and Dunham interview, 2007.

74. Dunham interview, 2007; and Mary Manning, "Area 51 Open to State Inspectors," *Las Vegas Sun*, April 28, 1995.

75. Warren Bates, "Classified Base Stays Unnamed," *Las Vegas Review-Journal*, May 5, 1995; *Frost v. Perry* and *Kasza v. Browner*, http://caselaw.findlaw.com/us-9th-circuit/1129437.html, accessed June 21, 2017; and Jonathan Turley, "Through a Looking Glass Darkly: National Security and Statutory Interpretation," *SMU Law Review* 53, no. 1, article 9 (Winter 2000): 205–49, https://scholar.smu.edu/smulr/vol53/iss1/9, accessed June 21, 2017.

76. Turley, "Through a Looking Glass Darkly"; and Susan Greene, "No EPA Personnel Cleared to Check Groom Lake Base," *Las Vegas Review-Journal*, April 21, 1995.

77. *Kasza v. Browner*; and Margaret A. Jacobs, "A Secret Air Base Hazardous Waste Act, Workers' Suit Alleges," *Wall Street Journal*, February 8, 1996.

78. Warren Bates, "Groom Lake Lawsuit Thrown out of Court," *Las Vegas Review-Journal*, March 7, 1996; and Keith Rogers, "Area 51 Burning Revealed," *Las Vegas Review-Journal*, September 3, 2007.

79. Dunham interview, 2011.

80. Ibid.; and Keith Rogers, "Documents May Help Former Area 51 Officer Land Settlement in Toxic Exposure Case," *Las Vegas Review-Journal*, February 21, 2016.

81. Dunham interview, 2011; and Rogers, "Area 51 Burning Revealed."

82. Rogers, "Area 51 Burning Revealed"; and Angus Batey, "Area 51: The Plane Truth," *The Telegraph*, June 18, 2011.

83. Keith Rogers, "Agency Gives OK to Some Area 51 Workers Seeking Compensation," *Las Vegas Review-Journal*, August 14, 2008; Keith Rogers, "Area 51 Worker Sees Hope in Supreme Court Ruling," *Las Vegas Review-Journal*, March 1, 2015; Fred M. Dunham Jr., transcript of testimony to Advisory Board on Radiation and Worker Health, meeting 54, day 2, Crowne Plaza Hotel, Redondo Beach, CA, April 8, 2008, 325–26.

84. Keith Rogers, "Sick Former Area 51 Worker Writes Obama," *Las Vegas Review-Journal*, June 3, 2012; and Carol A. Schoengold, William J. Brady, and Joe A. Stinson, "Census Report: United States Underground Nuclear Weapons Tests Personnel Review," DNA-6330F, vols. IV–VI, 1981–1992, Defense Nuclear Agency, Alexandria, VA, 1994.

85. Rachel P. Leiton, director, Division of Energy Employees Occupational Illness Compensation, Department of Labor, "Expansion of Nevada Test Site to Include Area 51," EEOICPA Circular 08-06, August 5, 2008; and Rogers, "Agency Gives OK to Some Area 51 Workers Seeking Compensation."

86. Jeffrey C. Gillen, official US Air Force biography, www.cannon.af.mil, accessed January 8, 2015.

87. Satellite imagery via NASA, Space Imaging, DigtalGlobe, GeoEye, and Soyuzcarta, 1988–2011; Dunham interview, 2011; and Rogers, "Area 51 Burning Revealed."

88. Keith Rogers, "Men Claim Top-Secret Retaliation by Air Force," *Las Vegas Review-Journal*, May 21, 2000.

89. Keith Rogers, "Ex-Area 51 Worker Says Commander Lied," *Las Vegas Review-Journal*, December 16, 2000.

90. Laura K. Donohue, "The Shadow of State Secrets," *University of Pennsylvania Law Review* 159, no. 1 (2010): 191–92n577; and Rogers, "Men Claim Top-Secret Retaliation by Air Force."

91. Rogers, "Men Claim Top-Secret Retaliation by Air Force"; and *Darby v. US Department of Defense*, 74 F, Appendix at 814 (9th Circuit Court, 2003).

92. Rogers, "Men Claim Top-Secret Retaliation by Air Force."

Chapter 9: Unusual Flying Objects

1. Frank T. Birk, biographical information via AFFTC History Office and SETP, August 1993; Mark Gamache, online résumé, accessed December 22, 2016; and Richard D. Colgren, online résumé, 2003.

2. Dennis Sager, biographical information, US Air Force, May 1999; and Dennis Sager, comments to author, February 25, 2000.

3. David A. Fulghum, "Groom Lake Tests Target Stealth," *Aviation Week & Space Technology*, February 5, 1996, 26–27.

4. Joseph A. Lanni, biographical information, US Air Force and SETP, 2006.

5. Trey Rawls, LinkedIn profile, accessed July 29, 2013; Greg Gilbreath, LinkedIn profile, accessed January 1, 2017; Alan Wigdahl, LinkedIn profile, accessed December 29, 2016; Author's Graphics Collection; Capt. Andrew J. McFarland, commander, Naval Test Wing, Pacific, "Farewell Letter" on the occasion of his retirement, June 19, 2020, Naval Air Warfare Center, Weapons Division, NAWS China Lake, CA; and Dan Javorsek, biographical information, US Air Force Operational Test and Evaluation Center, Kirtland AFB, NM, March 2021.

6. Nicholas J. Colella and Gordon S. Wenneker, "Pathfinder and the Development of Solar Rechargeable Aircraft," *Energy & Technology Review* (Lawrence Livermore National Laboratory, Livermore, CA), July 1994.

7. Jay Levine, "Morgan Recalls Solar Plane's Beginning," *The X-Press* 44, no. 2 (May 8, 2002): 4.

8. Adkins, "Vehicle Platforms in the Office of Research and Development."

9. Stuart Brown, "The Eternal Airplane," *Popular Science*, April 1994, 73–75.

10. Colella and Wenneker, "Pathfinder and the Development of Solar Rechargeable Aircraft."

11. Ibid.; and Michael J. Hirschberg, "To Boldly Go Where No Unmanned Aircraft Has Gone Before: A Half-Century of DARPA's Contributions to Unmanned Aircraft," AIAA-2010-158, presented at the 48th AIAA Aerospace Sciences Meeting, Orlando, FL, January 2010.

12. W. Ray Morgan, interview with author, February 17, 2015; and Adkins, "Vehicle Platforms in the Office of Research and Development."

13. Morgan interview; and AFP 11-6, "Administrative Practices: Nicknames and Exercise Terms," which lists HAVE RASH as a Science and Technology (S&T) program initiated by AFSC/TEX on February 8, 1983.

14. Adkins, "Vehicle Platforms in the Office of Research and Development."

15. Dunham interview, 2011; and Comments from ex-Lockheed employee who declined to give his name during discussion with the author at the National Atomic Testing Museum, Las Vegas, NV, June 2, 2012.

16. Morgan interview.

17. Greg Kendall, "Pathfinder Flight Test Log," August 1998, including data extracted from "HALSOL Final Report," AeroVironment, Inc., 1983; and Morgan interview.

18. Ibid.

19. Ibid.

20. Kendall, "Pathfinder Flight Test Log."

21. Ibid.; and Adkins, "Vehicle Platforms in the Office of Research and Development."

22. Colella and Wenneker, "Pathfinder and the Development of Solar Rechargeable Aircraft," 2–3; and Adkins, "Vehicle Platforms in the Office of Research and Development."

23. DARO staff, "Unmanned Aerial Vehicles (UAV) Program Plan," Defense Airborne Reconnaissance Office, Washington, DC, April 1994; and Adkins, "Vehicle Platforms in the Office of Research and Development."

24. DFRC Public Affairs, Fact Sheet: "Pathfinder Solar-Powered Aircraft," FS-034, NASA Dryden Flight Research Center, Edwards, CA, 2001.

25. Peck, *America's Secret MiG Squadron*, 175; AFP 11-6, "Administrative Practices: Nicknames and Exercise Terms," 1987; and "Red Hats Comprehensive Recall Roster."

26. John Prados, *How the Cold War Ended: Debating and Doing History* (Washington, DC: Potomac Books, 2011), 188–90.

27. Donovan, "Full Circle? The Transformation of Dedicated Adversary Air Training in the USAF," 45.

28. Ibid., 45–51.

29. Ibid.

30. Benjamin S. Lambeth, "The Winning of Air Supremacy in Operation Desert Storm," RAND Paper P-7837, 1993, 1–4; and Daryl G. Press, "The Myth of Air Power in the Persian Gulf War and the Future of Warfare," *International Security* 26, no. 2 (2001): 5–44.

31. Richard G. Davis, "On Target: Organizing and Executing the Strategic Air Campaign Against Iraq," Air Force History Support Office, Bolling AFB, Washington, DC, 2002, 173; Kevin Burns, biographical information via SETP; Daniel N. Dixon, biographical information, www.cvw8.navy.mil/dix.htm, accessed October 17, 2007; and "Red Hats Comprehensive Recall Roster."

32. Thomas A. Bussiere, "General Merrill A. McPeak: Leadership and Organizational Change," School of Advanced Airpower Studies, Air University, Maxwell Air Force Base, AL, June 2001, 1–26.

33. Thomas C. Horne, memorandum for HQ AFMC/XPMS, "413 TS Unit Emblems," with attachments, Unit Insignia files, AFFTC History Office, n.d. (circa 1992).

34. Brown, "Searching for the Secrets of Groom Lake," 52–59; Robert N. Polumbo, biographical information via USAF Air Reserve Command, Robins AFB, GA; and William Elliott, "Unofficial Groom Lake Chronology," via personal communication, October 30, 2000. Several independent sources identified the YF-112C pilot as Woody Nolan, who served as Red Hats operations officer (July 1997–May 1999) and subsequently as commander (June 1999–May 2000).

35. Luftwaffenmaterielkommando, "MiG-29 Flight Manual," GAF T.O. 1F-MIG29-1, September 30, 1994.

36. Tyler Rogoway, "How to Win in a Dogfight: Stories from a Pilot Who Flew F-16s and MiGs," Foxtrot Alpha, February 3, 2015, http://foxtrotalpha.jalopnik.com/how-to-win-in-a-dogfight-stories-from-a-pilot-who-flew-1682723379, accessed February 22, 2015

37. Ibid.

38. Ibid.

39. Ibid.

40. Donovan, "Full Circle? The Transformation of Dedicated Adversary Air Training in the USAF," 65.

41. Organizational chart, "53 Test and Evaluation Group, Detachment 3," February 2003; and USAF Fact Sheet, "Det 3, 53d Test and Evaluation Group," October 2005.

42. Office of the Director, Operational Test & Evaluation, "Live Fire Test & Evaluation," in *DOT&E FY2003 Annual Report* (December 2003), 304; and Rogoway, "How to Win in a Dogfight: Stories from a Pilot Who Flew F-16s and MiGs."

43. Rogoway, "How to Win in a Dogfight: Stories from a Pilot Who Flew F-16s and MiGs"; and Associated Press, "German MiGs, Missiles to Be Tested at Eglin," *Northwest Florida Daily News*, April 30, 2003.

44. Sighting report, http://www.n105tb.co.uk/N105TBsite2a_files/page314.htm, accessed March 13, 2007; and "Introduction," in "MIT Reports to the President 2002–2003," http://web.mit.edu/annualreports/pres03/05.00.html, accessed March 13, 2007.

45. Piotr Butowski, "Sukhoi's Latest 'Flanker,'" *Combat Aircraft* 9, no. 3 (2008): 52–55.

46. Phil Drake, posting as Stealth Spotter, "Su-27s in the USA," December 29, 2016, http://area51trips.blogspot.co.uk, accessed January 1, 2017.

47. Darren Boyle, "Is This Proof America Is Preparing for War with Russia? US Plane Is Spotted in a Mock Dogfight with a Russian Jet above the Top Secret Area 51 Base," *Daily Mail Online*, January 17, 2017, http://www.dailymail.co.uk/news/article-4127690/US-Russian-fighter-jets-mock-dogfight-Area-51.html#ixzz4W9LDHA5j.

48. Fred Clifton, posting as fulcrumflyer, September 1, 2007, http://www.abovetopsecret.com/forum/thread233946/pg2.

49. Guy Norris, "Fatal Nevada Crash Involved Foreign Aircraft Type," *Aerospace Daily & Defense Review*, September 11, 2017, http://aviationweek.com/defense/fatal-nevada-crash-involved-foreign-aircraft-type; and Douglas Wickert, "Risk Awareness: A New Framework for Risk Management in Flight Test," presented at the Society of Experimental Test Pilots 62nd annual symposium, Anaheim, CA, September 27, 2018.

50. Steve Davies, "Classified Air Force MiG Squadron to Disband in Wake of Commander's Death?," draft copy of proposed article, April 2022; and Steve Davies, *10 Percent True*, episode 34, "What Happened to 'Doc' Schultz?," YouTube video, May 7, 2022, https://www.youtube.com/watch?v=zidJB6qxlKs, accessed May 8, 2022.

51. Matthew Wallin, "US Foreign Policy toward Russia: An Overview of Strategy and Considerations," American Security Project, Washington, DC, November 2017; and Patrick Kingsley, "The Ukraine Crisis: What to Know about Why Russia Attacked," *New York Times*, March 1, 2022.

52. Jeremy Page, "China Building Airstrip on Spratly Islands, Satellite Images Show," *Wall Street Journal*, April 16, 2015; and Luis Martinez, "Chinese Jets Come within Several Hundred Feet of US Plane over South China Sea," ABC News, May 27, 2017, https://abcnews.go.com/International/chinese-jets-hundred-feet-us-plane-south-china/story?id=47664699, accessed June 3, 2017.

53. Office of the Director, Operational Test & Evaluation, "T&E Resources," in *DOT&E FY2015 Annual Report* (January 2016), 405.

54. Office of the Secretary of Defense, PE0605117D8Z: Foreign Materiel Acquisition and Exploitation, March 2014; Air Force Budget Appropriation; Research, Development; Test & Evaluation, exhibit R-2A, RDT&E, Project Justification: PB 2013 Air Force, Project 667500: Foreign Materiel Acquisition/Analysis, February 2012.

55. Chong, *Flying Wings & Radical Things*, 234–35; and Allen Samuel, "RTM for Composite Missile Airframe Production," presented at the Workshop on Closed-Mold Manufacturing of High-Performance Composite Missile Structures, Institute for Defense Analyses, Alexandria, VA, May 16, 1995.

56. Michael T. Miklos, "Field Artillery, the Ascending Branch of Force XXI," School of Advanced Military Studies, US Army Command and General Staff College, Ft. Leavenworth, KS, 1995, 90.

57. Erik Seedhouse, *Virgin Galactic: The First Ten Years* (Chichester, UK: Springer-Praxis, 2015), 47; and Allan Netzer, "Airborne Data Acquisition and Relay System," presented at the International Telemetering Conference, Las Vegas, NV, November 4, 1991.

58. John M. Hoffman, "Aircraft Accident Investigation, F-16C (86-0359), 9 August 1990," Air Force Flight Test Center, Edwards AFB, CA, October 26, 1990.

59. Ibid.

60. Dunham interview, October 7, 2011.

61. Hoffman, "Aircraft Accident Investigation, F-16C (86-0359), 9 August 1990."

62. Descriptive Summary: Program Element 0207160F, Tri-Service Standoff Attack Missile, Department of Defense, February 1994.

63. L. Martin Kaplan, *Department of the Army Historical Summary, Fiscal Year 1994* (Washington, DC: Center of Military History, US Army, 2000), 103–03; and Evan L. Mayerle, comments posted on Secret Projects Forum, March 14, 2006, https://www.secretprojects.co.uk/forum/index.php?topic=121.0.

64. Bradley Graham, "Missile Became a $3.9 Billion Misfire," *Washington Post*, April 3, 1995; US Government Accountability Office, "Missile Development—Status and Issues at the Time of the TSSAM Termination Decision," GAO/NSIAD 95-46, 1995. 3; and US Government Accountability Office, "Precision Guided Munitions Acquisition Plan," GAO/NSIAD-96-144, June 1996, 8.

65. James F. Peltz, "Secret Northrop Missile Racks Up Sky-High Losses," *Los Angeles Times*, February 15, 1994; Bradley Graham, "Missile Became a $3.9 Billion Misfire"; US Government Accountability Office, "Missile Development—Status and Issues at the Time of the TSSAM Termination Decision," 5–7; US Government Accountability Office, "Termination Costs Are Generally Not a Compelling Reason to Continue Programs or Contracts That Otherwise Warrant Ending," GAO-08-379, March 2008, 13–16; and Anita Latin, LinkedIn profile, accessed September 12, 2016.

66. Boeing News Release, "Boeing Unveils Bird of Prey Stealth Technology Demonstrator," October 18, 2002.

67. Paul Proctor, "New Markets on the Horizon," *Boeing Frontiers* 1, no. 7 (November 2002); "Combat Survivability Unit Hands Out Awards," *National Defense*, April 2002; and "MDC to focus on Phantom Works," *Flight International*, August 22, 1995.

68. Boeing News Release, "Boeing Unveils Bird of Prey Stealth Technology Demonstrator."

69. David A. Fulghum, "Advanced Stealth Appears in Boeing 'BOP' Prototype," *Aviation Week & Space Technology*, October 28, 2002, 36–38.

70. Rudy Haug, Doug Benjamin, and Joe Felock, "Boeing Bird of Prey," presented at the Society of Experimental Test Pilots 50th annual symposium, Anaheim, CA, September 30, 2006.

71. Doug Benjamin, "Black Planes, Blue Sky," presented at the Los Angeles County Air Show, Lancaster, CA, March 24, 2018; and Peter W. Merlin, "Bird of Prey—an Innovative Technology Demonstration," Black Projects, May 11, 2007, www.dreamlandresort.com.

72. Haug et al., "Boeing Bird of Prey."

73. Frederic A. Madenwald III obituary, via SETP, August 2012; and Haug et al., "Boeing Bird of Prey."

74. Haug et al., "Boeing Bird of Prey"; and Benjamin, "Black Planes, Blue Sky."

75. Ibid.; and David Desmond, email to Shawna Mullen, Society of Experimental Test Pilots, "Nomination of the Bird of Prey Pilot Team for a Retroactive Kincheloe Award," July 16, 2007.

76. Benjamin, "Black Planes, Blue Sky"; and Haug et al., "Boeing Bird of Prey."

77. Ibid.; and Desmond email.

78. Haug et al., "Boeing Bird of Prey."

79. Ibid.

80. Ibid.

81. Ibid.

82. Peter W. Merlin, "Testing Tailless Aircraft Technology Demonstrators," presented at the 2nd Annual AViation History Symposium, Antelope Valley College, Lancaster, CA, February 21, 2009.

83. Thomas P. Ehrhard, "Unmanned Aerial Vehicles in the United States Armed Services: A Comparative Study of Weapon System Innovation," PhD diss. submitted to Johns Hopkins University, June 2000; and US Air Force, "The US Air Force Remotely Piloted Aircraft and Unmanned Aerial Vehicle Strategic Vision," 2005.

84. John Boatman, "USA Planned Stealthy UAV to Replace SR-71," *Jane's Defence Weekly*, December 17, 1994; and Thomas P. Ehrhard, *Air Force UAVs: The Secret History* (Arlington, VA: Mitchell Institute Press, 2010), 12–17.

85. Ehrhard, *Air Force UAVs*, 12–17; and Bill Sweetman, "Focus Aircraft: HALE/MALE Unmanned Air Vehicles Part 1: History of the Endurance UAV," *International Air Power Review* 15 (2005): 63–69.

86. John Ranelagh, *The Agency: The Rise and Decline of the CIA* (New York: Simon and Schuster, 1986), 666–67; and Ehrhard, *Air Force UAVs*, 12–17.

87. Ehrhard, *Air Force UAVs*, 12–17; and David A. Fulghum and John D. Morrocco, "CIA to Deploy UAVs in Albania," *Aviation Week & Space Technology*, January 31, 1994.

88. Martin C. Faga, director, National Reconnaissance Office, "Report to the Secretary of Defense and Director of Central Intelligence Regarding NRO Restructure," January 8, 1990; and Ehrhard, *Air Force UAVs*, 12–17.

89. Ehrhard, *Air Force UAVs*, 12–17; and Sweetman, "Focus Aircraft: HALE/MALE Unmanned Air Vehicles Part 1: History of the Endurance UAV," 63–69.

90. Sweetman, "Focus Aircraft: HALE/MALE Unmanned Air Vehicles Part 1: History of the Endurance UAV," 63–69; David A. Fulghum, "Long-Term Stealth Project Gets the Ax," *Aviation Week & Space Technology*, May 24, 1999, 77–78; "High-Altitude Atmospheric Research Platform Information Package," Lockheed Corporation, Burbank, CA, February 1990; and Peter W. Merlin, "RQ-3A DarkStar UAV (Tier III Minus) Flight Log," August 2000, NASA Dryden Flight Research Center Historical Reference Collection.

91. David A. Fulghum, "Lockheed Martin Has Revealed a New Stealthy UAV," *Aviation Week & Space Technology*, September 22, 2003; Comments to author by former Skunk Works employee Jay Tweed, October 2003; and Tyler Rogoway, comments on AviationIntel.com, July 16, 2012, accessed January 4, 2013.

92. Author's observations and comments from Skunk Works employees at the Los Angeles County Air Show, Fox Field, Lancaster, CA, March 24–25, 2018; and Chris Pocock, "Skunk Works Reveals Stealth UAV Demonstrator," AINonline, March 26, 2018, https://www.ainonline.com/aviation-news/defense/2018-03-26/skunk-works-reveals-stealthy-uav-demonstrator, accessed March 30, 2018.

93. Eric D. Knutson, Joseph M. Wurts, and Michael H. Pohlig, "Unmanned Aircraft," United States patent D382,851, August 26, 1997; and Guy Norris, "More Details Emerge about Lockheed Martin's Pioneering X-44A," *Aviation Week & Space Technology*, April 9–22, 2018.

94. Sean Kearns, "Experimental Aircraft May Be on Horizon," *Antelope Valley Press*, July 11, 1999; and Alan Brown, "X-44 Talking Points," NASA Dryden Flight Research Center, Edwards, CA, April 2000.

95. David A. Fulghum and Bill Sweetman, "US Air Force Reveals Operational Stealth UAV," *Aviation Week & Space Technology*, December 4, 2009; Bill Sweetman, "New Air Force Team's Shadowy Role," *Aviation Week & Space Technology*, December 5, 2012; and David A. Fulghum and Bill Sweetman, "New Details: RQ-170 Payload Lost in Iran Is Identified," *Aviation Week & Space Technology*, January 2, 2012. Some patches made for the Desert Prowler flight test team feature design elements and colors associated with Groom Lake organizations, including the Red Hats. Handwritten on the back of one patch was the date "12/13/05"; a former Lockheed Martin Skunk Works employee claimed these emblems were carried on the aircraft during its first flight.

96. David Axe, "Stealth Drone's Secret Pacific Missions," War Is Boring, December 7, 2013, https://medium.com/war-is-boring/stealth-drones-secret-pacific-missions-3f12eee5c0d1, accessed December 12, 2013; Joseph Trevithic and Tyler Rogoway, "Details Emerge about the Secretive RQ-170 Stealth Drone's First Visit to Korea," War Zone, January 28, 2020, https://www.thedrive.com/the-war-zone/31992/exclusive-details-on-the-secretive-rq-170-stealth-drones-first-trip-to-korea, accessed May 3, 2020; Chief, Advanced Programs Division (ACC/A8Z), memorandum to chief, Basing Division (ACC/A5B), "30RS Unit Move," November 22, 2010; Chief, ACC/A5B, memorandum to vice commander, 432nd Wing, "30RS Movement Directive Request IAW AFI 16-403," November 30, 2010; and 432nd Wing History, "Rebasing Movement of the 30th Reconnaissance Squadron," 2010.

97. Ed Darack, "The Drone That Stalked Bin Laden," *AIR & SPACE / Smithsonian*, April 2016; and David Axe, "Iran Knows the Secrets of America's Stealth Drone," May 24, 2014, https://medium.com/war-is-boring/iran-knows-the-secrets-of-americas-stealth-drone-f3fc9b2c087a, accessed May 26, 2014.

98. Amy Butler, "Lockheed Unveils Secret Polecat UAV Design," *Aviation Week & Space Technology*, July 19, 2006.

99. Ibid.; Bob Dunn and Melissa Dalton, "Revolutionary Unmanned Demonstrator Unveiled at Farnborough Air Show," *Lockheed Martin Aeronautics Star* 7, no. 2 (2006); James Skeen, "Hush-Hush Warplane Exists," *Los Angeles Daily News*, July 20, 2006; and Amy Butler, "Not to Be Left Behind," *Aviation Week & Space Technology*, July 24, 2006.

100. Graham Warwick, "Lockheed Confirms P-175 Polecat UAV Crash," FlightGlobal, March 20, 2007, https://www.flightglobal.com/news/articles/lockheed-confirms-p-175-polecat-uav-crash-212700/, accessed March 27, 2007; and Amy Butler, "Road Kill: Polecat UAV Has Been Labeled a Total Loss after December Crash," *Aviation Week & Space Technology*, March 19, 2007, 44.

101. Robert K. Ackerman, "Air Force Researchers Set Stratospheric Goals," SIGNAL, February 2001.

102. Ibid.

103. Stephen Trimble, "Over the Horizon," FlightGlobal, July 4, 2005, https://www.flightglobal.com/over-the-horizon/61523.article.

104. Northrop Grumman Public Affairs, "Northrop Grumman Airborne Antenna Offers Better Look at Ground Targets," *Microwave Journal*, May 26, 2004.

105. Ibid.; and Jeffrey P. Massman and Thomas P. Steffen, "Low Cost All Metal Additively Manufactured Wideband Antenna Array Modules," AFRL-RY-WP-TP-2020-0097, Air Force Research Laboratory Sensors Directorate, May 2020.

106. Robert K. Ackerman, "Flying Eye in the Sky," SIGNAL, March 2007.

107. Jonathan D. Bartley-Cho and Joseph A. Henderson, "Design and Analysis of HiLDA/AEI Aeroelastic Wind-Tunnel Model," AIAA-2008-7191, American Institute of Aeronautics and Astronautics, presented at the 26th AIAA Applied Aerodynamics Conference, Honolulu, HI, August 18, 2008; and Robert C. Scott, Thomas K. Vetter, Kevin B. Penning, David A. Coulson, and Jennifer Heeg, "Aeroservoelastic Testing of a Sidewall Mounted Free Flying Wind-Tunnel Model," AIAA-2008-7186, American Institute of Aeronautics and Astronautics, presented at the 26th AIAA Applied Aerodynamics Conference, Honolulu, HI, August 18, 2008.

108. Bill Sweetman, "Under the Radar: Signs of Secret USAF Aircraft Programs," *Aviation Week & Space Technology*, December 3, 2012, 29; HQ USAF briefing by Maj. Gen. Dave Scott, AF/A5R, "Anti-Access / Area Denial Challenges," October 6, 2010; Alex Sansone, LinkedIn profile, accessed January 1, 2017; and Bill Sweetman, "Big Wing: Evidence Suggests Northrop Grumman Won Classified Contract to Develop New Stealthy UAV," *Aviation Week & Space Technology*, August 29, 2011, 46–47.

109. Guy Norris, "Groom Boom: Major Construction at Secret Groom Lake Site Paves Way for Flight Test Expansion," *Aviation Week & Space Technology*, October 29, 2007, 45–46.

110. Vincent J. "Van Gogh" Chioma, LinkedIn profile, accessed December 10, 2020; Travis J. "Fromo" Higgs, LinkedIn profile, accessed June 20, 2020; and Josh Lane, LinkedIn profile, accessed December 13, 2020. Some information was derived from the author's collection of Area 51 memorabilia (hereinafter called Author's Graphics Collection), which included artwork, logos, embroidered emblems, coins, decals, hats, T-shirts, jackets, coffee mugs, drinking glasses, beer steins, plaques, certificates, and similar items displaying an association with organizations, programs, projects, missions, or other activities. All such unclassified items were expected to eventually enter the public domain (and thus public scrutiny) and were therefore subject to prior approval by competent program security authorities.

111. Sweetman, "Big Wing: Evidence Suggests Northrop Grumman Won Classified Contract to Develop New Stealthy UAV," 46; and Amy Butler and Bill Sweetman, "Return of the Penetrator," *Aviation Week & Space Technology*, December 9, 2013, 20–25.

112. Guy Norris, "USAF Unit Moves Reveal Clues to RQ-180 Ops Debut," *Aviation Week & Space Technology*, October 24, 2019, 18–21; Colville McFee, "Opening Doors to the Future: 427th Reconnaissance Squadron Ribbon-Cutting Ceremony," April 26, 2019, https://www.beale.af.mil/News/Article-Display/Article/1825752/opening-doors-to-the-future-427th-reconnaissance-squadron-ribbon-cutting-ceremo/, accessed October 31, 2020; Joshua Williams, LinkedIn profile, accessed September 29, 2016; Matthew Genelin, LinkedIn profile, accessed September 29, 2016; Col. Ernest John "Dragon" Teichert, commander, 53rd Test Management Group, "53rd Wing Test and Evaluation," 53D Wing Instruction 99-101, June 2016; Michael "Gus" Deaver, LinkedIn profile, accessed September 29, 2016; Brian Owen, LinkedIn profile, accessed September 29, 2016; Jeff Pendley, LinkedIn profile, accessed July 3, 2017; Jennie Swiechowicz, LinkedIn profile, accessed July 12, 2017; Davies, "Classified Air Force MiG Squadron to Disband in Wake of Commander's Death?"; and Author's Graphics Collection.

113. Steve Trimble and Guy Norris, "Possible Photo of Highly Secret RQ-180 Aircraft Surfaces Online," *Aviation Week & Space Technology*, November 1, 2020; and David Cenciotti, "Mysterious Aircraft Spotted over Philippines Strikingly Similar to Mystery UAS Photographed over California Last Year," *The Aviationist*, September 5, 2021, https://theaviationist.com/2021/09/05/mystery-aircraft-philippines/?fbclid=IwAR0CRHxL0fJZHAn-vy-qVCUXXq_sikFqnvIJQfNGyG4OxCLxqyCjSomlWvnE, accessed September 6, 2021.

114. Nicholas Schmidle, "Getting Bin Laden," *New Yorker*, August 8, 2011.

115. Sam Yao and Dale Abildskov, "Low-Radar-Cross-Section OH-6A Helicopter Tail Rotor Blade," Army Air Mobility Research and Development Laboratory, April 1974.

116. E. F. Buckley, "RCS Measurement—Weathered LRCS OH-6A Infrared and Ultraviolet Detection," Army Air Mobility Research and Development Laboratory, 1977.

117. David W. Lowry, Melvin J. Rich, Saul Rivera, and Thomas W. Sheehy, "Structural Concepts and Aerodynamic for Low Radar Cross Section (LRCS) Fuselage Configurations," Army Air Mobility Research and Development Laboratory, July 1978.

118. Matt Graham, ARC Discussion Forums, February 3, 2010, http://www.arcforums.com/forums/air/index.php?/topic/200876-some-pics-from-army-flight-test/&page=4, accessed February 11, 2010.

119. Ibid.; and John F. Hagen, commander, Army Engineering Flight Activity, memorandum for commander, US Army Aviation Systems Command, "Memorandum of Effort Report, EH-60A Direction Finding Accuracy Kit Testing," AEFA Project No. 87-09-5," November 15, 1989.

120. Marvin L. Hanks, director, Army Aviation Technical Test Center, memorandum for commander, US Army Aviation Systems Command, "Memorandum of Effort, Support of the Technical Measurement and EMC/EMI Qualification Effort of the EH-60A Helicopter Equipped with a Direction Finding Enhancement Kit and Extended Range Fuel System," AVSCOM Project 87-09-7, TECOM Project 4-CO-230-00-012," February 4, 1991; and Matt Graham, ARC Discussion Forums.

121. Susan Greene, "Ex-Worker Describes Stealth Copter," *Las Vegas Review Journal*, February 26, 1995; Keith Rogers, "Stealth Craft in bin-Laden Raid Has Nevada Ties," *Las Vegas Review Journal*, May 7, 2011; David A. Fulghum, "US Black Programs Stress Lean Projects," *Aviation Week & Space Technology*, February 6, 1995, 18–20; and Author's Graphics Collection.

122. Jason L. Galindo, "A Case History of the United States Army RAH-66 Comanche Helicopter," Naval Postgraduate School, Monterey, CA, March 2002; Sikorsky Archives, "RAH-66 Comanche," https://www.sikorskyarchives.com/RAH-66%20COMANCHE.php, accessed November 12, 2020; and Boeing, "Historical Snapshot: RAH-66 Comanche," https://www.boeing.com/history/products/rah-66-comanche.page, accessed November 12, 2020.

123. Sean Naylor, *Relentless Strike: The Secret History of Joint Special Operations Command* (New York: St. Martin's, 2015).

124. Ibid.; and Marcus Weisgerber, "Mission Helo was Secret Stealth Black Hawk," *Military Times*, March 29, 2013.

125. Naylor, *Relentless Strike*.

126. Garrett M. Graf, "I'd Never Been Involved in Anything as Secret as This," *Politico*, April 30, 2021, https://www.politico.com/news/magazine/2021/04/30/osama-bin-laden-death-white-house-oral-history-484793, accessed May 2, 2021; Keith Rogers, "SEALS Trained for bin Laden Raid in Nevada Desert, Magazine Says," *Las Vegas Review Journal*, August 6, 2011; and Schmidle, "Getting Bin Laden."

127. Jim Wilson, "The New 'Area 51,'" *Popular Mechanics*, June 1997.

128. Ibid.; NASA, "X-33 Advanced Technology Demonstrator Program Final Environmental Impact Statement," NP-1997-09-02-MSFC, vol. 1, NASA Marshall Spaceflight Center, September 1997; Corey Bluemel, "It Is Rocket Science, Green River Is the Site for University Rocket Launches," *Emery County Progress*, July 3, 2007; and Joe Bauman, "Expert Says NASA Had to Cancel X-33," *Deseret News*, March 21, 2001.

129. Yahya A. Dehqanzada and Ann M. Florini, "Secrets for Sale: How Commercial Satellite Imagery Will Change the World," School of Social Sciences Research Collection Paper 2325, Singapore Management University, February 2000; Christopher Lavers, "Origins of High-Resolution Civilian Satellite Imaging," *Directions*, January 24, 2013; David DiBiase, "Early Space Imaging Systems," in *The Nature of Geographic Information*, Pennsylvania State College of Earth and Mineral Sciences, https://www.e-education.psu.edu/natureofgeoinfo/node/1900, accessed January 21, 2017; and Graham T. Richardson and Robert N. Merz, "High-Resolution Commercial Imagery and Open-Source Information: Implications for Arms Control," in *Arms Control and Disarmament Agency Intelligence Brief* (Washington, DC: Bureau of Intelligence, Verification and Information Management, May 13, 1996).

130. "Russian Satellite Returns EO Images," *Space Daily*, April 7, 1998, https://www.spacedaily.com/news/eo-98a.html, accessed May 13, 2000; Associated Press, "Satellite Images of Area 51 Are Being Put on the Web," *New York Times*, April 18, 2000; and Transcript of Department of Defense news briefing by Kenneth H. Bacon, assistant to the secretary of defense for public affairs, Washington, DC, April 18, 2000, http://www.defenselink.mil/news/Apr2000/t04182000_t0418asd.html, accessed January 14, 2017.

131. Michael A. Dornheim, "Groom Lake Base Revealed in Sharp, New Satellite Images," *Aviation Week & Space Technology*, May 1, 2000, 58–61; and Michael Dornheim email to author, May 5, 2000.

132. Congressional Record, "Security and Commercial Satellite Imagery," in *Proceedings and Debates of the 106th Congress, Second Session* (Washington, DC: US Government Printing Office, 2000), vol. 146, part 6, 7740–7741.

Chapter 10: National Asset

1. Bussiere, "General Merrill A. McPeak: Leadership and Organizational Change," 40–46.

2. AFFTC/HO staff, *History of the Air Force Flight Test Center, 1 October 1992–30 September 1994*, vol. 1, *Narrative*, AFFTC History Office collection.

3. David Eidsaune, LinkedIn profile, accessed March 29, 2012; Michael T. Brewer, official biography, US Air Force, accessed July 24, 2009; Michael Brewer, LinkedIn profile, accessed June 12, 2017; Roderick L. Cregier, LinkedIn profile, accessed November 16, 2015; Charles Knofczynski, LinkedIn profile, accessed April 14, 2016; and Doug Joyce, "Doug Joyce Awarded AIAA Associate Fellow at AIAA 48th Aerospace Sciences Meeting," *Aerospace New England* 47, no. 2 (March/April 2010): 3. In an April 2005 letter, nominating Pete Winters for the prestigious SETP Doolittle Award, retired major general Peter W. Odgers used the term "the National Classified Test Facility" rather than the more generic "a national classified test facility."

4. AFI 38-101, "Manpower and Organization."

5. Roderick L. Cregier, LinkedIn profile.

6. Charles Knofczynski, LinkedIn profile; Ron "Batta" Schwing, LinkedIn profile, accessed August 4, 2017; Sean Borror, LinkedIn profile, accessed November 16, 2015; Alan Wigdahl, LinkedIn profile; and AFI 38-101, "Manpower and Organization."

7. Charles Knofczynski, LinkedIn profile; David Eidsaune, LinkedIn profile; and David R. Zorzi, "The Numbers Tell the Story," *Armed Forces Comptroller*, Winter 2012.

8. AFI 38-101, "Manpower and Organization."

9. Benjamin A. "Alvin" Drew, LinkedIn profile, accessed September 4, 2014; Mike Tarlton, LinkedIn profile, accessed November 16, 2015; Travis J. "Fromo" Higgs, LinkedIn profile, accessed June 30, 2020; Roderick L. Cregier, LinkedIn profile; Ron "Batta" Schwing, LinkedIn profile, accessed August 4, 2017; and Air Force Instruction 13-212, vol. 1, Nellis Air Force Base ADM A, "Range Planning and Operations," 98th Range Wing, Nellis AFB, Nevada, January 2007.

10. Terry Tichenor, LinkedIn profile, accessed June 9, 2011.

11. Keith Colmer, LinkedIn profile, accessed March 17, 2014; and Vincent Chioma, LinkedIn profile.

12. Scott Heritsch, LinkedIn profile, accessed July 3, 2017; and Sean Borror, LinkedIn profile.

13. Duane Harmon, LinkedIn profile, accessed November 18, 2015; Jeff Parks, LinkedIn profile, accessed September 18, 2015; David Hiltz, LinkedIn profile, accessed November 18, 2015; Ron "Batta" Schwing, LinkedIn profile, accessed August 4, 2017; and Alex Sansone, LinkedIn profile.

14. Jason Dotter, LinkedIn profile, accessed December 20, 2016; James Lomax, LinkedIn profile, accessed December 1, 2020; Doug Hool, LinkedIn profile, accessed December 3, 2020; and Raymond Marshall, LinkedIn profile, accessed March 31, 2021.

15. Douglas D. Russell, "Welcome to Det 3, 53d Test and Evaluation Group," 53rd TEG web page, accessed October 7, 2005.

16. Davies, "Classified Air Force MiG Squadron to Disband in Wake of Commander's Death?"

17. Aerospace Vehicle Flight Report and Maintenance Document, AFTO Form 781F, CH-3E, Serial No. 62-12581, November 1968–September 1991, Air Force Flight Test Museum collection; *World Airpower Journal* 30 (Autumn/Fall 1997): 14; Andreas Parsch, email to author, November 8, 1997; Author's Graphics Collection; and US Air Force, "HH-60G PAVE HAWK Fact Sheet," February 2004.

18. John T. Coffindaffer, LinkedIn profile, accessed June 27, 2017; Lynne Nimocks, curriculum vitae in *Real-Resumes for Aviation and Travel Jobs*, ed. Anne McKinney (Fayetteville, NC: PREP, 2002), 97; and Author's Graphics Collection.

19. Sedric Pennington, "Air Force Receives Modified Black Hawk Helicopter," *Redstone Rocket*, September 13, 2011; Marcus Weisgerber, "Sikorski Pitches Area 51 Security Helicopters to Guard ICBMs," Defense One, March 1, 2017, https://www.defenseone.com/business/2017/03/sikorsky-pitches-area-51-security-helicopters-guard-icbms/135782/, accessed June 22, 2017; and Aaron Gregg, "Boeing Wins $2.4 Billion Air Force Contract for New Helicopters to Guard Nukes," *Washington Post*, September 25, 2018.

20. Scott Morrison, LinkedIn profile, accessed April 11, 2010.

21. Robert Gendreau, LinkedIn profile, accessed February 12, 2016; George N. Coleman III, "Air Force Weather—Our Heritage, 1937–2012," Air Weather Association, July 2012, 11-15, 11-23, and 11-28; John "Hank" Henry, LinkedIn profile; and AFI 38-101, "Manpower and Organization."

22. AFI 38-101, "Manpower and Organization"; and Author's Graphics Collection.

23. Zorzi, "The Numbers Tell the Story."

24. Rich Fillman, LinkedIn profile, accessed January 5, 2015; and AFI 38-101, "Manpower and Organization."

25. Craig Ness, LinkedIn profile, accessed June 4, 2016; Fillman, LinkedIn profile; and AFI 38-101.

26. Sean Haglund, LinkedIn profile, accessed February 12, 2016; Joseph DeMaria, LinkedIn profile, accessed January 15, 2016; and Alec B. Legg, online résumé, March 8, 2017, https://www.postjobfree.com/resume/acy6rf/civil-engineering-dod-quincy-mi-49082, accessed April 20, 2017.

27. Secretary of the Air Force, "Installation Geospatial Information and Services (IGI&S)," AFI 32-10112, September 2018; and AFI 38-101, "Manpower and Organization."

28. Douglas Lautner, assistant fire chief, Det 1, AFEREG, "Communication: The Key to Effective Change Management," an applied research project submitted to the National Fire Academy as part of the Executive Fire Officer Program, July 1999; and Jackson, "Change Mismanagement."

29. Wally Simmons, LinkedIn profile, accessed April 13, 2016; Eric Schomburg, LinkedIn profile, accessed April 14, 2016; Jamie Massaro, LinkedIn profile, accessed June 17, 2016; Jason Zarudny, LinkedIn profile, accessed June 17, 2016; and Christopher Ellis, LinkedIn profile, accessed August 24, 2016.

30. Robert Cox, comment in response to article by Christopher Francis, "MSgt. Behling vs. PODS, Continued . . . ," FrancisP@ge blog, September 18, 2007, http://francispage.blogspot.com/2007/09/msgt-behling-vs-pods-continued.html, accessed October 5, 2011.

31. CMSgt. Jason L. France, USAF bio and LinkedIn profile, accessed April 15, 2016; Juan Garcia, LinkedIn profile, accessed December 21, 2016; Code of Federal Regulations (CFR), Part 32—National Defense, Part 851, revised as of July 1, 1978; and Contract No. F42650-02-C-7010, NTTR CSOW, Annex B, Rev. 11, February 6, 2013, copy available in USAF FOIA Library.

32. "2016 Fact Book: Strengthening Our Experience, Capabilities, Morale, and Overall Mission Efficiency," Air Force Office of Special Investigations 43, no. 1 (Spring 2017); and Rick Doty, posted to 4450th Tactical Group USAF Facebook Group, December 28, 2021.

33. Dallas Croft, LinkedIn profile, accessed December 18, 2020; John Leary, LinkedIn profile, accessed August 24, 2016; Christopher Ellis, LinkedIn profile; Don Tuma, LinkedIn profile, accessed August 24, 2016; Tiffany Pasenen, LinkedIn profile, accessed August 24, 2016; John Danko III, LinkedIn profile, accessed March 7, 2017; and Jason Lively, LinkedIn profile, accessed March 7, 2017.

34. Donald S. Wear, online résumé, circa 2011, accessed April 18, 2017; Jeffrey C. Gillen, Air Force biography, accessed January 8, 2015; Author's Graphics Collection; AFI 38-101, "Manpower and Organization"; and John Ingle, "Med Group Squadrons Begin New Chapters after Redesignation," 82nd Training Wing Public Affairs, Air Force Medical Service, August 27, 2019.

35. Lawrence R. Benson, "History of Air Force Operational Test and Evaluation (OT&E) Mission, Organization, and Policy," AFOTEC Special Study AD-A259-658, December 1992, 30–32; AFOTEC Instruction 99-103, "Conduct of Operational Test and Evaluation," November 2004; AFOTEC, "Test Director's Toolkit," April 2010; and AFOTEC, "Operational Test and Evaluation (OT&E) Guide," 9th ed., Kirtland AFB, NM, November 2013.

36. Matthew R. Buehler, biographical information, http://www.reno.gov/home/showdocument?id=47386, accessed May 14, 2016: and Jeffrey H. Wilson, LinkedIn profile, accessed April 27, 2016.

37. Leona C. Bull, "JT3 President Pete Winters to Address AVBOT," Antelope Valley Business News 14, no. 7 (July 2002); JT3 Public Affairs, "Irreplaceable: JT3 Founder Orv Ramlo Takes His Final Flight," Inside JT3 8, no. 2 (June 2017); and Odgers letter.

38. Stephanie M. Smith, "Air Force Test Center (AFTC) Year in Review: 1 October 2017–31 December 2018," 412TW-PA-19267, Air Force Test Center History Office, Edwards AFB, CA, June 2019; and JT4, LLC, "Won and Done!—J-Tech II Contract Changes," Inside JT4 1, no. 1 (August 2018).

39. Mary Ann Hourclé, ed., "Audit Report: Advanced Test Facilities," Report 93-079, Acquisition Management Directorate, Office of the Inspector General, DoD, March 1993; Frank N. Lucero, "The USAF Single-Face-to-the-Customer (SFTC) Concept," International Telemetering Conference Proceedings, vol. 30, International Foundation for Telemetering, 1994; and Martin Welch and Mike

Pywell, "Electronic Warfare Test and Evaluation," AG-300-V28, NATO Advisory Group for Aerospace Research and Development, December 2012.

40. Office of the Secretary of the Air Force, "Electronic Warfare Test and Evaluation Process—Direction and Methodology for EW Testing," Air Force Manual (AFM) 99-112, March 1995; T&E Board of Directors, "Master Plan—Electronic Combat T&E Consolidation," Department of Defense, Washington, DC, March 1996.

41. Office of the Secretary of the Air Force, "Nevada Test and Training Range," AFM 13-212, vol. 1, addendum A, July 2020.

42. David Sorenson, *Shutting Down the Cold War* (New York: St. Martin's, 1998), 1; Congressional Record, "Defense Base Closure and Realignment Commission Report to the President," *Proceedings and Debates of the 102nd Congress, First Session*, vol. 137, no. 118 (Washington, DC: US Government Printing Office, 1991), 13, 25, 33–34; Congressional Record, "Defense Base Closure and Realignment Commission Report to the President," *Proceedings and Debates of the 103rd Congress, First Session*, vol. 139, no. 123 (Washington, DC: US Government Printing Office), 9; and Christopher M. Schnaubelt, "Making BRAC Politically Palatable," *The Hill*, March 15, 2017.

43. AFFTC/HO staff, *History of the Air Force Flight Test Center, 1 October 1992–30 September 1994*, vol. 1, *Narrative*, AFFTC History Office collection, 32–33; William W. Dobbs, memorandum for Col. Wesley J. Heidenreich, AFDTC/XRE, "Electronic Combat (EC) Test Capability Consolidation Briefing," October 4, 1993; and AFFTC/HO staff, *History of the Air Force Flight Test Center, 1 October 1994–30 September 1995*, vol. 1, *Narrative*, AFFTC History Office collection, 218–28.

44. Michael Kometer, LinkedIn profile, accessed August 11, 2017; 413th Flight Test Squadron Change of Command Ceremony program, August 6, 1998, author's collection; and 412th Test Wing, "413 FLTS Fact Sheet," http://www.edwards.af.mil/pewte/flight.html, accessed December 7, 1999.

45. Netzer, "Airborne Data Acquisition and Relay System," 2; 412th TW/CC, memo to Northrop Grumman Advanced Technology and Development Center, "Statement of Capability (SC) F95-12-12, Advanced Simulation Training Initiative (ASTI) C-130 Program," AFFTC JON A9408900, December 20, 1994, cited in *History of the Air Force Flight Test Center, 1 October 1994–30 September 1995*, AFFTC History Office, 607; and AFFTC pamphlet, "The 413th Flight Test Squadron: Full Service Electronic Warfare and Avionics Test and Evaluation," AFFTC History Office collection, n.d.

46. Paul Lewis, "Raytheon to Offer Active Antenna Options for F-15," FlightGlobal, September 30, 2002, https://www.flightglobal.com/raytheon-to-offer-active-antenna-options-for-f-15/45089.article, accessed October 3, 2010; David Donald, "Raytheon Continues Upgrades of F-15 Eagle Radar," AINonline, September 17, 2010, https://www.ainonline.com/aviation-news/defense/2010-09-17/raytheon-continues-upgrades-f-15-eagle-radar, accessed October 3, 2010; Nomination of the Pioneers of Stealth National Aviation Hall of Fame Spirit of Flight Award, http://www.pioneersofstealth.org/NAFH%20Award%20Writeup.pdf, accessed December 23, 2015; and Author's Graphics Collection.

47. Event program, "413th Flight Test Squadron Inactivation Ceremony, Edwards AFB, CA," May 6, 2004; Daniel Richards Jr., LinkedIn profile, accessed December 10, 2020; Appropriation/Budget Activity FY 2014, PE 0604256F: Threat Simulator Development, Department of Defense, Washington, DC, April 2013; and US Government Accountability Office, "Electronic Combat Consolidation Master Plan Does Not Appear to Be Cost-Effective," GAO/NSIAD-97-10, July 1997.

48. Holmes & Narver, "Central Nevada Supplemental Test Area Facility Records," prepared for Atomic Energy Commission, Nevada Operations Office, September 1970.

49. Holmes & Narver, "Summary Report: Central Nevada Test Area Demobilization and Restoration Activities," NVO-152, prepared for Atomic Energy Commission, Nevada Operations Office, December 1974.

50. Edward E. Tilzey, Bureau of Land Management, description of Base Camp and Halligan Mesa, from "Special Nevada Report," section 6.1.1.3, Science Applications International Corporation and Desert Research Institute, SAIC doc. DE-AC08-88NV-10715, September 1991; US Bureau of Land Management (BLM), "45 CFR, Public Land Order No. 6591, Nevada, Withdrawal of Land for Air Force Communication Site," April 11, 1985; Environmental Protection Agency, registration information, "USAF Communication Site, HWY 6 and Tybo Road," RCRAINFO—NV0001012590; and BLM, right-of-way for USAF Halligan Mesa access road, ROW N-42984.

51. Department of the Air Force, "Draft Environmental Assessment for Land Withdrawal and Expansion at Base Camp, Hot Creek Valley, Nye County, Nevada," November 2004; BLM, "Public Land Order No. 7630, Extension of Public Land Order No. 6591, Nevada," April 11, 2005; and Email correspondence with Gary Sellani, and information from his website, https://www.lazygranch.com/basecamp.html.

52. US Department of Energy, "Nevada Test Site Guide," DOE/NV-715, Rev. 1, March 2005; US Department of Energy, "Aerial Operations Facility, Nevada Test Site," DOE/EA-1334, December 2000; US Department of Energy, "Final Environmental Assessment for Aerial Operations Facility Modifications, Nevada Test Site," DOE/EA-1512, October 2004; Zach Rosenberg, "Satellite Images Reveal Secret Nevada UAV Site," FlightGlobal, December 7, 2011; and Keith Rogers, "You Know Area 51, but Just What in the World is Area 6?," *Las Vegas Review-Journal*, March 5, 2016.

53. Vincent C. Breslin, "History of the 37th Fighter Wing, 5 October 1989–31 December 1991," in AFFTC/HO staff, *History of the Air Force Flight Test Center, 1 October 1992–30 September 1994*, vol. 1, *Narrative*, 12th Air Force, Tactical Air Command, May 1992; Vincent C. Breslin, "History of the 37th Fighter Wing, 1 January 92–8 July 1992: Closeout," in AFFTC/HO staff, *History of the Air Force Flight Test Center, 1 October 1992–30 September 1994*, vol. 1, *Narrative*, 12th Air Force, Tactical Air Command, August 1992.

54. Leland Johnson, "Tonopah Test Range—Outpost of Sandia National Laboratories," Sandia Report SAND96-0375, March 1996; Robert L. Manhart, "Technical Manual: Tonopah Test Range Capabilities," Sandia Report SAND81-1871, November 1982; Todd Culp, D. Howard, and Yvonne McClellan, "1993 Site Environmental Report: Tonopah Test Range, Tonopah, Nevada," Sandia Report SAND94-1292, November 1994; Peter W. Merlin, *Images of America: Tonopah Test Range* (Charleston, SC: Arcadia, 2021); and US Air Force, "Final Environmental Assessment for the Declassification, Demilitarization, and Disposition of the F-117 Nighthawk, Tonopah Test Range, Nevada Test and Training Range," November 2017.

55. Radio intercept by Joerg Arnu recorded on June 18, 2021.

56. Don Snyder, Bernard Fox, Kristin F. Lynch, Raymond E. Conley, John A. Ausink, Laura Werber, William Shelton, Sarah A. Nowak, Michael R. Thirtle, Albert A. Robbert, "Assessment of the Air Force Materiel Command Reorganization," RAND, 2013, iii–xiii.

57. Ibid., 7–12.

58. Jeffrey R. Mayo, "Security Procedures for Inadvertent or Unauthorized Tracking and Sensor Acquisition of Low Observable and Sight-Sensitive Programs," EAFB Instruction 31-17, November, 2005.

59. Keith Estes, "'Pelicans' Participate in Red Flag Exercise," JaxAirNews, March 30, 2016, http://jaxairnews.jacksonville.com/military-jax-air-news/2016-03-30/story/'pelicans'-participate-red-flag-exercise, accessed October 3, 2016; and Author's Graphics Collection.

60. Keith Rogers, "Family Offered $5.2 Million for Land Next to Area 51," *Las Vegas Review-Journal*, August 28, 2015.

61. United States District Court, District of Nevada, *United States of America v. 400 Acres of Land, More or Less, Situated in Lincoln County, State of Nevada, and Jessie J. Cox et al.*, "Commission's Findings of Fact and Conclusions of Law," case no. 2:15-cv-01743-MMD-NJK, document 656, filed May 29, 2020, 14–15.

62. Keith Rogers, "Family Rejects Air Force's $5.2 Million Bid for Land near Area 51," *Las Vegas Review-Journal*, August 31, 2015; Keith Rogers, "Groom Mine Owners Call Fed Disingenuous," *Las Vegas Review-Journal*, September 9, 2015; David Walterscheid, chief, East Branch, Real Estate Transactions Division, Installations Directorate, Air Force Civil Engineer Center, Lackland AFB, TX, email to [DELETED] September 10, 2015, via Sheahan family; and Jennifer Miller, assistant secretary of the Air Force for installations, official statement, September 10, 2015, via Sheahan family.

63. Rogers, "Family Rejects Air Force's $5.2 Million Bid for Land near Area 51."

64. Ibid.

65. Rogers, "Family Accuses Air Force of Lowball Price Estimate on Land It Seized near Area 51," *Las Vegas Review-Journal*, October 24, 2016; and Glenn Meek and Kyle Zuelke, "Government Takes Family's Land near Area 51," October 16, 2015, http://www.lasvegasnow.com/news/government-takes-familys-land-near-area-51, accessed November 4, 2015.

66. Meek and Zuelke, "Government Takes Family's Land near Area 51."

67. Tyler Rogoway, "Family Demands to Know How a 200-Pound Antique Anvil Disappeared from Area 51," *The Drive*, May 10, 2017, https://www.thedrive.com/the-war-zone/10100/family-demands-to-know-how-a-200-pound-antique-anvil-disappeared-from-area-51, accessed June 3, 2017.

68. Tyler Rogoway, "Family Says Land Overlooking Area 51 Is Worth $116M—USAF says $330k," War Zone, December 6, 2016, http://www.thedrive.com/the-war-zone/6359/family-says-land-overlooking-area-51-is-worth-116m-usaf-says-330k, accessed December 10, 2016.

69. Ibid.; Keith Rogers, "Air Force Decides to Condemn Private Land near Area 51," *Las Vegas Review-Journal*, September 10, 2015; "Last, Frustrating House on the Range," *Air Force Magazine*, September 3, 2015; and

Andrew Craft, "Family Fights Government in Land Dispute near Area 51," Fox News, December 13, 2016, http://www.foxnews.com/science/2016/12/13/family-fights-government-in-land-dispute-near-area-51.html, accessed December 15, 2016.

70. Jerry Hendrix and James Price, "Bombers: Long-Range Force Projection in the 21st Century," Center for a New American Security, Washington, DC, June 2017.

71. John A. Tirpak, "Pay to Play; Get 'em While You Can; Black Diamond in the Rough; 50-Year Trainer . . . ," *Air Force Magazine*, January 2017, 11; DoD staff, "Quadrennial Defense Review Report," Department of Defense, Washington, DC, February 2006; and Bill Sweetman, "LRS-B: Why Northrop Grumman Won Next US Bomber," *Aviation Week & Space Technology*, October 30, 2015.

72. Susan A. Poling, GAO general counsel, decision on protest by the Boeing Company regarding award of LRS-B EMD and LRIP contract to Northrop Grumman, GAO File No. B-421441, Government Accountability Office, Washington, DC, February 2016.

73. Jeremiah Gertler, "Air Force B-21 Raider Long-Range Strike Bomber," Congressional Research Service, Washington, DC, November 2019; Joseph Trevithick, "The B-21 Raider: All the Names the Air Force Decided Against," War Is Boring, September 22, 2016, https://warisboring.com/here-are-the-names-the-air-force-didnt-pick-for-the-b-21-raider/, accessed January 21, 2021; and Abbé Reuter, AFTC Systems Engineering Division chief, briefing slides, "Edwards Reunion 2019," approved for public release, unlimited distribution, 412TW-PA-19224, April 2019.

74. 412th Test Wing Public Affairs, "420th Flight Test Squadron Reactivated to Support B-21 Raider Testing at Edwards," media release, October 4, 2019; Adam Goodpasture, LinkedIn profile, accessed August 3, 2021; John A. Tirpak, "New B-21 Raider Being Accelerated with Overlapping Development and Production," *Air Force Magazine*, April 28, 2022.

75. Marc V. Schanz, "Rethinking Air Dominance," *Air Force Magazine*, July 2013.

76. Jeremiah Gertler, "Air Force Next-Generation Air Dominance Program: An Introduction," IF11659, Congressional Research Service, Library of Congress, October 5, 2020; and Department of Defense, exhibit R-2, RDT&E Budget Item Justification: PB 2020 Air Force, Appropriation/Budget Activity 3600: Research, Development, Test & Evaluation, Air Force / BA 4: Advanced Component Development & Prototypes (ACD&P), PE 0207110F/Next-Generation Air Dominance, February, 2019.

77. Gertler, "Air Force Next-Generation Air Dominance Program: An Introduction."

78. Ibid.; Development & Prototypes (ACD&P), PE 0207110F / Next-Generation Air Dominance, February 2019; and Steve Trimble, "The Nearly Decade-Long Story That Led to NGAD Flight Demonstrator," *Aviation Week & Space Technology*, September 21, 2020.

79. Theresa Hitchens, "Aerospace Cos Wary of Digital Design Revolution," Breaking Defense, November 11, 2020, https://breakingdefense.com/2020/11/aerospace-cos-not-ready-for-digital-design-revolution/, accessed January 25, 2021.

80. John A. Tirpak, "Brown: NGAD Will Be a Multirole Fighter," *Air Force Magazine*, June 16, 2021, accessed June 19, 2021; and Alderson Court Reporting, stenographic transcript, proceedings of the Airland Subcommittee, United States Senate Armed Services Committee, "Hearing to Receive Testimony on Modernization Efforts of the Department of the Air Force in Review of the Defense Authorization Request for Fiscal Year 2022 and the Future Years Defense Program," Washington, DC, June 22, 2021.

81. Greg Hadley, "NGAD Price per Tail Will More Than Double That of F-35," *Air Force Magazine*, April 27, 2022.

82. Mark Gunzinger, Carl Rehburg, and Lukas Autenried, "Five Priorities for the Air Force's Future Combat Air Force," Center for Strategic and Budgetary Assessments, Washington, DC, 2020.

83. Gen. Mark A. Welsh III, "A Call to the Future: The New Air Force Strategic Framework," *Air and Space Power Journal* 29, no. 3 (May/June 2015): 3–9.

84. Brian W. Everstine, "Program Giving Companies More Access to Classified Info," *Air Force Magazine*, January 2021; Ellen M. Lord, undersecretary of defense for acquisition and sustainment, memorandum for Defense Industrial Base, "Special Access Program Contractor Portfolio Establishment," December 15, 2020; Marcus Weisgerber, "Is Lockheed Building the Air Force's Secret Fighter?" Defense One, October 20, 2010, https://www.defenseone.com/business/2020/10/lockheed-building-air-forces-secret-fighter/169408/, accessed January 23, 2021; and Sweetman, "Updated Facility Office Grows Secret USAF Role."

85. Valerie Insinna, "Defense Aerospace Primes Are Raking In Money for Classified Programs," Defense News, November 3, 2020, https://www.defensenews.com/industry/2020/11/03/defense-aerospace-primes-are-raking-in-money-for-classified-programs/, accessed January 25, 2021; and Steve Trimble, "Northrop

Financial Filing Reveals $444 Million Classified Sale," *Aviation Week & Space Technology*, January 28, 2021.

86. Department of the Air Force, SAF/AQ, "Building the Digital Force," Biennial Report 2019–2020.

Postscript: . . . And All That Is Hidden Shall Be Revealed

1. Patrick G. Eddington, Christopher A. Preble, and Seamus P. Daniels, "Bad Idea: Overclassification," Defense 360, Center for Strategic and International Studies, December 6, 2019, https://defense360.csis.org/bad-idea-overclassification/, accessed September 9, 2021.

2. Alec Schuldinger, "Learning to Keep Secrets: The Military and a High-Tech Company," in *Secrecy and Knowledge Production*, ed. Judith Reppy, Occasional Paper 23 (Ithaca, NY: Cornell University Peace Studies Program, 1999), 90.

3. Thornton "TD" Barnes, email to author, September 30, 2010; Mark Memmott, "There It Is! Area 51 Revealed in Declassified CIA Report," National Public Radio, August 16, 2013, https://www.npr.org/sections/thetwo-way/2013/08/16/212549163/there-it-is-area-51-revealed-in-declassified-cia-report, accessed August 17, 2013.

BIBLIOGRAPHY

Aronstein, David C., and Albert C. Piccirillo. *Have Blue and the F-117A: Evolution of the "Stealth Fighter."* Reston, VA: American Institute of Aeronautics and Astronautics, 1997.

Barnes, Thornton D. *CIA Station D: Area 51*. Danbury, CT: Begell House, 2021.

Barron, John. *MiG Pilot*. New York: McGraw Hill, 1980.

Blazek, Patrick A. *Nighthawks: Insider's Guide to the Heraldry and Insignia of the Lockheed F-117A Stealth Fighter*. Atglen, PA: Schiffer Military History, 1999.

Casper, John H. *The Sky Above: An Astronaut's Memoir of Adventure, Persistence, and Faith*. West Lafayette, IN: Purdue University Press, 2022.

Crickmore, Paul F. *Lockheed Blackbird: Beyond the Secret Missions*. Oxford: Osprey, 2004.

Crickmore, Paul F. *Lockheed's Black World Skunk Works*. Oxford: Osprey, 2000.

Crickmore, Paul F., and Alison J. Crickmore. *F-117 Nighthawk*. Osceola, WI: MBI, 1999.

Chong, Tony. *Flying Wings & Radical Things: Northrop's Secret Aerospace Projects and Concepts, 1939–1994*. Forest Lake, MN: Specialty Press, 2016.

Davies, Steve. *Red Eagles: America's Secret MiGs*. Oxford: Osprey, 2012.

Ehrhard, Thomas P. *Air Force UAVs: The Secret History*. Arlington, VA: Mitchell Institute Press, 2010.

Fuller, John G. *The Day We Bombed Utah: America's Most Lethal Secret*. New York: New American Library, 1984.

Grant, Rebecca Grant. *B-2: The Spirit of Innovation*. Falls Church, VA: Northrop Grumman, 2013.

Griffin, John. *The Pioneers of Stealth*. Morrisville, NC: Lulu, 2017.

Johnson, Clarence L., and Maggie Smith. *Kelly: More Than My Share of It All*. Washington, DC: Smithsonian Institution Press, 1985.

Kleyla, Helen H., and Robert D. O'Hern. *History of the Office of Special Activities (OSA) from Inception to 1969*. Washington, DC: Central Intelligence Agency, 1969 (declassified under authority of the Interagency Security Classification Appeals Panel, March 1, 2016).

Lovick, Edward, Jr. *Radar Man*. Bloomington, IN: iUniverse, 2010.

Merlin, Peter W. *From Oxcart to Senior Crown: Design and Development of the Blackbird*. Reston, VA: American Institute of Aeronautics and Astronautics, 2008.

Merlin, Peter W. *Images of America: Nevada Test Site*. Charleston, SC: Arcadia, 2016.

Merlin, Peter W. *Images of America: Tonopah Test Range*. Charleston, SC: Arcadia, 2021.

Merlin, Peter W. *Images of Aviation: Area 51*. Charleston, SC: Arcadia, 2011.

Merlin, Peter W. *Unlimited Horizons: Design and Development of the U-2*. Washington, DC: NASA, 2015.

Merlin, Peter W., and Tony Moore. *X-Plane Crashes*. Forest Lake, MN: Specialty Press, 2008.

Miller, Jay. *Lockheed Martin's Skunk Works: The First Fifty Years*. North Branch, MN: Aerofax, 1994.

Murray, Frank. *OXCART Convoy: How They Got to Area 51*. Charleston, SC: CreateSpace, 2013.

Naylor, Sean. *Relentless Strike: The Secret History of Joint Special Operations Command*. New York: St. Martin's, 2015.

Paglen, Trevor. *Blank Spots on the Map: The Dark Geography of the Pentagon's Secret World*. New York: Dutton Books, 2009.

Peck, Gaillard R. *America's Secret MiG Squadron*. Oxford: Osprey, 2012.

Pedlow, Gregory W., and Donald E. Welzenbach. *The Central Intelligence Agency and Overhead Reconnaissance: The U-2 and OXCART Programs, 1954–1974*. Washington, DC: Central Intelligence Agency, 1992.

Peebles, Curtis. *Dark Eagles: A History of Top Secret US Aircraft Programs*. Novato, CA: Presidio, 1995.

Pizzo, Sam. *As Good as It Gets / A Man of Many Hats*. Memphis, TN: Tommy Towery, 2008.

Pocock, Chris. *50 Years of the U-2*. Atglen, PA: Schiffer, 2005.

Pocock, Chris, and Clarence Fu. *The Black Bats: CIA Spy Flights over China from Taiwan, 1951–1969*. Atglen, PA: Schiffer Military History, 2010.

Rich, Ben R., and Leo Janos. *Skunk Works: A Personal Memoir of My Years at Lockheed*. New York: Little, Brown, 1994.

Richelson, Jeffrey T. *The US Intelligence Community*. Boulder, CO: Westview, 2016.

Sorenson, David. *Shutting Down the Cold War*. New York: St. Martin's, 1998.

Stafford, Thomas P., and Michael Cassutt. *We Have Capture: Tom Stafford and the Space Race*. Washington, DC: Smithsonian Institution Press, 2002.

Sweetman, Bill. *Inside the Stealth Bomber*. Osceola, WI: Motorbooks International, 1999.

Westwick, Peter. *Stealth: The Secret Contest to Invest Invisible Aircraft*. Oxford: Oxford University Press, 2019.

INDEX

413th Flight Test Squadron, 383, 445–447
1007th Air Intelligence Service Group, 34, 108–112, 125
1129th Special Activities Squadron, 99, 102, 143, 146, 154, 173, 175
4070th Support Wing, 46, 52, 116
4450th Tactical Group, 227, 288, 289, 294, 300–303, 307, 308, 451
4477th Test and Evaluation Flight/Squadron, 225–227, 235, 244, 382
4602nd Air Intelligence Service Squadron, 42
6513th Test Squadron, 232–234, 236, 236, 238–240, 245, 283, 288, 326, 356, 371, 380–383
6516th Test Squadron, 283, 473

A

A-12 accidents, 120–126, 136–138, 143–145, 146–152, 171
A-12 convoy, 83, 102, 103
A-12 cover plan, 99–101
A-12 maximum speed and altitude, 142
A-12 pole model, 81–86
A-12 retired, 172–174
A-12 sonic booms, 127
A-12 struck by missile debris, 170
A-12T trainer, 118–120, 153
Abbey, Richard S., 130
Abel, Tom, 289, 297, 301
Aboulafia, Richard, 460
Abraham, James G. "Jim," 36
Abrams, Richard "Dick," 287, 289
Ackerman, Tom, 238
Acosta, Roberto "Bob," 380
Adham, Walid, 202
Adkins, Charles N., 373–375, 378, 379
Adler, Fred, 310
Adolph, Charles E. "Pete," 193
Advanced Airborne Reconnaissance System (AARS), 402, 403
Advanced Simulation Training Initiative (ASTI), 446
Advanced Tactical Cruise Missile (ATCM), 272–279, 311
Advanced Technology Bomber (ATB), 324–326
AeroVironment, 373–379
AFEREG, Detachment 1, 448, 478

AFFTC (Air Force Flight Test Center) U-2 evaluation, 15, 33, 88, 89
AFFTC Detachment 3 established, 283, 474, 475
AFFTC X-15 support, 87–89
AFMC reorganization, 452
AFOSI (Air Force Office of Special Investigations), 42, 119, 125, 149, 150, 296, 439, 478
AFOTEC, 288, 441, 478
Aggressors, 212, 216, 221, 222, 225, 384
AGM-86B ALCM, 272, 273
AGM-129A ACM, 280
AGM-137 TSSAM, 391–394
aircraft accidents chronological list, 479–481
Akaka, Daniel K., 424, 425
Allaire, William W., 68, 185
Allen, Andrew L. "Drew," 476
Amundson, Maynard, 108, 173
Andersen, Roger, 145
Anderson, James, 151, 169
Anderson, Leslie B. "Skip," 214, 220, 221, 287, 288, 290, 291, 293–295, 301
Angle, Theodore E. "Ted," 113, 116, 176
Andrews, Carroll O. "Andy," 62
Andrews, John, 354
AQUATONE, 13, 17, 18, 21, 22, 31–37, 44, 49, 50, 54, 59–64, 71, 77, 78, 98, 134, 251, 347
AQUILINE, 177–183, 251
Area 6, 405, 449, 450
Area 12, 135, 185, 186
Area 13, 68, 69, 79, 357–360
Area 15, 184
Area 51 airspace intrusions, 72, 74, 96, 97, 133–134, 264
Area 51 cattle deaths, 252, 253
Area 51 designated, 78, 471
Area 51 helicopter support, 112–116, 432–434
Area 51 K-9 patrol, 135
Area 51 land withdrawal, 74
Area 51 RCS range, 78–82, 84–87, 118, 139–142, 155
Area 51 runway construction, 90–92
Area 51 transferred to USAF, 250, 472
Area 52, 450–452
Area 58, 447–449
Arthur, Walter E. "Pete," 330
Ashcraft, Robert G., 193, 198, 203

ASPA, 324
ATDC (Northrop Grumman), 413, 414, 463
Atkins, Allen, 264, 311
Atkinson, George W., 176
Atkinson, Rick, 326
Atomic Energy Commission (AEC), 16–22, 33, 34, 38, 42, 50, 64, 67–70, 73, 74, 78, 79, 83, 84, 89, 90, 98, 101, 103, 226, 253, 346, 364, 365, 447, 465, 466, 477
atomic testing (blast damage to Area 51), 63, 73
atomic testing (evacuating Area 51), 68, 70, 117, 185
atomic testing (fallout on Area 51), 18, 38, 63, 68–70, 73, 98, 184, 185
atomic testing (planned shots near Area 51), 184, 185
AURORA, 346, 457
AZANA, 180

B

B-2 stealth bomber, 324–326, 346, 413, 456
B-17G radar test bed, 62, 63
B-21 Raider, 457, 460
Babbitt Housing, 94, 96, 97, 108, 284, 285
Baber, Jerry W., 259
Bacalis, Paul N., 150
Bacon, Kenneth, 424
Baggerly, Charles "Bags," 227
Bailey, Gordon C. "Beetle," 113, 116, 150
Baird Atomic, 39, 135, 151
Baird, Lou, 193
Baker, Abner L., 143
Baker, Lloyd, 62
Bald Mountain, 61, 88, 89, 112, 113, 326, 340, 345, 432
Baldwin, Ed, 256, 286
Baldwin, Richard "Dick," 166
Bamberger, John "Jack," 334
Bargen, Richard, 345
Barham, Bob, 302
Barkeley, Richard T. "Rick," 330
Barnes, Pete, 289, 291, 300, 301
Barnes, Thornton "TD," 347, 465
Barnett, Arville G., 203
Barnette, Howard, 279
Barnoski, John J., 380
Barrett, Burton S., 108, 149
Barrett, Dave, 330
Barrett, William T. "Billy," 220
Barta, Philip "Tin Man," 227
Base Camp auxiliary airfield, 447–449
Base Realignment and Closure (BRAC), 444, 445
Bash, Jeremy, 421
Batista, Tony, 272
Beall, Christopher, 346
Beall, Robert J., 331
Beasley, Luther, 62
Beaulieu, Daniel, 144
Beech B200C King Air, 321, 331, 338, 339, 356, 396, 400, 419
Beech B350C, 339
Beech BE1900C, 338, 339
Beech, Stanley, 244
Beech Twin Bonanza, 15–17, 32, 92, 331
Beerli, Stanley W., 59, 60
Beesley, Jon S., 238, 288, 297, 301, 303–305, 308
Behling, Bradley, 438
Belenko, Viktor Ivanovich, 223, 224, 229
Belt, Robert B., 382
Bendell, Anthony "Bugs," 133
Bender, Gary L., 418
Benezet, Louis, 345
Benjamin, Douglas A., 397–401
Bennett, Robert, 150
Berg, Russell A., 49
Beswick, Keith L., 119, 159, 161, 259, 262, 263, 265–268, 270, 287, 289
Betts, Austin W., 98
BIG SAFARI program, 328
Bikle, Paul F., 33, 88
Bilbray, James, 353, 368
Bimmer, Mike, 330
Bird of Prey, 349, 395–401, 406
Birk, Frank T., 371
Bissell, Richard M. "Dick," 13, 15, 16, 17, 20–22, 24, 30, 33–36, 39, 42, 44, 47–51, 64, 77, 80, 82, 85, 90, 98, 107
Black Bats (ROCAF 34th Squadron), 186, 187, 189
Blackhats (Communications Squadron), 356, 438, 478
BLACK ROSE, 447
BLACK SHIELD operation, 143, 169–174
Bloomcamp, Frank W., 215, 216
BLUE BOOK, 53, 54, 346
Blue, Eugene A., 68
Boatwright, James F., 344
Bochum, Gary, 276
Boesch, Eugene F., 368, 369
Bohanon, Lorris M. "Larry," 105
Bolden, Charles F., 350
Bollens, Ross, 276
Bolstad, Terry, 322
Bonasso, Vincent G., 392
Bond, Robert M. "Bobby," 239–242, 259, 262, 272, 304, 310
Bongiovi, Robert P., 258
Borror, Sean L., 430
Boucher, Robert J. "Bob," 373, 375
Bowlds, Theodore F. "Ted," 292
Boyce, Ed, 122, 123

Boyd, Albert, 33
Boyd, John, 231
Bradfield, Edward N., 245, 269
Brandon, Frank, 203
Bray, James F., 40
Bridges, Roy D., 288
Briest, Paul W., 46
Briggs, Loran D., 34
Briglia, Frank A., 177, 179
Bristow, Billy, 146
Broadaway, John W., 338
Brooks, Alexander N. "Alec," 374, 375, 377
Brooks, Stanley P., 331, 332
Brothen, Arthur D., 331
Brown, Alan C., 256, 262, 285, 286, 294
Brown, Billie, 122
Brown, Brad, 300
Brown, Charles Q., 460
Brown, Harold, 323, 325
Brown, James E. "JB," 380
Brown, James W. "Billy," 40
Brown, Melvin H. "Hugh," 238
Brown, Scot, 386
Brown, Stuart, 354
Browner, Carol M., 362
Bruskert, Donald, 185
Bryan, Richard, 344
Bryant, David R., 238
Bryden, William "Bill," 31
Brysselbout, Frank, 283
burn trenches, 361, 365, 366
Butler, Derrick L., 339
Brzezinski, Zbigniew, 270
BSAX, 309–311, 323, 324
Buckner, Vernon, 25
Bukowski, Grace, 345
Bunker, Howard G., 40
Burchby, Dale, 318
Bureau of Land Management (BLM), 34, 341, 342, 345, 353, 354, 447–449
Burgeson, Harold E., 108, 144, 153, 154, 176
Burke, William, 77
Burns, Joe Lee, 212, 217, 221
Burns, Kevin P., 380, 382, 383
Burton, Richard "Dick," 263, 276, 291, 292
Bush, George H. W., 222, 294, 349
Byers, Floyd W., 330
Byzewski, Clem, 135

C

C-54 accident, 40–42
Caldara, Joseph D., 40
Calico, Forrest W., 176
Cammo Dudes, 351, 363
Campbell, Ernest D., 253
Campbell, Glenn, 340, 351–355
Campbell, William J., 323
Canterbury, William M., 52
Cantrell, Richard C. "Dick," 255, 256, 285, 305
Cappuccio, Frank, 408–410
Carco Air Services, 94, 175, 181, 327, 329
Carl, Marion, 210
Carney, Jerry, 67
CAROUSEL operation, 143
Carpenter, Adelbert W. "Buz," 346
Carr, Gerald, 247
Carr, Milton R. "Bob," 224
Carson, Johnny, 275
Carter, David L., 120
Carter, Jimmy, 270, 323
Carter, Marshall S., 130
Carter, Melvin, 70
Casey, William J., 298
Cashen, John, 256–258, 309, 311, 317, 413
Casper, John H., 222, 234, 238
Cassidy, Jennifer, 415
Cassidy, Thomas J., 193, 194, 197, 201, 203
Casto, Earl, 113, 114
Cates, Allen, 189
Cawthon, Michael E., 297
Celniker, Leo, 256
Central Intelligence Agency (CIA), 13, 15, 17–22, 24, 30, 32, 34, 36, 39, 40, 42, 44, 47, 49–51, 53, 54, 57, 60, 62, 64, 65, 67, 71, 74–77, 79, 85–87, 89, 90, 93, 97–99, 107, 108, 110, 112, 127, 129, 131, 132, 136, 139–141, 143, 145, 146, 149, 150, 152, 154, 156, 159, 161, 167, 172–174, 176–183, 186–189, 191, 209, 213, 215, 221, 222, 224, 228, 247, 249–251, 253, 254, 263, 284, 298, 327, 328, 341, 347, 373, 374, 378, 379, 402, 421, 422, 465, 471, 472
Ceplecha, Christopher S., 382
Chambers, Robert, 334
Charters, Pat, 276
Charyk, Joseph V., 107, 154
Cherbonneaux, James W., 181
Chioma, Vincent J. "Van Gogh," 414
Chope, George, 147
Christ, David L., 177, 180
Christie, Thomas, 231
Christman, "Pop," 25
Cibello, Victor G., 103
Cisek, Terry M., 330
Citizen Alert, 345
Civil Engineer Squadron, 437, 438
Clark, Robert, 66

Clayton, Bob, 284
Clement, Bob, 367
Clements, Ed "Pigpen," 217, 221, 232
Clendinning, Thomas B., 52
Clifton, Fred R. "Spanky," 384–386, 388
Clinton, William J., 362, 365, 423
Cohen, William, 369
Colby, William E., 248, 249
Coleman, J. Randall, 256
Coleman, Randy S., 263
Collins, Kenneth S., 108, 114, 119, 121–126, 169, 172, 174
Combs, Henry G., 24, 28, 81, 229, 256, 286
Combs, Richard, 330
COMMANDO RAIDER operation, 187
COMPASS ARROW, 402
Compton, Keith K., 109
Conehead Bar, 284, 356
Conley, Philip J., 238, 283
Connolly, Thomas F., 210
Connor, William M., 42
CONSTANT PEG, 225, 230–232, 380, 382
Constellation commuter fleet, 93, 94, 175
Cooke, Claude E., 80
Cornell, Donald A., 321, 322
Cowan, Maynard W. "Bill," 68
Cowley, Martyn B., 375
Cox, Robert, 438
Creech, Wilbur L. "Bill," 293
Cregier, Roderick L. "Trash," 428, 476
Crowder, Ira C., 135
Croxall, Karen, 345
Cruikshanks, Colin, 305, 306
Cruz, Frank, 25
Cunningham, Charles, 244
Cunningham, James A. "Jim," 39, 64, 80, 91–93, 100, 101, 124, 131
Curd, James, 147
Current, Edward K., 72, 74
Curtin, Robert F., 375, 376
Curtis, George C., 279
Cuthill, Fed J., 191, 193, 195, 197–200, 203, 204, 208, 209

D

D-21 accident, 161
D-21 first flight, 159
D-21 specifications, 155
D-21B accidental release, 163–165
D-21B captured by China, 168
D-21B copied by Russia, 167
Dahle, E. O., 184, 185
Dake, Theodore "Ted," 114, 176
Damaskos, Nick, 139

Dana, William H. "Bill," 112
Daniell, J. Rus, 129, 229, 254
Darby, Forrest, 368, 369
Dark Knights, 451, 452
Davis, Blair J., 108, 169
Davis, Loren W., 67
DC-3 radar test bed, 62, 63
Death Valley Forty-Niners, 9
DeButts, John, 276, 284
Delacroix, Benjamin, 139
Delap, John E. "Jack," 46
DeLauer, Richard, 280
DeMoss, James "Jimmy," 251
Dempsey, Thomas E., 455
DenMar Technical Services, 413
Dertien, Evan C., 476
Desert Prowler, 406
Detachment G, 71, 221
Deuel, James, 49
DFE kit, 418–420
DFOULS ("Damn Few Of Us Left Society"), 175, 176
Dionisi, Steve, 245
Dixon, Daniel N., 382
DKCRYST, 374, 379
Dobbs, David L., 346, 347
Dobbs, William W., 445, 476
Donnell, Al, 19, 20
Donohue, Donald J., 111, 121
Donohue, Elwood P., 123, 124
Doran, Gerald V., 253
Dornheim, Michael, 424
Down, Harry W., 203
Downie, Donald C., 64, 67
Doyal, Mike, 276
Drabant, Robert E. "Darth," 231, 232
DRAGON LADY, 34
Dreamland, 134, 217, 222, 239, 250, 284, 392, 429, 434
Dry, Jim, 263
Dryden, Hugh L., 54, 55, 88, 100, 101
Du, Miranda, 454
Duckett, Carl E., 140, 150, 174, 248
Duffy, Patrick E., 476
Dulles, Allen W., 13, 18, 34, 52, 154
Dunaway, Glendon K., 47
Dunham, Fred M., 284, 341, 349, 351, 355–357, 363–366, 392
Dunn, Craig P., 304, 368, 446, 476
Dunn, James, 304
DYCOMS (P-100), 301, 326, 444
Dye, Kevin, 367, 369
Dykes, George, 41
Dyson, Norman K. "Ken," 263, 265, 267–271, 287, 312, 314–318, 320, 322

E

Ealey, Marvin, 243
EARNING (R-12/SR-71), 131
Easter, John R. "Russ," 263–265, 269, 288, 291, 312, 320, 321
Eastham, James D. "Jim," 118, 121, 126, 129
Eckman, Philip K., 374, 378
Eclipse Program, 330–335
Eddinger, Thomas, 258
Edwards, Lloyd A., 215
Edwards, Marshall L., 103
EG&G airlift operations ("Janet flights"), 327–330, 333, 335–337
EG&G cover for Project 51 activities, 79, 84
EG&G Groom Lake radar test range, 77–87, 155, 219, 220, 278, 279, 301, 442–445
Eidsaune, David W., 476
Eisenhower, Dwight D., 13, 17, 33, 74
Electronic Warfare range, 443–447
Elliott, Richard G., 19
Ellis, Peggy, 323
Ellis, Richard H., 323
Ellis, Robert O. "Bobby," 223, 225, 243
Elsner, William "Bill," 258, 320
Engel, Richard L., 427
Engle Act, 342, 353
Englund, David B., 274, 320
environmental lawsuit, 360–367
Environmental Protection Agency (EPA), 253, 362, 368
EQUINE, 62, 63
Ericson, Robert, 61, 62
Ermer, Herbert A., 256
Ervin, Sheree, 276
Estey, Richard H. "Dick," 276
Everest, Frank K. "Pete," 33
Everly, Walter K. "Keith," 446

F

F-19 rumored designation for stealth, 306, 307
F-22 Raptor, 404, 429, 430
F-101 accidents, 152–154, 171
F-117A accidents, 295–299, 307
F-117A declassified, 307, 308
F-117A developmental testing, 287–296, 301–305
F-117A evaluation by British RAF, 305, 306
Faga, Martin C., 403
Farley, Harold C. "Hal," 287, 291–294, 300, 301
Farris, Clayton D., 40
Fasolas, Guy R., 40
Fees, James R. "Jim," 228, 229
Feightner, Edward L. "Whitey," 208
Felock, Joseph W., 397

Feng Hai-tao, 186, 190
Ferguson, Brint, 86
Ferguson, David L., 213–215, 218, 221–223, 229, 233, 234, 238, 242, 263, 276, 287, 291, 293–295, 298, 301, 304, 305, 315
Ferry, John M., 34
Field, Peter B., 218
Fields, Kenneth E., 19
FISH, 75, 76
Fisher, Dean, 244
Fitzgerald, William, 353
Flax, Alexander, 150
flying saucer, 75, 347, 349–351, 403
Flynn, LeRoy, 25
Ford, Michael W., 382
Foreign Technology Division (FTD), 191, 193, 202–204, 209–211, 213, 215, 217–219, 223, 224, 228, 229, 231, 236, 237, 242, 256, 346, 385
Foss, Warren, 133
Foster, Jim, 208
Fout, Paul, 138
Fox, William J. "Bill," 270, 271, 276, 277, 279, 355, 356
Frank, Robert S. "Bevo," 245
Freedom Ridge, 340, 351–355
Freienmuth, Karl S., 331
Frick, Glenn F. "Pappy," 212, 216, 217, 225, 226
Frisina, Andrew J., 181
Fronapfel, Thomas, 361
Frost, Helen, 360
Frost, Robert, 360
Frye, Fritz, 25
Fubini, Eugene, 154, 323
Fugnit, Michael, 416
Fulkerson, Bob, 345
Fulkerson, Glenn C., 24, 28, 67, 151
Fuller, Dan, 284, 302
Fussell, James, 145
Fylling, Chris, 264

G

Gaines, John H., 40
Galloway, Ben, 243, 244
Gardner, Trevor, 18, 30, 33
Garrett, Benjamin F., 11
Garvin, Louis A., 46
Gates, Robert M., 407
Gavette, Leon, 81, 103
Geary, Leo P., 78, 109, 130–132, 161, 166
Geisler, Francis K. "Paco," 222
Gemlich, Stephen, 146
George, Melvin F. "Mel," 65
Gerhart, John K., 130

Ghost Hawk (HH-60U), 434
Ghost Riders, 372
Ghost Squadron, 432–434
Gibbs, Jack A., 48, 67
Gibson, Bill, 164, 165
Gibson, Edward, 247
Gibson, Miriam, 164
Gilbert, William W., 209
Gilbreath, Gregory P., 372
Gilleece, Peter G., 207, 208
Gillen, Jeffrey C., 366
Gilliland, Robert J. "Bob," 120, 136
Gilmore, Richard A., 73
Gilmour, Warren, 255, 256
Gilson, Annie, 453
Girard, Ronald L., 175
Glaser, Lewis E., 354
Goatsucker Inn, 284
Godin, Eugene B. "Gene," 243
Goetzinger, Carl, 276
Goff, Teddy A., 203, 208
Goldfein, David, 458
Goodpasture, Adam E., 457
Goodwin, William A. "Bill," 135, 151, 171
Gorbachev, Mikhail, 380
Goudey, Ray, 28, 31, 44, 46, 49, 263, 265, 269–271, 276
Grabb, Arthur, 244
Grace, Frank G., 60
Grace, John W., 220
Graham, Matthew S., 418–420
Graham, Ralph H., 302–304, 476
Gravance, John "Jack," 276
Green Ghosts, 432
Green, James C., 122
Green, Jesse E., 209
Green, Larry, 314
Green, Steven A., 392
Greene, Murphy, 176
Greenpeace, 342
Greenway, Gilbert C., 17
Gregory, Lloyd D., 123
Grey Butte RCS range, 257
Greystone Office Park, 367
Griffin, John M., 258, 325
Grimm, Ralph E., 258, 312
Groom Lake auxiliary airstrip, 10, 11
Groom Lake gunnery range, 10, 11
Groom Lake prehistory, 9
Groom Lake selection as U-2 test site, 16–18
Groom Mine discovery, 9
Groom Mine radioactive fallout, 12, 13
Groom Mine and Sheahan family, 10, 12, 13, 98, 342–345, 453–455

Groom Mine Wheeler expedition visit, 8–10
Groom Mountains land withdrawal, 341–346
Groom, Robert W., 9
Gross, Courtlandt S., 107
Gross, Robert, 30
Grothe, Mark J., 331, 335
Grubbs, Kenneth K., 304
Gulli, Joseph, 103
Gum, Wilmer L. "Lou," 300
Gurin, Peter, 141
GUSTO, 75–77, 403

H

Haen, David B., 220, 226
Hagen, John F., 418, 419
Hajizadeh, Amir Ali, 408
Halaby, Najeeb E., 101, 107, 120, 131
HALSOL, 373–379
Hamilton, Ronald, 243
Hampton, Morgan C. "Clark," 329, 332, 333, 336
Hanes, Horace A., 130
Hangar 18 at Groom Lake, 284
Hanks, Carl, 164
Hanks, Fred F., 40
Harbison, Glenn, 284
Harnage, Oren B., 102
Harris, David A., 430, 476
Harris, Rama, 333, 334
Harris, Ron, 143
Hartley, Frank W., 159, 165, 166, 168
Harvey design study, 253–255, 259
Harvey, Francis A. "Frank," 24, 25, 56, 103
Haug, Rudy, 396–400
Haupt, Raymond L., 52, 108
HAVE BLANKET, 238
HAVE BLUE, 246, 251, 259–271
HAVE BOXER, 235, 236
HAVE BRIDGE, 191, 211, 223
HAVE COAT, 236–238
HAVE COFFEE, 193, 214
HAVE DOUGHNUT, 193–202
HAVE DOWN, 235
HAVE DRILL, 202–209
HAVE DRY, 215, 216
HAVE FERRY, 202–209
HAVE FIREMAN, 236
HAVE GLIB, 209–213, 218, 233, 238, 250, 251, 328
HAVE HEAT, 219
HAVE IDEA, 213–218, 220–222, 231, 233, 235, 243, 244, 247, 251, 283, 288, 328, 380, 382
HAVE JEEP, 219
HAVE LEMON, 212

HAVE LIGHTER, 235, 236
HAVE LIME, 212
HAVE LIST, 219
HAVE LOAN, 382
HAVE OUT, 219
HAVE PAD, 229–232, 239
HAVE PHOENIX, 380, 382, 383, 390
HAVE PRIVILEGE, 209–211
HAVE RASH, 375
HAVE RIDE, 224
HAVE UP, 234, 235
hazardous waste, 360–367
HB1001 accident, 268, 269
HB1002 accident, 270, 271
HBJAYWALK, 21
Headquarters Squadron Section, 427–429
Heath, Hugh C., 256
Heatley, Charles J. "Heater," 225
HEAVY TEA, 186, 187
Heckathorn, Richard "Dick," 276
Heidenreich, Wesley J., 445, 446
Heilmeier, George H., 254, 265
Helmantoler, William L., 41
Helms, Richard, 168, 174
Henderson, Earl, 243
Henderson, Everett J., 193
Henrichsen, Chris K. G., 302
Heritsch, Scott, 430
Herman, Carl, 25
Herr, John, 302
Herring, Hal, 176
Hertford, Kenner F., 42
Hewitt, Loyd A., 122
Hibbard, Hall, 30
Hibbs, Bart D., 374
Hickey, Herbert J. "Skip," 258, 265, 290, 313, 317, 320
Hicks, Robert, 392
Higer, Matthew W., 476
Higgs, Travis J. "Fromo," 414
Hildebrand, Richard R., 193
Hod, Mordechai, 204
Hodge, Ray, 244
Holbury, Robert J., 99, 102, 105, 108, 112, 113, 120, 123–125, 133, 137, 138, 144–146, 476
Holder, Kenneth G., 331
Hollingsworth, Dave, 238
Holmes, James M., 460
Holmes & Narver, 53, 77, 88
Holwager, David E. "Popeye," 243
Hopeless Diamond, 255, 256, 272, 323
Hopper, Cecil W., 135
Horan, Bud, 225
Horne, Thomas C., 383

Horner, Charles A., 309
Horner, Richard, 30
Horton, William "Bill," 276
Hosmer, Brad, 287
Hostage, Michael, 457
Hough, Richard "Dick," 25
House 6 Bar, 108, 134, 284
Houston, Jerry B. "Devil," 203
Houston, Larry, 188, 189
Howard, J. Daniel, 307
Hruda, Richard J., 40
Hubbard, Boyd, 119, 125, 127, 133
Hudson, Robert M., 476
Huff, Gerrald D. "Huffer," 225
Hughes 500P quiet helicopter, 187–189
Hughes, Patrick, 381
Huglin, Henry C., 130
Humann, Charlie, 329
Hunerwadel, Hugh P. "Pat," 67
Hunt, Mike, 346, 347
Huston, Vincent G., 18
Hutchins, Robert, 193
Hutchison, Dan, 284
Hyatt, Ed, 12
Hycon Manufacturing, 39, 40, 47, 49, 64, 155, 166
Hyland, Arlow K. "Butch," 237, 238, 244

I

IBIS DAWN, 447
IBIS HAMMER, 447
IBIS MUNIN, 447
IBIS TROUGH, 447
Imirie, Joseph S., 120
Indian Springs RCS range, 61, 65, 75–77
Inlow, Roland S., 247, 248
Intelligence Squadron, 435
International Space Station (ISS), 249
IRON MAIDEN operation, 143
Iverson, Ronald W., 221, 225, 230, 231
Izold, Michael A., 339

J

Jacks, Roger L., 271
Jackson, Gene, 217, 221
Jackson, Willie B., 331, 335
James, Bruce, 310
Janet flight call sign origin, 177
Jantzen, Milt, 272, 279
Jarboe, James F., 64, 65, 67
Jarvi, Dennis W., 320, 322
Jaspers, Gregory R. "Crash," 440, 476

Javorsek, Daniel "Animal," 372
Jeffrey, Arthur F., 138
Jimenez, James A., 382
Johnson, Bob, 25
Johnson, Clarence L. "Kelly," 14–19, 23–25, 27–31, 33, 42, 44, 49–51, 55, 67, 75–78, 82, 85, 86, 90, 91, 93–95, 101, 103–107, 109, 116, 118, 120, 123–125, 129, 131, 132, 136, 139, 141, 143, 145, 150, 152, 154–162, 166–168, 173, 174, 176, 229, 254–256, 259, 265, 296, 329, 349, 403, 477
Johnson, Lyndon B., 131, 132, 146, 152, 169
Johnson, Maurice B. "Duke," 203
Joiner, Ernest L. "Ernie," 24, 25, 27–29, 56
Joint Range Support Services, 441, 442
Jones, David C., 249
Jones, Jesse R., 203
Jones, Karl M., 304, 356, 476
Jones, Thomas V., 309, 324, 326
Jones, Tom, 262, 272
Jordan, Fo, 135
Jordan, Joe B., 193, 195–197, 201
Joyce, Douglas A., 282, 326
JT3 LLC, 338, 339, 441, 442
J-Tech contract, 441, 442
Jumper, John, 395
Junker, Corbin J., 329
Junker, Jack, 284

K

Kabat, Jules, 87, 135
Kallman, Richard P., 103
Kaminski, Paul G., 280
Kammerer, Dorsey G., 15, 19, 20, 24, 83, 103, 118
Kammerer, Mike, 263–265
Kane, Tom, 258
Karnes, Tom, 243, 244
Kasza, Stella, 363
Kasza, Walter S., 360, 362
Keator, Norman D., 238
KEDLOCK (AF-12/YF-12A), 129, 131, 347
Keesee, Richard G. "Rick," 243
Kelly, Connie Jo "CJ," 324
Kelly, John R., 108
Kelly, Mark, 460
Kelly, Rick, 343
KEMPSTER, 139, 140
Kendall, Frank, 456, 457, 460
Kennedy, John F., 94, 98, 100, 114, 129, 131
Kennett, Douglas J., 354
Kent, Art, 125
Keys, Jim, 225
Keys, Ronald E., 232

Kiefer, Eugene P., 100
Kier, David A., 403
Killian, James R., 75
Kimbel, Bruce K., 123
KINGFISH, 76
King, Weldon "Walt," 169, 171
King, William L. "Les," 375
Kinsey, Robert N. "Ma," 331, 332
Kirkpatrick, Lyman B., 97, 98, 341
Kissinger, Henry, 187, 189, 228
Klein, Richard E. "Dick," 284, 285, 296, 356
Kleyla, Helen, 22, 50
Kleyla, Robert L. "Bob," 186
Klinger, Robert T. "Bob," 24
Klingon cloaking device, 227
Knapp, George, 347–349
Knauber, Leo V. M., 49
Knoche, Enno H. "Hank," 250, 472
Knofczynski, Charles W., 428
Knowles, Harold F., 181, 182
Knox, Fred D., 238
Knutson, Eric D., 405
Knutson, Martin A. "Marty," 47, 52
Koester, Allen R. "Ray," 274, 275
Kolinsky, Robert, 416
Koon, Ralph E., 52
Koopman, Walter K., 135
Kotapish, William, 176
Koziol, Benedict J., 26, 67
Kratt, Jacob "Jake," 47, 52
Kreimendahl, Rodney H., 40
Kuhn, Fredolin W., 448, 449
Kulikowski, Stanley F., 193, 199, 203, 215, 242
Kunkle, Ron, 354
Kuramoto, John, 230

L

LaBlue, Al, 288
Lamothe, Lloyd G. A., 189
Land, Edwin, 13
Landavazo, Joel E., 243
Lane, Joshua A., 414
Langford, Del, 332
Lanni, Joseph A., 372
Larsen, Thane, 328, 329
Larson, Gerald D., 193, 198
Larson, Kermit H., 68
Laskowski, Joseph J., 238
Lauritsen, Henry G., 185
Law, Thomas, 138
Lawrence, Gerald B., 343
Layton, Ronald J. "Jack," 108, 114, 153, 154, 169, 170, 174

Lazar, Robert S., 347–350
Lear, John, 348
LeBailly, Eugene, 150
Ledford, Jack C., 108, 120, 126, 145, 154, 159, 176
Lehan, Paul, 67
Lehnhoff, Ruth, 333
Leitch, Andy, 343
Leiton, Rachel P., 365
Leitzel, Marvin R., 163, 164
LeMay, Curtis, 34, 44
LeVier, Anthony W. "Tony," 14, 16, 17, 19, 23, 24, 27–31
Lewallen, Gary, 225
Lewis, Tom, 135
Lien, Arthur, 46
Lincoln County sheriff, 351, 353
Linder, Isham, 302
Linn, Kenneth "Kenny," 304
Lipe, Walter A., 203
Lissaman, Peter B. S., 374
Little A'Le'Inn, 350
Livesay, Meade, 310
Lockheed Aircraft Service Company (LASC), 229, 230, 329, 330, 334, 335
Lockheed California Company, 373
Lockheed Georgia Company (GELAC), 274, 275, 279
Lockheed Missiles and Space Company (LMSC), 166, 272, 274–276, 279, 280, 311, 331
Lockyer, Allen, 411
Locus, Silvan S. "Stan," 256, 309
Logistics Readiness Squadron, 436, 437
Long-Range Strike-Bomber (LRS-B), 456, 457
Loschke, Robert C. "Bob," 256, 268, 269, 286, 290, 303, 305
Losh, Thomas C., 329
Love, Michael V. "Mike," 214, 221
Lovick, Edward "Ed," 65, 76, 139–141, 256
Lovrien, Clark E., 208
Lu Wei-heng, 189
Lucus, Evander, 203
Luther, Charles J., 222
Lyon, Don, 243

M

MacCready, Paul B., 373
MacDonald, Luther D., 65
Madenwald, Frederic A., 397
Mad Hatters, 414, 415
Madison, Richard "Dick," 262, 263
Magic Dragon, 186, 187
Maglieri, Domenic J., 127
Mahoney, James D. "Tony," 382
Ma Jiesan, 168

Makholm, James L., 329, 335
Malone, George E., 288
Manta UAV, 404–406
Marks, Michael D., 302
Marr, William H., 18, 19, 40
Marshall, Raymond S., 431
Martin, Edward F., 256, 258
Martin, Harry, 135
Martin, Marvin L. "Roy," 238
Masiello, Thomas J., 476
Matheny, James D. "Thug," 241
Matye, Robert L. "Bob," 23, 28, 30–32, 44
Maunder, David P., 312–314, 316–318, 320–322
Mauro, Frank, 409, 410
Maus, Stewart A., 331, 333–336
Mayerle, Evan L., 393
Maynard, Wayne, 263, 276
Mayo, Robert "Kobe," 217, 221
McCabe, George, 147
McClain, Larry D., 251, 252, 268, 283, 287, 290, 312, 356, 476
McCloud, Bill, 87
McCone, John A., 126, 131
McConnell, Landon B., 47, 48, 50, 51, 476
McCoy, Frederic E., 34–37, 48, 52, 63, 476
McGirr, Page, 305
McIninch, Thomas P., 177
McKay, Jim, 88
McKeown, Ronald E. "Mugs," 203, 207, 208
McMahon, John, 110, 378
McMillan, Brockway, 124
McMillion, Alva E., 135
McNamara, Robert S., 131, 132, 154
McPeak, Merrill A. "Tony," 383, 427
McQuillan, Richard "Dick," 237, 244, 445, 446
McRaney, Michael, 343
MD-21 accident, 161
Meathrell, Randy, 298
Meathrell, Richard H. "Dick," 287, 289
Mecchi, Richard R., 331
Medical Group, 440, 441
Medlin, Steve, 252, 253, 343, 350
Mehaffey, Robert, 189
Meierdierck, John H. "Hank," 46, 181–183
Meighan, William, 276
Merkl, Eldred D. "Don," 274, 292, 293, 302
Merlette, Suzie, 297
Merlin, Perry, 65
Meschko, Edward T. "Tom," 230
Methlie, George J., 379
MGM-137 TSSAM, 391, 393
MiG-17 Fresco, 190, 191, 202–214, 221, 222, 225, 227, 229, 231, 234, 238, 243

MiG-19 Farmer, 222
MiG-21 Fishbed, 191–202, 212–218, 220–222, 225–234, 236–238, 240, 243, 244, 380–382, 384
MiG-23 Flogger, 227–232, 234–237, 239–241, 243, 380–382, 384
MiG-25 Foxbat, 223–225
MiG-29 Fulcrum, 384–386
Miles, Marvin, 150
Military Air Transport Service (MATS), 37, 39, 40, 42, 49
Miller, Allan, 356
Miller, Dave, 244
Miller, David F., 342
Miller, Herbert I. "Herb," 13, 16–20, 86
Miller, Jennifer, 454
Miller, Mark, 276
Miller, Richard "Dick," 263, 265
Minion UAV, 404
Minotaur UAV, 404
Mission Support Group, 436
Mitchell, Daniel B., 108
Mitchell, Samuel A. "Sam," 251, 252, 283, 476
Mitzner, Kenneth M., 256
Mixson, Marion C. "Hack," 52
Mohrhardt, Robair F., 193
Mon, Donald D., 11
Monesmith, Burt, 30
Montgomery, Frederick D., 46
Montoya, Patrick E., 109
Moonflower project, 305, 306
Moore, William, 185
Moore, William G., 229
Moore, Robert, 253, 254
Moorman, Thomas S., 362
Moreira, William J., 203
Moreland, Huey H. "Hugh," 212
Morgan, Darwin, 449
Morgan, Walter R. "Ray," 373–379
Morgenfeld, Thomas A., 218, 225, 230, 235, 287, 289, 294–296, 299, 301
Moro, John E., 302
Morris, Michael C., 203
Moseley, Roger A., 238, 288, 294, 295, 297–299, 301–303
Mountain, Roger, 356
Mubarak, Hosni, 228
Muellner, George K., 237–239
Mulhare, Ross E. "Mule," 307
Mullan, William A., 103
Mullaney, Pat, 308
Mullen, Michael, 421
Mullens, Sid, 289
Muller, Alvin D. "Don"/"Devil," 217, 221, 222, 225

Mullin, Robert E., 46
Murphy, Joe, 176
Murphy, Robert F. "Bob," 25, 27, 28, 40, 56, 60, 256, 262–266, 286
Murray, Donald, 315, 316
Murray, Francis J. "Frank," 108, 112, 134, 156, 157, 169–174
Myers, Charles E. "Chuck," 253

N

N-327 XST model, 256, 257
N-345 BSAX design, 311, 323
Nagel, Steven R., 222
National Advisory Committee for Aeronautics (NACA), 54, 55, 61, 62, 255
National Aeronautics and Space Administration (NASA), 75, 87, 88, 99, 100, 105, 109, 112, 127, 132, 188, 214, 247–249, 261, 275, 286, 288, 318, 350, 366, 379, 401, 404, 406, 412, 413, 422, 423
National Classified Test Facility, 427, 428, 431, 439, 442
National Reconnaissance Office (NRO), 107, 124, 150, 154, 156, 166, 177, 247, 248, 402, 403, 464
Navy SEALs, 416, 421
NC-130H airborne test bed, 446
NDB Trucking Company, 361, 436
Nebeker, Alfred L. "Lynn," 328, 329, 334
Nelson, Byron "Buck," 306
Nelson, Douglas T., 102, 108
Nelson, Norman E. "Norm," 125, 256, 265, 286
Neptune Spear operation, 416, 417, 421
Neuwohner, Charles E. "Chuck," 238
Nevada Test and Training Range (NTTR), 385, 388, 404, 421, 428, 429, 431, 435, 438, 439, 441–447, 453, 455, 460
Nevada Wildlife Federation, 343
Newell, Robert T., 232
Newmiller, Carl, 135
Newton, Cyrus W., 135
Newton, Richard D., 21, 22, 24, 34, 35, 40, 70, 476
Next-Generation Air Dominance (NGAD), 457–460
Next-Generation Bomber (NGB), 455, 456
NICE GIRL exercise, 172
Nix, John B. "Tack," 292
Noce, Jim, 96, 133
Nolan, Robert C. "Woody," 383
Nole, Jack D., 60, 70, 71
Norton, Garrison, 30
Noyes, Cadwallader V., 177
NT-43A (RAT-55) radar test bed, 413, 430, 431
Nuttbrock, Dennis L., 244
NYLON CARPET, 363

O

Oberle, Joseph L. "José," 225, 227, 235
Ochal, Terry, 453
O'Donnell, Terence J. "Terry," 40
O'Donnell, William, 149
O'Driscoll, Mary, 344
Ogilvie, William G. "Bill," 276
OILSTONE, 34
O'Keefe, Timothy F., 232
O'Loughlin, Mary Beth, 302
Olson, Carl, 80
O'Neil, Dawson R. "Randy," 212, 216, 217
Operations Group, 429
Operations Support Squadron, 434, 435
Orr, Verne, 326
Orris, John, 331
Oshiro, Fred K., 256, 310, 311
OSTIARY, 58
Overholser, Denys, 255–257, 273
Overstreet, Carl K., 47
Owen, Mark, 258
OXCART pilots, 108
OXCART termination, 172–174
OXCART water survival training, 113, 114

P

PACER SPRITE, 289
Pack, Warren, 334
Padjet, Richard "Dick," 25
Palay, David D., 338, 339
Pape, Ed "EJ," 297
Papoose Lake, 68, 340, 347–349
Pappas, George M., 40, 41
Paradise Ranch, 18, 25
Parangosky, John, 81, 107, 110, 143, 146, 155, 177
Park, William C. "Bill," 105–107, 111, 115, 116, 118–120, 131, 132, 136–138, 146, 157–161, 263, 265, 266, 268, 269, 276, 287, 328, 329
Passon, Ray, 272, 274
Patnode, Arthur, 136
Patterson, Bill, 262
PAVE MOVER, 309
Payne, Fred, 109
Peck, Gaillard R. "Evil," 212, 217, 226, 235, 244
Pedersen, Dan "Yank," 207, 208
Pemberton, James "Jim," 331, 332
Pendleton, Wayne, 86, 87
Perdzock, John, 410, 411
Pereida, Mathew, 453
Perkins, Roland L. "Cy," 71, 108, 138

Perko, Kenneth, 254, 258, 265, 310, 311
Perry, Edward A., 53
Perry, William J., 258, 270, 272, 309, 311, 323, 394
Peters, F. Whitten, 368
Petersen, Forrest, 88
Peterson, Howard B., 329
Peterson, Ray B., 125
Pezzini, Bob, 135
Phantom Works (McDonnell Douglas / Boeing), 395, 396, 398, 455, 456, 459, 463
Phiffer, Harry, 87
Pinaud, Joseph H. "Joe," 113, 115, 116, 176
PINWHEEL operation, 143
Pirozzi, Philip C., 382
P-ISR UAV, 413–416
Pittman Station, 283, 473
Pizzo, Samuel E., 108, 135, 169
Placak, Oliver R., 38, 70
Plowshare project, 117, 184
Plummer, Jim, 166
plutonium, 38, 67–69, 357–359
Pocock, Charles L. "Charlie," 328–335
Pogue, William, 247
Pohlig, Michael H., 405
Polecat (P-175), 408–410
Polumbo, Robert N. "Mumbles," 383
Possenriede, Ken, 461
Postai, Mark F. "Toast," 238
Power, Thomas S., 30
Powers, Francis G. "Frank," 36, 37, 51, 75, 89, 346
Prabhakar, Arati, 457
Press, Michael "Bat," 216–218, 231
Pro, Philip, 362, 363
Proctor, William, 60
Proffitt, Ron, 331
Project 51 construction, 78, 80
Project 56 safety experiments, 38
Project 57 safety experiment, 67–70, 357–360
Project 274 (AQUILINE), 180
Project M277 (AQUILINE), 180
Project Grace, 386
PS-22 operating location, 289, 300, 305, 309
Purcell, Edward M., 65
Putt, Donald, 15

Q

QUARTZ, 402–404
Quick Kill (AN/MPQ-47) radar, 219
Quiet One (Hughes 500P), 187–189

R

Radant, Milt, 310
Radkey, Robert L., 374
RAH-66 Comanche, 420, 421
RAINBOW project, 65–67, 77
Ralston, Joseph W. "Joe," 259, 285
Ramspott, Larry, 184
Randolph, Gary L., 150
Range Directorate (Range Group), 439, 440
Rangers (Cammo Dudes), 363
Raschke, Edward K., 329
RATSCAT range, 256–260, 269, 325, 413, 417
Rawls, Michael T. "Trey," 372
Rawson, Ed, 82
Ray, Walter L., 108, 119, 146–152, 176
Ready, John K. "Jack," 218
Reagan, Ronald, 305, 325, 326, 344, 345, 380, 402
RECHARTER, 180, 181
recreational drinking, 356, 357
Red Eagles, 225–227, 231–233, 236, 238, 241–244, 355, 380, 382–385, 390, 431
Redfa, Munir, 192
Red Hats, 220–225, 229–245, 263, 267, 283, 284, 287, 291, 293, 303, 326, 330–334, 355, 356, 371, 372, 376, 378, 380–390, 431
REDLIGHT, 347
Reed, Jack G., 163–165
Reedy, Jack, 24
Reeves, Ed, 330
Reeves, James, 69
Reid, Harry M., 343–345, 367, 368
Reukauf, Paul, 286
Reynolds, Grant, 345
Reynolds, Richard V., 424
Riedenauer, Robert L. "Bob," 276, 297–299
Reiser, Donald, 177, 179
Rethman, Vincent C., 193
Reynolds Electrical and Engineering Company (REECo), 18–21, 24, 42, 50, 53, 68, 78, 80, 84, 90, 91, 94, 135, 176, 358–360, 365, 368, 437, 447, 448
Rhoades, Maynard R. "Dusty," 149
Rice, R. A. "Bud," 103
Rich, Benjamin R. "Ben," 229, 246, 254, 256, 258, 259, 261–263, 265–267, 269, 270, 272–281, 287, 292, 293, 296, 309–311, 323, 324, 329, 347
Richard, Robert B. "RB," 329, 334
Richardson, Elmer, 193
Richter, Rick, 176
Rifai, Radfan, 202
Ritland, Osmond J. "Ossie," 13, 16–18, 20, 30, 48
Rittenhouse, John, 344

RIVET HASTE, 212
Robbins, Jay T., 124
Robbins, Robert D., 418
Roberts, Joe M., 236
Robertson, Gary, 208
Robertson, Phillip O. "Phil," 46, 56
Robinson, Doug, 227
Robinson, George W. "Robbie," 175
Roche, James, 395
Rodgers, Franklin J. "Frank," 65, 78, 85
Rodreick, Denise, 220
Rogers, Keith, 369
Rogers, William, 228
Rohlfs, Albert F., 141
Roper, Will, 459
Rose, Wilburn S. "Billy," 57
Ross Aviation, 94, 327
Roussell, Richard J., 137, 138
Rowe, Frank, 263, 276
RQ-170 Sentinel, 406–408
RQ-180 (P-ISR), 415, 456
Ruiz, Connie, 353
Rupard, Hal, 163–165
Rural Coalition, 345
Rush, Kenneth, 248
Rusk, Dean, 131
Ruths, Donald R., 276, 277

S

Saavedra, Ruben, 66
Sadat, Anwar al-, 228
SADDLE SOAP, 19
Sager, Dennis F. "Bones," 371
Sampson, Janet, 176
Sampson, Richard A. "Dick," 176, 177, 476
Sam's Place, 252, 284, 317, 355–357, 425, 438
Sanders, Gilmore L., 175, 476
Sangl, Donald, 354
satellite imagery (commercial), 423–425
Satellite Reconnaissance Advanced Notice (SATRAN), 110
Saunders, Herb, 176
Savage, Paul, 244
Savidge, Thomas W., 238, 244
Saxman, John B., 231
Scamardo, Samuel J. "Sam," 113, 138
Schaefer, Carl E., 476
Schalk, Louis W., 105–109, 111, 116, 117, 119–121, 126, 129, 131, 132, 136
Scherrer, Richard C. "Dick," 254–256, 262
Schneider, Frederick W., 113, 116, 150

Schroeder, Bill, 255
Schultz, Eric E. "Doc," 388, 389, 431
Schultz, Gary, 350, 351
Schultze, Charles L., 146
Schumacher, Robert "Bob," 31, 36
Schwartz, George N., 476
Schwartz, Norton, 407
Scofield, Richard M., 302, 312, 313
Scoot-n-Hide shed, 284
SCOPE BARN operation, 172, 173
SCOPE COTTON operation, 146, 172
SCOPE LOGIC project, 152
SCORE EVENT, 251
Scott, Russell J., 108
Scoville, Herbert "Pete," 107, 136, 154
Seamans, Robert C., 223
Seamons, Rudy, 318
Secord, Richard V., 228
Security Directorate, 439
Seiberling, John, 344
SENIOR BOWL, 161–168, 175
SENIOR CEJAY, 324, 325
SENIOR HIGH, 258, 272, 274, 276, 309, 311
SENIOR ICE, 324
SENIOR PEG, 323–325
SENIOR PENNANT, 391
SENIOR PROM, 274–281, 283, 286, 287, 323, 356
SENIOR TREND, 276, 279, 283–309
SensorCraft, 410–413, 416
Seto, Edward I., 203
Setter, Louis C., 46, 63
Severinsen, Arve, 375
Sexton, Patrick J., 332, 335
Seymour, Robert L., 108
Shamu, 315, 319, 326
Shane, Maxine, 345
Shapira, Daniel "Dani," 192, 193, 202, 203
Sharp, James C., 148
Sharp, Norman, 165
Sharp, Patrick S. "Pat," 212, 267, 282, 283, 312, 326, 356, 375, 401
Shawler, Wendell H., 203, 209–211, 215
Shea, Richard T., 333
Shikaka, 416
Shingler, Herbert I., 46, 70
SHOEHORN, 347
Short, Raymond, 148
Shreve, James D., 68
Siefke, Stan, 305
Sieker, Robert "Bob," 31, 66, 67
Sierra Club, 343
Silas Mason Company, 18, 19, 53
Silent, Harold C., 40

Simon, Attila "Ted," 329
Simon, James S., 153, 154
Sinclair, Richard F. "Dick," 193, 215, 242, 243, 331, 332
Singel, Robert D., 247, 248
Singleton, Curtis F., 276
Sinnett, James M., 395
Site I, 15, 17, 18
Site II, 17, 18
Site 4 complex, 226, 393
Skliar, William L. "Bill," 108, 119, 144
Skougard, Roger, 122
Skunk Works (Lockheed / Lockheed Martin) ADP, 14, 15, 50, 75, 77, 106, 136, 143, 155, 156, 168, 229, 254–269, 272, 274, 275, 278, 279–281, 286, 287, 289, 306, 310, 311, 323–325, 329, 335, 373, 404–409, 411, 419, 456, 461
Skylab space station, 247–249
SKYLARK operation, 138, 139
Slater, Hugh C. "Slippery," 108, 135, 146, 150, 169, 173, 175, 476
Slater Lake, 135, 219, 220, 253, 284
Slay, Alton D. "Al," 251, 258, 262, 263, 272, 274
Slemon, Charles R., 130
Sloan, Peter, 296
Slusher, Bill, 354
Smalley, Daniel M., 339
Smith Arthur E., 123
Smith, Arthur L. "Pete," 331
Smith, Daniel H., 189
Smith, David "DL," 212, 217, 221
Smith, Donald D., 253
Smith, James, 150
Smith, John "JC," 207
Smith, Paul E., 25, 103
Smith, Robert W., 343, 344
Smith, Roger J., 215, 216
Smith, Stephen R. "Steve," 311
Smith, Walter T., 175, 181
Socci, Charles A., 203
Sorell, John, 392
Sorlie, Donald M., 52, 67, 191
Southwood, Dave, 305, 306
Sparks, Gordon R., 330, 335
Special Projects Flight Test Squadron, 372, 429–431
Spencer, Keith, 113
Spurgeon, Jerry, 243, 331
SR-71 Blackbird, 132, 146, 150, 152, 154, 157, 161, 168, 172, 176, 181, 182, 224, 254, 263, 286, 329, 346, 403
STABLEMATE, 223
Stafford, Thomas P., 222, 223, 233, 234, 250, 324
Staggs, Coy V., 113, 114, 116
Stanks, Thomas J., 103
Stanley, John, 262

Star, Moe, 256
Starbird, Alfred D., 20, 42
Starcher, Jack, 135
Staten, Kenneth E., 259, 265, 273, 285, 310
Station D (Flight D / Detachment D), 34, 36, 79, 251
stealth helicopter, 416–421
Stewart, Michael C., 307
STINGRAY, 456
Stockman, Hervey S., 47
Stoldal, Bob, 342
Strategic Defense Initiative (SDI), 346
Strauss, Lewis, 17, 18
STRAY CAT, 110
Strickland, John W. "Bill," 57
Stroface, Joseph F., 203
Stubben, Mark A., 476
Stump, Ronald, 135
Sturdevant, Charles "Chuck," 256
Su-7BKL, 211
Su-22 Fitter, 234, 235, 383
Su-27 Flanker, 386–389
Suits, Norman L., 211–217, 221, 222, 270, 271
Sukach, Christina, 388
Sullivan, Dennis A., 193, 198
Sullivan, Dennis B. "Denny," 108, 111, 120, 134, 144, 169, 170, 172, 174
Sun Pei-zhen, 186
Swain, David O., 395
Swalm, Thomas S., 203, 208
Swanson, Andree, 368
Swanson, Dane C., 380
Swanson, Mike, 405, 409
Swarts, Robert F. "Bob," 259
Sweidel, Davis N., 46
Sylvester, George H., 274
Syphers, Ronald W., 193, 237, 242, 243

T

TACIT BLUE, 282, 311–324, 326, 327, 349, 371, 390, 391, 406
TACIT GOLD (Sea Shadow), 309–311, 395
Tackabury, Paul D., 238, 301, 303
TAGBOARD (Q-12/AQ-12/D-21), 154–168, 174, 175, 254, 255, 347, 402
Tarver, Jim, 87
Taylor, Bill, 256
Taylor, John A. "Ashby," 238, 245
Taylor, Rufus L., 173, 174
Teague, Foster S. "Tooter," 203, 207, 208
TEAL DAWN, 280
Tellep, Dan, 272, 274
Teller, Edward, 348
Templeton, Horace A., 132
Thatcher, Margaret, 305
Thomas, Clarence, 147
Thomas, Ralph W. "Bill," 175, 176
Thomas, Richard G. "Dick," 312–314, 316–320, 322, 323
Thomas, William R., 146
Thomas, William W., 113
Thompson, Odis, 135
Thomson, Donald G. "Don," 193, 203, 204, 230, 235, 237, 238, 244
Tichenor, Terry D., 429
Tikaboo Peak, 355, 426, 434
Tilley, James W. "Jim," 238, 239, 476
Tonopah Test Range (TTR), 226, 227, 232, 236, 238, 243, 271, 288, 302–305, 307, 308, 330, 336, 338, 355, 359, 368, 380, 382, 393, 407, 427, 428, 448, 450–452
Torick, Ray, 160, 161
Total In-Flight Simulator (TIFS), 312, 313
Trapp, Charles E. "Charlie," 112–116, 149, 150
Traver, Holly, 284, 302
Travis, Joe, 350
Travis, Pat, 350
Tri-Service Standoff Attack Missile (AGM-137 TSSAM), 391–394
Trout, Edgar L., 276
Tucker, Robert C., 193
Turley, Jonathan, 360–363
Twigg, John K. "Jack," 258, 262, 270, 312, 316, 317, 320, 321
Twining, Nathan F., 33, 34
Twinting, William T. "Ted," 193, 198
Tymczyszyn, Joseph J., 120

U

U-2 accidents, 57, 60–62, 64–67
U-2 cover story, 54, 55
U-2 first delivery to test site, 23, 24
U-2 flight testing, 27–33
U-2 maximum altitude, 56
Ufimtsev, Pyotr, 256
UFO (unidentified flying object), 53, 54, 227, 346–351, 355, 371, 424
Uhlig, Edward R., 141
UPWIND operation, 152
Urolatis, Edwin J., 40
Urquhart, George, 256
USS *Pueblo*, 170
Utah Test and Training Range (UTTR), 273, 422, 428, 442, 444

V

Van Compernolle, Robert A., 78
Vanderhorst, Daniel R., 322, 323
van Ee, Jeff, 343
Van Norman, Charles V., 230, 244
Van Oss, Donald G. "Gary," 258
Van Sambeek, Ed, 244
Van Voorhis, Roy A., 339
Van Winkle, Wayne E. "Rip," 329
Varnadoe, James, 89
Vensel, Joe, 88
Vito, Carmine A., 47
Vogel, Ed, 342, 343
Vojvodich, Mele "Mel," 108, 119, 126, 137, 138, 144, 145, 169, 174, 299
VOLANT CAT, 229
VOLANT QUILT, 229
Voron drone, 167
Vortman, Luke, 185
Voyles, James H., 41
VP-45 patrol squadron, 452, 453
VX-4 test squadron, 193, 201, 207, 208, 218, 230, 391, 431
VX-9 test squadron, 431

W

Waaland, Irving T. "Irv," 256, 309, 311
Waddleton, Thomas R., 67
Walker, Joseph A., 109
Walker, Robert S., 354
Wallace, Kenneth M., 380
Wallis, John R., 164, 289
Walter, Alonzo J. "Lon," 108
Walters, Bill "Flash," 113–116
Walterscheid, David, 454
Watertown Airstrip designated, 33, 469
Watson, Kenneth "Kenny," 255
Weapons Test Range (WTR), 236
Weaver, Bill, 158
Weaver, Charles, 70
Webb, John S., 331, 332
WEDLOCK (M-21), 156
Weeks, Jack W., 108, 121, 122, 125, 128, 169–172, 174, 176
Weinberger, Caspar W., 325, 344
Weiss, Werner H., 79, 90, 96, 98, 99, 108, 146, 476
Welch, John M. "Mike," 203
Welch, Ray C., 237
Welsh, Mark A., 461
West, Scott, 368
Western Shoshone, 345, 346

Weyenberg, Keith, 392
Wheelon, Albert D. "Bud," 136, 140
White, Ed, 119, 124, 125
White Hats (Services / Force Support Squadron), 438
White, Robert M., 88
White Sides hill, 200, 340, 352–354
White, Wes M., 276
Whitley, Alton C. "Al," 300
Wiechman, Alan R., 395, 396, 455
Wigdahl, Alan, 372
Wiggins, Lloyd G., 103
Wilcox, Robert E., 96
Wilder, Lee, 87
Wilkerson, Pete, 25
Williams, Arnie, 176
Williams, David "Dave," 258, 265, 272
Williams, Gordon E., 240
Williams, Robert, 305
Wilson, Charles E., 43
Wilson, Dick, 135
Wilson, Houser, 108, 109
Wilson, Jim, 370, 421, 422
Wilson, Normal E., 203
Wilson, Roscoe C., 75
Wimberly, Charles L., 123, 125
Wineteer, Lawrence D. "Larry," 276
Wingate, Leo K. "Kent," 276
Winham, Paul E., 40
Winters, Charles P. "Pete," 211–216, 240, 283, 287, 290, 302, 441, 442, 476
Winters, James, 276
Wirt, Leslie S., 188
Wise, William H., 130
Wisneski, James H., 238, 240–242
WMK Transit Mix, 91
Woodruff, Seth R., 16, 17, 19, 20
Worden, John, 375
Worthington, Patricia R., 365
Wuest, Willys D. "Bill," 173, 176
Wurts, Joseph M., 405

X

X-15 rocket plane, 87–89, 109
X-273 experimental demonstrator, 372
X-1800 experimental survivable testbed, 256
XST, 255–259, 309, 310

Y

Yancey, William R. "Bill," 44, 46, 47, 51–53, 58, 116
Yates, Ronald W., 445, 446
YF-24, 372

YF-45D, 431
YF-110B, 195, 196, 213, 215, 233, 234, 238
YF-110C, 233, 234
YF-110D, 234, 237, 238
YF-110E, 382
YF-110L, 382
YF-110M, 382
YF-112C, 383
YF-112D, 383
YF-113A, 203, 205, 206, 207, 209
YF-113B, 235, 236, 238
YF-113C (HAVE PRIVILEGE), 210
YF-113C (HAVE PHOENIX), 382
YF-113E, 229, 235, 238, 239
YF-113G, 371
YF-113H, 382
YF-114C, 203, 206, 209–211, 213, 215, 238
YF-114D, 213, 238
YF-116A, 382
YF-117A, 291–295, 297, 298, 300, 301, 304, 309
YF-117D, 318

YF-118G, 395, 397, 400
YF-220, 372
Yitzhak, Yossi, 202
Yoshii, Mich, 24
Yost, Ed, 284
Young, David D., 108
Young, G. Lewis, 123
Yucca Flat Aerial Operations Facility, 449, 450
Yu Chuan-wen, 187
Yuletide Special Operations Area, 101, 123, 133, 134

Z

Zaloga, Thomas "Tom," 237, 244
Zarrella, Tim, 133
Zedeker, C. C., 193
ZIPPER project, 447
Zorzi, David R., 428, 436
Zubon, Nicholas R. "Nick," 151
Zuckert, Eugene M., 118